The Best of
Russian Life

Vol. 1: History and Culture

Edited by
Paul E. Richardson

Russian Life
BOOKS

ISBN 978-1-880100-68-4

Russian Information Services, Inc.
PO Box 567
Montpelier, VT 05601-0567
www.russianlife.com
orders@russianlife.com
phone 802-223-4955

Contents

Introduction
Paul E. Richardson

*W*hen we first came up with the idea for this book, the task seemed easy enough: cull through 15 years of back issues of Russian Life; select the best stories; re-edit them; publish them in a single volume.

Little did we know.

It turned out that many fine stories published in the magazine over the last decade and a half simply did not work in a book format. First, stories had to be strong in a text-only presentation, which ruled out features that relied heavily on photographs or illustrations. Second, stories had to be somewhat timeless. Many stories we published a decade ago (or even two years ago) are interesting as historical artifacts, yet they would not work well in a volume that seeks to have a more enduring relevance. Finally, stories had to be published before the end of 2009.

However, even given these few qualifications, the number of fine stories that we felt were worth re-presenting was still huge. We therefore decided to split the work into two volumes. The first volume, this one, includes stories more focused on history and culture, the second volume is comprised of biographies. Taken together, this two-volume publication offers a surprisingly comprehensive and broad view of Russian culture, history, society... and life. We hope it will serve well as both a reference volume (thus the index) and general reader that you can dive into at any point and savor an enjoyable story.

For this history volume, we have published the stories in roughly chronological order, based on the historical date of most relevance to the article (indicated on the first page). In many cases, this was a considerable challenge, because subjects often covered a broad swath of history and could not be easily pinned to a single date. Nonetheless, we picked a date we felt to be defensible. For the handful of stories at the end of this volume that deal with the modern day, we used the date the story was reported. For the biographies volume, the stories are published in alphabetical order by the subject's last name. In both cases, the current juxtaposition of stories creates new and interesting connections and their presentation in a text-only format makes them somehow new again.

The texts that appear in these two volumes are very much the same as the original articles that appeared in the magazine. There has been some style editing to introduce consistencies and to reinforce standards we have developed over the years. But there were very few corrections of fact needed, and relatively few edits of the texts to account for temporal variables like prices and anniversaries.

For me personally, it was a great pleasure to re-read these stories, rediscovering features I had not thought about for many years. I thank all of the authors for granting their permission to have their stories re-appear in this new format. If you would like to find out more about any author in this volume, please visit our website, where we try to keep all authors' biographies up to date. You can also see what else that individual may have written for the magazine, and where else they are published.

Sadly, our records do not indicate who the translators were of some earlier stories, and we apologize to translators whose work is going unrecognized. Where we do know the translators, we have indicated this.

Finally, special thanks are due Kate Reilly-Fitzpatrick for enduring the difficult organizational work involved in a work of this magnitude. I am equally grateful for the work of staff editors Maria Antonova, Mikhail Ivanov, Tamara Eidelman, Darra Goldstein, Lina Rozovskaya, Robert Greenall, Scott McDonald and Maria Kolsenikova; without their input and contributions (and, yes, translations) over the years, this volume could not have happened.

Paul E. Richardson

Very Old Ladoga
Vasily Latenko

Just 120 kilometers from Russia's northern capital lies the small village of Staraya Ladoga. Like St. Petersburg, Staraya Ladoga was once a capital – not of imperial Russia, but of ancient Rus. And in 2003, when St. Petersburg heralded its 300th birthday, Staraya Ladoga quietly observed its 1250th.

*R*ussia," wrote the historian Vasily Klyuchevsky, "is a country of forests and vast, slow-flowing rivers." In Staraya ("Old") Ladoga, Klyuchevsky's words ring true. Along the banks of the wide, slow-flowing Volkhov river, stretches the aesthetically perfect silhouette of an ancient Russian city. The panorama of kremlin walls and church domes is untainted by Soviet architecture.

Staraya Ladoga owes its birth and prosperity to the watery "road from the Varangians to the Greeks," which connected Scandinavia and the Baltic to the Black Sea. The exact date of the town's founding is unknown, but archeological excavations suggest that it happened no later than 753.

In the early Middle Ages, at the place where the Volkhov River flows into the Ladozhka, a Scandinavian outpost sprouted up – it later became known as Ladoga. The Varangian guests were a mixture of racketeers and merchants. They built their towns on the shores of the rivers Volkhov, Lovat, Dnepr and Volga so that they had a place to store their booty, receive furs as tribute from Finns and Slavs, and rest along the long road to Constantinople.

In the eighth and ninth centuries, Ladoga was the capital of the Slav-Varangian state, Russia's progenitor. Here, at the confluence of the rivers Volkhov and Ladozhka, ruled the Viking leader Rurik, founder of Russia's first royal dynasty. Prince Oleg the Prophet, one of the Rurikids, met his end here. According to an episode immortalized in the Chronicle (and which became widely known through Alexander Pushkin's "Song of Oleg the Prophet"), a soothsayer warned Oleg that he would die because of his favorite horse. So Oleg abandoned the animal, only to later die after being bitten by a snake that slithered out of the dead horse's skull.

For several centuries, Ladoga played a role later given to St. Petersburg – an administrative center on the outskirts of Rus, a window into Europe. Russia's first stone fortress was built here, as were six stone churches, two of which still stand today.

In the twelfth century, Ladoga was something of a suburb of Novgorod, a link in the chain of forts which protected that city from its enemies. In 1114, a stone fort with walls eight meters high and two meters thick was built here. Half a century later, in 1164, Ladoga withstood a siege by the Swedish army. After calling on Novgorod for help, Ladogans drove the Swedes to the estuary of the river Voronega and there crushed them. Legend has it that, in memory of this victory, the church of Saint George the Victor was built under the fortress' ramparts.

In the fifteenth century, four new churches were built in Ladoga – St. Peter, Simon, Vasily Kesariysky and the Birth of John the Baptist. The fortress was rebuilt into a pentagonal shape and multi-storied towers up to seven meters wide were added, including the quadrilateral Gates Tower, which was the only entry into the kremlin. The following century, Boris Godunov rebuilt Ladoga after the end of the Livonian War (1558-1583). The walls built then, along with the adjoining "Earth City," still stand today. Ladoga was one of the first wood-and-earth fortifications in Russia and, until the eighteenth century, it protected northwest Russia from invaders.

But high, thick walls did not save Ladoga from troubles within Rus itself – after devastating Novgorod, Ivan the Terrible's *oprichniks* paid Ladoga a visit as well. Having hardly recovered from this, Ladoga was drawn into the intrigues of the Time of Troubles. In 1609, beckoned by Tsar Vasily Shuysky, Swedish troops, together with Russians, liberated northwest Rus from the forces of the Second False Dmitry and brought their victory to Moscow. For this, Sweden was rewarded with the town of Korela and its surrounding district, which included Ladoga. In June 1611, joint Novgorodan-Swedish rule was established in the land of Novgorod. Order was maintained by Swedish military garrisons, deployed in border forts, including Ladoga.

But Swedish occupation of Ladoga did not last long. In early 1617, Muscovy, ruled by Tsar Mikhail Fyodorovich Romanov, signed a peace treaty with Sweden in the village of Stolbovo, situated halfway between the town of Tikhvin, occupied by Moscow, and Ladoga. According to the treaty, Ladoga and Novgorod were returned to Moscow. Yet the border with Sweden was still very close – along the river Lava. And here the Swedes established an outpost.

Ladoga had a central role in Peter the Great's Northern War. The main forces of Peter's army were gathered here before the campaign of 1702-1703. Fourteen regiments led by Boris Sheremetyev set out from Ladoga to assault the Swedish fortress of Noteburg (Oreshek) – the military campaign that brought victory against Sweden and led to the founding of the new capital – St. Petersburg.

In 1704, 12 kilometers north of Ladoga, Novaya ("New") Ladoga was founded. Peter ordered that all of Ladoga's administrative offices be transferred there, along with some of the town's citizens. This was when the ancient capital of Russia got its offensive prefix – Staraya ("Old"). From that point on, Staraya Ladoga became a historical backwater.

But this fate also "saved" Staraya Ladoga. It left standing an incredible number of ancient architectural wonders and makes this town no less important than any of the towns of the "Golden Ring."

Get Thee to a Nunnery

You will need a full day to get at least a brief glimpse of all of Staraya Ladoga's sights. The town covers about two square kilometers and includes over 160 monuments of historical and cultural importance.

The sights stretch along the left side of the road connecting Novaya Ladoga to Volkhov. The first is the famous burial mounds, one of which is thought to contain Prince Oleg the Prophet. From the mounds you can take in a beautiful view upriver of Ladoga's monasteries and kremlin.

Further on are the cemetery and nineteenth century Alexeevskaya Church and the Church of John the Baptist (1695). Closed by the Soviets, the churches reopened in 1991.

Behind these is Uspensky Monastery with the pre-Tatar Church of the Assumption of Our Lady, along with a collection of nineteenth century buildings – stone walls with towers, private cells, the refectory, the laundry-house and others. The monastery was a rather infamous involuntary home for two famous Yevdokias. From 1718 to 1725, Peter the Great's first wife, Yevdokia Lopukhina, who plotted against him, was locked up here. From

1754 until her death, Yevdokia Andreevna Gannibal, the unfortunate
first wife of Abram Gannibal, Peter the Great's Ethiopian favorite and
Alexander Pushkin's great grandfather, was held here. Yevdokia Dioper had
been married to Gannibal against her will and had cheated on him. She was
tried, and jailed for 11 years in the monastery.

Staraya Ladoga's main tourist attraction is the pentagonal kremlin,
which has been restored to the way it looked at the end of the seventeenth
century. Inside the fortress is the Church of St. George (1165) which
contains fragments of pre-Tatar frescoes. The small, four pillar church with
three apses is constructed of alternating layers of limestone and brick. In
1445, on the orders of Archbishop Yefimy Vyazhishchsky, the Monastery of
St. George was built around the church.

In 1646, the church was elevated to the status of Cathedral of all
Ladoga. But 100 years later, in the first half of the eighteenth century, the
monastery closed and St. George Cathedral became a parochial church.
In the nineteenth century, stone vestibules, belfries, new windows, doors
and roofing were all added to St. George's. In the twentieth century, it
was restored to its original appearance. If you visit the church today, you
are likely to be led about by its exotic tour guide – a young man sporting a
leather jacket and an earring.

Nearby, the wooden Church of Dmitry Solunsky houses a small museum
of peasant life. To the south of the kremlin stands Nikolsky Monastery, with
its seventeenth century Nikolsky Cathedral, nineteenth century Church of
Ioann (John) Zlatoust and eighteenth century private cells.

Formally, these landmarks were made a historical-architectural
and archaeological museum-reserve some 20 years ago. But, in reality,
Uspensky Monastery was turned into a home for children with handicaps.
The locals, who previously worked on the state farm, are now idle, and
thus permanently drunk. Signs of prosperity and labor are absent. There is,
however, a snack-bar selling cheap port, the retro-Soviet "Ladya" cafe, and
a very modest regional museum, opened hurriedly on the eve of the town's
jubilee, and housed in a wooden, nineteenth century merchant's home.

Everywhere a Rurik

Today, Staraya Ladoga is home to just over 2,000 souls. The houses
are all pretty and wooden, but also aging and decrepit. A natural, pastoral
appearance is spoiled somewhat by the wooden fences – all painted brown

in the heat of anniversary fever – and old garages. As in all big villages, the center of Staraya Ladoga is the square in front of the administration building and the local House of Culture. Ladoga also has a school, an information-entertainment center, and some shops.

The economic infrastructure is still in the development stage. In July 2003, the Duke Rurik café opened. Here you can feast on "Chicken Ladoga-style" (50 rubles) and "Duke's Delight" (a 75 ruble pork chop). The local hotel, also Duke Rurik, can accommodate up to 56 persons and rents out televisions at 50 rubles per day. There is also a hotel Ladya, which calls itself "a hotel of average comfort level."

To get to Staraya Ladoga by car you take Murmanskoye highway. Where the road forks for Staraya and Novaya Ladoga, there is a very cheap fish market, where you can buy nice whitefish and salmon. Inexperienced customers are easily spotted and vendors will try to sell you fish at triple the price, so be sure to haggle.

To get to Staraya Ladoga by public transport, take a suburban train from Ladozhsky or Moskovsky train station in St. Petersburg to Volkhovstroy Station – about a two-and-a-half hour ride. Then take bus 23 from the train station square.

You can also visit Staraya Ladoga with a tour bus – there are one- and two-day tours available from travel agencies in St. Petersburg. But no matter how you get there, Staraya Ladoga is a treat worth savoring. RL

November/December 2003

The Celebration of Summer
Tamara Eidelman

*M*any centuries ago, the existence of those living in Eastern European lands was ruled by the rhythms of the seasons. The most important events involved changes in the natural world. The arrival of every new season was a magical moment, where cosmic forces burst to the surface, taking on a special significance and determining much of what was happening in the present and what would happen in the future. In this perpetual cycle of natural elements and phenomena, the Sun plays a tremendous role.

When the Sun's power is at a minimum, Earth is covered with snow and it was believed that ancestral spirits walked its surface, potentially coming into contact with the living, who may thus be able to find out what the future holds. This is at the end of December, a time when it was customary to dress in strange, animal costumes, to prepare foods fitting for a wake (or rather, *pominki*, in Russian) and leave them out for the departed to come and feast. Those who took part in the magical processions that went from house to house singing songs were rewarded with generous gifts of food – a mystical token of future prosperity and wealth.

When the Sun regained its power and winter gave way to spring, ceremonies had to be conducted that would magically reinforce the power of the Sun and help nature awaken from its slumber. This is the origin of the *bliny* consumed during Maslenitsa, and the bonfires on which winter was burned in effigy, as well as the vast number of rituals to prepare livestock, peasant homesteads, and even the tools with which the land would be cultivated.

And then, when the Sun came into its full strength, summer made its entrance. The most important events of the year began to take place. Deep beneath the soil, from the seeds cast upon the ground, ears of grain started to erupt; the next harvest came to life; the power of nature was reaching its zenith. The magical force of flowers, grasses and trees proliferated and it was believed that water sprites, having spent most of the year asleep under

TRANSLATION: NORA FAVOROV

ground, came to the surface and swung from tree branch to tree branch. The magical denizens of the woods – snakes, bears, wood goblins – were awake.

The task of people in all of this was to support the great force of Nature, to conduct the required rituals without which the natural cycle cannot exist. And so, on the night of July 6-7 (according to the present calendar), when the sun shines with its greatest force, night is short and days are amazingly long, rituals were observed that called upon the great elements of fire and water to help mankind.

During the first hours of July 7 (June 24 before Russia switched to the Gregorian calendar), peasants set tremendous bonfires and jumped over them, bathed naked in rivers, sang and danced around the fires, and rolled tremendous burning wheels that were then pushed into the water. Fire and water prevailed: the fiery wheels were like symbols of the Sun and those who danced and sang in circular *khorovody* around the bonfires also suggested the Sun's circular path. Fire and water were united, a joining akin to the principle of the masculine and feminine. Indeed, throughout the ages, vast numbers of couples came together on this night – a time when anything goes.

Ten centuries after the birth of Christ, Rus became a Christian nation. But this did not alter the pagan foundations of peasant life. It is believed that there were remote places where people contrived to openly profess paganism up until the fourteenth century, not allowing churches to be built or priests to enter their communities. Gradually, however, the church managed to spread its influence over virtually the entire territory of Rus. The peal of church bells could be heard everywhere in the country and church holidays became the most important events in the lives of both rural and urban populations.

But in the countryside, under the surface, life still followed the unhurried and unchanging courses set through thousands of years of pagan tradition. Ancient beliefs molded themselves to fit new ways of life. Veneration of ancestors in December became associated with Christmas, feasting on pancakes during Maslenitsa became the final frolic before the deprivations of the Great Fast leading up to Easter. Springtime agricultural rituals were performed on the Thursday of Holy Week.

And what about the summer celebration of the elements? It just so happened that this day coincided with the birthday of John the Baptist, who had foretold the coming of Christ and christened the Savior in the Jordan River. The magical powers of water were thus given a Christian "basis." But the nature of the celebration – known as Ivan Kupala, from the verb *kupatsya*, to bathe – remained the same. Whatever view village priests may have taken, bonfires were still lit, peasants still swam naked, and couples went off into the woods. And, of course, everyone knew that, during this magical night, trees and grasses began to speak, that this was the only night of the year when the fern flowered – a plant that could be used to locate treasures sleeping underground, in the kingdom of the dead.

In the nineteenth century, when ethnographers started to study and describe Russian village rituals, they were struck by how many pagan beliefs had survived almost unchanged over the millennia. Peasants, often unaware of the ancient meaning of their rituals, and sincerely believing themselves to be true Orthodox Christians, nonetheless were following the practices of their pre-Christian ancestors. The ancient gods were still around; they had merely been transformed into Christian saints. For example, the protector of beasts and wealth – Veles – had become St. Vlasy, the protector of livestock. Others became spirits – wood goblins (*leshiye*) or house goblins (*domovoy*) – the reality of which no one doubted. During Ilya's Week in August, the Biblical prophet Ilya traveled across the sky in a rumbling chariot – the explanation behind thunderstorms. As late as the nineteenth century, people brought bulls to church on St. Ilya's Day, not realizing that the bull had always been the animal associated with Perun, god of thunder. In 1925, peasants in Leningrad Province decided to appease nature just as their ancestors had done. Hoping for a good harvest, they tied a young girl to a tree in the forest, offering her as a bride to the lord of the forest – the bear. Fortunately, times had changed and the poor girl was saved before her groom had a chance to make her acquaintance.

And what about Ivan Kupala? Even today, everyone – both in the city and the country – knows about this holiday, largely thanks to Gogol's dark tale "St. John's Eve," in which a fern flowers and an evil witch forces a village youth to kill an innocent baby. Everyone remembers that Ivan Kupala is a time for lighting bonfires and swimming naked. Some use this night as an occasion for high-society gatherings and wild parties; others mark it with more folkloric celebrations. These observances are marked by a certain artificiality, as are many attempts to "revive" ancient rituals.

Of course, today many rituals have been completely forgotten. It seems unlikely that there are still farmsteads where women rise at dawn on the Thursday of Holy Week to circle their houses naked, using juniper branches to sprinkle livestock and farm tools with water. And it is hard to imagine that on New Year's Eve there are still men who hide behind pastries while their wives pretend not to see them, a rather simple act of wizardry intended to ensure tall and healthy crops in the coming year. But many rituals refuse to give way to the onslaught of modern life. There are still places where people dress up and go caroling on Christmas, and while observance of the Great Fast (Lent) is far from universal in Russia, *bliny* are prepared during Maslenitsa even by those who do not consider themselves Orthodox Christians.

And, of course, in any part of the country, at any natural spring considered a source of holy water, one can find a little church or chapel. But then, nearby, you will always also see a tree with its branches covered with colorful ribbons – left by pilgrims who are acting out an ancient pagan ritual of leaving offerings to the water spirit. In June, during the Orthodox holiday, Trinity Week, some will go to church while others will decorate their homes with birch branches, since this is the time, also known as "Green Yuletide," when *rusalki* swing on them. The details of such rituals may have been forgotten, but their essence – the great power of the natural elements – will probably never die. And St. John's Eve will remain an eerie and majestic moment of transition, even for those who know nothing of how their ancestors marked this night.

July/August 2006

Suzdal
William C. Brumfield

*F*or many of its thousands of visitors, Suzdal is the essence of enlightened tourist development in Russia. Bucolic, quaint, well-restored and beautifully picturesque, without the decay and disorder that often characterize farming areas in rural Russia, Suzdal seems the perfect setting of a bygone era, a community immune from the march of time.

In fact, this impression has been carefully cultivated for the sake of tourist revenue. More than one American guest has commented on the similarities between this small Russian town (population slightly over 12,000) and Colonial Williamsburg, in the state of Virginia, which also attempts to create an impression of life from the distant past on the background of a few preserved architectural monuments. To be sure, much more has survived of medieval Suzdal than of eighteenth-century Williamsburg, yet the notion of a national shrine where an illusion of the past can be preserved for masses of tourists is shared by both.

The Town that Time Forgot

Suzdal is by no means unique in the antiquity of its monuments; yet among surviving ancient Russian towns, Suzdal is rare in having almost no other existence apart from tourism. Indeed, Suzdal was so lost in time that it did not even have regularly scheduled bus service (to the district center of Vladimir) until 1956. During the 1870s, town authorities interested in progress and growth tried in vain to have a railroad spur built from nearby Vladimir. Ironically, their failure ensured that Suzdal's greatest resource, its ensemble of architectural monuments, remained relatively unspoiled at a time when other medieval centers suffered from unregulated development.

There are many anecdotes about the fabled twentieth-century isolation of this once powerful medieval settlement, with its shuttered, abandoned churches and monasteries. Some of these buildings found prosaic uses, for storage and as places of detention. Others witnessed more dramatic events.

In the spring of 1943, after their defeat at the battle of Stalingrad, Field Marshal Friedrich von Paulus and other high-ranking members of the German Sixth Army were brought to isolated Suzdal where they eventually met with prominent German communists for discussions about a post-war German socialist state. Paulus later wrote about these meetings, but one can only imagine the effect of this quiet town on the German "guests."

According to a recent study of Suzdal by Yury Belov, Suzdal had been designated by the USSR Academy of Architecture to receive funds for restoration as early as 1941. The onslaught of war interrupted these plans, but at least the idea of Suzdal's resurrection had been introduced as a matter of national importance. These ideas would be realized in the 1960s with the designation of Suzdal as a major national site for historic preservation in the interests of tourism. In no small part, this recognition was due to the dedication of local historians and musuem workers such as Vasily Romanovsky, who founded the Suzdal Museum in 1921-22, and Aleksey Varganov, who became the director of the museum in 1931 and maintained a passionate enthusiasm for the town until his death in 1977. Under daunting conditions, the commitment by museum workers to the cause of preservation stemmed from an understanding of Suzdal's rare architectural and cultural heritage at a time when such interests were often considered useless and even subversive of the new Soviet order.

Early Settlement

What is it about Suzdal that inspired such devotion on the part of preservationists? Although it was soon eclipsed by other medieval centers, Suzdal was one of the earliest settlements in the Russian heartland. The first mention of the town occurs under the year 1024, but there were undoubtedly settlements there in the ninth and tenth centuries. By the early eleventh century, representatives of political and religious authority from Kiev extended their control into this agriculturally rich territory, making it an object of dispute among warring princely factions. By the turn of the twelfth century, the Kievan Grand Prince Vladimir Monomakh had created a new citadel for Suzdal and had endowed its first Orthodox cathedral, apparently the earliest major brick structure in the entire territory of northeastern Rus.

In the middle of the twelfth century, Suzdal was part of the domains of Yuri Dolgoruky, the founder of Moscow. He, in fact, made it capital of the powerful Rostov-Suzdal principality. Yuri's son and successor, Andrei Bogolyubsky, preferred neighboring Vladimir at the expense of Suzdal (changing the region's center to the former, whence the region became known as Vladimir-Suzdal), but the next ruler, Vsevolod III (half-brother of Andrei), undertook an extensive repair of the Suzdal cathedral in 1194 (and, in the thirteenth century, Suzdal was made the capital of the Suzdal principality). This proved to be a temporary measure, however, and in 1222 one of Vsevolod's sons, Yury, razed the brick cathedral in Suzdal and erected a magnificent new white stone structure dedicated to the Nativity of the Virgin. During the 1230s, the rich decoration of the interior was complemented by frescoes and a few mosaics near the altar. This cathedral withstood the sack of Suzdal by the Mongols in 1238, even though the interior was completely pillaged. In 1281 and 1293, Suzdal was again subjected to devastating Mongol raids. From the early 1200s until the middle of the following century, Suzdal was an independent principality. But, over the course of the fourteenth century, its power waned with the rise of Moscow.

Through decades marked by plague, famine, and invasion, the Suzdal Nativity Cathedral stood, until 1445, when a raiding force of Kazan Tartars took the town and set fire to the cathedral interior. This so weakened the roof vaulting that the upper part of the building collapsed. Not until 1528-1530 did Moscow's Grand Prince Vasily III undertake to rebuild the cathedral as part of his campaign of restoring the ancient heritage of the Russian lands under the protection of Moscow. During this reconstruction, the remaining stone walls were uniformly lowered to the level of a "blind" (i.e. solid) arcade at the top of the first floor, while the upper structure and the drums beneath the five cupolas were rebuilt of new brick, in the style of large Muscovite churches.

Fortunately, much of the original thirteenth-century limestone carving was preserved, including the ornamental columns of the arcade band as well as the carved lions and female masks (implying the sacred image of the Virgin Mary) that decorate the cathedral at its corners and along its facades. This emphasis on the ornamental function of carved stonework stands in contrast to the array of religious images on the surface of other stone churches built in the Vladimir area by Vsevolod III at the end of the twelfth century. However, the Suzdal cathedral has images of its own covering the surface of the great "Golden Doors" of the west portal (around 1233), and on a later pair of doors within the south portal (around 1248). The depiction of religious scenes and Orthodox saints in the panels of both portal doors were executed by applying gold foil onto copper plate. Miraculously, these valuable artifacts survived the turbulent and often destructive events inflicted upon the cathedral.

Still More Tribulation

The seventeenth century was a time of further trials for the Suzdal area. During the Time of Troubles, after the death of Tsar Boris Godunov in 1605, Suzdal authorities tried to proclaim loyalty to the rapidly changing rulers in Moscow, but this did not spare the town from the depredations of marauding bands of Lithuanians, who came to Moscow in support of various Polish claimants to the throne. Indeed, it was a Suzdal nobleman, Prince Dmitry Pozharsky, who raised an army that would eventually rid Moscow of the Polish occupiers and create the security necessary for the founding of the new Romanov dynasty.

Yet even after the establishment of peace in Moscow, Suzdal met with further travail: Crimean Tartars raided the town in 1634, and the plague, or "Black Death," struck in the 1650s. But despite these setbacks, there were sufficient funds to commission a new set of frescoes for the interior of the Nativity Cathedral. It would appear that the Orthodox Church succeeded so well in maintaining its sources of income that, in 1646, residents of the town complained bitterly to Tsar Alexei about the church's abuse of economic power at the expense of the town. After another fire swept through Suzdal in 1719, the upper part of the cathedral underwent repairs that gave it a baroque appearance; but that changed yet again in 1748, when the cupolas gained their great flaring onion shape, and a sloped roof was placed over the rounded gables. The cathedral remained in this form until the 1950s, when a major restoration brought back the curved roof line of the sixteenth century, while retaining the eighteenth-century onion domes.

Vasily's Churches

In a sense, the entire history of Suzdal can be seen through the history of its Nativity Cathedral. We can also see how attitudes toward the preservation of such great monuments varied over the centuries. Suzdal, however, has many other landmarks of antiquity, especially its monastic institutions, whose history occasionally rivals that of the cathedral itself for drama and mystery. Among the most beautiful is the Intercession, or Pokrovsky, Convent, founded in 1364. On entering the convent, now returned to the Orthodox Church, one passes underneath the expressive forms of the Annunciation Gate Church, completed around 1515. This intricate brick structure with three small cupolas is interesting not only in itself, but also because it reproduces in miniature the general outline of the main convent church, dedicated to the Intercession of the Virgin and built by command of Moscow's Grand Prince Vasily III in 1510-1514.

The Intercession Church, constructed of bick and painted white, has ornamental features typical of fifteenth-century Muscovite architecture, such as the pointed *kokoshniki* on the roof; yet it also has details typical of early Suzdal architecture, such as blind arcading on the facade and a row of rounded gables, or *zakomary*, at the roofline. One of the most intriguing aspects of the cathedral is a polygonal bell tower at the southwest corner. It originally had a chapel on its second floor and, although the upper level was rebuilt in the seventeenth century, it may have been one of the earliest examples in Muscovy of a brick tower with a conical roof.

All of the structures described above were commissioned as votive churches by Vasily III and his first wife, Solomonia Saburova, in supplication for the birth of a male heir. Tragically, in 1525 the looming dynastic crisis compelled Vasily, with the support of the church, to anull his marriage to Solomonia, who entered this same convent whose churches had arisen a decade before in supplication for the birth of a son. (Not until his second marriage, to Elena Glinskaya, did Vasily finally gain a heir, Ivan IV, subsequently known as "the Terrible.") Solomonia was only one among many women of high position who were subsequently compelled to take the vows in this convent. Others included Anna Vasilchikova (one of Ivan the Terrible's wives) and Peter the Great's first wife, Evdokia Lopukhina.

A number of Suzdal's monasteries received significant patronage from members of the tsar's family, as well as from wealthy nobles and merchants. The larger ones initiated massive expansion, such as the great walled citadel and twelve towers of the Savior-St. Yevfimy Monastery in Suzdal, built in the 1660s. The monastery, founded in 1350, possessed over 10,000 serfs in the late seventeenth century, and may have attempted to imitate the Moscow Kremlin in its fortress design. Indeed, over the past three decades, both Russian and foreign film companies have used the red-brick walls of this monastery as a substitute for Moscow's fortress. The largest tower, 22 meters in height, provides an imposing entrance with its size and ornamental facade.

As the burial place of Prince Dmitri Pozharsky, who died in 1642, this monastery had the character of a secular shrine and was much used for purposes of state at the turn of the eighteenth century. The monastery's main church, dedicated to the Transfiguration of the Savior, took its present shape at the end of the sixteenth century, although it was subsequently modified many times. The bright, colorful frescoes that cover the interior were painted in 1689 by a group of masters from Kostroma. Alas, this monastery also has its macabre secrets. In the 1760s it was designated as a place of incarceration for "deranged criminals," a number of whom seem to have been only foolish enough to publicly express negative opinions about the autocratic regime. Records show that several of these unfortunates were held without trial for many years in the monastery isolation cells.

At present, Suzdal, with its colorful parish churches and monasteries, seems remote from these darker pages in its history. Yet large numbers of tourists continue to visit the quiet streets marked by ancient churches, as well as the popular open-air museum of wooden architecture, consisting of log structures brought from other regions and reassembled in a small "village." Whatever the artificial elements of Suzdal as a tourist complex, with its large hotel hidden from view, the town's distinctive monuments from a turbulent past deserve to be seen and enjoyed in their current peaceful setting.

December/January 1998

May the Steam Be With You
Nick Allen

Two dozen naked men, jostling and groaning as they are fanned with belching steam and lashed with clumps of leafy birch twigs, may not sound like a discovery of health, spirituality and inner calm. Yet the wise owls of the banya (steam bath, plural: bani) will tell you that this centuries-old ritual unlocks multitudinous secrets of physical and mental well-being, not to mention wide tracts of the Russian soul.

*E*ach week, hundreds of thousands of men and women retreat into the swirling steam of *banya* houses across Russia, from Moscow's marble-columned showpieces, to modest huts with log-fed stoves on country allotments from Kaliningrad to Kamchatka, intent on a purging experience that will see them through the trials of the coming days.

"Civilization is far away, you're in your little *banya*, the birch branches are flailing, the steam is gushing – it is a pure song of joy," said Alexander Burnyashev, an office manager who drives five hours on the weekend to his dacha cottage to escape the rat race in the capital.

As the winter months close in, *banya* season booms in the city. A few seasoned veterans agree to join this writer on a tour of the city's public steam baths. Armed with some basic know-how, a pair of flip-flops, and a felt hat to protect hair and ears from singing, I set out to plumb the nebulous depths of the *parilka* steam room and the Russian soul.

In the 1990s, more than half of Moscow's city-owned *bani* closed down; by 2003, only four of the remaining 33 were municipally-owned; the rest were privatized.

Our first port of call is to be the Seleznyovskiye *bani*, located near the Novoslobodskaya station on the metro ring line. It is supposed to be a leap right into the big league – these hallowed halls pride themselves on the city's hottest steam, coldest plunge pool and most dedicated following, led by Grisha "the executioner" (so nicknamed by foreign guests on account of his unusual *banya* attire).

Best laid plans. A friend calls on the eve of the visit and explains that Seleznyovskiye is temporarily closed, due to a business dispute. It is not the kind of *razborka* (settling of accounts) that led to the murder of one of the owners here a few years ago, but the bloodless variety to be settled in court.

"We'll meet instead tomorrow, at 10 AM, at Krasnopresnenskiye *bani*, by the steps where Otari Kvantrishvili was shot dead," he offers, referring to the Georgian boxer and reputed underworld boss whose days ended at this place of leisure in a 1994 sniper ambush.

Setting aside uncomfortable chapters of criminal history that shadow Moscow *banya* culture, it is typical rush hour the next morning, a Sunday, at this upscale facility near the 1905 metro station and White House government building. A stream of patrons in the male wing pays 600 rubles ($20) for two hours of steaming, plunge pool diving, and the socializing and moments of private reflection that round out the experience.

Flushed men sit in the six-seat changing cabins drinking tea and beer, and snacking on pickled garlic or heaps of shrimps from the café between forays into the *parilka* steam room. The daily tensions of chilly Moscow are left outside and the air hums with chatter and laughter, as friends and colleagues discuss business, families, lovers and car repairs.

"*Na par!*" ("To the steam!") echoes across the room. The *parilka* cleaning ritual has been finished and fresh steam has been prepared. The *parilka* was swept clean of leaves and aired by opening a ventilation window, to reduce humidity. Then water, often mixed with aromatic oils or even beer, is bucketed onto tons of red-hot blocks of pig iron, heaped inside the gas-fired oven.

At this stage, the temperature can soar to 43° C (110° F) and humidity up to 90 percent. The secret of good steam is finding the right balance between the heat and humidity, where the air is moist enough to draw a good sweat, but dry enough to provide a penetrating warmth. This combination is what sets the Russian *banya* apart from the dryer Finnish sauna or the milder Turkish steam bath. Oil extracts from mint, pine tree or eucalyptus are thrown onto the wooden walls to evaporate, and the clients are summoned.

A small stampede ensues, with patrons squeezing through the *parilka* door and into the shimmering haze beyond. The blanket of heat is filled with masochistic promise. Barely have you found a seat on one of the crowded wooden decks inside this four-by-eight meter box (the higher you go, the hotter it gets), than you start to ooze sweat. The toxins absorbed over the last week are relentlessly drawn out through your pores.

A reverent silence falls on the room as the new steam descends. Chatting is frowned upon at this stage of the process. The men bow their hatted heads and sweat.

When the scalding onslaught abates, the *parilka* starts to buzz with conversation and the thrashing noises of the *veniki* – tied clumps of birch, oak, eucalyptus or prickly juniper branches which are whacked about the torso and limbs. Novices find this a startling part of the ceremony; veterans will tell you that it stimulates circulation, removes dead skin and has a mildly antiseptic effect, along with other skin-toning benefits.

"The *venik* gives its healing power to your body – basically it is a massage instrument," said Igor Yevdokimov, a specialized *venik* maker from the Vladimir region. Yevdokimov believes that a higher calling led him to spend his days binding twigs and shoots, crooning to them lovingly as a gardener would converse with his plants.

With the first sortie into the *parilka* completed, you duck under a cold shower or take a dip in the plunge pool, large enough at the Krasnopresnenskiye for a quick swim before you climb out, either to repeat the whole process, or to retreat to your cabin for a break.

WHICHEVER OF MOSCOW'S public steam houses you visit, you will generally find yourself among an unpresuming and welcoming – or at least non-interfering – community. As the expression has it, "there are no generals in the *banya*," meaning no one is likely to bother you and start barking instructions.

But it is not an exclusively Russian pursuit – foreign visitors soon succumb to its power.

"I continue to go, because the *banya* seems to reach me in body and soul. It is like exercise in that it strengthens me, especially my internal organs, and I sweat the impurities out of my body," said Bryon MacWilliam, an American writer who has seldom skipped his weekly sessions in Moscow over the past seven years.

"As for the soul," MacWilliam said, "conversations in the *banya* tend to be more sincere, the exchange more real, and people tend to be kinder, less aggressive – I'm just happy."

The practice has also stood the test of time. For centuries, the *banya* was an integral part of Slavic pagan rites of birth, marriage and death (as well as simple hygiene). One of the earliest recorded descriptions is found in the Russian Primary Chronicle of 1113, where the apostle Andreas tells of fascinating rituals he witnessed at wooden bathhouses as he journeyed up the river Dnepr, deep into Slav lands:

> They warm them to extreme heat, then undress, and, after anointing themselves with tallow, take young reeds and lash their bodies.
>
> They lash themselves so violently that they barely escape alive. Then they drench themselves with cold water and thus are revived. They think nothing of doing this every day and actually inflict such torture upon themselves voluntarily.

The process has changed little in 900 years, apart from the omission of tallow and the fact that it involves rather less ferocity than Andreas described. The *banya* has latched on to some part of the Russian soul and will not let go. Tellingly, there is a quote attributed to the poet Alexander Pushkin, who, reputedly enthusing about its rejuvenating and warming effects after a long journey, once described the *banya* as a Russian's "second mother."

As MAY BE deduced from some of the stories, *banya* culture has its share of shady and criminal associations. Traditionally, deals are celebrated here, alliances are consolidated, enmities bridged and spheres of influence divided amidst the unifying steam, often in the seclusion of the smaller private *banya* complexes that some facilities offer.

Visit the famous Sandunovskiye *bani* ("Sanduny") off Neglinnaya ulitsa, behind the Bolshoi theater, and you will observe a large number of top-of-the-range black Mercedes. Visitors to Moscow will generally be referred to Sandunovskiye for their first taste of Russian steam. For 800 rubles, you can languish amidst the nineteenth century décor and bathe in a marble pillared pool area. There are private cabins, but, between steamings, patrons mainly sit on long benches under ornate ceilings with antiquated saloon lighting.

The Sandunovskiye *parilka* is much like that of other well-rated *bani*, with a loyal clientele who take pride in their *banya* home. A Chechen businessman sits with his eight-year-old son Hussein, who was gently introduced to the custom at an early age. "Dad first brought me here to cure a cold," Hussein said, "now I always come with him."

At most any *banya*, it is not uncommon to see children as young as four scampering around the lower *parilka* levels.

Hussein's father hears I have not yet tried the individual *venik* treatment offered as an extra by the "*banshchik*" staff attendants. He promptly asks duty *banshchik* Yura to initiate me as his guest.

I am told to lay on the upper bench as Yura throws a half tub of water into the oven. Having topped up the steam, he sets to work on me with two birch branches – thwacka thwacka thwacka – settling into a smooth but firm alternating rhythm up and down my body, front then back. He also uses the *veniki* as paddles to keep me cocooned in a cloud of near-scalding steam.

After a couple of minutes, I start to balk at the heat, so Yura sends me for a dip in a large wooden tub of 4° C water. The biting cold knocks the wind from me. "Stay under for 30 seconds," Yura admonishes, "then sit in the *parilka* for five more minutes and you'll notice the difference."

As I emerge from the tub, my skin starts to prickle, as if electrified. I duck back into the *parilka* as instructed, then finish the session with a swim under the columns and statues in the pool room.

As they leave the *banya*, glowing guests are offered the traditional farewell: "*s lyogkim parom*," which, loosely translated, means "may the steam be with you."

Despite the luxury of the Sanduny, there is no difference between the procedure here and elsewhere, just different packaging and prices. In the male wing of the *banya*, at least, it is the expurgation of aches and stress and the social bonding that matters most.

"It is in the blood of every Russian man to like the *banya*, vodka, women and black bread," grins financier Andrei, when asked why he goes.

The women's *banya*, it seems, is a different matter. One occasional visitor described it as "a lot less gregarious [than the men's side], kind of closed in on itself, silent, almost a Zen affair – if it weren't for all the cosmetics lying around."

A regular, 25-year-old interpreter Maria Golubyeva, finally settled on the Seleznyovskiye *bani* for her sessions after some unsatisfactory visits elsewhere, most memorably to the female wing of the Krasnopresnenskiye.

"The women there were walking around in expensive high heels, drinking expensive tea," she recalled. "It was not exactly a fashion show, but they were certainly showing off to each other. Me and my American friend obviously did not fit in and were just ignored."

The women's section generally tends to be a little stricter on protocol: all talking is frowned upon in the *parilka*. Use of *veniki* is discouraged and not popular anyway, as they are hard on delicate skin. Many of the women prefer instead to smooth on honey while in the *parilka*, a process said to work wonders for the skin and nerve cells.

In the washing and changing area, they busy themselves with facial masks, scrub treatments and other synthetic and natural products, including a hair care shampooing treatment using a mix of oats and *kefir*-soured milk. Tips and advice are traded freely. "Most people know each other and the women's side is normally really nice," Golubyeva said.

MALE OR FEMALE, there comes a point when every *banya*-goer feels ready to graduate to more advanced individual paraphernalia, such as a slatted wooden *parilka* seat, or a more striking "*kolpak*" felt hat.

A trip to a *Banya* trade fair at Moscow's VDNKh Exhibition Park covers all the bases. The annual event draws *banya* devotees and manufacturers of the full range of accessories: gloves to avoid palm blisters during frantic *venik* sessions, aromatherapy lotions, numerous varieties of honey, deluxe *banya* units the size of railway sleeper compartments (self-contained with shower and heated marble seats; hermetically sealed for installation in private apartments, starting at $15,000).

Near to VDNKh is the next point on our *banya* city tour: Astrakhanskiye *bani*. It is one of Moscow's plainer *bani*, at 170 rubles a session. The *parilka* here is about the same size as the Krasnopresnenskiye or Sanduny, but is claustrophobic, with more than 40 people packed in the chamber when the steam is fresh.

The premises are battered yet functional, reminding that the *banya* is first of all a place to get clean. Astrakhanskiye is one of the few *bani* in Moscow where the plunge pool is mildly chlorinated.

THE NEXT WEEK leads to the Varshavskiye *bani* in southern Moscow, for the Monday night coed session, which costs 250 rubles for two and a half hours.

Many of the patrons are hard-core naturists who, after 1991, embraced new freedoms to share their love of the *banya* in communal sessions.

"I come not just for the naturist element," said Igor, a 49-year-old engineer. "The mixed *banya* is simply more relaxed."

As in the separate male and female wings elsewhere, peculiarities of each naked body are of little consequence here. Beer bellies and sagging breasts are wholly irrelevant. The only thing that matters is a shared zeal for good steam and a chance to relax. The gathering is entirely free from sexual connotations.

"Aaah, cleansing through atonement," pants one guest as he clambers into the heavy veil of heat on the top deck. Alexander, a 55-year-old accountant, is visibly relieved at the satisfied reaction. This is one of his first sessions as a trainee *banshchik* and Olga, a regular with 25 years of *banya* experience, instructs him how to air the room and make fresh steam.

"You should clean that up," she said, pointing at a pool of sweat on the upper deck. "Otherwise when people stand up here they inhale the steam and microbes it gives off – not everyone may be healthy in the *banya*."

Left to carry on, Alexander admits there's an overwhelming amount to take in. "You have to do this 15 or 20 times to know everything," he said, his brow furrowed with concentration as he flips ladles of water through the oven door into the red inferno, careful to avoid spillage on the outside brickwork, which would give off an unwelcome smell of burned stone. *"Na par!"* he calls timidly, and in they rush.

ONE CANNOT HELP wondering at the health effects of such sudden hot-cold climactic changes on the body. *Banshchik* Yura of the Sanduny recalls a few cases where people collapsed with heart problems in the steam room and needed ambulance treatment.

"But it was usually because they drank too much alcohol," he said. "You shouldn't drink in the *banya*."

At no *banya* visited did the staff admit to any fatalities, at least not from heart attacks. Kvantrishvili's assassination at *Bani na Presne* is a different matter. The older *banshchiki* recall the incident but shift awkwardly, cast their eyes downward and mumble something about "the mafia."

The specialized newspaper *Russkaya Banya* promotes the policy of everything in moderation for a healthy experience, and is adamant about the positive benefits of the hot-cold contrast and the massaging properties of the *venik*.

"It is medically proven that the effects of generous steam have a benevolent impact on the cardiovascular system. The invigorating surge of oxygen through capillaries to the nerve cells expels harmful substances and residues."

But the paper also notes that sweating and thermo-regulatory reactions apply extra strain on the body, so the pastime is not recommended for people with heart conditions or pregnant women.

Overindulgence can be harmful. Nikolai, a 30-year-old *banshchik* at the Krasnopresnenskiye, spends two days on, two days off, working long shifts tending the oven and earning extra money administering *veniki* workouts. Prolonged exposure to the steam is taking a toll on his body, he said, requiring him to undergo treatment for heat-damaged tendons and generally depriving him of the pleasure he used to get at the *bani*. "But what can I do?" he said. "I have a family to feed."

THE LAST STOP on our *banya* tour is Seleznyovskiye, which has finally re-opened. The price has recently risen, but all is forgiven in that first dash into the legendary steam. And, of course, there is Grisha "the executioner," a 43-year-old carpenter and regular Sunday visitor who worked here as an administrator in the 1980s.

Grisha's fame stems from his untiring, expert production of steam. There may not be any generals in the *banya*, but in the male wing there can be squabbles over how to tend the oven – just watch a group of men making a camp fire together and you'll understand.

"*Na par!*" Grisha calls out. The *parilka* fills up instantly and, for protection, Grisha dons a black hood with eyeholes (whence his nickname) before he ascends to the upper deck, where he uses a large paddle to fan gusts of scalding steam onto rows of pleasurably tormented patrons. After five minutes of groaning, the recipients salute his labors with a ripple of applause and grateful "*spasibos.*"

The plunge pool in winter seems barely warmer than the cold tub at the Sanduny. Remembering Yura's tip, I force myself to stay in longer than common sense dictates and my nerves scream their predictable response. Then I scramble out, feel the electricity, and know what it is to be alive.

January/February 2004

The Battle on the Ice
Tamara Eidelman

One of the most famous battles in Russian history took place on April 5, 1242. On the frozen surface of Lake Chudskoe (a large body of water between Russia and present-day Estonia, called Lake Peipus by Estonians) the Novgorodians soundly defeated the forces of a Livonian knightly order that was attempting to extend its influence into Rus. A young prince by the name of Alexander led the Novgorodian forces. Two years earlier, this prince had been given the surname Nevsky, after he defeated the Swedes on the banks of the Neva River. At the time, no one would have guessed that this young, energetic, clever, and ferocious knight would become one of the best-known figures in Russian history.

Even during his lifetime, Nevsky enjoyed great renown. At a time when Rus had suffered one defeat after another by the Mongol Horde, someone who had defeated first the Swedes and then the Livonians was bound to garner great respect. Furthermore, Alexander, who became a Grand Prince in 1252, was able to establish good relations with the Horde, and that immediately gave him great authority in the eyes of his subjects.

After Nevsky's death, the church lost no time extolling the achievements of the prince who died having "performed great labors for the Russian land, for Novgorod and for Pskov, throughout his reign giving his life for the True Faith." Soon he was declared a saint in the Orthodox Church.

It became a tradition for Russian princes and tsars to consider him their patron, to see in him a model protector of country and faith. The whims of fate allowed Nevsky's popularity to endure after the 1917 Revolution as well, despite the fact that, during the first post-revolutionary years, any monarch was automatically anathema to the new authorities.

Ten years later, however, Stalin's iron-fisted hold on power demanded a new ideological basis, and in the 1930s there was a gradual turn toward old imperial values. Officially, of course, nothing had changed. The revolutionary phrases, the communist ideology were still obligatory. But

TRANSLATION: NORA FAVOROV

there were a few rulers from Russian history who could now be mentioned without invective.

Stalin suddenly needed not only revolutionary firebrands as national heroes, but rulers who consolidated their power by any means – that was what attracted him to Peter the Great and Ivan the Terrible. But there was another subtle shift in ideology. Internationalism and the idea of world revolution was relegated to the shadows, but Russian patriotism and the military exploits of princes who had throttled foreign enemies were brought to the forefront.

In essence, what appealed to Stalin about Alexander Nevsky was the same thing that had appealed to the bishops of the Orthodox Church many centuries ago. They had liked that this prince had halted the advance of a Catholic order into Russia and had refused to unite with the Pope in the struggle against the Mongols. For this they forgave him his cruelty to the Novgorodians, whom he forced to submit to the Mongols and to pay them tribute.

No one remembered how Nevsky had ingratiated himself before the khans of the Horde and how he had invited punitive detachments into Rus and, motivated by a desperate thirst for power, pitted them against his own brother. It was Nevsky who did not allow the unification of those princes who had attempted to continue their struggle against the Horde. At his request, troops led by the "Tsarevich" Nevryui [a Mongol prince] were sent into Rus, nipping resistance in the bud and destroying the enemies of Prince Alexander.

All this was inconsequential, barely notable in comparison with the great deed – the crushing of the Livonian Order on Lake Chudskoe.

In the 1930s, Nevsky turned out to be useful to Stalin. This prince had stopped the Livonians, and, as Fascism grew in Germany, citizens of the USSR were reminded that the members of the Livonian Order were German.

Nevsky had not been able to establish good relations with the Novgorodians. The freedom-loving, self-governing townspeople had thrown out the prince – he was too eager to interfere in their business. This, despite the fact that Alexander had saved the city from Swedish invasion. Two years later, the tables were turned, and the townspeople had to bow down before Alexander with a plea that he defend them against the Livonians. On Lake Chudskoe, Alexander clearly demonstrated that the

interests of Novgorod were of little concern to him. He positioned the
Novgorod militia at the center of his battle formation – lightly-armed foot
soldiers, flanked by his cohort. The wedge-like formation with which the
Livonians attacked – the renowned "pig's snout" – hit the Novgorodians
hard, and they began to retreat with losses. At that point, the Prince's
men attacked from the flank. It was an ingenious military move, said
some. Others responded that Nevsky had just wanted to put the despised
Novgorodians in harm's way, rather than his own men.

Fifteen years later, Alexander again came to Novgorod with his cohort
in order to force the townspeople to submit to a census being conducted
by the Mongols. Everyone understood that a merciless collection of an
exorbitant tribute would follow the census, and they were prepared to resist.
Nevsky applied force, executing the most intractable *boyars* and cutting off
the noses and ears of others. The free city was forced to bow down before
the Horde. A desire for peace in Rus, said some. An effort to break a free
city, responded others.

In the standoff between the ruthless prince and the independent
city, Stalin's sympathies naturally were with the prince. The cult of the
commander-defender was restored. Sergei Eisenstein's 1938 film put
the finishing touches on Nevsky's rehabilitation. In it, the marvelously
handsome Nikolai Cherkasov (who also later played the lead in Eisenstein's
Ivan the Terrible) sallies forth to smash the Fascist, or rather the Livonian
forces (it was hard to tell), outfitted in an embroidered white shirt and
under the admiring gaze of the simple folk.

No historian can shatter the myths created by a cinematographer.
However many attempts are made now to knock Nevsky from his pedestal,
to show the contradictions in his personality, the cruelty and deception
of his policies, or at least to question whether or not Nevsky's actions
represented the only correct course for the time, they are all thwarted by
the fine figure of Cherkasov on the ice of Lake Chudskoe.

Perhaps people are comforted by the thought that Rus once had a
remarkable, noble, and brave defender. But it is difficult to understand
why – among the many rulers Russia has had – they choose to extol and
adore one who beat some neighboring powers and ingratiated himself with
others. The battle on Lake Chudskoe, it appears, was greatly exaggerated by
generations of chroniclers and historians. It was just one of many clashes in
the struggle for influence in the Baltic region between princes of Northern

Rus and the Livonian Order. But then there is one difference: the music of Prokofiev, which swells as we hear Cherkasov triumphantly pronounce, "He who comes to Rus with a sword, will die by the sword."

March/April 2006

Alexander Nevsky is a very ambiguous and complex historical figure, revered by the church, endlessly investigated by historians, and relentlessly exploited by politicians. Greater detail on the debate surrounding Nevsky and his role in Russian history can be found in a course of lectures by the excellent historian Igor Danilevsky, "The Russian Land through the Eyes of Contemporaries and their Offspring (12-14th Centuries)," published in 2000 in Moscow (in Russian only, unfortunately).

The Tver Uprising
Tamara Eidelman

*T*he rebellion against the Mongol Horde that took place in Tver in 1327 is one of the landmark events of Russian history. In the fall of that year, a delegation of *baskaks* (tribute collectors) headed by a Horde magnate named Cholkhan arrived in the city. At the time, Tver was one of the richest and most powerful cities in Rus, and its history up to this point very much resembled that of Moscow – its neighbor and rival.

Before the Mongol invasion (1237-1240), neither Tver nor Moscow was particularly prominent. When the forces of Batu Khan swept over the lands of Rus, its richest cities – Vladimir, Suzdal, and Kiev – bore the main brunt of the invasion. Moscow and Tver suffered, but to a lesser extent. Later, when Rus had become a vassal of the Khans, no one paid much attention to these minor towns. This allowed the principalities at the center of Rus to come into their own.

These towns saw a growth in commerce and a resurgence of stone construction, and, during the first decades of the fourteenth century, both Moscow and Tver expanded and grew richer. Alas, this mutual growth had unfortunate consequences. The two powerful principalities were located quite close to one another and the princes of Moscow and Tver became mired in protracted and destructive conflict. This conflict involved mutual affronts, military clashes, and, of course, competition for allies.

Before long, a rather curious alignment of forces took shape. Rus' mighty neighbor, the Great Lithuanian Principality, which had many ties to the principalities of Rus and was growing stronger by the day, became Tver's main ally. In the fourteenth century, Lithuania, which was led by strong and energetic princes with forces that had been hardened in battle with Livonian knights, was in the ascendant. The Lithuanian Principality was not under Mongol domination, and many Russian lands were happy to submit themselves to Vilnius to avoid paying tribute to the Horde.

TRANSLATION: NORA FAVOROV

As hard as it may be to believe in this day and age, in fourteenth-century Lithuania state documents were written in Russian. Furthermore, Lithuanian princes were happy to intermarry with the princely families of Russia. In those days, they calmly turned a blind eye to the religious differences between the two nations – the Lithuanians were still pagans and for them, one religion was as good as the next.

During the 1320s, Tver and Lithuania were bound by extensive commercial, military and family ties. The princes of Moscow, however, had supporters that were every bit as powerful. Moscow's Prince Yuri Danilovich exhibited exceptional diplomatic abilities. In fact, he so overwhelmed the Horde's Khan Ozbeg with gifts and charm that he was offered the Khan's sister Konchaka in marriage. Prince Yuri lost no time taking advantage of his new family ties, and with the help of one of the Horde magnates, launched a military campaign against Tver. His forces, however, were defeated and his wife was taken prisoner. She soon died in captivity.

It is not clear what benefited Yuri more – his marriage or his wife's death. In any event, he immediately accused Prince Mikhail of Tver of poisoning the Khan's sister. This did not end well for anyone involved. Mikhail of Tver was brutally executed by the Horde. Several years later, his son and heir Dmitry ran into the Prince of Moscow while visiting Sarai (the seat of the Horde) to show his respects to the Khan. Dmitry did not resist the urge to cut down Yuri, whom he saw to be his father's killer. Dmitry also never made it home. He was executed for daring to raise his sword in the Khan's presence.

As a result, in 1325 both principalities wound up with new rulers. In Moscow, Yuri's brother, Ivan Danilovich (who would later come to be known as Ivan Kalita), took the throne. In Tver, Dmitry was succeeded by his brother, Alexander Mikhailovich. Two years after the tragic deaths of the two rulers, everything was calm, but the aforementioned arrival of the *baskaks* in Tver in 1327 stirred up old animosities.

Those who traveled to each principality to collect tribute naturally expected assistance from the local prince. It was in the princes' interest to ensure that the money, livestock, and people required by the Horde were collected as quickly as possible. Throughout the collection process, the *baskaks* lived in the prince's palace and were entertained at the prince's expense. In this instance, the collections proceeded smoothly until

Cholkhan's men tried to take a cow from a local sacristan, who called on other locals for help.

This is how the rebellion started, and at first Alexander tried to reason with his subjects. Once it became clear that he would not succeed, he decided to join them, although he certainly knew that the Khan's rage would fall on him personally. He supported the rebels and even advised them to burn down his own chambers, where the Mongols had sought shelter. When it was all over, there was nothing to do but await the retribution that was sure to come. It came, however, from an unexpected quarter: Moscow.

Ivan Kalita had decided to use the uprising as a pretext for wreaking vengeance on his rival. Tver was defeated and Alexander fled to Pskov, but Kalita pursued him there as well. Moscow's army besieged Pskov and demanded that the fugitive be handed over. The Pskovians refused. At this point, Kalita sent Moscow's Metropolitan in under the city walls with a threat that the entire population would be excommunicated. Not wishing to endanger his supporters, Alexander fled once again, this time all the way to Lithuania, where he remained for several years, until he managed to obtain a pardon from the Khan that enabled him to return to Tver. But it was not his fate to die of old age. Kalita could not leave his neighbor in peace. He convinced the Khan that the Prince of Tver was again fomenting rebellion. Alexander was summoned to Sarai and executed.

After these sad events, Tver still managed to maintain its standing for a time, in part thanks to the fact that Lithuania's Prince Algirdas – one of its most renowned rulers – was married to a princess of Tver. But within a few decades Tver was forced to accept the role of "younger brother" to its rival Moscow, in other words, its vassal.

And what about Moscow? In sharp contrast to Tver, Moscow's power and prestige were on the rise. Ivan Kalita had won the confidence of his Mongol patrons, who charged him with collecting tribute not only from Moscow's own lands, but from the other principalities as well. This laid the foundation for Moscow's initial wealth. Ivan Danilovich's epithet – Kalita, or "money bags" – was well deserved; there is evidence to suggest that some of the tribute he collected never made it into the Horde's coffers. For this, centuries of Russian historians have sung his praises. And deservedly so: he not only orchestrated Moscow's ascendance and Tver's decline, but he bestowed several decades of peace on Rus, as the Horde stopped coming to collect tribute itself. Whether Rus found it any more pleasant dealing with Muscovite tax collectors than Mongol ones is another question.

But it is worthwhile reflecting on the following question: just who did more to bring peace to Rus – Ivan or Alexander? It was the Tver uprising that led the khans to decide they wanted nothing more to do with strife in Rus. The Golden Horde was having troubles of its own and was beginning a period of fraction, feuding, and conflict. It was much simpler to assign the obedient Prince of Moscow the task of collecting tribute than to deal with potential rebellion. Who should take credit for this – the pliant Kalita or the brave Alexander? Historians are unanimous in their exaltation of Kalita. All we can do is repeat the words of poet Naum Korzhavin:

> *Your face was repulsive*
> *Your character low*
> *But in hindsight progressive*
> *Were the seeds you did sow.*

November/December 2007

Kremlin Ghosts
Tamara Eidelman

*C*ould anything be more ordinary than the Moscow Kremlin?

We Muscovites have lived alongside our Kremlin for so long that it is difficult to remember when we first saw these massive red walls, when we first heard the mysterious names of its towers, when we first tried to imagine what the Tsar-Bell would have looked like in the bell-tower, or what the firing of the Tsar-Cannon would have sounded like. Later in our lives, the cupolas of the Kremlin cathedrals fixed themselves in our memories, along with the chimes of Spassky Tower, whose clanging became associated with the clinking of champagne glasses, and with Red Square, where everyone has strolled at least once ...

Yet, if you look more closely, you can see an entirely different Kremlin, one which is gone forever, but which cannot leave, because its ghosts are too tightly bound to this place.

THE GROUND ON which the Kremlin stands guards many secrets. We should not rush to learn them too quickly, but should submerge ourselves slowly. Perhaps it is best, therefore, to begin by circling the Kremlin walls from the outside. Walking beneath these majestic red walls, a whole world begins to unfold before you.

You begin to understand why this particular place was selected a millennia and a half ago (or more) by the first inhabitants, people who had no inkling that, many centuries into the future, they would be known as Muscovites. Their shadows are faded now: they did not leave behind any chronicles, legends or memoirs. But we can certainly grasp what drew them to this high hill on the banks of a river. Being close to a river meant life, and one dared not distance oneself for very long. Yet one also had to settle on a high riverbank to avoid the spring snowmelts. Back then, they were even bigger than today's and could easily lead to catastrophe – a settlement on a low-lying riverbank could be simply swept away.

We don't know exactly when the river began to be called the Moskva ("Moscow"), and we don't even know what this word means. Its root – "va" – means water in the Finnish tongue, so it is most likely that the earliest settlers were Ugro-Finns.

One can also deduce that living on a hill conferred another advantage – there was an excellent view from here, meaning it was easy to see approaching boats from a long way off, the better to prepare for meeting both friends and enemies.

Walking around outside the Kremlin walls, we stop in front of Borovitsky Tower, not far from the Moscow river. We feel the faint breath of the past, and it is easy to imagine how, where there is now a loud and busy street, there once grew a thick forest ("*bor*" in Russian), from which this tower took its name. The earliest residents of the Kremlin hill lived surrounded by this forest, and only a few wooden remnants of the settlement are still with us today. The discoveries of archaeologists working on Manezh Square and in the Historic Passage have made this place a paradise for diggers of the past. But, alas, this paradise is almost completely lost: much that is ancient – including ancient timbers from the once ubiquitous *bor* – is securely entombed under newer construction.

As we gaze at the river, the phantoms of a later era arise. As late as the nineteenth century, the Neglinka river (now channeled underground) still flowed where today's Alexander Gardens are laid. And a water-filled moat stretched along the Kremlin wall in front of Red Square, connecting the Neglinka and Moscow rivers. Therefore, if we walk through Alexander Gardens to Kutafya Tower and enter the Kremlin through the gate here, we can imagine how, at one time, the people of this hill lived on an island, accessible only by bridge.

But the Kremlin did not immediately become an island. We know that its wooden fortifications were raised in the twelfth century, perhaps even earlier. Yet we also know how easy it was to breach them, mainly because they were redone and reconstructed many times. At first the walls were oaken. Then, in the fourteenth century, under Prince Dmitry Donskoy, they were of limestone, which became the trump card in Moscow's battle for supremacy with Vilnius, capital of the great principality of Lithuania.

No matter how strange it seems today, in the fourteenth century, Lithuania was a state closely connected with the Russian land. It was even called "The Great Principality of Russians and Lithuanians," and a large portion of its residents spoke Russian. The Vilnius court had close family ties to the rulers of the Russian lands. In the 1360s and 1370s the powerful Lithuanian ruler Olgerd could rightly stake a claim to being the unifier of Rus – he was married to a princess from Tver; his troops defeated the Mongol Horde at Siniye Vody; he had vast territory under his control, populated with Orthodox Slavs who spoke in Russian dialects.

The white walls of the Kremlin, erected in 1366-67, were the main obstacle keeping Vilnius from becoming the capital of Rus. Lithuanian troops marched on Moscow three times, and three times they failed to take it, because they did not have the power to storm the stone fortress. The furious Olgerd ordered the scorching of the *posad* – the trading settlement surrounding the Kremlin. But the fortress did not surrender.

Only at the end of the fifteenth century did the walls we see today appear. They were built by Italian masters, so that today, when Russian tourists visit Bologna, they are often shocked to see buildings which remind them of their familiar Kremlin. Yet before the end of the fifteenth century, these walls were much more severe looking. Only in the seventeenth century were the walls decorated with elegant caps, turning the walls from fearsome military fortifications into something more typical of a fairy-tale castle.

The walls conceal their fair share of history and secrets. If one believes the legends, there are countless empty spaces and secret passages in them, which archaeologists say are quite difficult to find. There are even those who still hope to find here the priceless lost library of Ivan the Terrible.

The library of Ivan the Terrible was actually created by Ivan's grandfather, Ivan III (1462-1505). His second wife was Sofia Palaeologue, a cousin of the last Byzantine emperor, who brought to Moscow the library of her ancestors. Its contents are more or less known: it included the most valuable books of the ancient and medieval worlds, many of which are known today in name only. This library is absolutely priceless, but remains undiscovered to this day. It is known that, in the sixteenth century, Ivan the Terrible read many of these books. But what happened to them subsequently is a mystery. There are several places where this library could be hidden. One of them is the Kremlin.

If we bid farewell to this phantom forest and fortifications, then other shadows rise before us. Cathedral (*Sobornaya*) Square is the heart of the Kremlin, but what we see here is only the tip of a huge iceberg.

Prince Ivan Kalita, who, in the fourteenth century made Moscow wealthy and strong, began construction on the first Assumption (*Uspensky*) Cathedral, in the same place where the current masterpiece of Aristotle Fioravanti stands. The original cathedral, which collapsed in an earthquake at the end of the fifteenth century, held huge ideological significance. It was very important for Kalita to show that Moscow was the most important city in Rus. So he built a cathedral with the same name as the main cathedral in Vladimir, the town with which Moscow was vying for supremacy.

> *Ivan Kalita (1325-1340) was a famous Moscow prince. He is associated with Moscow's rise to primacy, because he attained the trust of the Mongol Khan and was granted the authority to collect tribute from all of Rus. Thus, the tax-collecting prince was also able to enrich himself, which is how he got his nickname – "Kalita" – which means "moneybag." The proceeds from his collection of tribute allowed Ivan Kalita to begin construction of stone buildings in Moscow, which was important for increasing the prestige of the princedom and for strengthening relations with the Orthodox Church, whose support was vital at that time.*

But the construction of this cathedral was not important only to Kalita. Metropolitan Peter – then the head of the Orthodox Church – shared his interest. Peter's formal residence was Vladimir, but he really had no desire to live in this decaying city, which had been overrun by the Mongols. Several cities vied to become the Metropolitan's new home, and Moscow was victorious in large part because of its construction of Assumption Cathedral. But just as the cathedral was nearing completion, the Metropolitan died. He was entombed in the cathedral and his grave became a site of pilgrimage for believers from all over Rus, in the process raising Moscow's position and esteem. The first cathedral no longer stands, but, just to the right of the altar in the current Assumption Cathedral, one can still see the modest tomb of Metropolitan Peter.

Fioravanti, the architect of Assumption Cathedral, was Italian, and he wanted to build a Renaissance cathedral in Moscow. But Ivan III had no interest in innovations from abroad. For him, like for Kalita a century and a half before, it was more important to underscore the primacy of Moscow over all other Russian cities. Fioravanti was therefore sent to Vladimir, that he might be inspired by that city's Assumption Cathedral. The Moscow cathedral we see today therefore recalls its twelfth century Vladimir predecessor in many respects. This knock-off is an example of ideological propaganda, fixed in stone.

The Kremlin's Assumption Cathedral has always been considered the religious center of Russia. If you look and listen carefully here, you will see and hear the rustling of ghosts from many centuries gone by. For over half a millennium, all of Russia's rulers were crowned in this cathedral, even during the period when they had to come here from St. Petersburg. We can imagine the young Tsar Peter (the future Peter I) in the square before the cathedral with his half-sister Sofia, who had the courage (or perhaps the arrogance) to publicly address the people here and entreat them to save her from her malicious relatives. It was an unusual thing in Russia at the end of the seventeenth century; an unmarried woman was not allowed to leave her *terem* (chamber).

> *Peter I (1682-1725) succeeded to the throne after his half-brother Fyodor. But, in 1682, Peter was just 10 and too young to formally assume the throne. As a result, a battle over the throne ensued between the relatives of his father's first wife (the Miloslavskys) and relatives of his mother (the Naryshkins). The battle turned bloody and finally a compromise was reached to jointly crown Peter and his half-brother Ivan. But, in reality, power was in the hands of Peter's energetic and strong-willed half-sister and regent, Sofia. In the Kremlin museum today, you can see the two-seated throne of Peter and Ivan, which had a hidden window, through which Sofia, hidden behind the throne, could proffer advice to her two young charges. Later, when Peter I had grown and taken power into his own hands, he banished Sofia to Novodevichy Monastery for the rest of her life, after she failed in a coup attempt while Peter was out of Moscow.*

The former German princess Sofia-August Friedrich Anhalt-Herbst came here after her succession to the throne as Catherine II. For the empress, having overthrown and murdered her husband, Peter III, it was very important to show that she had been transformed from a German princess into a true Russian tsarina. Coronation in the heart of Russia, in Moscow's Assumption Cathedral, held a special significance. And it is no accident that, after her coronation, Catherine undertook a lengthy pilgrimage to various monasteries in the Moscow region, even walking to Trinity-Sergiev Lavra, the largest Orthodox monastery. What Catherine (who, not long after this, received the appellation of "the Great") dreamed up, she usually accomplished. Indeed, this German woman, who was miraculously extracted from an impoverished German principality, was accepted by all, even the simple folk, and her rule became one of the greatest not only of the eighteenth century, but of all Russian history.

It was here, in Assumption Cathedral, in 1894, that Nicholas II, the last Russian tsar, was crowned. He arrived here for a festive ceremony that was followed by what should have been a huge, celebratory public fête on Khodynskoye Field, but which turned into a horrific bloodbath costing hundreds of lives. Thus, the day of the last coronation became a bloody and dismal event, an omen of the Romanov dynasty's forthcoming tragic conclusion.

Alongside Assumption Cathedral is another architectural masterpiece – Archangel Cathedral, built by Alevisio Novi, another Italian architect. He was allowed a bit more creative freedom, and he succeeded in raising a building that brought together aspects of the Orthodox Church and a Renaissance palazzo. It may be that Novi was allowed to depart from general canons since this church carried less ideological significance – it was the "family tomb" of the Russian princes and tsars. Still, the legends and dramas of the past are palpable throughout this building.

It is easy to be overwhelmed by the many tombs crammed inside Archangel Cathedral. And there is much that could be told about each one of them. But we can give our attention to just a few.

To the right of the entrance, in the far corner, a person is entombed who you will not find on the list of Moscow's rulers. It is Prince Vladimir Andreyevich of Serpukhov. He was Dmitry Donskoy's cousin and fought alongside him on Kulikovo Field. As a young prince, Vladimir Andreyevich was put in charge of the Zasadny Regiment,[1] and, for almost the entire battle, had to impatiently wait for his moment to engage the enemy. Beside him was the experienced commander Bobrok-Volynets, who held the prince back until finally, just before nightfall, it was decided that the moment had arrived. The Zasadny regiment, with its fresh troops, struck the Mongols with a mighty blow, insuring the Russians' victory. Later, however, Dmitry Donskoy's relations with his brave and energetic relative deteriorated. The Moscow prince suspected that his cousin had his eye on ruling Moscow. This, however, did not keep Vladimir Andreyevich from being buried alongside his royal relatives.

....

1. Troops held in reserve for a sudden assault.

Dmitry Donskoy (1359-1389) is the Moscow prince whose name is associated with the rise of Moscow in the second half of the fourteenth century. He received his nickname – "Donskoy" – for his victory over Mamay Khan's troops at Kulikovo Field in 1380. Kulikovo Field is located at the place where the river Nepryadva flows into the river Don. It was the site of one of the largest battles in medieval Russia. The unified forces of the Russian princes demolished the Mongols. Two years later, however, Khan Tokhtamysh burned Moscow and re-established Mongol control over Rus. Yet the significance of the Kulikovo battle was still huge. After this battle, the authority of the Moscow principality rose sharply, strengthening the independence of its leaders from the Mongols.

Archangel Cathedral is the burial place of princes and tsars. But one emperor also lies here: the young Emperor Peter II, the spoiled youth who fate determined would last just three years on the throne. In 1730, at the age of 14, and on the day he was to be married in Moscow, he died of smallpox. Instead of his wedding, the Kremlin witnessed his burial.

In the very center of Archangel Cathedral are the relics of Prince Dmitry, which the Church has declared a martyred saint. For us, he is interesting as one of the most mysterious figures in Russian history. Prince Dmitry was the son of Ivan the Terrible and his last (seventh) wife, Maria Nagaya. After Ivan's death, his son Fyodor, from his first marriage, ascended to the throne; Dmitry and his mother were exiled to Uglich. Tsar Fyodor did not have any heirs, and his half-brother Dmitry was officially considered the next heir to the throne.

Tsar Fyodor was a weak, indecisive, devout, God-fearing man. Some accused him of having a weak mind, others thought that he was simply not interested in earthly, material things. He was completely absorbed by religious thoughts, conceding all of his powers to his brother-in-law, the energetic and intelligent Boris Godunov. The young Dmitry, however, apparently shared his severe father's disposition. He dreamed of getting out of Uglich, and, in the winter, made snowmen in the shape of the boyars whom he blamed for his confinement, then proceeded to chop their heads off.

In 1591, the 10-year-old prince died under mysterious circumstances. An investigative commission found that he had an epileptic fit and cut himself in the neck with a knife that he had been playing with. But soon rumors flew that the youth was stabbed by the all-powerful Godunov, who himself dreamed of taking over the throne. If we recall the history of this unlucky and lonely young boy, which fate chose to be the last of the Rurik dynasty, then here, standing by his remains, we can feel the powerful breath of history. The death of Prince Dmitry set in motion one of the most fascinating, but also one of the most horrible, periods in Russian history: the Time of Troubles.

> *The Time of Troubles (1598-1613): After the death of Ivan the Terrible in 1584 and of his son Fyodor in 1598, the Rurik dynasty (begun in 1462) came to an end. The tsarina's brother, Boris Godunov, was chosen for the throne. He was a wise, energetic and enterprising leader, and expended much effort to bring a normalcy back to Rus, which had been brought to ruin under Ivan the Terrible. But Godunov's rule turned into a succession of endless disasters. Rus was assaulted by a horrific famine, a fire destroyed half of Moscow, and there were countless revolts. In Poland, an imposter, the fugitive monk Grigory Otrepyev, asserted that he was the Prince Dmitry, son of Ivan the Terrible, miraculously saved from murderers sent to Uglich by Godunov.[2] He managed to attract thousands of serfs and Cossacks to his cause. He actually ruled Moscow for nearly a year, after which he was murdered as a result of a boyar conspiracy. During the Troubles in Moscow, elected tsars came and went, with the Cossacks playing an influential role. Polish troops attacked Russia, as the Polish King Vladislav also staked a claim to the Moscow throne. The Time of Troubles came to an end in 1613, with the selection of Mikhail Romanov as the new tsar.*

Fourteen years after the youth's death, his body was brought from Uglich and ceremoniously interred in Archangel Cathedral. Thus did Boris Godunov try to bring an end to the rumors of the miraculous survival of the prince. But Godunov died shortly thereafter.

Recalling Prince Dmitry, we immediately sense the shadow of another Kremlin ghost, Chudov Monastery, which for hundreds of years stood inside the Kremlin walls (opposite the Senate building). Indeed, Ivan the Terrible was angered by its elders, who, according to the tsar, instead of praying were actively involved in politics. It turns out that the tsar's suspicions were not misplaced. Just a few decades after his death, a fugitive

---

2. It is actually a disputed historical fact whether Otrepyev was the False Dmitry, though this version of events was that chosen by Pushkin and Mussorgsky in their influential artistic renditions.

monk from the monastery, Grigory Otrepyev, returned to the Kremlin in the guise of Tsar Dmitry Ivanovich, supposedly saved from murderers sent by Boris Godunov. Just over 300 years after the False Dmitry's death, the monastery itself died. Under orders from the new Bolshevik government, it was torn down brick by brick.

Alongside the two grandiose cathedrals are Annunciation Cathedral – the private chapel of the Russian tsars, and the Faceted Palace – the place for luxurious diplomatic receptions and celebrations. And here another ghost rises before us, that of Ivan the Terrible himself. It turns out the tsar was not allowed to enter the family cathedral – not because of the blood he spilled across Russia, but because of his many marriages. And so a special addition was attached to Annunciation, so that the tsar could "attend" the services there.

There are also the ghosts of the foreign ambassadors, scurrying to a reception with the tsar in the Faceted Palace and looking out with wonder on the cupolas of the cathedrals. Some ambassadors were convinced that the cupolas were made of solid gold, even though they were simply covered in a thin gold leaf.

And nearby are more and more shadows, of tsars and tsarinas, of rebels and imposters, builders and monks ...

The Kremlin itself barely escaped becoming a ghost. At the end of the eighteenth century, the architect Vasily Bazhenov was so carried away by his plans for the new Senate building that he decided to destroy the Kremlin cathedrals. It is not clear what we should thank for their salvation – the wisdom and caution of Empress Catherine II or simply her dislike of Bazhenov, whom she suspected of dangerous masonic ties. Just over two centuries later, a similarly unlikely miracle saved St. Basil's Cathedral, which stands on the other side of the Kremlin walls. Stalin wanted to destroy it to make it easier for tanks to pass through Red Square; only the courage of preservationist Peter Baranovsky saved it.

Near St. Basil's, another phantom rises before us, one from a less distant age, from the time when Lenin and other top communists lived in the Kremlin, when the two-headed eagles were torn from the Kremlin towers, replaced by five-pointed ruby stars. It was a time when, on Red Square, under the Kremlin walls, a crazy, asiatic monument was raised to the successful revolution, and its leader was not allowed to rest in peace, but was put on permanent display in a public mausoleum.

This leads us into another, even more horrific era, when the Kremlin became a fortress, separating the Leader from his people. In the Stalin era, entrance to the Kremlin was closed, for not only were governmental offices located here, but it was also the residence of the Leader himself. The inner circle of the party, which also lived in the Kremlin, severely warned their children to hide if ever, heaven help them, they should see Stalin; and they were never under any circumstances to meet his gaze. No one knew what the Great Leader of All Times and Peoples would do, whether he would simply chat with a mischievous child of one of his close associates, or whether he would order the child arrested – all sorts of things happened.

We don't know how many horrible memoirs of the last century were overheard by Kremlin walls. That time is shrouded in strange legends – some sound reasonable, others, simply fantastic. And it could well be that the more fantastic ones are actually the more reasonable ones. Who can know?

Kids who were children of Narkom and Politburo members lived in the Kremlin and played at making pretend governments (what else would you expect?). Soon, a few of them turned up missing. Their worried mothers feared the worst: accident or suicide. Then, one of their husbands – a leading Party boss – calmed his wife with these sickening words: "Do not worry, our son is in prison." The kids were lucky – in a few years, they were allowed to return home.

The infamous NKVD boss Lavrenty Beria took his last free steps across the Kremlin cobblestones. Legend has it that, on that summer day a few months after the death of Stalin, when Khrushchev decided to arrest the all-powerful head of the secret police, Khrushchev had a secret understanding with the commandant of the Kremlin. As soon as Beria's car had driven through the Kremlin gates, the grates were suddenly lowered, so that the car following Beria, which carried his bodyguards, was blocked from entry. It was the end of one historical era and the beginning of another.

Nearby is a monument to the Brezhnev era: the huge, awkward Palace of Soviets, in complete dissonance with the ancient buildings that surround it. And yet, this crazy box of glass and concrete has become a part of history as well, occupying a slice of people's memories and casting a shadow onto us from the past. For it was here that Party Congresses were held to decide the fate of the country. Soviet leaders walked up and down these staircases;

Gorbachev and Yeltsin gave speeches here; it was here, as strange as it may seem, that *perestroika* began.

Today there are still places in the Kremlin that are almost always closed off from the prying eyes of mere mortals. State cars race by at high speed, flying to someplace in the heart of the Kremlin. Only later, on the television news, do we find out that, in St. George's Hall, one of the most famous sections of the luxurious Kremlin Palace, there was a regular meeting of officials.

The life of the capital continues outside the Kremlin. But the ghosts of centuries past have not disappeared. They are still here; one only has to listen attentively to understand what they are trying to tell us.

May/June 2004

In the Footsteps of St. George
Murad Agdzhi

*T*hese days, the Moscow boss who doesn't have a picture of St. George on his office wall – a place of honor until once reserved for Soviet leaders – is rare indeed. From times of old, churches and streets have been named after him, and bronze sculptures have depicted him killing the dragon with a spear. All but forgotten in the Soviet era, George's image is now plastered all over the city. But how and when did George receive a Moscow residence permit? And what do we really know about him?

Since 1380, Moscow has related to George as a bringer of victory. Prince Dmitry Donskoy carried his icon onto the field of Kulikovo, the Russians' first victory in their attempt to escape the Mongol yoke. Soon afterwards, a sculpture of a mounted soldier, fragments of which are preserved to this day, appeared on the main tower of Moscow's Kremlin. Then, in 1497, Prince Ivan III had George's image engraved on Moscow's great seal, and the horseman became part of the city's life once and for all. But at that time, Muscovites were not yet calling him George. Instead, they spoke of the "rider," whose name was Mikhail.

According to Eastern church tradition, the horseman was always depicted looking to the right, in accordance with the rules of *posolon*, or turning. In the West, by contrast, he looked to the left. In the Time of Troubles, St. George succeeded in exposing a western pretender to Muscovy's throne, who, out of ignorance, had a left-facing horseman engraved on his seal. Needless to say, the first documents gave the imposter away.

Since those difficult times, a prayer has arisen about the Moscow horseman connected with the miracles he wrought. Or perhaps there were other reasons. In any case, gradually, over the course of the eighteenth century, he acquired a new name: *Georgy Pobedonosets* (George Bringer of Victory).

Still, it was only in Moscow that he was known as George. Elsewhere, he was the *Velikomuchenik* (Great Sufferer) or *Strastoterpets* (Passionate

Sufferer). In general, the saint has an amazing number of names. The Moslems call him Jirjis, Khyzr or Keder; the Turks – Jargan or Gyurdahi; and the Slavs – Gyurgi, Yuri, Yegory, Yezhi or Irzhi. In other countries he is known, variously, as George, Georg and Jose.

But he is most revered among the Ossetians. Like Moscow's Saint George, the Ossetian saint is a horseman, but there the resemblance ends. The latter is a grey-haired old man on a three-legged winged horse – *Uastyrdzhi*.

Quite possibly, this is the most ancient image of Saint George. Which would mean that he already existed – before his birth. This apparent paradox can be explained in the following way. The culture of the Ossetians (or the Alan, as they used to be called) is very old. Their roots are in Persia and Tibet, and there, long before the birth of Christ, legendary heroes – youths in the image of old men – were already well-known. After the Ossetians learned about Christianity, ancient spiritual values were simply supplemented by the new ones.

This practice of combining traditions is natural and results in invisible links of time and culture. For example, the Slavs call George the "beast driver" and even "farmyard god." At the same time, they see in him features of Yarila and Yarovit – ancient fertility gods. For the Moslems, his exploits are also linked with the name of Allah. And finally, he contains qualities of the ancient eastern characters Khadir and Ilias – bringers of immortality and wisdom – who in turn passed on these qualities to George.

Wherever you look, there is a different St. George. Yet, at the same time, he is always the same. The explanation for this lies in his depth and universality, which is portrayed beautifully by an icon located in the Moscow Historical Museum. There, Saint George stands in prayer to God, holding his own severed head in his hands. It is impossible to think of a stronger image. In it, strength of soul and loyalty to faith, life and death – all the universal themes – come together.

As with any great legend, a secret historical record is concealed behind the literary images. But to understand its meaning, it is necessary to first go over the events of the story.

In a certain Eastern town, a huge dragon crawls out of the swamp and starts rounding up the young people. Finally, the turn of the ruler's daughter comes round. She sits down by the road in tears, awaiting her fate. Riding by, George sees her and decides to stay and face the dragon. But when the monster finally appears, George sets aside his weapon and begins to pray. And before the eyes of the amazed maiden, the dragon bows down before the soldier without touching him. Thus, George carried out his feat – he proved that the word is stronger than the sword, for the word was "God."

However, over the years, new "details" have grown up around the legend of Saint George, and its original meaning has been forgotten. For example, in the thirteenth and fourteenth centuries, the warrior took on the role of a hired killer. He was sat on a horse and instructed to kill the dragon, in other words, to break one of the Ten Commandments. But it was not for killing that George originally attained sainthood. At about the same time or a bit earlier, in one culture George became the patron saint of cowherders, in others – a symbol of ploughmen. The saint's image is honored in both the Christian and Muslim worlds. Everyone tries to make him their own.

Of the details of Saint George's life we know only the sketchiest details. He came out of Cappadocia, in the east of Asia Minor, which at one time was part of Armenia. For his time, George was a very educated man, as well as being a Christian missionary. His fate is mysterious. He died very young, but in spite of the more than one and a half millennia that have passed, his memory lives on.

Some believe that St. George was executed by order of the Roman Emperor Diocletian (ruled 284-305 A.D.) during his famous persecution of the Christians. However, it seems more likely that the Roman emperor had never even heard of George, much less executed him. Evidently, the "Diocletian" version of his death came about after the appearance of the First Church of Rome, in 494 A.D. At about this time, church leaders started to distort the saint's life story by way of bringing him closer to the history of the Roman church.

By this time, George's name was already much revered among Christians. This both frightened and at the same time fascinated Roman church leaders. Suffice it to say that Pope Gelasii of the aforementioned First Church of Rome banned the existence of the saint. So, just what was it about George that so embarrassed the church fathers?

From all the available evidence, it appears that the modern Christian church with its crosses, cathedrals and icons began with George himself. Before this, i.e., before the 4th century, Christianity (including the version practiced in Rome) was completely different. People prayed in synagogues, men were circumcised and everything was carried out with extreme secrecy and ceremony.

So what prompted George to introduce these innovations? Back in the last century, a certain Professor Kirpichnikov analyzed virtually all existing versions of St. George's life in his famous work *St. George and the Bold Yegory*. As a result, he came to the firm conclusion that one must search for George's origins in Asia Minor, paying special attention to the Caucasus. This is also where, in his view, one should look for George's persecutor and for the site of his execution. As to the "official" chronicle of George, which portrays Diocletian as George's persecutor and George's tomb as being located in the Palestinian town of Lidda, Kirpichnikov's conclusion is unequivocal: "Impossible!"

Even though Kirpichnikov came closest to figuring out the mystery of St. George, even he never fully deciphered it. For he neglected one very important event in the history of Europe – the Great Resettlement of Peoples, which occurred during George's lifetime.

From the second until the fifth centuries, the vast European steppe was slowly settled. At that time, Europe was totally subjugated by the *kipchaki*, or steppe people, who held sway not by power of arms but by power of spirit. Unlike the Europeans, they were not pagans. They worshipped a god called *Tengry*, the eternal blue sky, and the religion of the steppe was called *Tengranstvo*. Its symbol was the cross. Icons, iconostasis and temples appeared in the region as early as the fifth to third centuries before Christ.

And this is exactly what St. George's exploit is all about. He was the first European to familiarize himself with the Tengranian religion – and he assimilated their rites into Christianity.

One may well ask where this all took place. After all, George came from Asia Minor, but the steppe is a different territory altogether. Yet there was one point of overlap where they could have met and where George could have accomplished his immortal deed – the area near the city of Derbent in the Caucasus. This place was called "the Huns' passage." This was the crossroads between eastern and western cultures between the third and fourth centuries, when the Huns settled there

At approximately the same time, the first European, George, showed up at the camp of the Huns. It took him a few years to get to know the *kipchaki*. And then, according to documents, the Huns killed the young preacher, tying him to the tail of a wild horse, which they sent galloping along the sea shore. The chronicler Favst Busand, who recorded eyewitness accounts which later served as the basis for the legend of St. George, described it all in a rather detailed manner in the fifth century.

Another well-known historical fact practically ignored by historians is that the Huns' flags contained other symbols besides the cross. Namely, the image of the dragon, which, by the way, the Turks considered to be their forefather.

Let's look at the legend again. The dragon came from the swamp. This corresponds with reality: the Huns could have reached George's homeland only from the North, from the Kurinskaya Lowland, which, especially after the spring floods, often resembled a permanent swamp.

The maiden whose life George defended actually symbolized Armenia. For Armenia was the first both to conclude a union with her powerful *kipchaki* neighbors and to accept the cross that George brought from the steppe. Archeological evidence indicates that the first Christian temples were built in Armenia in the shape of a cross (just like the ones built on the steppe). Up until the fourth century A.D., the cross was never used as a Christian symbol.

This alliance between Armenia and the steppe people was mutually advantageous. According to both historical documents and legend, the Armenian tsar defeated the Persian shah with the help of steppe horsemen, and, as a result, Armenia attained independence. Starting in 301 A.D., Christianity became the official religion of Armenia. Ever since, the Christian cross has been called *Georgievski* – the Cross of St. George, and in the Caucasus, the straight cross, encrusted with precious stones and gold just as it was on the steppe, is considered to be St. George's symbol.

Thanks to the manuscript of Favst Busand, St. George's grave has been located. It is in Dagestan – in the mountains on the shores of the Caspian Sea, not far from Derbent. The grave is well-preserved. For centuries people took good care of it and came here to pray.

According to one of the legends, George is considered the eternally young guardian of the spring of life. Next to the grave, in a sacred forest, there is a cave with a healing spring, where mothers come if they lose their milk. Legends of non-Caucasian peoples confirm this fact. Serbian and Latin tales tell us that George's influence helped a mother to breastfeed her three-month-old son. The overwhelming majority of legends also mention the sacred forest next to St. George's grave.

There is also a special note in the legends that, by order from a tsar, George was buried on top of the highest mountain and not far from the sea. All this information is contained not only in European, but also Persian, Turkish, and Islamic legends about St. George.

Now we also know the warrior's real name – Grigoris. He was the grandson of Armenia's Enlightener, who was also called Grigory. According to Kirpichnikov, "St. George and St. Grigory are often mixed up, given the assonance and occasional abridging of both names."

So, it appears that the mystery is solved. And while St. George's image – large and small – now appears on everything from billboards to bus tickets, for most Muscovites, he remains little more than an eye-catching symbol. It is nonetheless important to remember the legend, and the true history, of the capital's adopted patron saint.

August 1997

Knights of the Don
Elena Pugachyova

The Don steppes in Southern Russia are a special place. In ancient times, the paths of trading caravans, religious pilgrims and nomadic peoples all criss-crossed here. The ancient Greeks thought that the waters of the Don separated the continents of Europe and Asia. They established their northernmost settlement in the river's lower reaches. The Slavs had their southernmost settlement here.

*A*ncient tribes migrated from west to east and east to west through this steppe corridor, bordered by seas and mountains: Sumerians, Scythians, Bulgars, Goths, Pechenegs, Polovtsians, Khazars. Every tribe sought to oust its predecessors from the banks of the Don, to drive them from the rich pastures, the lands teeming with fish and game. At the same time, the victors invariably interbred with the vanquished, inheriting elements of their culture.

The Golden Horde established their rule over the Don steppes in 1237. But this was only a small part of their vast empire: the Mongols ruled over lands stretching from China to Lithuania. They imposed an excessive tribute on Rus, devastating its southern principalities.

Over time, locals found that they could hire some of the Horde to protect themselves from the rest of the Horde. By the middle of the 1400s, such mercenary-protectors came to be called "Cossacks," a word some believe was derived from an old Tatar word for "horsemen."

Some time earlier, in 1380, at the Battle of Kulikovo Field, ancestors of the Cossacks (that is, a group that split off from the Mongols) apparently fought on the side of Rus, earning accolades from the Great Prince of Muscovy, who "generously rewarded and thanked the Host and ordered that the Cossacks' be permanently compensated." This first reference to the Cossacks indicates that theirs was a military organization, that they spoke the language of Muscovy and that they were Orthodox believers.

TRANSLATION: PAUL E. RICHRRDSON

So who were these Cossacks, and when did they appear on the Don? As it turns out, these are not esoteric historical questions, but the basis for heated political discussions, even today.

When historians seek to underline the Cossacks' innate independence, they place their roots back before the Slavs. Scythian or Polovtsian heritage is said to be responsible for their exceptional military skills, superior horsemanship, cunning, bravery and love of freedom. Their traditional clothing – pointed headwear, baggy trousers with *lampas* (strips of fabric covering the vertical seam) – are also said to be derived from the Scythians.

Yet, when historians want to assert Cossacks' subservience to the Russian State, their appearance is linked to criminals, lackeys and impoverished peoples fleeing the Russian heartland. But would such persons really have decided to move to an entirely uninhabited place, surrounded by enemies?

Some propose that the Cossacks are descended from Slavs who lived in the Don region and who, prior to the arrival of the Mongol-Tatar Horde, were subservient to Kievan Rus. This hypothesis could explain why the Cossacks came to the aid of the principality of Muscovy, why they spoke Russian and accepted Orthodoxy. Yet it is also not improbable that the Cossacks were members of the Golden Horde who, at the decisive moment, defected to Muscovy.

There are still other versions of history. But no matter which hypothesis is closest to the truth, Lev Tolstoy's words will always ring true: "the borderlands gave birth to the Cossacks."

Borderlands

In the fourteenth to sixteenth centuries, Russia's southern border was not a distinct line with firmly-set boundary posts. Instead, it was a wilderness – a huge expanse of disputed territory, big enough to swallow up modern day Utah, Colorado and Kansas. When it departed, the Golden Horde left behind islands of influence: the Khanates of Kazan, Astrakhan and Crimea. The impregnable Turkish fortress of Azov stood at the mouth of the Don, barring access to the sea. Nomadic Nogays and Kalmyks roamed the steppes. And it was here that the Cossacks lived, fought and made peace with their multinational neighbors.

The Cossacks eventually created an Orthodox republic – the Don Host (so named from the eighteenth century onward). Its roots were along the banks of the Don and its tributaries, where they built villages

– *stanitsy* (plural of *stanitsa*). Gathering in their main towns, the Cossacks came together in public meetings (known as the "*krug*," or "circle") to elect their leader – the *ataman*, with different Cossack groups lobbying for their candidate. Collecting on the square (the *maydan*), the Cossacks would cry out "*lyubo!*" if they approved of a candidate, "*ne lyubo!*" if they disapproved. New elections were held approximately every year. Women and children were not admitted into the *krug*, and Cossacks could lose their right to participate in the *krug* if they committed certain offenses (e.g. drunkenness). In any event, each *stanitsa* selected their *ataman*, who would then decide issues related to local administration. For military actions, a campaign *ataman* was elected, yet he gave up that authority as soon as he returned to the Host.

The *esaul*, the *ataman's* right hand aide, was also elected at the *krug*. For deciding important military matters, the campaign *ataman* conferred with a council of experienced, brave and respected elders. The executive power structure of the Don Cossacks also included a clerk and a translator – back then, educated people were not easy to find in the Don basin.

The *krug* decided on matters concerning the entire Host: declaration of war, terms of peace, creation of new *stanitsy*, reception of foreign embassies, trials of serious criminals. The most severe sentence was reserved for thieves and traitors: "*в куль, да в воду!*" ("into a sack and then into the water!")

The historian Mikhail Budanov concluded in 1886 that "the Don host had a government, which, albeit imperfect, was a government, for it issued decrees and orders which had authority throughout the entire Cossack territory; it imposed fines. In other words, it had jurisdiction. The Don host had 'career troops,' i.e. a military staff of sorts. It had sea troops, marine troops, cavalry, and foot soldiers."

Priests were also elected by the *krug*. However, the majority of *stanitsy* did without priests and churches. Marriages and births were not blessed in church ceremonies. In the early period of Cossack history, relations between men and women were perhaps best characterized by the proverb: "*отцов, как псов, а мать – одна*" ("men are numerous, like dogs, but there is only one mother"). Bachelor Cossacks, who were the majority in the early period, lived together in large groups. They split up tasks of fighting and hunting equally amongst themselves and had an economy of sorts – however primitive, which was based on shared ownership. For this reason, they called one another *odnosum* – "of one mind."

The Cossacks also had their own code of honor: "a mixture of virtues and defects peculiar to a people who lived like bandits," wrote historian Vasily Sukhorukov. "They were greedy in their looting and furious in their attacks on enemy territory. Yet the Cossacks lived together as brothers, disdaining thievery amongst themselves. But robbery committed against other parties and especially the enemy was wholly expected."

In conditions of constant military threat and uncertainty, it was difficult to create a stable society. It was dangerous to undertake major construction projects – a *stanitsa* often consisted merely of half-underground huts – *zemlyanki*. Responding to the Crimean Khan, who threatened destruction of all the towns on the Don, the Cossacks wrote: "Why should you travel so far to plunder? We are not a rich people; our villages are modest, woven of wattle fences and encircled by thorn bushes. And taking them and removing us would require a thick head, for we have strong arms, sharp sabers and accurate arquebuses. And we do not have large herds of horses or cattle to cede to you on the path of your plunder." So often subject to attacks, the Cossacks saw no point in tending the land or animal husbandry. Just going hunting or fishing, they risked running into troops from Azov or Astrakhan, of being pierced by nomads' arrows.

Grants from Moscow's grand princes and tsars – in the form of money, wine, gunpowder, swine, cloth and bread, along with the results of military plundering, formed the basis for the Cossacks' subsistence. Each winter and summer, the Host sent an embassy to Moscow to receive their grant. At the same time, the Cossacks were very protective of their independence from the Moscow grand princes and tsars. If the summer or winter embassy was led by the campaign *ataman*, then, upon his return to the *stanitsa*, he was removed from power and the Cossacks selected a new leader. Thus would all of the promises the *ataman* made in Moscow be annulled.

At first, the Cossacks were not required to serve the tsar, and their willful activities turned out to be a quite valuable diplomatic tool for Russia. In response to the residents of Azov, whom the Cossacks "would not allow to drink from the waters of the Don," Tsar Ivan IV ("the Terrible") claimed he was powerless: "they live on the Don outside our control and flee from us." To the Nogay Prince Yusuf, who was suffering under Cossack attacks, Ivan complained: "These lackeys of ours, they have done much evil in our lands and fled into the wilderness."

But Ivan's complaints were merely a feint. The tsar was in fact planning to employ the Cossacks in battles against his enemies. In 1552, Ivan IV turned his gaze toward one of the islands of Mongol influence in southern Russia. An army of 150,000 Russians and just over 1,000 Cossacks gathered near Kazan. The siege lasted for three months. In the end, the Cossacks stormed the walls and were the first to enter the city. Ivan's troops battled for a short time and the city fell.

Legend has it that, after the storming of Kazan, Ivan the Terrible wanted to bestow something on the Cossacks, but they refused riches. Instead, they asked that the tsar grant them the Don and all of its tributaries. He apparently agreed and his decision was confirmed in an official deed. (If this in fact happened, it is likely that the deed was rescinded by Peter I.)

Soon after this, the Crimean Khan, Nogay Prince and Astrakhan Tsar, all of whom had become anxious about Russian military successes, joined together in a military alliance against Russia. Cossack historian Evgraf Savelyov wrote thus of the 1554 conquest of Astrakhan: "While the Muscovite troops were still plying the Volga and a portion of them had landed and were moving slowly along the right bank of the river, the Cossacks, who comprised the forward troops, inflicted such a defeat on Yamchurgeya, the Astrakhan Tsar, that he left the city, fled to the steppes and hid at Azov." Later, the Cossacks turned back an attempt by Yamchurgeya to retake the city and suppressed an anti-Russian mutiny.

Siberian Conquest

The route to the Caspian was now open for Muscovy, and trade with Southeast Asia grew. Caravans traveled up and down the Volga, from which the Cossacks often extorted payments for passage. One of the leading Cossack-pirates of this time was *Ataman* Yermak. But this is not what made him famous.

In 1582, Yermak, who was headquartered in Perm, came to the attention of the Stroganov family – rich merchants and proprietor of the Urals region. First used by the family for defensive measures, Yermak was later outfitted with cannons, powder and provisions worth 20,000 rubles, to lead a detachment of 840 Cossacks to battle against Khan Kuchum, to conquer Siberia and bring back some of its riches.

Kind to supporters and vengeful to opponents, Yermak moved deep into the Asian heartland. On October 26, 1582, there was a decisive battle between this handful of Cossacks and tens of thousands of Tatar troops, resulting in the capture of Kuchum's capital, Isker. Yermak's success was not simply due to technically superior firepower. "Only a group of audacious and brave souls, unbroken by the weight of the Russian State, could do what they did, in such a spectacular way," wrote author Valentin Rasputin.

Knowing that the Cossacks could not hold the newly-won lands alone, Yermak requested of Ivan IV that he take Siberia under his protection, which the tsar did after Yermak's envoy presented him with an unprecedented bounty of furs. The tsar lavishly rewarded the Cossacks and bestowed on Yermak the title Tsar of Siberia. Significantly, he also gave Yermak a chain mail coat, and sent 300 musketeers (who arrived too late and under-provisioned). The heavy armor was to play a fateful role: in August 1585, Yermak drowned in it while trying to escape from a skirmish with the Tartars. True enough, the *ataman* was no longer young, and he was wounded and would likely not have survived his swim across the raging river. But in songs and tales – by nature symbolic – the hero's death is bound up with the tsar's gift.

Over the next 60 years, the Cossacks continued to lead Russia's drive across a largely unpopulated Siberia. They even reached North America (indeed, the Native American Yupik people adopted the word *kass'aq* to mean "white man"). The fact that Russia today is the world's largest country, that it stretches from the shores of the Baltic to the Pacific, is connected with the history of the Cossacks.

In 1584, the powerful despot Ivan the Terrible died and was succeeded by his feeble son Fyodor, who ruled for 14 years, overseen by a regency council increasingly dominated by his brother-in-law, Boris Godunov. Godunov rose to the throne after Fyodor's death, which ended the Rurik bloodline. Implicated in the death seven years earlier of Ivan's young son Dmitry, Godunov's name was also connected with the enserfment and impoverishment of the people, which was exacerbated by extremely cold winters and drought in 1601-2. Whole villages of devastated peasants fled from famine and enslavement to the Don, expanding the Cossacks' ranks. When landlords demanded the return of their "property," the Cossacks simply replied: "there is no extradition from the Don."

Time of Troubles

Due to migration into and within the region, the Cossack Host was no longer as unified as it once had been. Cossacks who had property of some sort and who lived in settlements, were called "domestics" [*domovyty*], in contrast to the homeless poor, who were called "the hungry" [*golitba*]. The former supported the Russian throne, the latter sought to destabilize it.

A new arrival to the southern steppes was the former galley slave, bandit and Cossack, Ivan Bolotnikov. In 1606-1607, he led an uprising that demanded that the "miraculously saved" Tsarevich Dmitry be returned to the throne (in fact, this False Dmitry had ruled for less than a year and been overthrown and murdered in a palace coup which put Vasily Shuysky on the throne). The uprising encompassed all of southern Russia, including the lower and middle Volga. Bolotnikov led his ranks of *golitba* Cossacks, peasants, and *streltsy* (sharpshooters, or Kremlin guards) to Moscow. The Don Cossacks, who had supported the First False Dmitry, took Bolotnikov's side and supported the new pretender, Peter, as well. As the great Russian historian Vasily Osipovich Klyuchevsky wrote, "during the Time of Troubles, the Cossacks brought great harm to the State, attacking it alongside Polish troops."

While the False Peter did not succeed in taking the throne, Bolotnikov's uprising was crucial in destabilizing Russia (Bolotnikov himself was caught and killed in 1608). A Second False Dmitry arose and soon the situation in Russia was on the verge of collapse: Shuysky was deposed in 1610; a handful of *boyars* took over and offered the throne to Poland's King Wladyslaw, as a way to head off False Dmitry II; Sweden invaded from the North, thinking they could dislodge the Poles and take the Russian throne. Then the Cossacks changed sides and united with a broad popular army that was marching on Moscow. But the alliance was short-lived. When the Cossacks murdered one of the uprising's leaders, the army fell apart. But, fired by a missive from imprisoned Patriarch Hermogen, the movement was resurrected by the merchant Kuzma Minin and Prince Dmitry Pozharsky, who laid siege to Moscow and captured the Kremlin in October 1612.

The newly-crowned Tsar Mikhail Romanov demonstrated his favor for the Cossacks, while at the same time trying to control them, restraining them from constant conflict with the Azov Turks. Azov, today a small town in Southern Russia, once occupied an important position in the Ottoman Empire. From this base, the sultans planned to seize territory along the

Don and Volga and in the Caucasus, as a means to reestablishing control over the Khanates of Kazan and Astrakhan. The fortress of Azov was equipped with the latest in fortification technology, and the Azov Turks felt secure enough to conduct constant raids on Cossack settlements. In 1637, the Don Host had finally had enough and decided "to go out and cut down the infidels, to take the city and plant the Orthodox faith within its walls." They succeeded.

"The hatred of all Christian peoples does not disturb my sleep," said Sultan Murad II, "but the Cossacks have caused me sleepless nights." The five-year occupation of Azov cost the Host – which withstood 24 sieges – some two-thirds of its population. Tsar Mikhail, whose foreign policy in the South was one of cautious defense, feared war with Turkey, and, upon the advice of an Assembly of the Land, would not assume protection of the fortress. The Cossacks were commanded to abandon the fortress, leaving the conquest of Azov to Mikhail's grandson.

The Petrine Era

Within a few decades, a new revolt ripened on the Don. Its leader was Stepan (Stenka) Razin. His father was an escaped serf and his mother a captured Turk. He was well educated for his time, intelligent and, most importantly, extremely charming. "Wild courage was reflected in his well-proportioned and lightly-pockmarked faced," wrote historian Nikolai Kostomarov. "There was something authoritative in his gaze; the crowds saw in him the presence of some irresistible, supernatural force."

Having traveled widely around Russia, Razin knew first-hand that many people were drowning in poverty and lawlessness, dreaming of retribution. But that was not Razin's primary imperative. Having spent years sacking towns along the Caspian and chased out of Persia, Razin was first and foremost a plunderer and thief; his political/military aspirations were surely secondary. Between 1667 and 1671, the Razinites murdered nobles, boyars and merchants, while promising the "dark masses" freedom and readily accepting them into their ranks.

By the summer of 1670, Razin had captured Tsaritsyno, Astrakhan, Saratov, and Samara and was moving steadily up the Volga with some 20,000 troops. But through tactical and strategic errors, despite wide popular support, Razin suffered a crushing defeat at Simbirsk and was captured by Cossack forces loyal to the tsar, who delivered him to the capital, where he was questioned by Tsar Alexei, tortured and killed. The old rule, "there are no extraditions from the Don," apparently now had its limits.

After the Razin uprising, the Don Cossacks were required to swear their allegiance to the Tsar. Peter I, who came to power just over two decades after the Razin uprising, insisted on the Don Cossacks' complete subservience. And most were ready to give it. While the "poor" Cossacks preferred a barbaric freedom on the Don, the "domesticated" Cossacks sought greater stability. In conditions of constant military threat, their economy, trade and professions had hardly developed; education and medicine were absent.

Tsar Peter I was, however, ready to help the Cossacks take on their enemies insofar as it meshed with his own goals. He understood that the Turkish fortress at Azov threatened not just the Cossacks, but Russia as well. Azov was taken in 1696. But the Don Host lost many men in the bloodletting, and needed an influx of new members. Yet they could not get them the old way: Peter decreed that all who had fled from serfdom to the Don must either return to their point of origin or risk being sent to hard labor. Peter also set limits on Cossack fishing of the Don, on cutting down forests, and confiscated all salt-boiling pots. Dissatisfaction with these restrictions led to a prohibition on the establishment of new *stanitsy* without "the highest level of approval." "So, is this why we fought for the tsar?!" the Don Cossacks grumbled.

A new uprising was not long in coming. It was led by Kondraty Bulavin, an advocate of old Cossack rights. In 1707, the revolt encompassed the Don, Ukraine and the Volga basin. Yet the most influential parts of Cossackdom did not support Bulavin. Surrounded by his enemies, he shot himself (or was shot). Pockets of resistance and various sieges were eventually eliminated within a few years. Some 600 Cossack families that were unable to reconcile themselves to the loss of freedoms were led by Ignaty Nekrasov in an emigration first to the Kuban and then to Turkey, where they founded a religious-ethnic community. (In the twentieth century, descendants of the Nekrasov Cossacks returned to Russia and continue to live there in isolated communities.)

Meanwhile, shortly after the Bulavin betrayal, Peter had to contend with a Cossack infamy on an even greater scale. The Ukrainian Cossack and Hetman Ivan Mazeppa, long a favorite in Peter's court, in 1708 betrayed the tsar by throwing his lot in with Sweden's King Charles, who was leading a – at that point – successful invasion of Russia. But the tide turned; after a brutal wintering over in Ukraine, Charles was defeated at Poltava, and the Ukrainian Cossacks loyal to him fled into the wilderness or were brutally executed as traitors.

Despite these events, Peter I granted the Cossacks self-government, but within strict limits: the head *ataman* was to be designated by the Russian emperor, and Cossacks were required to serve in the Russian army. The affairs of the Don Host came under the management of the State Military Collegium (analogous to the modern Ministry of Defense). In the main Cossack city of Cherkassk, a military affairs office was established, presided over by the *ataman* and his clerk, along with six elders. The main task of the elders was the search for and return of fugitives. Aside from this, they oversaw all military, judicial, administrative and financial affairs within the confines of their region (*okrug*). And the military *krug* lost its power. The history of a free people ended; the history of a "military-agricultural estate" began.

Settling Down

Peter I's reforms affected the personal, daily lives of the Don Cossacks. Implanting official Orthodoxy, the Emperor forbade civil marriages and divorces, as well as cohabitation with prisoners – all Cossack customs. Ending the practice of paying grants, Peter required the Cossacks to take up farming. As it turned out, the lands of the Don proved quite fertile (a cubic meter of Don soil was sent to Paris as a soil standard). By the end of the eighteenth century, the Don Host was sending bread to Russia as well as exporting it abroad. Vineyards and winemaking also took hold, as did animal husbandry; the Don Cossacks proved themselves particularly adept at horse breeding.

Trade began to develop. Russian, Ukrainian and even Turkish, Italian, French and Persian merchants began traveling to Cherkassk. The Cossacks sold grain, wine, fish, meat and livestock. Up until the end of the eighteenth century, one could buy slaves at the Cherkassk market. Yet Cossack commerce likely presented a rather motley picture, as described by Nikolai Gogol (writing about the Zaporozhets Cossacks): "Wide satin trousers stuffed into holey boots, a velvet caftan covers a dirty shirt that is all in tatters, a gold belt shone on an old *sormyge* [outerwear] and, instead of a raincoat on powerful shoulders, there flutters a Persian carpet or a Turkish shawl." (Peter sought to impose European lifestyles and clothing, and thus allowed the Cossacks to wear any clothing they obtained as booty from military campaigns.)

The tsars and tsarinas that followed Peter on the throne in the eighteenth and nineteenth centuries sent the Cossacks into wars with Turkey, Persia and the nations of the Caucasus. The famous quote of Napoleon, "Give me 20,000 Cossacks, and I will conquer the whole of Europe, and even the whole world," was a hard-won lesson from his defeat in Russia. "One must give the Cossacks their due," Napoleon said. "It is largely to them that Russia owes its success in this campaign. They are, without a doubt, the best light cavalry in the world."

Serving in the ranks of the Russian army, the Cossacks crossed all of Europe, traversed deserts, scaled mountain ranges. These "falcons of the Russian steppes," as the Germans called them, were the first to enter Berlin, Milan and Paris. But the old ways remained: "Plunder had always been a prime motive for the Cossacks at war," wrote Mikhail Sholokhov in his novel, *Quiet Flows the Don*. "...Back in the days of the German war, when the regiment had been ranging over the rear areas in Prussia, the brigade commander – a general of some merit – had addressed the twelve squadrons drawn up before him and, pointing with his whip at a small town lying amid the hills, had said 'Take it and the town is yours for two hours. But when those two hours are up, the first man caught looting goes to the wall!'"

There are of course opposing accounts. An eyewitness wrote of the Cossacks' entry into Berlin in 1760: "Several thousand Cossacks and Kalmyks came down the street. They had long beards, fierce glares and mysterious weapons: bows, arrows and pikes. The sight of them was frightful and at the same time majestic. They went through the city in a quietly and orderly fashion and billeted in villages, where apartments had been apportioned for them."

The borders of the Russian state expanded. The region of the Don Host was no longer on the front lines, but in the rear. No longer fearing attack, the Cossacks began to build permanent housing instead of earthen hovels. These homes – *kureny* – were built with the annual flooding of the Don in mind. They were set on high, stone foundations, which raised the upper rooms above any floodwaters. The main floor was surrounded on its perimeter by a balcony, to which boats could be tied up during flooding.

The better off and more influential Cossacks built palaces in Cherkassk no less grand than those which shimmered in the capital.

The rich, thriving capital did not please Russia's central powers. It is not without reason that Pushkin called Cherkassk a "degraded city." Too much there reminded one of its independent past. What is more, the Cossacks themselves continually did things to remind the Powers that Be of their rebellious nature.

In 1773-1775, Russia was shaken by the peasant revolt led by the Don Cossack Yemelyan Pugachev, a charismatic fugitive and the most successful in a prolific line of Peter III pretenders (Peter III was the tsar and husband of Catherine II, who was deposed and murdered in 1762). While the main body of the Pugachev revolt was led by Yaik (Ural) and Volga Cossacks, the Don Cossacks joined the revolt as a reaction to an effort to move them to the Caucasus for defense of the new, more southerly border. The Don Host threatened to secede; they did not want to part with their historic center of Cherkassk. At the same time, however, the fortress-like capital of Cossackdom was becoming crowded and was repeatedly inundated by the flooding Don.

Early in the nineteenth century, it was decided to move administrative functions of the Cossack Host elsewhere, to a new capital: Novocherkassk. But the decision went unimplemented until *Ataman* Matvey Ivanovich Platov personally got behind it. After affirming the plan for Novocherkassk with Tsar Alexander I, the *ataman* ordered all of the Cossacks of Cherkassk to move and start construction of the new Cossack capital. But the majority resolved to stay put. According to the Don historian Yevgeny Savelyov, the *ataman* then ordered that Cossacks who refused to move to Novocherkassk would be flogged on the main square until they agreed.

The Whirlwind-*Ataman*, as Platov was called, became famous in the Russo-Turkish War. In 1774, Khan Devlet-Girey, a vassal of the Turkish sultan, sent out 20,000 Tatars against the Cossack troops of Platov and Stepan Larionov. The 1,000 Cossacks withstood 10 attacks before reinforcements from the regular army arrived. In the report on the Russian forces' victory, it was stated that, "among the enemy dead were two sultans, one prince of Kokand, several notable men, and over 500 common troops, all buried on the battlefield. Our losses were not great, specifically: 8 killed, 15 missing in action, and 54 injured." The famous poet and warrior Denis Davidov wrote, "If someone should find himself in a similar situation, then let him remember the heroic feat of the young Platov, and his weapons will be showered with success. Fortune is not always blind; it may elevate a difficult battle to the level of glory attained by the venerable hero of the Don."

Platov was a hero and a tyrant, one whose strong, contradictory nature was reminiscent of Peter I. And the capital he built echoes a young St. Petersburg, with its wide avenues, strictly planned streets and buildings designed by the best European architects.

Novocherkassk was in fact the personification of the Cossacks' new fate. Warriors, farmers and businessmen alike all built homes and civic institutions intended to show themselves off as cultured, educated people. At the end of the nineteenth and start of the twentieth centuries, they opened up schools, a university and *gymnasium*. They founded theaters and museums. Don writers, composers and painters began to be widely known.

At the start of the twentieth century, the region of the Don Host was divided into nine districts (*okrugs*), with district administrations subordinated to the war ministry. Each village (*stanitsa*) elected a village administration, which convened public assemblies. At such assemblies, every Cossack (excepting women and children) had the right to speak on matters before the assembly, or to introduce proposals. Decisions were taken by simple majority. Business affairs comprised a large part of the assemblies, including the allotment of land and improvements to the village, sorting out family disputes and prosecuting petty thefts. The village administration was also responsible for equipping those Cossacks who were sent into military service. Cossacks served with their own horses, arms and uniform equipage. But if a Cossack was poor, then the administration saw to his outfitting.

Cossacks began their military service at the age of 18, with three years of training and drilling in the *stanitsa*. Between the ages of 21 to 33, they served within the ranks of the regular Cossack forces, which were divided up into military units that existed both in peacetime and in times of war. Between the ages of 33 to 38, Cossacks served in the reserves and could be called up in times of war. At the age of 38, a Cossack went into retirement. If a family had just one wage-earner, he was not subject to service, and there were deferments for completion of school or university education. (Typically, however, the parents of Cossacks preferred their sons to serve rather than to study.)

Just before the start of the First World War, there were some three million people living in the region of the Don Host, about half of them Cossacks. The remainder were industrial workers, miners, peasants who moved there from Central Russia, Ukrainians and Jews – all people whom the Cossacks called outsiders (*inogorodniye*), and whom they treated with great suspicion. Outsiders had fewer rights and could not take part in the land allotments. This contradiction was subsequently to play a fatal role.

Wars and Revolution

In the First World War, several call-ups emptied the Don *stanitsy*: old Cossacks and untrained youth were both drafted to the front. After the February 1917 revolution, Cossacks returning from the front began to reformulate their local administrative bodies. In Novocherkassk, an all-host *krug* was called and they elected a new *ataman*, the first since the time of Peter: General Alexei Kaledin. It was hoped and assumed that he would be able to control the brewing unrest on the Don.

After the October coup, a Bolshevik military-revolutionary committee was formed in Rostov, which included several "outsiders." The Kamenskaya *stanitsa* Cossacks (Bolsheviks) were led by Fyodor Podtelkov, who was supported by 11 cavalry regiments, five batteries, one mounted "hundred," and one battalion. The entire Don Cossack contingent at that time consisted of 60 cavalry regiments, 37 batteries, 126 mounted "hundreds," and six battalions. A delegation sent by Podtelkov met with the Kaledin government and demanded the swift transfer of power to the revolutionary committee. Kaledin refused, and the Cossack resistance became a critical spark inciting Civil War. Within a few days, Bolshevik troops from Moscow, Petrograd and other cities, combining their forces with Podtelkov's, broke through into Novocherkassk. The Cossacks, tired from war, did not offer significant resistance. Kaledin resigned from the position of *ataman* and shot himself.

On the Don, as elsewhere across Russia, the Bolsheviks set about enforcing their rule with violent and confiscatory actions, which in turn pushed the Cossacks to revolt.

Summary execution of 62 old Cossacks in Migulinskaya stanitsa, executions in the Kazanskaya and Shumilinskaya stanitsas (former Khutor atamans, Cavaliers of St. George, sergeant-majors, respected

*village judges, school administrators and other bourgeoisie and Khutor
counter-revolutionaries) – over six days over 400 people were shot."*
– Mikhail Sholokhov in a letter to Maxim Gorky.

The Cossacks elected a new *ataman*, Pyotr Krasnov, who declared the
sovereign state of The All-Powerful Don Host and created a unified Don
Army from the various isolated, insurgent detachments. And, in order to
repulse the Bolsheviks, he concluded a treaty with Germany. At first, the
Cossack-German alliance routed the Bolsheviks. But victory was to be
short-lived; a split soon opened up in the Host along the long-familiar lines
of the *golitba* and *domovyty*. Sholokhov, in Quiet Flows the Don, wrote
about it this way:

*In April 1918, a great division took place on the Don: northern
Cossacks returning from the front left with the retreating Red Army
soldiers; southern Cossacks chased them down and pushed them back
within the borders of their region....*

*The decisive division of the Cossacks into northerners and southerners
happened in 1918, but its roots can be traced back hundreds of years,
when the less prosperous Cossacks from the northern regions – who
lacked the fertile soil as was found near the Azov sea, who were neither
wine growers, nor rich in hunting or fishing skills – broke away from
Cherkassk, and took up raiding in Russian lands and became the most
reliable recruits for every sort of rebel, from Razin to Sekach.*
[Book 3, Part 6, Chapter 1]

By the end of 1918, Germany's failure in war and the abdication of
Kaiser Wilhelm left the Cossacks on their own and vulnerable to Red Army
attacks; support from Britain, France and the U.S. was inconsistent and
insufficient. "Now," Krasnov said, in a speech before the delegates of the
Military Krug, "armed with rifles and machine guns, the Don Cossacks are
fleeing without a fight, surrendering their native villages and farms to the
enemy for desecration; the Reds are capturing officers and leading them off
to be shot or to suffer in the Red Army. All sense of a command structure
has been lost, and officers no longer have the trust of their soldiers. Today,
entire hundreds are going over to the Reds and returning with them to
murder their fathers and brothers. We no longer have a unified and strong
Don army." Shortly thereafter, Krasnov resigned.

In January 1919, a decree signed by Yakov Sverdlov, head of the Central Committee of the Communist Party, called for de-Cossackification: "Carry out mass terror against rich Cossacks, exterminating every last one. Confiscate bread and collect all surpluses at the indicated locations; and not just bread, but all agricultural products." In order to save themselves from complete extermination, the Cossacks fought on, and were widely-portrayed as a chief enemy of Red Forces. "The blood which is now flowing on the Southern Front," wrote the Cossack Filipp Mironov, commander of the pro-Red Cossacks, "is shed in vain and in excess and is being spilled out to the satanic guffaws of Vandals, resurrected from the Middle Ages and the Inquisition to carry out their evil designs."

In the end, the Cossacks were vastly outnumbered and outgunned. At the end of 1919, military *ataman* Afrikan Bogayevsky issued an evacuation order. The 1920 All-Russian Congress of Working Cossacks notwithstanding, the Don Host for all practical purposes ceased to exist in that year, with many Cossacks leaving Russia for Turkey, France and elsewhere. Those that remained in the Soviet Union fell under the sentence of de-Cossackification: Cossacks were forbidden from following their customs, going to church, wearing traditional clothing, from even calling themselves Cossacks. They were tossed from their homes, which were given to people from other regions.

Beginning in 1927, under Collectivization, the property of all peasant farmers was confiscated by *kolkhozes*. Sholokhov wrote Stalin about the process of Collectivization on the Don: "*Kolkhozniks* and individual farmers alike are dying from hunger. Adults and children are eating everything imaginable, but none of it intended for human consumption: beginning with carrion and ending with oak bark." Stalin wrote a thank you telegram to the writer and some measures were taken. But the general strategy – to enslave the farmers – was unchanged.

During the Great Patriotic War (WWII), the majority of the remaining Soviet Cossacks fought in the ranks of the Soviet Army. Cossack formations comprised more than 70 military units. "The Germans can be stopped in the South!" wrote the paper *Krasnaya Zvezda* in 1942. "They can be hit and smashed! This was proven by the Cossacks who, in trying conditions showed themselves to be brave, fearless fighters for the Motherland and became a threat for the German invaders." But it was an unequal fight and the enemy drove on to the Volga.

After their defeat at Stalingrad, the Germans swiftly retreated from the Volga. But, comparatively speaking, they began to resist more strongly in the regions bordering the more westerly Don River. In point of fact, since the outbreak of the war, the Cossacks were first in the ranks of anti-Bolshevik forces within the Soviet Union. Several *stanitsy* greeted invading German troops with bread and salt – traditional signs of hospitality. Some Cossacks even created detachments on their own initiative and went over to join the enemy.

At the beginning of the war, some of the Cossacks who emigrated in the 1920s (including the afore-mentioned General Krasnov) expressed their willingness to join the Wehrmacht in its fight against the USSR. In Germany and other occupied countries, the Cossacks were deployed as a national-liberation movement, whose leader, Vasily Glazkov, proclaimed to the Cossacks: "The valiant German Army is crossing the Cossack borders and entering the territory of our Cossack lands. We now know that our Cossack population will be truly glad to greet the German soldiers as liberators from the long years of the Moscow Yid-Bolshevik yoke." Hitler declared the Cossack and Caucasian units to be "equal partners" with the Germans and authorized their use both in the battle with the partisans and on the front lines, in the USSR, in Italy and the Balkans.

But, inevitably, Nazi Germany approached its denouement. Cossack troops were in the vanguard of Soviet troops that drove the Germans back to the West. In open battles, the Cossacks fighting on the side of the USSR prevailed over the Cossack-Fascists.

Post-War Adjustments

After the war and after Stalin's death, relations with the Cossacks changed somewhat – they were no longer considered to be "enemies of the people," and they, as many political prisoners, began to return from exile. But a good number of Don Cossacks, fearing new repressions, considered it wise to forget their roots. Others could not forget that the Don lands had once belonged to them, and they decided they could not let their children forget this.

The Cossacks' modern revival began during *perestroika*. In 1990, a Union of Cossacks of the Region of the Don Host was founded. A *krug* was called for Rostov-on-Don, in order to declare "the Civil War at an end." In 1992, the State officially recognized the Cossacks' right to exist and to reinvigorate their way of life, their cultural traditions and their way of military service. Yet, once again, a split soon became evident among the Cossacks: some were loyal to the new Yeltsin administration, others aligned themselves with the opposition. (In 1993, some members of the new Cossacks took part in the storming of the White House, were arrested for this, then amnestied.)

In 1997, Cossacks who agreed to cooperate with central and local organs of power were officially accepted into service, to perform a range of official functions, from battling criminal elements in cities and towns, to freeing prisoners in war zones. They are called "enrolled" Cossacks, and are distinguished from "public" Cossacks, who oppose the Powers That Be. In 2006, a new Federal Law came into force, whereby only official, "enrolled" Cossacks are allowed to fulfill government functions, as assigned to them. "Public" Cossacks are forbidden from wearing uniforms and symbols that distinguish them as such.

Meanwhile, many observers see the "revival" of Cossack traditions to be nothing more than opportunist nationalism by modern pretenders – seeking to claim an anachronistic and heroic past with which they have no direct link. Indeed, some Cossack leaders have been aggressively xenophobic in their remarks, if not their actions.

These are but the latest wrinkles in the complex, six centuries of Don Cossack history within – but never quite a part of – Russia. Ever at the borders of society – literally and figuratively – the Cossacks have been at once prized and reviled for their independent streak, which has borne both great successes and great infamy. As the Cossacks seek to resurrect their identity in a society that has long since lost the need for a cavalry, they will surely struggle against countless stereotypes and historical ghosts, drawing deeply upon the battle-hardened experience in their 600-year history.

July/August 2006

The Little Water of Life
Paul E. Richardson & Mikhail Ivanov

There cannot be not enough snacks,
There can only be not enough vodka.
There can be no silly jokes,
There can only be not enough vodka.
There can be no ugly women,
There can only be not enough vodka.
There cannot be too much vodka,
There can only be not enough vodka.
— A Russian toast

*I*t could be argued that 1998 was the 600th anniversary of the arrival of vodka in Russia. One nineteenth century source on Russian culture, food and folkways notes that "it can probably be supposed that vodka appeared here no earlier than 1398, when the Genoese began shipping vodka to Lithuania and acquainted us with the pernicious drink."

If this is the case, then it took several decades for this "pernicious drink" to take root in Russia. For most contemporary experts cite the mid- to late-1400s as the time when vodka began to be distilled in Russia. Within another 100 years, the state was starting to move in and set up a monopoly over the production and sale of vodka that would last – but for a thirty-year hiatus – for the next four centuries. Over that period, vodka has come to play a vital role in Russian culture, in the financing of the Russian state, and, sadly, in the destruction of families and individuals due to alcoholism, abuse and accidents.

The Russian Drink
Many nations of the world have a singular drink that they have come to be identified with and that has come to be identified with them. For the French it is wine; the British and Germans have beer; the Japanese

have sake; the Norwegians have aquavit. And, for Russians (and Poles, Belarusans, Finns and Ukrainians), it is vodka.

Perhaps no other spirit would have been so compatible with the Russian soul. The subtle lithesomeness of wine, best taken in the open air with fine cheese and warm bread, is a bad fit with Russia's long winters and short growing seasons. While beer has enjoyed popularity in Russia through the ages, it is simply not a "serious enough" drink. It does not pack enough punch to unleash true feelings and passions.

But vodka, so pure and purposeful, so ideal for warming the despondent soul in February or for cooling passions in August, is a feast or famine sort of drink. One would expect something like vodka to arise from a northern culture with a communal peasantry, where long winters and tortuously short growing seasons meant back-breaking labor intermitted only by community-building social feasts and drinking bouts. What is more, the unique ability of vodka (unlike wine or beer or even mead) to act as an accompaniment to any manner of feast or food (whatever is on hand), plus the fact that it can be distilled from any type of grain or organic matter (again, whatever is on hand), makes it all the more welcome. And, when it was discovered that the best vodka resulted from filtering with birch charcoal (not oak or pine, but birch, the tree of the Russian taiga), well, what more need be said?

The Birth of Vodka

Actually, the first Russian drink of choice was *myod* – mead. Made from honey (also known as *myod* in Russian), of which Russia has always had in plentiful supply, *myod* is referred to in Russia's earliest written document, *The Primary Chronicle*. It was this drink which Rus' Grand Prince Vladimir was probably thinking of when, in 986, he rejected Islam as the state religion for Russia (because it prohibits consumption of alcohol) with the well-known line, "For the Rus, drink is joy; we cannot be without it!" Vladimir instead embraced the more permissive Christianity imported from Byzantium.

Vladimir's Rus also imbibed of other fermented beverages, e.g. beer (*pivo*), wine (*vino*) and many types of *kvas*. But distilled beverages did not come to Russia or Europe until many centuries later. The process of distillation, which can be traced back at least to Mallorca at the end of the thirteenth century, moved slowly north into Europe in the fourteenth and fifteenth centuries. As the previously cited nineteenth century source (*The Russian People, Its Habits, Ceremonies, Legends, Superstitions and Poetry*) indicated, it was Genoese merchants who likely brought the first distilled spirits (then referred to as *aqua vitae*, or water of life) to Russia.

At first, the new elixir was referred to as *zhiznennoy vody* – literally "living water" or "water of life," and used as a balsamic, for medicinal purposes. The process of distilling vodka (a name, which means "little water" or "dear water", and may well have been borrowed from the Polish *wodka*) in Russia seems to have begun in the early 1400s – in 1426 visiting Genoese merchants demonstrated distillation for the Grand Duke of Lithuania and, a few years later, a Russian delegation of clerics went to Italy, visiting monasteries famous for their distilling. Rye, wheat and barley were the principal raw ingredients, and vodka was actually referred to in its various incarnations as wine. Ordinary vodka was called "simple wine" (*prostoye vino*), with the best type being "good wine" (*vino dobroye*). Of a higher sort was *boyarskoye vino* – boyar's wine. Better still was "double wine" (*vino dvoynoye*), which was an extra-strong vodka.

Originally, vodka was not a neutral spirit. The crudity of early distilling processes meant that many impurities remained in the vodka and had to be masked by other, more pleasing flavors. Indeed, Faith and Wisniewski, in their book *Classic Vodka*, suggest that distilling in Russia derived from the widespread practice of extracting pitch from pine logs by boiling them in large pits – they cite as evidence that the verb *smolit* long meant both the production of pitch or alcohol. Cover the pit, capture the steam and one could produce a poor form of alcohol and pitch in one process.

In Elena Molokhovets' famous cookbook for new housewives, first published in second half of the nineteenth century, she listed dozens of recipes for preparing vodkas, from baked vodka to peach pit vodka to vodkas flavored with raspberry, pepper, allspice, roses or cherries. Other sources list infusions such as cinnamon, lemon, saltpeter, bison grass (making the famous *Zubrovka*), juniper, rowan berries, black currant and others. And then there is the famous hunters' vodka. It is flavored with port, ginger, cloves, black and red pepper, juniper berry, coffee, star anise, orange and lemon peel and roots of tormentil and angelica. It can be purchased under the name *Okhotnichaya*. By the end of the last century, according to Faith and Wisniewski, there were over 100 different flavored vodkas sold in Russia.

As the process for distilling and filtering vodka became perfected (filtering with charcoal was not discovered until the 1700s), rye became the grain of choice as a raw material. About half of all Russian vodka was typically made from rye, with wheat and potatoes being less desirable fundaments. It was also soon discovered that multiple distillations (with dilution in between) led to purer vodkas, less burdened by congeners and odorous elements. By the 1700s, triple-distilling, together with birch-charcoal filtering, became the standard for finer vodkas, and made flavoring and infusion of vodka unnecessary. By the beginning of the twentieth century, the best Russian vodka was defined as that using Moscow river waters, distilled from grain (vs. potatoes) and diluted to a concentration of 40 percent.

The Tsars' Vodka

The growth of vodka distilling at the end of the fifteenth century was brought on by advances in distilling technology and new surpluses of grain, thanks to the introduction of crop rotation. Not surprisingly, at about this time, state and tsar began to take an interest in vodka's earning power. Whereas Grand Prince Ivan III (1462-1505) had completely forbidden the production of strong spirits, Tsar Ivan IV ("the Terrible," 1533-1584) built the first *kabak* (tavern) for his *oprichniky* (palace guard) in Moscow, on the Balchug. Tradition has it that Ivan saw Tatar *kabaks* during his siege of Kazan (1552), and he decided to use the same principal of state-owned distilleries/taverns as a way to control the trade in spirits while profiting from them. Still, Ivan IV did not love drinking, and he restricted drinking in *kabaks* (which spread throughout the country during his rule) to Holy Week, Christmas and "Dmitry's Saturday."[1] At all other times, public drunkenness could lead to a prison term.

Tsar Fyodor (1584-1598), who succeeded Ivan IV, led a drive to tear down *kabaks*. But Boris Godunov (1598-1605) recognized the economic value of the vodka trade and ordered expanded building of *kabaks*, even allowing vodka to be purchased and taken off the premises.

By the early 1600s, the smallest towns and villages had their *kabak*, often called a *kruzhechny dvor* (derived from *kruzhka*, the tankard used to measure wine, and *dvor*, meaning courtyard). The end result was rising drunkenness, which Tsar Mikhail (1613-1645), the first Romanov tsar,

....

1. Until 1769, an October holiday to remember those killed in Dmitry Donskoy's famous Battle of Kulikovo field; after 1769, the day was moved to August 29.

combated with limited prohibition. Like Fyodor, he moved to tear down the *kabaks*, establishing drinking houses where wine was sold only on the premises. The tide turned again with the ascension to the throne of his son, Tsar Alexis (1645-1676), who allowed the building of one *kabak* in every town (and three in Moscow), which eventually multiplied of their own accord.

Perhaps more significantly, Tsar Alexei codified and institutionalized the state's monopoly over alcohol production and sale in his famous Law Code of 1649. Private production was to be punished brutally and all revenues from the sale of vodka went directly to the royal coffers.

This arrangement would continue more or less unchanged for nearly two hundred years, until another round of reforms, in 1861, removed the state monopoly on vodka production and sales, replacing it with an excise system. This hiatus of state control lasted just 33 years, but that was enough for some enterprising individuals – most notably Pierre Smirnoff – to become rich in the distilling business. In 1894, the state again gradually began to impose a state monopoly that was fairly complete by the time WWI began.

Temperance, or not

During WWI, Tsarist Russia imposed a "dry law," which sought to keep army recruits sober enough to fight. And when the Bolsheviks stole power in 1917, they extended prohibition on ideological grounds, arguing that the tsarist state sought to keep its subjects docile through liberal distribution of vodka, which may not have been that far from the truth. Catherine II, as Stephen White notes in *Russia Goes Dry*, once supposedly commented that a drunken people is easier to rule. Vladimir Lenin, a teetotaler, saw alcoholism as a disease that would keep Russia from moving forward to communism. As White writes, Lenin said the proletariat, "had no need of intoxication, it derived its strongest stimulant to struggle from its class position and from the communist ideal; and what was needed was clarity, clarity and once again clarity..." In 1922, at the 11th Communist Party Congress, Lenin would declare that there would be "no trade in rotgut."

By December 1919, new laws were enacted to severely punish private production of strong spirits. Not that this was highly significant: according to White, at least a third of rural households were likely engaged in illicit distilling of alcohol in the 1920s. The government stepped up its anti-alcohol campaign for a time but eventually admitted defeat. In 1925, private homebrewing (the making of *samogon*) was allowed, as long as it was not intended for sale, while the state monopoly over production and sales continued. Henceforth, the battle against increasing alcohol consumption (by the late 1920s, White reports, the average urban family spent 14 percent of its income on alcohol) was mainly fought through education and propaganda.

Forced industrialization would put an end to this battle. Once again, a Russian leader chose to use revenues from vodka to finance growth and national defense. By the end of 1930, Stalin, now firmly in control, ordered expansion of vodka production. By the late 1930s, the strength of vodka (which had previously been kept at 20 percent) was allowed to rise to its "natural" level of 40 percent. As White writes, by 1940, "there were more shops selling drink than meat, fruit and vegetables put together." During the war, vodka was issued to troops as part of their rations.

Vodka and the State

Stalin's move is not surprising. Since Ivan the Terrible established the first *kabak* in Russia, the Russian state has used proceeds from vodka sales to further its domestic and foreign agendas. And the Russian public has repeatedly obliged the leadership by consuming vast amounts of vodka. In the nineteenth century, upwards of 40 percent of all state revenue came from alcohol duties and sales. In the twentieth century, toward the end of the Soviet era, some estimates put vodka sales at 15-20 percent of the value of all retail trade turnover. Obviously, the state could not afford to ignore this "lucrative" source of revenue – vodka production between 1940 and 1985 more than doubled (beer more than quadrupled and wine increased over eight-fold).

But the costs were very real. From the 1940s to the 1980s, consumption of alcohol quadrupled in the Soviet Union. One independent study cited by Stephan White estimated that 15 percent of the Soviet population in the 1980s could be called alcoholic. The effects on society are not hard to imagine, if painful to elaborate. White offers an exhaustive portrait of the social costs of increased alcohol consumption from the end of WWII to the present day: alcohol abuse became the single largest cause cited for divorce; by the late 1970s, life expectancy for Russian males had dropped to just 61 years; between 1960 and 1987, there was a population loss due to alcohol abuse in Russia of some 30-35 million persons; 74 percent of all murders committed in the early 1980s were committed under the influence of alcohol, as was the same proportion of rapes; in the early 1980s, 75-90 percent of absences from work were related to alcohol; economic production was said to drop by up to 30 percent following weekends and paydays; by one estimate, the economic losses from alcohol abuse in the 1980s were three times the amount taken in through taxes on alcohol.

Certainly, it would be wrong to associate the free availability of vodka as the singular cause of these societal abuses. Also at the root of this social malaise in the 1970s and 1980s was massive societal depression brought on by an untenable socio-economic system, by the "stagnation" and moral vacuum wrought by the empty promises and apathy of late sovietism. When you are living in a lie, escapism is a natural reaction.

But, long before the arrival of totalitarian communism, vodka had a dark influence on Russian culture. The state's dependence on revenues from alcohol sales have encouraged alcoholism and abuse for hundreds of years. As Adam Olearius, a member of the Holstein Embassy to Russia in the seventeenth century wrote, "the vice of drunkenness is prevalent among this people in all classes, both secular and ecclesiastical, high and low, men and women, young and old... None of them anywhere, anytime, or under any circumstances lets pass an opportunity to have a draught or drinking bout. They drink mainly vodka, and at get-togethers, or when one person visits another, respect is rendered by serving one or two cups of wine, that is, vodka."

Misha's Campaign

Fighting this vice (and repairing gashes in the social and economic fabric of the Union) was the impetus for Soviet President Mikhail Gorbachev's anti-alcohol campaign of the late 1980s. This attempt to make an alcohol loving (and dependent) country go cold-turkey (lucidly detailed in Stephan White's aforementioned book) was a vast political failure. It contributed perhaps even more than the loss of empire to the disdain with which Gorbachev is held in Russians' eyes. The campaign, which cut back on production and restricted sales and distribution of vodka as well as beer, wines and other spirits, succeeded in bringing about declines in official sales of vodka (cut by nearly half) and other alcohol products, as well as in actual consumption (estimated at a 25 percent decline between 1985-6). But the response from the public was increased production of *samogon*, which created a huge sugar deficit, increased deaths due to alcohol poisoning and decreased work efficiency by other means – huge numbers of Soviets were waiting in lines to get vodka or wine.

What is more, the campaign against alcohol consumption, insofar as it was effective, freed up purchasing power among consumers that would have otherwise been spent on alcohol. This, combined with the fall-off of revenues to the state from a decline in alcohol sales, contributed to massive shortages of all manner of consumer goods.

There were some gains, however, most notably in the health of the population. Life expectancies stabilized, birth and death rates dropped, alcohol-related deaths on the job and off went down and the birth rate went up. Divorces declined. But, as admirable as these changes were, the public was gravely dissatisfied with the means to these ends; Russians resented sobriety by government decree. And the government, for its part, was executing its anti-alcohol program unevenly, and on the sandcastle foundation of seven decades of socialist falsehoods. So it was little surprise that, as early as 1987, the cash-strapped Soviet government began relaxing many of its restrictions on sale and distribution. By 1990, White writes, the level of alcohol consumption had bounced back to its pre-campaign levels.

Enter the Market

As in many spheres, the disintegration of the Soviet Union and the collapse of the command economy changed the alcohol market radically. In the early 1990s, poorly executed "shock-therapy" reforms subjected the population of the Soviet Union and then Russia to a prolonged bout with hyperinflation. The state needed medicine to keep the beleaguered population at bay. Cheaper vodka was one answer. According to a report by the Rand Corporation and Moscow's Center for Demography and Human Ecology, between 1990 and December 1994, consumer prices in Russia increased by 2,020 times for all goods and services, by 2,154 times for food products but by only 653 times for alcoholic beverages.

The other supposed answer was "free" vodka. In 1992, Russian President Boris Yeltsin signed a decree abolishing the 68-year-old state monopoly on the production, import and sale of vodka. It was replaced by a system of free production and trade of hard liquor based on licensing. This was a very Russian solution to the problems of the monopoly – to completely overturn the status quo rather than tinker with it. The *Financial Times* predicted at the time that "the lifting of the state monopoly on vodka is political suicide for a country where economic and other difficulties provoke the people's desire to drown them in wine."

After state control over the production, import and sale of vodka was loosened, distillers, importers and retailers (in the form of kiosks), sprouted like mushrooms after a rainstorm. By the late 1990s, according to renowned alcohol expert Igor Serdyuk, there were some 1,300 licensed vodka "players," and some 250 vodka brands were registered with *Rospatent*.

Foreign Vodkas

One absurdity, played out in other consumer spheres with the opening of the market, was the mass influx of Western vodkas. Consumers in the land that invented vodka began flocking in droves to international favorites like Finlandia, Absolut and Smirnoff. But the state, hard pressed to protect local producers (and knowing a good tax base when it sees it) started introducing severe licensing and excise taxes on imports.

Another problem brought on by the influx of imports was exemplified by the Smirnoff vs. Smirnov dispute. Internationally-known Smirnoff vodka is a trademark and recipe that, over the course of this century, passed from emigre descendants of nineteenth century vodka baron Pyotr Smirnov to now be owned by the huge distilled spirits company IDV. But, when IDV decided to go into the Russian market (returning Smirnoff to its homeland, so to speak), it ran into one Boris Smirnov, a former KGB agent who founded a "Trade House of Pyotr Smirnov's Descendants" and started producing "Smirnovskaya" vodka. The trademark dispute over the right to use the name of Pyotr Arsenievich Smirnov and the title of "Purveyor to his Majesty's Imperial Court," raged for nearly a decade before being settled in 2004.

The True Costs

The liberalization of the alcohol market also opened up the bottom side of the market, letting in a flood of cheap, fake and often downright lethal vodka. According to the Russian Academy of Sciences, by 1988 the combined death toll from alcohol poisoning, cirrhosis of the liver and alcohol-induced violence and accidents was down to 179 deaths per 100,000 – a level not seen since 1965. But by 1995, with the failure of Gorbachev's anti-alcohol campaign and the collapse of the USSR, according to government data, this rate had climbed to nearly 500 deaths per 100,000 (by way of comparison, the U.S. rate for 1995 was 77). In teh late 1990s, *Nezavisimaya Gazeta* estimated that 43,000 Russians died each year from vodka poisoning alone. In 1997, the total number of alcohol poisonings from fake wine and vodka (both fatal and nonfatal) in Russia reached 90,000.

According to estimates by the Russian Health Ministry, alcohol consumption in Russia reached 15 liters of pure alcohol per year for every man, woman and child in 1996. (Health Ministry experts concluded that, assuming most children were not drinking, adjusted adult consumption was 18 liters of pure alcohol – i.e., the rough equivalent of 38 liters of 100-proof vodka per person, per year, vs. eight liters per adult per year in the U.S.).

As noted above, in the past the Russian state benefited from (and perhaps encouraged) such excess consumption. Yet that is not the case now. Budgetary proceeds from the alcohol business have plummeted to an all time low of 3 percent, whereas in Soviet times, the infamous *pyanye dengi* (drunken money) accounted for one-third of the Russian budget. The reason? Money that should have come to the state in the form of taxes has been ending up in the pockets of bootleggers or corrupt state officials.

In today's Russia, vodka supports entire regions. The republic of North Ossetia's economy is reputedly based largely on sales of illegal spirits smuggled into Russia from Georgia. Former North Ossetian president Askharbek Galazov allegedly funded his entire election campaign with money from spirit trafficking. Then there are the many "charitable" organizations, like the National Sports Fund and the Russian Orthodox Church, which allegedly exploited their privileged, duty-free status to make a killing importing and reselling wine and/or spirits.

Dragon in the Bottle

Thus did it become apparent that "free" vodka was dangerous and "cheap" vodka had some very significant social and economic costs. Pressed by immediate economic concerns (months-long wage arrears, namely to the army), in 1993 President Yeltsin issued a decree restoring the "state monopoly" on alcohol production. But this was easier said than done. Once the green dragon (a Russian folk idiom for alcohol) was out of the bottle, it was virtually impossible to put it back in.

For one thing, the means to the end is different from past crackdowns. Yeltsin's "monopoly" is nothing like that of the Soviet era. It is largely one of licensing and other regulatory measures, such as excise stamps and banning alcohol advertising from TV. There are mandatory tax points at distilleries to control "illegal leaks of spirits and vodka" from factories. Special excise stamps were introduced on alcohol (although all attempts to make them technically fake-proof have been in vain). A regional registry of all licensed alcohol producers and traders was compiled. In September 1997, Yeltsin dedicated his radio address to vodka, explaining to Russians that the government's success in bringing the alcohol market to heel is important not only for preserving the nation's health but also for maintaining a stable budget and paying pensions on time (a reality that many observers did not appreciate).

Little by little, the new measures have started to pay off. Two or three years ago, as much as 90 percent of Russia's alcohol market was widely believed to be "in the shadows." Today, this figure is down by nearly half.

Stamps Chez Luzhkov

One new trend may hold further hope for regulating the vodka market. Cities and regions have set up control policies of their own – not unlike State Liquor Control Boards in the U.S.

Moscow, for one, passed a resolution requiring an additional type of bar-code stamp on alcohol production. All vodka transported into the city and region must pass through a network of special "unitary enterprises" for quality testing and bar-coding. While the State Antimonopoly Committee spoke out against this measure, calling it a barrier to free competition, Mayor Luzhkov and his retinue proceeded anyway.

Moscow was following the example set by Tatarstan, whose authorities introduced a state "monopoly" on the production and sales of hard liquor. In Arkhangelsk, a system was introduced requiring regional quality certificates for all vodka sold within the region's borders. Needless to say, there are special fees for certification services. In Voronezh, all vodka producers must supply their products to the Voronezh Alko enterprise, which operates under the dependable cover of the local administration. These local authorities do not hide their desire to beef up local budgets and support local vodka producers at the expense of outsiders, and under the pretext of keeping out poor-quality vodka.

But there is a problem with this new, increased local control over vodka production and sales. It will increase prices in the shops. Which, in turn, will increase the price gap between legal and illegal vodka. The danger is that higher prices on "safer" vodka may once again turn Russians to cheaper, fake vodkas.

Six hundred years after it first appeared in Russia, vodka continues to play a pivotal role in Russia, challenging both policymakers and health providers. While the specific issues may have changed somewhat over the centuries, the general tensions have not. Russia cannot base a modern economy on revenues from alcohol. But it is a hard reality to avoid after so many hundreds of years of relying on the "green dragon." All the more so since vodka is become such an inalienable part of Russian culture and cuisine.

It is surely true, following the Russian saying, that there "can be too much vodka." The question is whether there can simply be "enough" vodka, and how much that is.

April 1998

Islands of Mystery
Maria Antonova

Strange things always happen with Solovki," wrote Dmitry Lebedev in response to my letter, "one needs to be careful."

I emailed Lebedev when I decided I absolutely had to visit the Solovetsky Islands in 2008. Lebedev is the unofficial coordinator of the Northern Seafaring Fellowship, a group of enthusiasts involved with several volunteer projects on Solovki. They run a free Seafaring Museum and are constructing a wooden replica of the eighteenth century ship that Peter the Great used to sail the White Sea.

"I'd like to come and work on the islands," I wrote, "what can I do to help out?"

Two days later, I received a call from the International Fund for Animal Welfare (IFAW). "Do you want to come to Solovki the day after tomorrow?" asked Maria Vorontsova, the fund's director in Russia. "Someone from the Natural Resources and Environment Ministry was supposed to go, but cancelled at the last moment. We already have a ticket."

I was already on a plane bound for Arkhangelsk when Lebedev's email hit my inbox. Nevertheless, he was right: you must be careful of what you wish for.

THERE ARE TWO ways to reach the islands. One involves a long train ride to Kem, a gloomy seaside town in Karelia where some of Pavel Lungin's movie, *The Island* (*Остров*), was filmed. From there, travelers endure a bumpy, three-hour boat journey to the Solovetsky port. Inexplicably, the trip didn't take as long in the nineteenth century. According to some monastery accounts, Solovetsky monks who went to the mainland to buy food and sell salt made the crossing in just over two hours.

In order to save time, our group is taking the second, "bourgeois" way: the connecting flight through Arkhangelsk. From Arkhangelsk, we board a tiny, lightweight Antonov jet, where passengers have to be distributed equally on both sides of the plane to prevent tipping. The vibration makes speaking feel like you are sitting inside a drum.

IFAW has a number of projects around Russia, one of which is sponsoring studies of beluga whales off the coast of Bolshoy Solovetsky Island. Over time, the whales have become yet another natural attraction on the islands. Over 30,000 visitors come to the archipelago every year to admire its heritage of austere northern Orthodoxy, to learn about the horrific Soviet prison, and to breathe the salty air of the White Sea that surrounds this unique ecosystem.

We wait by the plane's cargo opening, from which a young man is handing out suitcases like he's selling potatoes from a truck. "Zhenya, if you damage my luggage, you're in big trouble," one female passenger says half seriously before accepting her bag and disappearing into the morning mist.

SEVERAL HUNDRED LOCALS live on the islands. For the most part, they live in the village of Solovetsky, the settlement that surrounds the Solovetsky Kremlin. Some inhabit simple, century-old wooden houses, others live in apartment blocks left behind from various Solovetsky eras: the prison, the military settlement, the seaweed harvest, the museum. The tourist mecca period came last.

As it became possible to purchase housing here in the 1990s, the boundary between "local" and "tourist" was blurred. Many families live in their island flats in summer and return to live in a big city during winter. Former Moscow classmates have bumped into each other here after losing touch for decades.

MANY OF THE buildings on Solovki are testaments to the faith and endurance of the monks that first inhabited this remote archipelago in the fifteenth century, seeking spiritual and physical isolation from the world. For at least the first 100 years, it was a desolate outpost with only wooden structures.

In the sixteenth century, the monastery also became a northern point of defense against enemy ships, and eventually its importance, both spiritual and military, was recognized by Russia's rulers, who gave it considerable support. Although the monks bravely fought foreign intruders, they also proved feisty to Moscow on several occasions, the most tragic of which was the "Solovetsky sitting" in the 1670s. Rebelling against Patriarch Nikon's reforms, the monastery refused to submit to tsarist diplomats. When troops stormed the monastery walls after a blockade lasting eight years, few monks were spared.

Armed with not much more than time, their health, and what the island provided naturally, the monks completed a number of amazing infrastructural projects. One is a 1220-meter-long dry-stone dyke. The dyke snakes across the water, connecting Bolshoy Solovetsky with Bolshaya Muksolma Island, where the monks had cows and farmland. According to monastery accounts, Zosima, one of the three original monks on the islands (the other two were Savvaty and Guerman), forbade the keeping of animals on the main island. The dyke/causeway was engineered by a monk and former peasant, Feoktist.

We spot a boat with two men in it as soon as our captain, Vladimir Danilovich, drops us off at the dyke. "I wonder what they are doing," says biologist Nadezhda Cherenkova, our guide. "If they are harvesting seaweed, we need to report them to the station – they are poachers in a protected area."

Bolshaya and Malaya Muksolma are renowned for the abundant seaweed near their shores. Malaya Muksolma is one of three official harvesting areas for the Arkhangelsk Seaweed Factory, an enterprise that receives in its raw material from Solovki. Seaweed harvesting was a main source of income for locals in the 1970s. Now, most harvesters are from other parts of the country; some from as far away as Moldova. Locals are unimpressed with the 45 cents they can get per harvested kilo; it's much easier to earn a living renting out a room to tourists during the summer.

The two lost souls in the boat are seasonal workers from Arkhangelsk. Apparently, they caught the wrong current off of Malaya Muksolma. Small wonder, as they are hopelessly drunk. One introduces himself as Vanya Fortochkin, and presents us with a starfish hanging onto life in a crummy plastic bag. If they are poachers, they are unsuccessful ones. Nadezhda rolls her eyes and goes back to describing for us island wildlife and history.

DURING OUR TIME on the islands, we occasionally saw points where the islands' various interest groups collide. Nadezhda and her husband Alexander, an ornithologist, are both from Moscow, but have lived on the islands for over a decade. Like IFAW, they want the archipelago to be recognized as a UNESCO World Heritage Site of mixed status, which would protect all of the islands' ecosystems, not just cultural landmarks such as the Kremlin on Bolshoy Solovetsky Island.

But if this happens, the Arkhangelsk Seaweed Factory will likely close. Most of the pharmaceutical and cosmetic products made at the factory are produced from Solovetsky seaweed.

When I meet the factory's director, Yelena Bokova, in Solovetsky village, she complains that locals have gotten used to easy money from tourism, that they have forgotten how to work. To her, the monastery is but a prop – a remnant of the past that gives Moscow historians access to an easy life on museum salaries. "They come here and spend their entire lives guarding a rock," she says sarcastically.

Just a few locals are "unspoiled" by tourism mania, preferring the grueling labor of seaweed harvesting. As Bokova and I talk, boats pull into Solovetsky port and music is playing. It is a prelude to the Solovetsky Regatta, an event that brings tourists to Solovki from all across the country. Bokova sighs. Many years ago, there was a harvesting site right next to the port, she says, but it was closed after workers started to use harvesting boats to take tourists for rides.

In the summer, the port is alive late into the evening. Days are so long during the summer, in fact, that they never really become nights. The sun dips toward the horizon, giving the islands a pink-orange glow, then rises again. During our three-day stay on Solovki, the wee hours of morning were only delineated by the silence that filled the village around midnight, and the local cows that floated eerily past our hotel at 1 AM, clanging their cow bells.

THE NEXT DAY we take the boat to Beluzhy Cape, named after the white beluga whale that has congregated there for decades. Scientists from Moscow's Shirshov Oceanographic Institute study the animal from a watchtower. Belugas come here to have offspring in June, after the ice melts. In July, brown baby belugas swim alongside their white mothers. In a month, the colony will migrate away from Solovetsky shores.

"Nobody knows why they come here," says Vladimir Baranov, one of the scientists on the tower. "There is a small spot [of sand] that is just four square meters, and all of the whales try to rub their bellies on it," Baranov says, "it's a ritual they repeat over and over again."

Baranov looks like a pirate but talks like a philosopher. While his colleagues peer toward the horizon with binoculars, he stands behind them, listening to whale chatter through headphones. The animals make clicking sounds to "see" the surroundings with their built-in sonar. To communicate with one another, Baranov says, they whistle. "We have their alphabet already, now we are trying to put together a dictionary of what all of the signals mean," Baranov says matter-of-factly, but I am rather sure he is making a joke.

Scientists from the Shirshov hope to one day mount a camera over the spot where the Belugas congregate. Simultaneously monitoring their behavior and language would bring greater understanding. Observation through diving was fruitless, as the Belugas are easily spooked. And the last thing the scientists want to do is scare the whales into leaving these feeding grounds altogether, endangering their survival.

This Beluga tribe is one of only five or seven such pods in the White and Bering Seas, researchers say, and is the only one in the world that comes so close to the shore. Monastery accounts don't mention Belugas on the Solovetsky coast, but the animal was widely hunted in tsarist times for its prized skin – a carriage on display in St. Petersburg's Hermitage Museum has a roof made of beluga leather.

Attached to one of the poles of the watchtower is a faded, plastic toy horsehead. Baranov tied it there to recall the legend that Savvaty and Guerman came to the islands on "a white horse," a beluga. The horsehead is also the mascot for this team of Moscow scientists, who live in a secluded campground all summer. The campground is their *skete* ("cell, hermitage"), where they mark time by the tides and celebrate birthdays by presenting each other with stones from the nearby beach.

The "birthday garden" in front of their wooden kitchen building looks a lot like a graveyard.

STONES ARE EVERYWHERE on Solovki – witnesses to an era of repression and monuments to lives that ended in the Solovetsky prison camp. Gulag memorials in several Russian cities, including Moscow, are boulders from these islands, site of the first Soviet camp for political prisoners.

Yury Brodsky is Russia's most dedicated chronicler and historian of the Solovetsky Prison. He started collecting evidence and archival information in the 1960s, and published a book on the subject in 2003, full of former inmate accounts, correspondence, photography, and the chilling story of the country's exemplar prison. His archive holds over five thousand images, and he has travelled around the country extensively to interview former *zeks* (prisoners).

Brodsky likes to speak broadly about historic trends, noting that a prison was projected as part of the monastery as early as the sixteenth century. Even in their planning stages, the Kremlin walls had cells, and inmates were held in the basements of the Uspensky and Spaso-Preobrazhensky cathedrals. The first inmates were the non-possessors (*nestyazhateli*) – Orthodox believers who were against ecclesiastical land ownership.

"There was a prison in the genes of Solovki," Brodsky says. The genetic inheritance was establishment of Solovetsky Prison in 1923. Over the next ten years, a million people went through its system, including some of the dedicated Bolsheviks who worked to establish the prison in the first place. Most of those sent here were politicals being isolated from the body politic. Most did not receive any trial; their fates were decided at various semi-official committees.

Brodsky explains all of this as we stand atop of Sekirnaya Mountain. Like any other Solovetsky site, this mountain has at least a dual significance. The view from here is beautiful, and the elegant white church doubles as a lighthouse – a small glass cabin on top of the belltower houses a powerful projector that guides passing ships. But in the prison camp period, this church served as a lock-up, a punishment cell where prisoners often died after enduring cruel torture. On the second floor, inmates stripped to their underwear awaited execution.

The Solovetsky Prison Camp laid the groundwork for the Gulag system. Here, the system of labor, punishment, and identity erasure was perfected through trial and error. Looking at the archipelago through the lens of this era is difficult and wearying. It seems so much easier to forget, to stop questioning why history unfolded along a path that was so bloody, uncompromising, and illogical. Brodsky has dedicated half of his life to this study and it has clearly worn him down. He is concerned that prison history will be swept under the carpet.

Nearby are several neat stacks of logs. "The monks have chopped down a building where female inmates were held before their execution," Brodsky says. He is opposed to how the monastery is commemorating prison victims selectively, putting Orthodox crosses over mass graves where Jews and Catholics are also interred, for example. The museum, a secular organization, is also not representing the atrocities adequately, he says, "their position is to collect the material without judging it, to find something positive in the prison camp period."

This period ended in 1933, when prisoners were sent to other labor camp projects, such as the Norilsk Nickel mine and factory beyond the Arctic Circle.

IT IS SATURDAY, the Orthodox holiday of Sts. Peter and Paul. I want to get the monastery's perspective, but Father German, who has the authority for such discussions, is ill. Instead, I meet with Pyotr Boyarsky, a well-known Arctic explorer and one of the people who signed a public letter this summer in favor of handing over the entire archipelago to the Orthodox Church. The letter has much of the community, especially the museum staff, up in arms.

As we stand next to the monastery gates after the holiday service, Boyarsky is listing the things he is not happy about on Solovki. To him and many Orthodox believers, Solovki should be first and foremost a spiritual pilgrimage center. Instead, irresponsible development is turning it into a commercial and recreational spot.

This year, there is yet another unwelcome guest on Solovki: Ministry for Emergency Situations troops are camping out in green tents on a site where mass graves used to be, preparing for exercises on Sekirnaya Mountain. Their heavy trucks are tearing up what remains of Solovetsky roads.

"Tourism is out of control, there are helicopters flying, women are bathing in the Holy Lake in bikinis, there is advertising everywhere, there are unnecessary regattas, there are so many people – everywhere!"

Boyarsky points to a crowd of people headed in our direction, but then we both realize that these are not drunken tourists but the Procession of the Cross, making its turn around the Kremlin in celebration. We both laugh at his mistake as he accepts greetings and congratulations from passersby. The priest showers us with holy water, and, for a moment, the joyous singing and smiles on everyone's faces ease the complexities of Solovki.

LATER IN THE day, our group is standing, waiting for the tiny Antonov plane to take us back to Arkhangelsk. The airport may be the only place on Solovki where all the different classifications of archipelago visitors come together: pilgrims who bunked in monastery dormitories, backpackers who have just broken camp, moneyed Muscovites who have stayed in a new hotel, monks on monastery business to the regional capital, journalists leaving more confused than when they arrived. We have all come to Solovki with our own motivations, and are leaving with very different experiences.

These islands will ever be a mystery beckoning all comers, not unlike that patch of sand where Belugas rub their bellies without knowing why.

I know I will be back for more.

January/February 2009

Two Cities: A Tale
Vasily Latenko

*H*ave you ever been to a city with a river running through it?

Of course you have. But have you ever been to a city, where, because of historical circumstances, the river has become an international border, dividing the city in two? Imagine for a moment that Paris used to be one city, but then split in two, with France on one side of the Seine and Germany on the other. Or imagine Budapest being split once again into Buda and Pest. Nonsense, you say.

And yet, this is exactly what happened to the Estonian town of Narva, founded on the left bank of the Narva river, and the Russian town of Ivangorod, which sits on the right bank.

The two towns have changed hands throughout history, now in Sweden, now in Lithuania, now in Estonia, now in Russia. But they always traveled through history as a pair, residing in the same country or empire. Then, in 1991, the Soviet behemoth stumbled, fell, and Narva and Ivangorod were set into opposing camps. On May 1, 2004, when Estonia joined the European Union (having joined NATO a month previous), modest Narva became the European city closest to Russia's second capital, St. Petersburg, just 147 kilometers away. Ivangorod, across the river, stayed in Russian hands.

It is a rather unassuming international border. After all, the Narva river is less than 200 meters wide at this point. Or, as historians are fond of writing, the two towns are just "a gunshot away" from one another. Not a propitious fact, but then let us start from the very beginning.

Border Towns

The oldest known inhabitants of this land – in the middle Stone Age – built themselves wooden houses on the left shore of the river, where Narva stands today. In the Novgorod Chronicle, Narva is first mentioned in 1171, as the town of Rugodiv. Ivangorod is the younger sibling, having been founded in 1492, when Ivan III ("the Great"), Prince of Moscow, built a fortress here – one of Rus' first defensive fortifications. Ivangorod is also mentioned in fifteenth century German documents, which call the town "counter-Narva."

In the early part of the thirteenth century, Estonia was taken over by the Danes (1220-1346), who transformed Narva – then a fishing village named Narvia – into a stronghold between northern Estonia and Russia. The first Danish fortress here was probably made almost entirely of wood. Russians burned it down at the end of the thirteenth century.

In the mid-fourteenth century, the region became part of the Livonian Order. Then, two hundred years later, during the Livonian War, Narva and Ivangorod were captured by Russia, which held them from 1558-1581. Narva and Ivangorod were occupied by Sweden from 1581-1590 and 1612-1704, and they were turned into strong fortresses on the Russian border. The bastions built then have partially survived to this day.

As a result of Peter the Great's victory over Sweden in the Northern War, Narva and Ivangorod fell under Russian rule in 1704. The two towns were actually unified into one, with Ivangorod becoming "the Ivanovskaya side" of Narva. Russian rule over Narva lasted until November 28, 1918, when Narva was occupied by Germany during the allied intervention against the Bolshevik revolution.

In 1919, both Narva and Ivangorod were part of an independent Estonia, which ended in July 1940, when Estonia (along with Lithuania and Latvia) was forcibly absorbed into the USSR. Just over a year later, Germany again occupied the towns. They were liberated in 1944, and the border between Soviet Russia and Soviet Estonia was established along the river Narva. Thus, when Estonia regained its independence in 1991, the international border separated the two towns for the first time into two different countries.

United by Vodka

Throughout history, Narva and Ivangorod have always lived as a husband and wife, fighting and then reconciling. But they have always lived together, even today, as they find themselves on different sides of the barbed wire that guards this international border. Every day, Narvanians go to Ivangorod and Ivangorodians go to Narva, joking as they go: "I guess I'll go take a walk to NATO!"

It only takes a half-hour to cross the Russian-Estonian border. The walk is all downhill from the bus station in Ivangorod. There is an exquisite view here of the Narva ramparts, built by the Swedes in the fourteenth and fifteenth centuries, now dotted with Russian fishermen, who are happy to sell you fresh pike, perch, and, when they are in season, lamprey – considered a delicacy by locals on both sides of the river.

After the transit point, you come onto a bridge full of vans and trucks – many countries, especially those in Scandinavia, use Estonia to transit into Russia. The bridge is quite interesting; in Soviet times it was officially baptized The Bridge of Friendship, joining the Republic of Estonia with Leningrad Region. Before the river was a border, daring youths would jump from the bridge into the raging river – a feat all the more difficult because, not only is the river 20 meters below the bridge, but there are huge stones to avoid. Today, no one jumps from the bridge. Anyone brave (or foolish) enough to do so would face hours of interrogation from border guards.

According to official statistics, some 4,500 persons travel from Ivangorod to Narva every day. That is 30 percent of Ivangorodians and more than five percent of Narva's population of 70,000. Russians cross the border, carrying into Estonia vodka, cigarettes, and clothes, which they sell quickly and at a nice markup – Russian prices are lower than those in Estonia. Such trafficking helps Ivangorodians make ends meet: the average salary in Ivangorod is just R2-3,000 ($70-100) per month, so smuggling is widespread.

"I walk to Narva every day," said Yelena, a barmaid at a café in Ivangorod. "I take along sweaters and vodka. We live badly. What can I say? Young people either become drunkards or leave to study in Petersburg, from where no one wants to return home. Pensioners make up a little less than half of [Ivangorod's] population of 12,000."

In Yelena's café, they are playing an Estonian radio station. Meanwhile, Narva's Russian-speaking residents watch mostly Russian channels; few Russian Narvanians have learned Estonian, and fewer still like Estonian TV. There are very few ethnic Estonians in Narva, so all signs in the town are in two languages.

Narvanians walk to Ivangorod in the same numbers every day as those going in the opposite direction. Their purpose is to buy the same things – alcohol, tobacco and lower-priced food. A typical purchase consists of a liter of vodka, a box of cigarettes and cereals. In the last few years, businessmen, counting on shoppers from Narva, have opened enough food stores in the Russian town to feed three or four Ivangorods (or one Narva).

Not surprisingly, this cross-border trade is the town's major source of income. Of Ivangorod's 5,000 employed, some 2,400 work in services, while just over 1,000 work in industry. The latter has been on a gradual decline since 1992. Today, the only flourishing factory is one started in 2000 – it produces alcohol. Everything here, it seems, turns on vodka.

And what about Narva? On the left bank of the river, the standard of living is a bit better, but still quite far from prosperous. German journalists traveled around the new EU countries in 2003 and published an article in *Hamburger Abendblatt* under the headline, "Narva: A Look into the European Abyss." "When Estonia joins the EU next year," they wrote, "Narva will probably be the ugliest and the most unkempt town of the new Europe."

German journalists may have laid it on too thick, but the fact remains that neither of these divorced spouses are doing very well. Outwardly, Ivangorod is the least attractive. The main street, ulitsa Gagarina, is lined with two-story houses, a dilapidated Palace of Culture, small shops, a food and clothing market... and that's about it. Narva, meanwhile, has modern supermarkets and clean streets. But external appearances can be deceiving. Both towns suffer from high unemployment, low salaries and bleak economic futures.

It is never easy living on the frontier.

Selling the Fortresses

Narva and Ivangorod might have remained a province "forgotten by people and God," if not for their impressive historical past, which lives on in the form of the awesome fortresses situated here. Both towns dream wildly of developing tourism, yet neither has been able to get moving forward.

Still, there is plenty for tourists to see here.

"In the Northwest, there is nothing else like this," said Gennady Popov, director of the Ivangorod Fortress-Museum. (Popov, by the way, lives in Narva and works in Ivangorod.) "In Koporye, the fortress is a tiny, puny little thing, not to mention Staraya Ladoga. There is no other fortress like ours anywhere in Russia. Yet it does need to be restored. In 1994, when restoration work was stopped, we needed $5 million for 10 years of work. Today we would need even more, because back then they did not do conservation. The state will never allocate that amount of money."

But even in its current state, the fortress is impressive: fortified walls several meters thick, with churches inside the walls. Visitors are transported centuries back in time.

Tour guide Sergei Nikitin speaks with evident pride of the Ivangorod fortress. "There are known cases, when, early in the twentieth century, Narva grammar-school students never returned from explorations of the fortress's passageways – so little had they been studied." He points to a beautiful church. "This is Assumption Church; Catherine the Great came here. The son of the poet Pushkin, Alexander Alexandrovich, was commander of the fortress regiment here; one of Pushkin's ancestors was governor of this fortress. The lives of many great people are connected to this fortress."

We walk to a redoubt on the fortress, where guns once fired on attackers. An Estonian flag flutters in the breeze. A Russian flag also once flew here. But its flagpole is now naked. The flag, Nikitin says, not entirely convincingly, is being restored. Others say the flag was simply stolen.

Later, Nikitin recalled how he found an article in *Rossiyskaya Gazeta* with a photo of Vladimir Putin visiting the fortress in 1992. "He then worked in Petersburg City Hall and came here. This is my, it could be said, scientific discovery," he jokes.

One cannot help thinking that a plaque with "Putin Was Here" is just around the corner. Anything to promote the fortress.

Artists are in fact trying to help the struggling Russian town, promoting its tourism potential. Last year, the Mariinsky Theater performed the opera *Prince Igor* in the Ivangorod fortress.

"This didn't do anything for the museum," Popov said. "Tickets were $75, so they brought about 200 people from Petersburg themselves. For us, it didn't do anything. Except five biotoilets remained after their visit. Besides, I think that for *Prince Igor*, the Fortress of Ivangorod is not a suitable decoration. He was a pagan, yet the opera was performed with Orthodox churches in the background."

The Mariinsky's press officer, Oksana Tokranova took another view. "Such fortresses as the one in Ivangorod are unique," she said. "All over the world, they are used as stages for performances. At *Prince Igor*, during the performance of the opera, real horses grazed, crosses were burned, the feeling from what was happening was incredible."

This year, the Mariinsky will be back – to perform the ballet The *Fountain of Bakhchisarai* in the Ivangorod fortress. Popov grumbled his disapproval. "*The Fountain of Bakhchisarai* should be staged in the Crimea," he said. "For our fortress, *Boris Godunov* would be more appropriate – he is the one who stormed it."

But Putin and Godunov alone cannot develop tourism. Real action is needed, not stop-gap or *ad hoc* benefit performances.

Deputy head of the Ivangorod municipality, Alexei Shantsev, said the main obstacle to tourism is geographic: the city is located in the border zone. "It is impossible to enter the city impromptu," he said. "[A foreigner] has to inform the authorities of his visit 10 days prior and get a permit. We need less control. We have been working with European partners, for example, with the Finnish town of Kotka. We would like for Finnish tourists to be able to visit us by sea. [The Narva river empties into the Gulf of Finland just 14 km away.] Also, the lack of infrastructure is an obstacle: there is just one working hotel in town, Vityaz. It was built in 1980, for the Olympics. It has just 60 rooms. These combined problems scare investors off, since their investments would not likely have a swift return."

The Narva fortress, across the river, is no less picturesque. It houses the Narva Museum, with exhibits on the Middle Ages and the era of Peter the Great. In addition, the castle has one modern collectable which is slowly gaining in historic value. It is the monument to Vladimir Lenin which used to stand in the center of Narva. After Estonia won its independence in 1991, town authorities did not have the nerve to destroy their Lenin, so they moved him to the fortress. And there the stone leader stands today, pointing toward Ivangorod's medieval walls, or maybe just toward Russia.

Not all that is of interest in Narva is from antiquity. For instance, there is a bilingual memorial plaque celebrating the visit to the town by Czech writer Jaroslav Hasek. It was installed by the Society of Beer Lovers Named For The Good Soldier Svejk, Hasek's best-known character. The plaque reads: "'On the corner of May street I saw a lovely scene. A policeman was trying to pull apart a fight between a fat boar and a stray, bearded goat. That's all I saw in Narva...' (Jaroslav Hasek, December 1920)"

Unfortunately, Jaroslav Hasek wrote very little about Narva. In addition to the phrase on the plaque, he wrote: "...They are driving us across the bridge, and two more kilometers through the town, which civil war has marked significantly. A long strip of unfilled trenches crosses the square – for the edification of posterity, and also for the purposes of sewage, which is here at about the same level of development as it was hundreds of years ago, when German crusaders were building this city."

Not far from Hasek's plaque, another writer is honored. Alexander Pushkin never visited the town, but a bust of him was unveiled here five years ago nonetheless. Locals joke that, if you look at the monument from the side, you can see that it resembles the mayor of Narva at the time the bust was installed.

But there is plenty more to Narva. In the town center, there is the City Hall, built in 1668-71 in the style of Dutch city palaces. In Soviet times, the City Hall housed the Palace of Pioneers (the Soviet youth organization). Today the building stands empty. But they are talking about moving the mayor's office here soon.

And, of course, you can always bring a pole and drop a line in the Narva river to catch an international dinner. For 300 years, this river bound these married cities together, as war and history repeatedly conspired to change their nationality. Now the river stretches between the married couple, separating them like generations of accumulated differences. The divorce, it seems, is quite final. Visitations, however, will continue indefinitely.

November/December 2004

An End to Heresy
Tamara Eidelman

On December 4, 1505, in the Moscow Kremlin's Chudov Monastery, Archbishop Gennady of Novgorod breathed his last. One would think that the death of an aged monk would be of little significance, yet the actions of this man had serious repercussions on Russian history. Approximately 20 years before Gennady's death, unusual priests came on the scene in Veliky [Great] Novgorod. They began to harshly attack the Orthodox Church, accusing its priests of acquiring too much wealth and of making appointments to church positions in exchange for money – a sin condemned by Holy Scripture.

Following this line of thinking, the rebel priests concluded that the priests who had attained their office by sinful means could not administer the sacraments, and that therefore the entire church service had no meaning. On top of that, these wandering preachers denied the sanctity of icons and cast doubt on the Holy Trinity – a central article of Christian faith.

We do not know whether or not the Novgorod heretics actually said the things their opponents accused them of. All we have are denunciatory speeches, primarily those of Archbishop Gennady himself. Given the duration and zeal of his efforts to expose the heretics, it can be presumed that his enemies enjoyed broad support among Novgorodians. And this is not surprising. The birthplace of the heresy was a major commercial city. Throughout Europe, it was enterprising and tightfisted merchants who first refused to meekly submit to ecclesiastical prescriptions. They were also the first to be bothered by ecclesiastical opulence. They had no desire to give up their hard-earned money to the Church.

At the end of the fifteenth century, Western Europe was full of heretics. In Germany, young Martin Luther, destined to initiate the struggle against the power of the Catholic Church, was coming of age. But across Russia, things were absolutely calm. The Orthodox Church enjoyed the support both of the rulers and of their subjects and was confident in its authority.

TRANSLATION: NORA FAVOROV

The exception was Novgorod – the most "European" of Russian cities. Here, some people appeared and questioned this authority. And Gennady did everything he could to silence them. After a multitude of wrathful sermons were directed at them, the heretics were convicted. They were seated backwards on horses and led around the city as the faithful spat upon them. Birch helmets were placed on the unfortunate dissenters' heads and then set on fire. Any who managed to survive this punishment fled to Europe. And that should have been the end of it.

Should have. Instead, this was only the beginning. It turned out that some of the heretics had not in fact fled. Somehow, they mysteriously turned up in Moscow, in the Kremlin, in the royal chambers. For 15 years, there had been supporters of the heresy among Grand Prince Ivan III's closest confidants, first and foremost two prominent diplomats, the brothers Ivan and Fyodor Kuritsyn. The fact that Ivan Kuritsyn was better-known by his pagan name, "Wolf," bothered no one. Back then, it was not unusual to practice two faiths. But the fact that the Kuritsyn brothers discussed sinful priests and the impropriety of Church wealth – that was a source of displeasure to many.

But there was nothing to be done. Ivan III was the sovereign and, having unified Rus and refused to pay tribute to the khans of the Golden Horde, he would brook no arguments. He had won the right to call himself an autocrat. He invited Italian craftsmen to Moscow to rebuild the Kremlin cathedrals and palaces and now it was evident to all what a great ruler lived here. Ivan married Sofia Paleolog, the niece of the last emperor of Byzantium. In so doing, he won the right to appear with Byzantine symbols of power – the orb and scepter. Who could raise objections with such a sovereign? There was no longer room in the country for both a strong sovereign and a strong church. The Church hierarchy was left with no choice but to pray for the preservation of its status.

Help for the priests came from a completely unexpected quarter. One of the strongest supporters of the heresy was the daughter-in-law of the Grand Prince: the Moldavian Princess, Yelena Stefanovna, widow to Ivan's eldest son. The young woman exercised great influence, primarily as mother to Dmitry, the royal grandson. Ivan III so loved young Dmitry that he officially named him heir to the throne. Yelena Stefanovna's support must have made life for the heretics significantly easier at court. It may even have been she who pointed out to Ivan how advantageous their teachings were for him (challenging the power of the Church).

Nonetheless, Sofia Paleolog, the second wife of the Grand Price, did not accept the young daughter-in-law's privileged position. She had a son by Ivan named Vasily, and Sofia made every effort to ensure that Vasily would inherit the crown, not Dmitry. After lengthy and convoluted intrigues, Sofia and Vasily were victorious over Yelena and Dmitry. The latter were expelled from court and confined to a dungeon. This was a triumph not only for Sofia, but also for Archbishop Gennady, who had been unsuccessfully trying to convince Ivan III to break with the heretics.

Gennady and his loyal ally, the renowned Bishop Joseph Volotsky, spared neither actions nor words to convince the Grand Prince to switch sides. One argument proved decisive. Volotsky, who had for years argued the supremacy of ecclesiastic authority over secular authority, suddenly sent Ivan a missive declaring that the right to punish heretics, and by extension to interfere in Church dealings, must belong to the sovereign. The nimble mind of Ivan III immediately saw how well this arrangement could serve him. Supporting the heretics would inevitably lead to the sovereign taking over the Church's wealth and revolutionary changes to religious life. But an alliance with Gennady and Joseph opened up another course for the Grand Prince: the Church would remain strong and wealthy, but would openly recognize the supremacy of the State and promise to serve it. Ivan decided that a strong Church as ally was better than a weak and looted Church.

In 1504, to the delight of Gennady and his supporters, the Holy Synod definitively denounced the heretics. Wolf Kuritsyn and his followers – referred to in official documents by scornful diminutives such as Mitya Konoplev and Ivashka Maksimov – were burned inside a log structure on the Moscow River. A certain Nekras Rukavov first had his tongue cut out and then was taken to Novgorod and burned there.

This was, perhaps, the only burning of heretics in medieval Rus. Until the schism of the seventeenth century, the church remained completely tame. Yelena Stefanovna was fortunate. She died quickly in prison. Her son, Dmitry, on the other hand, outlived his grandfather and spent many years in confinement during the rule of Sofia Paleolog's son, Vasily III.

During the last years of Archbishop Gennady's life, he was accused of taking bribes (forcing him to leave Novgorod). But in December of 1505, as he lay on his deathbed in Moscow, he must have taken pleasure in a sense of duty well done. How could he know that the tsars of Russia would not need a strong church for long? Each successive ruler gradually deprived the clergy of rights and privileges; two centuries later, Peter the Great placed the church under the full control of the State.

November/December 2005

St. Basil's: The Stuff of Legend
Andrei Yurganov

The story of Vasily the Blessed does not tell us why his name superceded the iconic Red Square cathedral's official name... Perhaps the personal victory of one holy fool over evil is more memorable than a distant military battle.

*I*f you walk up into Red Square from the north on a snowy winter morning, you will be treated to a breathtaking sight. Like a colorful toy resting in the palm of this cobblestone field, the Cathedral of St. Vasily (Basil) the Blessed climbs into view, its jeweled domes looking more like a circus attraction than a national shrine. Perched high above the Moscow river, flanked by the stolid, gothic towers of the Kremlin fortress and the creeping commerciality of GUM, the church radiates an architectural self-confidence that is at once appealing and awe-inspiring. It is so amazingly out of place, and yet so perfectly set.

Interestingly, this icon of Russian culture was not always the multicolored baroque wonder we see today. Originally, the church was much less bright, more calm in tone. A sixteenth century visitor would have seen only red brick and white stone, star-shaped blue and yellow rosettes on the facets of the tent tower, and onion domes covered with tin sheeting (there were also eight small onion domes perched on the tines of the eight-pointed star that divides the central tent-roof chapel). It was only during the seventeenth century that the church took on the color and appearance with which we are now familiar.

What is more, the true name of this church is not St. Basil's, but the Cathedral of the Intercession on the Moat. Built between 1555 and 1561, it superceded (and incorporated) the Church of the Trinity that Ivan had ordered built in commemoration of the sacking of Kazan on October 1-2, 1552, a battle begun on the important Orthodox holiday of the Intercession of the Virgin. Thus the first part of the church's name. The second part of its name refers to the moat which once flowed below the church.

How is it that this name, connected with one of Rus' most important military victories, was cast from popular usage? The answer lies in a saint buried in one of the cathedral's eastern chapels. This chapel is dedicated to the *"yurodivy"* ("fool in Christ") Vasily (Basil), who died just weeks before the storming of Kazan in 1552.

Who was this man? The Chronicles recount Vasily's rather odd acts: he gave alms to a rich merchant instead of a poor one, he threw stones at the homes of the righteous and kissed the homes of the corrupt. He was repeatedly beaten for breaching public order, he was humiliated and often stoned by children. The life of this *yurodivy* was full of misfortune and misery, for no contemporary was supposed to know his main secret.

A *yurodivy* is one "touched," a fool for God, a saint whose outward derangement belies a hidden fight with the devil – a fight beyond the capacities of an ordinary man. The life of a *yurodivy* was one of the hardest in Russia. In fact, there are no more than 30 such *yurodivy* recorded from medieval Russia, and each knew he was doomed to die in misery and shame.

During the day, the *yurodivy* would "play" with the devil, then at night pray for God to forgive his tormentors. The *yurodivy* forsook normal reason for Christ's sake and gained the ability to see through the devil's plans, resist them, and daily pursue the devil while making a mockery of him.

In one of his recorded miracles, "Vasily the Blessed" is said to have seen "with the supreme reason of the saintly spirit" the image of the devil hidden behind an Icon of the Virgin which hung above the Varvarskiye Gates in Kitay-Gorod. Vasily ordered his disciple, a *dyak* ("scribe") to destroy the icon, reputed to have miraculous powers. The *dyak* dared not, so Vasily himself broke the icon with a stone. He was set upon by an irate crowd and promptly arrested. In court, the *yurodivy* declared that "this devilish miracle [the icon] was meant to lull the believers into temptation." The image of Satan was uncovered behind the icon; the painter was executed and Vasily was released.

Whether one believes such apocryphal tales, it was bold prophecies that distinguished the *yurodivy*, and Vasily was renowned for his courage and prophetic gifts. In particular, he is reputed to have predicted the devastating fire of 1547 (which may not have been so miraculous, given how susceptible the medieval town of wood was to fire).

The English traveler Giles Fletcher, who visited Russia during the reign of Boris Godunov, wrote: "In addition to monks, they have special eremites there whom they call holy men... They walk completely naked, even in winter in hard frost... with long hair... They are thought to be prophets and men of great holiness and thus are allowed to speak up freely without any limits even of the very highest himself [God]. If such a man blames someone... no one argues and they just say that the accused deserves this because of his sins." Fletcher noted that Vasily "dared to blame the late tsar [Ivan the Terrible] for his cruelty and all the oppressions he inflicted upon his people." It was a charge Ivan was susceptible to accepting in the repeated bouts of cruelty and repentance throughout his life. Indeed, Vasily was revered by the tsar, who, along with Metropolitan Macarius, attended Vasily's funeral on August 2, 1552.

And yet, the story of Vasily the Blessed does not tell us why his name superceded the official name, connected though it was with the victory over the Tatars at Kazan. Even if the memory of this saint was sacred, why would this national victory be less so? Perhaps the personal victory of one holy fool over evil is more memorable than a distant military battle.

As it is, we know all too little about the battle at Kazan. Too little we can take as fact, that is. In the "Short Chronicle of the Kazan Tsardom," the author tells of the storming of Kazan by the Russian army in 1552, but also combines real facts with folkloric fantasies. Tsar Ivan the Terrible is portrayed in the language of fairy tales as a flawless, ideal man: "And quite wise he was, and persistent, and strong in his body, and light on his legs like a snow leopard; and in every undertaking he was like his grandfather [Ivan III]." The tsar prays for the whole Orthodox people, confident in a long-awaited victory. The Russian warriors are similarly portrayed in hyperbolic fashion: "All the warriors, those holding spears and the cavalry men – they breathed like fire in Kazan with bravery and with wrath..." Meanwhile, the Tatars are depicted as barbarians who pillage Rus and torture Christians, "putting hot coals in their sandals." The Tartars "took along tall wives and strong girls whom they taught the art of field battle and how to shoot and defend the city's fortress walls; they even made them wear armor."

Yet, for all his patriotic fervor, the Chronicle's author still shares his admiration for the defenders of Kazan. In the chapter, "On the Fall of the Brave Residents of Kazan," he sings praises to the heroic deeds of the enemy: "Each Kazan resident fought with a hundred Russians, and sometimes even with two hundred." Nor does the chronicler hide the fact that Russia's sack of Kazan was followed by the destruction of mosques, murders and atrocities.

The attitude towards Tatars in Russia has always been mixed. True, in the minds of the Russians, the Tatars adhered to an alien faith; they were Muslim. Thus, their political power could not be totally accepted by an Orthodox country not ready to forget its Kievan Rus heritage. Yet, since 1472 and the reign of Ivan III, the threat of Tatar domination had all but subsided and the khanates bordering Rus' southern lands (e.g. Kazan, Astrakhan and Crimea) were largely subsumed by internal intrigues, for a century fluctuating between being allies, adversaries and vassals of the strengthening Muscovite state.

The khanate of Kazan was particularly rife with internal struggles for succession after the death of Safa-Girey in 1549. Ivan, who initially sought to secure Rus' southern flank through alliances with the khanates, elected to intervene in Kazan, in 1551 placing on the throne there Shah Ali, protected largely by troops from Moscow. But Ali did not sit well with either his protectors or his vassals, and within a year he was ousted. This time Ivan sought to put a Muscovite governor on the throne. Not surprisingly, this raised the ire of not only Kazan Tatars, but also those in neighboring Crimea, which attacked Muscovy from the southwest. The Tatar forces were repelled by the Tula militia and the path to Kazan was opened. Ivan laid siege to the fortress city for two months, before German engineers blew a hole in the walls that led to the sack.

It took Muscovy five years to pacify the region, but the victory in Kazan was hugely significant, opening the empire's expansion to the South and effectively ending (but for a dangerous episode in the Time of Troubles) the Tatar threat. Shortly thereafter, the khanate of Sibir and the Nogai horde both pledged their subservience to Ivan, who in 1556 went on to conquer the Astrakhan Khanate, opening the full length of the Volga to Russian dominance.

So it was that the seizure of Kazan came to symbolize the growing power of Moscow, the vanquishing of the "infidels," and the confirmation of Ivan IV's righteousness in proclaiming himself not just grand prince, but "tsar" in his 1547 coronation. The Church of the Intercession was to embody this glory and achievement, to stand as a grand symbol of Rus' Eastern Empire.

Interestingly, for all of its exterior grandeur, the Cathedral of the Intercession is remarkably small and close in its interior. While its external appearance could not but attract the attention of all (particularly given its commanding position in Red Square – at the time of its construction and until the completion of the Ivan the Great Bell Tower, it was the tallest structure in Moscow), its interior chapels are so small as to accommodate only small services of four or five persons. It gives the appearance more of a family church for the tsar, an elite cathedral for the few "chosen ones."

Ostensibly, it appears that the builders and architects allowed themselves some creative freedom in the construction of this national monument. The architects Barma and Postnik Yakovlev created a new type of church, using as its central unifying element the amazing tent-roof (*"shatyor"*) structure first employed in the Church of the Ascension at Kolomenskoe (commissioned, incidently, by Vasily III on the occasion of the birth of his son, Ivan IV).

Ivan ordered Barma and Yakovlev to raise a stone church consisting of eight chapels adjoined to the existing Trinity Church. A monument to the warriors who gave their lives for their homeland, several of the chapels were to be named for Saints Days which coincided with important battles against the Tatars. Yet, instead of eight, the craftsmen built a total of nine chapels, perhaps, it is argued by some, because they envisioned greater symmetry in nine than in eight, guided, as one medieval chronicle has it "by spiritual reason."

That the architects' vision was correct is clear. The tent-roof chapel (which is the Church of the Intercession from which the assemblage of chapels derives its name) is a powerful central axis, uniting the eight onion domes of the other chapels, each with its own image, yet each somehow resembling the others. Contemplating the church, one is struck by an overall harmony that embraces the distinctive characters of each of the elements. While it appears at times asymmetrical from various angles, with different sized and shaped cupolas, if viewed from above, it is readily apparent that it is perfectly symmetrical, with three chapels across in any direction, vertical, horizontal or diagonal.

Nonetheless, apparently such creative freedom was not the norm, particularly as the Orthodox Church under Metropolitan Macarius was seeking to regularize liturgies, practices and even architecture. Some, including the tsar, regarded Barma and Postnik's revisionism as inadmissible in an Orthodox tsardom (making doubly odd the myth that Ivan had their eyes gouged out so that they could not again make anything so beautiful). The church may well have been the first Russian architectural monument which triggered public polemics – about which we can only guess from the scarce fragments extant in the Russian Chronicles. Yet the polemics were perhaps not rooted only in a debate over the artistic merits of the Cathedral of Intercession on the Moat.

Three years after construction began on St. Basil's, the *udelny* (regional) prince Vladimir Andreyevich began construction of another important church employing tent-roof architecture. It was the Church of Saints Boris and Gleb in Staritsa (now the site of New Jerusalem monastery; the church was torn down about a century later to make room for new construction). And it was completed and consecrated on May 2, 1561, when the remains of the two most revered of Russian saints were transferred there – a month *before* the dedication of the Cathedral of the Intercession on the Moat.

Could there have been some rivalry behind the building of the Boris and Gleb church concomitant to the completion of the Cathedral of the Intercession? The dedication inscription in Boris and Gleb by the Staritsa prince offers a clue: "To parents, in obedience."

Whom could Prince Vladimir have had in mind? Of course, in the first place he was referring to his father, Andrei Staritsky, who raised the revolt against Yelena Glinskaya, mother of then child Ivan, since become Ivan IV. Yet because Prince Vladimir's mother Evfrosiniya Khovanskaya was still alive at the time of the construction, then why the plural "parents"? As it turns out, the reference is to Vladimir's father as well as to the Grand Princes Vasily II ("The Dark") and Ivan III, grandfather and father of Tsar Ivan IV. Thus did Vladimir seek to elevate his own lineage on a level with that of the tsar, as if to say "we all come from the same stock."

In one of his polemical letters to his confidant (and later opponent) Andrei Kurbsky, the tsar averred to this incipient rivalry and questioned the lines of succession: "And why would Prince Vladimir be the head of the state? Wasn't he born from the fourth regional prince?... What is his merit before the state? What is my fault before him?" Perhaps not surprisingly, by the end of the decade, in 1569, Prince Vladimir and his family fell victim to Ivan IV's paranoid delusions, forced to drink poison at the tsar's command.

Nearly four hundred years later, Joseph Stalin, in many ways Ivan the Terrible's historical *doppelgänger*, slated the Cathedral of the Intercession on the Moat for destruction, to share the ignominious fate of Konstantin Ton's Savior's Cathedral. Yet, by virtue of the miraculous intervention and temerity of the architect Konstantin Baranovsky, who protested against the barbaric plan of Stalin's "enlighteners," it survived. In yet another legend surrounding the mythic cathedral, tales abound of Baranovsky having barricaded himself in the church with a machine gun. Baranovsky's heroic defense of the sacred monument (which was only polemical) cost him several years in Stalin's camps.

Perhaps it is inevitable that such a significant national monument would become shrouded in mysteries and legends. Thankfully for our modern edification, this amazing cathedral has outlasted them all (as well as nearly half a millenium of Russian rulers), proving itself to be a monument to "spiritual reason" which simply cannot be destroyed.

November/December 2001

Alexandrovo Sloboda
Tamara Eidelman

*T*oday, Alexandrova is a two-hour ride from Moscow by commuter train. That two hours does not exactly fly by; through the window, all you see is forest and the occasional little village. But if you listen hard to the rattle of the wheels, you can begin to understand what a remote place Alexandrova Sloboda must have been more than four hundred years ago, in the sixteenth century, when the fate of Russia was being decided here.

At first, this was just a village that sat amidst the favorite hunting grounds of Grand Prince Vasily III – it was he who ordered a palace built on the banks of the Seraya River. Time passed, and Vasily's son, Ivan IV, ascended the throne of the Muscovite Principality. The boy became Grand Prince at the age of three. At that time, no one foresaw that he would become a bloody tyrant and the first Tsar of Russia, Ivan the Terrible.

We do not know how often the young Ivan visited the village. In any event, it is well known that he loved to hunt and he undoubtedly spent time there. Probably his anxious and troubled soul felt safe and secure in this place, nestled amidst a dense forest. From his youngest years, Ivan lacked safety and security. As a child, he had lost his father at age three and his mother at eight. As a small boy, he was forced to sit for hours as foreign ambassadors were received and pronounce words he could not understand. As a depraved adolescent, with no one in charge of his upbringing, he was surrounded by people trying to ingratiate themselves with him and not daring to stop him when he threw cats from the roof. At the age of thirteen, he ordered his first execution.

Later, the young tsar had burned indelibly on his imagination the sight of Moscow in flames and wild, riotous crowds. Still later, Ivan became the Reformer Tsar, who, over the course of ten years, in conjunction with wise counselors, completely restructured the system of government in the country. And yet, throughout it all, terror resided in Ivan – at first latent and then breaking through the surface with increasing frequency. There

TRANSLATION: NORA FAVOROV

was the terror of the *boyars*, who, he was certain, had poisoned his mother, dooming him to a lonely childhood. There was the terror of conspirators, the conspirators who had killed his first-born, dropped into water by his nursemaid – surely no accident. There was the terror of evil-doers, the evil-doers who had driven his beloved wife, Anastasia Romanova, to her grave. Again, there was no evidence of this, but that made the sight of her in a coffin all the more sinister. There was the terror of the *voyevods*, the military leaders who were losing battles. There was the terror of friends and comrades in arms, of those who were helping him and, surely, dreaming of getting rid of him…

The only way to rid himself of that terror was to take all power into his own hands. But the greater his power, the more terrified he became, and the more frequent was the thrust of the dagger and the fatal potion. He could stand it no longer and so, in December 1564, he understood what he needed to do.

One terrible December day, the residents of Moscow learned with horror that the tsar had disappeared. For people of those times, life without the tsar was the same as death, and Muscovites understood that something dreadful was coming. Meanwhile, the Terrible One was on his way to Alexandrova Sloboda. This place was to shelter him, to help him find loyal followers. He ordered that his father's palace be reconstructed and made into a luxurious residence. From here he sent word to Moscow that he was renouncing the throne. On the banks of the Seraya River he waited to see what would happen next…

Swarms of Moscow residents, including those very same *boyars* whom the tsar had accused of betrayal, made the long trip to the Sloboda (Russian for "settlement or village"), and got down on their knees, begging the tsar to return. This story is often pointed to as an example of Ivan's hypocrisy. However, the tsar was more than serious about what was happening. During those days, he was deeply upset and it is known that he lost all of his hair from stress.

After receiving universal assurances of loyalty, Ivan announced that, all the same, he was handing his kingdom over to the *boyars* and leaving himself just a widow's share – an *oprichnina*. This word, which had traditionally referred to the share of land a widowed Grand Princess would be left with after her husband's death, took on a whole new meaning under Ivan. He put the lands around Alexandrova Sloboda under his total control, control exercised by his *oprichniki*, loyal servants of the tsar who dressed in black and rode with dog's heads and brooms hanging from their saddles. The symbolism was clear: they would sniff out, gnaw at and sweep away betrayal.

Thus began the bloodiest seven years of Ivan's rule, a period in which Alexandrova Sloboda held a prominent place. Here Ivan feasted – and his guests never knew whether they would return home with a rich reward or perish from a poisoned goblet. Here the feasts were interrupted by hours of prayer (there was a reason that during Ivan's reign remarkable churches were either built or reconstructed in Alexandrova). Ivan Vasiliyevich liked to pray for the forgiveness of his sins together with his close associates and then descend into the palace's depths with Malyuta Skuratov, the head of the *oprichniki*, to torture his unfortunate prisoners.

And it was here that the tsar, on deciding to marry yet again, arranged a viewing of two thousand *boyar* daughters, from among whom he chose Marfa Sobakina (the real-life, ill-fated heroine of Rimsky-Korsakov's opera, *The Tsar's Bride*), who died two weeks later. And it was here that he married Princess Dolgorukaya and, the very next day, having concluded she was not a virgin, he put her in a carriage and ordered that the horses be driven into the river. And it was from here, from Alexandrova, that the tsar's troops rode out to crush and destroy Veliky Novgorod, which to Ivan was a city of traitors.

Seven years later, in 1572, when Ivan understood that the *oprichniki* had acquired too much power, he began to fear them as well. He dismantled the *oprichnina* and forbid any mention of the word, on pain of death. Nonetheless, he continued to spend time in Alexandrova Sloboda. The high walls of the Alexandrova Kremlin must have still seemed trustworthy. And this was where the aging tsar committed one of his most dreadful crimes. Ivan struck his own son with a staff, mortally wounding him – he perished within a few days. After this, the tsar repented and spent a long time praying for forgiveness. Toward the end of his life, he visited the Sloboda less and less frequently. He was fated to die in Moscow, perhaps at the hands of conspirators after all.

The palace in Alexandrova Sloboda gradually sunk into disrepair. During the Time of Troubles (1598-1613), it was used as a fortress. Decades later, the palace was dismantled, the churches were rebuilt and a monastery was placed where the tsar's residence had stood. Who knows? Perhaps here, in the monastery by the river, there were prayers of repentance for sins committed in the Sloboda... And across the river, in the area known as the *posad*, the settlement of merchants and artisans, there lived almost two thousand people. The *posad* gradually flourished and grew. By the end of the eighteenth century, it had earned the right to be called a city.

The main street here was – and remains – the road from Moscow. It had been a long time since the tsar's cortege traveled down it, although people still traveled it to buy the goods produced by Alexandrova's skilled ironsmiths. At the end of the nineteenth century, a railway line past the city was completed and trade became even brisker. Today, it is not just Ivan the Terrible who is the subject of Alexandrova's museums. You can visit a museum devoted to the daily lives of merchants and see the home of a prosperous nineteenth century resident, even enjoying tea served according to the customs of bygone days.

But Alexandrova never became a big industrial city. In 1913, when the Tsvetaeva sisters, one of whom was fated to become a great Russian poet, spent a summer in Alexandrova, what drew them there was the peace and quiet. Today, in the marvelously displayed, but, alas, dilapidated museum of Marina Tsvetaeva in Alexandrov (the town's current name), you can breathe in the atmosphere of the pre-war and pre-revolutionary years.

Only the names of a few streets recall the times of Ivan the Terrible – Streletskaya (Musketeer) Street, Starokonyushennaya (Old Stable) Street, Hunting Meadow. You just have to pronounce these names and it seems that detachments of *streltsy* are marching through the streets of the quiet town, that horses are being led from the stables to the palace, where the tsar himself is whistling for his kennelman and galloping off to hunt...

Fortunately, however, in Alexandrova all is quiet.

November/December 2005

Bolotnikov's Rebellion
Tamara Eidelman

*T*here are places on Earth where every structure, every hill speaks to you of ages past. Sometimes there is only a solitary voice. Sometimes there are many voices, rising out of the recesses of time, joining together into a chorus. One voice usually sings the solo, but this does not mean that the others could not sing as intriguing a song.

In Kolomenskoye, the solo is sung by the Church of the Ascension, the graceful sixteenth century wonder, reaching skyward like a fairy-tale castle. But as soon as you enter Moscow's Kolomensky Park, you see that you are in a place that resounds with the voices of many different eras.

The most distant voice reaches us from the primitive past. Not far from the museum, where later the village of Dyakovo would stand, an ancient encampment has been unearthed. We do not know how many centuries its people lived here or what fate befell them. The evidence seems to indicate that they were Ugro-Finnic – the most ancient settlers of these parts. Maybe they were already calling the river that flowed past them the Moskva, not knowing that later a great city would take its name. They lived on a bend in the river. Today, the vast expanse of Moscow can be seen from here, and, in the distance, another amazing sight – Tsaritsyno Palace and park. For those who settled here two or three millennia ago, this place provided an ideal vantage point from which to keep an eye on the river, which was the only way into these wooded wilds. From the tall hill, you could see anyone coming from a great distance, be they traveling merchants or unexpected enemies.

Millennia passed. A few dozen kilometers from the village of Dyakovo, a city began to grow. During the fourteenth century, its local princes began to prosper. They built themselves a palace outside their city, in the village of Kolomenskoye. Today, there is nothing left of the original palace beyond a few entries in the official records of land ownership. Yet, walking through the park today, it is possible to imagine oneself an illustrious ruler – perhaps

TRANSLATION: NORA FAVOROV

the artful and thrifty Ivan Kalita or the brave Dmitry Donskoy. What did they do here? Did they come here to relax? To pray? Were they dealing with Affairs of State? We know that the forces of Dmitry Donskoy passed through Kolomenskoye on their way back from Kulikovo Field. Did the Prince stop here to rest or did he hurry home? We can only guess.

Over the next two centuries, Muscovite princes developed a special fondness for Kolomenskoye. Even today, one senses a remarkable calm here, despite the fact that it is only five minutes to the metro, that nearby there are major thoroughfares, cars, and factory smokestacks. Here there is a peaceful park, a quiet river, sky and open spaces, the likes of which one rarely finds in a large city. It is not surprising that, when Prince Vasily III ordered that a church be built here in honor of his first born, a gallery was constructed around it so as to create a special place for the sovereign to sit and admire the river and forest. At the time, no one knew that the church that was so remarkable for its elegant airiness, the Church of the Ascension, was being erected to honor a child that would grow up to be one of the cruelest tyrants of Russian history: Ivan the Terrible.

After Ivan died, he left behind a devastated and blood-drenched country, as well as two sons who were barely capable of ruling. After Tsarevich Dmitry died under mysterious circumstances in Uglich and after the sickly Tsar Fyodor passed away, the Rurik Dynasty came to an end. Boris Godunov, one of the *boyars*, became tsar. This marked the beginning of the Time of Troubles, an era of hunger and exceptionally cruel winters, of *boyar* tsars and false pretenders. After a daring nobleman, talented poet and fugitive monk, Grigory Otrepyev, became tsar, passing himself off as Dmitry, the son of Ivan the Terrible who had been thought to perish, it seemed that anything was possible.

The False Dmitry managed to hold the throne for a year before he was murdered by conspirators led by the *boyar* Vasily Shuysky. Rumors immediately spread that the tsar had survived, and the Poles started promoting a new pretender – False Dmitry II. These rumors reached the Cossack hinterland, and the Cossacks stirred up small landowners, who were unhappy that Vasily Shuysky had proclaimed himself tsar. The story of the survival of "Tsar Dmitry" was also believed by one Ivan Bolotnikov, who, at the time, was making his way home across half of Europe. And what was not to believe? He had after all seen the tsar alive, with his own eyes.

By the standards of any time, Bolotnikov lived an amazing life. But at the beginning of the seventeenth century, a fate such as his was truly remarkable. In his youth, he had fled the estate where he was a serf to join the Cossacks. He was then captured by the Crimean Tatars and sold into slavery to Turkey, where he became a galley oarsman. He was again captured, this time by the Venetians.

In 1606, Bolotnikov was freed from captivity and made his way to Poland, where, at the palace of George Mniszek, he met the "true" Tsar Dmitry. Never mind that this second false Dmitry was actually a Polish puppet by the name of Molchanov. Bolotnikov apparently believed in him and was dispatched by "Dmitry" to Muscovy with a wad of money, to clear the path for his "return" to the throne.

Bolotnikov arrived in Putivl in the summer of 1606. There, Grigory Shakhovskoy, the petty nobleman who had been a favorite of the first False Dmitry, was so impressed with Bolotnikov that he appointed him "royal *voyvode*," or commander in chief, of the brewing rebellion. Soon Bolotnikov found himself at the head of a raging revolt, which spread from the towns and villages in the south and which pursued Shuysky's fleeing *boyar* forces to the very gates of Moscow. By October of 1606, the capital was under siege and the rebel camp was at Kolomenskoye.

Bolotnikov was in Kolomenskoye a little more than a month. While there, he built an *ostrog*, a little wooden fortress, from which he sent out his messengers and tried to assemble fresh forces, seeking to win over the city's inhabitants by sneaking leaflets into the city that urged slaves to kill masters and merchants, promising that they would inherit their riches. Indeed, the propaganda worked; popular sympathies were leaning toward the rebels. But then, in the middle of November, one of Bolotnikov's leading generals unexpectedly defected to Shuysky with his sizeable forces. It was a crippling blow.

In the middle of a decisive battle, another of Bolotnikov's leading commanders went over to Shuysky. This second major defection sent the rebels into disarray: on December 2, 1606, at the village of Kotly, between Kolomenskoye and Moscow, Bolotnikov's forces were decisively crushed. They fled back to Kolomenskoye, where Shuysky barraged the *ostrog* for three days, until Bolotnikov and the remnants of his forces beat a hasty retreat.

Bolotnikov remained at large until October of 1607, regrouping his forces for a final battle at Tula, where he was captured. The unrepentant former galley slave was taken to the distant northern town of Kargopol, where he was blinded and drowned in a river. Did a vision of the white wonder of the Kolomenskoye chapel or the Venetian canals pass before his eyes before he died? We will never know.

Calm returned to Kolomenskoye. The *ostrog* built by Bolotnikov was demolished and all traces of the time his troops spent there were destroyed. After a few more decades, the tsar of the new Romanov dynasty – Alexei Romanov – took up residence in Kolomenskoye. Historians write about Tsar Alexei's love for beauty, and a wooden palace was built here that came close to being one of the wonders of the world. Today, the only thing left of the palace is a small replica in the museum and recollections about a special enclosed walkway leading from the palace to yet another church, Our Lady of Kazan. The walkway was built to enable tsaritsas and tsarevnas to attend service without exposing themselves to the gaze of strangers.

During the century that followed, there were few signs of life in Kolomenskoye, as the capital had been moved to St. Petersburg. From time to time, tsars and tsarinas would visit here, pray, wander the grounds, or even build themselves suburban palaces. Nonetheless, not much was happening. The voices of history were quiet. It was not until the 1920s, when Peter Dmitriyevich Baranovsky began work on a museum, that history again began to sing here.

Baranovsky's contributions to Russian historical architecture are enormous; he is responsible for restoring or saving countless monuments of Russian history. It was he, for example, who put a stop to plans for the destruction of St. Basil's Cathedral on Red Square during the Stalin era.

As a result of Baranovsky's efforts, Kolomenskoye has been transformed into a remarkable museum. Now, voices that long emanated from these grounds are joined by other voices, as remnants of Russia's wooden architectural traditions were transplanted here. There is a wall from the Cossack *ostrog* fortress in Bratsk, built during the exploration and conquest of Siberia – a distant relative of Bolotnikov's *ostrog*.

Peter the Great, who, like Dmitry Donskoy, passed through Kolomenskoye with his army after an important battle – the Battle of Poltava – also spent some of his childhood here. This is remembered through a cabin that has been transported here from Arkhangelsk, where the young tsar also spent time.

A wooden gate from a seventeenth century monastery was brought here from the shores of the White Sea. And the ancient villagers of Dyakovo received a gift from their contemporaries in the Don steppe – the famous stone figures known as *kamennye baby*.

It would seem an impossible mix – churches from the sixteenth and seventeenth centuries, primitive settlements, ancient sculptures, oak logs associated with Peter the Great, wooden structures from various periods. But here it all seems to fit. The ground under Kolomenskoye breathes history and voices from the past merge into a harmonious symphony.

November/December 2006

Steeped in Tradition
Mikhail Ivanov

In true Orthodox fashion, not a la German.
Not weak like water, or a children's drink
But rich in Russian flavors, full of aroma and strength
The fragrant tea is poured in an amber-like stream
— poet Pyotr Vyazemsky

*I*n 1638 Tsar Mikhail Fyodorovich ordered his *boyars* to taste a "foreign herb" sent to him as a gift by Khan Altyn. Three hours later, the boyars returned with the following report: "We tried everything. The herb is solid, hard to chew and bitter tasting."

Mikhail Fyodorovich's immediate reaction was to take offense at Altyn Khan, who had dared to give the tsar such a worthless, bitter herb. But he relented when the khan's emmisary informed him that this herb had to be steeped in hot water. After he drank the tea, Tsar Mikhail found words to praise the "bitter herb."

Russian culture is steeped in a rich collection of tea-related rites and proverbs. It is ever easy to find a pretext for a tea party here: tea is drunk "after the road," "after the bath house," to spark a conversation or establish a business contact. Indeed, it is hard to overstate the social value of tea in Russia.

Thick volumes have been written about the healing and rejuvenatory properties of tea. Tea with red wine (and fresh jam on the side) helps ease symptoms of the common cold; applying a handkerchief soaked in tea to your eye can help sure a stye; strong black tea with dry brown bread is the classic people's antidote against diarrhea.

Still, this love affair with tea is some three centuries old in Russia. Between the time of Tsar Mikhail and the mid-1800s, tea consumption in Russia was hampered by the long trade route between western Russia and China, which made tea an expensive taste.

This changed when transportation and trade improved, such that by the turn of the century Russia ranked second in the world for tea consumption. Between 1901 and 1910, tea imports averaged 69,555 tons per year. By 1913 (often cited in Russia as the "exemplary" year for many economic indices), tea imports totaled 75,807 tons.

In 1917, revolution, economic isolation and civil war caused tea imports to plummet by nearly half – to 52,301 tons. But Russians were so "addicted" to their tea habits that the Bolshevik government had to do something. In 1918, the Sovnarkom signed the Decree On Tea, establishing rules for tea distribution and pricing. A governmental body, *Tsentrotchai*, was created and charged with tea procurement and distribution. Needless to say, imports of tea (as with most other items) collapsed: in 1918, 9,640 tons were imported, in 1919, the figure fell to 13 tons, slowly climbing to 924 tons by 1924. With the arrival of NEP in 1928, some 15,946 tons of tea were imported. By 1940, tea was being grown in Soviet Georgia and southern Russia, which, combined with imports, pushed total packaged tea in Russia to 24,545 tones, or about one-third of their pre-War levels.

Imports again fell during WWII, but domestic output provided a "survival level" of tea for the Soviet Army and the war-stressed population. Since then, tea has been a part of Russians' special hoard of food products, set aside for the worst of times (known by the Russian acronym "NZ", for "untouchable stock").

At war's end, domestic tea production and imports totaled 17,432 tons, rising slowly in the post-war era to 57,973 in 1958 and 79,000 tons in 1986 (just surpassing 1913 levels).

But alas, this plenty was not to last. Between 1986 and 1997, economic reform and the break-up of the Soviet Union and wars in Georgia and Chechnya (which borders Krasnodar region) led to an 80 percent decline in domestic tea production. Imported teas also disappeared from store shelves. A pop song of that era lamented: "The neighbor went on a drinking binge/ They are on strike at his factory/And there is no tea – only one pack is left."

By the mid-1990s, imports began to rise once again, this time organized by private entrepreneurs rather than the state. Igor Lisinenko founded Maysky Chai ("May Tea") and quickly became the world's largest importer of tea from Sri Lanka. "Such a product like tea is loved in our country," Lisinenko said in a 1998 interview. "And Russians will always buy it, even in hard times."

Indeed, tea is firm rooted in Russians' hearts. In an opinion poll conducted in 2001 by *Russian Food Market* magazine, half of the respondents named tea it as their favorite non-alcoholic beverage (only 31 percent named coffee). A recent review of the Russian tea market by *Dengi* magazine revealed that half of Russians drink at least five cups of tea a day.

Today, supply has been allowed to meet demand. Per capita annual consumption of tea in Russia is estimated at 1.1 kilograms, putting Russia in second place worldwide, behind Great Britain, where the figure is 4.1 kg per capita. But, according to *Vitrina* magazine, consumption in Moscow and St. Petersburg is considerably higher – about 2.5 kg.

In 1998, according to the State Customs Committee, Russia imported 148,800 tons of tea, and may have risen to around 160,000 tons in the last two to three years. Said Alexander Voronov, head of the information center at Maysky Chai: "This figure has stabilized and didn't change even during the 1998 crisis, when Russians relinquished many of the products they came to like. But not tea."

The main source of tea drunk in Russia, according to the Russian Tea and Coffee Association, is India, which supplies about 87,000-89,000 tons (Russia is the world's largest importer of tea from India), while Sri Lanka exports some 33,000-35,000 tons with other countries – Georgia, Indonesia, China, Kenya and Turkey – making up the balance.

Some 60 percent of the market is controlled by three importers: Maysky Chai, Unilever, Grand and Orim Trade. Another 20 companies (like the Russian firm Nikitin) cover another 20 percent, with about 200 smaller firms, including producers of exclusive brands, supplying the remainder. In a 1999 poll by the Komkon group, the preponderance (36.6 percent) of respondents named Maysky Chai as their favorite brand, followed by Brooke Bond (29.8 percent), and the resurrected Soviet brand "Indian Tea with an Elephant" (27.99 percent).

While many younger and middle-aged Russians have become "corrupted" by tea bags, the majority of Russians of all ages (82 percent in a recent Russian Food Market poll) said they still prefer loose tea. In fact, tea in bags accounts for just 4-6 percent of the tea market here, preferred largely by twenty- and thirty-something managers and students (those for whom time is more valuable than traditional tea rites). Thus, tea in bags is often called *ofisny* "office" tea. Either way, black tea is still the dominant tea, with over 94 percent market share.

"**EVERYBODY DRINKS TEA** in Russia but few know how to drink it right," said Maysky Chai's Voronov, whose center tries to teach the "right" way to prepare the beverage. For one, Voronov said, water should be taken off the heat as soon as the first boiling bubbles appear. Waiting longer makes the water hard and impacts negatively on flavor. This is a difficult condition when one is using an electric kettle, one interjects. To which Voronov replies: "And who says an electric kettle is a good thing for tea?!"

Of course, the most authentic way to make Russian tea is to boil water in a samovar heated from its inner tube by burning coals, or, better yet, by burning pine cones (which adds an exquisite aroma to the smoke). "Russia without samovars," said Pyotr Stolypin, prime minister under Tsar Nicholas II, "is not Russia."

The samovar (the name means "self-boiler") is thought to have been "invented" in 1746. It may have been partially derived from similar devices used by the Mongols. But others argue that it is a hybrid, combining the old Russian *shitenik* (a teakettle-like device that had to be lifted and poured) and the Dutch *bouilliotte*, which had a spout like a modern samovar, and examples of which were brought back from Holland by Peter the Great. Samovars quickly gained huge popularity, particularly in bone-chilling St. Petersburg, where it became necessary to keep a hot pot of tea on all day long. Today, samovars are not the central home appliances they once were in Russian homes. They are more likely to be found at the dacha, where there is more time and patience for preparing the beloved beverage in the traditional manner.

IF FORGING SAMOVARS became an art form over the centuries, two hundred and fifty years of tea has also had an impact on other areas of the arts. Famous Russian artists such as Boris Kustodiev and Vasili Perov have made tea drinking subjects in their paintings. The works of Gogol, Pushkin, Tolstoy and others are littered with poignant and romantic scenes around tea drinking.

More recently, there have been several notable cinematic tea references. In the Soviet blockbuster film *Man with a Rifle*, a soldier comes from the front to talk to Lenin, only to bump into him in the long corridors of Smolny while toting around an empty teapot, looking for hot water. In another wildly popular film, *White Sun of the Desert*, the dozing hero, Fyodor Sukhov, has an idyllic dream of himself, his wife and the harem of wives he is protecting, all sitting around the samovar. Finally, in *Come Tomorrow*, provincial simpleton Frosya Burlakova has come to the capital to conquer Russian opera. But at a restaurant, she surprises her host and waiter by ordering seven glasses of tea, because "this is exactly how much tea" she drank every night back in Siberia with her mother.

Of course, one may wonder how wise it is to have tea at night, especially in such "Burlakovian" quantities, given the drink's caffeine level. But then decaffeinated tea has about as much of a market in Russia as non-alcoholic vodka. After all, if the French can have their requisite nightcap of *cafe noir*, why not Russians their *chyorny chai*?

In fact, tea has always been consumed in huge quantities here. In the nineteenth century, Russian *kuptsy* (merchants) in *traktirs* (public houses) would pat their generous guts and order up tea *s polotentsem* – with a towel. Why with a towel? Why to hang about their necks so that they could wipe away the sweat when gulping down hot tea by the glass.

Of course, no discussion of Russian tea rituals is complete without a mention of the distinctive tradition of drinking tea from a glass set into a metal *podstakannik* (glass holder). Film director Nikita Mikhalkov once recalled how he taught Italian actor Marcello Mastroianni how to drink tea the Russian way when Mastroianni was starring in Mikhalkov's movie *Ochi Chyorniye* (Black Eyes). Russian men sip their steaming tea from a tall glass placed in a *podstakannik*, and the teaspoon is never removed from the glass. Instead, you curl your finger through the handle of the *podstakannik* and your thumb pressed the teaspoon against the glass.

There is really no explaining this tradition, dangerous as it may seem to the tea drinker's eye. Which, according to the popular Russian joke, makes this an ideal way to ferret out a Russian spy. Just offer the suspected spy a mug or cup of hot tea. Sure enough, a well-trained Russian spy will remember to remove the teaspoon before drinking, like a good foreigner. Yet he is sure to give himself away by closing his eye when he takes a sip.[1]

September/October 2001

1. Maysky Chai company contributed information for this article, and some statistics were derived from the Russian magazine *Tea & Coffee.*

The Bering Strait
Tamara Eidelman

The strait that runs between the easternmost point of Asia and the western extremity of the Americas is not particularly wide – 35 kilometers at its narrowest point and 86 at its widest. But, if you consider how harsh nature is here, how forcefully the two oceans – the Arctic and the Pacific – batter one another as they meet here, how long the sunless winters endure, how quickly the cold summers flit by, how ice floes drift through the cold, grey water, you might feel that you are faced with an insurmountable barrier dividing two worlds.

But, in fact, that is not how it was. During distant, primeval times, on several occasions the earth rose up and a bridge was formed linking America and Asia. This is how the ancestors of today's Chukchi, Eskimos and Aleuts made their way from Siberia to Alaska and then spread throughout the Americas. Then another thousand years passed, and the land bridge disappeared under the oceans. Two worlds were again divided. True, it is known that, during especially cold winters, when the Arctic froze over, the denizens of Chukotka set out toward the East and made their way to the not-so-distant lands of America. It is said that they do so even today.

Nonetheless, for thousands of years, most people on Earth did not suspect that there was a place where Asia and America met. Native Americans and the peoples of Siberia lived their separate lives, never straying far from their habitual hunting and fishing grounds. Even after the New World appeared on their maps, Europeans had only the vaguest ideas about its northern extremities. What they knew of Asia was that, in the Far East, there was the vast and mysterious China, and that somewhere in the vicinity was the fairy-tale land of *Jipangu* – Japan. The remaining boundless expanses of Asia seemed like nothing but endless taiga, wandered by strange, fur-clad peoples. God only knew where this taiga ended.

Exploration of the Americas and Siberia was first driven by the desire for gold and spices. Who needed cold lands covered with ice and snow?

TRANSLATION: NORA FAVOROV

The Conquistadors advanced beyond Columbus's foothold into Central and South America, in search of Aztec and Inca gold, hoping to find the fabled land of El Dorado. A little later, about a century after the discovery of America, the Cossacks, serving the tsars of Moscow, started to move east through Siberia. Kilometer by kilometer, they explored one river after another. Rivers were the roads into the impassable taiga. They provided sustenance, and along their banks were built tiny wooden fortresses – *ostrogs* – from which eventually sprung wealthy Siberian cities.

In the seventeenth century, as English colonists were settling in along the eastern coast of North America, Russian Cossacks were pushing east across Siberia. They were not after gold, but furs, which in fact were worth their weight in gold and the primary source of pride and wealth for the tsars. But one need only look at a map to see that gradually fur ceased to be an end in and of itself. Early on, the Cossacks had conquered enough territory to bury Moscow in fur, yet the expeditions pressed forward.

Today, flying over Siberia, one can imagine how endless the vast stretches of forest and tundra must have seemed to its explorers, how insignificant they must have felt and how powerless they were in the face of wild Asiatic nature, where summers are marked by debilitating heat and it is hard to breathe from the swarms of gnats, where winters are unimaginably cold, where the rivers are so wide they look like seas, and where the trees grow so tall they seem to touch the heavens. Some were driven here by thirst for personal gain, some were fleeing the law, others were hoping to be pardoned for past crimes, and some simply liked the free life, far from state authority. By the mid-seventeenth century, Cossack expeditions had conquered most of Siberia and were approaching the Far East.

What brought Semyon Dezhnev – the man for whom the easternmost cape in Asia is named – to this place in 1648? He was born in a village not far from Veliky Ustyug, in northern European Russia. How did he wind up serving in a Cossack detachment, in search of walrus grounds in Chukotka and surrounding areas? Did he think about what a vast expanse separated him from the house he was born in? Or did his previous life seem to him something absolutely unreal, a thing of the past?

What qualities did Semyon Dezhnev and his commander, Fedot Popov, possess? Were they insanely brave or insanely irresponsible when they decided to set out over the ocean in seven small ships called *kochi*? Why did they fail to turn back when two of the *kochi* were smashed on the rocks and two others disappeared? Why did they stubbornly head forward, rounding the cape that they called the Large Stone Nose? They certainly did not suspect that they were passing between two continents and that later this would become Cape Dezhnev.

What did Dezhnev think when he realized that only 12 men remained alive out of the entire expedition and that all of his commanders had perished? Did he grieve over his lost comrades? Did he rejoice that all the honors would fall to him? Was he wondering how he would survive yet another unbearable winter or how they would sail up the Anadyr River, against the current, to places already settled by Cossacks?

We can only guess at the answers to these questions. However, despite the amazing feats of the Cossacks, toward the beginning of the eighteenth century, Eastern Siberia was still a land of mystery. It more or less belonged to Russia, but no one was quite sure exactly where these possessions were and where this land ended. In 1724, when Peter the Great wrote instructions for the First Kamchatka Expedition, he issued an order to verify whether the lands north of Kamchatka were truly called America. The straits through which Semyon Dezhnev and Fedot Popov's *kochi* had sailed a half century earlier had seemingly vanished. A new expedition was setting out, and it was being led by someone who had little in common with his Cossack predecessors: Vitus Bering (1681-1741), a Danish-born sailor who had "served in the East Indies," as he was recommended to Peter, before entering into the service of Russia.

What had compelled Bering to leave his native Denmark and set out for Russia, which must have seemed to him no less alien and distant a place than Chukotka had seemed to the Cossacks? Perhaps he dreamed of achieving success that would have been out of his grasp had he remained at home. From the reports of his contemporaries, it appears that Bering was not someone capable of decisive action. Everyone remarked on his piety, meekness, and humility – rare qualities in a trailblazer. Nobody mentioned daring. It all seemed to boil down to the simple fact that Bering painstakingly and dutifully followed orders. If the Russian emperor commanded him to clarify whether the lands of America were north of Kamchatka, then that was what he had to do. Although, if we think about it, perhaps in the calm and thorough execution of this orders, which were unprecedented in sweep, lies the very essence of daring, the daring of a man who twice crossed all of Siberia in order to study its eastern reaches.

But once Bering set out on his expedition, it took three years for him to reach the Far East and bring all the equipment needed there. Only then did the ships set sail. The First Kamchatka Expedition (1725-30), as it later turned out, skirted Kamchatka and Chukotka and passed through the strait that would later be named for its "discoverer." But neither Bering nor his crew understood what they had done. They merely made certain that there were no American lands up ahead, and then they decided to turn back, afraid that their ships would be damaged by ice.

In 1733, Bering was once again sent on a mission. Now his goal was no less than a study of the coast of the Arctic Ocean and an expedition to America. Again, years were needed to reach the Far East. During this time, several detachments under Bering's command would attempt to reach the north via the rivers of Siberia. Two of his commanders were tried for "conduct unbecoming." What offenses had they committed on the banks of the Ob? Some died, others were somehow delayed in their travels, and for several years they could not manage to set sail before the approach of winter. Could Bering have been dragging his feet on purpose?

But Bering did progress toward Kamchatka and in 1741 he was sailing the North Pacific. By then he had turned 60 – a ripe old age in those days. The commander complained to those around him that he no longer had the strength to carry out his mission, but he nonetheless continued to walk, ride, and eventually sail onward. Bering's ships reached the coast of America, charted the Aleutian Islands – and then became lost. The ships were not able to find one another in unknown waters amidst a terrifying autumn storm. Bering's ship turned back and, in the fall of 1741, after lengthy travail, stopped at an island that is also now named for him.

It was here that the exhausted commander ended his days. He died standing in a pit half filled with sand – he had climbed into it in an attempt to save himself from the cold. Did he feel pride and satisfaction at having carried out his mission to pinpoint the location of the American coast, a mission ordered by a tsar who had long since died? Did he have a premonition that the sea, the strait and the island would all bear his name? Did he reminisce about Copenhagen or the warmth of India? Or, closing his eyes and gradually weakening, did he just listen to the relentless crashing of mighty ocean waves?

September/October 2006

Salt in their Wounds
Valentina Kolesnikova

*N*early every ruler on the Russian throne withstood large or small popular revolts. In the days of old, people mainly protested abuses of power by the tsar's minions, turning to the tsar himself for help and justice, believing that the tsar knew nothing about the evil or cruel actions of his servants.

There have been many reasons for popular uprisings throughout Russian history. But a special place among revolts is occupied by those concerned with life's simplest necessities, such as salt, bread, matches, and honey. The demand for and prices of these items fluctuated, but the people's relationship to them was constant and unchanging throughout centuries of Russian history. These necessities became a unique barometer for the political and economic life of Russia. For example, before World War I was declared in 1914, the people already knew that war was inevitable, not because they followed the movement of the world's political powers, but because matches and salt disappeared from the markets. Exactly the same thing happened on the eve of World War II. In former centuries, rising prices or the imposition of some kind of limit on salt, bread, matches, honey, or vodka evoked furious protests from the broadest segments of the population.

It was because of these things – salt, bread, honey, and vodka – that a huge revolt flared up in Moscow on June 12th, 1648, later spreading to Pskov and Novgorod. The reason for the revolt was the growing shortage of and the high taxes levied on these everyday necessities. These taxes were the veritable drop that overfilled the cup of patience among the people. There were already taxes on everything, but the people took the taxes on salt, bread, and honey as theft by the tsar's representatives, who kept inventing new schemes to line their pockets by stealing from ordinary Russians. The rebellion of 1648, which has entered historical text as "the Salt Rebellion," was all the more meaningful because it occurred during the reign of one of the most sensible and peaceful Russian statesmen – Alexei

Mikhailovich, who for his devotion and his gentle and kind disposition was called "*Tishayshy*" - "the quietest."

Obviously quite a bit of exaggeration is contained in this designation. It is more representative of the people's wish for such a tsar, than of the actual features of Alexei Mikhailovich. However, much in the tsar's personality does deserve a great deal of respect: he really was very devout, observed churches rites and orders and tried to live with Christian reserve. These qualities turned out to have a large influence on official business and his day-to-day interactions with people, especially the *boyars* to whom he granted the opportunity to help lead the country. He had a remarkable statesman's mind: central power was strengthened under his reign, the rights of peasants were formalized, Ukraine, Smolensk, and various northern lands were united or reunited with Russia. In many ways, Alexei helped pave the way for the reforms of his son Peter I: he didn't reject innovations that came from the West, while at the same time he believed in the old ways.

Alexei took over the throne when he was only 15 years old. At this age, he couldn't rule the kingdom without the help of guardians and advisors. When Alexei was still a baby, his father, Tsar Mikhail, chose the *boyarin* Boris Morozov to be the boy's guardian, educator and tutor. Mikhail did not see through Morozov's external façade of pleasant and amiable manners, peaceful well-wishing and wisdom to the cunning, jealous, greedy and immoral person that Morozov really was. Even the young Alexei couldn't see his true face: he was sincerely devoted to Morozov, respected and esteemed his tutor with endless devotion, and thought of him as the best of the boyars.

When Alexei became tsar, Morozov was made first magnate in the kingdom. On Morozov's advice, Alexei chose the daughter of the *boyarin* Miloslavsky, Maria, as his wife. The Miloslavskys were among Morozov's closest relatives. But Morozov didn't stop at this: after a year he himself married Anna, sister of the young Maria, and in so doing became a relative of the tsar. Thus, he was able to give important posts in the kingdom to his relatives and closest friends, among whom were courtiers like Pleshcheyev, Trakhanyotov, Chistov, infamous extortionists, bribe takers, and oppressors. The Morozov-Miloslavsky clan was like a herd of predators; they shamelessly robbed Russia and her people by taking advantage of the trusting young tsar.

The people, who respected and loved Tsar Alexei, refrained for a long time from complaining about the tsar's relatives, who were crushing them under the weight of heavy taxes. Only when the clique levied their taxes on the most basic necessities – salt, honey, bread, and vodka – did the rebellion erupt in Moscow. Crowds of people broke into the homes of the *boyars*. The residences of Morozov, Miloslavsky, Trakhanyotov, Pleshcheyev and Chistov were ruined and destroyed. The latter three were killed; Morozov and Miloslavsky hid in the tsar's palace, whence the rebelling crowds headed, demanding of Tsar Alexei that he turn the two scoundrels out and give them a well-deserved punishment. Though the tsar defended them, he found out about the crimes of his former favorites, in whom he had had so much faith. In Moscow the rebellion ended bloodlessly: the people believed in the tsar who promised to restore justice. In Novgorod and Pskov the people rebelled longer and Tsar Alexei was forced to send troops to suppress the insurrection – not without bloodshed.

And so the rebellion of 1648 came to an end. The reign of Alexei Mikhailovich was destined to live through another, even more terrible rebellion – a full-fledged peasant revolt under the direction of the popular leader Stepan Razin. But some good unquestionably came from the salt tax revolt. It is widely believed to have been responsible for Tsar Alexei's promulgation of the famous Law Code of 1649, which, for the first time, systematized existing laws and regulations. It would be the foundation of Russian law for the next two centuries.

June/July 1998

Fighting Mankind's Worst Enemy
Yelena Utenkova

Some 450 years ago, just a few months after the 16-year-old Grand Prince Ivan IV ("The Terrible") crowned himself tsar, a horrible fire leveled Moscow. Since that time, Moscow has burned to the ground 12 more times and large parts of it have been destroyed in over 100 instances.

Nikolai Gogol said that, in Russia, there are two great disasters – roads and fools. Alexander Koryukhin, head of the information division of the Moscow Firefighters' Association, argues that there is a third – fires.

In 1996, fires killed 17,000 people in Russia and caused R27 trillion ($5.4 bn) in damage. On average, some 600 fires break out every day, killing two people every hour.[1] In 1996, in Moscow alone, 21,696 fires were registered, with a death toll of 416 persons and damages estimated at more than R74 billion.

For Whom the Bell Tolls...

As these statistics indicate, fires in Russia are serious business. And so they have been throughout history. In ancient times, Russians built their homes primarily of wood, packed together like sardines in a can, so that, when one house caught fire, a whole village could go up in smoke. For a long time, Moscow did not even have a fire brigade and the residents themselves had to put out fires. Everyone pitched in – in fact, refusal to help in fighting a fire was punishable by corporal punishment and imprisonment. However, the means for extinguishing these fires were so primitive and the people so ignorant that, after large fires, great cities were often reduced to fields. As was the case with Moscow 13 times over the last 450 years.

1. By way of comparison, in 1995, according to the U.S. Fire Administration, there were some 260,150 structure fires reported in the U.S., working out to some 700 building fires per day (there were also nearly 600,000 non-structure-related fires), which killed 1,588 persons and caused $4.2 bn in damage.

In pre-industrial Russia, when fires broke out, people were warned by the ringing of an alarm bell. One could tell what part of the city was burning by the sound of the bells – the louder the sound, the more important the place. At the end of the seventeenth century, Tsar Aleksei Mikhailovich published a special decree: "If the Kremlin catches fire, the bells should automatically be rung three times. Soon the bells in the rest of the city and both ends of the Spassky will ring, but softer..."

The last great fire in Moscow occurred in September 1812, during the war against Napoleon. French troops took over the city after almost all its residents had fled. On the very next day, a devastating fire broke out. The center of Moscow was reduced to ashes. Out of the 9,000 Moscow houses existing at that time, some 6,500 were destroyed. To this day, no one knows for sure how the fire started. According to one version, the residents themselves set their city on fire to deny Napoleon the spoils. Another rumor has it that the French occupants were to blame. While yet another, echoed by Tolstoy in *War and Peace*, has it that "the mother of Russian cities" burned because any empty city, left without supervision, must burn.

Every Boy's Dream

Russia's first fire patrols were established by Tsar Alexei on April 17 (April 30, new style), 1649, in Moscow. They not only put out fires, but sought to ensure fire safety in the tinder-box capital.

In the 1720s, construction of Russia's first fire depots began. In cities throughout Russia, fire towers sprang up – imposing structures second in height only to church towers. From lookout points on these towers, the whole city was spread out below like a picture book – any large fire was readily visible.

Under Alexander I (1804) the first special firefighting detachment was created, "for dispatching night watchmen and forming a special team of firefighters made up of retired soldiers no longer capable of serving at the front." Service on this team lasted 25 years (the same as for military conscripts). Since then, Russian firefighters have been a subdivision of the military, though this service is now voluntary.

The first fire charter in Russia came out in the middle of the nineteenth century, and, from that time on, firefighting has been a highly respected occupation. The royal family took Russian firefighters under its wing, and the journals *Pozharnoye delo* (Fire Business) and *Pozharny* (Fire) began publication. A special firefighters' uniform was introduced. It was one of the most beautiful in the Russian empire. The *braidmeister* (the head of a fire brigade) wore a gilded bronze helmet with the army's coat of arms, along with a dress half-caftan of dark green cloth, embroidered with silver thread, a chrome sword and boots. An ordinary fireman would wear a bronze helmet and a gray half-caftan, with light blue shoulder straps. Their shining helmets made a strong impression. Young women engaged to firemen were the envy of their friends. And, of course, almost all young boys dreamed of growing up to be firefighters.

In general, in large cities where fire departments were created by order of the tsar, such departments flourished. But, in Russia as a whole, the state of fire prevention was far from satisfactory. The USSR's National Firefighting Service was inaugurated on May 24, 1918, when Lenin signed a decree on "the organization of government firefighting measures." This day was later chosen as the firefighters' professional holiday.[2]

New Times, Old Problems

In the summer of 1997, a group of American firefighters from Los Angeles got a first-hand look at how difficult the firefighting situation is in Russia, when they visited Moscow to observe their Russian colleagues on the job. According to Koryukhin, of the Moscow Firefighters' Association, the Americans were unanimous in their conclusion that firefighting conditions in Russia are much worse than in America. There are a variety of reasons for this.

First, according to data from the High Technical School of the Interior Ministry (MVD), five percent of all Russian apartments have been turned into small warehouses. Residents store gasoline, lacquer, old newspapers and magazines, and other flammable items in their apartments. This is compounded by the growth in crime, which has led Russians to make their apartments into impenetrable fortresses. Corridors on each floor are closed in by armored doors. Apartments are equipped with state-of-the-art locks, often more secure than bank vaults. At times, firefighters have trouble breaking into a burning apartment when dwellers need urgent help.

Second, economic hardship and a decline in social order has taken its toll. The fire equipment in many apartment buildings is obsolete or out

---

2. And the day was celebrated on May 24 throughout the Soviet era. In 1999, on the 350th anniversary of Tsar Alexei's decree, the annual day was changed to April 30.

of order. Alarm signals don't work, hoses are not connected and cars are parked on top of hatches where firefighters hook up their equipment. In Moscow, 50 percent of firefighting equipment is obsolete, and the situation on a national scale is even less encouraging.

And yet, somehow, Moscow's firefighters seem to cope. On February 25, 1996, Moscow experienced its worst fire in ten years, when a warehouse of the Moscow Pneumatic Tire Factory burned. Over 15,000 square meters of space was destroyed, containing enough rubber, sulfur and chemical reagents to make a million tires. Material damage was estimated at more than R50 billion ($10 mn) and could have been much more, had the fire spread to nearby residential areas. Fortunately, firefighters managed to contain the blaze, even though they lacked the special foam-generating equipment needed to extinguish hot rubber (on which water is virtually useless).

Moscow firefighters do have one unique and advanced piece of firefighting equipment in their arsenal, however. It is a special helicopter that can be used to extinguish fires 24 hours a day, and, according to Koryukhin, it made a deep impression on the recent U.S. visitors. The helicopter can take an especially heavy load, and its shape enables it to fly up to balconies and roofs to pick up fire victims. As the Moscow firefighting team has only two fire ladders which can reach up as high as the 22nd floor (and even they cannot be completely unfolded in windy weather), a helicopter which can both drop off firefighters and extinguish fires with airborne water cannons comes in handy.

Third, Russians are not taught fire safety. Nor do they respect fire security rules. According to Koryukhin, the state has not developed a coherent system of fire awareness, whereas all foreigners are well informed about how to behave during a fire. While all Russians can recall the childhood motto that was the basis of their "anti-fire education" – *Spichki detyam ne igrushka* ("matches are not children's toys"), this is about as far as the "education" went. "Therefore," Koryukhin said, "I can't cite a single example over the last few years when foreign citizens have suffered in a fire." The comparative figures are indeed startling: in Russia, there are some 78 deaths per 1000 fires; in the U.S., that number is 2.4.

Finally, there is the effect of the Russian penchant for drinking binges, and the rising tide of alcoholism. Russia now has an annual, *per capita* hard alcohol consumption rate of 14 liters. This means more accidents, more drunks falling asleep without putting out cigarettes, and more "holiday fires" that get started from unextinguished cookout fires – the number of forest fires in Russia has virtually doubled as compared to last year.

Shortages of qualified personnel, while not a problem at present, do loom on the horizon. For now, salaries of firefighters are competitive ($170 to $190 per month, plus a so-called 'Luzhkov bonus' of $35 – named after Moscow's popular mayor), and the Higher Engineering and Technical School (the fire school) has no problem finding recruits. But if the government has its way and tax benefits for servicemen are abolished, enrollment could drop drastically.

Privatization also awaits. Since the Russian army is short of personnel, firefighting units are gradually and painstakingly being switched to a contract system. As the last fire-servicemen finish up their tours of firefighting duty, the end of an era approaches. It is less than certain that there will be a wealth of candidates volunteering to take on such a dangerous job for a relatively small salary.

As it is, many fire-fighting teams are forced to respond to alarms by sending only two or three people, instead of the seven specified in the charter.

With Moscow expanding every year, a firefighting squad often arrives as much as ten or twelve minutes after a fire is reported. In a move to remedy this situation, in 1991 the Moscow government developed a program to increase the number of firefighting units. Over the first three years, this program was fully implemented, but last year only four units were set up, instead of the twelve planned. This year the situation is even more "complicated."

Playing with Fire

As if they didn't have enough to worry about, Russian firefighters are plagued by false alarms, a traditional "distraction" of disturbed people and children. Over the first three months of this year, there were 2,937 false alarms in Moscow – almost 20 percent of the national total. Unfortunately, Russian lawmakers have not yet passed a law which would allow such people to be fined, even though the technology exists to pinpoint the source of any alarm call. If the call comes from a child, emergency operators explain that they will call the militia, who will fine his parents. As a rule, this works. But such measures do not work with adults.

Firefighters must also deal with bomb threats, which caused particular problems last summer. Then, a rash of false bomb threats occurred in connection with the deteriorating situation in Chechnya. False explosives were planted at airports, railway stations and in administrative buildings.

Arson is also a problem in Russia, accounting for 7 percent of all fires (in the U.S., the number is considerably higher, around 20 percent). Criminals will set fire to anything. And the infamous *razborki* (settling of accounts) between rival crime groups has added fuel to fire statistics. Even the U.S. embassy has been a victim of arson. Last year, a middle-aged woman visited its consular section, poured gasoline on the floor and set it on fire. Security guards rushed to extinguish the flames, while the perpetrator walked out and disappeared in the crowd. To this day, her motives are unclear. Maybe she was denied a visa, firefighters joke bitterly.

An Historical Puzzle

In addition to the distant anniversary of the Great Fires of 1812 and 1547, this year also marks the anniversary of a more recent fire. Twenty years ago – in the winter of 1977 – a devastating fire broke out in Moscow's centrally-located Rossiya Hotel. The blaze spread from the 5th to the 22nd floor, with some 1,000 people trapped by the flames. Saving these victims proved to be extremely difficult, because the fire stairs only reached up to the seventh floor. As a result, 42 people died, including five firefighters. Another 52 were injured. The list of victims included such VIPs as the deputy foreign trade minister of Bulgaria and two Bulgarian trade counselors. The cause of the fire is still unknown.

Komsomolskaya Pravda, the popular daily newspaper, recently published a feature article that speculated on the possible causes of the disaster. The newspaper suggested that the fire may have been the result of *razborka* between the two rival law enforcement bodies at the time- the KGB and MVD. Another version has it that the Rossiya was set ablaze by dissidents protesting the Soviet regime, because delegates of a Communist Party plenary session were staying in the hotel at the time.

And finally, there is a version steeped in superstition. It turns out that the hotel was built in 1967 on the site of a torn-down orthodox cathedral. Ten years later, in 1977, the disastrous fire broke out. Another ten years passed, and then, in 1987, a TV set in a room caught fire. The guest fled in panic without informing hotel management and the flames spread.

Although the fire was quickly extinguished, one woman died of asphyxia and one man received lethal burns. Therefore, according to the article, the hotel employees were awaiting the winter of 1997 with anxiety, hinting at some kind of divine retribution for spiritual sins.

While each of these versions seems wilder and more improbable than the next, TV investigations of the disaster hit closer to home. Had the firefighters been issued with more efficient equipment, the reports suggested, the casualties would not have been so high. As for the spark which set the Rossiya burning, its source, as with so many other fires in Russian history, will probably remain a historical puzzle.

Between ill-informed and careless citizens, insufficient funds and recruitment problems, Russian firefighters today are in an unenviable position. But, in spite of all the difficulties, statistics shed a ray of hope. Over the first three months of 1997, the number of fires in Russia decreased by 15.4 percent in comparison with the same period last year, while the number of fire-related deaths decreased by 27.5 percent. Still, in that same time period, 116 people lost their lives. And, unless the Russian government magically comes up with more money to pump into fire safety and educational measures, it seems likely that "mankind's worst enemy" will continue to cause deaths in Russia – deaths which are all the more tragic because so many might have been prevented.

July 1997

Dawn of the Russian Navy
Lev Pushkaryov

*P*rior to 1696, it would have been an exaggeration to say that Russia had a fleet, let alone that she was a sea power. There was no regular navy with weaponry, no system of acquisition or staffing, no military service, training, uniforms, no centralized system of command and supplies.

However, the eastern Slavs had a millenium of maritime tradition. It began in the fifth century B.C. in the Black Sea and later spread to the Mediterranean, where Kievan ships sailed with the Byzantine fleet. Novgorod merchants and colonizers, meanwhile, reached Spitzbergen and other remote northern lands.

Setbacks like the Tatar yoke, which destroyed Russia's shipbuilding industry, put the country behind naval powers like England and France, which were able, unlike Russia, to expand their territories without fear of attack. It was only with the appearance of a will to modernize and reform Russia and strengthen her international standing, in the person of Peter the Great, that Moscow began to seriously consider building a navy.

"Invaders came from the East, South and North," explains Admiral Kasatonov, deputy commander-in-chief of the Russian navy and head of the Marine Historical-Cultural Center. "In this very specific situation it was difficult to create those state institutions which would have strengthened central power, and when the tsar's power was strengthened, the need arose for Russia to expand its foreign ties, which would also strengthen its statehood."

Peter the Great's love of boats stemmed not just from state interests, but began in childhood, when he found and restored a little old wooden boat on his father's estate at Izmailovo. In 1688, already tsar, he built a flotilla on Pleshcheyevo Lake at Pereslavl-Zalessky, which became a kind of research center for the new navy.

Peter did not restrict himself simply to building a navy, however, but strove to instill a maritime spirit in the whole of society. Marine sports clubs were set up, and naval training courses introduced for nobles. Russia's shipbuilding industry was relaunched in Arkhangelsk in 1694.

Perhaps most important of all, Peter made sure that this spirit entered the country's cultural life, and nowhere more so than in its new capital and chief port, St. Petersburg, founded in 1703.

Seamen were soon a substantial part of St. Petersburg society, and were gladly invited to court festivities. St. Petersburg quickly turned into a vital trading port on the Baltic and the navy's main base. All these things formed in the public consciousness the image of the sailor as a defender of the fatherland and the navy as one of the main bulwarks of that defense.

Numerous decrees and rescripts by the tsar on the building of the fleet and formation of crews for its ships spread throughout the country the idea of serving and defending Russia on the sea. In fact, in just a little over 20 years time, the navy developed to such an extent that it had a decisive effect in Russia's Northern War with Sweden (1700-1721), setting the stage for Russia's growing influence on European diplomacy and security.

Peter the Great personally saw to it that the idea of a victorious Russian fleet developed in people's minds. He used every means imaginable to arouse an interest in and respect for the fleet, like saturating the book market with books about sailing.

Another characteristic of the Petrine era was the glorification of the fleet by the clergy in church. Feofan Prokopovich, a preacher and publicist enlisted by the tsar to articulate his reformist ideas, mentioned in only his second sermon the building of naval ships. His essay, *A Word in Praise of the Russian Fleet* (1720) is especially revealing. In it, the preacher lists with great enthusiasm the benefits which Russia would receive from the creation of a navy: "We stand over the water and watch as our guests sail to us, while we ourselves are not capable of this. It's just like Tantalus in the fables standing in the water and yearning. And thus even our own sea is not ours."

The image of the victorious fleet penetrated the theater of the day. In the play *Russian Glory*, written for the coronation of Peter's wife, Catherine I (a year before his death), Neptune helps Russia create an "unprecedented fleet," which "frightens everyone."

The successful sailor became a literary hero of the Petrine era. In *The Story of the Russian Sailor Vassily Koryotsky*, the reader meets an "expert in the business of navigation:... he knew everything there was to know on the science of sailing, on the seas, where islands, shelves, shoals, rapids, winds and heavenly planets were. And for his knowledge he was senior on ships, and was highly revered by all senior sailors..." The victorious sailor-hero became a model to be imitated.

The sea also made its way into poetry. In his *Three-Language Primer*, Fyodor Polikarpov compared the words of a fool to the sound of the sea.

Of course, literature, theater and religious sermons formed the opinions of mostly the higher echelons of St. Petersburg society. Naval dress, in particular sailor's uniforms, became fashionable, and the city's inhabitants imitated hardy sailors, subconsciously adopting their behavior, vocabulary and customs.

But a much greater change in the mentality of St. Petersburg society originated from the successes of the Russian fleet in the Northern War. After vanquishing the Swedes, the victorious navy returned to port to celebratory artillery salutes. Thousands of Petersburgers lined the Neva embankments to see the Russian and captured Swedish ships glide home. Special documents and engravings depicting the various sea battles were dispatched throughout Russia.

Engravings by artists like Pikart and Schoenebeck infused the public consciousness with ecstatic images of the victories and of the new northern 'Paradise,' as people came to call St. Petersburg. In fact, all contemporary engravings of the city were filled with navy ships, reflecting joy that the city was rising proudly, where "ships from all corners of the earth cram in droves into her rich harbors..."

These engravings (of which there are about 100) decorated the tsar's chambers and the homes of grandees. They were displayed in extravagant frames and loudly adorned with bright moire ribbons in crimson, azure and green, and thus could not fail to garner attention.

Alexander Pushkin was to later write that "Russia entered Europe like a ship entering the water to the sound of axes chopping and cannons firing..."

But Russia did not just enter Europe loudly – her navy enabled her to become one of Europe's great powers. Henceforth, almost none of Europe's problems were solved without at least Russia's indirect participation. Whether it was the 150-year guarantee to the Kingdom of Denmark, Russia's role in the many Balkan crises, or establishing a presence in North America, it all began in 1696, with the navy that Peter built.

October 1996

Secret Mission
Nikolai Pavlenko

*I*n 1696, returning to Moscow after their victory over Turkish forces at the fortress of Azov, Peter the Great's soldiers were honored with ceremonial cannon fire and public verse. Though full of his triumph over the Turks, Peter was worried that, since he had failed to conclude a peace treaty with them, the Turks might wait for a propitious moment to restart hostilities.

With that in mind, in the Spring of 1697, Peter, then just 25 years old, decided to send a Russian mission abroad, in order to both secure Holland's assistance in any future conflicts with Turkey, and to apprentice himself and his men to Holland's superior shipbuilders. Peter the Great, with his much-documented appreciation for all things foreign, was eager to upgrade his country's military might by securing the talents of foreign military experts and arms.

Russia sent a 250-man strong mission to Holland, headed by three plenipotentiary ambassadors: Franz Lefort, Fyodor Golovkin, and Prokofy Voznitsin. Among the personnel were 62 security men, translators, physicans, cooks, and 35 young noblemen who desired to go abroad and acquire shipbuilding and navy skills.

In order to avail himself of all possible freedoms abroad, Peter decided to travel not as the Russian Tsar but simply as a private individual, Peter Mikhailov, heading a group of volunteers. Since no tsar before him had ever crossed Russia's borders, the situation was really quite unique: the 25-year-old tsar was the *de facto* leader of the delegation, but his true name and status were not to be mentioned (under punishment of death). In the eyes of outsiders, the mission was represented as under the guidance of the three Russians ambassadors.

In reality, of course, Peter gave written instructions as to the goals and tasks of the Great Embassy, such as the need to hire shipbuilding and navy experts, buy blacksmith's and carpenter's tools, paper, lead, paint and complete other tasks. Yet, and this may explain why, in the end, Peter's

Embassy was not totally successful, the tsar's instructions failed to explain exactly how his ambassadors were to secure new allies in the war against the Turks. The absence of these and many other important details may be somewhat due to the fact that in his role as a "volunteer," Peter was unwilling to issue exact orders himself.

Why did Peter choose to hide his true identity? One could make an educated guess that, besides Peter's wish to hide his temporary absence from Russia from the Turkish government, Peter had always felt ill at ease amidst all the pomp and circumstance expected from heads of state: the rigid rules of social etiquette were of little interest to him. As *kurfurstinnen* (Electress) Sofia of Hannover and her daughter, Sofia-Charlotte of Brandenburg, described him, "Peter was a talented, knowledgeable and hard-working man, capable of performing many different tasks, save using a knife and fork in the proper way."

But most important, Peter was eager to learn how to build ships, and it was clearly incompatible for one of his royal rank to perform manual labor. Traditionally, the tsar was forbidden from engaging in any sort of physical labor whatsoever.

On March 25, 1697, the grand procession crossed the Russo-Swedish border, entering Riga, the capital of Livonia, then in the possession of the Swedish crown, on April 1. In order to continue on with their journey, the Russians had to replace their sledges with carts, and Riga's merchants, who had them over a barrel (and were suffering from a famine), did not hesitate to cheat them by any and every ruse. In a letter home, Peter described the merchants as "cursing and snarling for every penny." Peter, meanwhile, used the week spent in the capital to carefully examine the city's fortress, to the warranted suspicion of the Swedes. On the whole, Peter's experience in Riga was something he preferred to forget – his next contact with Sweden would be in war, and he would cite his rude reception in Riga as one of his excuses for beginning that Great Northern War.

From Sweden, Peter made his way via Poland to Konigsberg, where he met up with Frederick III, the *kurfust* (Elector) of Brandenburg. Aside from their mutual love of carousing, the two heads of state tried to strike up a military alliance. But negotiations dragged on for nearly a full month (May 24-June 22), due mainly to Frederick's insistence on including a clause on mutual assistance, guaranteeing that, in case one state was attacked, the other would instantly come to its aid. The Russians feared that such a clause would raise Swedish suspicions, to the detriment of Russia's international interests. To be sure, having no peace treaty with Turkey in the South, Russia was not in a position to complicate its relations with the powerful Swedes in the North.

But, realizing that in order to secure one ally Russia might be forced to alienate another, the two parties agreed on general, verbal assurances that, should one power be threatened, the other would come the first's assistance. Both monarchs "shook hands and kissed." Russia was on her way to creating a stable geopolitical program.

On August 18, 1697 Peter arrived in the shipbuilding town of Zaandam, bypassing Amsterdam. Peter lost no time in familiarizing himself with the world of Dutch shipbuilders. He bought some shipbuilding tools and rented a small house adjoining the house of a blacksmith who had worked for Peter in Moscow. He enjoyed spending time examining local warehouses, workshops and shipyards, displaying natural talent for the work. According to one Dutch source, "Peter was a very clever and inquisitive person who often embarrassed local specialists with questions that were too difficult for them to answer. His memory was matchless. Moreover, he was a very smart artisan, who was always surprising locals by doing things better than they did."

For a number of reasons, mainly due to the speed with which gossip can travel, Peter failed to conceal his true identity, though he did his best to blend in with his surroundings. In Holland, working as a volunteer in the Zaandam shipyards, he even dressed in the same outfit as the other workers – a red flannel jacket and canvas trousers. But, of course, nothing could hide his distinguishing height – six and a half feet tall – and his distinctive nervous tics.

Peter did not enjoy being the center of attention, but he could not escape the curiosity of local people, who came from far and wide to see the Russian tsar working as a common shipright. Annoyed by the crowds which followed him, he wanted nothing more than to be left alone and to work in peace. In order to appease Peter, the local *burgomaster* issued a special decree ordering severe punishment for all those who showed disrespect to the foreign guest. But this was not enough and Peter was forced after just one week to move from Zaandam to a more private shipyard in Amsterdam.

The Russians learned a great deal at the Dutch shipyards, receiving upon the completion of their two-month course of study a certificate from shipbuilding expert Gerrit Claes Pool to the effect, for example, that "Peter Mikhailov has proved himself a diligent and smart carpenter, and in the area of shipbuilding has acquired knowledge and skills comparable to our own."

The Holland experiment proved a success, but Peter was not satisfied; he wanted to learn still more, so he decided to go to England, home of the world's best ship designers.

In London and later in Deptford, a borough of Southeast London and site of some major shipyards, Peter got the chance to acquire the profession of a shipbuilding engineer in earnest. Peter spent four months in England, meeting with all manner of professional people and visiting sites of educational interest. He visited London factories and workshops, in which his fancy for watchmaking became a marked skill. He indulged his love of astronomy at the Greenwich Royal Observatory and visited the British Mint, planning to buy Russia one of England's newly invented coining presses. He also made a trip to Woolwich, the center of military industry, Oxford University and many other educational British sites.

While Peter was working in England's shipyards and visiting English industrial and educational establishments, his ambassadors were unsuccessfully negotiating with the Dutch in Amsterdam and the Hague. Not only did the Dutch turn down Russia's proposal to pool battle forces, but also refused to provide Russia with a loan to cover high military expenditures. Even the Russian ambassadors' promises to grant Dutch merchants extensive privileges in the silk trade with Iran and Armenia proved futile. "They do not want give us nothing," Lefort wrote in his broken Russian.

Peter, meanwhile, had been engaged in personal, *tet-a-tet* meetings with William, Prince of Orange, who was simultaneously *Stadholder* of Holland and King William III of England. Both in Amsterdam and in London, the two had met and developed feelings of mutual admiration and respect. But Peter could not find common ground other than a mutual animosity for Louis XIV, King of France.

Thus, after returning from England to Amsterdam, Peter decided to go to Vienna, to try to prevent Austria, Russia's ally in the war with Turkey, from striking a separate deal with the Turks. This time Peter took onto himself the responsibility of directing negotiations, but again to no avail. The peace was to everyone's benefit but Russia's (Peter had not yet secured the access to the Black Sea that he sought), and Austria was starting to get concerned about Louis XIV again. Having no other choice, Peter decided to make a trip to an age-old enemy of Turkey (and another sea power), Venice, to build an anti-Turkish coalition and to inspect Venetian warships.

But this was not to be. As he was about to depart for Venice, Peter received intelligence that four regiments of *streltsy*[1] had mutinied and marched on Moscow. He cancelled his voyage to Venice and headed with haste for Moscow. But, on June 24, in Krakow, hearing the good news that the mutiny had been suppressed, he decided to slacken his pace and take some time to strike up new, and rewarding acquaintances.

On July 31, Peter met Augustus II, Elector of Saxony, recently become King of Poland. The two leaders were of the same age and similar dispositions and quickly became good friends. Besides much time spent relaxing together, they secretly discussed the possibility of an anti-Swedish alliance and even a surprise attack to wrest the Baltic provinces from Sweden. These discussions did not end in the form of a written treaty, instead "both monarchs gave each other their word of honor and parted." They even exchanged their clothes as a gesture of friendship. So, a year and a half after starting out, on August 25, 1698, Peter quietly returned to Moscow in the Polish king's baggy costume.

Earlier, on June 3, 1698, four vessels arrived in the Russian port city of Arkhangelsk, bearing a motley crowd of sailors, infantry troops and shipbuilders totalling 672 people. Among them were 26 captains, 35 lieutenants, 33 navigators, and 345 sailors. Another ship brought to Russia more than 15,000 handguns, various tools, exotic animals and birds. In all, Peter recruited over 750 foreigners, especially Dutchmen, to serve in Russia, promising to subsidize passage, provide advantageous employment, and assure religious tolerance and separate law courts. Unfortunately, Peter's hospitality did not extend to Jews, whom he considered parasitic.

In conclusion, while Peter's main political goal, to secure alliances in the prosecution of further war against Turkey, had not been achieved, the trip was not wasted. Besides many new skills and much new knowledge, some time later Russia formalized verbal commitments to join forces in fighting against Sweden, inaugurating the Northern Alliance, made up of Russia, Saxony and Denmark. The war with Sweden that ensued would last twenty

....
1. Permanent, regular regiments that took their name from their chief weapons, muskets.

years and open up Russian access to the Baltic Sea, leading to the founding of St. Petersburg at the mouth of the Neva river.

Most significantly, for Peter himself, his time abroad served to crystallize his plans to quickly, and brutally, bring Western customs and technology, but not belief systems or ways of governance, to Russia. Unlike the majority of his countrymen who viewed foreigners with fear and distrust, Peter was determined to use Western ideas to improve Russia. It would be a long and inconclusive struggle for the energetic monarch.

March 1997

The New, New Year
Tamara Eidelman

September 1, 1700 was a day when a very important event did not take place.

For centuries, the first of September had been a day of celebrating the New Year in Russia. It seems counterintuitive now, but it was quite logical, actually. August was when the most important agricultural activities of the year were completed. And if some unfortunate event or bad weather conditions stopped people from collecting crops, it meant almost certain death from starvation. So peasants worked very hard to bring in the crop.

Of course, peasants did not work on St. Elias Day – August 2 (or July 20, old style). This day for religious ceremonies had pagan roots, in the annual celebrations of the god Perun, who was said to drive his chariot across the skies making thunderous noises, a common enough occurrence in the tempestuous days of early August.

On St. Elias Day, peasants brought gifts to church – not too unlike pagan offerings of atonement, perhaps – beseeching the saint to keep their fields from being ruined by rain or storms. They brought fruit, flowers and vegetables. Quite often they also sacrificed an ox, an animal long associated in many cultures with the gods of storm and tempests.

But as soon as this celebration was over, everyone hurried back to work. It was important to prepare food for the long winter ahead, to collect crops, to bring in the hay. There was no time to spare. Of course, if you were rich, you hired someone to help out for the month; if you were not, you asked for help from family.

By the end of August, the heavy work was done. You could finally relax. Logically, it really was more like the end of the year than December – at least for peasants. You thanked the people who helped you and often left a small part of the field unharvested – another pagan rite: an offering to the god Veles, to beseech him for good crops in the coming year.

TRANSLATION: NORA FAVOROV

Early September was a rare time in Russian villages: peasants could afford to eat meat. This was due to economics (meat did not last as long then) and superstition (feasting somehow magically ensured that there would be enough food for the winter). So cows and pigs were slaughtered and huge celebrations ensued. Even though medieval Russia did not yet know vodka, people also drank a lot of *medovukha*, made from honey. These feasts were a celebration of the New Year. And even though townspeople did not have to work in the fields, they still followed the old traditions, knowing that their prosperity depended on good crops and the amount of cattle which God (or pagan spirits, as the case might be) would send them.

It was like this until the time of Peter the Great. In 1697-8, Peter, who had always had a keen fascination with things western, led a secret diplomatic mission to Europe – The Great Embassy. In order that he could avoid the complications of court protocol, Peter traveled under the name of Peter Mikhailov. Of course, everyone knew that this tall, strange tsar was masquerading as a junior officer, but officially they could not know or recognize him as tsar. It gave Peter immense freedom.

As soon as Peter returned to Russia he began "westernizing" everyday life. And the young tsar did not brook any resistance. *Boyars* who came to welcome him home were subjected to a painful and humiliating procedure: Peter cut off their beards. At that time in Russia, a man without a beard considered himself to be naked, emasculated, even homosexual (a mortal sin). Western dress, which many thought to be unusual and indecent, became mandatory. Parties were organized where people were required to bring their wives and daughters (springing them from the confines of the *terem*) and allow them to dance with other males – shock upon shock. Guests even smoked – something previously associated with the Devil. It is therefore not surprising that many Russians began to whisper that the tsar was the Antichrist.

On September 1, 1699, everyone as usual celebrated the New Year. But then, just three months later, they were ordered to celebrate the New Year again, on January 1, as was the tradition in the West.

As a sign of good beginnings and good cheer, congratulate one another on the New Year, wishing good fortune in business and prosperity for the family. In honor of the New Year, commit to decorating a tree in order to amuse the children, and ride down hills on sleds. Adults shall not engage in drunkenness and brawling –

there are plenty of other days for this. Whosoever does not celebrate on the New
Year, shall be subject to the rod.

It is somewhat ironic to think that Russians would need to be threatened
with the rod to get them to celebrate. But clearly not everyone was accepting
of change.

As it turned out, on September 1, 1700, what would have been the New
Year was instead the occasion for a new war – against Sweden, in order
that Peter, pursuing his naval passions, could obtain for Russia an outlet
to the sea. Peter changed the calendar and New Year's was not celebrated
on September 1. Henceforth, the year would begin with the traditional
celebration of Christ's birth (which actually had long ago been crafted to
coincide with and overshadow the pagan holiday of the Winter Equinox)
and not the Creation of the World.

People were confused, and, since it was rather dangerous to contradict
the tsar, they cancelled their celebrations. At least in cities. In villages, the
tradition of celebrating the New Year in September held on for some time.
The break was painful at first – especially as it was but one of many Petrine
changes. But, by the nineteenth century, January first and Christmas trees
(*yolkas* – something else Peter had much admired abroad) were popular
throughout Russia. Peter had won, except on one detail: people drink a lot
on New Year's. In fact, there used to be a saying – "to go under a *yolka*" –
meaning to visit a tavern.

September/October 2005

The Life and Times of the Russian Peasant House
Nancy Cooper Frank

Constructed from a sturdy framework of interlocking, axe-hewn logs, the Russian peasant's house – the *izba* – did a respectable job of keeping rain and snow out and the stove's warmth in. But like any dwelling, no matter how simple, it provided much more than shelter. Rituals, customs, and beliefs, as well as the sometimes elaborate decoration of the *izba* (plural: *izby*), reflected the many meanings and functions its inhabitants attached to it.

Log houses dotted the Russian countryside for centuries. Even now, many wooden buildings in Russia retain something of the spirit of old-fashioned izby, echoing their silhouettes and carvings. The peasant's log house also lives on in literature and art. Calling up so many facets of traditional rural life and lore, it remains part of the cultural landscape.

By the second half of the eighteenth century, when researchers started taking an interest in them, the oldest *izby* still standing probably dated from early in the eighteenth century. Certainly the pedigree of extant log houses reaches much further back, but it is not clear how much the details had changed since earlier eras. In any case, the *izby* that have come down to us follow basic principles of log construction long used in Russia for all kinds of buildings, in town as well as village.

Folk traditions in architecture persisted the longest and flowered into the greatest variety of forms in the European Far North. This region had the luck to escape the physical and cultural disruption of Mongol occupation. The population consisted of peasants who were not serfs and who only paid a land-tax to the state. Wood was plentiful. Nineteenth-century movements in other parts of the country to reform and rationalize the layout of villages left the North untouched.

In Central Russia, a fence enclosed the peasant's house and assorted agricultural buildings. But in the North, stables, cattle-sheds, haylofts, and agricultural storage rooms were often joined under a single roof with the family's living space. (The stronghold-like farmsteads of Siberia represented yet another regional variation.) The combined house-and-covered-yard arrangement made sense in the harsh climate.

Naturally, the size of the *izba* depended on the prosperity and size of the household, which might be a nuclear or multi-generational family, or a set of brothers with their wives and children. In any case, the northern "huts" in particular could be massive. Sometimes the living quarters and the more extensive covered farmyard were joined end-to-end in one elongated rectangle. Or the farming and living sections met at a right angle, forming an "L." In the two-story *koshel* or "basket" house, the ridge of the roof marked the divide between the living quarters and the agricultural spaces. The *koshel* was recognizable by its asymmetrical roof: a steep, short slope covering the house proper, and a longer slope stretched over the enclosed farmyard.

In all regions, the presence of a stove defined a habitation. The word *izba*, related to the verb *istopit* "to heat [a stove]," referred both to the structure as a whole and any heated room within it. A simple house had only one of these multi-purpose rooms used for cooking, other domestic tasks, eating, and sleeping; a larger one could have two or more. In a "smoky" (*kurnaya*) *izba*, smoke from the stove rose through the room above head level to collect under the high, trapezoidal ceiling and escape through a slit. These chimney-less or "smoky" houses continued to be built until the mid-nineteenth century, co-existing with chimneyed houses.

Restorers have salvaged a scattering of peasant log houses, mostly from the nineteenth century, along with log churches and other structures, and have transported many of them to regional open-air museums. One of the richest ensembles graces the island of Kizhi on Lake Onega. There are also notable collections of folk architecture in Novgorod, Suzdal, and near Irkutsk, to mention a few. Equipped with stove, cooking pots, brass icons, looms, brightly painted spindles, shelves for sleeping and built-in benches, some of the exhibits look ready for their next tenants. Handsome as these houses are, their present museum-piece status can only hint at the role they once played in everyday life. Fortunately, many of the rituals, customs and beliefs centering on the dwelling were documented in the nineteenth and early twentieth centuries, with some supporting archeological evidence for earlier periods.

The Creation of the World

As in cultures around the world, so in traditional Russian peasant society, building a place to live was symbolically equated with the creation of the world. Putting up a house meant constructing a cosmos – an ordered, sacred space – so it demanded special rituals. As in the Chinese art of *feng shui*, there were unlucky and lucky spots. Prudent builders avoided a site exposed to invisible dangers, such as a place where a road had once run, where a house had burnt down, or where a bathhouse (haunt of evil spirits) had stood. Sometimes divination with bread or grain helped determine the proper site. Peasants took similar care, for both practical and symbolic reasons, to choose unblighted, "living" wood, cutting trees down in the fall and allowing them to season over the winter.

Erecting a house was a communal effort punctuated with feasts for all the helpers. There was food and drink all around after the first interlocking row of logs was set in place, and again to celebrate the raising of the matitsa – the main ceiling beam. The builders enjoyed the third communal meal after they'd put the topmost roof beam – the *konevaya slega* or "horse-beam," in place. For good measure, one more meal marked the completion of building.

These feasts harked back to much earlier house-foundation rites based on animal sacrifice. Archeologists have found horse skulls and chicken heads under the log frameworks of houses in medieval Novgorod. Back in those days a ceremonial meal would have accompanied the sacrifice. It was a practice derived from ancient beliefs that the world emerged from the body of a slain human or animal. By analogy, the cosmos that was the new dwelling grew from the creature that donated its spirit to the house. Later, for example in Vladimir province, a small tree placed in the ground at the building site sometimes filled the role of sacrificial victim.

Centuries after builders had ceased to bury horse skulls under house foundations, the main roof beam was still called the "horse beam." This is just one way in which the sacrificial beast of long-forgotten foundation rituals lived on in generations of peasant houses.

Both decorative carvings and words used for parts of the *izba* strengthened the identification of the house with a living thing. It was at the same time human-, animal-, bird- and tree-like, a hybrid creature or an entire microcosm of creatures.

The *izba* frequently appeared as a living being in the work of "peasant poet" Nikolai Klyuyev (1884-1937), who soaked up the lore of his native Olonets region in Northern Russia, along with everything from Eastern mythology to avant-garde artistic currents of Moscow, St. Petersburg and points West. Klyuyev's house could wear the most exotic of colors, becoming a "peacock-*izba*" standing "beneath a fiery baobab." But at the core of Klyuyev's image of the *izba* stand Russian folkways and folk speech related to building. For example:

На бревенчатых тяжких лапах	*On timbered, cumbersome paws*
Восплясала моя изба.	*My izba broke into a dance.*

The Russian word for "paw" (*lapa*) appears in the building term *v lapu* describing an arrangement of interlocking logs, trimmed so that their ends didn't project. So, yes, an *izba* could stand – if not dance – on four "paws."

The Russian language gave the *izba* a "forehead" (*chelo* for gable) and a "helmet" (*shelom*, a name for the hollowed log covering the top roof beam), even eyes (*okno* "window" is etymologically related to *oko* "eye"). The roof was home to a flock of "magpies" (*soroki*), the fat wooden pegs holding the "helmet" log in place. Below these roosted two rows of "chickens" (*kuritsy*): tree trunks with one root left intact, jutting out at the bottom of either side of the roof to support other elements of the nail-less roof.

Capping the main roof beam and crowning the front gable was the *konyok* ("little horse"), often carved in the shape of a horse's head, or two horse's heads facing in opposite directions, or a bird. The *konyok* was identified with the house as a whole, again recalling a sacrificial creature imparting its life to the structure. Many researchers, notably archeologist B.A. Rybnikov, have also considered the *konyok* to be a solar symbol, remnant of myths depicting horses or birds drawing the sun across the sky. Aware of this interpretation of the *konyok*, Klyuyev turned the *izba* itself into a solar steed:

Солнце избу взнуздало –	*The sun bridled the izba –*
Бревенчатого жеребца,	*The timbered stallion.*

Just below the *konyok*, hanging down from the tip of the gable, a decorative board typically displayed a rosette that appears to have been another solar symbol. On either side, carved boards covering the ends of the eaves also bore solar discs. Together, the three circles represented the sunrise, the sun at its zenith, and sunset. Through these symbols, the sun lent its life-giving and protective powers to the house.

The house needed protection from malignant forces. The doorway was particularly vulnerable, so sometimes people buried talismans or sacred writings under it. A Klyuyev poem alludes to this custom, invoking the protection of a copy of the popular religious legend "The Dream of the Mother of God" buried under the threshold.

Moving in was fraught with danger. Before crossing the threshold of their new home, the family released an animal – often a cat – or a rooster inside. Behind this custom lingered the idea that establishing a new home somehow invited or required a death, in particular that of the head of the household. The animal deflected the danger onto itself.

Inside, the most important parts of the *izba* were the stove and the "red corner" – the *krasny ugol* (*krasny* "red" originally meaning beautiful). Life in the house revolved around these two "centers," which invariably stood diagonally across from each other.

The "red" corner was the icon corner and functioned as the domestic altar. It had pre-Christian origins as a sacred space, but any specifically Christian household rituals tended to center on it. The stove had immense practical significance, of course, for cooking as well as for heating. Reverence for the stove derived from pre-Christian belief in the sacredness of the hearth. In folk speech and rituals, the stove could stand for the house as a whole. The "red" corner was associated with light, the sun, and the directions east and south; the stove was associated with darkness, the earth, and the directions west and north.

The "red" corner was considered a primarily masculine realm. At the family table, the head of the household took his place nearest the icons. The stove corner, in contrast, was also called the "woman's corner" (*baby ugol*). Here women cooked, spun and did other work. In a kind of sympathetic magic, to aid a difficult childbirth, the door to the stove as well as the doors, windows, and gates to the house were flung open.

As the Russian expression had it: "The stove is our own mother" (*Pech nam mat rodnaya*). The "mother-stove" in Klyuyev's poetry naps, "snores in the half-darkness," hums to herself, worries about keeping the house warm.

Upon entering a new dwelling, a family immediately attended to the two "centers" of the house. The man set the household icon or icons in place. The woman of the house performed the moving-in rituals for the stove, which included lighting the fire for the first time, or transferring coals from the old stove to the new. Sometimes she started preparing a pot of kasha in the old house, and finished cooking it in the new.

Another symbolically important part of the house was the *matitsa* (etymologically related to *mat*, "mother"), the main ceiling beam. Like the stove, it could stand in for the dwelling as a whole in rituals. The matchmaker from the prospective groom's family didn't cross under the *matitsa* of the bride's family house until after a particular point in the prenuptial negotiation ceremonies. A bride touched the stove and the *matitsa* of her husband's house. Travelers touched the *matitsa* before setting off.

A resident spirit, the *domovoy*, watched over the house from his favored haunts under or behind the stove, under the floorboards or up in the attic. As house spirit, the *domovoy* had close affinities with the animal who in earlier times was thought to lend its spirit to the house. He was often associated with horses, his favorite animal, or roosters, his favorite bird. The *domovoy* liked to be addressed as "grandfather" or as "master" (*khozyain*) of the house; he was both an ancestor figure and a shadowy double of the head of the household. Essentially benign, he grew testy when he or his house suffered neglect. When moving, the family had to make a special point of inviting the *domovoy* along, or it would have no peace. In short, the *domovoy* embodied the protection and continuation of the dwelling, the household and the family along the male line.

Life Becomes Art

Grandfather *domovoy*; the custom of carrying the hearth-coals from the old house to the new one; carvings following folk motifs: all of these represented the continuity of past and present. Yet the world of the Russian *izba*, including the appearance of the house itself, was hardly immune to change. As William Brumfield notes, the traditional carvings grew more intricate and profuse during the eighteenth and nineteenth centuries, at the same time that the influence of urban architecture increased.

Newfangled flourishes, such as "baroque" curves on window surrounds, appeared and people started adding paint to carvings. In central Russia, raftered roofs, replacing the complicated and distinctive Russian nail-less roofs, became more and more common from the first decades of the nineteenth century on. When plank gables replaced log gables, carvers lavishly ornamented the gables as if to compensate for the plainness of the planks. Lower prices for glass allowed bigger windows. Changing the look even more, some log buildings were clad with boards.

While outside forces were helping to change peasant houses, another, opposite trend gained strength. The second half of the nineteenth century saw a growing interest in folk architecture and craft among Russia's educated classes, making the peasant hut a symbol of national pride and identity. Architects working in wood built everything from schools to hospitals to restaurants to summer cottages unmistakably, if loosely, inspired by the traditional peasant hut.

Expeditions to record and preserve old log buildings formed a part of a broader rediscovery of native traditions. Professional and amateur scholars documented oral literature, beliefs, rituals, and customs, including those that illuminated the role of the dwelling. The influential art critic V.V. Stasov promoted folk-inspired architecture and investigated the pre-Christian symbolism behind such features of house decoration as the *konyok*. For Stasov and many others in the nineteenth century, the study and adaptation of folk art and architecture offered a way to bridge the gap in Russia between folk and "high" culture.

Members of the artist's colony of Abramtsevo, inaugurated in 1875 by industrialist Savva Mamontov and his wife Elizaveta Mamontova, collected, studied and drew inspiration from folk crafts of all kinds, including log architecture and woodworking. The grounds around the main house filled up with pavilions and workshops designed in a stylized "neo-Russian" folk idiom. *Izby* of the Russian Far North – along with the log churches of that region – received special attention because they represented the "purest" and oldest building traditions. In the 1890s, in another estate that became an influential artists' colony, Princess Maria Tenisheva had guest cottages built to look like northern log houses.

In art, the *izba* had a dark and a bright face. In village scenes by nineteenth-century realists, clusters of brown huts radiate a humble and subdued charm at best. Interiors show darkness and poverty if not outright squalor, though sometimes there are glimmers of domestic beauty, in details such as embroidered linen towels carefully hung on the wall for a special occasion. In fin de siecle and early twentieth century modernist art, on the other hand, gaudy and festive log houses crowd out somber ones.

If the newer approach was less realistic in some ways, it also represented an attempt to capture the aesthetic spirit of peasant decorative arts. For example, the illustrator Ivan Bilibin put a good deal of imagination into his fairy-tale *izby*. It was an imagination fired by his pilgrimages, in the first decade of the twentieth century, to the far North, where he studied traditional artifacts, including buildings and their carvings. A strong strain of interest in folk and "primitive" objects, including the *izba*, continued to run through the teens and twenties. In this vein, a vibrant stage design by Natalya Goncharova for an unknown production (1913-1914) features an *izba* surrounded by its individual elements – doors, windows, details of carvings – shuffled, skewed and magnified to dwarf the house itself.

Both Klyuyev and his fellow "peasant poet" Sergei Yesenin approached the *izba* as an esoteric text made of symbols passed down over generations. In a lyric essay of 1920, Yesenin wrote: "The red corner, for example, in an *izba* represents the dawn, the ceiling – the vault of the heavens; the *matitsa* – the Milky Way." If the horse was a symbol of "aspiration" in Egyptian, Greek and Roman mythology, wrote Yesenin, "only the Russian peasant got the idea of placing it [the horse] on his roof," turning his house into a chariot. Where others saw a prosaic, earthbound hut, both Yesenin and Klyuyev saw a symbol of striving after the infinite, an inheritance from nomadic Scythian forebears.

In Klyuyev's apocalyptic vision, the *izba* united earth with the heavens, the human sphere with nature, and Russia with the world. After the Revolution, it was also supposed to link the rural past with an imminent "peasant paradise" – a dream that had collapsed by the time of his execution (for membership in a nonexistent anti-Soviet organization) in 1937. Klyuyev's *izba* also had a more personal, intimate connection to memory and the past, in poems written after the death of his mother. In "Songs of the *Izba*," the house and all the beings it shelters – the "orphaned" stove, the painted and carved animals, the *domovoy*, the saints on the icons – mourn the death of their mistress. In an echo of folk beliefs, she returns to her house one last time after death to bless it.

For the "village prose" writers of the 1960s and 70s, rural wooden houses evoked powerful but vanishing ties between the past and the present. Their work is haunted by ruined or involuntarily abandoned *izby*, conveying a cultural and spiritual loss that resonates quite independently (as Kathleen Parth has argued in *Russian Village Prose: The Radiant Past*) of the controversial nationalist views expressed by members of this school. In Valentin Rasputin's *Farewell to Matyora*, an old settlement must make way for a hydroelectric station. One of the villagers thoroughly cleans her *izba* one last time before seeing it off with prayers, as if paying her last respects to a loved one.

More recently, the *izba* has cropped up in the work of Siberian-born French writer Andre Makine. In his 1995 *Dreams of My Russian Summers*, the narrator retraces the fortunes of his family from just before 1917 to just after the fall of the Soviet Union. Makine's Siberian log house (there are actually two of them in the story, but their identities merge) is a dark, fusty, "wrinkled," sagging hulk. But it keeps its inmates alive and imbues them with its own stubborn vitality, its dogged genius for survival. The following passage refers to a period of famine in Siberia the early 1920's, as experienced by the narrator's French great-grandmother and grandmother:

> *It was above all the izba that saved them. Everything in it had been conceived to resist endless winters, bottomless nights. Even the wood of its great logs was imbued with the harsh experience of several generations of Siberians. Albertine had sensed the secret breathing of this ancient dwelling, had learned to live closely in tune with the slow warmth of the great stove that occupied half the room, with its very vital silence.*

At the end of the tale, Makine's *izba* lingers on in the courtyard of a Soviet-era apartment block and is threatened with demolition. (There's some hope, though; the apartment dwellers have banded together, in a "support group, or whatever," as one character carelessly reports, to try to save it.) It is pushing two centuries, above the normal upper limit for a heated log structure. But the image of the *izba* in Russian culture has lived much beyond this span and shows no signs of disappearing.

March/April 2002

Feast Amid Carnage
Tamara Eidelman

*B*y the summer of 1709, Russia and Sweden had been at war over lands along the Baltic coast for nine years. The battle would rage for another twelve.

This endless Northern War completely changed the face of Russia, since it drove Peter the Great to build countless factories, enlist hordes of soldiers (placing a crushing burden on the entire country), revamp taxation (to increase revenues, of course), change the way the country was administered, and create a new educational system.

After the Northern War, neither Russia nor Sweden were ever the same. Russia became an empire with mighty ambitions, while Sweden turned its back on the struggle for international influence and relinquished its standing as the strongest country in northern Europe, which it had been throughout the seventeenth century. Instead, it gradually transformed itself into a peaceful, prosperous state that minded its own business.

There was actually a joke told in Soviet times: A man is brought into the KGB and asked, "Is it true you're dissatisfied with Brezhnev?"

"Oh, no, of course not," the man replied. "If I'm dissatisfied with anyone, it's Peter the Great. If only he'd lost the Battle of Poltava, we'd all be living in Sweden now."

Russia, as we all know, did not turn into Sweden, and the Battle of Poltava remained the most famous moment of the Northern War. It was extolled during Peter's reign, but its true glorification was assured, of course, by Alexander Pushkin, in his poem *Poltava*:

> *Collide with crashing, swing and hack;*
> *And, flinging corpses head on heap,*
> *Hot balls of iron hurtle, leap*
> *Into the stumbling ranks and thud,*
> *And plough the ground and hiss in blood.*
> *Swede, Russian – stabbing, splitting, slashing,*

TRANSLATION: NORA FAVOROV

Commingled uproars, drumbeats, clashing,
Groans, hoofbeats, neighing, cannon's boom,
And universal death and doom.

[...]

But triumph's near, hurrahs are shouted:
We've broken through; the Swede is routed!
O wondrous hour! O glorious sight!
One onrush more brings headlong flight.
The cavalry pelts off, pursuing,
Swords dull with slaughter, and the chewing
Of death lies black upon the field
Like locusts on a summer's yield.

Exultant Peter – proud, vivacious,
His eyes aglow with martial fame.
And his triumphal fete is gracious:
Amidst the cheering troop's acclaim
He bids the lords beneath his scepters,
Both Swede and Russian, to his tent;
And gaily mingling prey and captors
Lifts high his cup in compliment
To the good health of his "preceptors."[1]

Pushkin had ambivalent feelings about Peter the Great, but in *Poltava* he is the embodiment of courage and nobility. The famous story of the feast arranged by Peter after the battle was seen as emblematic of the tsar's magnanimity. The feast was not a figment of Pushkin's imagination – it is a historical fact, and descriptions of it were published as early as the eighteenth century.

Under Catherine the Great, a merchant from Kursk by the name of Ivan Ivanovich Golikov was sent to Siberia for corruption in the vodka trade – not a rare offence. Shortly thereafter, an amnesty was announced in honor of the unveiling of a monument to Peter, the famous Bronze Horseman. After that, Golikov saw Peter as his benefactor and began to compile materials for a biography. The result of this effort was a multi-volume work that depicted Peter as the greatest, most majestic of all Russian rulers. Naturally, Golikov also described the feast that followed

1. Translation by Walter Arndt (*Alexander Pushkin: Collected Narrative and Lyrical Poetry*, Ardis, 1984)

the Battle of Poltava. It is possible that Pushkin used this description as his source.

> The monarch ordered Prince Menshikov to bring all the captured generals and commissioned officers into the tent. The monarch, standing bareheaded at his little table, received them with great warmth. After kneeling before his majesty, they presented him with their swords.
>
> At three in the afternoon, the great sovereign, turning to the captives, said with a smile: "Yesterday my brother Charles promised you would dine in my camp today, and, although he did not keep his royal word, we will see that it is so, and for this I ask you to share a meal with me." And so that this ironic, one might say, greeting would not be so hurtful to them, he ordered that each of them immediately be returned his sword.
>
> And during the repast, as they were drinking to the health of his majesty and all his royal house and victorious arms, cannon fire sounded continuously.
>
> His majesty turned to his courtiers and, after pouring a glass of wine, said: "I drink to the health of my instructors in the art of war."
>
> "And to whom," asked Rehnskold, "might your majesty, be so good as to refer with such a fine name?"
>
> "You, Messrs. Swedes," said the sovereign.
>
> The repast continued until five in the afternoon, after which the indefatigable sovereign sent Prince Golitsyn with both his guards regiments, and also with the Lieutenant General Bour and the ten cavalry battalions under his command, to pursue the Swedes, who had fled to outside Perevolochna.

YEARS, DECADES, CENTURIES passed. The Battle of Poltava continued to be perceived as a great victory that ended in jubilant celebration. The very word "Poltava" was sure to evoke Pushkin's melodious lines.

Toward the end of the twentieth century, the Swedish historian Peter Englund wrote a book entitled (in Russian) *Poltava: The Story of One Army's Defeat*. Here, the story of Poltava is told from the Swedish perspective. It turns out that Swedish archives hold a multitude of previously unknown documents associated with Charles XII's campaign in Ukraine and with the Battle of Poltava. The Swedish soldiers were Lutherans, and from childhood they had been taught to read the Bible, so, unlike their Russian counterparts, they were literate and wrote countless letters home, many of which have survived to the present. Englund studied these letters and painstakingly culled a multitude of fascinating details from them. The Swedish generals also left behind memoirs, which gave us a new description of the tsar's feast:

When the Swedish commanders had symbolically acknowledged defeat by relinquishing their weapons, the tsar invited them to a feast with the Russian generals. They all went into a second spacious tent that had been sewn of expensive fabrics of Chinese and Persian manufacture. Carpets were placed over the earth, which was crimson with blood. Hands were gallantly kissed; the tsar himself poured the vodka. The meal began and everyone raised toasts to the health of the tsar, to his family, to the glory of his arms and so forth. Cannons fired in salute, and the Swedes and Russians conversed courteously, partook of the fare, and exchanged compliments. An atmosphere of civility and courtesy reigned around the festive table, which groaned with dishes. Against a backdrop of universal gallantry, just one [Russian] Lieutenant General stood out – Ludwig Nikolaus von Hallart, who was upset about the harsh treatment he had been subjected to in Swedish captivity after the Battle of Narva. The situation was growing heated, but it was diplomatically diffused by Menshikov; intervening, he asked that the Swedes pay no attention to Hallart's tirades: "The Lieutenant General just had a little too much to drink." The festive meal on the field of battle was then able to continue, even as anguished soldiers continued dying.

The field of battle was dreadful to behold. Approximately 9,000 dead and dying, hordes of wounded (surely more than 4,000 and probably no fewer than 10,000), as well as countless multitudes of doomed horses lay scattered about over a relatively small space – in the field, in the bushes, under trees, in ravines, in short, everywhere. The fortifications were turned into burial mounds, hollows became mass graves. Where the fiercest fighting had taken place, corpses obscured every inch of ground, creating a sort of carpet over the earth. For example, near the third redoubt there may have been as many as 1,000 bodies covering an area equal to approximately 250 square meters. Anyone who surveyed this nightmare probably saw and heard what has been described by the many witnesses of other battles. In the distance, the earth was moving as if it were alive. This was the countless wounded, writhing in convulsions of pain, a lacerated carpet covering the earth. The air was filled with an unsettling, pulsating, mournful groan that would fade only to again intensify, but in any event was never silent. It was the moaning and crying of tens of thousands of maimed and dying. In the center of the field, where the apocalyptic general battle had played out, dead bodies were heaped one on top of another in a disorderly pile.

SO THIS IS how Poltava looks from the twentieth century – generals cynically feasting, while around them thousands writhe in pain, sacrificed to the cause of two rulers' imperial ambitions...

But there was a third party to the Battle of Poltava, one that is usually forgotten. Charles XII had come to Ukraine expecting help from the Cossack *hetman* Mazeppa, who had betrayed Peter and evidently hoped, with help from the Swedes, to revive Cossack freedoms that the Zaporozhian Cossacks had given up a half-century earlier. Mazeppa is one of the main figures featured in Pushkin's *Poltava* – an old man who falls madly in love with the young daughter of his enemy, Kochubei, kills her father, brings misfortune on his land, and ultimately loses not only power, but his beloved. For readers of *Poltava*, Mazeppa is never a terribly engaging figure – just a treacherous old man. But in the era of Ukrainian *perestroika* one suddenly began to hear that Mazeppa could be viewed not as a traitor to Peter's interests, but as someone fighting for an independent Ukraine (or at least for Cossack independence).

So it was not only Russian and Swedish soldiers who suffered and died on the fields outside Poltava, but Cossacks as well. This fact has been little remembered over the past 300 years, although not all forgot it. Nikolai Ivanovich Kostomarov, who grew up in Ukraine, was one of the nineteenth century's most prominent Russian historians. Although he spent his life as a historian of Russia, he also studied Ukraine, or "Little Russia" as Russians then called it. He wrote a book about Mazeppa. It also includes a description of the Battle of Poltava.

When the prayer service was concluded, the tsar invited his brothers-in-arms to a feast that was being served inside the tent... Eminent Swedish captives – generals and colonels – were also invited to the feast. They brought [Charles' chief counselor, Count Carl] Piper in during the feast and sat him down at the table as well. The tsar treated all of his captives affectionately, personally returned Field Marshal Rehnskold his sword and praised him for courage and the faithful execution of his duties. Although the other captives' swords had been taken away, the tsar immediately graciously returned them. "Gentlemen," Peter addressed the captives, "My brother Charles invited you to dine in my tent today, but he did not keep his royal word; we will keep it for him and we invite you to dine with us." Raising his goblet of wine in toast, Peter exclaimed, "I drink to the health of my brother Charles!" Then, to the sound of cannon fire, Peter raised a toast to the health of his teachers.

"Who are these teachers?" Rehnskold made so bold as to ask.

"You, the Swedes," the tsar replied.

"Fine thanks your majesty has shown to your teachers," said Rehnskold.

...By order of the tsar, beginning at four o'clock on the morning of the following day, they began to dig graves to bury the dead. The entire army was assembled at the site. Two graves were prepared, and at 6 o'clock the sovereign arrived... The usual burial rites were performed over them... and the tsar bowed low to the ground three times before the dead and was the first to throw earth into the grave with his own hand. Other commanders followed his example... After the funeral ceremony had been completed for the Russian dead, Peter ordered that the enemy bodies be given a ceremonial burial, assigning captive Protestant ministers to perform this task...

...The Swedish commanders were placed in the custody of Russian grandees... and all others were placed with Russian officers in accordance with the ranks of the Swedish captives, right down to the non-commissioned officers and rank-and-file soldiers. They were all sent to Russia several days later. The worst fate befell the Little Russian followers of Mazeppa, who were captured, or, in most cases, turned themselves in once they saw that the Swedes had lost. Nordberg, who witnessed this first hand, says that they were subject to the most horrible torture, their arms and legs were broken, their mutilated bodies where tied to wheels and publicly displayed, while others were hung or impaled on pikes... We cannot absolutely refute Nordberg's account, since the savage punishment of rebels and traitors against the tsar was the custom under Peter.

So what is Poltava – the triumph of a great tsar, a battle that changed the geopolitical balance in northern and eastern Europe, the tragic loss of thousands of soldiers, or a failed attempt by Ukraine to liberate itself?

Probably it is all that, which is what makes it so interesting, because people of every period see something of their own in it.

May/June 2009

The Museum of Ballet
Yaroslav Sedov

There's still a half-hour before curtains-up, but all approaches to the Mariinsky Theater are blocked by traffic. And there's no way to get there from our city-center hotel but by car: it's a 15-minute walk to the metro, and, while trams do run right past the theater, they do so only irregularly.

*W*hat's playing?" asks the taxi driver. The photographer and I start to explain that today is an historic occasion, because the legendary choreographer and one-time Mariinsky dancer Yury Grigorovich, formerly head of the theater's ballet company, had brought his new theater, which he founded in 1996 in Krasnodar, after leaving Moscow's Bolshoi Theater, to St. Petersburg for the first time. Over the last few years, Grigorovich's new theater has taken on almost all of his major works, and today is performing his celebrated *Spartacus*. The driver listens carefully, nods politely, and then asks: "How many acts?" Three, we tell him; he thinks for a moment, then says: "That means it'll finish about 11 o'clock. Good. There won't be any traffic jams then, so I can do several runs to hotels."

The Mariinsky Theater is one of St. Petersburg's most famous symbols, alongside the Bronze Horseman, St. Isaac's Cathedral, and the raised bridges over the Neva during June's White Nights. Founded in the 1740s, it is one of the world's oldest theaters, mentioned in the same breath as La Scala, Covent Garden, the Grand Opera, Comedie Francaise, Moscow's Bolshoi and Maly and another St. Petersburg theater, the Alexandriinsky, all of which helped shape their countries' national theatrical traditions.

In this, the Mariinsky has played a particularly high-profile role: it is the cradle of classical Russian opera and ballet, which even today make up a large chunk of the world's most popular repertoire. It was for the Mariinsky that Mussorgsky, Rimsky-Korsakov and Tchaikovsky wrote their operas; it was here that Marius Petipa staged *Sleeping Beauty*, and his protégé Lev Ivanov premiered *Swan Lake* and *The Nutcracker*. It was here that Fyodor

TRANSLATION: PETER MORLEY

Shalyapin made his name, and here that Mikhail Fokin began the quest that would end with the triumph of Serge Diaghilev's Ballets Russes in Paris.

All this history resonates on approaching the Mariinsky's emerald building on Theater Square. The square was a center of entertainment in the city as early as the middle of the eighteenth century: here, masked balls and equestrian contests were held, carousels whirled, and markets and fairs traded. On the site of the current Mariinsky was a wooden circus, which in the middle of the nineteenth century was given the status of "Imperial" and rebuilt by Albert Cavos as a stone building that often staged fairy-tales in musical and dance form. After the fire of 1859, Cavos rebuilt the circus in just one year, but as an opera theater named Mariinsky, in honor of Empress Maria, wife of Emperor Alexander II.

The Mariinsky enjoyed its golden age in this building. Walking through its showcase front-of-house halls – joyous, but with no theatrics; decorated in quiet shades of pearly gray, white, and light blue; adorned with majestic crystal chandeliers – you could easily think you are not in a theater foyer, but the living quarters of the Winter Palace. This is actually not that far from the truth, as the Mariinsky Theater was a public salon for the Court in the late nineteenth and early twentieth centuries. Protocol dictated visits by heads of state and personal guests of the tsar's family, and even everyday performances had the impression of a court ritual.

The management of the imperial theaters molded their cast of performers, directors, artists, and composers with as much care as the jewelers who selected diamonds for imperial finery (though influential *prima donnas* such as the ballerina Matilda Kshesinskaya would refuse to play by the rules and simply dispose of any functionaries who got in their way). The singers and ballerinas were frequently compared in high-society talk and newspaper columns – but then how else could sublime mastery of Italian *bel canto* or bewitching virtuoso ballet technique be described if not in these terms?

This era introduced a number of inventions into everyday theatrical use, including the famous 32 fouettés first used by Pierina Legnani in *Cinderella*, the celeste – a small keyboard instrument which mimics the sound of bells – which Tchaikovsky made part of his *Nutcracker* orchestra, new electric stage machinery, and so on. But the Mariinsky's most important achievement was the Russian national opera repertoire created by Rimsky-Korsakov, Tchaikovsky and the "Mighty Handful," and the revelations of Marius

Petipa that nourish ballet to this day: in *La Bayadere*, *Sleeping Beauty*, and *Raimonda*, Petipa subjugated dance to the principles of symphonic music, developing choreographic combinations as composers use themes and leitmotifs.

At the turn of the century, artists of the World of Art movement tried to break into theatrical art, but the Revolution forced them to continue their quest in Europe. However, the Mariinsky was able not only to cling onto its traditions in the Soviet era, but also to create powerful new currents in musical theater, such as "choreographic drama," or ballet renditions of drama; diametrically opposed abstract forms, combining traditional ballet and the avant-garde; the ballet of Yury Grigorovich, which merged both ideas; as well as expressionist experiments by opera directors.

"It Used to be Red"

At the administrative entrance where honored guests and the press enter the Mariinsky Theater, everything is confusion. The photographer and I elbow our way through in search of the press secretary. Ahead, all is laughter, cries of greeting, and swinging television-camera lights. When we reach the lit-up space, we see why: Yury Grigorovich, suntanned and smiling, in an elegant dark-blue suit, is greeting every guest personally. Next to him is his wife, former Bolshoi prima ballerina Natalia Bessmertnova. "Yura, you see – I came specially from my dacha just to look at you," flirts the famous 1960s prima ballerina Ninel Kurgapkina, Rudolf Nureyev's helper for his Paris *La Bayadere* and now working with the Mariinsky's most famous current ballerina, Ulyana Lopatkina.

To the public, performances by Grigorovich's theater are grand and showy; to the man himself, they are highly labor-intensive. Four runs of daily performances, with three works in each: *Spartacus*, *The Nutcracker*, *The Golden Age*, and *Romeo and Juliet*. The hall is packed at prices that, for St. Petersburg, are sky-high, starting at 1,500 rubles (about $50); there are VIPs from St. Petersburg and Krasnodar – as well as Defense Minister Sergei Ivanov and his U.S. counterpart, Donald Rumsfeld, who gave *Spartacus* a standing ovation. The dancers and their teachers applaud excitedly, swapping opinions, and then there is endless back-slapping backstage.

Then comes night-time scene-changing and lighting rehearsals, followed by a run-through with the cast the next morning, as there's no other time. We invite ourselves to one of the rehearsals – otherwise we won't be able to get an interview with Grigorovich, whom everyone is after.

"Please don't take any pictures," Grigorovich frowns. "Half of the artists are in rehearsal costume, and will only be marking their steps." But he relents when he finds out we are not from television.

"Let's get down what I have to tell you quickly, because later you'll have to wait for an hour and a half while we run through the big scenes. I danced at the Mariinsky for seventeen years, and began directing here. Then I headed this theater's ballet company, and exactly forty years ago I moved to Moscow to head the Bolshoi Ballet. The productions we took on tour I created in Moscow and my versions were never part of the Petersburg repertoire. Of course, I get very nervous and am acutely aware of my responsibility. I hope that our performers will give the audience a new insight into these works, and that the experienced Petersburg public brings out artistic revelations from the dancers."

I turn off my recorder. But the stage is not yet ready for the rehearsal, and Grigorivich, unfettered by "protocol," carries on. The famous brocade curtain slowly descends. "You know it used to be red?" Grigorovich says. "Yes, that was how Alexander Golovin designed and made it. But the color scheme was so strong that my teacher, Simon Virsaladze – a master of staging whom I worked with for many years, made a blue version to match the fittings of the hall. Golovin's red curtain is still used as a decoration during concerts."

We ask whether Grigorovich will have to make any changes, given that the Mariinsky stage is six meters narrower than the Bolshoi's, and that the auditorium is more compact and has two more balconies.

"No, no", he smiles. "But because of this, the performances will make a special impression here. Every member of the audience will feel as though they are part of a festival, but also as though the performance is being staged just for them."

When the rehearsal starts, everything becomes clear: If Moscow's Bolshoi is a theater for large-scale ballets with casts of hundreds, then the Mariinsky is for soloists, and its stage seems to put them into extreme close-up.

From 1964, when Grigorovich left the Mariinsky Theater to head the Bolshoi Ballet, to the beginning of the 1990s, the St. Petersburg company was essentially a choreography museum, preserving and demonstrating the best ballet of nineteenth- and twentieth-century ballet stagings, as well as impeccable dance technique. This era in the theater's history is symbolized by the program "An Evening of Old Choreography," comprising surviving fragments of nineteenth-century ballets with sets and costumes stylized from old paintings by the artist Igor Ivanov. (A shortened version can be seen in the widely available video recording *A Night of Classical Ballet*.)

The *prima donna* of St. Petersburg ballet in those years was Irina Kolpakova, the last pupil of Agrippina Vaganova, founding mother of the Russian academic school. Kolpakova executed even the most difficult combinations of steps with brilliant ease, rather like a *bel canto* soprano with virtuoso coloratura passages. Kolpakova's fellow soloists included ballerinas of various styles, each of whom could easily have been the leading lady of another company: the temperamental virtuosi Gabriella Komleva and Alla Sizova, both electric actors of incredible stamina; the poetic Elena Yevteyeva, whose dancing revived the image of the featherweight ballerinas of the Romantic era; the radiant Svetlana Yefremova, who brought a ray of sunshine to the stage; the lyrical Lyubov Kunakova, whose fluid dancing exuded the placidity, strength and good-nature traditionally associated with the Russian character; and the unique Galina Mezentseva, the most brilliant personality of the 1970s and 1980s, whose dancing lines and interpretation fused strict Petersburg academism with twentieth-century schools from avant-garde to expressionism and existentialism.

Today, one can hear snatches of foreign conversation in the Mariinsky's labyrinthine backstage corridors, or run into renowned dancers or choreographers from Europe and America on their way to a rehearsal or discussing some project or other – the aging walls with their peeling paintwork and the shabby old furniture are the only reminder that this is Russia's oldest theater.

The Mariinsky has always been a significant international player. Some of Europe's top artists worked here, such as Verdi, who wrote one of his finest operas, *La Forza del Destino*, as a commission from the theater. Wagner's operas received their Russian premieres here. In turn, Mariinsky alumni such as Shalyapin, the choreographer Georgy Balanchivadze – better known by the name he adopted in America: George Balanchine – and many others blazed trails in opera and ballet around the world in the twentieth century.

In asserting itself as a major center for contemporary musical theater, the Mariinsky has recently been preparing for a massive overhaul of its historical home and for the construction of a new building. The upheavals associated with this preparation and the often heated discussions surrounding it have proved to be no less entertaining than the dramas which unfold on its stage.

A Window on Europe

The 1988 appointment of Valery Gergiev as artistic director marked the beginning of a new era for the Mariinsky Theater. Gergiev's main interest is in opera, which assumed primary importance with his arrival. But Gergiev radically changed every aspect of the life of the theater, as a result of which Petersburg ballet has undergone equally striking changes.

Crowded into the beautiful if cramped (for 150 journalists, at least) foyer before the premiere of *The Nutcracker* – staged not by a choreographer, but the artist Mikhail Shemyakin – we looked forward to a rare discussion with Gergiev about ballet rather than opera. Gergiev was delayed: some said he had arrived at the theater in the morning, others that he had just got there. While we waited, we swapped thoughts on Gergiev's career and the influence it has had on the Mariinsky Theater.

Gergiev's rise began at the Leningrad Conservatory, in the class of Ilya Musin, the guru of the Russian conducting school. At the age of 23, Gergiev won the Soviet Union's National Conducting Competition and the Herbert von Karajan Competition in West Berlin, where he was supported by jury member Tikhon Khrennikov, then the influential head of the Union of Composers of the USSR. Khrennikov also arranged for Gergiev to conduct the premiere of his ballet, *The Hussar's Ballad*, in St. Petersburg. It was with this work that Gergiev made his debut at Moscow's Bolshoi.

"Do you know how funny his debut was?" recalled one journalist who saw the performance. "He was so nervous that he frightened the orchestra to such a degree that the musicians had to stop at one point. Thankfully, the show was just a normal performance, and no-one noticed."

After the 1988 death of Yevgeny Mravinsky, legendary principal conductor of the Leningrad Philharmonic, his post went to Yury Temirkanov, then artistic director of the Mariinsky Theater (which, from 1935 to 1992 was actually known as the Kirov Theater). Temirkanov's position at the Mariinsky was taken by Gergiev, who immediately made plain his intention to strengthen the theater's standing worldwide, and stunned the Russian public with his workaholism, unbelievable by the standards of the time. Putting on half a dozen new opera productions a season became the norm for the Mariinsky, which began to restage all of Prokofiev's main operas. Gergiev gave the Russian premiere of Wagner's *Parsifal*, and over the course of several years put on the whole of the *Ring* cycle. He also became friends with Placido Domingo, who performed in Mariinsky productions and gala concerts, and introduced about a dozen singers onto the European stage, who became principals at top theaters worldwide. The theater became home to opera festivals dedicated to Mussorgsky, Rimsky-Korsakov and Prokofiev, as well as the annual *Stars of the White Nights* in the summer. There were also regular tours abroad – to the joy of poor Russian artists and pragmatic European managers (because frequently it works out cheaper to bring a ready-made production from Russia than to put together a new staging in Europe).

But Gergiev does not confine himself solely to running the Mariinsky Theater. Somehow, he manages to combine this work with duties as principal guest conductor at the Metropolitan Opera in New York, director of festivals in Rotterdam and Mikkeli, and annual appearances at the Salzburg Festival – the most prestigious in Europe – as well as numerous individual projects. New additions to this list are made regularly, the most recent including the Moscow Easter Festival and the extended musical celebration of St. Petersburg's 300th anniversary. Unsurprisingly, discussions of the quantity of Gergiev's work and its effect on the quality of his conducting are a continual topic amongst arts aficionados.

Reviews of Gergiev's performances and concerts include both those which credit him with an unbelievable temperament and interpretational genius, and thorough critical dissections of his work. From this we can surmise that some of the conductor's performances make a very strong impression on the public. But working in a hurry is one of his trademarks: for the most part, the program of the Moscow Easter Festival sounded fussy and one-paced, in which individual works were ignored and secondary details were given overdue prominence. On occasion, Gergiev operas have a patchwork feel: in important vocal scenes he muffles the orchestra, while giving himself free rein in instrumental episodes. Even at the Salzburg Festival, with one of the world's top orchestras and first-class singers at his disposal, it seemed that the ensemble's musicianship was a real burden: Gergiev wanted to lead and to shine, but the perfidious operatic genre continually demanded that he give the limelight to his cast. Possibly for this reason the conductor takes more pleasure in the symphonic repertoire, which he can interpret as he wants. And in opera Gergiev is at his best dealing with Wagnerian epics, in which the voices, like orchestral instruments, are intertwined into the musical fabric.

Gergiev's fans excuse his defects by pointing to his exorbitant workload and organizational difficulties. And indeed, Gergiev thinks about these even during his most important performances, discussing them right before going on stage and on the way out of the orchestra pit. For him it is the most natural thing in the world to have several plans on the go at once, to talk with different people simultaneously, to be in a rush, to mobilize people, or to change his plans on short notice. Negotiations are for him as much of an art form as music, and he can discuss economic and political aspects of culture as animatedly as the theater.

Our press conference is a vivid example. Gergiev's tardiness – by a half-hour – is of course forgiven. What does it matter *when* we hear him? We have to spend all day in the theater in any case. Immediately after the conference, there is a rehearsal on stage, and then the performance. Gergiev is forgiven for barely listening to questions in an attempt to save time: his first answer is a long rambling monologue covering everything that could be asked and everything he considers necessary.

The problem is not that Gergiev combines being an artist and a businessman, but that he often substitutes one for the other. For example, he invested huge effort into bringing a veritable galaxy of stars and famous ensembles together for St. Petersburg's 300th anniversary, rather than finding real artistic ideas for the occasion. He staged a remake of Diaghilev's *Saisons Russes* at Paris' Le Chatelet theater rather than coming up with his own equivalent. He attempts to make artistic projects into social and political events, and vice versa.

Because of this, Gergiev often falls into the trap of missing the obvious. The comic *Nutcracker*, with its stage so overflowing with Shemyakin's window-dressing that there was virtually no room left for the dance, is in itself not a problem: the production made its mark. But Gergiev failed to notice that the premiere coincided with the 120th anniversary of the birth of the legendary Anna Pavlova, the ultimate symbol of St. Petersburg ballet. And he did not use this as a reason for an artistically "exclusive" project.

Similar omissions can be seen in Gergiev's strategy for the development of the Mariinsky Theater, which he has turned from Russia's leading theater, with its own aesthetic traditions, into a peripheral European theater. On Gergiev's watch, directing and staging have fused Russian opera with the language of foreign theater. But with a couple of exceptions, no productions in this sphere have been artistic revelations or examples of cutting-edge trends. Musically, St. Petersburg has still not consolidated its position in world opera: appearances by leading foreign (even Russian) singers are still rare events, rather than everyday occurrences. Unlike Europe's top theaters, for all its global ambitions, the Mariinsky cannot guarantee that the listed performers will necessarily be playing – or even that the performance will be the one advertised. It has become the custom in Russia for everything to change not half a year in advance, but a month or even a week before the event, which makes it very difficult for respectable people who plan far ahead to rely seriously on the theater.

But Gergiev's most paradoxical achievement is that his various musical activities have made him into a newsmaker whose image bears little or no relation to the artistic logic of what he does. It is of great interest to the Russian public that the conductor did not tell former Culture Minister Mikhail Shvydkoy why he advocated American architect Eric Owen Moss' avant-garde project for renovating the Mariinsky building before suddenly rejecting it, and whether his wife accompanies him on his numerous long trips abroad, and how many children he has. Gergiev's life has become a more significant performance than any of the operas he conducts.

Hollow Victories

The ballet company has been just as actively involved in the process of Europeanization. Its work at home, which produced fascinating original repertoire, has been virtually abandoned in favor of intensive, wearisome foreign tours and the transfer to the Mariinsky's stage of foreign, twentieth-century classics of choreography. In these years, the company has hurriedly come to grips with all the main works of George Balanchine, the ballets of Jerome Robbins, and older works by living classics such as Roland Petit, William Forsythe, and John Neumaier.

"Of course, it's very interesting to work with the world's best choreographers, producing especially for you," said Andrian Fadeev, one of the company's best young dancers, and the only artist who has managed to work with all of the famous directors whom the Mariinsky has invited in recent years. "But, at the same time, such a large theater needs an artistic leader who defines the main direction of its development. Also, it's important for young artists to look up to the masters of the older generation who provide a model of performance style."

Today, Petersburg ballet's best-known masters, its standard bearers – the ballerinas Irina Kolpakova and Alla Sizova, the choreographer Oleg Vinogradov, and dozens of renowned young artists such as Yelena Pankova, Larisa Lezhina, and Anastasia Dunets – live and work in Europe and America. In their place, the Mariinsky Theater has founded an annual ballet festival which showcases top dancers from Europe and America.

At the same time, the Mariinsky has launched some ambitious plans, trying to polish its crown jewels by reconstructing *Sleeping Beauty* and *La Bayadere*, those nineteenth-century choreography encyclopedias created for its stage by Marius Petipa. Ex-Mariinsky dancer Sergei Vikharev and artist Andrei Voitenko have tried to recreate the original design, staging, steps, and gestures from recordings by former Mariinsky director Nikolai Sergeyev. After the Revolution, Sergeyev took his recordings to London, and they subsequently ended up in the Harvard Theater Collection, which generously gave the Mariinsky all the materials it needed.

The result was a performance of a fundamentally different type of ballet. In twentieth-century editions of *Sleeping Beauty* and *La Bayadere*, the most important thing is classical dance. Russian choreographers tried to underscore that Petipa used physical motifs like composers use musical themes. Therefore the pantomime "conversations," showpiece entrances of extras and demonstration of sham miracles in Soviet editions only emphasized the dance scenes.

In the reconstructed productions, everything is turned on its head. These are ballet processions, in which classical dance comes out of ceremonial rituals. The characters in their heavy costumes do not stand out against the monumental, detail-heavy scenery, but are rather swallowed up by it and look like component parts. All of the extras are dressed just as gaudily as the soloists. This style looks like carnival *kitsch* from a circus presentation or pictures in a fashionable nineteenth-century magazine. Petipa – angling for success with the Petersburg public – largely copied these *kitsch* shows in works based on Spanish, Hungarian, and Egyptian fairy tales, set to the fiery can-cans of Cesare Puni.

These reconstructions ought to have been a sensation – the ballet equivalent of the discovery of Troy or the raising of the Titanic – but instead were met with suspicion. Russian dancers and balletomanes wondered whether a precise reconstruction was possible when the recording system captured only the outermost points of the movements, without showing how they were executed. Critics suggested that such reconstructions ignore points of reference and, eventually, destroy the basis of the ballet school: the dance combinations which have come down to us, passed from artist to artist – from leg to leg, as it were – authentic and tested by time for artistic "durability." And what was brought out of the archives was dubious.

But another problem was more obvious. The current artists were unable to create the impression of an old-fashioned dance style fundamentally different from the style they are used to. Petipa's ballets demand worldly chic and lively, artistic movement. When Matilda Kshesinskaya, Nicholas II's favorite and the grande dame of the Mariinsky Theater, performed the episodic role of Little Red Riding Hood in *Sleeping Beauty*, dressed in a short skirt and apron, and Petipa's strapping daughter Maria came on as *Cinderella*, this created a comic effect in itself. Petipa's physical efforts and stylistics remained behind the scenes, in the rehearsal rooms and exercises that the public never saw, while the action on stage appeared effortless.

The previous generation of Petersburg ballet dancers – artists such as Irina Kolpakova, Gabriella Komleva, and Galina Mezentseva – were able to stylize old-fashioned performance practice even in Soviet editions of Petipa's ballets. For today's artists to perform a version which is much closer to the original nineteenth-century production is almost impossible. They are used to dazzling audiences with their unique physical gifts and head-spinning technical tricks, but have more difficulty enchanting them with artistry and a sense of style. They put in huge amounts of energy, dance fussily and heavily, commit lots of errors, and look nothing at all like the characters in the performance.

But even when the company is on form and dancing error-free, it does not follow the laws of theater psychology. The dancers are more like colors or musical timbres in the on-stage action than they are characters, and, as a result, the airy, impressionist *Chopiniana* and the graphic "Dance of the Shades" from *La Bayadere* are indistinguishable from each other. The amusing game interludes from *Don Quixote* appear unnatural. The artists have no way to understand brilliant stylistic scenes (such as *La Bayadere's* monumental pantomime dialogs, which Petipa staged in European classical style), and therefore execute them formally, like schoolchildren at an exam. The current successes of the Mariinsky are predicated not on demonstrations of a unique Russian dance style, but merely on having a number of good dancers and on the scale of the theater's productions.

January/February 2005

By Axe, Rope and Bullet
Dasha Demourova

In May 1744, Tsarina Elizabeth imposed a ban on the death penalty. It was the first such ban in Russia and it lasted sixty-nine years.

Pagan Rus did not know the death penalty as such, but tribes did engage in private vendettas. Blood feuds were later replaced with a system of fines that varied by social rank.

The Charter of Dvina (1389) is the first written Russian law that mentions the death penalty. The penalty was imposed only for the third incidence of theft.

In the Charter of Pskov (1467), the death penalty was enacted for the crimes of treason, theft from churches, arson, horse stealing, and three convictions for theft. The absence of murder from the list is easily explained: it was more profitable to impose fines for murder than to apply the death penalty.

In the *Sudebniks* ("Codes of Law") of 1497 and 1550, the list of crimes punishable by death was significantly lengthened. It now included treason, robbery, murder, riot, surrendering a city, falsification of documents, arson, and more.

By the second half of the sixteenth century, punishment for crimes began to have the motive of deterrence, rather than simply punishing the criminal. This, combined with the cruelty of Ivan the Terrible's reign, led to the torturing of condemned criminals before they were put to death.

In the Penal Code of 1649, crimes covered by the death penalty again expanded. There were now 63 crimes punishable by death, including blasphemy, theft, treason and arson. Under Peter the Great (1696-1725), 123 crimes brought the death penalty. The methods of execution were regulated in detail and differed depending on their purpose: they were either aimed at torturing a criminal and making an example of him or at safeguarding society from the criminal.

Against this backdrop, Tsarina Elizabeth's decree of May 7, 1744, temporarily banning the death penalty, was a path-breaking reversal of centuries of state policy. A permanent decree abolishing the death penalty was issued in 1753.

Still, not all was as it seemed. Elizabeth replaced the death penalty with other (often horrendous) types of punishment (like beating and drubbing) that nonetheless lead to death. And, in the eighteenth century, the death penalty was often used extra-judicially, in response to peasant revolts.

The moratorium came to an end in the Penal Code of 1813, which introduced new systems of punishment, including the death penalty, deprivation of all political and civil rights (so called "civil death"), fines, etc. Rulers began to use the death penalty to rid themselves of political enemies. The execution in December 1825 of five Decembrists, aristocratic conspirators who attempted a coup against the tsar, shocked society. Noblemen were previously largely immune from the sentence of death.

At the Decembrists' hanging, the ropes tore, and the condemned, including Sergei Muravyov, fell to the ground. While Muravyov's injured leg ached severely, he moaned: "Poor Russia, they can't even hang a person properly here!"

The Penal Code of 1832 (introduced in 1835), restricted the death penalty to military crimes, treason and crimes committed during quarantine situations. In general, there were few death penalties in the nineteenth century, even revolutionaries and terrorists were rarely sentenced to death (Lenin's brother, Alexander Ulyanov, being a notable exception; in 1887 – he was hanged for conspiring to assassinate Alexander III).

Revolution changed everything. From 1905 on, the number of executions increased. Statistics show that, between 1826 and 1905, 612 persons were executed, while between 1906 and 1912 there were 4,098.

Of course, these numbers pale in comparison to the victims of Lenin and Stalin's terror. According to official data, between 1921 and 1954 some 643,000 people were executed – this does not include victims of Gulag labor camps. While it is hard to estimate the exact number of people who perished during the first four decades of Soviet rule, the human rights group Memorial and other experts have credibly shown that over 20 million persons were executed, perished in the Gulag, or were murdered by state-imposed famine.

There was a rather "utilitarian" aspect to the death penalty in Russia during the twentieth century. Repeated reversals in policy gave an indication of what the leadership considered to be the gravest societal ills, while behind the legal façade political executions followed no rules.

After the February Revolution, the death penalty was immediately abolished (March 12, 1917), but on July 12, 1917 it was restored once again in an attempt to keep soldiers at the front from deserting. On October 26, 1917, the day after the Bolshevik Revolution, the new government prohibited the death penalty, while carrying out executions in secret.

On February 21, 1918, the death penalty was restored for certain groups of criminals (spies, hooligans, etc.). And in September 1918, the "Red Terror"decree was issued, proclaiming the penalty of death for all "counter-revolutionaries." Some 5,496 people were executed between June 1918 and February 1919. In January 1920, the death penalty was abolished again, on the initiative of Felix Dzerzhinsky, the secret police head, only to be restored again in 1922.

In the 1930-1940s, 42 crimes were punishable by death. After WWII, on May 26, 1947, the death penalty was replaced with a 25-year prison term, in consideration of peacetime. But, with the renewed threat of war (the Cold War), just three years later, on January 12, 1950, there was a new decree legalizing execution for treason, espionage and sabotage. On April 30, 1954, premeditated murder was added to the list of crimes punishable by death. And a decree of May 6, 1961 extended the death penalty for crimes of misappropriation and currency speculation. Less than a year later, on February 15, 1962, it was further extended to include murder of a militia officer, rape and bribe-taking.

Between 1962 and 1990, in the USSR as a whole, according to Anatoly Pristavkin, who was the head of the State Pardon Committee under President Yeltsin, 24,500 persons were sentenced to death and 21,000 executions were carried out. During this period, and throughout the Soviet era, the primary form of execution has been by gun.

After the collapse of the Soviet Union, the number of executions in Russia fell significantly. In 1990, just 76 persons were executed. In 1992, just one person was put to death. But, by 1995, the number was on the rise again (86), dipping somewhat in 1996 (53).

The Russian Constitution, ratified in 1993, stated that, in the future, the death penalty should be abolished, and that one can only be sentenced to death by a jury. On May 16, 1996 (252 years and nine days after Elizabeth's decree), Russian President Boris Yeltsin signed a decree that placed a moratorium on the death penalty – a requirement for Russia's entry into the Council of Europe.[1] Three years later, in June 1999, Yeltsin commuted the death sentences of all of Russia's death row inmates. While the Council of Europe insists that Russia must legislatively abolish the death penalty, that reality does not seem to be in the immediate future.[2]

Public opinion hardly favors such a move. In a nationwide poll conducted by Levada Center in March 2002, just 12 percent said that the death penalty should be permanently abolished; 12 percent favored the current moratorium; 49 percent said capital punishment should be reintroduced on the scale it was employed in the early 1990s; 18 percent said the use of capital punishment should be broadened. In February of this year, 42 percent of those Levada polled said they supported the death penalty for convicted terrorists.

May/June 2004

Postscript: In November 2009, the Constitutional Court of Russia extended the country's moratorium on the death penalty, "until the ratification of the 6th Protocol to the European Convention on Human Rights."

----

1. Executions, however, continued until August 1996. The last person executed was serial killer Sergei Golovkin, convicted in 1994 and shot August 2, 1996.
2. The current Penal Colde permits use of the death penalty for five crimes: murder with certain aggravating circumstances, attempted murder, terrorism, severe instances of torture or mayhem, genocide. Under military law, treason, espionage, desertion and sedition are punishable by death.

Tuber or Not Tuber
Semyon Ekshtut

> *"Ever since the Romanovs ascended to the Russian throne, from Mikhail Fyodorovich to Nicholas I, the government has been at the forefront of education and enlightenment. The people follow along, but often lazily and half-heartedly. And it is precisely this which constitutes the strength of our autocracy."*
>
> *– Alexander Pushkin*

Potatoes came to Russia long after they were a staple in the European diet. Introduction of the tuber to Russia is usually credited to Peter the Great, who became familiar with potatoes while learning the shipbuilding trade in the Netherlands, bringing back with him seeds with which to grow the plant in St. Petersburg. Another version has it that the potato came to Russia not only from the West but also from the East: via Kamchatka and Alaska, where the plant had long been locally grown.

According to the *Great Encyclopedia of Cyril and Methodius*, at first Russians thought that the edible part of the plant was the fruit growing on the potato bush after it blossomed, rather than the root growing underground. Hapless potato growers boiled the fruits and tried to eat them with sugar, but the taste was still so awful that they gave up on it. Apparently even Catherine served the wrong fruit of the potato plant to her husband Peter the Great after he gave her the "earthly apples" as a gift.

As was the case with many innovations in Russia, potato cultivation was imposed from above. In 1765 Catherine the Great directed the Senate to pass a decree and special regulations "On Potato Growing, Transportation, and Storage." In each Russian *gubernia*, potato growing was to be monitored by the local governor. Yet, even 25 years later, in 1790, German settlers were about the only potato growers in St. Petersburg and its vicinities.

In 1797, during the reign of Paul I, state officials in villages were required to "introduce peasants to potato cultivation." But Russian peasants are a conservative lot, and they were lukewarm about the mysterious root from abroad.

It took the iron hand of Tsar Nicholas I to break the peasants' passive resistance and introduce cultivation of the *kartofel* on a national scale. The effort began with so-called *udelnye* and state peasants. *Udelnye* peasants (from the word *udel*, a land plot allocated to members of the imperial family) worked on imperial plots and were the property of the imperial family. State peasants lived on state lands, and paid rent to the state, but were considered to be free individuals.

On January 1, 1838, the Ministry of State Properties was founded to manage state peasants. Count Pavel Kiselyov, holding the military rank of general (Nicholas I called him his "head of the general staff dealing with the peasantry"), was appointed the ministry's head. It was a tumultuous time for Russian farms. The years 1839-1841 saw bad harvests, and there was not enough grain even for seed crop, leading to a terrible famine. Thus, potatoes seemed a perfect way to spare peasants from starvation and Kiselyov became the tuber's main proponent.

Unfortunately, Count Kiselyov had many opponents at court. The famous countess Eudoxie Golitsyn, immortalized in verse by Alexander Pushkin, launched a vehement counterattack against Kiselyov, calling the potato a threat to Russian national traditions.

Admiral (and Count) Alexander Menshikov, one of the sharpest tongues in high society, excoriated Kiselyov, saying his potato reforms would further ruin the peasants. Menshikov never let slip an opportunity to gore Kiselyov. At that time Russia was waging a war in the Caucasus and Nicholas asked Menshikov whom he should send to the region to put down seven rebellious Caucasian villages. "If you are looking for someone who is good at ruining," Menshikov said, "then you can't go wrong choosing Count Kiselyov. If he ruined the state peasants, he could ruin those remaining seven villages just like that!"

The government's orders requiring potato cultivation on state and imperial property provoked the so-called "potato revolts," first of *udelnye* peasants (1834) and then of state peasants (1840-1841). The revolts took place throughout much of western Russia, including the towns and regions of Perm, Vyatka, Orenburg, Tobolsk, Kazan, Saratov, Ryazan, Moscow, Vologda, Olonets and Tambov. Ironically, today these are Russia's most important potato growing lands.

In one of its reports, the Third Department of the Chancellery of his Imperial Majesty [the secret police] wrote: "Ignorant allegations to the effect that the potato is a cursed fruit whose cultivation brought about God's refusal to bless the Russian land with fertility, were the cause of disobedience of peasants of the Moscow *gubernia*, who, in some villages, destroyed entire potato fields."

A highranking official in Kiselyov's ministry blamed revolts in the Saratov *gubernia* on "the ignorance and frenzy" of peasants: "That very ignorance and attachment to a free lifestyle inculcates in their minds the idea that every governmental measure aimed at improvement will result in the alienation of all of their rights and property; hence the reason for such stubborn resistance to potato growing in 1841."

State peasants feared that potato cultivation would lead to their further impoverishment or, just as bad, to their transformation into *udelnye* peasants. In the recent past, peasants had been forced to grow beetroot and then work in sugar factories to process the plants – taking them away from the land. Peasants in Saratov gubernia apparently feared that potato growing would encourage the land owners to build yet more "sugar factories" which, to quote Decembrist Nikolai Turgenev, the peasants "feared like the plague."

As the cited report indicates, religion and superstition also fed into the revolts. In one of the villages of the Vyatskaya *gubernia* some provocateurs spread the rumor that "the [Orthodox] faith is going to be changed, and that it was everything to do with potato growing."

Over 500,000 peasants took part in the potato revolts, ravaging potato fields, assaulting state functionaries and launching armed attacks against troops sent in to quell the riots. In some places, the most active insurgents were shot. For the State was determined to stay their "potato course." On August 25, 1841, the Executive Secretary of the Ministry of the Interior, Count Stroganov, sent Russian governors the following Ruling of the Sovereign: "His Majesty the Emperor, upon reading reports regarding cases of disobedience by some state peasants in connection with potato sowing, gave the following Supreme Order: culprits fit for military service shall be conscripted and those unfit shall work as serfs in Bobruysk [a city in present day Belarus]."

To borrow a phrase from Russia's revolutionary-democrat Alexander Herzen, potatoes were grown in Russia "the hard way."

IT TOOK ANOTHER decade for the potato to earn some respect in Russia and for the crop's cultivation to spread. In fact, by the second half of the nineteenth century, Russians had begun to adopt the potato as their own, even boasting homegrown brands at international exhibits. By the turn of the century, the potato was firmly planted in Russian cuisine and culture.

In the early decades of Soviet rule, the potato saved millions from famine during the Civil War and the lean years of WWII. In the 1940s, Muscovites even grew potatoes in small plots or gardens within the city.

And yet, the coercive element in potato cultivation persisted, albeit in a somewhat modified form. Every fall in the post-WWII Soviet era, high school, university and institute students, and even research fellows at scientific institutes, were required to spend one to one-and-a-half months on "*kartoshka* missions," helping collective farms harvest the potato crop. The army was also called in as "free labor" to dig and pack the tubers.

Actually, for servicemen, the work was a welcome change from military routine. But students were split: the lazy ones loved to go on *kartoshka* missions; good students regarded the "social chore" as a total waste of time. But for either, protesting would have been an ideological revolt rooted in a "misunderstanding of the Party and *komsomol* line," with the inevitable consequences for one's career. "*Kartoshka* dodging" was heavily frowned upon.

The most interesting solution was offered by film director Eldar Ryazanov, in his 1980 film *Garage*, a sharp satire on Soviet reality. In it, a respected professor of zoology joins his research fellows in packing potatoes at the potato warehouse. He then put his business card in every carton of potatoes, as proof of the quality of his work. "If they send me there," he says, "one who is paid R600 a month [a huge salary in Soviet times], then I must be fully responsible for the quality of my packing work." Some customers found his business card and called his research institute bosses to inform on the matter. From then on, the professor was left off the packing crews.

Of course, today, with the transition to a market economy, mandatory potato missions have stopped.

Free of all compulsory aspects or ideological imperatives, the potato is now free to simply be itself: a beloved side dish in Russian cuisine. A position it earned, needless to say, at no small price.

September/October 2000

Inside the Bolshoi

Yaroslav Sedov

*V*ery little escapes the fear of terrorism in our world today. And so, beginning this season, everyone entering the Bolshoi is thoroughly scanned and searched, as if they were boarding an airplane. Long lines of audience members snake between the theater's columns, waiting to pass through the metal detector and to open their bags; another line – replete with ballet stars, stagehands, journalists and guests – extends out the stage door. Following recent bombings and the fire at the nearby Manezh, no one thinks of protesting. The hum of conversation surrounds the entrances; jokes are made about how all are equal before the greatness of the Bolshoi.

Yet some are more equal than others. The heavy oak door opens and the line respectfully steps aside to let pass a small, elderly lady with grey hair and a piercing, searching gaze. She is Soviet ballet legend Marina Semyonova, a renowned teacher who trained generations of the Bolshoi's best dancers, and who this year celebrated her 96th birthday. Semyonova gave up her weekly classes only last year, but continues to work with individual dancers. To see her exchange cordial greetings, passing coolly through formalities and setting off down the corridor with a brisk, businesslike step, is to immediately understand what is meant by "regal simplicity" – perfect *beau monde* or theatrical society manners.

The Bolshoi Theater measures its history in ages. In each, the soloists, conductors, managers, staging traditions and even the architectural appearance of the building change. At times, the Bolshoi has been a yardstick; at others a theatrical backwater. It has been threatened with closure several times, but it has always been the country's principal theater, and not just because it is Russia's largest, both physically (the word *bolshoi* means "large" or "grand") and in the number of its employees (currently about 3,000, with 250 in the *corps de ballet* alone). No, the Bolshoi is Russia's principal theater because the state of the Bolshoi can be used to judge the cultural situation in Russia more broadly.

TRANSLATION: PETER MORLEY

Marina Semyonova's career coincides with the era in which the Soviet state turned the Bolshoi Ballet into its prima cultural showcase. The best dancers from all over the Soviet Union were invited to the Bolshoi; those that reached the pinnacle of artistry were pulled into the inner orbits of cultural and political power. Of course, this led to some disconnects: e.g. Bolshoi prima ballerina Galina Ulanova was held up as an example of the Soviet worker and public figure, but at the same time did not need worry about life's mundane problems. But if the stars were taken care of, the State also "took care of" all the fees received for ballet tours abroad – sizeable sums once the Bolshoi had been turned into a hot export commodity.

At first glance, it may seem strange that ballet could have flourished under the totalitarian Soviet regime, which sought to negate so much of what had come before it. Yet, notably, some of the earliest Soviet choreographers – Rostislav Zakharov, Leonid Yakobson, Kasyan Goleizovsky, Leonid Lavrovsky and, later, Yuri Grigorovich – succeeded through application of principles from the Imperial Theater.

Grigorovich, in fact, is responsible for opening a new chapter in Russian ballet. Following his *Stone Flower* and *Legend of Love* at the turn of the 1950s, he proposed a new form of ballet, in which the dance – using modern flexible movements – shaped the plot, rather than the other way around. Moreover, the Grigorovich era was remarkable for the huge number of brilliant dancers – including Maya Plisetskaya, Nina Timofeyeva, Natalya Bessmertnova, Vladimir Vasilyev, Yekaterina Maksimova, Lyudmila Semenyaka, Alexander Godunov, and Nadezhda Pavlova. In previous eras, there had been only one or two stars of this calibre at any one time. These dancers combined textbook technique with cutting-edge (for the time) repertoire and audacious aesthetics that at times all but contradicted traditional ideas about ballet. In short, they showed that the Russian school, combining elements of the French, Italian, and Danish, was not only viable, but could also strike out in new directions on its own, and that Russian dancers could perform anywhere – from the Paris Grand Opera, where Rudolf Nureyev created a new repertoire, to Hollywood, where Mikhail Baryshnikov made a career starring in musicals.

With Gorbachev's *perestroika*, ballet was freed from having to propagandize Soviet achievements. Now, however, it had to defend itself as an art form, and resist attempts to turn ballet into show business. The artistic goals and problems of Russian ballet were further challenged by problems with facilities. Decades of neglect meant that colossal restructuring was needed at both the Bolshoi and St. Petersburg's Mariinsky Theater. Beginning in the mid-1990s, the Bolshoi gradually became an enormous complex whose main building – the historical theater – seemed to be constantly being readied for "unprecedented reconstruction." Staff and management also underwent fundamental (and repeated) changes.

Experts and the public have viewed all of this with ambivalence. In recent years, barely a month has gone by without some media discussion of impending changes, be they in personnel or infrastructure. The Bolshoi has remained Russian culture's leading newsmaker.

Perhaps to distract from discussions about reconstruction, the Bolshoi lured 24-year-old Mariinsky star Svetlana Zakharova to the capital for the start of last season (2003/2004). Zakharova thus became not only a Bolshoi prima ballerina, but in essence the "new face" of Russian ballet, with both the press and theater fans obsessively following her every move. Official visitors are escorted to Zakharova's performances: when she debuted in *Giselle*, then-Prime Minister Mikhail Kasyanov brought along his French counterpart, Jean-Pierre Raffarin; Zakharova also danced a triumphant opening night when the Bolshoi went on tour to Paris.

Zakharova's status at home equaled her international fame as one of Russia's most popular young stars, someone who dances all the leading roles in the top theaters of Europe and the U.S..

But apart from all the usual ceremony around Zakharova's performances, there are also interpretative discoveries confirming that, if anyone can take Russian ballet into new aesthetic territory, it is this ballerina. We were granted the rare opportunity to attend her rehearsals and see these discoveries being made.

The Rule of Unpredictable Failures

The Bolshoi's legendary stage and its multi-tiered golden auditorium are isolated from the outside world by walls that are two meters thick. It feels like being inside a fortress of art, where no distractions are allowed or anticipated. Performers say that appearing on the stage of the Bolshoi is a critical examination – but one that offers great rewards.

"It's not about the thickness of the walls, because the Kremlin's are even thicker," said Konstantin Ivanov, one of the Bolshoi's most aristocratic ballet princes. "And it's not about the legends, because all old theaters have them. The reason is the perception of greatness which makes you stop and ask yourself: 'Who are you? What are you worth? What have you accomplished your life?' I had the same feeling in the Vatican. The closer I got to St. Peter's, the clearer these questions became, and I felt like a little grain of sand. At the Bolshoi, though, this doesn't overwhelm you – it mobilizes you. You feel that you're part of something important, no matter which show it is. You understand that this is historic, just because it's taking place in the Bolshoi. Someone in the audience may be there for the first and only time, having dreamed about it all their life. Your performance forms people's impressions of the theater."

Watching stagehands industriously fetching pieces of staircases, walls, ships, and rocks from the hidden depths of the building, it seems as though the performance has already begun – scenery is being put in and taken out, and the lights in the wings create rainbows, highlighting everything around them in color. At performances in honor of the backstage workers, the curtain is sometimes left raised so that the audience can see the scenery being changed – and every time it gets a round of applause.

Now, though, it's different – as though we are seeing it for the last time. In February 2004, Bolshoi General Director Anatoly Iksanov published the latest detailed timetable for reconstruction of the theater building. In 2005 it will be closed for five months, and in 2006 for the whole year, during which time the company will have to perform on the New Stage or be on tour. Backstage, meanwhile, walls dating from 1853 and even 1825 will be taken down – although arguments are raging about the best way to do this. For all the years of planning, no-one has produced a satisfactory explanation as to why such massive reconstruction is needed.

Theater employees smile when we ask, looking at the peeling paintwork, whether the building is *really* so decrepit that it needs immediate salvaging. For more than 30 years, people have been saying that the Bolshoi is on the brink of collapse. In the 1970s, for the theater's 200th anniversary, some wooden beams were replaced in the auditorium. Shortly afterward, it was noticed that the new beams had begun to rot, but that the 200-year-old ones were in the same condition as ever.

"The building has survived thanks to its integrity and the durability of its 'skeleton'", says Alevtina Kuznetsova, the theater's chief architect for more than 50 years. Kuznetsova talks passionately about previous reconstructions and unrealized projects, about acoustic secrets, about how the building's foundations contain still-unstudied materials, and other marvels. The more she talks, the less clear it becomes why partial demolition followed by reconstruction is being proposed, rather than just the repair of this amazing building.

The official answer is that the stage and the stage equipment are obsolete. But the Bolshoi's equipment has been being improved and fitted into the original walls – be it introducing electricity, computer networks, etc. – for two hundred years, and nothing prevents this from continuing. The current management thinks that this is not enough, though, and the Bolshoi's stage is being asked to do things for which it was not designed – such as rapid changes of large amounts of scenery, which needs "pockets" (spaces the size of the stage from which ready-to-go sets can be brought on-stage in three seconds) that the theater does not now have. But such shows are just another form of theater. To reconstruct in this way a building meant for fly scenery is like turning a tape-recorder into a CD player.

Former Bolshoi Deputy General Director Dmitry Rodionov used to be in charge of technical services at the theater, before leaving last year for a more senior position. "The theater has a real communications problem," Rodionov said. "It has miles of piping and cabling. Also, much of the stage equipment has outlived itself – it is kept going by the inventiveness of the staff, who continually fix things, repair things, adapt things. You can work like that forever, but it's very risky. We call it 'the rule of unpredictable failures' – you never know what is going to fall apart, or when."

Reserved and taciturn, Rodionov argues every point strongly. But even he is enthused when talking about the theater's technical equipment, which he knows inside out and backwards. He can barely contain his excitement when comparing the impressive and controversial reconstruction – as well as the financial figures being quoted – with the vital everyday problems which the projects ignore. For example, unlike other theaters around the world, the Bolshoi has not reconstructed its set warehouses for many years, and, as a result, many priceless sets and props have been destroyed. To this day, no-one knows how many and which Tchaikovsky, Mussorgsky, and Verdi autographed scores are stored in the Bolshoi's nooks and crannies, or how many recordings – audio and video – there are of rehearsals and performances which could be released to public acclaim and delight.

The Bolshoi has unparalleled workshops which combine old techniques of theater art with cutting-edge engineering solutions. Here they make wonderful sinew strings, the best pointes in Russia, and the best tutus in the world. But the current management neither looks after them nor gives them basic support. The workshops (located next to the Federation Council, Russia's highest institution of state power) lack ordinary showers and air-conditioning systems. While dancers (including world-famous stars) run up and down staircases and corridors decorated with "picturesque" peeling paint – the workshops produce beautifully-cut handmade costumes to order at one-third the cost of anywhere else in the world.

Sylph Search

These conversations hung in the air as we moved from the old building to the Bolshoi's auxiliary wing, which opened last year and is home to rehearsal spaces and a warren of offices, including the press service, photo service, administration, and reception rooms for directors and their deputies. The spacious six-story building feels like the corporate headquarters of a company that wants to show off its wealth. One is not supposed to think about how much the silent lifts, marble steps, sliding glass doors, quality furniture, and lamps cost. Men in expensive suits and girls in fashionable pantsuits scurry along the corridors; weary dancers in rehearsal clothes drag bags full of shoes and props, rushing to get to the hall as quickly as they can.

According to the theater's charter, the Bolshoi is primarily an artistic, not a commercial, foundation, creating productions and performances in order to develop the cream of Russian and global traditions, to educate people, and so on. The Bolshoi is one of Russia's cultural crown jewels, and as such gets state financing not through the Ministry of Culture, but directly from the Ministry of Finance. It is a line item in the country's budget. In recent years, however, the Bolshoi's management has actively pushed for the theater to become a more commercial enterprise.

Why doesn't the Bolshoi invest its "artistic capital"? This is a question which perplexes many observers, who have watched as the theater puts on expensive, but artistically dubious, commercial productions. Bolshoi legend Yuri Vladimirov – the first man to dance the fearsomely difficult role of Ivan the Terrible and now a ballet coach at the theater – reflects on this with surprise when we speak with him during a break in a rehearsal with Spanish dancer Igor Yebra Iglesias, who has come for coaching in the part of Ivan before an appearance in the Kremlin; the Bolshoi's new management has sent its production of this ballet – based on Prokofiev's music and Eisenstein's film, with stunning choreography by Grigorovich and sets by Simon Virsaladze – to the Kremlin Ballet.

"Nowhere else has the opportunities – the schools, the large troupes, the workshops" that the Bolshoi does, Vladimirov says, and, for him, it is a shame to see the strengths built up in the past being ignored in favor of "wasting our energy on questionable experiments."

Indeed, the Bolshoi's main "commodity" is its unique identity. The theater world may change, but this identity can always be sold for the highest price. So why have the businessmen now working as consultants and sitting on the theater's Board of Trustees ignored this?

The reason is probably that, as board member and former State Duma deputy Professor Konstantin Remchukov put it, they see the Bolshoi Theater as an "international corporation with international ambitions" – and have made themselves "managers of a large enterprise called the Bolshoi Theater with the whole world, not just Russia, as its market."

But theater management is fundamentally different from business management, because the aims of artists and large producers contradict each other. The concepts of artistic value and originality are inseparable: the more original the artistic "product," the more expensive it is. In industry, on the other hand, production efficiency is all-important: The larger the factory, the more profitable it is to produce goods *en masse*. So the logic of conceiving of the Bolshoi Theater as a "corporation" demands a management mindset focused on mass production, not individual artistic pieces. Such an institution does not need artists whose work has to be supported by the managers – this model does not allow for artistic tasks. The clearest formulation that the trustees have come up with for the theater's future goals is: "Put its income in order, put its expenditure in order, then define its development strategy and find funds to implement it."

So what is to be developed? "Tours must be financially supported, staff have to be found," Remchukov says. "For example, to entice a star to come here. Maybe there won't be enough money in the budget, so the businessmen will get together, like in football, and we'll get, say, Ronaldo at the Bolshoi Theater." In other words, artists – if there are any left – will be workers to be hired and fired.

Superficially, this looks like the general practice abroad, where most performers work with different theaters on a contract basis – but in substance it is completely different. The Russian theater market is not like, say, the European one, where there is a network of theaters of various categories, each of which encompasses a number of equal performing spaces and companies working in similar conditions. By signing contracts with different theaters in turn, the performers effectively form one large company. Formally, the performers and production team meet anew for every show, but actually each show involves more or less the same performers – which over time creates well-organized companies.

In Russia, however, there are just two important professional centers for opera and ballet – the Bolshoi and the Mariinsky. Directly copying foreign models is therefore not viable. The Bolshoi derives its authority not from borrowing people and shows, but from its own "products": and not just stars such as Anastasia Volochkova, but its artists, producers, workshop employees – all of whom have unique skills honed inside the theater. As a team united by common goals, they have maintained Russia's authoritative – sometimes definitive – position in world theater since Diaghilev.

Playbill

The Bolshoi's success has always been due to its company's know-how – its ability to perform original, multi-act ballets and operatic shows that don't just look like a mish-mash of different tricks, but progress in a well-ordered, logical way, allowing for the musical-theater environment and the rules of the dramatic arts.

Looking at the theater's playbills for the last few seasons, it is clear that the number of performances showcasing the Bolshoi ballet's individual style is much narrower than it could and should be. Grigorovich's legendary *Spartacus* and *Legend of Love*, those symbols of the Bolshoi – or, if you like, part of its brand – play just three or four times a season. There are two versions of the romantic masterpiece that is *Giselle*, which saved the Bolshoi from oblivion in the middle of the twentieth century, but the better of the two – Simon Virsaladze's production with its sophisticated pastel sets – is squeezed onto the New Stage, despite being designed for the open spaces of the old building's large stage. And on the main stage is Vladimir Vasilyev's version, with its distorted versions of the familiar dances and mise en scene, and Sergei Barkhin's stage design – all sandy drapes and funny little tassels, and primitivist trees in the second act that are irritatingly careless and turn the action into a tedious parody of itself.

Russian classical repertoire fares better. The emotional *Nutcracker* is staged as a New Year's boat journey to a silver star, with showy dance movements and captivating drama for the main and support characters. The Bolshoi's *Sleeping Beauty* is one of the best twentieth-century versions of this classic ballet, as Grigorovich and Virsaladze stress its musicality, rather than the glitz of the Imperial theater, while keeping Marius Petipa's basic choreography. The impressionistic design – shot through with sophisticated pearl-colored shading – creates ghostly images of an overgrown castle. The eroded contours of the columns and arches, the patterns traced by the branches and the park's decorative fences – like ink-prints on silk – carry echoes of Petipa's intricate dance lines and are just as inventively varied as the themes in Tchaikovsky's score. *Swan Lake*, meanwhile, is not a fairy-tale with a happy ending, but a tragic poem with a hero who breaks the laws of natural harmony, inevitably leading to an apocalyptic *dénouement*.

As magnificent as the film *Cleopatra*, the old favorite *La Bayadere* includes stunning scenic dances with fairies, parrots, and fans, wild ritual fire dances with daggers and drums, as well as airy dances of shades in white tutus, descending from the heavens in a long line. It is the Bolshoi's version that reproduces Marius Petipa's first St. Petersburg production. The brilliant *Don Quixote* is loosely based on Cervantes' great picaresque novel, but showcases all of Alexander Gorsky's virtuosic dances – a symbol of the bravura Moscow ballet style.

All of these wonderful productions, however, were done many years ago, while today the theater does not have a clear artistic development concept. Over the last few years, the company has brought to the stage French choreographer Roland Petit's old version of *The Queen of Spades* – made for Mikhail Baryshnikov, and not considered one of Petit's great successes – and masterpieces by Georges Balanchine (prompting unfavorable comparisons with the Mariinsky), and revived Petipa's classic *Raimonda*, which should be in the repertory of any self-respecting ballet company in any case. And that's it. Out of respect for the theater we will pass lightly over the management's pride in Alexei Ratmansky's comical *The Limpid Brook* (a parody show with circus-like costumes, but lacking a circus wit and inventiveness), and *Romeo and Juliet*, dressed up by British director Declan

Donellan in jackets and contemporary skirts, with schoolboy exercises and modern dance from Moldovan choreographer Radu Poklitaru.

Of course, no organizational model guarantees artistic discoveries, but the right conditions can be created – in other words, a distinct artistic school can be developed and a strong permanent troupe brought together, with technical support and a repertoire policy allowing the artists to improve their skills and grow from performance to performance. In other words, make the artist lead the sponsor and the administrator, not vice versa.

Semenyaka

We're now approaching – with some trepidation – the doors of the ballet class where we have a meeting with one such artist, Lyudmila Semenyaka, one of Russian ballet's most enchanting stars, the twentieth century's best Princess Aurora, a favorite in Europe, America, Argentina, Japan, Australia, and Russia, and now the Bolshoi's head coach. Semenyaka danced various versions of all the classical leads – Aurora and Princess Florina, Odette/Odile and Giselle, Sylphide, Kitri, Nikia, Raimonda, and many more – and is the only ballerina to have taken main parts in all of Yuri Grigorovich's productions.

Semenyaka's style was called ballet *bel canto*: She executed the most virtuosic of passages with grace and precision, making it look like a theatrical game with whimsical changes of rhythm and unexpected accents slotted deftly into the classical picture of the role. When she came on stage, it was as though an electric shock ran through the audience, illuminating everything around her and daring you to tear your eyes away from her movements. Semenyaka elevated her life force into a key conception of beauty for ballet; a condition of emancipation from human nature more beautiful than the highest high art; beautiful and terrible at the same time. Semenyaka brought a vibrant edge to even the most tranquil scene; when she let rip you could almost feel some awesome forces at work – like when a string speaks from any sound resonating nearby.

In the 1970s, when theatrical types were strictly limited, Semenyaka was one of the first ballerinas to play different types of roles at the Bolshoi. At the beginning of the 1990s, when most dancers got into the custom of performing any role, and performance practice leveled out, Semenyaka was again a pioneer, this time in stylization.

Semenyaka's career had no downs. She reached her peak in the Gorbachev era, and became a ballet symbol of *perestroika* at a 1987 gala concert at Kennedy Center in Washington heralding Gorbachev's historic meeting with Ronald Reagan. In 1989, in recognition of Semenyaka's status as a Russian ballet symbol, the Culture Fund held one of its first charity events – a benefit concert for the dancer in the Moscow Conservatory's Tchaikovsky Hall. Instead of the pomp and crcumstance traditional on such occasions, there was a tasteful program, including the first performance in Russia of excerpts from ballets by Balanchine and Roland Petit.

Semenyaka retired as a performer only a couple of years ago. She performed at the Contemporary Drama School, making the show *Fine Medicine for Melancholy* – staged for her by Iosif Raikhelgauz – a sell-out every night for two seasons. She is still a favorite guest on a number of radio and television programs and talk shows about the arts. But her main love is still ballet, whose secrets she passes on in the rehearsal room to new ballet stars, to the *corps de ballet*, and to students – from graduates to little girls coming in for a consultation lesson before joining the school.

When we open the door at the appointed time, in the middle of the room is a simply yet elegantly dressed lady, animatedly explaining something to a ballerina copying her magisterial gestures. And then, moving to the corner of the room, she executes several light jumps, segues into an impetuous turn, and finishes the phrase with five pirouettes. We break into applause. Semenyaka looks over and bids us welcome: "Come in, sit down. We were just about to go through the whole passage from the start without stopping."

Listening to Semenyaka's pithy stories, all interesting details and polished phrases, is almost as engaging as watching her dance. We are interested above all in her biography, in how she combined the Moscow and St. Petersburg ballet traditions in her dance, following in the footsteps of her great predecessors, Marina Semyonova, Galina Ulanova, Nina Timofeyeva, and Yuri Grigorovich. She talks about her regular trips to Moscow as a student at the Vaganova Academy, to participate in concerts at the Kremlin Palace of Congresses. There were lots of these concerts as part of various festivals, and these trips worked the children into a state of joyous agitation while still on the platform at Leningrad's Moscow Station with their parents.

"Usually it was during the winter, with wet snow and frost that made your eyelashes longer," Semenyaka smiles. "Winter in Moscow was dry, with crisp snowflakes. There was a friendly atmosphere around us – just like Lev Tolstoy described it, with pies, sweets, and all these enticing smells. The adults were mainly concerned with our being warm, and made an effort to buy us something tasty. So in my earliest memories, Moscow is a fairy tale city. Sure, we had come to work, and were well aware of that, but people were so kind to us – we were taken to the Kremlin with its cake-like cathedrals. So, for us, it was a process of getting to know the city, not just work."

Semenyaka moved to Moscow after the First International Competition for Ballet Dancers in 1969, which changed the destiny of everyone who took part in it. The competition was rich with sponsorships and became a national event, like the first Tchaikovsky Competition. Semenyaka was thoroughly prepared for the competition, and passed a qualifying competition, during which she was spotted by Galina Ulanova. And thus was her fate decided. After the competition, she was invited to the Bolshoi Theater. There was great personal happiness for her too, as she married the leading dancer, Mikhail Lavrovsky. "I got everything at once – the theater and the feeling of a family which had created its history," Semenyaka said. "And Galina Sergeevna [Ulanova], for whom my husband's father, the ballet-master Leonid Lavrovsky, had created works, became my teacher."

As Semenyaka talks, it becomes clear that the chief principle in an artist's training – and the foundation of the Bolshoi school's life – was a combination of uncompromising professionalism and warm, familial tenderness and attention. A shining example of this was Semenyaka's teacher Nina Belikova, who trained several generations of St. Petersburg's top dancers. "She had a rare gift as an educator and a mentor," Semenyaka remembers. "From her we acquired not just professional habits, but lessons on how to live our lives. She looked after us like a mother, and solved all our problems; she made sure we were dressed properly, that we ate properly. She was part of her students' destiny, fought for them, and more than once showed that she had been right to rate their potential so highly."

This educational style is fundamentally different from accepted practice around the world today, where teachers just give lessons and take no interest in their pupil's personal or professional destiny. Belikova knew everything about her profession – she was a pupil of Vaganova herself, the founding mother of the Russian classical school, and inherited and developed Vaganova's system for developing a dancer's personality. She was able to size up a child's potential and teach him or her how to work.

In all likelihood, victory at the competition did not turn Semenyaka's head, but rather inspired her to go on and do more. She confessed that, after being invited to the Bolshoi, she was not nervous so much about the great theater as about meeting with Ulanova. The first show in which they danced together was *Swan Lake*. Semenyaka's debut was well-received, and the whole cast applauded her on the stage afterwards. But the most important thing was Ulanova's approval. "It wasn't frightening – it was important," Semenyaka explains. "Galina Sergeyevna represented for me the very peak of ballet, and here I was approaching her. I was conscious that, in any case, I had come out of the same school as she had, and I think this helped her to start a conversation with me that we could both understand. We began work on imagery, and, in fact, on personal development. Ulanova for us was an entire ballet universe that raised ballerinas – who in turn became for a new generation of audiences what she had been for her audiences."

Although Semenyaka has always been interested in stylistics, she said that the current fashion for authenticity is not her sphere. Clearly, whatever text she studied – whether Sylphide with Elsa-Marianna von Rosen, Balanchine, or parts for Grigorovich's ballets – she studied in microscopic detail; but above all for her it was important to convey the image and idea of the style, the dramatic foundations of the production. When preparing Michel Fokine's *Swan Lake*, she said she wanted to create an independent artistic space – to find out what could be done in that miniature after Maya Plisetskaya. Semenyaka rehearsed with Ulanova, studied various versions, and attempted to imagine the quintessence of her concept of this miniature – not to reproduce an antique costume, but to make a contemporary tutu resemble it; not to overdo the details, but emphasize key bodily moments; the *pas de bouree* of the dying swan; the hand movements typifying the image and the era when the number was created.

"This approach came about as a result of the understanding of the ballerina in the original sense," Semenyaka says. "A genuine ballerina is not just mistress of her art, or a sparkling personality. She is above all a channel for harmony and the highest sense of her profession. A ballerina is like a priestess whose gestures are sacred, because they show the secrets of the universe – which is played out in lots of ballets, for example *Bayadere*.

The ballerina has no right to execute even one step that does not have a whole set of conditions for the existence of her art behind it. This set of conditions should be as obvious in the ballerina's dancing as generations of magnificent ancestors are in an aristocrat's family tree."

So how does this understanding of the ballerina's "mission" fit with the conditions in which ballet exists today – thrown into the harsh world of business and competition? Semenyaka's answer is measured, but optimistic. "Dance is not music and not philosophy: Only in a certain culture can it be raised to the status of a spiritual height," she said. "And if these conditions disappear, then dance can be kept at this height only thanks to individual, auspicious moments or significant figures. For example, Petipa convinces me that ballet is great art, but, let's say, many fashionable contemporary stagings will be unwatchable after a while. But dance will always keep developing, and ballet must be protected. Ballet for me is on the same level as the art of the word, because it can express thoughts, create harmony and an integral map of the world. It's a language, an artistic system.

"Business and all its categories are now taking root in ballet – but in Russia theater, including ballet, there is not just entertainment. Here it takes on the role of a vital space for the human soul, permanently pulsing, struggling, searching. I am not used to typifying the theater as being 'in crisis', 'fractured,' or 'in turmoil'. It's not economics, where you have crises. In theater you have spiritual ups and downs, reflecting the era it is living through. But so much has been done by our theater throughout its history that it seems to me that it has enough spiritual strength to last forever – to feed generations to come."

Semenyaka cites her pupils as an example – contemporary young artists, well adjusted in life but no strangers to such an interpretation of the ballet world. Closest to her is obviously Svetlana Zakharova, who, despite her tender years, is already a master and has achieved much. Semenyaka says that, for her, working with Zakharova is the same as playing on a Stradivarius for a violinist. But just as she is preparing to tell us how this is so, Zakharova walks into the room for the rehearsal we have come to see, and the conversation breaks off – or, more precisely, it becomes a professional dialogue between the two ballerinas.

The New Face

One of a new generation of performers developing new dance aesthetics, Ukrainian-born Svetlana Zakharova graduated from the Vaganova Academy in St. Petersburg, and gained recognition for her interpretations of lead roles in various Mariinsky Theater productions, including *Giselle*, *Serenade*, and *Sleeping Beauty*. In choreography from different eras and demanding different stylistic approaches, she bewitches her audience with the flowing lines of her dance, her phenomenal virtuosity, and her aristocratic style. No wonder, then, that she is an established favorite with audiences around the world, in demand at top theaters everywhere. But although Zakharova is now a reference point for other professionals in global performance practice, she continues to develop her own style. In the rehearsal we saw, Semenyaka helped Zakharova to hone dance phrases, pushing her to make a statement as a superb interpreter.

Zakharova made her first Moscow debut as the Egyptian princess Aspicia in French choreographer Pierre Lacotte's production of *The Pharaoh's Daughter*, based on Marius Petipa's ballet of the same name. The ballet tells the story of a British explorer who hides from a sandstorm in a pyramid. He falls asleep, and dreams that the mummy in the pyramid has turned into the pharaoh's beautiful daughter, and he himself into an Egyptian. The various personages in the resulting magnificent court show do not so much dance as parade in luxurious costumes and jewels.

Lacotte filled out Petipa's original work with virtuoso combinations of fiendishly difficult little steps, and, just before Zakharova's debut and the filming of the shows, he came to Moscow and edited her part to account for her individuality and phenomenal technique. The result was that an experiment in theatrical stylization became a living, breathing performance.

Zakharova executed Lacotte's dance hieroglyphics with great artistry and calligraphic precision, prompting comparisons to the coloratura soprano parts in which goddesses and priestesses express their passions in *bel canto* opera. Rather than being the prima donna of common imagination about the stage manners of the stars, Zakharova emphasized the sophistication of the St. Petersburg style. Tall and slim, she turned the dance now into captivating lines reminiscent of the contours of Nefertiti, now an Egyptian beauty in flowing clothes, now an exotic flower waving in the breeze. Her princess was a romantic heroine, and Zakharova herself a promising actress, able physically to convey shades of amorous trembling, fears, and doubts.

In other words, Zakharova had the authentic, subtle Imperial Ballet Style which Lacotte was looking for. Fused with Muscovite emotionality, this style provided the Bolshoi Theater with creative breakthroughs throughout the twentieth century, from Marina Semyonova's manifestos and Galina Ulanova's psychological discoveries, to Lyudmila Semenyaka's exquisite stylistics.

In *La Bayadere*, Zakharova brings the spirit of classical high tragedy – which Petipa made great use of when creating the work – to the festive atmosphere of a sumptuous work based on a fairy tale. She plays the story of the dancer's love for the warrior Solor and her rivalry with the king's daughter not as a daily conflict, but as an insoluble contradiction between human passions and the calling of a priestess, who must dedicate all of her energies to sacred mysteries. The result of the tense dramatic scenes in the first two acts, when Zakharova combines austerity and emotion in a regulated series of expressive poses, is just as important and compelling as the renowned *Dance of the Shades*, when the heroes converse with the next world like in Dante's Divine Comedy.

Zakharova's debut in Yuri Grigorovich's *Swan Lake* was understandably eagerly awaited: Who else could discover something new if not a ballerina who had triumphantly danced the role of Odette/Odile in just about every other version of the ballet? Interest was stoked further by the fact that Grigorovich's decidedly tragic version differs fundamentally from most other interpretations – fairy tale, festive and gay, occasionally affecting, but far from conceptual.

Zakharova attempted to fit in to the Bolshoi's production, while retaining where possible the bodily movements she found for other versions. While emphasizing Odette's victimhood and uncompromising nature, in individual scenes Zakharova gave her the naiveté and charm of a fairy tale princess, combined with the nervousness and ethereal nature of a beauty from the decadent Symbolist era. To Odile's phantasmagoric appearance, Zakharova added the manners of a seductive high-society lady. Many of her movements during the performance were so beautiful in themselves that they could be admired regardless of whether or not they were had any interpretative basis. And although connoisseurs noted the unusual accents with rapt attention, it was clear that even when Zakharova performs a repertoire role without changing anything, the usual *mise en scene* takes on a new interpretation, seemingly dreamed up just before.

Zakharova has had the opportunity to work with many of the world's ballet companies, but has preferred to stay in Russia, going abroad only on tour. In breaks during the rehearsal, we asked Zakharova what she particularly values in the Russian theatrical atmosphere and the way in which Russian theaters work. She said that, above all, she loves the possibility to "live" each performance, not just work through them. In Europe, there is a widespread tendency to put on shows in blocks, with, say, 20-30 performances of *Swan Lake* in a row. This is convenient for the ballet company, but if the dancer puts all her emotions into the performance and does everything she planned, then she doesn't want to touch that role again for some time afterward – the part should be approached at a different stage, with different feelings. Then it will be a revelation.

We asked Zakharova if she, like Semenyaka, felt that the theater was like home. She took up the theme eagerly. "Home is where my family is," she said. "We've all moved to Moscow now – my parents, my brother, who have nothing to do with ballet, but have learned what's what over the years. And home is also where I can work with people whom I trust and who become as dear to me as my relatives. In St. Petersburg this is my favorite coaches, Olga Moiseyeva – to whom I owe my formation as a ballerina – and Yuri Fateyev, who mainly works with male dancers but worked on the Balanchine ballets with me. In Moscow, of course, this is Lyudmila Semenyaka, whom I'm working with now. We met last season, when I came to dance *Giselle*, and then the Shades from *La Bayadere* for Marina Semyonova's birthday concerts. I asked Lyudmila to help me prepare for these performances, and realized that this is the person at the Bolshoi who is closest me as a teacher and mentor. She is a wonderful professional, and a great ballerina. Not long ago, I watched a video of her dancing at about the same age as I am now, and I was stunned. It was filmed thirty years ago, but looks completely contemporary. She thinks in a contemporary way, but most importantly feels what the dancer wants but cannot always express. She doesn't dictate the interpretation, but helps to bring out the individualism in it."

Zakharova picks out *La Bayadere* as one of her particular favorites. She first performed in the ballet at the Paris Grand Opera, after which she was acclaimed as a star of world standing. Many years before, it had been her first show at the Academy, and she danced the Shades for her graduation exam. "When I arrived at the theater," she says, "Olga Moiseyeva asked me, 'What do you want to dance?' Without thinking, I said, '*La Bayadere*'. She looked at me all surprised – 'Really? Well we'll see.'" The three acts of this ballet – so varied in terms of their emotional content, acting demands, and dance character – requires great balletic skill and artistic maturity. Zakharova has virtually all the versions of *La Bayadere* in her collection, including the Natalya Makarova version, which she danced triumphantly in New York.

But her collection has even more versions of *Swan Lake*, from Russian and European to Chilean and Brazilian – probably a couple of dozen in total, the most extravagant of which, by ballet-master Derek Dean, was in London's Royal Albert Hall, which holds an audience of several thousand. The audience is seated in a kind of amphitheater formation around the stage, on which there are not 32 swans like in normal theaters, but 64. Watching these equal, synchronized dancing lines from above is unbelievably impressive. The soloists have to dance around the edge, trying to face all of the audience in equal measure. Even the duets are constructed so that the dancers turn 360 degrees and face the whole audience during them. The orchestra is placed above, and the conductor sees you on a television. And when this whole "stadium" applauds, it is a wonderful feeling.

Zakharova confesses to having been afraid, as it was her first appearance abroad with the Bolshoi Theater. But when it became obvious that the performance was a success, she felt unbelievably proud that the performances had been of such a high class. One month later, Zakharova returned to Paris to dance *Giselle* with the Grand Opera's own ballet company, and was again well-received.

Zakharova laughs when asked whether the Grand Opera's stars are jealous of her success. "No, we all learn from each other," she says. "They were all curious and supported us when we did *The Pharaoh's Daughter*, which French ballet-master Pierre Lacotte choreographed using very difficult small steps that are not typical for Russian ballet. And after the show they came and were amazed: 'How do you manage it? It looked so beautiful!' That's the best thing – your colleagues recognizing that you have mastered their style."

The ballerina said she tries to master the company's style – to fit in and not look like an "outsider" – everywhere she goes, and she says that this is due to her Russian training. The Paris version of *Giselle* is different from Russian versions, and Zakharova's partner, Laurent Hilaire, one of the Grand Opera's established stars, suggested that she "do it your own way, like you usually do" – but she learned the French version anyway. But Zakharova also has to blend in with unfamiliar shows at the Bolshoi Theater; the most challenging, but also most rewarding, was Grigorovich's *Swan Lake*. Odette remained the same, with just a few tweaks to subtleties – Zakharova always dances this part as she was trained in St. Petersburg. But Odile is different everywhere. At the Bolshoi she is ambiguous, many-faced, mysterious; attractive and repellent; acting not of her own accord, but by the will of some evil genius. "I want her dance to be as bewitching as Mona Lisa's smile," Zakharova says. "Recently, in the Louvre, I spent ages looking at this picture again, and now I'm working out how to make the same associations on stage."

Zakharova talks about her work so enthusiastically that the break comes to an end all too soon. As we leave, we ask whether she feels she has become part of the Bolshoi Ballet after one season. "I felt that from the very start," Zakharova smiles. "Everyone accepted me with genuine good feeling – from the stars to the stagehands. They understood that I had come to work hard. And I hope that my performances bear out my right to dance here."

November/December 2004

Postscript: Closed for reconstruction in 2005, the theater was found to have serious structural problems and that it was 75 percent unstable. After some $730 million and six years of work, the theater was set to reopen in late 2011 with a performance of Glinka's opera, Ruslan and Ludmila.

The Magical World of the Russian Circus
Masha Nordbye

Oy, how I love the Tsirk", bellows Alexander Frish, a charismatic and eccentric performer who has been clowning around in the Russian Circus for over 25 years. Frish calls the circus "the universal language of joy and laughter that lets us all become children again." The circus is indeed a magical world, full of vibrant artistry, precision and grace. It is a highly respected art form that, in Russia, is taken as seriously as the theater and classical ballet.

It is also one of the country's most popular forms of entertainment – over half the Russian population attends at least one circus performance a year. More than 50 permanent circus buildings (more than in the rest of the world combined) are scattered in cities stretching across Russia, from Moscow to Siberia. From the capital, the Russian State Circus Company, Rosgostsirk, oversees 40 circus collectives, 15 tent circuses, nine animal circuses, circuses on ice, and the Circus of Lilliputians – in all comprising over 3,000 artists who perform in traditional single-ring circuses throughout Russia and more than 25 countries each year.

The circus is one of the world's most ancient performing arts. Circus Maximus, founded in 329 BC, continued operating until the Roman Empire fell in the fifth century. When Russia adopted Byzantine Christianity in 988 AD, it imported many of the arts and customs from Constantinople as well. One thousand year-old frescoes painted inside Kiev's Sofia Cathedral depict musicians, dancers, and even a man holding a long wooden pole, with a young boy ascending to the small square platform at the top.

By the eleventh century, Russian *skomorokhi* (the origin of this word is uncertain; some think it derives from the French *searamouche*, a comedic-musician) acted as wandering minstrels, roaming the countryside, singing and playing music. Russian carnivals, the *baraban*, also traveled with tumblers, dancers and performing bears, staging acts at local markets and fairs. They were especially popular during holidays and harvest times, and even performed at monasteries.

By the thirteenth and fourteenth centuries, many tournaments were organized around horse competitions. At jousting and riding events, participants dressed in brightly decorated costumes. The pantomimist developed silent theatrical skits when his voice could no longer reach the larger audiences. Even the art of clowning originated at these types of festivals. (Clowns were eccentric, from the Latin, meaning "off center.") By acting comical and boisterous, the jester could entice crowds over to a particular booth or attraction. For amusement rides, crude wooden Ferris wheels were constructed; the first carousels or merry-go-rounds used real horses.

The performing arts had became so popular by the seventeenth century that the Russian Church (alongside Patriarch Nikon's many strict reforms in 1648) decided to ban all forms of public entertainment. The Church regarded performers as partners with the Devil, whose function was to entice the audience to sin. Needless to say, the religious ruling did not have much effect. Peasants joked that they would merely repent after a performance and be forgiven anyway. And the aristocracy built their own theaters at home, hiring visiting troupes. One of Tsar Alexei's (1645-1676) primers even described a jester who was at court with trained dogs and bears.

Peter the Great (1689-1725) began his reign by overturning the Church edict banning amusements. He allowed open entertainment spots to be built all around his new capital of St. Petersburg, and even permitted women to perform. Peter especially loved the *shuti*, or jokesters, and court functions frequently included theatrical spectacles. Fireworks were set off in the Summer Gardens, and the Swan Canal had a tiny boat for Peter's favorite court jester.

During the reign of Peter's daughter, Elizabeth I, an article in a St. Petersburg newspaper described performances made by trained bears, strongmen who lifted logs with their teeth, and rope walkers who danced on lines tied between trees on the grounds of the Royal Palace. Rope walking originated with traders who, to demonstrate a rope's strength and durability, would string it between two trees and then hang and step on it. Tightrope, highwire and ladder balancing later evolved from these common merchant demonstrations.

In the eighteenth century, the horse was a central feature of everyday life. It was Peter the Great who initiated construction of the city's first "horse factories." Their main purpose was to get horses ready for manège showings (and wars). Many of the upper classes had their own manege rings, and dressage was even studied in school. It is no wonder, therefore, that equestrian events played a central role in that era's public entertainment, and in the evolution of the modern circus.

The First Circuses

In 1768, the first modern circus was created in England by Philip Astley, a former cavalry officer turned trick rider. He named his spectacle "circus," from the Latin, meaning circle or ring. (The Russian word *tsirk* stems from the French *cirque*.) Astley's circus consisted mainly of trick riding, tumbling and wrestling events that were all performed inside a 42-foot-wide ring – the ideal width for his exhibitions of horsemanship. His popular circus performed throughout Europe.

It was one of Astley's horsemen (and later rivals), the dashing Charles Hughes, who first introduced the circus to Russia. In 1793, when Hughes brought his equestrian troupe to perform before the Empress Catherine II at the Imperial Court, it caused an immediate sensation. Catherine the Great was so taken by Hughes and, of course, his horses, that she rewarded him with a private circus and, so the story goes, with her intimate favors as well. (In the same year, Hughes' pupil, John Bill Ricketts, introduced the modern circus to American audiences in Philadelphia.) Over the next decade, the circus became so popular that, by 1811, an amphitheater was built in Moscow to accommodate 5,000 spectators.

By the mid-nineteenth century, other circus entrepreneurs, mainly from France and Italy, had established circuses in many of Russia's major cities. On November 22, 1845, the Cirque Olympique gave its first performance on Merry-Go-Round Square (today's Theater Square) in St. Petersburg. It was run by the Italian equestrian, Alessandro Guerra, who had the nickname Il Furioso, for his tempestuous style of trick-riding. Set within a large, wooden, rectangular-shaped building, Olympique had six Ionic columns marking the portico entrance. To survive the cold, dark St. Petersburg winters, the space was well-heated, well-lit and comfortably decorated; there was even a coffee house set up next door.

Over 40 performers were decked out in lavish European-style costumes, and the beauty and talent of the female equestriennes particularly guaranteed the tour's success. Crowds utterly adored the panneau ballerinas who (while dressed in tutus) stood and balanced on 'flat wooden saddles' as their trotting horses pranced around the ring.

Just one year later, the success of the Cirque Olympique was unexpectedly undermined when another prominent circus came to town, the Cirque de Paris. (By this time, St. Petersburg was a bilingual city and French the language of the court.) At the heart of the company was Paul Cuzent, considered one of Europe's finest horsemen. Their wooden circus building opened near the Alexandrinsky Theater (today's Pushkin Theater) off Nevsky Prospekt. This circus radiated a greater feeling of intimacy, with carpeted corridors, fragrance burners and an elegant parlor atmosphere. Cirque de Paris also incorporated many novel acts into its show, including magicians and animal trainers.

With the two circuses vying for attendance, Guerra got Count Orlov – whose family had helped sponsor Hughes' debut – to contribute money so that his Cirque Olympique could hire new, eye-catching Parisian acts. Meanwhile, Cuzent's three beautiful sisters – Armantine, Pauline and Antoinette – enticed audiences with their ravishing costumes and remarkable equestrienne skills. Prince Konstantin Nikolaevich, a member of the royal family, was said to have succumbed to the charms of Antoinette, who was already wedded to the circus' producer, Jean Lejars. The Circus battles ended three months later, when the Cirque Olympique conceded defeat and moved on to perform in Vienna.

Tsar Nicholas I, reflective of his strict censorship of artistic expression, wasted no time in reigning in the competitive circus wars. As soon as the Cirque Olympique left town, the once foreign-owned circuses were put under complete state control. The Management of Imperial Theaters acquired the two circus buildings, and Cuzent's Cirque de Paris was grandly renamed the Cirque de la Direction des Théâtres Impériaux. Nicholas personally signed all authorizations, approved programs, and even delegated performers' salaries and vacation times.

In addition, Nicholas thought it was high time that his country's Imperial Circus had more Russian performers. So, in 1847, Nicholas ordered the creation of the world's very first circus school, which included classes in horsemanship, trick-riding and acrobatics. There were already schools for drama, music and dance; France's famous Marius Petipa, who redefined classical ballet, was the ballet master of the Imperial Dance School. Meanwhile, the tsar ordered the demolition of the Cirque Olympique; in its place, an even grander building was erected.

The Imperial Circus, which premiered to the public on January 29, 1849, cost a whopping 216,000 rubles. It was a large stone, classically-designed complex, filled with crimson velvet seats, chandeliers and gas-light candelabras. Paul Cuzent, now the circus' director, filled the luxurious interior with the first grandiose pantomimes. One, The Alta Blockada, included a choir, a troupe of 22 Cossack horsemen, and over 100 enlisted men from the Imperial Army. After the building caught fire on January 22, 1859, Alexander II invited the famous architect, Alberto Kavos, to rebuild it. The following year, on October 2, the new structure reopened as the Mariinsky Theater (the Kirov from 1935 to 1992), now to display operas and ballets.

Shortly before Nicholas I's death in 1855, another circus building was constructed on Admiralty Square, and was leased to visiting companies. Here, in 1861, aerial master Jules Léotard was honored with standing ovations. As early as 1828, newspapers told of a Flying Indian who performed on elevated cords in Astley's circus. But the flying trapeze act is credited to this Frenchman who, in 1859, began to swing and somersault from one trapeze bar to another in the Cirque Napoleon in Paris, wearing the first "leotard." In Russia, Léotard was banned from wearing his signature full body tights by the Imperial Censors and was forced to wear a costume of black pants and white shirt. With this new craze, single trapezes were hung from the underside of hot air balloons or on moving, horse-drawn floats. For a while, performers even flew through paper or burning hoops. The great leap forward came in the 1880's, when flyers began to do tricks to catchers and return back to the trapeze board.

Over a century later, Russia's Flying Cranes would tour the world as one of the greatest aerial acts of all time. The act's producer, Vil Golovko joked that "I was baptized on the trampoline when I was seven months old." Taking five years to perfect a routine before a single performance, the ten flyers combine extraordinary trapeze and acrobatic skills and utilize all aspects of the net and trapeze, creating an exquisite aerial ballet. Soaring to the *Ride of the Valkyries*, the Cranes are a Wagnerian poem in motion.

Russian circus performers often create their acts around a story. The Cranes' act was first inspired by a popular Russian folk song (*Cranes*, sung by Mark Bernes) commemorating WWII. (The popularity of the 1957 war film, *The Cranes Are Flying*, also influenced the act.) It is about friendship and sacrifice, about the spirits of fallen soldiers turning into white cranes and flying away, their souls released to heaven. The only female in the act plays the last of the fallen cranes, and is courageously rescued so that peace may prevail. In 2003, a new generation of The Flying Cranes made their debut in Moscow's Tsirk Nikulina.

The Golden Age

By the late nineteenth century, it was fashionable to visit the circus of Gaetano Ciniselli, an entrepreneur from Milan. (Ciniselli first performed in the Cirque Olympique.) His first circus building, built in 1877 along the Fontanka Canal, still houses today's St. Petersburg Circus. The Ciniselli Circuses were the center of performance activity up to the 1917 Revolution, and were mainly filled with trick riding events and wrestling matches (the wrestlers later became circus strongmen).

In 1883, the Brothers Nikitin constructed a two-ring, outdoor circus on Khodinsky Field in Moscow that held 15,000 spectators. (Ten years earlier, P. T. Barnum had opened the first three-ring circus in America.) Over the next few decades, the Ciniselli, Nikitin and Salamonsky families went on to establish circuses in cities all around the country, from Kiev and Kazan to Yaroslavl and Novgorod.

During this time, the clowns, who were originally brought in as mere comic relief, soon developed a more meaningful and humanistic connection with the masses. Since the eleventh century, Russian mimes – or *vatagami* ("in support of the masses") – had been poking fun at the upper classes. By the end of the 1800's, the clowns were also supporting public views of opposition to the tsars.

Nowhere in the world were circus performers as politically active as in turn-of-the-century Russia. The circus became a haven for protests, where uncensored sketches depicting the tumultuous state of tsarist Russia were tolerated. Since the circus was the most popular form of entertainment available to the common man, the clown began a tradition of activist social comedy, and took every opportunity to satirize the tsars, landowners and merchants. The most popular clown of the time, Vitaly Lazarenko, once even protested on stilts through Moscow's Red Square.

On occasion, the performers did get in trouble. For example, Lazarenko was once banned from performing after staging a skit on the 1905 revolution. A sign was posted: "Banned by the city of Orinberg. Vitaly Lazarenko. After 5 pm he is forbidden to perform any longer because of words he spoke on the 3rd of September at the circus, concerning his views on the Russian Constitution." Later, however, Lazarenko performed before soldiers on the front lines during WWI.

The Durov brothers, Anatoly and Vladimir, were among the most beloved circus performers in Russia, and quite creative dissenters. Born of nobility, their mother, Alexandra, was said to have disguised herself as a Hussar and fought against Napoleon. First sent off to military school, the brothers later ran away and joined the circus. They went on to become outstanding clowns and animal trainers. The brothers established a highly effective approach to animal training that had a profound impact on animal acts around the world. "All my knowledge and all my heart are for the people," said Vladimir who, in 1927, celebrated 50 years of work in the Russian Circus. The Durovs went on to found one of Russia's first circus dynasties; today, the fourth generation of Durovs performs in the Russian circus, and Moscow hosts the famous Durov Animal Theater for children.

"Galai, would you like to go to the circus today? If so, we'll expect you at 6:30 p.m. If not, lend me your season pass; Ivan and I are going."

This note to a friend was penned by the writer Anton Chekhov, who adored the circus. In his newspaper column, "Fragments of Moscow Life," Chekhov spoke out against social inequities, and much of his material was based on what he saw at the circus. One day, a group of merchants stole a performer's pig and roasted it. They never asked the performer for the pig, but just gave him money afterwards with a slice of roasted pork. Chekhov wrote of the incident "as the trampling of human dignity in a society where money has become God."

One of Chekhov's short stories was titled *Kashtanka*, named after one of Vladimir Durov's favorite dogs. He even modeled the clown in the story after Durov. After viewing a circus performance in 1885, Chekhov wrote: "Moscow is terribly addicted to swineishness. During one of Durov's performances, he presented a pig reading the papers. The pig was offered a variety of papers, but indignantly refused each of them in turn, grunting suspiciously all the while..." (the pig apparently knew that the papers were highly censored and that there was absolutely nothing worth reading).

This act would have been censored in any theater, but, cleverly, without written dialogue, such circus skits could not be subjected to official censorship. Once, in Odessa, Vladimir Durov came out into the ring with a green pig. At the time, Odessa had a very anti-semitic mayor, Admiral Zelyony (whose last name translates as "green"). Everyone immediately burst into laughter. Durov was reprimanded, so he then showed up in the ring wearing a padlock on his mouth. The audience understood again, and Durov got around the censors.

Bring in the Soviets

In a letter to Chekhov, the novelist Alexander Kuprin (many of whose short stories centered around circus life) expressed his wishes concerning the future of the Russian Circus. "Will I ever live to see the day when, on our circus posters, instead of foreign management, one will find Russian names? I know they will create a repertoire no worse and certainly much better and more original than the foreigners have, because our muscles are stronger, fate has not bypassed us without courage, and we have patience enough and laughter! Oh, the Russians can laugh better than anyone in the world, because our laughter is a very special kind."

Kuprin's wish came true at the onset of the 1917 Bolshevik Revolution, when all foreign directors fled the country and the Russian circus was left to itself. Appropriately, Karl Marx was quoted: "...on seeing a fearless acrobat in bright costume, we forget about ourselves, feeling that we have somehow risen above ourselves to reach the level of universal strength."

A whole new era of Russian producers emerged to cultivate native performers. Circus troupes toured the country and, continuing their political role, encouraged the masses to cheer on the new Union of Soviet Socialist Republics. On September 22, 1919, Vladimir Lenin signed a decree nationalizing the Russian circus. Thus did the world's first government-run circus organization, Soyuzgostsirk, begin operations. The first performance of the Moscow State Circus took place a week later.

During these revolutionary years, some of Russia's finest writers and directors – Chekhov, Gorky, Eisenstein and Stanislavsky – focused their attention on the circus. Lunacharsky, the head of the Circus House, rallied: "Here it will be possible to have fiery revolutionary speeches, declarative couplets and clowns doing caricatures on enemy forces." Poet and playwright Vladimir Mayakovsky wrote skits for the new state circuses. One of his most famous was *Moscow Burning*, about the burning of the tsar and aristocracy, releasing Moscow to the people.

> *Comrade Circus, where's your grin?*
> *Here's a sight to tickle us.*
> *Look and see who's trotting in*
> *The Dynasty of Tsar Nicholas ...*
>
> *Don't forget about 1905,*
> *A year of undying glory and fame*
> *When the dream of the land came alive.*
> *And revolutionary ideals set aflame.*

Maxim Gorky pronounced: "I love this popular form of amusement to distraction." He wrote the play, *The Lower Depths*, and even got the famous bear trainer, Ivan Filatov, to play the Baron. The clown Lazarenko later studied with the avant-garde theater director, Vsevolod Meyerhold. Another famous director, Konstantin Stanislavsky, during a Moscow Art Theater season (entitled Merry Evenings), had his actors depict various circus artists in pantomime. Stanislavsky loved impersonating a circus horse trainer by dressing up in black leather boots, breeches, and a top hat. He often exclaimed: "the circus is the best place in the world!"

The young Soviet circus began to blossom in 1927 with the creation of Moscow's School for Circus Arts, the modern world's first professional circus school, founded to provide a consistently high standard of training. Today, at hundreds of circus schools throughout Russia, students can train for up to four years, studying all facets of circus life. During their final year, they create their own acts. Once the act is approved, the Circus Board helps provide everything from costumes and equipment to animals and special effects.

The Circus Today

Even though the automobile, train and airplane eventually surpassed the horse for modes of transport, horse acts remain an essential element of the circus (after all, the circular arena had originally been designed for horsemanship). So, the Russians turned back to their traditions for creating new equestrian numbers, such as the Djigit horsemen who perform stunts on fast, galloping horses. Today, the Djigits are an exhilarating part of many a Russian circus performance.

The green-eyed and silver-maned Tamerlan Nugzarov, who comes from the northern Caucasus, stems from three generations of circus performers. "I learned everything from my father," explains Nugzarov, "as he learned everything from his; now my sons carry on the Djigit tradition." Tamerlan's father was a Cossack horseman; and, today, the Nugzarov family carries on their heritage with dazzling, unparalleled horsemanship. The 12 horses gallop at full speed around the ring, while riders perform tricks both atop and beneath their mounts. The act culminates with a stunt rider jumping through a hoop of knives. "This is nothing," Tamerlan attests. "In my opinion, the hardest injuries are those to the soul." Nugzarov's awe-inspiring act was awarded a Gold (first prize) at the annual International Circus Festival in Monte Carlo.

In 1996, Moscow began hosting an International Festival of Circus Arts on Red Square. Circus acts from around the world competed on 13 rings in every genre, from juggling, acrobatics and animal acts, to high-wire and trapeze. The winners received a "Golden Bear." The Russian Circus All-Stars also made a special appearance, which included The Flying Cranes, the famous juggling Ignatov family, Nugzarov's Galloping Djigits, and Nikolai Pavlenko, one of the world's preeminent tiger trainers. Pavlenko has created an animal extravaganza like no other in the world. He stands inside the cage with 17 wild Sumatran tigers, whose names range from Masha to Tony, and takes them through a spine-tingling performance of a lifetime. (Today, even though animal acts are no longer as popular with international audiences, the Russian Circus still respects its long-standing animal traditions.) Appropriately, the festival's first prize was awarded to the act, Noviye Russkiye – the "New Russians" performed stunts while dressed in coat and tails, symbolizing the country's *nouveau riche* generation.

In 2003, as St. Petersburg was fêted on its tercentennial, the St. Petersburg Circus celebrated its 125th anniversary at its current location. Today, the facility also houses a Circus Museum (established in 1928) and research library of more than 100,000 historical circus items. In Moscow, Russia's second oldest circus, built in 1880, originally held the Ciniselli and Salamonsky Circuses. It later became known as the *Stary* (Old) Circus on Tsvetnoy Bulvar. Today, the independently-run Old Circus has been renamed Tsirk Nikulina, after Yuri Nikulin, one of Russia's most popular comedic artists, who became the circus' director in 1984. (Nikulin died in 1997; today his son Maxim carries on the directorship.) The *Novy*, or Bolshoi "New" Circus, opened in 1971, and sits perched atop Sparrow Hills, near Moscow University.

Nikulin had performed in the circus during most of the Soviet era, and always tried to overcome hard times with the help of humor. Starting in 1936, he began collecting jokes and, eventually filled two volumes with over 10,000 of his favorite anecdotes. "Laughter is beneficial to the human body." Nikulin surmised. "When smiling, giggling, bursting into laughter, a person, without even suspecting it, keeps himself healthy."

With the fall of Communism and the formation of the Commonwealth of Independent States, Rosgostsirk has had to regroup considerably. Without major state subsidies, there has been a large revenue loss; and, many highly skilled performers have left Russia for other circuses and theater acts abroad. But, considering that this ancient performing art has already survived a millennium of turbulent Russian history, the circus is sure to carry on. "Even though this is a time of great transition in Russia, a time when old styles are giving way to new," explained St. Petersburg Circus Artistic Director Alexei Sonin, "the circus is one tradition that is sure to remain as important to Russia as it has for centuries; it is truly a part of the Russian soul."

Minutes before the lush velvet curtains part, the backstage area glistens with sequined bodies and the sheen of stretching muscles. These performers dedicate their lives to creating a world of fantasy that everyone can enjoy. The language they speak is without words; their beauty, courage and skill bridge the gap between generations, nations and cultures. Their message of awe, love and laughter goes straight to the heart.

The renowned Russian "Sunshine Clown," Oleg Popov, has been working in the Circus for over 50 years, and could have retired years ago. But he prefers to keep on working. "What happens," he reflects, "is that a fine speck of sawdust enters your bloodstream and stays there for life. The magic never ends!"

January/February 2004

A Tumultuous Century Begins
Tamara Eidelman

*I*n January 1805, the New Year's edition of the newspaper *Moscow News* opened with a poem that readers must have read with great interest and feeling. After welcoming in the New Year, the author went on to talk of his hopes:

> *In humility and with reverence,*
> *I welcome the emissary of the Heavens,*
> *And with affection,*
> *The flow of tears trickling down my face,*
> *Addressing myself to the ineffable,*
> *I pour out prayers of the heart.*
> *I, a young son of this time, ask*
> *That what is to come be not as it was,*
> *That tranquility will be glorified,*
> *That all peoples will have peace.*
> *I pray that everywhere a lovely calm will take root*
> *And that human blood shall not flow,*
> *That the plagues of dissension, malice, war, depravity, revolt and sedition*
> *Will cease to orbit the throne,*
> *That the Powers That Be shall not tear at one another again,*
> *And that all the Sons of the Earth*
> *Shall embrace one another with tenderness,*
> *And that everywhere Love shall reign!*

Well, people always dream of peace and happiness at New Year's. But, with the arrival of 1805, this was particularly true. In Europe, as it turned out, Peace *had* finally arrived. The wars of bloodletting, which had begun with the French Revolution and continued through Napoleon Bonaparte's ascent to power, had been over for a year. In 1804, for the first time since 1792, the European nations did not war. And of course everyone hoped that things would stay this way for good.

In Russia, life was also getting much better. True enough, there was a war on with Persia, but it was so distant – in some kind of far-off Caucasian region – and military actions proceeded so slowly that one could easily forget about it. Most in the empire experienced the sweet taste of internal and external peace.

Russia, true enough, had not had an active part in the wars against France. However, the echo of the European battles did resound east to Moscow and St. Petersburg – people here were appalled by the atrocities of the French revolutionaries, they cried at the murder of Louis XVI, they were surprised by the initiative and energy of the young Corsican Bonaparte, who had come to power so suddenly. What is more, in the preceding decades, Russian troops had certainly seen action. The Empress Catherine had warred several times with Turkey, expanding her possessions along the Black Sea; she had participated in three partitions of Poland and warred with Sweden.

So war was something familiar, as was delighting in the successive victories won under the Russian standard. The impetuous Emperor Paul, who finally ascended to the throne after waiting many years for his mother to pass on, rushed headlong into adventurous military actions – sending the Russian Navy into the Black Sea and sending Alexander Suvorov at the head of Russian troops into the Italian and Swiss Alps (a much more distant locale than some strange Caucasian adventure).

Paul, despite the shortness of his reign, managed to make friends with the Corsican Bonaparte, to have a falling out with England (Russia's former ally), and even to send a detachment of troops to the East – to help the Corsican (or, more correctly, the First Consul of the French Republic) to conquer India.

Now, in 1805, all of these stormy events were in the distant past. Paul I had expired in his bedroom in Mikhailovsky Fortress, from an unexpectedly aggressive "illness," the consequences of which could be seen in the gross disfigurement and bruising of his body, and on his face, which was twisted in the hideous grimace of one who had been strangled. The fact that the emperor had been murdered was clear to everyone. But no one was shocked by it – a new, wonderful time was approaching.

In 1801, to general jubilation, the attractive young Emperor Alexander Pavlovich – Alexander I – ascended to the throne. He restored liberties to the nobility which Paul had trampled, promised to carry out multiple reforms, called back the soldiers who were humbly advancing toward India, and reestablished good relations with England. Wasn't all this splendid?

And yet, in the ensuing four years, it had become clear that the young tsar was in the grip of melancholy (hardly surprising for a person who had a hand in his father's death), that he was indecisive and feared carrying out the planned reforms. Yet he was still a good fellow and was loved by all.

In a word, one could hope that life was becoming calm and happy, that people would life peacefully and normally.

In Moscow, someone was selling a newly published book: "on lengthening the human lifespan, or a means for attaining the highest levels of health, happiness and a ripe old age; the most reliable ways to preserve one's health, to treat all manner of illnesses, with descriptions of causes and of medicines available all around us; ways to protect oneself from lightning during a thunderstorm. Paperback price: two rubles."

The book's price is rather high, but then who can afford *not* to learn how to live to a ripe old age, while remaining healthy and happy, while also learning how to protect oneself from lightning during a thunderstorm? The American Benjamin Franklin invented some kind of marvelous lightning rod a half-century before, but surely there must be something simpler and less strange than putting a metal rod on the roof of your house. Judging by the fact that the advertised book was reputedly going through multiple reprints, there were plenty who sought ways to lengthen their happy and healthy lives.

If life did not always go along happily, it was enough that it should pass peacefully and full. The six-year-old boy Sasha Pushkin played in his parents' Moscow home, not suspecting that, in a few years, he would be sent off to study at the Tsarskoye Selo lyceum. And he probably as yet had no premonition of how quickly his soul would be consumed by an inexplicable desire to write poetry.

Another Sasha, this one Griboyedov, was 10 years old this year and his future was equally opaque. Who could know that he would one day write one of the greatest Russian plays of all time – *Woe of Wit* – and make a career as a diplomat, only to have his life cut short, beheaded in that same Persia with whom Russia was now warring?

The honored General Mikhail Kutuzov, who was well-tested in court intrigues, had for three years been enjoying a deserved rest at his estate. He had participated in more than his fair share of wars and diplomatic missions, and his many wounds – including two to the head – were a graphic testament to this. Kutuzov's continued service to the crown, however, was not helped by the fact that he had played a role – albeit not a major one – in the sentence handed down to Paul I. The new emperor's pangs of conscience compelled him to distance himself from anyone who reminded him of his sins. Tired, blind in one eye, Kutuzov could not possibly have suspected that the main events of his life were still before him.

In general, no one had the faintest clue of the changes on the horizon. People were born and died, were happy and sad, went about from place to place.

For sale: Home near the Arbat, at the entrance to Nikola na Peskakh, at number 84; 13 *sazhens* [91 feet] long; built over 14 years; with furniture; plaster walls; three huts in the yard; two outbuildings, one new; on a stone cellar; stable with 12 stalls; two icehouses.

Where had the owner of this house in the very center of Moscow suddenly decided to go? They had spent 14 years building this house, put in a stone cellar and two ice houses. They had a place to store their reserves. In hospitable Moscow, a place that reveled in its feasts, this was far from the least desirable of places. A stable which could hold 12 horses immediately evokes thoughts of luxurious equipage, of owners who loved to ride about the city. Where could they be off to? To Petersburg, to start a career? To one's estate, because they had squandered their money and could no longer afford to live in the city? Many years later, the heroes of *War and Peace*, the Rostov family, having spent their riches on endless parties and celebrations, entertained this very idea. Or perhaps the owner of the house at Nikola na Peskakh had gone abroad, in search of a quieter life?

People loved to travel in 1805. Laurence Stern's *A Sentimental Journey* and Nikolai Karamzin's *Notes of a Russian Traveler* were in fashion, and everyone who had means to do so ventured to distant lands – some out of curiosity, some on business. People of limited means sought ways to travel anyway they could. Thus, in the *St. Petersburg News* there was an announcement:

Individual departing at the end of this month for Berlin seeks a fellow-traveler paying their own way.

Traveling together is both cheaper and more fun.

Those staying at home were by no means bored. One could read. The capital's bookstores had a large selection, from *Universal Medical Guide* and *The Newest Russian Songbook* to the books of Rousseau or *Russian Werther* by some fellow named Sushkov, who had decided to offer the sad novels of Goethe to his countrymen. People could also focus on their children's education, since there were plenty of people seeking work as teachers. In any newspaper, you could find plenty of announcements like these:

Middle-aged woman, German, with excellent references and familiar with housework, desires a position in a manor home as housekeeper or nanny for children.

Young woman from a noble family desires to teach children to play piano.

Potential teachers and even those who pretend to the role of steward, as a rule underlined their knowledge of foreign languages. The capital was full of foreign language speakers; the most unusual people were tossed here by the European storms – milliners, chefs, teachers. So one can easily understand Mr. Miller, who calculatingly placed this ad:

Any woman, knowing how to speak, read and write in German, Russian and French, and desiring a position teaching children, may show up at the Miller Leather Factory, near the Gallernaya harbor in building number 709.

Obviously, many middle-aged women and young women from noble families who came to his door, and, upon verification, turned out to be not quite appropriate for the role of teacher...

The large cities burgeon, attracting people by legal and non-legal means. State Councilor Vasily Bestuzhev places an announcement in the lost and found:

Lost, four recruiting receipts, received for three and a half recruits, in exchange for serfs who escaped from a Simbirsk estate and were registered in Astrakhan as members of the bourgeoisie. It is requested that, if these turn up somewhere, they please be turned in to the proper authorities.

What happened to these four serfs, who were equivalent for some reason to three and a half recruits? How did they manage to escape from Simbirsk and get themselves to Astrakhan? And how did they manage to register as bourgeoisie – that is, to become citizens?

Judging by the advertisement, the escapees were captured and sent off to be soldiers. Vasily Bestuzhev was probably a relative of the five Bestuzhev brothers who, twenty years from now, along with other members of a secret society, would attempt to change the law on serfdom and pay for it with their freedom. The State Councilor, however, is apparently not troubled by moral dilemmas related to ownership of other people – for him finding the recruiting receipts is most important, so that he does not have to (heaven forbid) give the army other, better working and more settled serfs.

However, no matter how much the population changed and grew in the large cities, life was still very much in keeping with village traditions. There were not many activities beyond the boundaries of one's own home. Rich people might have their music salons or home theaters, balls or children's parties. And there were certainly theaters – both in Moscow and Petersburg – but they were not open to the general public. They were places of high society, where aristocrats met.

There were no museums. Those collections which decades from now would attract loads of tourists, were for now in private hands. Around Christmastime, Petersburgers were invited to experience a Nativity Play – a fairy-tale like puppet show. But all other activities took place within the walls of merchants' homes or noble palaces. Which meant it was quiet and calm on the streets.

Lost goods were brought by those who found them to the Police Department, were those who lost things had them returned to them. For instance, this is where you would go if you

Lost women's sable stoles and 2 wraps, one with silver and the other with gold tassels.

Of course, one had to present "proof of ownership." Even money was brought here. The individual who

Lost a red morocco wallet with 37R and camisole with 260R.

is asked to appear at the Police Department. Perhaps they want to ask the individual how he survived not only without his wallet, but also without a camisole? Has he perhaps been overdoing it a bit with visiting *kabaks* [taverns]?

BUT, OF COURSE, the peaceful course of this settled and well-adjusted life was to be rudely interrupted. Once again, there began to be talk about the villain Bonaparte, who had more or less declared himself to be Emperor of the French and was gathering up troops in France, near the city of Boulogne, in order to attack England.

By fall, even more distasteful things came to light. It turns out that the vile Bonaparte, instead of attacking England, turned on Austria, a long-time ally of Russia. The noble Russian Emperor Alexander had no alternative but to send troops in support of Austria's Emperor Franz II.

Groaning and rubbing his blind eye, Kutuzov leaves his village, flattered that he has been remembered, and accepts command of the Russian army. The autumn months pass quickly. But news does not travel quickly back to Russia.

Russian troops had, by November, already skirmished with French troops on German territory, and newspapers described the October victory of the British Navy over France at Cape Trafalgar, in which Admiral Nelson perished. The papers reported on his grand funeral, and on the inheritance he left his wife. But, out of common decency, they said nothing of his affair with Lady Hamilton. The casualties at Trafalgar were counted at 1,587, and it was observed that no naval battle had ever been so large or so bloody.

French, Russian and Austrian troops converged, but in Russia, as Christmas and New Year's neared, people continued to buy and sell homes, to hire domestic help, to search for things lost.

On November 25, the Academy of Sciences held a ceremonial meeting in honor of its 80th anniversary. Along with various other reports, there was one on essays submitted to the Academy's competition, announced the previous year. Of course, the majority of the essays did not satisfy the academics – not one eulogizing Alexei Mikhailovich, the father of Peter I, nor one exalting Minin and Pozharsky, who liberated Moscow from the Poles. The gold and silver medals were instead awarded to two works on a rather dubious theme: a glorification of Ivan the Terrible. Obviously, it took a huge expenditure of effort to endorse the actions of this bloodletting tsar, and for this the authors were duly rewarded.

The academics, ceremoniously gathered in Petersburg, did not know that five days previous there had been a horrific bloodbath near Austerlitz, which ended with the crushing defeat of Russian and Austrian forces – one of Napoleon's greatest victories. Emperor Alexander I, fleeing the field of battle and on his way home, decided to relieve Kutuzov of his command. The cunning general had preferred not to challenge the emperor about the deployment of Russian troops before the battle, and would now pay for it with disgrace. Of course, it was easier for the young tsar to blame everything on the decrepit old general than on his own interference. What is more, Kutuzov had seen Alexander crying after the battle, and a monarch rarely forgives something like that.

But it would be fully a month before Russia learned of this disaster. The newspapers printed news of various small battles, then about the arrival of the tsar back in Petersburg, and then, for some reason, about Austria's signing a peace treaty with Napoleon, and the recall of Russian troops. The first report of the horrific battle, and the indications of the huge losses on both sides, appeared only on January 2. Perhaps the newspaper publishers did not want to spoil their readers' holidays. Or perhaps the post really did move that slowly.

NAPOLEON'S CAMPAIGN IN Germany still lay in the future, as did new battles with Russian troops... and the Peace of Tilsit (1807), yet another humiliation for Alexander I. And it was still quite some time until 1812, to the Battle of Borodino and the burning of Moscow. But, after that, Russian troops would march all the way to Paris, and young officers, who had shown their bravery on the field of battle, would begin to wonder why the tsar did not want to eradicate serfdom, and whether he really was as beautiful and honest as they had thought previous, and whether perhaps they should use force to compel him to free the serfs and, if he refused, unseat him from the throne.

And the young Sasha Pushkin, grown and sent by his parents to study at the Lyceum, would begin to write poems. And Sasha Griboyedov would begin to write poems and plays, and to study Eastern languages, because the Caucasus would suddenly become an exceptionally important place for Russian policy.

But, for now, no one suspected any of this. Cavaliers of the Order of St. George – the most honored of military awards – made a request:

Boldly and in all humility we ask Your Imperial Majesty to bestow on Your Highness the special military award of St. George.

Tsar Alexander's Order of St. George, it should be noted, was to be for special bravery shown... at Austerlitz.

Citizens were preparing for Christmas and the New Year. The quibbling leather factory owner Miller could still not find teachers for his children. In the capital of St. Petersburg, someone is selling "a home with a milk cow and three young horses."

Someone, with knowledge of French and German, geography, history and arithmetic, offers their services to persons seeking a governor for their children or a steward for the home.

Young woman named Dobrozhanskaya, who knows how to sew and make lace, who also speaks German and French, seeks a position in a home in the city.

What will happen with the leather magnate Miller and his children, with the wonderfully educated "someone," and with the young Dobrozhanskaya? The whirlwind of the next decade has covered their tracks. The tumultuous nineteenth century has begun, and soon Trafalgar will no longer be neither the biggest nor the bloodiest of battles.

September/October 2005

The First Ambassador
Mary Claffey and Sara Sikes

On a brisk February day in 1810, forty-two-year-old John Quincy Adams was out for his daily constitutional, strolling with an American colleague along St. Petersburg's Neva River. Adams, in his role as the first American minister to the Court of Alexander I, had spent the morning writing in his small hotel on the Nevsky Prospect. A creature of routine, he ventured out despite the cold, and, while passing under a bridge along the quay of the Neva, he and his companion were "overtaken by the Emperor, who stop'd and spoke to us about the weather." Adams remarked later in his diary – a diary of over 50 volumes he kept faithfully for 68 years – that the Emperor "walks entirely alone, and stops and speaks to many persons whom he meets." Tsar Alexander was just 32 years old, but after succeeding his murdered father to the throne in 1801, he became one of the most powerful men in the world – his influence and wealth challenged only by Napoleon.

Adams had been formally presented to Tsar Alexander the previous fall, and they saw each other often at diplomatic functions, but after the chance encounter on the Neva they met frequently for exercise. They shared a polite aversion to the endless parade of balls, festivals, feast days, soirées, and sleigh rides – even the tsar could not escape the ritualized "dissipation" of St. Petersburg – and found rejuvenation in the outdoors. In the five years Adams lived in St. Petersburg, he records thirty-three unofficial meetings with the tsar, sometimes simply noting, "Met and spoke to the Emperor." During these walks they rarely spoke about official business. They discussed the weather and the merits of flannel underwear, and they debated when the ice on the Neva would break. While they avoided larger diplomatic issues of trade between neutral countries, the coming war between the United States and Great Britain, or Napoleon's bellicose push across Europe, Alexander and John Quincy enjoyed a close familiarity that would foster a positive relationship between their countries for decades to come.

Appointed to his post by President James Madison on June 27, 1809, Adams quickly wrapped up his work as a lecturer of rhetoric at Harvard College, a position he had held for just under a year. The eldest son of John Adams, the nation's second president, JQA (as he frequently signed his name) had already enjoyed a varied career when he received his appointment to Russia. Although at the time he deemed it "the most important of any [enterprise] that I have ever in the course of my life been engaged in," Adams was only at the halfway point of one of the most distinguished careers in public service in American history.

With an enviable resumé for any generation, John Quincy Adams' diplomatic career began at the age of fourteen, when his father was minister to the Netherlands during the American Revolution. His affinity for languages and particularly his fluency in French, his maturity, and a naturally discreet nature made him an obvious choice to accompany Francis Dana to St. Petersburg in 1781 as secretary and translator. Dana had been appointed by the Continental Congress to negotiate a treaty with Empress Catherine, but was unsuccessful in gaining recognition from the Court and returned after fourteen months. John Quincy was just 16 when he returned to the Netherlands, traveling alone through Finland, Sweden, and Denmark. John Adams acknowledged that, while his son's exposure to the world had been valuable, JQA needed to gain a formal education at Harvard. After following his father to The Hague, Paris, and London, John Quincy moved back to the small town of Cambridge, across the river from Boston, to complete his undergraduate degree and legal training.

After Harvard, John Quincy was rescued from a mediocre legal career when President George Washington appointed him minister to the Netherlands. His father subsequently sent him to the Court of Prussia in 1797, an appointment he reluctantly accepted, wary of any appearance of nepotism. Early in his career, the charge was difficult to dismiss, but John Quincy proved to be a far better diplomat than his father. At this time, JQA met and courted 22-year-old Louisa Catherine Johnson. They married in London and left for Berlin three months later. After he was recalled to the United States, Adams waited only a year before running and winning a seat in the U.S. Senate.

JQA's appointment to St. Petersburg came at a pivotal point in American history, and his was an extremely successful mission that strengthened U.S.-Russian relations and further defined American commercial trade strategies. Adams capped off his diplomatic missions in Europe with the successful negotiation of the Treaty of Ghent (which ended the War of 1812), and his appointment as minister to Great Britain, the highest diplomatic post for an American. He returned to the United States in 1817 to serve as secretary of state under James Monroe, and he was elected president in 1825. After losing a bid for re-election, John Quincy returned to Congress and served eighteen years in the House of Representatives. He died after collapsing on the floor of the House in 1848, at the age of 81.

> Head-winds, calm, rain. Whales, Porpoises, and a Gannet, a bird accustomed to the neighbourhood of land in these regions.
>
> – JQA Diary, September 5, 1809, aboard the *Horace*

As the church bells tolled noon on August 5, 1809, the Adams family sailed from Boston Harbor in a merchant ship outfitted for the journey. The *Horace* spent 80 days at sea and carried John Quincy, his wife Louisa, their youngest son Charles Francis, Louisa's sister Catherine, John Quincy's nephew William Steuben Smith, and two servants to Russia. They were also accompanied by two secretaries to the legation "but at their own expense." Adams' salary as minister was second only to the president's, but the expense of keeping even a modest household burdened them for their entire time abroad.

On their second day at sea, JQA reflected in his diary about his motives for accepting the commission – "That of serving my Country... stands foremost of them all; and though it neither suits my own inclination, nor my own private judgment, I deem it a duty to sacrifice them both to the public sense."

His wife Louisa bewailed her family's fate. She had packed up her life in just a month, leaving her two older children, eight-year-old George and six-year-old John, in the care of relatives in Massachusetts, not to see them again for six years. Louisa recorded in a memoir 30 years later, "Broken hearted miserable, *alone* in every feeling; my boy was my only comfort. I had passed the age when Courts are alluring. I had no vanity to gratify, and experience had taught me years before the meanness of an American Minister's position at a European Court." Their disparate feelings about John Quincy's career opportunities would plague their marriage for many years.

Louisa Catherine, the daughter of an American merchant raised in England and France, was an intelligent and witty woman who suffered from a delicate constitution and a shy nature. Just 34 when they sailed for Russia, Louisa struggled to keep up with John Quincy's rigorous schedule, with the exacting demands on a diplomat's wife, and with periodic depression. While he shone in St. Petersburg, she faded under the onslaught of parties, balls, and social obligations. Still, Louisa played the part. Her fluency in French, her musical and artistic skills, and a natural facility for the diplomatic dinner party – she excelled even when she despised it – made her a favorite among the diplomatic corps and the royal family.

For the Adamses, diplomacy was a family affair. Shortly after their arrival in Russia, even three-year-old Charles Francis was on display attending the Children's Ball, an annual event hosted by the French ambassador for the children of nobles and visiting dignitaries. Napoleon's emissary, the Duke de Vicence, was the most powerful ambassador at Court and lived almost as lavishly as the Tsar. "The Ambassador" – as the diplomatic corps always called him – set the tone for St. Petersburg's social events, spending one million rubles (about $350,000) a year on entertainment alone.

Louisa described the Children's Ball: "We took Charles, who I had dressed as an Indian Chief to gratify the taste for Savages." As little Charles entered the dance floor, "there was a general burst of applause when he marched in, at which he was much surprised." Following the dances, the children were fed a sumptuous dinner late into the night with "oceans of Champagne." Mothers were all obliged to stand behind their children's chairs in full dress. Charles appeared dutifully at these events in a variety of costumes – as Bacchus or the Page from Beaumarchais' *Marriage of Figaro* – but at the end of the evening when a lottery for expensive toys was held, Charles was always dragged away. John Quincy – strictly adhering to U.S. government policy – would not allow any member of the family to accept gifts.

...how congenial it is to my temper to find extravagance and dissipation a public
duty.
                                    – John Quincy Adams to Abigail Adams, February 8, 1810

During the summer of 1811, Louisa was nearing the final stages of
pregnancy. It was her eleventh – she had suffered seven miscarriages and
would have three more before her child-bearing years were over. Her
anxiety was compounded by the news of her beloved sister's death in
childbirth. Yet, despite their ever-dwindling finances and Louisa's tenuous
health, the "dissipation" continued in St. Petersburg. Just a week before
Louisa gave birth, John Quincy departed from Apothecaries Island in the
Nevka River, where the family was spending the summer, and made his
way to the annual Peterhof Fête. Arriving at about two in the afternoon,
Adams wandered through the grounds, watching hundreds of servants
and workers set up for the massive illumination and fireworks display. All
of St. Petersburg attended the annual event. Thousands of peasants made
their way on foot to watch the late summer festivities, while the nobles
arrived in handsome carriages. JQA noted that some even arrived in
"imperial yachts, under full sail and dress'd out in a full suite of colours."

After a dinner that included "fruits of all climates in profusion.
Cherries, Strawberries, raspberries, Apricots, plums, peaches, Oranges,
grapes and pine-apples," the company proceeded outside to view the
light displays. "There were three hundred thousand lamps, and sixteen
hundred persons employed to light them," followed by a 15-minute
firework display. Adams recorded in detail the light displays, the food, the
dancing, and the assortment of costumed nobles, but despite his attention
he was not as impressed with the spectacle as he had once been. "I was
present at this fête in the year 1782," he wrote. But, lacking recognition,
JQA and Francis Dana could only observe the Court alongside thousands
of Russian peasants. More than thirty years later, Adams' familiarity with
"all the principle individuals" dulled the glimmering spectacle. "The
company then was, I think, more numerous, and from my impressions
more splendid in dress," but upon reflection, JQA concluded that
"perhaps . . . their magnificence in dress was not so familiar and common
an object to me as it now is."

When Adams left at 1:30 in the morning, he "pass'd upwards of two
thousand as I presume on the road; and during the first half of the way

great multitudes of people returning on foot. The numbers of People who attended at this celebration, are asserted to be at least fifty thousand." Walking through St. Petersburg in the early hours of the morning, JQA discovered that by custom all bridges were raised at two in the morning for several hours to let vessels pass through. He did not reach home until nearly five AM.

> There is something in these enquiries about weights and measures, singularly fascinating to me.
>
> - JQA Diary, February 16, 1812

Adams' diplomatic salary was excessive by American standards. But at $9,000 a year, it barely covered the minimum standards for a diplomat in St. Petersburg, and every year John Quincy was forced to choose between gaining a reputation for parsimony or going into personal debt. He usually accomplished both. JQA wrote home to his parents to complain of the financial expectations for his household – they kept a frugal fourteen servants – causing his mother Abigail to send a letter to President Madison demanding his recall. As a testament to her influence, Madison sent recall papers to him the following spring, but Adams never acted on them.

Added to the cost of their household was the apparently routine practice of servants fleecing their employers. In January 1812, after moving twice to cut costs, Adams discovered that his steward had defrauded him. Just a day later, the Adamses were "obliged to dismiss the woman who furnished us with butter, milk and cream," when they realized that she had been providing them with three pounds of dairy while charging them for five. Within two weeks, Adams found "573 bottles of wine missing!" Just after he dismissed the steward, JQA learned that 15 months of bills had been left unpaid.

John Quincy had a sharp temper, but he was widely known as a generous and forgiving employer, clearly tolerating much from untrustworthy servants. The following month, he records in his diary, "I continue to be engaged so great a portion of my time in the most insignificant trifles of household economy, that it has become irksome to me, in the extreme. The closer I make my inspection, the more and more I discover of imposition, and of pillage, in every shape." As he kept closer watch on

household goods, Adams became intrigued with another question, that
of weights and measures. "This day I weighed some coffee sent from two
different places and found it short weight, about one pound to forty.... I
called at an English Mathematical instrument makers' to enquire if he
could make me an *arshine*,[1] with the English and French corresponding
measures, but he could not. I went also to a tinman's to inquire if he had
any measures of capacity, but he had none except a cup which he said
would hold a pound of water."

Adams' humble inquiries –   driven by thrift and a keen desire not
to be cheated –   began a decade-long investigation that concluded in
a definitive scientific work, *Report on Weights and Measures*. Submitted
to Congress in 1821, the report shows the depth of Adams' creativity.
It was at the time the most complete survey of its kind. Drawing on his
diplomatic experience, historical knowledge, and scientific inquiry, Adams
came to believe that a uniform system of weights and measures would
advance the cause of peace. He was struck by the sweeping uniformity in
the weapons of war and the continual disagreement about "the greatest
invention of human ingenuity since that of printing," the French metric
system. For JQA, the principle of uniformity as expressed in the metric
system needed only transparency and cooperative endeavor to further
peaceful human relations. It required no hard-fought legislation or
treaties between warring nations; the goal of peace could only be won by
peaceful measures. In the *Report*, Adams found it "strange" that mankind
"should use the same artillery and musketry, and bayonets and swords and
lances, for the wholesale trade of human slaughter" while refusing "to
weigh by the same pound, to measure by the same rule, to drink from the
same cup, to use in fine the same materials for ministering to the wants
and contributing to the enjoyments of one another."

While few read his report, Adams considered it his finest work and
adhered to its philosophy of uniformity and transparency in defining
American foreign policy. What began as a modest attempt to reconcile
household accounts grew into a deeply held conviction about peaceful
commerce and the proper role of government. Adams saw the future
in trade and commerce, and he understood that a uniform system of
measurement would offer a kind of *lingua franca* much like that used to
further diplomatic relations and amity among nations.

....

1. A Russian unit of length equal to 28 inches.

John Quincy Adams' enthusiasm for scientific inquiry was not limited to weights and measures. The man who would, years later, prove instrumental in the founding of the Smithsonian Institute, was thrilled by all things mechanical. In late October 1811, Adams visited a glass-making factory just behind the Monastery of St. Alexander Nevsky that manufactured looking glasses, decanters, wine glasses, tumblers, colored dishes, and vases. Adams declared their steam-powered polisher of looking glasses to be "an invention of prodigious effect" and lamented, "I wish I could visit a manufacture once a week, and spend three hours at every visit."

A few weeks later, Adams called on the Imperial Librarian, whose collection of curiosities included a number of manuscripts from England, even an annotated prayer book used by Mary Queen of Scots while she was in prison. JQA was unimpressed with the man's historical knowledge and recorded an incredible account of a "small Latin Bible written upon a soft and beautiful kind of vellum which he pretended was of human skin." Politely inquiring where such a book could be manufactured, the librarian could not say, but speculated that "it was done by the monks of the middle ages, and must be the kinds of infants who had died without baptism." Ever the diplomat, Adams only remarks, "I have yet some doubts with regard to this fact."

John Quincy kept to a rigorous schedule in his role as minister. Rising very early, he read the Bible, wrote voluminous correspondence to the U.S. State Department, walked three to seven miles, tutored his son Charles Francis, and attended with Louisa dinners and balls into the late evening. But with every free moment, JQA prowled St. Petersburg's bookshops and museums, its factories and schools, and found every opportunity to explore the "city of princes."

And thus accoutred I appeared before the Gentlemen of our party who could not refrain from laughter at my appearance.

– LCA Diary, November 12, 1809

Mrs. Adams' life in St. Petersburg followed a different trajectory. As one of the only foreign women accompanying her husband, Louisa was an oddity to many. Tradition reigned at Court and, in her first week in Russia, Louisa and her sister Catherine were expected to appear in lavish attire to be presented to the Emperor, his wife, and his mother. Dressed "modestly" in a silver-tissue hoop dress, a crimson velvet robe, a fur cloak, and a single diamond arrow pin, Louisa appeared before the royal family with just her court sponsor, Countess Litta, a dowager bedecked in diamonds. John Quincy did not accompany her. Louisa's fluency in French saved her from an otherwise awkward event, for though "the Emperor and Empresses spoke very kindly to us. I did not know a creature in the room." When asked by the American consul to dance a polonaise, Louisa "was much afraid I should blunder but I soon fell into the step and made out without mortifying my fastidious partner." She continued in "tolerable spirits," rejoining her husband for dinner with the Emperor, who ate on solid gold plates while the rest of the diplomatic corps dined on silver. The party ended at one in the morning, but "no one was allowed to depart before the Emperor.... I was glad to get home – All this was too much like a fairy tale."

Louisa's life of expensive gowns and late night parties was happily put aside when she gave birth to her only daughter in the summer of 1811. "O she grows lovely. Such a pair of Eyes!! I fear I love her too well." Louisa's devotion to her baby girl was all-consuming, in part because she never forgave herself for leaving her older children in America. In January 1812, Louisa returned to her social obligations, but noted that "after a long protracted confinement by sickness and anxiety I once again take my Station in the world for which I care so little." Baby Louisa was sick throughout the winter, as were her mother and Charles Francis. When Louisa took the child out for walks, the "superstitious Russians" would stop her in the street: "they all say 'that She is born for Heaven'." In February, the youngest Adams developed a high fever and was sick throughout the spring. The doctors believed the cause was connected to her teething. In late summer, doctors lanced the baby's gums in an effort to relieve her symptoms, but the small, weak child – just past her first birthday – was immediately seized with convulsions. On September 14, Louisa noted that "Renewed blisters, warm baths, and injections of Laudanum and Digitalis have been tried . . . with no favourable effect." The following day the child died, "as lovely an infant ever breathed the air of heaven."

The death of the younger Louisa Catherine Adams marked a tragic turning point for John Quincy and Louisa. While JQA threw himself into his work, negotiating trade rights for American merchants and keeping abreast of Russia's war with France (Napoleon invaded Russia on June 24, 1812; he began his retreat in October and finally left Russian territory on December 14), Louisa simply shut down. She ended her journal with "My child gone to heaven" and retreated from society as much as she was able, going through the motions of her social obligations, always longing for America. When she finally left St. Petersburg two-and-a-half years later, she wrote: "I scarcely can define my feelings. Much as I wish to see my Children, my heart is torn at the idea of quitting for ever the spot where my darling lays." But Louisa would find strength when she thought she had none. Louisa's dramatic departure from Russia and journey across Europe in the wake of Napoleon's army would become legendary in the Adams family, solidifying her reputation as a "well-traveled lady."

As early as the fall of 1810, JQA reported to the U.S. State Department that the Franco-Russian alliance[2] would probably not last. When war finally broke out 18 months later, Europe was not surprised. In March 1812, John Quincy met a preoccupied tsar on the Neva – *"il avance toujours."*[3] Breaking their usual silence regarding official business, Alexander confided, "war is coming which I have done so much to avoid." The tsar left soon after that for the frontier, to bolster the assembled forces. Their numbers were immense on both sides. JQA wrote in his diary, "there was in history, scarcely anything like it. It was like Romance. What it would come to [Alexander] knew not." John Quincy wrote to his mother before the year was out that Napoleon's forces were conquered by the two harshest Russian generals, "General Famine and General Frost…. In all probability the career of Napoleon's conquest is at an end." While John Quincy reported regularly to the U.S. the status of the war in Russia, he continually sought news on the war in North America, his main source being the American merchant ships docked in St. Petersburg.

In the spring of 1814, John Quincy Adams left Russia for Göteborg, Sweden, where he was to be one of several representatives negotiating a peaceful resolution to the War of 1812 (the American, not the Russian one). Tsar Alexander had been instrumental in bringing Britain and the U.S. to the negotiating table, although the British spurned his offer to host the conference in St. Petersburg. After arriving in Sweden, Adams

---

2. Created with the July 1807 signing of the Treaty of Tilsit.
3. He keeps advancing.

learned that the British had moved the negotiations to Ghent, a medieval city in present-day Belgium. The contentious talks lasted from August 8 to December 24 and were further complicated by lengthy news delays from the battles in North America. Famously, though the Treaty of Ghent was signed on Christmas Eve, the news did not reach American shores in time to prevent the Battle of New Orleans. A crushing defeat for the British, the battle propelled General Andrew Jackson to national fame, and eventually to the White House – he defeated JQA in the presidential election of 1828.

Weeks before signing the treaty, Adams came to the conclusion that five years in Russia was enough and he requested a recall. Although he enjoyed his schedule of study and diplomacy, John Quincy felt that he had done all he could in Russia on behalf of the United States. His work in Ghent was very successful and he knew he would be well received by the Madison administration. Adams hoped to be given the most coveted diplomatic post for an American, that of minister to the Court of St. James [Great Britain]. While awaiting news from the United States, he sent word to Louisa: "break up altogether our establishment at St. Petersburg.... and come with Charles to me at Paris, where I shall be impatiently waiting for you." She was "astonished" at JQA's instructions to sell the furniture, pack up his library, and keep a detailed accounting of her expenditures, not least because he had never trusted her with so much responsibility. But Louisa rose to the challenge and on February 12, 1815, "at five o'clock in the evening of Sunday, I bade adieu to the splendid City of St. Petersburg" in company with eight-year-old Charles Francis; Babet, a French maid; and two manservants hired for the journey.

> In Petersburg for five long years I had lived a Stranger to all, but the kind regards of the Imperial family; and I quitted its gaudy loneliness without a sigh, except that which was wafted to the tomb of my lovely Babe.
>
> – Louisa Adams "Narrative of a Journey
> from St. Petersburg to Paris," 1836

They began their journey in a carriage outfitted as a sleigh, but by the time they reached Riga on the Baltic coast they were "overtaken by a thaw, and I was under the necessity of staying four or five days, to get my Carriage fixed and to dispose of my Kibitka."

The party traveled east along the Baltic Sea coast, passing desolate villages and making extensive detours to avoid impassable roads. Aside from the near upset of the carriage while crossing over thawing ice, "no other incident occurred worth notice until we reached the frontier of Prussia." During the winter of 1815, rumor of Napoleon's return was everywhere and the battlefields of the previous winter could still be seen. All manner of hastily dug graves, shreds of clothing, piles of boots and even human remains lined the leveled roads. Louisa, decades later, vividly recalled that

> the Season of the year at which I travelled; when Earth was chained in her dazzling, brittle but solid fetters of Ice . . . the ways were rendered deeply interesting by the fearful remnants of men's fierry and vindictive passions; passively witnessing to tales of blood, and woes. Such are the graphic deleneations of War's unhallowed march.

After stopping for a week in Berlin while the carriage underwent much-needed repairs, they continued across Prussia, passing "small straggling parties of disbanded Soldiers, loitering home." Acutely aware of her vulnerabilities, Louisa would put on her son's "Military Cap and tall Feather, and lay his Sword across the window of the Carriage; as I had been told, that any thing that *looked* military escaped from insult." As they neared the French border, rumors of Napoleon's return or possible demise met them at every inn. Unbeknownst to Louisa – or even to John Quincy – they were headed directly for Napoleon's growing army and the last surge, later known as The Hundred Days. Fearful of impressment, Louisa's manservants abandoned her in Frankfurt. The only servant she found willing to journey with her into Paris was a fourteen-year-old boy, Dupin, who had served in the Russian campaign.

Just outside of Epernay, France, Louisa encountered Imperial Guards on their way to meet Napoleon. Upon hearing "the most horrid curses, and dreadful Language" from a number of women following the troops, Louisa quickly realized that she might be in mortal danger. Spurred on by the cries of the women – "Tear them out of the Carriage! They are Russians, take them out kill them!" – the soldiers turned their guns on the drivers, at which Louisa hastily presented her passports. When they realized that she was an American lady trying to reach her husband in

Paris, they shouted, *"vive les Americains,"* at which Louisa waved her handkerchief and responded *"vive Napoleon!"* to the cheering shouts of the soldiers.

After five weeks on the road, Louisa, Charles Francis, Babet, and Dupin arrived at the gates of Paris at 11 in the evening. Upon checking into the Hôtel du Nord on the Rue de Richelieu, they found "Mr. Adams not returned from the Theatre." He soon came home and was "astonished" at Louisa's adventure; "as every thing in Paris was quiet, and it had never occurred to him, that it could have been otherwise in any other part of the Country."

Louisa Catherine Adams had left Russia with a heavy heart. But as the years passed, she would regard her time in St. Petersburg, and particularly her departure, as formative. At JQA's side, she relaxed into a gracious, intelligent, and worldly woman, becoming a favorite in Washington. In 1836, having reached a kind of retirement, Louisa wrote the narrative of her travels and hoped that "perhaps at some future day" it would "serve to recall the memory of one, *who was.*" `

Distracted first by the negotiations and later by the pressing duties of a new post (he was indeed appointed ambassador to the Court at St. James in 1815), John Quincy did not immediately reflect upon leaving the "city of princes." He did, however, follow with great interest the movements of the Sovereign Prince of Russia. In March 1814, just before JQA left St. Petersburg, Alexander led the coalition armies into Paris. After Napoleon's forces ravaged Moscow, the tsar would have been forgiven had he exacted revenge on Paris. But his "moderation" and "humanity" impressed all of Europe. John Quincy wrote that he "may now truly be called the darling of the human race."

By the time Adams reached Ghent in June, Alexander was passing through the city on his way to the Congress of Vienna. Standing shoulder to shoulder amid a cheering crowd, John Quincy saw him riding with a suite of officers, "distinguished from them only by the greater simplicity of his dress... very few in the crowd knew him as he passed." Even after five years, Adams could not precisely call the tsar a friend –   his access at Court did not extend that far. But the two men's regard for one another was apparent to all at Court. Alexander's easy manner and John Quincy's unpretentious acceptance fostered a truly diplomatic relationship. Standing in the rain on that hot June day, JQA was struck by the tsar's "affability" and proudly declared to Louisa that he "has shown himself as great by his forbearance and modesty in prosperity as by his firmness in the hour of his own trial." Alexander did not see John Quincy in the crowd and Adams never saw the tsar again. They departed each other's acquaintance, but their shared spirit of diplomacy and temperance brought peace and prosperity to their nations for generations to come.[4]

September/October 2008

4. John Quincy Adams' complete diaries are available online at the Massachusetts Historical Society website: masshist.org/jqadiaries. The diary of his wife, Louisa Catherine Adams, is currently in production and will be published in a two-volume edition in 2011. Visit masshist.org for the new Adams Papers Digital Editions, a full text presentation of all previously published volumes. The Adams Papers is a documentary editing project dedicated to publishing the correspondence and diaries of the Adams family, including John, Abigail, John Quincy, Louisa Catherine, and Charles Francis.

The Decembrists
Vera Bokova

*I*n the early morning of July fourteenth, 1826, near the Peter-and-Paul Fortress in St. Petersburg, arrangements were being made for an execution.

The prisoners had been brought out of the dungeon well in advance; they had already drawn straws to decide who would be led to the platform first. They sat near it, with their hands and feet chained, watching nonchalantly as the gallows were built.

These were the ringleaders of the so-called Decembrist Revolt of seven months previous, an abortive uprising by liberal army officers, influenced by modern ideas that had swept through Europe in Napoleon's time.

There were five of them: Pavel Pestel, Kondraty Ryleyev, Sergei Muravyov-Apostol, Mikhail Bestuzhev-Ryumin and Pyotr Kakhovsky. All were officers and three of them (Pestel, Muravyov and Ryleyev) had fought in the Napoleonic War. Ryleyev was also a famous poet and publisher. The youngest of the convicts, Bestuzhev-Ryumin, was 24; the oldest – Colonel Pestel – had recently turned 33.

Before the massed formation of the guards battalions, to the sound of a military march and drum roll, the prisoners, dressed in long linen shrouds with hoods covering their heads, took their place at the gallows. But as soon as the trapdoors opened, something unexpected happened: three of the five ropes broke and the condemned fell into the pit below.

There is an ancient Russian belief that if a hanging is unsuccessful, it cannot have been ordained by God. The convict is immediately pardoned. On this occasion, the executioners thought of informing Tsar Nicholas I, but he had deliberately left for his summer palace that day. They decided to repeat the execution.

It turned out that there was no spare rope, so one of the men was sent to buy it, but it was early in the morning and all the shops were closed. It was some time before the execution could be continued.

All the while, the band played marches, and the convicts whose ropes broke still lay in the pit under the trapdoor. They were all injured.

"Poor Russia! Can't even hang anyone properly!" said Ryleyev when he regained the ability to speak.

Shortly afterwards, the deed was done.

The next day, in the center of St. Petersburg on Peter's Square, soldiers and townspeople said mass in thanks for "the liberation of the country from the conspiracy."

The prisoners' priest, Pyotr Myslovsky, did not go to the square. Instead, he performed a quiet requiem in his cathedral.

Thus ended the final chapter of the history of Russian secret societies, an important factor in Russian public life in the first quarter of the nineteenth century. Because Russia had no parliament, free press or freedom of speech, dissenters were forced underground. And with absolute monarchy, a complete lack of civil rights and freedoms, corruption, crime, bureaucracy and serfdom, there were plenty of causes for dissatisfaction.

The Napoleonic War of 1812-1814, in which Russia was one of the victors, brought the nation closer together and, at the same time, increased the desire for change. Societies like "The Salvation Union" and "The Prosperity Union" emerged between 1815 and 1820.

Most of their members were aristocrats, army officers who were dissatisfied with the existing regime and dedicated to reform. The societies were fractious and disorganized, constantly disintegrating and reforming. Still, they were united by their desire for a constitution and emancipation of the serfs.

This could be most clearly seen in a group of societies whose members called themselves "The Secret Union." They created a few notable draft constitutions, and, when reformist Tsar Alexander I promised constitutional rule, its members actively began propagating liberal ideas.

But Europe's 1820-1821 revolutions and upheavals forced Alexander I to crack down on the liberals his policies had spawned. Censorship and police persecution were increased. Some educational organizations were shut. All secret societies were prohibited by special decree, but some Secret Union members refused to comply.

In November 1825, Alexander died suddenly and all of Russia swore an oath of obedience to Konstantin, his successor. Yet no one knew that, a few years earlier, Konstantin had renounced his claim to the throne (this had been kept secret). The crown was passed to Konstantin's brother, Nicholas.

But in the confusion of this succession, rumors spread that Nicholas intended to usurp Konstantin's power. This short interregnum had a profound effect on several young members of the Secret Union, led by Ryleyev. These passionate and excitable men, including romantic writers like Alexander Odoyevsky and Nikolay Bestuzhev, decided the time was right to declare their constitutional aspirations and, with a bit of luck, to secure them.

The oath of allegiance to Nicholas was set for December 14, 1825. The conspirators decided to incite rebellion in a few brigades, bring them to the governmental buildings to shout "long live the constitution!" Then the conspirators would demand establishment of a constituent assembly to decide the future of Russia.

The plan was incoherent, and its participants' conduct incompetent. More like an armed demonstration than an uprising, the revolt was destined to be unsuccessful. A tiny group of troops gathered on Peter's Square, stood idly by the famous Bronze Horseman monument to Peter the Great for a few hours, and then were shot at from point blank range by troops loyal to the government.

Because the uprising took place in the month of December, everyone who had ever been a member of The Secret Union was henceforth labeled a "Decembrist."

The government's investigation lasted about half a year, and implicated almost 600 people. The breadth of the case surprised the government, and most of the arrested were quickly pardoned and freed. Others were demoted and transferred to the Caucasus War. Some 121 people were sentenced to various terms of *katorga* – hard labor – and exile to Siberia. Five were hanged.

As one of the exiled Decembrists, Mikhail Lunin, said: "In England I would have been a member of His Majesty's opposition, and in Russia I am a state criminal."

The exiled endured their hardships with a rare courage, dignity and truly Christian patience. Wives joined their husbands, though they had to leave their children – the authorities strictly prohibited bringing them to Siberia. The spouses also had to agree to a number of humiliating rules: to give up titles, property and civil rights; to obey the prison authorities; and to meet only infrequently with their husbands in the presence of a guard.

Eleven women gave up everything to share their husbands' exile. Princess Maria Volkonskaya, who followed her husband but left her son, explained: "My son is happy and peaceful; my husband is unhappy – my place is near my husband."

The poet Alexander Pushkin, who sympathized with the Decembrists, sent this poem with Alexandra Muravyova, one of the women who left for Siberia:

Deep in Siberia's mine, let naught
Subdue your proud and patient spirit
Your crushing toil and lofty thought
Shall not be wasted – do not fear it

Alexander Odoyevsky answered him:

The spark will flare into a flame
We shall not waste our crushing toil
Our people won't forget our name
When freedom comes to Russia's soil

When the term of hard labor was over, the exiled Decembrists were sent to different corners of Siberia. As such, they were often the only educated people for thousands of miles around. They considered it their duty to study the nature, climate and ethnography of their local areas. They ran schools, treated the sick, cultivated plants and spread the Christian gospel. Their memory is still honored in Siberia, and indeed elsewhere in Russia.

In recent years, though, historians have started looking at the Decembrists in a different light. At the peak of *perestroika*, Soviet literary journals published classified archives containing Lenin's many direct orders for execution of the Bolsheviks' opponents. At this, many Russians became disillusioned with their "revolutionary past" and some historical essays even questioned the justness of the Decembrist plot against a tsarist regime which, it was now considered, suited Russia much better than Bolshevism.

In any case, the Decembrists certainly influenced the revolutionary movement in Russia. Every Soviet student remembers Lenin's famous phrase: "The Decembrists woke up Herzen" (a famous nineteenth century Russian democrat, himself an inspiration to Lenin). And Odoyevsky's famous line, "The spark will flare into a flame" became the motto of the Bolshevik newspaper *Iskra* (The Spark), which Lenin edited for a time before coming to power.

But the difference between the Decembrists and the Bolsheviks was great. In fact there is a well-known Russian anecdote that starkly (if satirically) illustrates their disparate goals:

> In October 1917, a babushka sitting by a window in St. Petersburg asks her grandson: "What's all this fuss at the Winter Palace about?"
> "The Bolsheviks are taking it by storm."
> "What do they want?"
> "They want to see to it that there are no rich."
> "Strange people, those Bolsheviks. My father, a Decembrist, wanted to see to it that there were no poor."

What of the Decembrists' legacy, then?

While it would be an overstatement to say the Decembrists spurred the abolition of serfdom in Russia, it is important to note that they were the first to call for it. And this important measure (1861) impacted greatly on Russia's industrial development in the late nineteenth and early twentieth centuries.

And surely today, as Russia lives under a new, democratic constitution, one that, on paper at least, guarantees basic political and economic freedoms, some credit must be given the Decembrists. However naive and ill-prepared, the rebels, through their brave actions and crushing toil, certainly laid one of the first stones in Russia's road to democracy.

December 1995

In the Land of Magic Art
Mikhail Ivanov

Dear citizens and passengers! Under Article 171 of the Russian Penal Code, illegal entrepreneurship is punishable with a fine of up to 500 minimal salaries or up to a three-year prison term.

*T*he metallic, official voice droned from the loudspeakers of the packed *elektrichka* as the train pulled away from Moscow's Yaroslavsky train station. The objects of this dire warning – the ubiquitous train peddlers – were clearly unmoved. At each stop, more peddlers hop on board to work the cars and hawk their wares.

Dear passengers! I submit for your consideration a new shoe shine cream which will help your leather footwear survive the hard frost and street slush. If someone is interested, I will approach him.

While the shoe shine peddler walks the length of the car, a second merchant is already beginning his litany.

Dear passengers! Here is a unique glue which can stick together pieces of wood, metal, rubber and what not...

Potato peelers, cotton handkerchiefs, crossword collections, bottle openers, insider's tips for gardeners... You name it, they sell it on the *elektrichka* to dacha-goers and travelers. Luckily, one vendor offers a more mundane product – bottles of Yarpivo, a beer brewed in Yaroslavl, the terminus of this particular *elektrichka* route. Another offers a personal favorite: *sukhariki*, dried pieces of brown bread flavored with garlic – the ideal beer snack.

After my fifteen rubles end up in the pocket of the beer peddler, I realize I should have also bought one of the cheap bottle openers on offer (and, looking at my shoes, slopped from the muddy square at Yaroslavsky train station, some of the shoe polish would not have hurt either). Luckily, two empathetic fellow-travelers bustle to my rescue, popping open the precious Yarpivo with a well-practiced motion – prying it against the metal seat handle. Ah, the pleasures of collective travel...

AN HOUR AND ten minutes out, I disembarked at Abramtsevo station, my mood perfectly softened for the 15-minute walk to the famous estate. A wide, well-trodden path leads from the train station into a fairy tale forest smelling richly of pine and echoing the songs of a winter bird choir. A forested hill on the left shore of the Vorya river is overgrown with old-style dachas from the 1930s-1950s – typical summer homes of the intelligentsia elite. Throughout the Soviet era, the cultural aura of Abramtsevo and its rural atmosphere attracted many artists, such as Igor Grabar and Vera Mukhina. In 1932, a "House of Rest for Creative Workers" was opened in Abramtsevo and many Soviet cultural celebrities came here. The writer Leonid Leonov lived in the former dacha of painter Vasily Polenov; cinema star Lyubov Orlova rested and worked here with her husband, film director Grigory Alexandrov.

In fact, in the late 1930s, Abramtsevo was a prestigious health resort: the sanitarium of Narkompros (the Ministry of Education) was located on the grounds of the former estate. During the Second World War, a military hospital was located here. It was not until the 1950s that Abramtsevo was reopened as a museum.

SLOWLY, THE DARK forest gives way to the bright vista of a small river valley, accentuated by an immaculate snow. As you come out of the forest to the other, right shore of the river Vorya, you feel like a mole emerging into the sunlight. Cross the Vorya, climb a steep hill and you are standing at the iron facade of Abramtsevo Estate Museum.

Initially, the main purpose of my visit was to look at the nice samples of Russian *izby*. The local Teremok and the wooden Artist's Studio are stylized imitations of authentic peasant *izby*. But once I have arrived, a visit to the main mansion becomes unavoidable.

Abramtsevo Estate originally belonged to the writer Sergei Aksakov. His family lived here up until 1870 when, due to financial difficulties, the writer's daughter, Sofia Sergeyevna, was forced to sell the estate to the young industrialist Savva Mamontov for 15,000 rubles. Several rooms in the interior of the house still bear the imprint of the Aksakovs: family portraits, photos, furniture, a library and even the writer's desk are religiously preserved.

> ...We are looking into buying a village near Moscow. The thought that
> you, my dear friend, will occasionally be our guest makes our seclusion
> much nicer in our eyes...
>   – Aksakov to his literary idol and friend Nikolai Gogol
>   in the winter of 1843. By the fall, Aksakov had bought Abramtsevo.

The sixteenth century Chronicles of the Moscow State speak of "the empty site Obramok." An *obramok*, according to Vladimir Dal's dictionary, is a "frame or border," in this case the edge of a forest, a site on a hill. "Obramok" meant a hill amid thick forests, flanked on two or three sides by a stream or a river. Hence the name of this place – Obramkovo, which, at the end of the eighteenth century, became the phonetically softened "Abramtsevo."

The estate does not attract visitors for the beauty of its palaces or for splendid, European-style parks. Instead, there is the simpler, more sublime beauty of unpolished nature here. The ancient mansion where Sergei Aksakov lived from 1843 until his death in 1859 stands watch over the picturesque river Vorya.

> Прекрасно местоположенье:
> Гора над быстрою рекой
> Заслонено от глаз селенье
> Зеленой ощею густой.

"A great location, a hill upon a rapid river, a village hidden from the eyes by a thick green forest," wrote Aksakov in an 1843 poem. "The little village of Abramtsevo is a nice corner on the shore of the river Vorya, near Khotkovsky Monastery and not too far from the Troitse-Sergiyev Lavra," the writer's son Ivan later added.

Here in Abramtsevo the hospitable Aksakov hosted Gogol, Ivan Turgenev, the slavophile poet Aleksei Khomyakov and other cultural luminaries. Gogol (whose portrait hangs on the wall of the central mansion) visited Abramtsevo for the first time in 1849, and for the last time in 1851, just four months before his death. Gogol was deeply attached to Abramtsevo and Aksakov. It was here that he read a chapter from his second volume of *Dead Souls*, which he later burned. A copy of *Dead Souls* inscribed to Aksakov for the latter's birthday is kept in the mansion-museum.

Turgenev visited Abramtsevo often in 1854-5, and he and Aksakov became close friends. The two writers shared a fervent love for hunting and Turgenev agreed to contribute to Aksakov's *Hunting Almanac*, a collection of literary works on that theme.

Aksakov wrote his famous book *Notes on Fishing* (1847) here. The volume's bright yet simple language won him many fans, even among readers who never held a fishing rod. In Maxim Gorky's novel, *Life of Klim Samgin*, one of the heroes says: "You go read Aksakov's *Notes on Fishing* – it's addicting. An amazing book..." Aksakov's other books included *Family Chronicles, The Childhood Years of Bagrov the Grandson*, and *Memoirs*, which was highly praised by Turgenev and Nikolai Nekrasov.

Aksakov was an honest and candid writer: as he admitted, he did not "possess the gift of pure invention" and could "write only based on reality, following the thread of true being." He deprecated himself as a second-rate writer and felt his true vocation was to prepare the ground for "first class writers, great writers."

Perhaps it was fitting, then, that Abramtsevo – Aksakov's estate – became, after the author's death, one of Russia's most fertile grounds for artistic talent. Under the ownership of Savva Mamontov, the famous Russian entrepreneur and art patron who also initiated the construction of several historic monuments in Moscow (namely the Metropol Hotel), Abramtsevo became a flourishing center for Russian culture and the visual arts.

Savva Mamontov's father, Ivan, was an industrialist who built one of the first railroads in Russia, connecting Moscow with Sergiyev-Posad – home of Russia's most sacred monastery. Mamontov graduated from the Law Faculty of Moscow State University, was an avid theater-goer and a true lover of art. After his father's death, Mamontov took over the family railway business, as well as a factory in Mytischi and the Nevsky Ship Building Factory in St. Petersburg. Mamontov the younger also made his mark on the development of railways in Russia, overseeing the construction of the rail line from Vologda to Arkhangelsk, as well as the Donetsk railroad.

But Mamontov did not only focus on business. Gifted with many artistic talents, Mamontov sang and sculpted, and was a talented writer, playwright, actor and director. But his biggest talent turned out to be encouraging and nurturing other artists' creativity. Soon after acquiring Abramtsevo, Mamontov established there an artistic union which would be known as Abramtsevo's Artistic Circle. This community of artists fixed their minds on Russian history as a means to reviving Russian art and reflecting in it "the eternal search for a national note." Among the circle's members were Vasily Polenov, Ilya Repin, Viktor Vastnetsov, Mikhail Nesterov, Mikhail Vrubel, Konstantin Korovin, Valentin Serov, and the sculptor Mark Antokolsky. By any measure, it was an awesome collection of artistic talent – one that would have immense impact on the course of Russian art.

THE TOTAL ARTISTIC freedom and the warm atmosphere reigning in the Mamontov house, combined with the magnificence of the surrounding environment, were all conducive to the creation of artistic masterpieces. Polenov painted his famous landscapes here, Vasnetsov worked on his magical *Alyonushka*, Repin worked on his *Unexpected Guest*.

Last and certainly not least, in the canteen of the house, a young Valentin Serov painted a portrait of Mamontov's elder daughter, Vera – a painting which would become famous simply as *Girl with Peaches*.

The atmosphere in which this and other great works of art were created is religiously preserved at Abramtsevo. A copy of Serov's painting hangs in the self-same canteen (the original is the State Tretyakov Gallery), outfitted with the same mahogany chairs; in the corner, by the entrance to the red guest room, is the statue of the grenadier, made by Sergiyev-Posad craftsmen and painted by Serov. On the wall hangs a majolica saucer by Vrubel.

Mamontov did more than simply preserve the estate he had purchased, enlarging the old *usadba* considerably. In the park near the mansion, architect Viktor Hartman designed the Art Studio where Vasnetsov, Serov, Polenov and Repin all worked, but where, in later years, Vrubel reigned. In summer, this *izba* became a sort of dormitory.

Not far from this beautiful example of a Russian *izba* (with all the requisite wood carvings – a *konyok*, a *nalichnik* and so on), stands the magical Banya-Teremok, conceived by the architect Ivan Ropet. In fact this *teremok* is called a *banya* because it was built on the site of Aksakov's old bathhouse; it actually only ever served as a lodging. The interior features carved furniture designed by Polenov and his sister Elena.

As William Brumfield wrote in *A History of Russian Architecture*, "in its fanciful manner, the Teremok is a foretaste of the free-style, sculpted architecture at the turn of the century; and in this, it prefigures the design of the church at Abramtsevo, which unified the colony's creative diversity."

This Church of the Savior, more precisely "Savior-Not-Made-by-Hands" (*Spas Nerukotvorny*) exemplifies how concentrating the efforts of several artistic geniuses can create a true masterpiece. Vasnetsov designed the church and Polenov worked on the Icon of Christ the Savior above the entrance to the church. The museum guide makes a point of mentioning that the church was unveiled in 1882, on the day of Polenov's wedding to his wife Natalia.

Vasnetsov used the design of a twelfth century church near Novgorod, the Savior in Nereditsa, as his starting point for the Abramtsevo church. Yet he built on this tradition by incorporating into his design crafts and decor from different schools of architecture: stone carving typical of Vladimir, majolica decoration along the lines of Yaroslavl churches, and windows in the Moscow style. The church is small and cozy, and features the work of many artists: Repin worked on the Icon of the Savior, Polenov on the Annunciation Icon and *The Last Supper*; Vasnetsov painted the Icon of the Virgin (there is said to be a resemblance to the artist's wife and two-year-old child in the work) and that of Saint Sergei Radonezhsky, in addition to designing the mosaic-tile floor; Antokolsky created a bas-relief in stone of the head of John the Baptist.

In 1891, a small chapel was added to the northern façade of the church following the tragic death of Mamontov's son Andrei in his early 20s. Andrei was a talented youth who had graduated from the Moscow School of Art and Sculpture and Architecture and, together with Vasnetsov, painted the frescoes of the Vladimir cathedral in Kiev. He was buried in this chapel, as was Mamontov, who died in 1918.

As HARD AS it may be to believe, the contributions to Russian culture made by the Abramtsevo Art Colony go well beyond painting and church architecture. There were also contributions to woodworking, ceramics and the theater. Mamontov's wife Elizaveta, together with Elena Polenova (the artist's sister), worked actively in woodworking workshops Elizaveta set up here in 1885. Elizaveta's two major goals were to help peasants' children learn a profession – and thus secure additional sources of income (they were also given a full set of carving tools after graduating from a four-year course of training), and to revive dying folk crafts. Elena became artistic director of the wood-carving workshop.

Many of the furniture pieces created in Elizaveta's workshop – namely a desk given her as a birthday present by young craftsmen – now stand in the main mansion of the estate-museum. The success of the workshop was so great that wood carvings and furniture from Abramtsevo became very popular with the Russian intelligentsia; a cupboard made in Abramtsevo can be seen in the study of Anton Chekhov's house in Yalta.

In 1890, Mamontov established a ceramics workshop in Abramtsevo headed by technologist-ceramist P. K. Vaulin. Today, the estate displays Vrubel's amazing ceramic works – his colored sculptures unite form and colors into a singular expression of his chosen theme. Vrubel also created original stove tiles for the main mansion. Many of his other ceramic masterpieces, such as Sadko, Lel and the Snow Maiden, were inspired by the music of Rimsky-Korsakov.

Yet it was in theatrical stagings that the multifaceted talents of these great Russian artists all flowed together into a sparkling river of talent. The artists would often gather in the mansion's red guest room and read aloud the dramatic works of Pushkin, Lermontov, Tolstoy or Shakespeare. The local theater grew out of these readings, performing such works as Alexander Ostrovsky's *Snow Maiden*, with stage decorations by Vasnetsov.

While Mamontov was himself often the director of these productions, it was the cousin of Mamontov's wife Elizaveta, the young Konstantin Alexeyev (the future Stanislavsky), whose participation might be said to have been most historic.

"Usually, plays were held during Christmas holidays," Stanislavsky later recalled in an obituary to Mamontov read at a special ceremony at MKhAT in 1918. "Then, for a week or even two, the whole house was turned into theater workshops... In one room a canvas was unfolded for Vasily Polenov and he, helped by his young aide Konstantin Korovin, would prepare the decor for the first act. In the second room, Ilya Repin with an aide, say, Serov, would paint decorations for the second act. In the third room Viktor Vasnetsov and Vrubel would bustle... Savva Ivanovich Mamontov would write the first act of the play, whose staging was hastily prepared upstairs..."

How interesting it is to hear "helped by his young aide Konstantin Korovin..." from this vantage point in history, when the smallest sketch by Korovin could steal the show at any art auction ...

As I WALKED out of the mansion, overwhelmed by impressions, a group of rowdy high school students reminded me of my own teenage years as they shouted: "Let's go see the *izbushkha na kurnikh nozhkakh!*" The "*izba* on hen's legs" is a mystical house that figures in many Russian fairy tales; it is the "headquarters" of the witch Baba Yaga who, before entering the *izbushka* would pronounce the same incantation: "*Izbushka-izbushka* turn your back to the forest and your front to me."

This fairy tale corner of the *usadba* not far from the Teremok was conceived by Viktor Vasnetsov with so much taste that the little *izba* became inseparable from the surrounding landscape. The *izbushka* has been a place of mirth, imagination and games for many generations of Abramtsevo residents and visitors.

I departed Abramtsevo with a feeling of light sadness, mixed with regret. The young guys I watched climb the fairy tale *izbushka* were about the same age as my children and here I had neglected to invite along my daughter Yevgeniya – a student at the Stroganov Art School – to accompany me on this trip to the magical land of Russian art. Deep down, I guess I felt she would refuse the invitation, but then, that's no excuse. Initiation to culture, as they say, sometimes takes a bit of pressure.

It is a sad commentary on our times that most Russian teens know less about Viktor Vasnetsov than about the "heroes" on the tasteless video-voyeur reality TV-program here, *Za Steklom* (*Behind the Glass*). The program, which followed the lives of teens with hidden cameras, was recently cancelled due to TV-6's "financial difficulties."

How quick we are to savor the sweetest, lowest-hanging "fruits" of Western culture, only to find out too late that they have such a bitter aftertaste. How hard it seems to be to borrow the higher-hanging fruits, while building on our centuries-old cultural heritage. How quickly we forget our own folklore and the names of the talented ones who walked the pathways of Abramtsevo a century ago...

What set me ruminating on these "heavy" themes was a framed quote hanging in the mansion:

It was by Alexander Koshelev, a noted slavophile and editor of *Russkaya Beseda* who frequently visited Aksakov. He wrote these words even before Mamontov gathered together the artist's colony in Abramtsevo. They summarize well some of the tensions that have existed in Russian art and society for the last 200-odd years.

The *elektrichka* stopped abruptly during our return trip. Someone had pulled the emergency stop-handle because of a brawl in the neighboring car. The ticket controllers were calling for the militia, because a Russian "hare" (ticketless passenger) was trying to get off the train en route to Moscow without paying the fine. Needless to say, this woke me from my philosophical meanderings and led me to search frantically for my own round-trip ticket (which had cost me all of 48 rubles – $1.50).

In point of fact, these days it is pretty difficult to travel like a "hare" on the *elektrichkas* traveling in and out of Moscow. There are entry and exit turnstiles that open only on insertion of special, bar-coded tickets. It is a smart innovation borrowed by our railway system from Western Europe which, despite high initial costs, is surely paying for itself.

This is what I call "making the best use of what was developed in the West" to solve a specifically Russian problem – cracking down on unscrupulous passengers who would not buy a ticket unless state-of-the-art equipment forced them to. And it is an innovation that railway entrepreneur Savva Mamontov, would surely smile upon.[1]

March/April 2002

---

1. Ivan Rybakov's *In the Land of Radonezh* was an invaluable resource in the author's preparation of this story.

The Treasury of Russian Art
Maria Kolesnikova

*D*usty, nineteenth century homes line narrow, winding streets in Moscow's ancient Zamoskvoreche (literally, "beyond the river") region. It would be easy to get lost here. Thankfully, near Tretyakovskaya metro station there is a huge sign in Russian and English, pointing the way to the gingerbread building at Lavrushensky pereulok 10: the State Tretyakov Gallery. But even without the sign, an observant and careful traveler could follow the human trickle that daily leads to the statue of Pavel Tretyakov outside the museum's entrance.

Moscow's Tretyakov Gallery is often overshadowed by St. Petersburg's Hermitage Museum, which has a larger collection (over three million items) and a significantly more prominent international face. But the Tretyakov is Russia's cultural icon. Even the most artistically dormant Russians will stop in at the Tretyakov, if only to check whether the pictures they remember from school textbooks – Savrasov's *Rooks Arrived*, Shishkin's *A Morning In The Pine Forest* and Serov's *Girl With Peaches* – really exist. Less dormant souls will spend days here, marveling in their devotion.

The Tretyakov Gallery got its start when Pavel Tretyakov acquired two paintings in 1856: *Temptation*, by Nikolai Schilder and *A Skirmish with Finnish Smugglers*, by Nikolai Khudyakov. (Tretyakov bought some art before this, in 1854, but these two, in his own words, were the start of his collection.) The museum now counts over 140,000 drawings, sculptures and paintings, and six branches: the main exposition at Lavrushensky 10, twentieth century art at Krymsky Val 10, and four monographic studio-museums. The gallery opens over 20 exhibitions each year and public outreach programs include art classes for children, concerts and lectures.

The staff of the Tretyakov is its living soul, caring for the complex and growing collections with as much care and affection as Pavel Tretyakov himself. In fact, some of the staff have been working here since 1956 – the gallery's centennial – including two Deputy Directors: Lidia Iovleva, and Lidia Romashkova.

"The museum is an institution where people either stay for life or leave right away," said Romashkova, who is now Deputy Director for Coordinating the Conservation of Museum Assets, and who was the gallery's Chief Conservator until 2002. "It is lots of work with huge responsibilities and very modest pay."

Clearly, devotion of staff helped the Tretyakov endure the difficult twentieth century and enter the twenty-first with confidence. Snug and clean after a massive, nearly decade-long reconstruction that ended in 1995, the Tretyakov on Lavrushensky now boasts high-tech electronic information desks, modern, climate-controlled exhibition halls and lavatories with automatic water taps. But such modern amenities camouflage a long and difficult struggle not just to succeed, but to stay afloat.

"The spirit of Pavel Mikhailovich Tretyakov is guarding us," Romashkova said. Indeed, it seems a canon amongst the staff that Pavel Mikhailovich's good karma helped the museum survive the looting of the Civil War, bombings and evacuation during World War II, Soviet neglect and the recent transition to capitalism. "You can't go around Pavel Mikhailovich," she added.

The State Tretyakov Gallery started as a private collection by Pavel Mikhailovich Tretyakov (1832-1898), a Moscow merchant, who in the mid-1850s began collecting art. His first purchases included both Russian and foreign paintings, but soon he developed a vision for bringing together in one place a collection based on "the Russian school, as it is," in order, as he wrote in a letter to Lev Tolstoy, to comprehensively represent Russian art.

Tretyakov befriended the Itinerants (*Peredvizhniki*), a group of realist artists led by Ivan Kramskoy, whose views he shared and whom he supported through donations and acquisitions. By the end of the 1860s, Tretyakov had decided to set up a portrait gallery of Russian "writers, composers and figures of the art world," apparently influenced by the 1865 opening of Britain's National Portrait Gallery. He purchased many portraits by Kramskoy, Repin and Perov, and he commissioned others, including Kramskoy's portraits of Tolstoy and Nekrasov. Tretyakov's collection grew quickly. By 1872, he owned over 150 paintings and had to add a two story annex to his family's home in Lavrushensky pereulok, previously just a small house surrounded by an orchard. In a few more years, two more annexes were tacked on, turning the house into a suite of rooms surrounding an open yard.

From the earliest days, it had been Tretyakov's intention to give his art to the people, and he opened the gallery's doors to the public in 1881. After the death of his younger brother Sergei in 1892, Sergei's excellent collection of French art was added to the Pavel's collection. Shortly afterward, Pavel Tretyakov presented both collections to the city of Moscow. At that time, the Tretyakov brothers' gift numbered 1,287 paintings, 518 drawings, 9 sculptures, 75 paintings and 9 drawings by foreign artists, valued, according to the inventory, at 1.43 million rubles. After Pavel Tretyakov's death in 1898, the Board of Trustees decided to transform Tretyakov's house into a museum. Among many changes in 1904, the decision was made to add a distinctive, Russian styled decorative porch, designed by Victor Vasnetsov.

CONTINUITY RULES THE museum's operation, and the Tretyakov's conservators, who come and go in generations, embody this notion. Romashkova worked as a conservator for just under 45 years, including 19 years as Chief Conservator. "I came when the older generation was still there, the people who preserved the collection during the Revolution, and who kept it through the wild years of the Civil War, those who evacuated with it during World War II," Romashkova said. She still admires her teachers, eagerly sharing the stories she heard on what they had to endure.

In the aftermath of the October Revolution of 1917, the Tretyakov benefitted from having already been State Property for nearly two decades – this may have saved it from looting during nationalization. In fact, the Tretyakov collection had doubled in size by 1922 – as private art galleries were nationalized, most of their collections ended up in the Tretyakov. But revolution back-burnered a 1915 Duma Decree that set forth a plan for the museum's reconstruction. The plan was not revisited until the 1980s, by which time the walls were leaking and the roof was about to fall in.

During WWII, the Tretyakov was evacuated to Novosibirsk and Molotov (now Perm). Within a month of the war's start, on July 17, 1941, thirteen rail cars packed with national artistic treasures were heading for Novosibirsk. There, the collection was stored in boxes in the basement and lower floors of the half-constructed Novosibirsk Opera Theater.

Some of the art was impossible to evacuate from the gallery's building in Moscow, however, such as the statue of Ivan the Terrible (which weighs slightly under a ton), and most of the other large marble and bronze statues. These all stuck out the war in their home at Lavrushensky, covered in sandbags. The Tretyakov Gallery reopened on May 17, 1945.

"The older generation preserved the collection through the war and put it on display again," Romashkova said. "But my generation didn't have it easy, either." Moving house is like living through a fire, as the Russian adage goes. The gallery's second evacuation in half a century came with the long-needed reconstruction of the building at Lavrushensky 10. Romashkova led the effort as the gallery's Chief Conservator. "That was yet another evacuation, but even more comprehensive," she said. "Never before was the entire collection removed from the Gallery."

Reconstruction was long overdue. In the 1950s, by Romashkova's account, a gallery visitor – an engineer, warned the administration that one of the walls was about to collapse and that a protective shield had to be constructed. Then a chunk of plaster fell in right next to Repin's *Ivan the Terrible and His Son Ivan*, escaping the painting by a hair. The ceiling leaked, and the staff had to put pails and mops throughout the gallery.

Things got worse when the walls started seeping water. "We kept running, moving the pictures around, from one hall to another, drier one," Romashkova recalled. "It was horrible! We had to close many halls because they could no longer take visitors." Since most of the conservators are women, Romashkova had to recruit outside volunteers to save some of the larger pieces of art. She would approach male visitors and ask them: "Can you please move this statue a bit, it is under water dripping from the ceiling." She was never refused.

Despite the building's awful state, permission to close down the gallery was not easily won. It took years of complaints and visits to high offices by Tretyakov Director Yuri Korolyov, who took to carrying around in his briefcase a cut out chunk of corroded wiring from the walls, as well as photographs documenting the building's horrendous conditions.

The gallery was too important a landmark to close down – just unthinkable, the Soviet government insisted. International tourists and high profile visitors had to see the prized collection of Russian national art. But of course the gallery continued to deteriorate and Korolyov persisted.

Finally, in December 1982, the state agreed to close the gallery for reconstruction. But of course all of that art had to go somewhere. And so, in less than a year, a depository was built next door to the Tretyakov, on the site of a nineteenth century house destroyed during World War II.

With reconstruction, the museum staff could finally dream of getting things right, instead of making do with what they had. At the depository, they designed in larger rooms, huge doors and elevators, pull-out stands for pictures and easy-roll carts for large, self-standing works – all to make work slightly easier for the predominantly female staff. The Tretyakov also became the first museum in Russia to install a climate control system in both the depository and all of its halls – no more sweating walls in summer and iced-over windows in winter. No more exposing the great works of art to the merciless elements.

The depository connects to the main building via the second floor. This was a labor-saving detail during the evacuation – which actually did not take place until February 1986. But it did not help with some of the museum's bigger works. Alexander Ivanov's *Appearance of the Christ Before the People* would not fit through the passageway, and had to be rolled on a drum and carried through the street. But then it wouldn't fit in the depository's specially-designed, oversized elevators. So it had to sit on that building's ground floor for the entire reconstruction period.

The condition of Surikov's *Boyarynya Morozova* did not allow it to be rolled on a drum. It had to be carried out in a specially-made canvas envelope, eight people on a side. But the crew ran into trouble at the door: the painting was too big to go through. "We stopped and just stood there, at a loss as to what to do," Romashkova recalled. "And I thought, 'They took it out somehow during the war. It's the same door.' We started looking and discovered a covered up opening in the wall that had been made to take the painting out."

In the end, all obstacles eventually fell away, and construction began. Yet then arose a complication of a different kind: in 1991 the Soviet Union collapsed. Everything changed. "We managed to do a lot. We put in the building, did the ceilings, and we had the decoration remaining. And that's where the money ended," said Romashkova. But somehow the staff struggled on and eventually got the support they needed from the State to finish the job. In the end, instead of the planned five years, reconstruction took just under ten. In 1995, the Tretyakov reopened in a new post-Soviet reality it had yet to digest.

LIFE AT THE Tretyakov today is not easy, but it is more interesting than 15 years ago, said Lidia Iovleva, First Deputy General Director. Freed from the need to march in line with a State Ideology, museums can now work more independently, led by artistic value, and not the Party Line. "The freedom that we now have comes with more responsibility for what we are doing," Iovleva said, adding that gallery staff now feel even more accountable to society for preservation of the collection and for the projects they launch.

Yet new times have their own challenges, chief among them finding money. "This is not news for American and European museums," Iovleva said, "but we didn't have it before." Under the Soviet Union, the State paid all the bills. Today, the Russian government does cover the staff's modest salaries, utilities and building maintenance. But the Tretyakov is mostly on its own when it comes to raising money for new acquisitions and temporary exhibitions, where expenses run anywhere from hundreds of thousands to millions of dollars.

Following the lead of other international museums, the Tretyakov now has a Board of Trustees, as well as a Society for the Friends of the Tretyakov Gallery, made up of Russian and international companies, including DaimlerChrysler, Halliburton and Coca Cola, among others. There is even an American branch, established in 2002: American Friends of the Tretyakov Gallery, which combines fundraising with promotion of the gallery in the U.S. But individual membership is still modest. "Shortly after MOMA's reopening in New York, I saw people lining up to buy museum memberships there," Iovleva said. "We don't have that here yet." The growth of a middle class and the country's economic stability may mend this gap soon, along with tax incentives expected to be provided in a forthcoming Law on Art Patronage.

One of the bigger challenges the museum faces is expanding its collection. The State supports some new acquisitions, but purchases are becoming increasingly difficult in the wake of skyrocketing prices for Russian art. "We often have to chip in," said Iovleva. "Part of the money might come from the State, through the Roskultura agency, and then we find sponsors to cover the remainder."

Yet it is hard for the Tretyakov to compete at international art auctions, where prices run in the millions of euros. "But we do buy some pieces for several hundred thousand euros every year," Iovleva said. A recent example is the 2003 acquisition of a landscape by Karl Bryullov, which Tretyakov researcher Yelena Bekhtieva discovered on the island of Madeira, where Bryullov lived from 1849 to 1850. The gallery bought the painting for just over $200 thousand, with monies allocated by a special order of the president. Some of the new art also comes through donations, such as two works by Komar & Melamid and Grisha Bruskin, from the American Friends of the Tretyakov Gallery. Some contemporary artists donate works to the Tretyakov, at the museum's request, said Irina Lebedeva, Deputy Director and Head of Twentieth Century Art.[1] It works out well for both sides: it is quite prestigious for the artist to have his or her works in this "National Collection," and the gallery could not otherwise afford to purchase the art. For its 2006 anniversary, the gallery was expecting new additions to its collection, including *Julia*, a sculpture by Vera Mukhina, from the Russian government, and a collection of twentieth century art from the City of Moscow.

IN 2006, THE Tretyakov hosted more exhibitions than usual, including ones devoted to Russian Symbolism, fourteenth century drawings, French art, Whistler and Alexander Ivanov.

The gallery is also bringing back all of the collection's art from overseas. Foreign loans help the gallery raise money and the iron is hot. "Russian art is in fashion," said Iovleva. "On the one hand, this fashion is supported by the political and economic interest in Russia. On the other hand, Russian museums now have more freedom, and they've become more active in international exhibitions."

Some 213 Tretyakov paintings were included in the Guggenheim's much lauded RUSSIA! exhibit in 2005. "The impact [of RUSSIA!] was the same as after the first tour of the Kirov Ballet almost three decades ago, which introduced Russian culture to Americans," said Alexandre Gertsman, president of the American Friends of the Tretyakov Gallery. RUSSIA! attracted some 400 thousand visitors, breaking stereotypes about Russian art. "Generally, from the American perception," Gertsman said, "there are two main categories of Russian art: Russian icons and Russian

----
1. Lebedeva has since been promoted to the position of Director.

avant garde. This exhibition introduced American audiences to the whole stratum of Russian culture, showing the best of Russian art throughout nine centuries."

The Tretyakov continues to adapt to life in the free world – attracting sponsors, selling gallery-logoed souvenirs, sending exhibits abroad. And, as the Russian economy bathes in the stability brought by higher international prices for oil, the Tretyakov is setting a new, more ambitious goal: construction of a four-story building on Moscow's Kadashevskaya embankment. Still in the planning stages, the building would have a spacious hall for temporary exhibitions, a children's studio, an exhibition of Russian sculpture, (currently kept in the depository for lack of adequate display space), and fuller exhibition of the many Russian icons in the Tretyakov's collection.

The Tretyakov might be sprouting new branches, but it will never leave Lavrushensky 10, its hospitable home for 150 years. This, the long-serving staff say, is simply unthinkable.

May/June 2006

1861

A Gift for Young Housewives
Darra Goldstein

*E*lena Ivanovna Molokhovets was the author of Russia's most famous cookbook, *A Gift to Young Housewives*, first published in 1861. Little is known about her life. Born in 1831 into a military family in the far northern city of Arkhangelsk, she received a good education at a school run by the Imperial Educational Society for Noble Girls. With her husband, an architect, she had ten children. He seems to have been an enlightened spouse who was supportive of her writing. Molokhovets's old age coincided with the turmoil surrounding the 1917 Russian Revolution. She died in St. Petersburg in 1918.

Her cookbook, however, lives on. *A Gift to Young Housewives* went through 29 editions before being deemed too bourgeois for publication under the Soviet regime. Yet families who had a copy of Molokhovets's tome continued to treasure it, and by the 1950s the author had become almost a mythical figure – so much so that she was immortalized in a disparaging poem by the poet Arseny Tarkovsky. During the late Soviet years, when faced with food deficits, the joke-loving Russians often quoted Molokhovets's prescription to go down to the cellar and fetch a joint of meat to serve unexpected guests. Only in the late 1980s, under *perestroika*, were Molokhovets's recipes finally reprinted, and a new edition of her book appeared in 1991.

Until Molokhovets published her book, the only popular cookbooks were those written by Katerina Avdeeva, who had published four of them between 1842 and 1848. *A Gift to Young Housewives* differs from Avdeeva's volumes in that it goes beyond culinary matters to emphasize domestic life. Molokhovets equates an efficient household with a good family life and makes it clear that the responsibilities of a woman are moral as well as domestic. She guides young housewives through the pitfalls of domestic life, and her sympathetic understanding of the daily dilemmas of kitchen management endeared her to her readers and likely accounted for the enormous popularity of her book.

The first edition of *A Gift to Young Housewives* offered fifteen hundred recipes; by the twentieth edition of 1897, there were 3,218, beginning with soups and ending with recipes for fast days, when meat and dairy products were proscribed. The subheadings for the soup chapter alone reveal the book's extraordinary range: Hot Meat-based Soups; Meat-based Pureed Soups; Fish Soups; Butter-based Soups (without Meat); Milk Soups; Sweet, Hot Soups from Milk, Beer, Wine, and Berries; and Cold Soups. The soups are followed by an entire chapter devoted to their accompaniments. There is also an informative chapter on vegetarian cookery. Of greatest interest to the social historian, however, are the detailed sections on maintaining a household, including the treatment of servants, food storage, table settings, kitchen floor plans, etc. *A Gift to Young Housewives* offers great insight into the lives of middle- and upper-class Russians in the nineteenth century, as well as into the evolution of Russian cuisine.[1]

January/February 2006

1. Molokhovets' cookbook is available in English translation (by Joyce Toomre) from Indiana University Press, under the title *Classic Russian Cooking.*

The Spirit Wrestlers of Southern Russia
Maria Kolesnikova

*F*ew in Russia remember the Doukhobors, the pacifist Russian Christian sect championed by Lev Tolstoy over a century ago. In fact, even the name Doukhobor evokes little reaction.

"It sounds funny. Perhaps it is an evil house-spirit?" guessed Mikhail Grishin, 20, an engineering student in Rostov-on-Don. His grandmother, Maria Grishina, 80, a retired schoolteacher, does no better. "Doukhobor sounds like *doushegub* [murderer]," she said. Natalia Trifonova, a Rostov University professor, knows of the Doukhobors. "But they are all gone now," she noted. "To find them you should go to Canada."

In fact, the Doukhobors are not all gone. An estimated 40,000 still live in Russia and the countries of the former Soviet Union. About the same number live in Western Canada, and a few hundred live in the U.S., according to Koozma Tarasoff, a Canadian historian of the Doukhobors and author of 12 books and hundreds of articles about their culture. Scattered around Russia, Doukhobor populations are centered in the Tselina region in Rostov oblast, Cherns region in Tula oblast, near Blagoveshchensk in Amur oblast and the Mirnoye settlement near Bryansk.

Doukhobors (*Doukhobory* in Russian), literally means "spirit wrestlers." It was a name bestowed on the sect – which had previously been known as *Ikonobory* ("icon fighters") – by a Russian Orthodox Church priest (originally, the epithet was *Doukhobortsy* – "wrestlers against the Holy Spirit" – and intended as an insult, but the members of the sect changed it to the more positive *Doukhobory*, which implies a wrestling *with* the Holy Spirit). The sect has its roots in the 1650s, when Patriarch Nikon's reforms of the Russian Orthodox Church led to the *Raskol*, the Great Schism. Some of the schismatics, called *Popovtsi* ("priesters") sought a return to pre-reform traditions, eventually giving way to the movement known as Old Believers. Others, called *Bezpopovtsi* ("priestless"), argued for dispensing entirely with priests. Some went further still, rejecting icons, sacraments, the divinity of Christ and even the Bible. They became precursors of the Doukhobors, who developed into a distinct religious group by the early eighteenth century.

The notion of God within each individual is the cornerstone of Doukhobor belief. "This philosophy has no creeds and does not need any Bible, Church, icons, or priests to fulfill its needs," Tarasoff explained. "From this notion, we support the moral imperative that we cannot kill another human being – because then we would be killing the spark of God in us. The creation of a non-killing society is the essential quest of the Doukhobors."

Not surprisingly, Russia's tsars saw such pacifism as a threat, as something that could undermine social order and lead to rebellion. As a result, the Doukhobors suffered through centuries of persecution and three major resettlements. Under Tsar Alexander I, they were moved to Molochnye Vody, on the border between Ukraine and Russia. Under Nicholas I, they were exiled to Transcaucasia, along the border of Georgia and Turkey. There, in 1895, the Doukhobors refused to fight in Russia's war with Turkey, burning all their weapons in a symbolic protest against war and militarism.

The furious tsar ordered that the Doukhobors be scattered throughout Transcaucasia, "sending the father to one village, the mother to another and their children to yet a different village," according to Doukhobor lore. The Doukhobors pleaded for help. It came from Quakers in the United States, who shared many beliefs with the Doukhobors, most notably pacifism and anti-clericalism. And it came from the Russian writer Lev Tolstoy, whose own personal philosophy had, by this time, gravitated into non-violence. Tolstoy called the Doukhobors a "people of the 25th century." The Doukhobors, for their part, called Tolstoy "our father," after he donated $17,000 from the publication of his book *Resurrection* to help pay for emigration of some 7,500 Doukhobors to Canada in 1898. Despite this mass emigration, the majority of Doukhobors remained; many moved to Southern Russia after the Bolshevik Revolution in 1917.

MY QUEST FOR the Doukhobors takes me to Petrovka, a village in Tselina region, about 100 miles southeast of Rostov-on-Don. In 1921, some 4,000 Doukhobors were permitted to resettle here, establishing 21 villages (consolidated to 11 in the 1950s). Today, there are just six Doukhobor villages. Petrovka is the largest and it is by no means exclusively Doukhobor. Other inhabitants include Russian Orthodox, Armenians and Meskhetian Turks, who fled from Uzbekistan after the collapse of the Soviet Union.

Farther into the country, the asphalt road turns to dirt and cows mindlessly collaborate in the creation of a traffic jam. By the time I reach Petrovka, the dirt road has turned to mud.

Regional administrator Lyudmila Nikitina – my guide in Petrovka – offers a disapproving glance at my sandals as she dons her rubber boots. As we splash together through the mud, she explains that Doukhobors still comprise about half of the village's declining population of 300. "It's not as good as it used to be," Nikitina says. "Young people can't find jobs here and they have to leave."

I examine the streets of Petrovka, looking for traces of Doukhobor culture. Most houses appear to have porches bordered with columns, their whitewashed siding shyly hiding behind trees in the yards. On some, sheds and hen houses share a roof with the house itself. These are traditional Doukhobor homes. Newer ones use brick and have no porches. Some of the houses are well-kept; some are shabby; some are deserted. The streets seem empty, with only two or three middle-aged women digging in their gardens. There are few children and men.

We approach one of the women. "You are a Doukhobor, aren't you?" I ask. She seems proud. "Yes, I'm a pure-blood," she replies. She invites us into her house, to see a typical Doukhobor interior of three rooms with papered walls. "It's more fashionable today than whitewash, as prescribed by tradition," she explains. The house has painted floors, several wardrobes made in the 1970s, a television and lots of embroidery. It smells of ripe apples.

Our hostess is Tatyana Yuritsina, a social worker in Petrovka. "Doukhobors are the nicest, the most hospitable people," she says. "Now there are many refugees and many people of different religions here. But we have no trouble with them."

Yet, life carries on and the Doukhobors are changing. "We used to live without fences," Yuritsina says. "And the young, they don't want to follow Doukhobor traditions. Take my daughter. She's 25, and she won't listen to me, won't stick to the tradition." Yuritsina speculates that her generation may be the last of the "true Doukhobors," because only older members are clinging to their roots.

Many Doukhobors now marry outside the sect. Yuritsina's husband Vasily is Ukrainian; she says she met him in Rostov and brought him back to Petrovka. "I don't mind Doukhobors," he says. "They are people, just like everyone else. And the religion isn't important in the long run. You have to believe in God and not sin. That's all."

THE MUSEUM OF Doukhobor Culture and Worship is a small home dating to the 1950s which was turned into a museum in 1991, thanks to a donation from the local collective farm, Lenin Kolkhoz. It has a collection of Doukhobor artifacts and serves as a place of worship for a few of Petrovka's active Doukhobors.

Today, a dozen Doukhobor women have assembled in the living room, the largest room in the house. Its walls are adorned with embroidered towels and traditional costumes. A table in the far right corner holds a bust of Lev Tolstoy and albums with black-and-white photographs of community members. On the wall are portraits of two Doukhobor leaders, Lukeria Kalmykova and Peter P. Verigin.

The Doukhobor women greet us with a traditional hymn. They are wearing long skirts with fancy, embroidered aprons, colorful blouses and white kerchiefs. Some of their attire comes from their grandmothers; some was adapted from the contemporary clothing bought at a local market. It is the sort of clothing no longer worn in everyday life.

"If you dress Doukhobor-style and walk along the streets, people will look at you as if you were a savage," says Yevdokia Bulanova, 75, a Doukhobor who lives in the village of Khlebodarnoye, five miles from Petrovka.

The women in front of me walked to the museum wearing their regular dresses. They carried their traditional Doukhobor costumes in plastic bags, then changed at the museum, like schoolchildren for a class drama performance. But the reality is that they came here to perform, and they like it.

Their singing seems to erase years of worry and woe from their faces. They have a certain ethereal solemnity. The words of the hymns are hard to make out, enhancing the impression that they are protecting some hidden truths. But the explanation is more down to earth. Years of persecution made Doukhobors in Russia drawl their syllables when singing, so that outsiders could not understand their meaning, says Lyudmila Borisova,

66, a choir member and Doukhobor activist. "Canadian Doukhobors sing much faster," she says, "and one can actually make out the words." Once they have started, the women do not want to stop. Their singing goes on and on. They forget about their hardships, miniscule pensions, cows that need milking, or water that only runs out of the tap a couple of hours each day.

Petrovka's Doukhobor choir once was quite well known. Ethnographers came from Rostov and Moscow to record them singing their traditional hymns and psalms. The choir even toured Rostovskaya and neighboring provinces during the 1995-1998 centennial celebrations of Doukhobor heritage. But the choir doesn't travel anymore. "People are scattered," Borisova says. "We used to have a big choir, but now maybe only a dozen people remain." Some left the village, some are too old to travel, and some are dead.

"Young people don't come to our meetings," Borisova says. "They are busy working and don't have time."

Vera Guzheva, 44, is an exception. Guzheva, who lives in Taganrog, about 170 miles northwest of Petrovka, came to the meeting with her mother, Vera Safonova, who is 77. "My mother is a Doukhobor, but I'm not," says Guzheva. "Our generation doesn't even know who we are."

The other women at the meeting hiss in protest.

"I've lived in the city for 25 years, I am not a Doukhobor anymore," Guzheva responds.

"Who are you then? You are not a Ukrainian, you are not a Belorussian, you are a Doukhobor," Borisova asserts.

"No one in the city knows the Doukhobors. How will I explain to people who I am?"

"You don't need to tell them, you just have to know in your soul that you are a Doukhobor," Borisova says.

After moving to Taganrog, Guzheva had converted to mainstream Russian Orthodoxy, thinking it was more convenient than living as a Doukhobor. During her baptismal, the priest corrected her, saying that the right name of the religion she was giving up was Doukhobortsy, not Doukhobors, a fact she didn't know. "But in my soul I'm a Christian and a Doukhobor," Guzheva says.

Doukhobors in Petrovka nourish Doukhobor legends and revere names like Lukeria Kalmykova and Peter P. Verigin. They remember the rituals, and, during their meetings on major holidays – Christmas, Whitsunday, Easter and St. Peter's Day – they each read a psalm and then all perform a low bow, even though some of the women now need help standing up afterwards. But ask them to explain the essence of their belief and daily traditions, and they may give you a puzzled look.

There is an awkward silence when I pose this question while visiting the village of Khlebodarnoye. Yevdokia Bulanova finally speaks. "We have our *Zhivotnaya Kniga* [Book of Life], and you can read something about it there," she suggests. "Nadezhda, bring it here."

Nadezhda Trofimenko, whose home we are visiting, disappears behind the curtain separating the bedroom and living room, and returns with an old, leather-bound book, which she sets down carefully. "This is the principal Doukhobor document, here you'll find everything," Trofimenko says.

The Doukhobor *Book of Life* is the primary written artifact of Doukhobor heritage, which had been transmitted orally before 1899. Compiled by the Russian ethnographer Vladimir Bonch-Bruyevich while spending nearly a year in Canada transcribing Doukhobor psalms and hymns, the Book of Life preserves Doukhobor oral history and serves as a bible of their faith.

Dr. Vladimir Kuchin, 63, a researcher at Rostov-on-Don's Anti-Plague Institute, has lived in Rostov since 1958. He is a Doukhobor, and in his tiny studio apartment on the city outskirts, he archives a complete collection of the back issues of *Iskra* – the Canadian-published Doukhobor magazine. He also stores trunkloads of Doukhobor recordings and artifacts, which he has been collecting since 1975. He frequently contributes to local papers and to *Iskra*, and he said he is thinking about writing a book on Doukhobor heritage. But he must wonder whom he would be writing for. His own brother and sister have expressed no interest in their Doukhobor roots. And his parents, when they were alive, worried about his fervor for Doukhoboriana. "Dear son, why do you need all this?" they used to ask.

Kuchin's grandparents moved to the Tselina region in 1922. They were in their thirties; his father was 10 and his mother was 8 at the time. At first, people lived in sod houses – 30 people in each home. "Their life was hard, but full of wisdom, patience and good spirit," Kuchin says. When the Soviet state started putting up collective farms (*kolkhozy*), the first Doukhobor

Doukhobor Beliefs

The Doukhobors are a Christian sect that hold beliefs similar to the Quakers. While no short description can be a complete statement of any faith community's beliefs, some of the central tenets of the Doukhobors are:

• Their religious philosophy is based on the two New Testament commandments articulated by Jesus: "Love God with all thy heart, mind and soul," and "Love thy neighbor as thyself." They have many other maxims they adhere to; one of the most popular – coined by Peter Verigin – is "Toil and Peaceful Life."

• The commandment "Thou Shalt Not Kill" is of fundamental significance and dictates a life practice of pacifism and a rejection of military service.

• Allegiance to God supercedes allegiance to state or country.

• They believe that people are capable of divine reason and do not need intermediaries, such as priests, religious ceremonies, liturgies, churches or icons in order to experience God.

• They reject the literal interpretations of the Trinity, Heaven and Hell, original sin and the resurrection of Jesus Christ.

• They believe that bread, salt and water are the basic elements needed to sustain life and therefore of great religious significance. All Doukhobor meetings and important events are held in the presence of bread, salt and water.

• They avoid the use of alcohol, tobacco and animal products for food and stray from involvement in partisan politics.

• Historically, the Doukhobors have at times practiced communal living.

• The Doukhobors do not depend on the Bible or a psalter, and sing their hymns (many composed from the eighteenth century to the present) a cappella.

• Their traditional psalms, hymns and spiritual songs are compiled in *The Book of Life (Zhivotnaya Kniga)*.

kolkhoz – Obshy trud (Joint Labor) was set up in Petrovka, headed by Peter P. Verigin. There followed a *kolkhoz* named after the military commander Vasily Chapayev, and then six Doukhobor villages were united in another kolkhoz named after Vladimir Lenin. In 1928, Doukhobors in the Soviet Union dropped their stricture against army service. "There was no other way to survive," Kuchin says. For the most part, the Doukhobors lived an uneasy peace with the atheistic Soviet State. The government was tacitly permissive toward their religion, as long as the Doukhobors did not openly profess it.

Certainly many Doukhobors were imprisoned and exiled under Stalin. Kuchin recalls one story from Petrovka which reflects the insanity of the times. A villager, Fyodor Tomilin, made a chest for his little daughter's toys and instruments and decorated it with a newspaper clipping that featured, among other things, a picture of Marshal Mikhail Tukhachevsky, a prominent Soviet military leader arrested and executed in 1937 on trumped-up charges of treason. Some time later, another villager, Koozma Pereverzev, stopped by to borrow some tools. On his way out, Pereverzev said, "Such a young guy, and already a marshal." Tomilin had no idea what Pereverzev was talking about. Ten days later, Tomilin was arrested and accused of treason along with Tukhachevsky and his supporters. He was sentenced to 10 years in prison. Tomilin insisted that he did not have any idea who Tukhachevsky was, and that no one by this name lived in this village. Only after several years in prison, when he saw Tukhachevsky's photo somewhere else, did he understand what had happened.

In the 1960s, political liberalization allowed the Doukhobors to be open about their beliefs. "I left my home village in 1958, when I entered Rostov State Medical Institute," Kuchin says. "Even then I didn't conceal my religion from my friends."

Unfortunately for the Doukhobors, Kuchin's example was becoming more typical. The youth left the village for the cities, where they studied, worked, lived, got married and had children. Many married people outside their religion, often assimilating into Russian Orthodoxy. In bigger cities, like Rostov, Doukhobors no longer gather to sing psalms. "Canadian [Doukhobor] visits might stir people up," Kuchin says. "Some people would meet at Whitsunday, St. Peter's Day, and Christmas."

Kuchin says he used to go to Petrovka quite frequently, until his father died in 1999. But he does not go any longer. It is too painful. "The things that have been happening since the 1980s and 1990s are incredible and I can hardly find the right words," he says. "Prosperous Doukhobor villages in Tselinsky and Bogdanovsky regions have become hard to recognize. Suspicious strangers are buying up many homes; other houses are abandoned and falling apart, and yards and gardens are covered in thick weeds."

The Doukhobor cemetery is also covered with thick grass. There, Doukhobor graves, devoid of tombstones and crosses, are marked only by fences with people's names. Anna Sen and Tatyana Safonova lead me to the grave of the five settlers who died during the Doukhobors' first winter in Tselina region. These people are heroes, and a memorial plaque was placed over their grave in the 1960s.

Three years ago, Lyudmila Dorokh, a long-time director of the museum and one of the best singers in the Petrovka choir, told me, "We are losing our identity as a community and the Doukhobor culture here will be gone in several years." She is gone now, lying in this quiet cemetery. And her prediction is slowly coming to pass.

Certainly there are attempts to preserve Doukhobor culture in Tselina region. Canadian Doukhobors visited the museum several years ago and gave $200 for repairs. Regional authorities provided a tape recorder, so that locals might record Doukhobor psalms. "We are trying to preserve the Doukhobor culture, which is unique," says Lyudmila Nikitina, the regional administrator. "Once a year, we bring children from the local school to this museum for a history class, to tell them about the Doukhobor faith and traditions. I wish we could do more before it's too late."

On the way back to the village, we meet other women from the Doukhobor museum. They are walking home, carrying plastic bags containing their traditional costumes. They show us a recently built asphalt road, which gives Petrovka a new, better connection with the outside world, for better or for worse.

September/October 2005

1905: The New Year's Blizzard
Tamara Eidelman

"Whiteness, whiteness across the land, to the furthest corners…"
"Мело, мело по всей земле, во все пределы…"

*T*his famous Boris Pasternak line immediately comes to mind when one thinks of the last days of 1904. At that time, all across Russia it was cold and snowing heavily. On the twentieth of December, all the trains arriving at Moscow's Kursk Station (trains from the South) and Kiev Station (from the Southwest) arrived a full day late; trains coming from the West, into Brest Station, were 15 hours late. At some places in the steppes of Belorussia, the trains simply stood still, unable to get through the snowdrifts.

The city of Zhitomir – far from the northernmost point in the Russian Empire – was completely cut off from the outside world by drifting snow. And then there was Vladivostok: it was not enough that the city was located on the edge of the theater of military operations in the Russo-Japanese War; it was also miserably cold. "It is not the Japanese who are killing us," wrote a journalist from the Far East, "but the prices and the cold."

Cold… snow… the white blizzards blew… the snowstorms howled… and the citizens of the huge Russian Empire were muffled in luxurious fur coats or in pitiful "fish fur" frocks, trying to stoke their furnaces still hotter, warming themselves with a cup of tea or a tumbler of vodka.

In St. Petersburg, they lit special bonfires so that homeless tramps, cabbies awaiting passengers or benumbed passersby could warm up a bit. Local homeowners provided some wood… delivery men bringing fuel to the area were ordered by policemen protecting the fire to toss a few logs into the fire from their carts… soon huge flames blazed in the street, protecting some Petersburgers (for a short time at least) from the cruel frost.

Special teams roamed the city, gathering up people who were lying in the streets, no matter whether they were passersby who had fainted from the cold, or tramps who had drunk until their back teeth were floating. Anyone left on a snow-covered street was in mortal danger.

Yardmen everywhere worked ceaselessly. Every morning they shoveled the snow into massive piles. Toward the city's outskirts, these drifts sometimes lasted until spring; nearer the center, however, the snow was pushed into pits or into specially-constructed, heated boxes for melting the snow, through which flowed hot water exiting from *banyas*. Here, the snow melted quickly, shrouding everything in pearls of steam.

Horse-drawn trams were somehow dragged along their snow-clogged and ice-encrusted rails. Cabbies did not sit up on their seats, but stood on the sledges, in order that it would be easier to drive. People were even transported on special sleds across the Neva.

The snow-blanketed empire was huge and surprisingly diverse. Somewhere, troops marched. Soon they would travel the long path across the empire to battle with the Japanese. Relatives cried from the knowledge of how many soldiers were not returning from this war being fought God knows where for God knows what. Soon, Russia would echo with the strains of a new waltz, *In the Hills of Manchuria*. It would become one of the most popular Russian songs of its day: "The fields sleep, not a single Russian word is heard... A dear mother weeps, a young widow weeps, all of Russia weeps, cursing its fate and fortune..."

Somewhere, poets, artists and musicians were enjoying themselves. Like creative people everywhere, they foresaw the arrival of something terrible – perhaps even horrific. But, because of their typical carelessness, they preferred not to think about this. Or perhaps this foresight brought a certain poignancy and fatalism to life. It was good to spend time in fine restaurants or in the halls of the latest literary and artistic journals, talking endlessly about the fate of Russia, about one's amorous adventures.

Many of the great Russian poets of the twentieth century were already born. Anna Akhmatova was 15, Alexander Blok was 24, Osip Mandels'tam 13, Boris Pasternak 14. Sergei Diaghilev had already organized the "World of Art" exhibitions and was thinking about his future Russian Seasons performance in Paris. The architect Roman Klein was creating a beautiful new building for Moscow, at the request of Moscow University Professor Ivan Vladimirovich Tsvetayev – the Alexander III Museum of Fine Arts [the future Pushkin Museum]. In fact, in December 1904, the papers wrote about the completion of the seventh section of the museum. At that time,

Ivan Vladimirovich was tirelessly traveling to all of the great European museums, gathering an incredible collection of reproductions, in order that young people interested in the history of art, but who did not have the means to travel, could receive a proper education in Moscow.

It was a time of melodic verses, wonderful paintings, unusual music and fantastic theatrical productions. Against this backdrop, none were especially afraid of the arrival of something new. "Let the storm rage sooner!" cried this energetic generation, mimicking the popular young writer Maxim Gorky, who had so successfully described the lives of society's rejects.

In the snow-covered forests of Siberia, workers mined coal and gold, or drilled for oil. Peasants worried what the coming summer might be like, and how to make their stocks last until the new crop came in. Rich merchants accumulated their millions and frittered them away – some on the expansion of their businesses, some on the acquisition of strange, indecipherable paintings by unknown artists. When the children of the industrialist Shchukin were found to suffer from psychiatric maladies, Muscovites as one diagnosed the cause: this is what happens when you live alone and hang on your walls a painting called *Dance*, by some crazy French artist named Henri Matisse.

In the Winter Palace, the close and unlucky imperial family prepared for the New Year. Nicholas and Alexandra – loving and extremely interdependent – already had several daughters. And, in August of 1904, they finally gave birth to the long-awaited heir: Alexei, who turned out to suffer from a strange, incurable disease: hemophilia. Their domestic unhappiness was aggravated by the fact that, across the country, an increasing number of troublemakers were being uncovered. Yet, despite the best efforts of the police, they were not being captured. Of course, the tsar's family did not hear anything about the little-known socialist named Vladimir Ulyanov, who was writing malicious tracts under the pseudonym of Lenin. But he, of course, heard plenty about them and, preparing to ring in the New Year in the company of other political emigrants, dreamed of the day when he would be able to deal with his hated Romanovs.

No one in this huge and strange empire – not the intellectuals or the gendarmes, not the peasants or the gold barons, not the soldiers or the university professors – could have foreseen the abyss which would soon swallow them up and corrode their lives. For now, they more or less unsuspectingly readied for the coming holidays, hoping that 1905 would bring a change for the better. At the end of December, certainly, no particular improvements were apparent.

Russia had been fighting with Japan for nearly a year. Just recently, in December, the main base for Russian troops in Manchuria – the fortress at Port Arthur, which for many months had heroically fought off the Japanese – was surrendered to the enemy. Thousands of Russian and Japanese lives were lost at Port Arthur, and not just simple soldiers, but commanders as well. Vice Admiral Stepan Makarov died in March, when his ship hit a mine just as it was leaving the harbor. The main architect of the defense of Port Arthur, General Roman Kondratenko, was also felled, as was the superb artist Vasily Vereshchagin, who had ventured to the war in order to recreate it on his canvases. It turned out that all these deaths were in vain. Port Arthur was lost, and the war continued.

The papers transmitted colorful reports from the front. While there were no large battles during the winter, reports of losses arrived almost daily. What is more, in the final days of December, the Japanese began transferring arms and munitions to Port Arthur. Needless to say, this news did not fuel optimism for the coming year. One Japanese city did allocate several thousand yen for the upkeep of Russian prisoners, but this report, of course, did not evoke happiness. General Anatoly Stoessel, the commandant of Port Arthur, was still known in the papers as "the hero of Port Arthur, the soul of its defense, the leader of the brilliantly courageous troops, a man, whom, for these eight months, amazed an applauding world." For the public, however, it was increasingly unclear why this hero, despite the presence of "brilliantly courageous troops," and huge reserves, nonetheless lost the fortress. In just a short while, it turned out, Stoessel would be brought up on charges of treason. But for now, despite rumors and gossip, there were no official statements.

The flotilla under the command of Admiral Zinovy Rozhestvensky had left Kronstadt a few months previous and slowly but surely was making its way around Europe and Africa, hoping to reach Japan by the spring and strike a crippling blow. This particular military plan was criticized on many fronts, but the decision was nonetheless taken to send the ships, in order, with this unexpected maneuver, to bring about a swift end to the war. Meanwhile, the sailors prepared for the New Year's holidays.

It was not an easy journey and there had already been a diplomatic scandal, when Russian ships fired on some foreign fishing vessels, having concluded that they were about to attack. But now they were far from snow-laden Russia and heading into warmer waters. Little could they expect that a horrific defeat and almost complete annihilation awaited them in May at the Straits of Tsushima. Few of those who greeted the New Year aboard the flotilla, including Rozhestvensky, would ever see their homeland again.

Everywhere in Russia they were selling maps of military operations, in order that everyone could understand where this strange Manchuria was. Those who wanted to help the families of soldiers could purchase "artistic postcards of the Red Cross," which today we might call congratulatory cards. In the capital, there was an endless chain of humanitarian activities. Grand Duchess Yelizaveta Fyodorovna, who was tireless in her charity work, was the patron of one of the many blood donation depots for soldiers – located in none other than the Great Kremlin Palace itself. Blood donations flowed like a river.

For his part, Sergei Alexandrovich, the Grand Duke and Governor General of Moscow, and Yelizaveta Fyodorovna's spouse, was more interested in the struggle against political troublemakers and in other diversions not in keeping with his marital status. However, he of course could not but encourage his wife's humanitarian efforts. The relative success of this less than happy marriage would not continue much longer. Just a little more than a month into the New Year, Sergei Alexandrovich would perish from a bomb thrown by the terrorist Ivan Kalyayev. Yet Sergei Alexandrovich's widow was somehow strong enough to forgive the murderer, and even to visit him in prison prior to his execution. Yelizaveta, a future saint of the Orthodox Church, would die her martyr's death in 1918. Together with other members of the imperial family, she was shot and thrown into a Siberian mine where, apparently, she survived for a few days, trying to ease the suffering of the other wounded souls.

But at this time, of course, neither husband or wife knew of their future fate. But then who could have expected what was to come? The aridly severe Sergei Alexandrovich knew that revolutionaries were hunting him, and Yelizaveta Fyodorovna was, with each passing year, becoming increasingly occupied in prayer and mysticism, exceeding even her sister – the Empress Alexandra Fyodorovna – in this regard.

The pre-holiday period is an especially favorable time for charity work, since it can be combined with entertainment. On January 1, 2005, a benefit concert for Yelizaveta Fyodorovna's blood bank was held in the

Great Hall of the Moscow Conservatory. Petersburg was not left behind, however, holding a "patriotic exhibition, connected with military events in the Far East." On December 22-23, just before Christmas, there was to be a "grandiose, popular bazaar in the halls of the Noble Assembly." Some 50 benefit organizations took part, offering goods from Paris and London, Christmas toys, games and lotteries and, of course, buffets and kiosks with champagne – with music provided by military orchestras.

In Moscow, the Arbat Theater on Povarskaya ulitsa held benefit events, putting on plays with superbly appropriate names: *The Happy Month of May*, *Criminal Mother*, and *Kiss Me Dear*. These were followed by dances until 3 AM. All the monies from tickets were donated to help wounded soldiers.

The war was going on and on, and gradually became more or less "normal." And yet, Christmas and New Year's always give the impression of a holiday, of joy. At the end of 1904, just as now, regardless of everything, people wanted to be happy and celebrate. Streets in the big cities were brightly illuminated – gaslights were decorated with illuminati configured like stars or crowns, or simply with candles. The dark of winter was illuminated by a multitude of large and small fires.

Winter's parade of *troikas* began. For aficionados, there were whirlwind rides down city streets, preferably with a rosy-cheeked beauty beside you, seductively muffled in furs – for this, it is never too cold. The place you rented a *troika* in St. Petersburg was the Ciniselli Circus. Here, lovers of lively entertainment were engulfed in a fantastic Russian fairy tale. Coachmen waited alongside the circus building, dressed in Russian caftans and wearing *shapkas* with peacock feathers. Sleds were decorated and painted "in the Russian style"; horse harnesses were covered with decorative silver and, of course, their dashing about was accompanied by the sound of little bells. So that passengers did not freeze, the insides of the sleds were lined with carpets. These wonderful contraptions rushed about the city streets, voicing songs and the tinkling of bells, heading to some suburban restaurant or other where gypsies entertained.

Of course, far from all Russians were able to partake of such amusements. Simpler folk had their own way of preparing for the holidays. For one, trade increased. Hostesses began to prepare for the holiday table which, according to tradition, should overflow with abundance, in order to guarantee prosperity throughout the coming year. In Petersburg, crowds packed the largest dockside warehouses, which, for some reason, were called "brawls" (*buyany*). The Herring Brawl and Butter Brawl were both especially popular. Herring was unloaded from huge barrels into the boxes of peddlers, who then launched themselves into the city to ply their goods. At the Butter Brawl, despite the warehouse's name, a brisk trade was done in barrels of cognac. However, not all of the contents of the barrels made it to holiday tables – there were clever craftsmen who would drill holes in the barrels such that barrels sometimes lost as much as half their contents between the warehouse and the storefront.

At this time of year, there was energetic trade in every city center. The New Year's feast traditionally included pork. Pigs are an animal associated with fertility and growth, so they provided not only a tasty meal, but also one that portended of future riches. The feast included pies (*pirogi*) as well. In fact, in those families where village customs still held sway, the host gave the appearance of hiding behind the pies, then asked his wife if she could see him. She answered that she could not, because the "ears" were too high. This obviously superstitious exchange was intended to guarantee a good crop in the coming year.

Of course, Christmas was, at that time, a much more important holiday than New Year's, and people prepared much more for it. In Moscow, on the morning of December 25, festive services were accompanied by a cannon salvo, but on January 1 there were no cannons. Yet New Year's was nonetheless a holiday, and all civil servants were required to wear their holiday dress uniforms.

And then there were the presents associated with Christmas and New Year's and offered by merchants everywhere, for every taste. You could purchase musical instruments for your wife or children – guitars, Viennese accordions or simfonions. You could bring your beloved "Snow Lilies" perfume in order to correspond with the season. Or, on the other hand, you could purchase "Breath of Semiramid's Garden." And, of course, you could buy Christmas tree decorations anywhere – winged angels, gilded nuts and apples, candles... In short, everything that turned the holidays into a fairy tale, then as now.

Obviously, holidays were a time of vacation for students, and rest for their parents. The doors of theater, concert and exhibition halls were thrown open. The pre-New Year's schedule in 1904 was very familiar: *Traviata*, *Swan Lake* and *Sleeping Beauty* played at the Bolshoi Theater. At the Maly, as always, was Ostrovsky's *Sheep and Wolves*. In St. Petersburg, at the Mariinsky, *Traviata* was also on the schedule. Then, on the 2nd of January, after the artists had had time to rest from the holidays, they performed Wagner's *Tannhäuser*. Apparently, at that time, the Mariinsky was less conservative than the Bolshoi.

There were also simpler diversions. In Moscow, just before the holidays, a new aquarium was opened, consisting of 27 smaller aquaria. The scope of this enterprise was possible due to the patronage of Count Orlov-Davydov, who devoted eight thousand rubles to the project – a huge sum at that time. Twelve of the aquaria housed exotic fish and 15 others, placed closer to windows, where it was colder, were home for Russian fish, who were more accustomed to the local climate.

For those not interested in the calmer, more educational amusements, there were always public gatherings at the Manezh. They took place twice daily during the holidays: from noon until 5 PM, and from 7 PM until 2 AM. Apparently, there were plenty of people interested in celebrating. Consider the painfully alluring program: the opera *Askold's Grave*, performances of Gypsy, Russian, Ukrainian and international choirs, presentation of living bas-reliefs, performances of dancers, jugglers and acrobats, the couplet-poets Mr. and Mrs. Shukhman, African plays, Chinese magicians, the musical clowns Bim and Bom, balalaika virtuosos, an American carousel (whether this was the same as the advertised "American slides," we don't know), lotteries and feasts.

Serious people could skip going to see Bim and Bom or hearing the couplets of Shukhmans. They could instead take part, for example, in the activities of the Imperial Moscow Society of Nature Lovers. Their agenda had an important item: constructing tubers of saffron.

One can imagine how the public thronged to such a fascinating session. On the other hand, who knows? But at least nature lovers gathered a few days prior to the holidays. The Fifth All-Russian Congress of Surgeons, on the other hand, met in Moscow on the 31st of December and wound up their meeting only at midnight that day. Apparently, the surgeons were not in a hurry to get home to ring in the New Year.

So that is how December was – cold and snowy, full of news from the front and announcements of new and still newer events and amusements, a time when great works of culture were being created alongside the commission of great acts of villainy. And to everyone it seemed that this is how time would rush forward, mining coal and gold, harvesting grain, building homes... Someday, the war would end and life would take a turn for the better; the emperor would hand down some reforms, or perhaps even a constitution; everything would be fine.

Someone put an announcement in the newspaper, seeking "an intelligent woman with 8-10 thousand rubles in capital," to become the publisher of a respectable journal, which promises a good income. Why a woman, in particular? Perhaps the author of the ad thought that it would be easier to deceive a woman? In neighboring ads, a gardener with 17 years experience and excellent recommendations seeks work, while someone else offers subscriptions to the children's journal *Igrushechka* ("Little Toy"). And a Mr. Velitsyn is thinking, thinking hard in fact, about how to make life more just. He has published "The Triumph of Socialism," dedicated to all Russian socialists and offers it for sale for one ruble.

All of them – the schemer looking for "an intelligent woman," the experienced gardener, the publisher of *Igrushechka*, and Mr. Velitsyn – were seeking a long and happy life. If someone was not certain of the possibility for a quiet life in this snow-filled country, then he could turn to the Russia Insurance Company, which would insure "a trousseau for girls and a stipend for boys, capital for old age and, in the event of death, stipends and pensions for spouses." In 1904, some 81,142 persons insured their futures with this famous insurance company, and, in the coming year, RIC hoped to further increase the number of persons who felt more secure about their futures.

Yet the future was already closing in. It was less than a month before demonstrators in St. Petersburg would attempt to petition the tsar, only to be met by troops, gunfire and streams of blood. All of Russia would be covered with barricades. The revolution would begin. The bomb thrown by the Socialist Revolutionary Kalyayev would tear Grand Duke Sergei Alexandrovich to pieces; the Battleship Potemkin would revolt for God only knows what reason; factories and railways would go on strike; there would be shooting in Moscow's streets. General Rozhestvensky's flotilla would reach the Japanese island of Tsushima in May, heading from there directly to the bottom of the sea. The poets would continue to write their fine verses. Painters would create their canvases, on which masquerades at Versailles would alternate with mysterious Russian landscapes or tall ships from the time of Peter the Great.

And the blizzards and storms would gather greater and greater force, and, before we knew it, a shot would ring out at Sarayevo and the First World War would begin. The Russian tsar would thrice sign a decree on general mobilization, only to twice rescind it, unable to decide whether to begin the war...

The blizzard, in the end, would become bloody, sweeping away the tsar, along with his hemophilic heir, his wife and daughters, as well as, surely, the publisher of *Igrushechka*, Mr. Velitsyn, who dreamed of the triumph of socialism, the experienced gardener with 17 years' experience, the coupletists Shukhman, and the Grand Duchess Yelizaveta Fyodorovna. And, in a few years at the Lubyanka, in the building of the Russia Insurance Company, which had sought to guarantee everyone a peaceful and secure old age, they would install the NKVD. In the basements of this horrific prison, they would torture and kill countless souls. Those with a dark sense of humor would say that once this building had housed "RosInsure," before "RosHorror" took over.

But for now no one knew what was to come. In the courtyard, it was December 1904. The New Year would be here soon, and it was time to buy presents.

January/February 2005

The October Manifesto
Tamara Eidelman

> *Strife and unrest in the capitals and in many parts of Our empire fill Our heart with a great and heavy sorrow...*
>
> *We impose upon the government the obligation to fulfill Our inflexible will:*
>
> *1. To grant the population the unshakable foundations of civil freedom, rooted in the principles of the true inviolability of the individual, freedom of conscience, speech, assembly and union.*
>
> *2. To immediately have those classes of the population that are now completely deprived of elective rights participate in the Duma.*
>
> *3. To establish as a firm rule that no law shall come into force without the approval of the State Duma.*
>
> *We call upon all true sons of Russia to remember their duty to the Motherland, to help put an end to this unprecedented strife, and together with Us to devote all Our efforts to the restoration of peace and tranquility to Our native land.*

So many things had to happen in Russia before such words could be heard...

Tsars had, from time to time, thought about making changes to the structure of government. In the eighteenth century, Empress Catherine created electoral bodies for the nobility and for those living in cities, wishing to accustom her subjects to taking part in the running of the country. Yet the *tsaritsa* could not quite bring herself to give up her own absolute power. She foresaw too many perils down that path – memories of the Pugachev Rebellion and the savage forces it brought to the surface were still fresh.

At the beginning of the nineteenth century, Alexander I had dreamed of giving Russia a constitution, renouncing the throne, and settling somewhere in Germany, on the banks of the Rhine, with his wife. But these dreams remained just that.

As might have been expected, revolutionaries were often ready to take things farther than the rulers. In December 1825, young revolutionaries

TRANSLATION: NORA FAVOROV

filled Senate Square in St. Petersburg with the doomed hope of a
constitution, or perhaps even a republic. Later in that century, members
of the People's Will party embarked on a bloody hunt for Alexander II. In
1881, this tsar – who had freed the serfs and introduced trial by jury and the
Zemstvo, a local elected body – was killed by a terrorist's bomb.

One hundred years were to separate the fanciful dreams of Alexander
I and the moment when his great grand nephew, Nicholas II, signed the
October Manifesto and brought Russia an elected legislature – the State
Duma. The gulf between society and the authorities had been growing.
Students no longer wanted to attend the lectures of professors who held
conservative views. In educated circles, it was simply unseemly not to
sympathize with the revolutionaries. And the authorities were not shy
about the means they used to staunch the growing crisis. After a peaceful
demonstration carrying a petition to the tsar was shot at on January 9, 1905
(Bloody Sunday), there was an uproar: "Freedom, we want freedom!" These
words resounded in the hearts of workers, who refused to go to work, in
peasants, who burned their masters' estates, in lawyers, who defended the
revolutionaries, and in teachers, who instilled forbidden ideas in the minds
of their pupils.

It was as if the smoke of burning manor houses darkened the skies of
Russia, clouding and unsettling the mind.

In the fall of 1905, events reached a certain point beyond which people
were eager to move. Yet, at the same time, they were also afraid of the
abyss that lay beyond. By the end of September, the number of strikers
could be measured in hundreds of thousands. In October, life in Moscow
and St. Petersburg came to a standstill – the trams were not running, the
banks were closed, schools and universities were empty, newspapers were
not being published, the theaters were silent and city water ceased to run.
After the railroads ceased operation, the strike instantly spread to other
cities. The Minister for Railways came to Moscow in the hope of calming
the strikers, and had to drive his own locomotive back to St. Petersburg,
which, being a former railway engineer himself, he was able to do.

Stopped in its tracks, the country waited – what would happen next?
Rebellion, bloodshed, civil war? Dictatorship, punitive detachments, and
more bloodshed?

At this fateful moment, so much depended on the kind, simpleminded,
weak-willed Tsar Nicholas II. He, of course, fully understood the weight of

his responsibility. He simply did not know what to do. Ten months before, Nicholas had made the terrible mistake of giving his consent – either tacit or explicit – to fire on a peaceful demonstration. Now what was to be done? Make concessions to the revolutionaries? He was dead set against this. Troublemakers, bandits and criminals coming from Lord knows where. That was how Nicholas saw them.

Nicholas was completely convinced that Russia was made for autocracy. "I cannot squander a legacy that is not mine to squander," he said. How could he take a course of action that his great forebears had not allowed? And yet, how could the revolutionaries be stopped? As one of Nicholas' intimates put it, "the Sovereign, being a weak man, believed most of all in physical force" – a position not conducive to negotiation and compromise.

The tsar, it would seem, genuinely did not understand that normal people might want to limit his power. He, like many at court, was convinced that only miscreants or their weak-minded followers could oppose the authorities. The notion of dialogue between the authorities and society never took hold.

Yet by October a decision had to be made, and Nicholas pondered it in a state of agony. General Trepov, who had a great deal of influence over Nicholas, tried to convince him to introduce a dictatorship and bring troops into the capital. Count Sergei Yuliyevich Witte urged him to make concessions. Nicholas did not like Witte. This man was a great finance minister. He built railroads, introduced monetary reform, attracted foreign investment. But the tireless minister did not stop at that. He tried to increase the rights of peasants, creating entrepreneurial opportunities for them, and supported liberal reform – as a result of which he lost his post in 1903. But now Witte's time had come.

Nicholas did not want to give in to the strikers, but he also did not want bloodshed. He asked his relative, Grand Duke Nicholas, to take over as dictator, to which the latter replied that he could not turn down the tsar, but he also did not want to doom the nation. Therefore, his only option was to shoot himself. Perhaps these words were what tipped the scales. Grand Duke Nicholas, who had run to the Tsar with pistol in hand, soon left with royal orders to convey: Witte should draft a manifesto. Russia was to be given political freedoms, an amnesty, and a legislature.

It worked. The strikes came to an abrupt halt. Even the wave of violence from extreme nationalists, who were unhappy with the changes taking place, could not dampen the outburst of widespread jubilation. The country began to prepare for elections. Witte was appointed Prime Minister, but after only half a year in office, he would be sent into retirement. In another twelve years, the tsar would be overthrown. In thirteen he would be shot.

September/October 2005

The Tunguska X-File
Tamara Eidelman

There were three of us in the *chum* [teepee] – my husband Ivan and I, and the old man Vasily. Suddenly someone gave our chum a hard jolt. I was startled, cried out, and woke up Ivan, and we started to climb out of the sleeping bag. Again someone gave our chum a hard jolt, and we fell onto the ground. Old man Vasily fell on top of us, as if someone had tossed him up in the air. There was noise all around, someone was making noise and banging on the *ellyun* [the reindeer hide covering of the *chum*]. Suddenly it became very light, a bright sun was shining on us and a strong wind was blowing. Then someone fired a mighty shot, as if ice was exploding the way it does in the winter on the Katanga, and a dancing *Uchir* [tornado] immediately swooped down and grabbed the *ellyun*, started to twist it and spin it and then carried it off somewhere. There was nothing left but the *dyukcha* [frame of the *chum*]. I was scared out of my wits and started to go *bucho* [lose consciousness]; I saw the Uchir dancing. I cried out and immediately came back to life. The *Uchir* dumped the entire *dyukcha* on me and banged up my leg with one of the poles. I crawled out from under the poles and started to cry: the chest with the dishware had been thrown out of the tent and it was lying far away, opened and with many of the cups broken. I was looking at our forest and I couldn't see it. Many tree trunks were standing branchless, leafless. Many, many trunks were lying on the ground. Dry tree trunks, branches, and reindeer moss were burning on the ground. I looked around and saw some kind of clothing burning; I walked up and saw that it was our rabbit-fur blanket and the fur sleeping bag that Ivan and I slept in.

A bright summer night dawned and the fire began to die out. Instead of heat we started to have cold. We decided to move toward the Katanga. All around were wonders, horrible wonders. It wasn't our forest. I had never seen such a forest. It was some kind of alien forest – we had a thick forest, an old forest. And now in many places there was no forest at all. On the mountains, all the tree trunks were lying down, and it was light, and you could see everything off in the distance.

TRANSLATION: NORA FAVOROV

But you couldn't walk through the swamps at the foot of the mountains: some tree trunks were standing, some were lying, some were leaning, some had fallen on one another. Many tree trunks were burned, and the dried sticks and moss were still burning and smoking.

Such were the recollections of an Evenk woman named Akulina about the events of July 30, 1908 in the Siberian taiga. Today, a century later, all the eyewitnesses have passed on, yet, thanks to the dedicated work of scholars, we have their first-person accounts – and plenty of people saw and/or heard the strange explosion that resounded in the sky over the Podkamennaya Tunguska River (the headwaters of which Akulina refers to as the Katanga), a place extremely distant from any city or town.

If you can look past the stories which claim that the Tunguska became littered with doppelgängers – clones separated by several kilometers, or that the Evenk god Ogda flew across the sky, there is great similarity in the many accounts. Clearly there was a tremendous rumble; many people thought that an earthquake had begun; in several places, houses much sturdier than Akulina and her husband's *chum* were shaken and jolted; a bright fire flashed in the sky – some described it as shaped like a sphere, others, like a barrel and still others like a huge, fiery broom.

The fall of the Tunguska meteorite – if this was, in fact, a meteorite – remains one of the most alluring mysteries of the twentieth century, and the ranks of those wishing to solve it are growing rather than shrinking. There are countless explanations for what happened – some harebrained, some with a measure of science behind them. Perhaps a giant meteorite smashed into the earth in 1908, or perhaps it was an asteroid or a comet. Perhaps a tremendous gas bubble escaped from local swamps, or perhaps this was the crash of a spaceship from Mars... And of course the idea that the fire god Ogda may have been chastening people for their defiance has also yet to be disproved.

While each of these versions may have their merits, they all have a little problem. No one has yet formulated a theory that explains all the evidence that has been discovered in the taiga. Unanswered questions always seem to remain; there is always a lingering "but..." Perhaps this is why there is no end to the number of people involved in trying to finally eliminate all these "buts." Enthusiasts from Krasnoyarsk, physicists from Italy and the United States, authors of fantasy literature, geologists, and astronomers continue to grapple with this puzzle.

The human story behind the Tunguska enigma is no less amazing than the enigma itself. Why, after careers as a forest ranger, surveyor, revolutionary, and soldier, did Leonid Kulik suddenly decide to devote himself to the study of meteorites and organize several expeditions to the taiga between 1927 and 1939, expeditions that collected extensive evidence relating to the events of 1908? What motivated him? Perhaps he believed that the New World that was emerging after the revolution had to open uncharted expanses for knowledge and science? Or maybe in the 1930s the taiga was just a good place to hide – away from the bloody Terror and human wickedness? What did the members of Kulik's expedition talk about around the campfire in 1937 – and what were they afraid to talk about? What was foremost on their minds – finding a meteorite or news from home, where their families might disappear without a trace? Or was Kulik simply spellbound by the majestic and mysterious world of the taiga? In addition to his scientific articles, he described his investigation in verse.

The center of the impact I walked all around!
Like a fiery spray of incandescent gasses
And cold bodies
The meteorite smashed into a hollow
With its hills, its tundra, its swamp
And, like a spray of water,
After hitting the smooth surface,
It sent a shower
To all four corners,
And just like that a spray
Of incandescent gasses with a cluster of bodies
Penetrated the earth
And its immediate effect,
As well as
Its explosive reverberation produced
This entire picture of destruction.

Я центр паденья обошел вокруг!
Струею огненной из раскаленных газов
И хладных тел
Метеорит ударил в котловину
С ее холмами, тундрой и болотом
И, как струя воды,
Ударившись о плоскую поверхность,
Рассеивает брызги

На все четыре стороны,
Так точно и струя
Из раскаленных газов с роем тел
Вонзилась в землю
И непосредственным воздействием,
А также
Взрывной отдачею произвела
Всю эту мощную картину разрушенья

Did Leonid Kulik think of this crater as he lay dying in a German prisoner of war camp in 1942? Amidst the horrors of war, how distant the enigmatic tranquility of the taiga must have seemed.

And why, in the 1930s, was the young engineer and inventor Alexander Kazantsev suddenly gripped with the urge to write his first novel, *Flaming Island*? In it, a horrifying environmental disaster that threatens the entire planet turns out to be directly related to a cosmic accident involving, in Kazantsev's vision, the wreck of a Martian spaceship over the taiga in 1908.

Kazantsev's book had all the correct ideological trappings, with villainous American capitalists and Japanese spies pitted against Soviet scientists and soldiers. He was true to the party line to the end of his long life, and the novels he published in the 1970s were unbearably dull. But *Flaming Island* (*Пылающий остров*, which has not been translated into English) has a certain fascination – however diluted – largely thanks to the Tunguska mystery and to the novel's occasional flashes of inspiration, like the sending of space ships to Mars or the threat of planetary suffocation due to a burning atmosphere.

A new spike in interest in the Tunguska meteorite mystery came with its fiftieth anniversary in 1958. This is understandable. The Soviet system had softened a bit – not enough to allow political freedom, yet it was possible to accept and even romanticize "unusual behavior," escape from workaday life and city air, and, consequently, from official structures and ideologized behavior. This is one reason that one of the most romanticized professions at the time was geology, a pursuit that is not, it would seem, an easy one. The image of the geologist was not of someone elbow-deep in dirt who does not see home for months at a time, but someone who dons a sweater and a long beard, and spends time on expeditions, where he plays his guitar and sings around evening campfires. The very word "expedition" – whether geological, archeological, or paleontological – was captivating. An expedition meant freedom; an expedition meant an unusual, extraordinary life. And an expedition seeking to solve one of the great mysteries of our times was doubly alluring.

It is no coincidence that 1959 was the year that the Integrated Amateur Expedition came into being, an endeavor whose participants to this day are striving to solve the mysteries surrounding the events of 1908. The KSE (as its acronym reads in Russian) is made up of a combination of serious scholars and romantic dreamers, along with, of course, oddballs and ordinary people who simply enjoy backpacking through the taiga. You can laugh at them or shrug your shoulders, or you can admire their patience and persistence. But if you were to see the enthusiasm with which they describe how they lug their backpacks along "Kulik's Trail," as the path to the site of the disaster is now known, you would understand the absence of true mystery in most of our lives.

Maybe it really was Ogda flying over the taiga after all?

May/June 2008

The Victory that Wasn't
Tamara Eidelman

By the start of the summer of 1916, World War I had been going on for two years. For Russia, this meant two long years of heavy fighting, primarily against Germany and Austro-Hungary. Thousands of soldiers and officers already lay beneath the earth, and there was no end to the war in sight. Every day, long lists appeared in the newspapers:

Killed: Lieutenant Alfer, Lieutenant Bukreyev, Lieutenant Volobuyev, Lieutenant Gromov...

Died of wounds: Cornet Annenkov, Second Lieutenant Bauer, Major General Bitsyutko, Lieutenant Voytsekhovsky...

Wounded: Lieutenant Abramov (remained in the ranks), Captain Alexandrov, Lieutenant Andreyev...

Furthermore, while the first months of the war had been more or less successful for the Russian Army, 1915 brought stunning defeats. German forces broke through the front and occupied vast stretches of the western Russian Empire. The sense of national solidarity and desire to defend the country that had been felt by almost every Russian at the war's inception now gave way to bafflement and irritation. What was the point of this grueling war? Could it really be all for the sake of some obscure geopolitical interests, incomprehensible to the average Russian? And why was the war being conducted so incompetently?

The newspapers made every attempt to publish reports of amazing "acts of patriotism" and promote heroes like Second Lieutenant Kliopa, who was wounded nine times from 1914 to 1916.

"In August 1914, he received two shrapnel wounds. One of them tore off the phalanx of his left thumb. Another destroyed the nerve of the little finger on his

TRANSLATION: NORA FAVOROV

left hand. After the wounds were dressed, he remained with his unit. He then suffered three wounds: one in his hand, where a bullet ruptured a vein; a second in the abdomen; and a third from a bayonet. In 1915, a hit to his left leg crushed his tibia. With a bandaged leg, Kliopa took part in heavy fighting as the Russians were forced to draw back in 1915. In August, due to complications in the healing of his wounds after wading through a swamp, Kliopa went to an infirmary. He then returned to his regiment at his own request, despite the fact that he was not slated to go back. He had refused a non-combat assignment.

It is not clear whether this tale elevated the fighting spirit of other soldiers or increased their longing for the end of the war, which seemed ever more elusive.

Politicians increasingly hinted at treason and betrayal at the highest levels. Absurd rumors spread among the people: "The tsaritsa is German. She is obviously spying for her people. Her lover, Rasputin, is probably helping her." Who could convince them that Empress Alexandra, while she had indeed been born in Germany, had grown up in England and, since ascending the Russian throne, saw herself as a truly Russian and Orthodox sovereign? Who would believe that the Siberian peasant Gregory Rasputin – who through a strange twist of fate had wound up at court treating the hemophiliac heir to the throne – was seen by Nicholas and Alexandra as a holy person, and that they would not believe incriminating tales about him? The idea of an affair between the tsaritsa and Rasputin would have seemed to them a total absurdity.

Then, just when it appeared that the country was falling apart at the seams, things began to look up. By the beginning of 1916, the economy was improving. Russia's military command was starting to contemplate striking back at the German and Austrian armies. But, while the general command was focused on planning to strike at German forces (which were positioned along the upper half of the Eastern front), decisive actions taken further south, by the commander of forces facing Austro-Hungarian armies, changed everything.

Alexei Alexeyevich Brusilov was a distinguished officer from a venerable military family. In 1916, he was already over 60 and battle-hardened. The area he was commanding was not viewed as the primary focus of conflict – he was in charge of the Southwestern Army Group, which was battling the Austrians. But, during the summer of 1916, Brusilov's unexpected successes and the sudden advance of his troops thrust him into the limelight.

Suddenly, after a year of misfortune and reversals, the Russians were taking over town after town. Jubilation swept the nation. Newspapers proclaimed that "Vast numbers of telegrams are pouring into the Petrograd Telegraph Agency from different cities of the Empire, telling of church services held in celebration of the victories of our valiant troops. In many towns, church services were followed by military parades. Telegrams from loyal subjects come one after the other with expressions of patriotic fervor."

Renewed optimism was shared by Russia's allies, who had also been mired in heavy fighting. "With every day, news of Russian successes is more remarkable, more enthralling," was the sentiment expressed in English newspapers. In Paris, an official Russian communiqué was read at the matinee of the *Opéra Comique* and greeted by a rousing ovation. The audience stood for both the Russian anthem and the Marseillaise.

Newspaper advertisements in the summer of 1916 were an odd mixture of the realia of war and peace.

Now available: *War Silhouettes*, a collection by combat participant M. Lisovsky.

A new book by I.B. Smolyaninov, Camouflage (war stories).

The Triangle Company manufacturers all surgical and first aid supplies essential for infirmaries and hospitals.

Available for purchase: the best gift for the Russian soldier in captivity: powdered eggs.

At the same time, Heinrich Weiss & Company announced that it was discontinuing production of its line of elegant footwear:

All remaining stock is being sold at a 10 percent discount.

One can certainly understand Heinrich Weiss & Company – it was hardly a time for elegant footwear. What was there to dress up for?

But life went on. A new book was released: *Field Guide for the Young Naturalist*; advertisements announced the availability of

Garrett English locomotives, tractors, English oil engines, steam engine threshers.

And, despite the war, entertainment was still available. One could go to see the farce *Our Kept Woman*, or the comic play *War with Mother-in-Law*. An announcement offered the lease of

> Three or four marvelously-furnished large rooms in Petrograd with a view of the street and the option of a fully-equipped kitchen to a respectable gentleman.

(It also stated that the apartments featured electricity, telephone, and bathrooms. Evidently, these amenities were not yet to be taken for granted.) A man advertised his availability as a chauffeur, describing himself as "highly-cultured and free of all military obligations." "Healthful suppers" were advertised for those "who value their health." And summertime had come. A single man or woman wishing to get out of the city could rent a room in Gatchina (meals optional) with an "educated family."

The Brusilov Offensive raised hopes for better times to come. Soon, elegant footwear might again be appropriate and there would be no need to ship powdered eggs to prisoners of war.

Brusilov's armies marched through Galicia and needed reinforcements. But before the ponderous bureaucratic machinery was able to grasp the situation, before it was understood that reserves should be sent to the southwestern front, the offensive had come to a standstill. The front was quiet. Brusilov's hard-won successes had been squandered. This was the summer of 1916. Grishka Rasputin, who would be murdered in December 1916, had just a few months to live. Indeed, the centuries-old Russian monarchy was in its last months. It would fall in February 1917.

This was the last summer for quite some time that an educated family would be able to spend a peaceful summer at their dacha in Gatchina. What would happen to them in a year? Would they be caught up in the whirlwind of change? Would fate take them away from Russia forever? Would they die of typhus, as so many did during the Civil War? What would happen to the "respectable gentleman" renting the marvelously-furnished apartment? Would his dwelling be seized by revolutionary sailors? And whose side would the courageous Second Lieutenant Kliopa be on (assuming he lived another year and did not die of one of his many wounds)?

Would Captain Alexandrov and Lieutenant Andreyev recover from their wounds? Perhaps they would be killed by their own soldiers, whom they were urging to continue fighting a war that seemed long since lost. Or perhaps they would flee to the Don River, turning on their new Bolshevik commanders and eventually perishing on Civil War battlefields. And who would the highly-cultured chauffeur be driving now?

In the summer of 1916, catastrophe was just around the corner. For now, General Brusilov's armies were conducting their offensive. Their commander would go on to be put in charge of the entire Russian Army and would make one last futile attempt to organize an offensive. After the Revolution, he came out of a brief retirement to serve the Bolsheviks, dying in 1926 – in a country that looked nothing like the one he fought so hard to defend during the summer of 1916.

May/June 2006

When Things Fall Apart
Tamara Eidelman

February 18, 1917 (March 3, new style)
   Workers at the Putilov Factory in Petrograd go on strike.

The **Putilov Factory**, manufacturer of trains and munitions, was one of Russia's industrial giants. Founded in 1801 as a state factory, it was purchased in 1868 by the engineer Nikolai Putilov. After the revolution, it became the Krasny Putilovets [Red Putilov Worker], and in 1934 it was renamed for the recently-murdered Leningrad party boss, Sergei Kirov.

February 23
   Unrest flares up in bread lines. More and more of Petrograd's population is joining riots started by women tired of queuing for food.

> *A great throng of workers pours through a grimy working-class district. Another throng joins them from a side street. Lots of women, and they're the angriest of all. By the time they pass a one-story factory, they're a crowd of hundreds – they themselves don't know what they're doing. It's up in the air. Workers are watching them through the glass, through the ventilation windows. The crowd starts to shout.*
> *"Hey you, munitions worker! Outta' there! Come join us. Bread!"*
> *They stop by the windows to urge them on.*
> *"Enough, munitions worker! How can you work so long as we got these lines? Bread!"*
> *For some reason, the munitions worker doesn't care, he even walks away from the window.*
> *"Uncaring bitches! You're sittin' pretty, is that it? So, every man for himself? I'll tell you what – the glass! The glass!"*
> *The smashing of glass. A big guy, a foreman steps outside, without a hat.*
> *"What kind of fooliganism are you up to? We all have our own heads. You think we're making ourselves corn hoppers in here?"*
> *Someone launches a chunk of ice at him. "Your own head?"*

TRANSLATION: NORA FAVOROV

The foreman clutches his head.
The crowd guffaws.

March 1917
Alexander Solzhenitsyn

February 24-25

A general strike begins in Petrograd. From the memoirs of Pavel Milyukov:

> On February 23, when up to 87,000 workers at 50 enterprises went on strike because of the bread shortage, Protopopov asked Khabalov to tell the people that, "There is enough bread," and "The unrest has been stirred up by provocateurs." On February 24, 197,000 workers went on strike. Khabalov announced that "there should be no shortage of bread." Apparently "a lot of people are buying bread to store as rusks." The government decided to "delegate the problem of food to municipal authorities."

Pavel Nikolayevich Milyukov was an outstanding Russian historian and leader of the Constitutional Democratic Party, known as the "Cadet" party. March 1917, when he was appointed foreign minister of the provisional government, was the apogee of his political career. But by the end of April he was forced to resign because of what came to be known as the Milyukov Note, in which he promised the Allies that Russia would uphold tsarist commitments to prosecute the war against Germany to its conclusion. After the Bolshevik victory he left for the Don region – a destination for many fleeing Bolshevik control – and then went to Kiev, where he tried to negotiate with the German command, hoping to win their support against the Bolsheviks. These negotiations outraged the majority of Cadets and Milyukov stepped down as party chairman. Later, from emigration, Milyukov called on his comrades to accept the changes that had taken place in Russia and abandon any hope of a military overthrow of the Bolsheviks. He counted on the internal degeneration of Bolshevism and a rebirth of the empire. He died in 1943 in France.

Alexander Dmitriyevich Protopopov, who had been active in provincial self-government, serving in the *zemstvo* and as a district marshal of the nobility, was a member of the Octobrist Party and a deputy in the third and fourth Dumas. He was also active in many charitable organizations and the Russian Geographical Society and authored a number of technical books on the textile industry and agriculture. In 1917, he was Internal Affairs minister. He worked out a plan to prevent riots in Petrograd by dividing the city into districts and putting Guards units in charge of each one. During the final days of February, the other ministers wanted to remove Protopopov from the government, given his extreme unpopularity and the fact that his name alone was an obstacle to reaching agreement with the Duma. They were hesitant to do this, however, and merely announced that Protopopov had fallen ill. On February 28, the minister himself came to the Tauride Palace, where the Duma was meeting, and was detained. The next day he was imprisoned in Peter and Paul Fortress. After the Bolsheviks came to power, Protopopov was hospitalized with a "nervous disorder" and later moved to Taganka prison. In 1918 he was shot.

February 25, evening

A telegram from the tsar to Khabalov reads

Hereby command to put an end to riots in capital, impermissible in time of war with Germany and Austria.

Sergei Semyonovich Khabalov, the general in charge of the Petrograd military district in February 1917, attempted to put down the uprising, but his troops did not obey his commands. On February 28 he was imprisoned in Peter and Paul Fortress. In October 1917 the case against him was dropped, days before the Bolsheviks took power. In November, Khabalov was dismissed from the army, and in 1919 he left for the South of Russia. In 1920 he emigrated to Salonika, Greece. He died in 1924.

February 26

A clash takes place between revolting soldiers and troops loyal to the government. A February 26 telegram from Rodzianko to the tsar:

The situation is serious. The capital is in a state of anarchy. The government is paralyzed; the transport service has broken down; the food and fuel supplies are completely disorganized. Discontent is general and growing. There is wild shooting in the streets; troops are firing at each other. It is urgent that someone enjoying the confidence of the country be entrusted with the formation of a new government. There must be no delay. Hesitation is fatal.

Mikhail Vladimirovich Rodzianko was one of the founders and leaders of the Union of October 17, otherwise known as the Octobrist Party. In 1917 he was chairman of the Duma. Tsarina Alexandra had a strong dislike for Rodzianko, which complicated interactions between the Duma and the government. Via telegraph, he conducted negotiations with the Army Headquarters that culminated in the abdication of Nicholas II. He did not serve in the Provisional Government, remaining chairman of the Duma until it was dissolved in October 1917. After the Bolsheviks took over, he went to the Don region and became one of the founders of the White movement. He later emigrated to Yugoslavia and died in 1924.

February 27

Troops in Petrograd begin to support the rebellion. The Provisional Committee of the State Duma is created.

February 28

The tsar attempts to return to Tsarskoe Selo from Army Headquarters in Mogilev, a town in present-day Belarus, but he is unable to, because the railway lines have been blocked.

March 1

The tsar arrives in Pskov, where he hopes to find support from General Ruzsky, commander of the northern front.

Nikolai Vladimirovich Ruzsky, the general commanding the northern front in 1917, along with other commanders, put pressure on Nicholas II, forcing him to abdicate the throne. In April 1917, Ruszky was forced to step down for health reasons, although his resignation was probably also precipitated by the impact political turmoil was having on the army. He underwent treatment in the spa resort of Kislovodsk in the northern Caucasus, and in September 1918 was captured by the Caucasus Red Army. In October 1918 he was shot, after being forced to dig his own grave.

From the memoirs of General Brusilov:

I received detailed telegrams from headquarters reporting on the course of the rebellion and finally was called to a direct line by Alexeyev, who told me that the newly-formed Provisional Government had informed him that if Nicholas II refused to abdicate, it was threatening to cut off the army's food and munitions supply; therefore Alexeyev asked me and all the top commanders to telegraph the tsar asking him to step down. I told him that from my perspective this measure was essential and that I would immediately do as he asked and right away I sent a telegram to the tsar in which I asked him to renounce the throne.

Alexei Alexeyevich Brusilov was the general who orchestrated the renowned Brusilov Offensive in 1916. After commanding the southwestern front in early 1917, in May-June 1917 he was made Army Commander-in-Chief. He attempted an offensive that failed because the army was already in a state of complete disarray. He was removed from his post to make way for an advocate of harsher measures, Lavr Georgiyevich Kornilov. Brusilov lived in Moscow, and in 1920 he agreed to serve under the Bolsheviks. He died in 1926. Soviet historians have always held Brusilov in high esteem.

Mikhail Vasiliyevich Alexeyev was the son of a career soldier who advanced to the rank of general. After serving as chief of staff for the Commander-in-Chief, from March through May 1917 he was put in charge of the Russian army, in which capacity he attempted to halt its disintegration. Soldier self-governing committees were being established throughout the army, undermining discipline. Alexeyev believed that if such committees were being created, they should include officers, who would be able to influence the soldiers. After the Bolshevik takeover, he left for the Don region, where he was one of the founders of the White movement. He created the Volunteer Army, with whom he endured the difficult Ice March, a retreat across the frozen Don steppe in the dead of winter. He died of heart disease in September 1918 in Yekaterinodar (present-day Krasnodar). He was laid to rest in Belgrade.

March 2

The tsar decides to abdicate the throne. The rightful heir is his son Alexei.

Tsarevich Alexei Nikolayevich was the sole, long-awaited son of Nicholas II, born in 1904 after being preceded by four sisters. It soon became evident that the boy suffered from the incurable disease of hemophilia. Tsarevich Alexei was shot along with his parents and sisters during the earliest hours of July 17, 1918 in Yekaterinburg.

306 *Best of Russian Life: History and Culture*

The evening of March 2, at the train station in the town of Dno, where the tsar's train had been blocked from continuing, two envoys arrived representing the Duma: Alexander Guchkov and Vasily Shulgin.

Alexander Ivanovich Guchkov lived a life that was not at all typical of his time. He was born into a merchant family and went on to receive an excellent education at the universities of Moscow, Berlin, Vienna, and Heidelberg. He nonetheless chose a military career, which proved tumultuous. He served in the Guards, fought on the side of the Boers in the Boer War, found himself in China during the Boxer Rebellion, and was a representative of the Red Cross during the Russo-Japanese War. Guchkov's stormy nature manifested itself in his passion for dueling, a practice that was out-of-date by his time. He nevertheless achieved success as an entrepreneur and became a millionaire. Guchkov was active in politics and was one of the founders of the Union of October 17. In March 1917, he became Minister of War, but in April he was forced to step down together with Milyukov, with whom he shared the belief that Russia should continue to fight Germany. Guchkov remained active politically, feeling it was essential to oppose the Bolsheviks. He supported Kornilov, and was even arrested after Kornilov's 1917 rebellion was suppressed, but was released the following day. Soon after the Bolsheviks took over, Guchkov left for the Caucasus. He was the first industrialist to provide financial support to the White movement. In 1919, Guchkov went abroad to represent Denikin in negotiations with the Entente nations. Later, in emigration, Guchkov's independent nature prevented him from finding a place within any particular political party. He died in Paris in 1936.

Vasily Vitaliyevich Shulgin was one of the most extraordinary Russian conservatives. He was a proponent of extreme nationalistic views, but at the same time he did not fit the stereotype of a "rabid nationalist." He published a newspaper named the *Kievlyanin* [Kievan], where he defended the idea that Ukraine was a Russian land. A highly-cultured, well-educated man, he was nonetheless a stalwart advocate of absolute monarchy. An opponent of anti-Jewish pogroms, he nonetheless inflamed passions with his anti-Semitic articles during the infamous 1913 trial of Mendel Beilis, a Jew accused of ritual murder. After the February revolution, Shulgin first and foremost urged that strong central authority and the territory of the empire be preserved. When the Bolsheviks came to power, Shulgin, who was living in Kiev at the time, devoted his considerable energies and talents to supporting the White cause, which he saw primarily as a monarchical and Russian movement. After the conclusion of the Civil War he emigrated, however he spent some time in Russia during the 1920s, sneaking into the country illegally. In 1944, Shulgin was arrested in Yugoslavia and sent back to the USSR, where he was imprisoned in a labor camp until 1956. It is interesting that, by then, Shulgin's attitude toward Soviet rule had changed. He now saw in it a transformed continuation of the absolute monarchy in which he so fervently believed. Shulgin died in Vladimir in 1976 at the age of 98.

Nicholas gave Guchkov and Shulgin his signed abdication proclamation.

In the days of the great struggle against foreign enemies, who for nearly three years have tried to enslave our motherland, the Lord God has seen fit to send down on Russia a new heavy trial... In these crucial days in the life of Russia, We thought it Our duty of conscience to facilitate for Our people the closest union possible and a consolidation of all national forces for the speedy attainment of victory. In agreement with the Imperial Duma We have thought it befitting to renounce the Throne of the Russian Empire and to give up supreme power. As We do not wish to part from Our beloved son, We transfer succession to Our brother, Grand Duke Mikhail Alexandrovich, and give Him Our blessing to accede to the Throne of the Russian Empire... May the Lord God help Russia!

Signed: Nicholas

Pskov, March 2, 1917, 3 pm

Until the birth of Tsarevich Alexei, Nicholas II's younger brother, Grand Duke Mikhail Alexandrovich, had been considered heir to the throne. Until 1912, he had been second in the line of succession. However, when he married a woman of insufficiently exalted lineage (and on top of that a divorcée), Nicholas II revoked his right of succession and banished him from Russia.

There are several different accounts of Mikhail's demise. One has him being shot in 1918 together with the other Grand Dukes in Perm. It is said of him (and not only of him) that before being shot he took off his boots and threw them at his executioners with the words, "Wear them, kids, they are, after all, royal." According to another account, Mikhail was killed without trial along with his secretary. There is also a version that ends with the miraculous survival of Mikhail. Pretenders have appeared over the years claiming to be the Grand Duke.

One day after assuming the throne as the last Romanov tsar, Mikhail also abdicated:

> A heavy burden has been laid upon me by the will of my brother, who has given over to me the imperial throne of All Russia at a time of unprecedented warfare and popular disturbances.
>
> Inspired by the thought, which is shared by all the people, that the good of our native land is above all else, I have taken a firm decision to assume the supreme power only in the event that such is the will of our great people... Therefore, invoking God's blessing, I ask all citizens of the Russian state to pay allegiance to the Provisional Government, which is to be endowed with full power until such time as the Constituent Assembly, which shall convene as quickly as possible, takes its decision on the form of government as expressed by the will of the people.

March 3, 1917
Signed Mikhail
Petrograd

March/April 2007

The Body Politic
Roy Medvedev

Throughout its seventy-year history, the political health of the Soviet Union was seen, both in the West and in Russia, as a reflection of the personal health of its leaders. From Lenin's arrested vision to Brezhnev's slurred speech, the true health of Russia's communist leaders was a closely-guarded state secret, ever the subject of rumors, jokes and speculation. Only in recent years have secret archives been opened, so that information about past leaders' health could become available.

*I*n order to survive the many carnivorous power struggles endemic to climbing the political ladder in the Soviet Union and the current Russian Federation, virtually all Soviet and Russian leaders had to be vigorously healthy when they were young. The battles they engaged in, against ideological rivals and foes, required almost superhuman energy and efforts. Such demands on an individual's health were intensified by the fact that, once obtained, the totalitarian crown required a single person to tackle all the problems the country might face.

At the same time, the ideological nature of power, the absence of any natural methods of succession and the top man's multiple roles as head of state, head of Party and Commander in Chief meant that the leader could often stay in power until the end of his political, and physical, life. Once power was achieved, men usually held onto it long after their best years had passed.

In fact, absent free elections or an open political process, the country's political stability demanded immortality. Lenin's waxy corpse, the Muscovite Mecca of countless pilgrimages for the faithful, is a case in point. Eternal life was necessary because shake-ups in the Kremlin made people, both Russians and foreigners, nervous. In this new Egypt of undead idols, it was far easier to keep resurrecting a controllable mannequin, who could be counted on, than to train someone new.

The only Soviet leaders who did not die in office, Nikita Khrushchev and Mikhail Gorbachev, were both good old boys who harbored revolutionary tendencies. And both fell victim to the "extraordinary circumstances" of their own invention. Yet their fellow General Secretaries were determined to prolong, however artificially, the fading system which had given them so much. For the sake of unlimited power, with all of its obscene perks and pleasures, these men sacrificed their health, their ideals and, ultimately, their country.

Lenin is Always with Us

Vladimir Ilyich Lenin was no stranger to sacrifice. A dedicated revolutionary who worked non-stop for his cause and comrades, Lenin would eventually live to usher in the Revolution, but not to save it from those who would manipulate it to further their own ends. The very events that enabled him and his party to come to power would eventually take their toll on his personal health, reducing him, in a few years, from an active Bolshevik to an invalid.

During the October Revolution and the ensuing civil war in Russia, Lenin worked almost continuously under huge pressure. Society was re-fashioning itself in his image and Lenin's obligations to that society could not but exhaust him. He was everywhere at once: guiding, threatening, maneuvering, cajoling and, of course, leading the masses.

The Beginnings of Mortality

When he was just past 50, he began to show symptoms of cerebrospinal sclerosis. This disease was compounded by his grueling daily schedule, as well as the lasting physical effects of Fanny Kaplan's 1918 assassination attempt on his life.

Yet, in spite of his worsening condition, Lenin remained firmly in control as the idealized father of the Party, the one human being who could maintain a firm hold over the Party's numerous, quarreling and ambitious revolutionaries. Yet his illness became increasingly pronounced, and Lenin was forced to move to Gorki, a retreat near Moscow. He took up residence there on December 13, 1922. Hoping for a quick return to the Kremlin, he refused to give in to his doctors' wishes and retire from politics. During his first days at Gorki, Lenin worked several hours a day, but frequent and acute pains, as well as a heightening exhaustion, compelled him to limit his activity first to 15, and then 10 minutes a day. He used that time to dictate articles and letters to his devoted sister, Maria Ulyanova, and to his wife, Nadezhda Krupskaya.

In these final years, Lenin was especially concerned with the problem of naming a political heir. Lenin had achieved Party leadership because the people considered him to be the living embodiment of the Bolshevik cause, in all its flaws and virtues. But afterwards?

Stalin, among others, was acutely aware of the possibilities created by Lenin's death. To realize his goals, he, under the guise of Bolshevik loyalty and friendship, "protected" Lenin's failing health by severely limiting his movements, screening his contacts, and isolating him from the day-to-day activities and decisions of his comrades. Increasingly cut off from the political realm he had given so much to, Lenin's health continued to ebb.

Lenin lived, Lenin lives, Lenin will live!

This decline was aggravated on March 9, 1923, when Lenin suffered a severe stroke, or cerebral thrombosis. After Lenin's right leg and arm were paralyzed, his consciousness dimmed and he lost the ability to speak. Leading German and Swedish neurologists and hematologists were asked to treat Lenin. Special news bulletins were issued on a daily basis, keeping the whole country informed about Lenin's health.

By the autumn of 1923, Lenin began to show signs of improvement; he was able to communicate by means of gesticulation and he even regained his motor skills somewhat. Hopeful that Lenin would pull through, the entire USSR was shocked to hear of his death on the evening of January 21, 1924.

Exhibiting methods that would soon become ritual, Joseph Stalin was lead pallbearer of Lenin's coffin and spoke eloquently at the graveside of the man he had, slyly, helped to eliminate.

With Lenin safely dead, the path to power was clear.

Graven Idols

Stalin was notorious among his comrades for his mental strengths, for his seemingly tireless ability to work long hours and for his amoral appetites. Prone to arduous work days and nocturnal habits, Stalin usually rose late, then worked at his Kremlin office, nicknamed "the little corner," until 2 or 3 AM. Government employees, in fear for their lives and careers, only dared to leave their offices after he had.

Stalin had never been a particularly healthy man. Since childhood he had had to fight to stay alive. At the age of seven, he contracted smallpox. Yet he survived (his three brothers all died from childhood diseases). The disease left his face scarred, but he was alive. As he got older, he knew he was an unprepossessing sight, with his short stature and pocked face (he is also reported to have a withered left arm, for reasons that are in dispute, and an imperfect left foot, on which two toes were joined). At the age of 27, he was pronounced physically unfit for military service during a general mobilization. Still, he possessed a formidable intellect. And intelligence more often than beauty is a means to power. After rising to power, he would be seen only in specially produced photos or newsreels, which smoothed his pock-marked skin, hid his diminutive size and muscled his left arm. He was the distant but adored father of millions – millions whom he feared and loathed.

The Lion in Winter

Stalin's heavy pipe-smoking and drinking, combined with his ever-worsening paranoia and destructive habits, destroyed his precarious health. Besides arterial sclerosis and high blood pressure, he suffered from terrible headaches and increasingly numerous attacks of dizziness. Justly suspicious of all those around him, and fearing for his life, he avoided confiding in anyone or seeking medical treatment, unable to believe that anyone could, or would, help him. As his daughter Svetlana Alliluyeva wrote, "He knew and understood that he was hated, and he knew why."

Instead, he put his faith in his long-lived Georgian ancestors, hoping that he would follow in their footsteps. At the most, he sometimes dissolved iodine into a glass of boiled water, and drank that after dinner. This "medicine" of course, did not help him. In 1949, Stalin had a stroke which brought on a partial loss of speech.

Aware that he had to change his life somewhat if he was to live longer, Stalin stopped reporting to the Kremlin for weeks, preferring to work at the "Near" (in Kuntsevo) or "Far" (in Volynskoye) *dachas*, surrounded by his faithful lackeys: Georgi Malenkov, Lavrenty Beria, Nikolai Bulganin and Nikita Khrushchev. He spent the fall and early winter months at his southern residences, either in the Crimea or on Lake Ritsa, in the

Abkhazian mountains, avoiding his home near Moscow in the wintertime, because of respiratory difficulties.

Killers in White

In 1953, Stalin transferred his fear of doctors to the nation as whole, with the infamous "Doctor's Plot," when he had his (mainly Jewish) Kremlin doctors arrested on the contrived charges of having murdered a number of Soviet officials on Zionist orders. Unfortunately for Stalin, his new doctors, Russian to a man, did not know him or his medical history, and terrified, were unable to do anything. However, after so many years spent ignoring the advice of his physicians, it is unlikely that Stalin could have ever become truly healthy. His vile activities had taken their spiritual toll on his maligned body and soul.

In his brilliant biography of Stalin, *Stalin: Triumph & Tragedy*, Dmitri Volkogonov put forward the idea that "earlier disturbances of brain function had caused numerous cavities, or cysts, in the brain tissue, especially in the lobes." Volkogonov further suggested that "such changes would have been responsible for changes in the psychological sphere, making an impact on Stalin's despotic character and exacerbating his tyrannical tendencies."

The God Is Dead

Joseph Stalin's death on March 5, 1953 was a fitting cap to his grotesque existence. Following a late night party with his closest henchmen that lasted until 4 a.m., Stalin suffered a stroke while alone in his room in the early morning of March 2, 1953. Since his household staff was too terrified to enter his suite without being summoned, Stalin was left to lie, alone, in pain on his bedroom floor for almost an entire day and night. When, at 11 PM. on March 3, one of his bodyguards finally found the courage to check on his boss, he found him on the floor, pale and barely breathing.

The deathly farce continued, since, without Marshal of the Soviet Union Beria's permission, nothing could be done to help the Leader. But Beria, out drinking with one of his numerous conquests, was only found much later that evening. A victim of his own legendary bureaucracy, Stalin was left to suffer, surrounded by his helpless staff and children.

When Beria did arrive, he was drunk and belligerent. Either not willing to acknowledge what had happened, or hoping to use the Leader's death to propel himself to power, Beria screamed, "Can't you see Comrade Stalin is asleep, leave him alone!" He ordered Stalin's personnel to "let him rest" for the night, and then calmly left. Only the next day did Beria, sure that Stalin would not make it, allow the doctors to see him. By then Stalin was unconscious and Beria was already nominally in charge.

Revelations

Beria's power was, thankfully, short-lived, due to a timely coup organized by Nikita Khrushchev. Though Khrushchev seemed an unlikely choice for political maverick, given his history as a prominent Stalinist lackey and executioner, as well as the fact that it was he who wept the most at Stalin's passing, he turned out to be the politician who did the most to destroy Stalin's monolithic system.

During his ten years in power, Nikita Khrushchev never stopped surprising the world with his vigor and stamina. He could work 14 to 16 hours a day, never needing a break. He allowed himself to relax only during energetic hunting sessions.

He could speak at plenary sessions and party congresses for three to four hours at a stretch. People still remember how Khrushchev once delivered two reports in a row, standing on the podium for more than eight hours and taking only a short breather. When visiting the Stavropol region or Central Asian republics he spent hours in the scorching heat, with his bald head uncovered, inspecting cotton and maize fields.

But Khrushchev, with all his ill-planned reforms, and more importantly, revelations, was too dangerous for the loyal comrades to tolerate for long. He was exciting the masses too much, his "Thaw" was too threatening. The Party's past and future was in danger.

Therefore, his associates, led by Leonid Brezhnev, pensioned the 70 year-old Khrushchev off, citing "his old age and poor health." Vibrantly healthy before his humiliating dismissal, in exile Khrushchev turned into a sad, lonely old man, sick in body and soul.

From Ilyich to Ilyich

What an irony it is that Leonid Ilyich Brezhnev replaced Khrushchev "for reasons of health" while the former was still relatively young and healthy, but then himself hung on long after he was nothing more than a sick puppet, causing considerable damage to himself and his country.

When Leonid Brezhnev first come to power, at the age of 58, he gave no signs of his later chronic deterioration. In fact, he was originally thought to be the most handsome and physically healthy Politburo member. Even the Western media admiringly cited his well-cut suits and cheerfulness.

It was in the mid-1970s that Brezhnev's health began to show serious signs of dilapidation. In early 1975 he suffered a stroke and a heart attack. He could not speak for two months, and a paralysis of facial muscles wiped away his former attractiveness. Brezhnev's doctors managed to soften the aftermath of his illness, but by then he was quite another person. He became suspicious and a hypochondriac, his crafty intelligence weakened. On top of which, he suffered from insomnia, for which he chewed sleeping pills like candy, frightening his staff with his increasingly bizarre behavior. Trying to control him, they watered down his vodka and gave him placebos instead of his potent sleeping pills. This created a Catch-22 situation, as Brezhnev, frustrated by the weak pills and booze, ate and drank all the more. Doped up, he drove his sports cars with nary a care, almost killing himself and his terrified bodyguards. In his "second childhood," he soothed himself with drugs and alcohol at the state's expense.

By the early 1980s, Brezhnev could not move unattended. He also had a great deal of trouble speaking. Uttering long words was too difficult for him, making the state-controlled media dub and correct his mistake-ridden public speeches, in order to hide his true predicament from the Soviet people. All of which was to no effect, as cutting jokes about his terrible pronunciation, buffoonery and illness were legion.

Finally, on November 10, 1982, Brezhnev died of a heart attack in his sleep, putting both himself and his indolent nation out of their misery. Jeopardizing his country's future, Brezhnev had wasted his final years by remaining only marginally in control and dreamily prolonging his death-in-life existence.

The Mystery Man

Brezhnev was dead, but the Soviet Union still had a few years to go.

Yuri Andropov, Brezhnev's successor, had had a lot of trouble with his health even before he assumed power. He had suffered from diabetes since the age of 30 and, when he was 52, had a severe heart attack. His kidneys were in bad shape as a result of a case of *salmonella* contracted in China, and a case of Asian flu in Afghanistan.

But few people knew about the new General Secretary's troubles. While in charge of the KGB and as a Central Committee member, Andropov had demonstrated an exceptional capacity for work. He took no days off, and if he didn't finish reading all the papers brought to him during his work day, he took them home. He spent what little spare time he had listening to Russian classical music, visiting art exhibitions and reading American detective stories. Though the country's stagnating situation was having an adverse effect on Andropov's already enervated health, many people hoped he would last long enough to guarantee a continued stability.

His outward appearance, however, was deceptive. In the spring of 1983, one of his kidneys stopped functioning, and he had to undergo at least twice weekly dialysis treatments. Later that year, in September, he caught a severe cold while vacationing in the south. Immediately afterwards he was readmitted to the hospital, never to be discharged. For five months he ran the country from his ward by means of notes, letters, and telephone calls. He dictated documents and speeches to his aides, but received only a very limited number of his friends and colleagues. Mikhail Gorbachev, Yegor Ligachev, Dmitry Ustinov and Viktor Chebrikov were among his few visitors.

During these five months, Andropov very convincingly pretended to be recovering. He skimmed over huge amounts of documents and read new literary magazines, though he couldn't turn the pages without outside assistance. But his condition continued to deteriorate in late January 1984, and he died a couple of weeks later, on February 9.

From Bad to Worse

Still, the country hung on. Reflecting the USSR's weak heartbeat, the new leader of the nation and the party, 72-year-old Konstantin Chernenko, was a dying man. His diseases were legion, the most serious being emphysema. Chernenko could neither breathe, nor speak properly. At Andropov's funeral he could hardly produce a single phrase without pause. On coming to power, he spent several weeks during the spring of 1984 in the hospital, writing notes and letters for the Politburo's consideration. That summer he was taken to Kislovodsk, the best spa in Russia for lung problems.

But the place was unfriendly to Chernenko: the weather was cold and it did not stop drizzling for 12 days. At the spa, he contracted pneumonia and was immediately brought back to Moscow. Only in the late fall was he able to return to his Kremlin office, and then only for a period of two months. On top of which, he could not walk any longer, and had to rely on a wheelchair for transportation.

In January, 1985 Chernenko was readmitted to the hospital. Now, realizing how seriously ill he was, his peers no longer treated his notes and letters as directives to be strictly obeyed. Yet, opting for the devil they knew, the leadership gave Chernenko sufficient power to be satisfied. His supporters knew how problematic it would be to find a useful replacement.

The Soviet people suspected what was up, and rumors flew about the General Secretary's death. To quell them, it was decided to show him on television. A ward of the Central Clinical Hospital was disguised as a polling station where Chernenko was supposed to cast his voice for the Supreme Soviet election, now in progress. Everybody could see Chernenko trying, painfully, to put his ballot into the slot. Some time later, a new show was staged during which the Moscow party boss, Viktor Grishin, presented Chernenko with a deputy mandate. It was a sorry sight and no one was particularly shocked, three days later, when the news about Konstantin Chernenko's death on March 10, 1985 was made public.

The Healthy Face of Socialism

Unaware of Gorbachev's revolutionary plans for Russia, most citizens were simply glad to see a young, healthy man in charge for once. (Referring to the top leader's deaths in the early 1980s, Gorbachev wrote in his memoirs that, "All this was fraught with symbolic meaning. The very system was dying away; its sluggish, senile blood no longer contained any vital juices.")

Gorbachev, the first and last Soviet president, was blessed with exceptionally good health, enabling him to withstand all the tests of life. Gorbachev used to leave the Kremlin late at night with his face gray from fatigue, but the next morning he was back in his office full of energy.

On the other hand, Boris Yeltsin, Russia's first president and Gorbachev's greatest enemy and rival, was known both for his love of sports and his debilitating private lifestyle. After an energetic young adulthood of volleyball, Yeltsin systematically destroyed his health with rumored alcoholic binges (which allegedly brought on cirrhosis of the liver). He exacerbated the damage done to his body by playing tennis and refusing to take care of his weakening heart.

These grave problems were worsened during the 1996 presidential elections, in which Yeltsin, determined to hide the extent of his career-threatening illness from the press, his rivals and even his supporters, continued to campaign ferociously, almost killing himself and his country's chances for democracy.

In September 1996, with the elections won and after months of dodging the press, Yeltsin finally admitted to the world that he would be going under the knife for a heart bypass operation, which many specialists say he should have had years ago. Yeltsin's serious heart problems were amplified by the fact that he suffers from a condition in which his heart is unable to pump all the blood it needs. Given the president's age and health, it was a potentially fatal operation (some Western doctors initially gave Yeltsin just a 50 percent chance of survival, but, after he was forced to rest for two months, his chances were upgraded to 90 percent).

Throughout 1996, concerns for the president's health were mixed with voices from the press and parliament demanding his immediate resignation. After being assured that Yeltsin was in good health, and then giving him their votes, many Russians felt betrayed by how Yeltsin and his handlers had lied.

This feeling of betrayal was aggravated when, too soon after the November 5, 1996, quintuple bypass operation, Presidential Spokesman Sergei Yastrzhembsky went on record as saying that the 65-year-old President was making a wonderful recovery and would quickly return to the Kremlin as soon as he got over a "serious cold." Yet, within days, there came news that President Yeltsin had actually contracted double pneumonia, quickly putting an end to such optimism. (Handlers had said on the eve of the July 1996 election that Yeltsin had missed three days of events because of a "cold," when in fact the president had experienced a heart attack.) Russia settled down to wait and see. Would the President and his government survive?

As it turned out, Yeltsin shocked the world with his recovery, exuding his past vitality at the March 1997 summit in Helsinki with President Clinton. Gone was the elderly, haggard leader, caricatured in the press and Duma as a senile pawn, handing the state reins to shady advisors. By the middle of 1997, Yeltsin seemed to be revived, more decisive, willing to flex his political muscle, unwilling to take 'nonsense' from an uppity Duma.[1]

One Small Step for Democracy...

The authoritarian system is based not only on power, but also on a common ideology. The head of the system is the main interpreter of the current doctrine. He acts as both the political and the spiritual shepherd of society. It is not in the nature of such a "master" to surrender to time by aging gracefully or retiring peacefully; such heights of glory are not meant for mere mortals.

Democracies abide by other rules. No ideology enjoys the status of "obligatory"; doctrines and religions are separated from the State. There are opposition movements, free elections and an independent mass media, all of which, in concert, assure that the public learns about the abilities and strength of possible leaders, in order to judge their governing powers.

In the spirit of *glasnost*, Yeltsin's government has sought an image of openness and truthfulness. Yet Yeltsin, claiming issues of privacy and fearful of electoral repercussions, had to be forced by critics to reveal the true state of his health. Wisely, the press and the people recognized that, in a situation like this, "privacy" is reminiscent of the Soviets at their worst: secretive, deceptive and arrogant.

In a democracy, the truth, however unpleasant, will come out: perhaps not immediately, but eventually. And the truth is always the best medicine.

May 1997

---

1. In frail health, Yeltsin resigned from the presidency before the end of his term, on December 31, 1999, as a restul of which then Prime Minister Vladimir Putin became acting president. Yeltsin passed away on April 23, 2007.

Russian Lacquer Miniatures
Cherry Gilchrist

The road to Kholuy passes through stretches of open meadowland, brushing the edge of the forest and traversing marshy tracts until it swings around the last sharp bend and meets the broad River Teza. This is the end of the road. The silver sign of the Firebird welcomes the occasional visitor. The fine, but crumbling, church singles the town out as a place of historical importance. Substantial brick houses along the riverbank indicate that once rich merchants lived and traded here. The other houses in the village are traditional, brightly-painted wooden *izbas*, with carved fretwork around the windows and eaves.

But this is no typical Russian village: of its 1800 inhabitants, 300 are artists. Kholuy's roots as an artistic community stretch back to the thirteenth century. For hundreds of years, it was also an important trading centre. And, along with three other villages – Palekh, Mstyora and Fedoskino, it is now home to a unique art form, the Russian Lacquer Miniature.

The quality of Russian Lacquer Miniatures is widely-known around the world, yet even the average Russian knows very little about the art form. In Russian cities, cheaply-painted boxes are sold to tourists for a few dollars as "Lacquer Miniatures," and in the United States many people erroneously call them "Palekh boxes." Anyone can admire and enjoy a genuine lacquer miniature, but when you understand more about its history and the work that goes into it, then you truly begin to value it.

The history of the Russian Lacquer Miniature can be traced back to Russia's ancient past, yet it is a comparably young art form. It looks timeless, but was only fully established as a genre in the 1920s and 30s. There are two distinct chapters in the history of lacquer miniatures.

In the thirteenth century, the village of Kholuy and its neighbors, Palekh and Mstyora, were icon-painting centres, founded by monks who fled the Suzdal area to escape the Tartar-Mongol invasion. They made their way into remote forested regions about a hundred miles to the east, where they established three separate settlements. Over the course of the centuries, these three villages trained generations of icon-painters. The names Palekh, Kholuy and Mstyora became synonymous with schools of icon-painting, and their icons can often be found in museums and auctions today.

The icon-trading attracted commerce and fairs and markets arose. Kholuy, now the quietest of the lacquer miniature villages, was once the liveliest and probably the wealthiest. Major fairs were held there at least five times a year, with buyers and sellers arriving not only from far-flung corners of Russia, but from abroad as well. Cloth, furs, fish, *lubok* prints and anything and everything was sold here, along with the icons. Drunkenness, merry-making and quarrels abounded. One deep pool on the edge of the village is still known as "Turk's Lake," into which, it is said, a Turkish trader was hastily tipped after one quarrel too many. Old coins are regularly dug up in Kholuy gardens, and the fair still just about lives on in the memory of old folk, though it was suppressed in the 1930s.

The trade in icons fell into sharp decline at the end of the nineteenth century, partly because mass-produced printed icons were cheap and widely available. After 1917, religious painting was discouraged, putting the remaining icon-painters out of a job. Officially, icon-painting was now defunct. Unofficially, the tradition was carried on secretly; the former director of the Kholuy lacquer miniature workshop said he used to tip off artists when official visitors were coming, so that they could hide any icons in progress.

The second chapter in the evolution of the lacquer miniatures as an art form came after the Bolshevik Revolution. Dedicated artists who remained cast about for something into which to channel their talents. They tried painting carpets and china, without great success. Then, in Palekh, an artist named Ivan Golikov began to create the first lacquer miniatures. The miniature form actually sprang out of the icon tradition, since icons often contained a border of miniature paintings around a central subject. But now, instead of sacred themes, Golikov took the age-old legends and fairy tales of Russia for his subjects. He retained the use of tempera, egg-based paints, and much of the icon style. In particular, the richly-colored, gold-ornamented icons of Yaroslavl served as a inspiration, their horses and chariots, robes and palaces already almost suggestive of fairy tales rather than religious themes. But, significantly, Golikov changed from using wood to lacquered *papier mache* as a base.

This is where Fedoskino, the fourth Russian village comes into our story. Fedoskino artists argue that they were the first school of Russian lacquer miniature painting, since their workshop was originally set up in 1798. It was the brainchild of a merchant named Korobov, who realized that he could sell vast quantities of snuff boxes if he could make them both cheap and attractive. Many people could not afford the snuff boxes made of ivory, jade or other precious materials which were in vogue at the time. Using a process he discovered in Germany, Korobov began to produce little boxes of *papier-mâché*. He employed artists to decorate them, and he finished them in lacquer to produce a very durable and attractive finish. Over the course of time, many other beautiful but functional types of boxes were produced, as tea caddies, card cases and so on. And, since Fedoskino lay just north of Moscow, it was well-placed to serve the fashion-conscious clientele of the city.

The Fedoskino artists painted in oils from the start, and took their style from mainstream art, which at that time in Russia was very similar to Western art. They did begin to introduce a distinctly Russian flavor however, painting troikas and village scenes, and girls in national costume. They also began to concentrate more and more on the quality of the painting itself; it was no longer enough just to decorate a box. The workshop, a highly successful venture, subsequently passed into the hands of the Lukutin family, and remained as such until it became a cooperative in 1910. It has always retained its distinctive style, which is also now often characterized by an underlay of mother of pearl, or gold leaf. This gives the miniature an iridescent sheen, and an inner glow, and is particularly effective for bringing to life snow scenes, sunlight, and silken draperies.

Back in Palekh in the 1920s, Golikov gathered a small group of artists around him, and this founding group set the Palekh style securely in place for succeeding generations. It is, not surprisingly, very iconic, with beautifully detailed faces, and elongated figures poised in dignified stances. It consists of vivid colors, often including brilliant reds or blues, but always used with restraint on a background of black lacquer.

All the lacquer miniature schools generally use black for the outside of the box, and red for the inside, though they paint over the black to a far greater degree than the Palekh artists. Red equals life and beauty in Russian color symbolism, and the black expresses both the mystery and the sorrows of life. The black background helps the vivid miniature scenes appear as if they are floating in another dimension of time and space, drawing us into the intense world that they create. The gold of the delicate ornament, used to highlight detail and provide a decorative border, is a symbol of eternity. This trio of colors – red, black and gold – also forms the basis of color in other Russian folk art too, especially in the lacquered wooden ware of Khokhloma.

Kholuy and Mstyora followed Palekh into the painting of lacquer miniatures in the 1930s. There was some rivalry between the villages, as each was eager to define its own status, and over the course of the years all three villages have developed very distinctive styles and outlooks. Kholuy is dynamic and colorful, relying on contrast and a depth of perspective, and it often contains superb natural detail. Kholuy artists today show remarkable creativity, especially the talented 26 or so members of the Kholuy Union of Artists. Mstyora style is dreamy, with delicate, carefully-graded colors, and usually all of the background is painted over. Mstyora style needs a different eye; there is often less detail than in Palekh or Kholuy painting, but the overall effect is wonderfully harmonious.

So, despite the early start in Fedoskino, the genre of the Russian lacquer miniature with its four schools only really came to birth in the middle of the twentieth century. It remains a very Russian art form at its heart, with subjects drawn from fairy tales, historical legends, Russian landscapes and architecture, as well as festivals and scenes from old village life. The artists meticulously research their themes, if they are not within living memory. Sometimes flowers, animals, portraits, and non-Russian themes are painted, often with stunning results – but stray too far or too often from the Russian flavor, and the art weakens.

The artists of this genre go through a thorough training lasting five years. Each of the four villages has its own art school, and outsiders are welcomed as well as children born and bred in the villages. There is healthy competition for spaces, with about four or five applicants vying for each slot. In general, students do not pay tuition, though the schools are beginning to offer a proportion of fee-paying places simply to survive. Students must show not only a talent for art, but must also have excellent eyesight and good general health.

Contrary to popular belief, the lacquer miniature artists' eyesight does not typically deteriorate more than other adults, despite the fact that they carry out such incredibly detailed work (Painting fine gold ornament is especially taxing and is done with the finest of brushes.). They are taught so well that they work more with mind and hand than with the eye. In fact, lacquer miniature artists prefer not to work with magnifying glasses, as they like to see the whole of their composition at once. But students don't spend all their time in such concentrated work; they are also encouraged to work in charcoal, oils and watercolors, to draw from life, and to study the history of art as well. Much of their miniature training is acquired by copying from examples, so that they learn in a very disciplined and structured way. For their diploma, however, they must produce a completely original composition.

It is important to understand that lacquer art does not depend entirely upon original compositions. The word "copy" often has negative connotations in Western minds. But this does not mean something slavish and mechanical; it is rather the chance to recreate the work of a master. This approach is common in Easter art as well as in icon-painting, where the artist does not have to strive to be original. Some artists at the pinnacle of their profession only paint originals or "author's works," as they are described in Russian. Others will only ever paint existing subjects, drawing from a range of designs and repertoire. Altogether, this forms the body of the art, which has a life of its own and a strongly collective element. Even the most "original" artists usually meet in council in their union or co-operative to discuss their works – and criticisms are certainly made, especially if other artists feel that new compositions are spoiling or weakening the tradition. Artists who leave and settle elsewhere are rarely able to keep up the quality of their work; the members of the collective rely on each other, the spirit of the art, and indeed the "spirit of place" of their village.

Some years ago, the Soviet government tried to artificially create a fifth center of folk art in the industrial city of Lipetsk. Artists were tempted to re-settle there with promises of modern flats, bathrooms and running water (luxuries not available in the *izba*). Sadly, the experiment was a failure; nothing new or creative has emerged from Lipetsk, and it now turns out low quality miniatures for the tourist market. The artists who moved there could never return, and gradually they lost both their individual creativity and the vital link into the main body of the art.

The four lacquer miniature villages are each quite individual, set in beautiful countryside that is a source of inspiration to the artists. Intense sunsets, deep forests, spring floods, fall harvests and winter snows all fuel their imagination. The artists are rooted in the traditional life of the Russian countryside, with seasons for potato-planting and mushroom-gathering, berry picking and fishing. And, like most rural Russians, they have to make do for themselves, mending their homes and tending the vegetable plots. Women and men are both in the ranks of artists, sometimes even working as a husband and wife team, taking turns minding the children while the other paints.

Meanwhile, more than ten years after the lifting of state controls, lacquer miniature artists find the situation for selling their art to be quite fluid. Though some regret that they are no longer as financially secure as they once were, most prefer the creative freedom: they are no longer tied to a production quota, and can work as and when they please.

The four original state-run studios, one for each village, still function in various disorganized stages of privatization. Some artists work there on salary, while others are members of cooperatives or unions. Still others go it alone. Much depends upon their contacts, and the selling network that they find their way into. Thus, it is not always the best artists who are the richest.

The domestic market for this art form is weak, although recently record prices for lacquer miniatures have been extracted from tourists in St. Petersburg. The plain fact is that most miniatures find their way West; in Russia, only corporate customers such as banks regularly buy them. Once, museums were queuing up to buy the best lacquer miniatures, and none of the *real* masterpieces ever left the country. Now the museums do not have the funds for such purposes, and Russians with money would rather buy consumer goods than art.

This dissolution of control over production brought other challenges as well. In Fedoskino and Palekh especially, artists have split into many groups, some of them now in a difficult relationship with one another. But, on the whole, genuine aspiration and honesty is still at the heart of the tradition, and the studios still work with dogged persistence in extremely difficult market conditions. Each village has its own stupendously good museum, and exhibitions, celebrations and jubilees are common excuses to get together with artists and colleagues from the other lacquer centers and party at great length once the official speeches are over.

It is worth noting that the making of the *papier-mâché* and the lacquering and polishing of finished works is actually not done by the individual artists. Rather, it is done by another team of craftsmen, who are skilled, but who do not enjoy the status level of the artists. It is an interesting process in its own right, involving just the right type of cardboard, from which the *papier-mâché* is made, the "slow-cooking" of the *papier-mâché* for two or three months, and painstaking lacquering and polishing. Three or four coats of lacquer are applied before the artist begins painting the miniature. Afterwards, between seven and twelve coats must be applied, and each one dried and polished to achieve the right finish. The lacquer has to be made to just the right formula; untrained city artists producing "souvenir" boxes often slap on a couple of coats of floor varnish, and hope for the best. This will usually crack up within a couple of years, whereas properly lacquered works will survive, with only a little dulling, for centuries.

No genuine lacquer miniature is completed in less than three months from start to finish, and many will take a year or more. The simplest design will take the artist several days to paint; the most complex more than twelve months.

As the basis for the lacquer miniature, the traditional form of the box is still the most popular. Yet, as the art became finer and finer, so the utility of the box was largely forgotten, and the miniatures became collectors' items in their own right. Although the art of the miniature is the main focus, a miniature on a box is still evocative, like an exquisite treasure chest. Some of the old functional shapes have been retained, such as the 'inkwell' and 'cigarette case', but for decorative interest only. Artists often paint plaques and panels as well, and brooches have gained in popularity in recent years. They also occasionally paint wall panels and frescoes – on a completely different scale of course – and lovely examples of these can be seen in the restaurant in Palekh, and in the children's home in Mstyora.

It is often asked whether there is a Persian or Moghul influence in the miniatures. The artists themselves deny this, and it is more likely that there is a slight similarity of style, simply because of painting lively scenes on a small scale in vivid colors. Once, at a British art exhibition, Uzbeki miniaturists were painting in the tent next to some Russian lacquer miniature artists. A British interpreter was getting very heated as she defended her Uzbeki artists against the supposed crimes of their "thieving" former overlords, claiming that those Russians next door had "stolen" the tradition from the Uzbeks. The Uzbeki Minister of Culture, who happened to be present, gently put her right. He noted that they had actually sent some of their own Uzbeki artists to Palekh to train in miniature painting and production, having lost their own indigenous tradition some time back. With the help of this input from Russian artists, they are now trying to recreate their own style using Russian technique as a basis.

The creative potential of the Russian lacquer miniature can be tapped in unexpected ways. But at its heart, it remains a uniquely Russian art form, its little boxes dispatched across the globe as messengers from the soul of Russia, carriers of her magical tales and traditions.

November/December 2001

Blood for the Revolution
Alexei Kilichenkov

"...In the navy we see a shining example of the creative potential of the working masses, in this respect, the navy has shown itself to be a vanguard unit."

– Vladimir Lenin

At the end of June 1905, Russian society, which had still not cooled off from the crushing defeat by the Japanese at Tsushima Strait a month previous, was shaken by news of a mutiny. The impossible had happened – the crew of the Black Sea Fleet's powerful, brand new battleship, the *Prince Potyomkin of Tavridia*, had ousted its officers, set sail for Odessa and opened fire on the town.

The mutiny shook Tsar Nicholas II much more than the death of Baltic Fleet commander Admiral Zinovy Rozhestvensky at Tsushima. He wrote in his diary:

I simply can't believe it. God knows what is happening in the Black Sea Fleet. Three days ago the crew of the *St. George the Victorious* joined the *Potyomkin*... Everything must be done to keep discipline on the other ships of the squadron! Then we must punish the ringleaders heavily and the mutineers harshly.

With uncharacteristic mercilessness Nicholas gave the order to destroy the battleship. But harsh repressions against the rebels did not have the desired effect. In 1905-7, a wave of mutinies rocked naval bases in the Baltic, the Black Sea and the Far East, involving the crews of 22 ships and over 20,000 land-based sailors.

The unrest of 1905 had deep roots in the old Russian navy. In the numerous and modern vessels of the tsarist fleet built in the early twentieth century, all was far from well. Peasants and skilled workers came to the fleet with their centuries-old traditions and ideas, from a world full of clear-cut behavioral mores and spiritual absolutes.

Yet life in the navy confronted the recruits with a completely different, unknown world, one much more alien to them than the army. From their simple, beloved peasant *izbas* (cottages), they were plunged into a world of steel, electricity and steam engines.

The new sailors found themselves learning new ideas. The training schools for new specialists (electricians, radio operators etc.) became, in the words of revolutionary sailor P. Dybenko, "schools of revolution" – the new, conditional truths of new technology were accompanied by equally conditional revolutionary "truths." Many sailors developed split sets of values: their traditional peasant world view and abstract ideas forced on them from outside.

In addition, feelings of being cut off from real life, the sense of responsibility of each man before the whole crew and the privileges of foreign travel, good food and clothing encouraged an elitist spirit and made the navy a tempting target for the revolutionary opposition.

The authorities began to perceive the navy as a kind of powder keg beneath the foundations of Russian statehood. Defense Minister Rediger remarked that, "At present, the navy is not an element of strength, but an element of danger to the state. The security of the state requires its liquidation..."

However, such radical measures were not needed – the government managed to fend off the first onslaught of revolution. Indeed, it took the revolutionary parties some time to take root in the navy. The spontaneous Potyomkin mutiny actually served to thwart a general naval revolt then being planned by the Marxist RSDRP. The Kronstadt mutiny of 1905 was clearly not properly organized either. According to the 1926 chronicles *Uprising in the Baltic Fleet*, "a crowd of armed sailors poured out into the street and had a genuine *pogrom*: looting and setting fire to private houses and government buildings..."

One Black Sea Fleet sailor of the day pointed out in his memoirs:

...It is said that extremist parties had a powerful influence over us. I don't know who influenced who, but I was strongly influenced by the injustice of our leaders...

Many of these injustices came to light on the eve of the mutiny: on the battleship *Chesma* 10 sailors drowned due to the negligence of a watch officer, though no one was found guilty; on the *St. George the Victorios*, a midshipman used a dirk to strike a sailor who had been awarded the St.

George's Cross in the Japanese war, despite the fact that the sailor could not be subjected to corporal punishment.

The sailors usually targeted their anger carefully, and this sometimes led to very unexpected behavior. During the Black Sea revolt of 1905, sailors of the 32nd naval depot who had armed themselves and thrown out their officers, decided to hold a parade and prayers for the birthday of the Dowager Empress. "The prayers," said one of the participants, "were to prove that we were not a riotous rabble..."

Bloodshed Becomes the Norm

And yet, even in the early days of naval unrest, the mood could very quickly turn ugly. In the 1905 Kronstadt uprising, unexpected resistance from the Yenisey Regiment caused them to turn their frustrations elsewhere. They began looting and rampaging, killing any officer who came in their sight. Thus began the unhappy tradition of the mass murder of the officer corps, reminiscent of the killing of landowners during peasant revolts.

After constitutional changes, an uneasy calm returned. In fact, in 1909 a new naval "renaissance" began in Russia and a powerful ocean fleet was built. The process was only interrupted by the First World War.

In wartime, the situation in the navy remained relatively stable. Everything changed on the night of March 1, 1917. Sailors on the garrison island of Kronstadt (off St. Petersburg) reacted murderously to news of mass unrest in the capital. The supposedly "bloodless" February revolution began at Kronstadt and other bases with the mass murder of officers by sailors. Between March 1 and 4, 120 officers were killed and over 600 arrested. Events in the navy added a worrying note to the euphoria of the first days of the revolution, and became a threatening herald of the 1918-21 Civil War...

In Helsingfors (Helsinki), meanwhile, it took just the words "Deal with any disagreeable officers" from a neighboring vessel for ship of the line Poltava's otherwise calm sailors to turn nasty. Someone in the crowd even shouted: "Brothers, we need blood!.."

Often officers were killed not because they were cruel and unjust, but because, on the contrary, they had real influence over their crews and the revolutionaries saw them as a danger. At the funeral of Midshipman Bittenbinder of the torpedo-boat *Gaidamak*, meanwhile, the whole crew was present and many wept – while being terribly sorry for him, they considered him an inevitable victim of the revolution.

Vanguard of the Revolution

By the end of the February revolution, sailors had already crossed their Rubicon into a world of hatred and distrust. Officers looked at ordinary sailors as murderers, while the sailors feared vengeance from the officers should there be a reaction. From this point on, Kronstadt was a pro-socialist bastion, controlled by the soviets (worker's councils) and sailors' committees, where the Bolsheviks were the main influence.

Meanwhile, the lack of military activity at sea meant that sailors did not suffer from the fatigues of war as the soldiers did. As a consequence, they were much more eager to come to the defense of the revolution. Their characteristic cohesion and camaraderie turned them quite naturally into a mobile shock force. With a feeling of their own exclusiveness and superiority over land forces firmly instilled in their minds, sailors did not limit themselves to acting on orders from above.

For example, able seaman Malkov of the cruiser *Diana* decided of his own accord to close the newspaper *Birzheviye Vedomosti*. He remembered afterwards: "It was a nasty little black hundreds[1] paper, and kept slandering the Baltic sailors. I just went to see the Baltic crews, told the lads: 'It's time to close [*Birzheviye Vedomisti*], let's not stand on ceremony!...' Several volunteers appeared at once... when we came out of [the offices] I noticed the magazine *Ogonyok* next door... Another hostile magazine. We spoke to the lads, and decided to close it as well..."

Thus it was that Lenin singled out sailors' units, along with blue-collar youth "for participation everywhere, in all the most important operations..."

Sailors stood out in another way, too. They were mostly well-built, and wore uniforms which were distinctly memorable in comparison with the soldiers' grey greatcoats. Also, because of the traditional shortage of firearms in the navy, sailors were inclined to hang weapons on themselves. While from a purely practical point of view the presence of ammunition belts and grenades on the body was extremely uncomfortable, it certainly had a powerful effect on civilians.

---

1. The Black Hundreds (Chyornosotentsy) were hard-right, anti-semitic groups that were originally formed in opposition to the revolution of 1905.

And so, come October, sailors were again at the forefront of revolution. At the decisive moment, 10,000 sailors and 11 navy ships (including the famous *Aurora*, which fired the first shot in the revolution and is regarded as its symbol) arrived in Petrograd and took an active part in the overthrow of the Provisional Government, capturing key buildings like the telephone exchange, post office and the Admiralty. A composite unit of sailors was sent to Moscow to seize power, then to the Don, the Urals, Kiev, wherever the Bolsheviks opened a front.

Turning Against the Masters

The sailor had become a symbol of victorious revolution. Which is why the mutiny of Baltic sailors less than three years later, in the spring of 1921, came as a deep shock.

In fact, the situation in the Baltic Fleet by the beginning of that year was very similar to February-March 1917. Though the ships remained, the Civil War had left the fleet virtually useless for battle. The peasant-sailors aboard ship at Kronstadt awaited their demobilization with bated breath, and listened avidly to the news of peasant revolts like the Antonov uprising in Tambov.[2]

Most of all, sailors were unhappy about the injustices of the new authorities. Letters from home and stories told by colleagues returning from leave gave plenty of fuel for dissatisfaction. People were sick of the policies of "war communism," which had brought poverty and famine.

The apathy of the navy command also played a role – it made no attempt to react to these "injustices" or in some way revive the fading attraction of the ideas of the Bolshevik Revolution. This apathy merely strengthened sailors' discontent.

The revolt was triggered by the Petrograd city government, which did the (until then) unthinkable – i.e. use force to suppress worker unrest. News of the violence fell on fertile soil, and on March 1 the revolt began...

From the start, the sailors tried to emphasize the 'legality' of their actions. Order was kept in Kronstadt, and people were encouraged to continue at their posts. Their main slogan was "Power to the Soviets, not parties!" an attempt to prove that they were not rioters.

....

2. One of the largest anti-Soviet uprisings in 1920-1921. Antonov was Alexander Antonov, one of the leaders of the uprising.

This time, however, they miscalculated, and the country did not come to their aid. A change of course at the Party Congress and the introduction of the New Economic Policy deprived the revolt of its political base and *raison d'etre*. By the summer the mutiny had been virtually quelled – partly by delegates from that same Congress, as the media of the day triumphantly proclaimed.

This marked an end to the period of great upheavals, with the symbol of October consigned to the history books. Together with the rest of the country, the Red Navy entered a period of relative stability and renounced its revolutionary fervor. The authorities maintained a tough discipline designed to prevent a repeat of 1921.

And yet, some 55 years later, in 1977, the year of the 60th anniversary of the October Revolution, Captain Sablin of the Baltic Fleet ship *Storozhevoy* attempted to take his vessel to the West. He and his sub-lieutenant were captured and executed for treason. This time, Kronstadt's mutinous tradition was reversed – it was the officers, not the crew, who protested against the authorities of the day.

October 1996

For Whom the Bells
Dasha Demourova

On December 6, 1929, the Soviet government issued Decree No. 118, which forbade all bell ringing in the Soviet State and commanded that all bells be removed from church bell towers and melted down to help industry. Thousands of church bells were destroyed in the 1920s and 1930s. Yet even these repressions did not wipe out Russian bell making traditions.

The Baptism of Rus in 988 brought bells to Russia from Byzantium. According to one report, at that time there were just two bells in Kiev. Less than 50 years later, a multitude of bells were reported to have been in use not only in Kievan churches, but in those of other major cities as well. By 1066, bells were becoming war booty in conflicts between principalities. In the fourteenth century, bells began to be cast in Russia.

Bells have played a rather prominent role in Russian history. They were used as a call to worship, to chime the hours, to inform people about the death of a tsar or the beginning of a war campaign. In some places, bells were rung to announce the execution of a criminal, or the death of a bishop or other notable. Other bells sounded an alarm: the approach of an enemy or a house on fire. Certain church bells were rung to herald an important announcement from the tsar or a ruling body. Different church bells rung in different ways communicated to parishioners (who could not make a church service) which part of the service was being celebrated.

Even the earliest bells made in Russia normally bore information about the date of founding and the weight of the bell, as well as the name of the customer or person in whose honor it was cast; sometimes tsars, tsarinas and saints were also depicted on the bells. The master bellfounder was a very honorable position in Russia. Special services were held prior to a casting, at which the master asked for a blessing. Immediately after that, his apprentices would start a rumor circulating in the town – the more nonsensical, the better. This was based on the superstition that the further a rumor spread, the better the future bell would sound.

There are many Russian legends, tales, riddles and superstitions connected with bells. For example, it was believed that if one heard a bell ringing before starting work, it would bring good luck, but if a bell rang all of a sudden by itself, it signaled trouble. Bells were often treated like living creatures, punished with whips or having their clappers torn out. For example, the Uglich bell was held responsible for riots that followed the death of Ivan the Terrible's heir – Prince Dmitry – in 1591. Boris Godunov ordered that the bell's clapper and "ears" be cut off and that the bell be exiled to Siberia.

Some interesting church traditions were also connected with bells. On Easter Eve, the large bell in the Kremlin's Ivan the Great bell tower would strike at midnight, upon which signal the bells of all Moscow's churches would start ringing. During the entire week of Easter, anyone who wanted to ring a church's bells and celebrate Christ's resurrection was permitted to do so.

In Russia, unlike elsewhere, bells (at least since the fourteenth century) do not swing when rung. Only the clappers hang free. This gives bell ringers much greater control over the intensity and interval of impact, allowing for a wide variety of rhythmic patterns and combinations with the same bells (from funeral knells to joyful dances).

The seventeenth century was perhaps the greatest period in Russian bell culture. Production technology had improved and now even giant bells, like the 100-ton Tsar Bell, could be cast (the Tsar Bell on display in the Moscow Kremlin is actually the last of *four* bells which bore the name Tsar Bell; three previous Tsar Bells are no longer extant). The profession also advanced: by the end of that century, there were 150 bell ringers working in the Moscow Kremlin alone.

After Peter the Great lost nearly all of Russia's artillery in the battle with Sweden near Narva (1700), he ordered all churches, monasteries and convents to give one-third of their bells for recasting into artillery. The upside was that all these institutions sent the State the worst third of their bells, thus improving the quality of the ringing throughout the country.

In the beginning of the nineteenth century, Russian bells began to appear in America. After Russian traders founded settlements in Alaska, Orthodox churches were built and bells were brought from Russia and remain in the U.S. to this day.

Early in the twentieth century, there were about 200 bells in Moscow, including 39 giants. Only five of these survive (three are in the Kremlin and two are in Rostov the Great). No bell tower or belfry in Moscow managed to keep all its bells. After the October Revolution of 1917, removal and destruction of bells was a communist passion – perhaps a reflection of the historic personification of bells. By 1926, bell ringing could only be authorized by local authorities, not by church officials alone. The afore-mentioned 1929 decree banning bell ringing was intended to avoid the use of bells to call people to anti-Bolshevik actions. The atheistic government also had an economic interest in the non-ferrous metal. In 1920, authorities in Kostroma melted down bells to produce cauldrons for public dining-rooms (*stolovayas*). Many bells were turned into tractors.

It is therefore not surprising that the limited revival of the Orthodox Church which Stalin allowed during WWII did not lead to a revival in bell ringing – the bells were all gone. And ringing was still not allowed in any case.

By the end of the 1950s, the Thaw allowed reinstallation of some bells, and some sets were cobbled together from bells found in factories, theaters, people's homes or sheds and even in rubbish pits. Interestingly, at least one complete set of bells did survive the carnage. Harvard Professor Thomas Whittemore intercepted the bells from Moscow's Danilov Monastery *en route* to their being melted down. At his suggestion, American businessman Charles Crane purchased the bells from the Soviet government for the price of the bronze with which they were made. Crane had them transported to Harvard University and installed in a tower at Lowell House. For the past half century, these Russian bells have announced the beginning of term and the results of Harvard football matches. The possibility of returning the bells to Danilov Monastery next year and replacing the Harvard originals with replicas is being discussed.[1]

One other famous set of bells survived in Rostov, on the order of Anatoly Lunacharsky, an early Soviet Minister of Culture. When, in 1919, local authorities decided to melt down the Rostov bells, Dmitry Ushakov, director of the Rostov Museum, wrote to Lunacharsky, asking him to protect the bells. Lunacharsky visited Rostov, agreed that the bells were of great historical value and ordered them saved. The Rostov bells were silent

....
1. The bells were returned to Danilov Monastery in 2008.

until the late 1960s, when the government featured the Bells of Rostov in a recording.

Today, bell founding is experiencing a renaissance in Russia – an annual exhibition and sale in Yaroslavl presents works of contemporary casters from Voronezh, Tutayev, Kamensk-Uralsky and Moscow. Communities collect money to cast a bell (cost: $15 per kilo on average) and, as soon as the exhibition ends, the bells are sent to convents and Orthodox churches. There is also the Museum of Bells, the only one in Russia, situated in Valdai (400 km from Moscow), although there are many more bells in private collections than in museums.

November/December 2004

Saving the Chelyuskin

R.E.G. Davies

In 1932, the Soviet merchant ship Sibiryakov had attempted to sail across the Arctic Ocean to demonstrate that a Northeast Passage route was possible, linking European Russia with the Pacific Ocean ports in the Russian Far East. It was not successful; but its efforts suggested that, with the help of ice-breakers, the voyage was possible. Therefore, the following summer, another voyage was planned. It would turn out to be one of the most amazing stories of survival of the twentieth century.

*B*uilt in a Danish shipyard as the *Lena*, a ship quite similar to the Sibiryakov was commissioned and sailed to the ice-free port of Murmansk. There it was renamed the *Chelyuskin*, after the Russian explorer who had discovered the northernmost point of the Eurasian landmass. It was manned, in addition to the crew, by a scientific expedition, headed by the experienced Dr. Otto Schmidt, and a relief party for Wrangel Island – a remote outpost off the shores of Chukotka. Altogether, there were 112 persons on board the ship, which, skippered by Captain Vladimir Voronin, steamed out of Murmansk on July 16, 1933, escorted by the ice-breaker Krasin.

At first, the *Chelyuskin* made good headway. It crossed the Barents Sea without incident, except that, halfway across the Kara Sea, the number on board was increased to 113, when little Karina (named after the Sea) was born to a Wrangel Island family. Then, navigating north, to seek open waters from the pack-ice, the *Chelyuskin* sighted Uyedineniya Island, which had been mistakenly charted 50 miles away from its true position.

By September, the ship had sustained some damage to its hull, as it battled its way through the pack-ice, and the ice-breakers were not powerful enough to clear channels of open water. The relief party was unable to reach Wrangel Island, as the *Chelyuskin* was in the grip of the pack-ice most of the time. Only by keeping close to the Siberian shore was it able to make headway.

On October 3, eight people, the older ones and some who were ill, were taken ashore across the ice, near North Cape, by local Chukchi and their dog teams. This reduced the number on board to 105. Eventually, on November 5, when it was within sight of open water in the Bering Strait, the ship came to a halt. Trapped in pack-ice frustratingly close to its goal, the *Chelyuskin* could go no further.

Despite efforts of assistance by another ice-breaker, the Litke, the ship was helpless. Captain Voronin did his best to escape from the ice's grip, but strong currents forced the ship back the way it had come – to the northwest.

On February 13, 1934, just under seven months from when it set sail, the *Chelyuskin* gave in – the pressure of the ice stove in the ship's weakened hull and the it sank 75 miles from the nearest point of land: the small village of Vankarem.

Fortunately, passengers and crew had long since been preparing for this disaster. Everyone on board, except for one steward, who slipped off the icy deck and drowned in the frigid ocean, was able to get off the ship and to unload a substantial quantity of supplies, including food, oil, building equipment and materials – all intended for the community on Wrangel Island. They set to work and established a camp on the pack-ice.

The *Chelyuskin* had been well-equipped. In addition to a little Shavrov Sh-2 floatplane (used to reconnoiter the ocean and seek channels of open water), it had a good radio, and Dr. Ernst Krenkel was able to request help from Moscow. An emergency committee was set up immediately, under Politburo member Valerian Kuybyshev. Quickly realizing that any other method would be hopeless, he organized a relief expedition by air; and, as a wise precaution, Kuybyshev set up three separate units, calling upon the best Soviet pilots of the day to rush to the East.

Meanwhile, a twin-engine ANT-4 transport aircraft was already in the Chukotka area, at Anadyr, about 300 miles from Vankarem. In temperatures as low as -37° C, Anatoly Lapidevsky made many attempts to fly north (these flights alone would make a good adventure story), eventually reaching the *Chelyuskin* camp on March 5, 1934, and evacuating twelve people – all the women and two children, including little Karina. Lapidevsky could not risk another trip, as the aircraft was the size of a DC-3, and could have crashed through the ice during the approaching spring thaw.

Unit No. 1 of the main rescue operation was comprised of Polikarpov R-5 training/ambulance biplanes, led by Squadron Commander Nikolai

Kamanin. They went via the Trans-Siberian Railway, and then more than 2,000 miles onward by ship, to reach the Chukotka area, south of Anadyr, on March 21. Of this team, pilots Pivenstein, Demirov and Bastanzhiev could not get through, and the latter two were lucky to survive. Their aircraft crashed 20 miles outside Anadyr and they had to trudge back, half-starved and half-frozen, through the deep snow to the base in Anadyr. But Kamanin, with Vasily Molokov, veteran of many Siberian survey flights, got through to Vankarem.

Unit No. 2, under the command of V.L. Galyshev, was made up of aircraft already in Siberia, providing regional airline service to Yakutsk. These were metal-built Junkers-F13s, of German design, but built under license in Moscow. They were able to fly the whole distance from Khabarovsk, in appalling conditions of terrain and climate, often using improvised airstrips. Galyshev's aircraft broke down at Anadyr, but Mikhail Vodopyanov, another veteran Siberian flyer, and Ivan Doronin, were able to join Kamanin at Vankarem on April 11.

Unit No. 3 took an entirely different route. The pilots, Sigizmund Levanevsky and Mavriki Slepnev, headed west, by rail and ferry, to London, then by ship to the U.S. and onward to Alaska. At Fairbanks, the Soviet trading organization AMTORG purchased two Consolidated Fleetster cabin aircraft from Pan American Airways. With two American mechanics, they headed for Chukotka.

Therefore, by April 11 – two months after the *Chelyuskin* had sunk – six aircraft were gathered in the Vankarem-Cape North area. They were two R-5s, two F-13s and two Fleetsters. Also, on April 2, Mikhail Babushkin had flown in from the ice-camp in the *Chelyuskin*'s diminutive Shavrov Sh-2, which had been salvaged and repaired.

Between April 7 and 13, 1934, in an historic shuttle service between the ice-camp and Vankarem, all 104 survivors of the ill-fated *Chelyuskin* were brought to shore. It had not been easy, as the ice campers had to build several airstrips, because the pack-ice was breaking up.

Some of the campers were evacuated in enclosed stretchers under the wings of the R-5s. Molokov alone brought out 39, and Kamanin 34. On April 6, Otto Schmidt, who had fallen seriously ill with pleurisy, insisted, along with Captain Voronin, on being among the last to leave. Molokov brought him out on April 11, and Slepnev took him back to Fairbanks, via Nome, in the relative comfort of the Fleetster cabin. Schmidt was accompanied by Dr. Nikitin, and committee representative G.A. Ushakov, who had flown in with Slepnev and Levanevsky.

From Vankarem, the weaker survivors were flown in stages to Providenia, the port where the ice-pack first receded in the spring. Some went by dogsled, and the strongest even walked part of the way. Two ships, the *Smolensk* and the *Stalingrad*, collected the 104 passengers of the *Chelyuskin* and brought them to Vladivostok. Their journey back to Moscow on the Trans-Siberian was interrupted by celebrations at almost every station – the course of the rescue having been reported extensively in the Soviet press.

But the biggest celebration was in Moscow, where the *Chelyuskin* survivors and their rescuers where honored in a great parade – the equivalent of a New York ticker-tape welcome – and greeted by Stalin, Kalinin and the entire Politburo. Everyone associated with the *Chelyuskin* adventure was decorated with the Order of Lenin, and a new title was bestowed on the seven pilots who fought their way through to the ice-camp. They became the first Heroes of the Soviet Union.

This was the first time the advantages of aviation were instrumental in saving the lives of anyone at sea. And it was possibly the first time in history that aircraft had rescued anyone – on land or sea – from certain death.

July/August 2004

Postscript: In 2006, the Chelyuskin-70 Expedition announced it had found the remains of the ship at the bottom of the Chukotka Sea. Its claims were verified the following year.

A World Apart
Samuel Scheib

*T*o say that the Park Pobedy (Victory Park) station is deep is to say that the Moscow Metropolitan is just a good way to get around. Mounting the escalator, one immediately recalls the posters in the metro showing a station attendant, young, blond and cute in her blue uniform. She smiles beguilingly and the text reads "*Yest Vykhod.*" There is an exit.

This is reassuring. The escalators, among the fastest in the world, whisk passengers along at almost a meter per second. So quick are they that, in 2003, six German tourists were hospitalized when the speed of the steps tripped one, who knocked over the other five. Speed notwithstanding, it still takes exactly three minutes to ride from top to bottom. If you begin listening to an average pop song as you mount this monster, the tune will end right as its teeth spit you out at the other end.

The station serves its namesake, once the grounds where Napoleon and his army staged before entering Moscow, and is now home to a complex of museums, memorials and parks. As a trainload of passengers arrives, there is a collective gasp, a buzz that runs throughout the car. Park Pobedy gleams. The walls and floors are orange, gray, and white, representing the colors of Russia's first military order. The marble has been smoothed and polished to a metallic luster.

On the occasion of Victory Day, most of Moscow seems to be heading to Victory Park to watch the fireworks. As the train empties into the hall, there is the rarest of sites: thousands of Muscovites, mouths agape, staring in wonderment at a metro station. A foreigner turns to his Russian companion to ask why Russians are acting this way.

"Because we have never seen it before," he replies, stunned himself.

The Moscow Metropolitan has been operating for seventy years. That is 70 years of people leaning against its walls while waiting for friends and lovers; 70 years of vapor exhaled by millions of daily passengers; 70 years of *slyakot* (dirty slush) brought in on Muscovites' muddy winter boots;

70 years of washing and scrubbing that still makes Moscow's one of the cleanest undergrounds in the world.

The stations that opened in 1935 are still remarkable today: a repository for acres of granite and mahogany, orlets, porphyry and semi-precious stones like onyx, and 23 varieties of marble. Its designers intended to overawe citizens of and visitors to the capital of the world's only socialist state, just as seventeenth century architects did with the mirrored halls of Versailles, and nineteenth century visionaries did with the neo-classical muscularity of Washington D.C. But as impressive as these stations are, time has dulled the oldest of them and Moscow has reared generations of citizens on their storied platforms. For tourists, the metro is an object of fascination. For Muscovites, it is an unapologetic part of the everyday.

It was fitting that Victory Park station was completed just in time to usher Moscow up to Victory Park to celebrate Victory Day. The capital's very first metro line was completed just in time for another holiday eight days earlier in May. Standing among a throng of Muscovites in 2003, gushing at the wonder their country had produced, it seemed possible to understand for just a moment what it must have been like when the Red Line opened for official viewing on May Day 1935.

Socialist Showpiece

It is an interesting what-might-have-been to consider how the Moscow Metropolitan would have looked had the imperial government of Nicholas II been responsible for its first stations. The Moscow city council had discussed the possibility of building a metro as early as 1900, but the unlikely alliance of the Imperial Archaeological Society and the Archbishop of Moscow, fearful that construction would damage the city's ancient churches and other structures, weighed in against it.

With the existing transportation system overwhelmed by the rapidly growing capital, the council revisited the idea again in 1930 and immediately received the endorsement of the Central Committee of the Communist Party. However a tsarist metro might have looked, it is certain that a cash-strapped autocracy would not have spent lavishly on a system to largely serve the working class.

The metro became the most visible salient in Stalin's war of industrialization carried out on his backward nation. Gigantomania is the term-of-art applied to the first and second Five Year Plans by the economist

Nicholai Basili, who chronicled 20 years of Soviet power in *Russia Under Soviet Rule*. Every plant, Basili wrote, had to be "bigger than the greatest in the world," regardless of whether or not such massive projects made any economic sense. Magnitogorsk was a massive steel works built to be larger than those of Gary, Indiana – at the time the world's largest steel producing center. The assembly building of the Chelyabinsk tractor factory had the greatest area of any building in the world, large enough to contain 21 soccer fields, with enough room left over to build dressing rooms for the players. Azbest had the world's largest open cut asbestos mine.

It only made sense, therefore, that Moscow, the head from which sprung this pathology of vastness, would have its own super-project. Experts from London, Paris, and New York advised Soviet authorities against building an underground. Such construction is always difficult, but never more so than in a place like Moscow, where geologists had no idea what would be found under the city's ancient streets. In a city that had only a few thousand automobiles, the experts said, the money would be far better spent on ground level transit.

But of course, the metro was to serve purposes far greater than just transportation. The unprecedented depth of the stations would make them ideal as bomb shelters in the event of war. But, more importantly, the metro would also be a showpiece of what *homo sovieticus* could accomplish.

In many regards, the foreign experts were right. Moscow's foundations proved to be unstable and unpredictable – significantly different from what the country's experienced coal and asbestos miners were accustomed to. The cut-and-cover method (an open trench is dug from street level and then covered afterward) had only limited usefulness, given Moscow's famously long winters. When miners hit a quicksand deposit, its contents drained from its natural cavity into the mineshaft, removing the support from buildings above ground. Similarly, water deposits flooded the mines. To counter these problems, engineers devised a method of chemically freezing the material around the shafts so that miners could then excavate it like any rock.

The freezing process created its own problem. The walls were frozen to between 10 and 14 degrees Fahrenheit. The concrete in use at the time set best in summer temperatures of 60° or above and not at all below freezing. The concrete had to be heated in order to dry, which meant engineers had to add a layer of insulating material between the ice and the warmed concrete. All these additional steps made the battle of the metro one fought in inches but ultimately measured in miles. Expense piled on top of expense.

Kolya's Mine

Workers began excavating the first shaft in 1932, but progress was slow. In early 1933, with an opening date set for the 1934 anniversary of the October Revolution, Stalin assigned his energetic lieutenant, Nikita Khrushchev, to oversee construction. It was a daunting assignment: a rapidly approaching deadline, and he answered to Stalin. "When we started building," Khrushchev later remarked, "we had only the vaguest idea of what the job would entail. We were very unsophisticated. We thought of a subway as something almost supernatural. I think it's probably easier to contemplate space flights today than it was for us to contemplate the construction of the Moscow Metro in the early 1930s."

Khrushchev had considerable mining experience and was a tough taskmaster. He may have missed the original November 1934 opening date, but he made remarkable progress. A German writer visiting Moscow in the summer of 1934 recalled that, in "every quarter of the city, the earth shook with the ringing of hammers, the banging, bumping and screeching of single-bucket excavators, concrete mixers and machines that turned out mortar." Once the arduous task of excavating and construction was complete, the architects and designers were called in.

There was no template for how the stations would look, but by the early 1930s the modernists were falling out of favor and socialist realism was becoming the standard for the arts. In architecture, that meant a return to classicism. Doric and Corinthian capitals, coffered ceilings, apses, and colonnades created a visual link with the great civilizations of the ancient world. For the Palace of Soviets station, architects Dushkin and Lichtenberg reached back even further in time. The ceiling of this shallow station is held up by Egyptian columns, capped by lotus leaves that form the shape of stars on the ceiling. One wag called it the "150-meter alley of palms."

The importance of this station, now called Kropotkinskaya, cannot be understated. It was to serve as a foyer for the actual Palace of Soviets, the greatest building in the world, which was to be crowned with a 100-meter tall statue of Lenin – more than twice as tall as the Statue of Liberty. A competition to design it went through several rounds before settling on a final design. The drawings are impressive, but construction never progressed beyond pouring the foundation (which kept sinking in the soft ground). As the intended seat of power for the nation, this planned building lent great significance to the station underneath it. VIPs came to see it before it was opened. The ever-astute Lazar Kaganovich praised it saying it was "just like a railway station," while the portly Kliment Voroshilov observed that "it looks just like a restaurant." Both missed a more appropriate connection. The Egyptian theme was a distinct variation from the style typical of stations of this time, and one must wonder if its architects were connecting it with the Pharaoh-Tsar Stalin.

A month before the metro opened, some English journalists were invited to view the Palace of Soviets and Komsomolskaya Square stations. A Mr. Eden noted that "[the Soviet Union] has used the rich experiences of Europe and America, but taking all the positive and discarding all the negative. The metro was built with purely artistic taste." He was especially taken with the Palace of Soviets station, comparing it favorably with the best stations in London, Charing Cross and Piccadilly Circus. "The metros of the capitals of the world," he continued, "will all be compared against the Moscow Metropolitan."

In Moscow there were two days of holidays to commemorate the opening of the metro to the public. On May 14, citizens carried banners through the streets bearing a message that would echo in the 2003 ad campaign: *Yest Metro* (There is a Metro). The next day, according to *Pravda*, when the metro officially opened, "the holiday continued when hundreds of thousands of Muscovites filled the metro beginning at dawn, taking a fantastic journey in the radiant, underground palaces, and, full of the unforgettable impression, exited onto the street." All told, 372,337 people passed through the metro on its first full day of operation.

Among the signs present, one read, "The best metro in the world is built." Of all the things its architects and designers got right, the most important is that riders never feel like they are in a tunnel. That is something that no other metro can boast, least of all London's, which feels every inch a tube.

Dark Corners

The mosaics, paintings, relief sculpture and statuary of the Moscow Metropolitan offer a short course in Soviet history – the children's version. The workers reading *Iskra*, the competition between the Ural and Donbas miners, the happy farm girls collecting wheat or riding tractors – none of the iconography smiling from the walls and ceilings of this lovely web of concrete and steel betrays the fact that the metro was incorporated in the trio of horrors of Stalin's reign: collectivization, industrialization, and the Great Terror.

The metro was built in a very Russian way: under coercion. Passing the Russian Baroque architecture along the rivers and canals of St. Petersburg, there is nothing there to intimate the pain of the serfs who built it under Peter the Great's sword, or to memorialize the many who died in the process. So it is with the metro.

Yet there *are* distinct differences between the metro and other Stalinist construction projects – most distinguished by their remoteness. Approximately 100,000 laborers died building the distant White Sea Canal. John Scott, an American working in desolate Magnitogorsk, reported untrained, underfed, and exhausted men falling from scaffolding to their deaths. The gold mines of Siberia's Kolyma were frigid slaughterhouses where thousands died extracting the precious metal. But Moscow was anything but remote. And its builders were not political prisoners.

Yet the metro *was* a product of Soviet industrialization, a period as famous for the grandeur of its projects as it was infamous for its leaders' cavalier attitudes toward both resources and human lives. One of Scott's more potent observations was that "Russia's battle of ferrous metallurgy alone involved more casualties than the battle of the Marne."

As the superintendent of metro construction, Khrushchev took enormous risks. He pushed his crew of 70,000 relentlessly. Shifts ran to 48 hours without rest and Khrushchev ignored engineers' warnings that tunnels would collapse. Flooding and fires, and casualties, were common. But, unlike the situation with prison laborers, whose plight would not be told for decades, these stories were hailed in the pages of *Pravda* as "heroism in service to a great cause."

Moscow in the early 1930s had little automobile traffic and was still struggling with shortages of food and housing. Arguably the city's residents had greater need for basic necessities than for a shiny new underground train, so surface transportation would have been a more prudent use of funds. And the frequent accidents added to already high construction costs. In 1934 alone, 350 million rubles were spent on the metro. For perspective, 300 million rubles were spent on consumer goods for the *entire* Soviet Union during the entire first Five Year Plan.

Funding for massive industrialization projects came largely from grain exports. Activists were sent into the countryside to "invite" the peasants to join collective farms. One activist recalls a gathering: "I called a village meeting, and I told the people that they had to join the collective, that these were Moscow's orders, and if they didn't they would be exiled... They all signed the paper that same night, every one of them. Don't ask me how I felt and how they felt. And the same night they started to do what the other villages of the USSR were doing when forced into collectives – to kill their livestock." Another activist remembered that every peasant "had a greasy mouth" from the feast that ensued. It turned out to be a last supper.

The images of healthy farmwomen that adorn the metro bear little resemblance to the skeletal figures then occupying the countryside. Writer Boris Pasternak visited some villages in the early 1930s and later described what he saw as "inhuman, unimaginable misery, such a terrible disaster, that it began to seem almost abstract." The collectivization of the peasantry is one of the saddest episodes of the Soviet century. While grain was sold abroad to buy material and machines, millions starved to death at home. Some of that blood money certainly fell into the coffers of Metrostroy, the organization responsible for building the metro system. It is interesting to note that, before coming to Moscow, Khrushchev was a crucial figure in collectivizing Ukraine, the corner of the Soviet Union that suffered most from starvation. Despite being named for Kaganovich, and later Lenin, Khrushchev's presence is never far from the metro.

Industrialization marks the first half of the thirties, the Great Terror the second and the opening of the metro neatly straddles the two. The Terror is the third dark corner in the metro's storied past. No one was imprisoned in the metro, nor tortured there. But, given the security organ's preference for surprise arrests, many were taken in the metro. One author writes of being escorted "through the circular upper concourse of the Byelorussian-Radial subway station on the Moscow Circle Line, with its white-ceilinged dome and brilliant electric lights, and opposite us, two parallel escalators, thickly packed with Muscovites, rising from below." Solzhenitsyn made his way to the Gulag through the metro.

Second Generation

The next round of stations opened in 1937-38 and expanded the vocabulary of the earlier stations with some standout results. The lighting in Sokol is brilliant. It has a single line of stanchions that emerge from the benches around their bases, only about four feet on a side, and spread out to the width of the ceiling. Between each of the flowering pillars is a white dome lit by fixtures mounted on the elaborate crown molding just inside the cavity.

This crop produced two stations that are still among the most famous. Mayakovskaya was one of the deepest stations at the time. This is another of Dushkin's stations. Instead of the thick pylons that held up most other stations, he used thin columns faced with corrugated stainless steel and embellished at the bottom with red orlets, a decorative stone from the Urals. Between the steel ribs of the station are false cupolas with mosaics made from smalt, a type of colored glass. The depictions of the cast – the workers, soldiers and farmers that are the stuff of proletarian art from Berlin to Magadan – flying airplanes, parachuting, and so forth were based on a series of drawings by the artist Alexander Deyneka.

Mayakovskaya was so beloved that it was reproduced for the 1938 World's Fair in New York, where it won the grand prize in architecture. It would later show up in a painting of Stalin's 1941 meeting held in that station to mark the anniversary of the October Revolution, while the Nazis were poised at the edge of Moscow.

When tourists have time to see only one station, they see Revolution Square. This station, yet another by Dushkin, has 80 larger-than-life statues of the cast crammed under red marble arches. The figures all look terribly uncomfortable. One worker is holding himself up by his jackhammer, a soldier by his rifle. The student could not have studied very long in the pose he presents. Just two stations away is Baumanskaya, designed by Boris Iofan a few years later, that also has a series of bronzes. These are smaller-than-life, but the chests on some of the men are so puffed up that the figures seem to burst from their confines. This is conjecture, but with the large men greatly restricted and the small ones strutting about, it leaves one to wonder if Dushkin and Iofan had something to say about their times.

With Hitler's attack on the Soviet Union in 1941, the Soviet Union shifted to a war economy. As yet another signal of the importance of the Moscow Metro, it was the only major project that was undisturbed by the war. Several new stations were completed in 1943 and 1944 and these carried on the incremental changes made during the 1937-38 group. Stalinskaya (1944) is difficult to describe, but is defined largely by geometric patterns and a great variety of colored stone. Paveletskaya is probably the most elegant station in the metro. Its long colonnade of white marble holds a white vaulted ceiling. Where the arches meet, there is a golden shield with a hammer and sickle. It is uncluttered and calm.

Naturally, war themes were incorporated. At Izmailovsky Park, a sculpture of the beautiful partisan Zoya Kosmodemyanskaya stands guard posthumously, while behind her, small friezes of machine guns hanging from trees top the columns. Then there is Novokuznetskaya, a dizzying display of workmanship. A bas-relief cornice runs the length of the station, showing what must be the entire Red Army in action. A series of brightly colored mosaics dot the elaborately decorated ceiling. Between the narrow passageways to the trains are six-foot tall marble benches with carved scrolls for arms. This station is almost overwhelming and typical of what was to come after the war.

Postwar Boom

The ring line was part of the original 1931 plan, but no one then could have imagined the power that the USSR and Joseph Stalin would hold when it was eventually built. This line was the apotheosis of both. There seems to be no standard for what these stations should contain, as long as it was expensive. Taganskaya has gorgeous, light blue ceramic murals. Novoslobodskaya is breathtaking when riders stream past its dozens of internally illuminated stained-glass windows. The red ceramic molding of Kievskaya alone is worth stopping to see, but it also has its own didactic renderings of the cast, and even one of Peter I, the only image of a tsar in the metro known to this author.

The post-war round of station construction reached its apogee with Komsomolskaya. By adding steel supports, its architects expanded the height and width of its arches; this expansive station could contain any two previously built stations. The baroque arcade of white marble columns holds a barrel-vaulted ceiling covered with portraits of Russia's greatest heroes based on illustrations by Pavel Korin: Alexander Nevsky, Dmitry Donskoy, Kutuzov, Suvorov, Lenin, and two frames of Stalin. These characters are illuminated by chandeliers the size of compact cars. Louis XIV would have felt right at home here, awaiting the next train.

After Stalin's death in 1953, Khrushchev clawed his way into power. The Soviet Union had not yet recovered from the war and the need for frugality would mark many of Khrushchev's building projects. In reply to the housing shortage, he ordered the construction of thousands of five-story concrete apartments. These poorly built, "temporary" structures, many of which are still in use today, came to be called *khrushchoby*, a play on Khrushchev's name and *trushchoby* (slums).

Underground, Khrushchev established a bland template for station construction that was used for decades, usually at distant suburban stations: a long, square hall lined with square columns, covered in tile with the occasional ornament. That is all. These stations were made in the cut and cover method and passengers who lived near them probably felt lucky they were at least out of the weather – some stations in this era (Pionerskaya, Fili, Studencheskaya and others) were built even more cheaply, outdoors at ground level. It is said that Khrushchev's insistence on building more, if cheaper, stations, came from his 1959 visit to the United States and his horror at seeing the glutted L.A. freeways.

By the time Khrushchev was removed from office in 1964, the metro was serving 3.2 million riders per day, a considerable increase from its first years of operation. He added more than 17 miles of track and dozens of stations during his tenure, so he can be forgiven if some look stingy. But he should be credited for one other contribution to the metro. After Khrushchev's 1956 secret speech, the two mosaics of Stalin on the ceiling at Komsomolskaya were removed, as was his statue from the central hall of Kurskaya. Stalinskaya became Semyonovskaya, and Zavod imeni Stalina became Avtozavodskaya. But, more significantly, there was less worry now about being "taken" on the way to work. "The fear is gone." Khrushchev said. "That is my contribution."

Onward

Flush with oil money in the 1970s and 1980s, the sturdy, expensive style of the 1940s and 1950s came back in vogue. The neo-Stalinist stations of this period call to mind the bulky, gaudy cars rolling out of Detroit at that time. The barrel vaulted ceilings, heavy chunks of marble and granite, and *kitsch* were back, often with peculiar results. Aviamotornaya (1979) has a gold foil ceiling and a statue of what appears to be angels – odd in an atheist state. Shosse Entuziastov (1979) has a fist breaking its chains, an immediate reminder to American visitors of the Black Power movement.

There are some exceptions. In Ploshchad Ilyich (Ilyich Square, 1979) for example, the massive square red marble stanchions support the ceiling over a floor of gray, black and red granite. At the end of this somber station is a portrait of Lenin. This station has much calm and dignity and is a tribute far more dignified than the crushing ceremony surrounding the waxen corpse on Red Square.

Through decades of turbulence, including the wild years of industrialization, the greatest war the country has ever seen, imperial expansion, the space age and the Cold War, construction continued on the Moscow Metropolitan. As a testament to the metro's significance, Russia continued building even as the Soviet Union collapsed and the country faced seemingly untenable economic circumstances.

Many of the stations built in the 1990s and into the twenty-first century are innovative and grand, set pieces with what came before. Chkalovskaya resembles a space station with its green plastic lights bridging gray marble on either side of the arched roof. Vorobyovy Gory (under repair from 1984 to 2002) always provided a nice view, sitting as is does on a bridge over the Moscow River. Its large windows are now contained in a renovated, modern station brimming with sleek silver and grey paneling. And the station that began this narrative, Park Pobedy is emblematic, a beautiful addition to a system that is rich and deep. With history, that is.

November/December 2005

The Year Soaked in Blood
Tamara Eidelman

In 1937 the New Year fell on Friday, a workday. So everyone worked. Building socialism and fighting foreign and domestic enemies apparently left no time or energy for frivolous celebrations.

The country had been living with a six-day work week for several years. Mondays and Fridays, to say nothing of Sundays, were declared vestiges of the pre-Revolutionary past. Now there was the first day of the *shestidnevka* (the six-dayer), the second day of the *shestidnevka*, etc. The 6th, 12th, eighteenth, 24th, and 30th of each month were designated as days off. The only month when you could rest on the 1st was in March, to make up for the missing fifth day off in February.

But on that first day of 1937 you were at least allowed to decorate a holiday tree, a tradition that had been renounced in previous years. Legend has it that Stalin was quite taken with the Moscow Art Theater performance of Mikhail Bulgakov's *The Days of the Turbins*, and that he was enchanted by the Christmas tree decorated on stage by the Turbin family, whom history had slated for destruction. After watching Bulgakov's play several times, at the end of 1935 the Great Leader permitted his people to once again decorate holiday trees.

On the other hand, his decision may have had more to do with the fact that he had a little daughter at home, a child who had lost her mother to suicide in 1932. Whatever the case may have been, by the dawn of 1937, the most important holiday tree in the country had been installed for the second year running in the Hall of Columns of the *Dom Soyuzov* (House of Unions). Of course, the holiday being celebrated was not Christmas, but New Year's.

The Soviet people were supposed to rejoice and have fun. After all, they had so many causes for jubilation – the creation of *kolkhozes*, the construction of factories, the establishment of socialism and, of course, their own Great Leader and Teacher, Comrade Stalin.

TRANSLATION: NORA FAVOROV

The front page of *Pravda* on January 1, 1937, did not read "Happy New Year," as one might have expected. These times operated according to their own unique logic; the headline read, "The Great Helmsman is Leading Us."

The Helmsman had indeed steered quite a course. Nobody had taken the time to calculate how many millions had died of hunger during collectivization. Nobody had dared ponder how many millions were rotting away in camps or had simply been shot without trial.

Perhaps Joseph Vissarionovich himself had stood before the New Year's tree reflecting on how many enemies of the people he had already managed to destroy as he admired the sparkling of its many lights. Soon he would find out the answer: on January 1, newspapers called on "all Party and Soviet organizations and all Bolsheviks, whether Party members or not, to provide all possible assistance to those carrying out the general census of the population."

The census was set to take place on the 6th – the first day off of the New Year. The census results were shocking. It turned out that the population had suffered a horrific decline, a genuine demographic catastrophe. But none of this appeared in the newspapers. Instead, it was announced that the census had shown an increase in the well-being of the Soviet people.

And the Soviet people rejoiced in their well-being. There was the rejoicing of the collective farm workers who had been sent to prison for scavenging the fields for stray ears of grain. There was the rejoicing of the industrial workers who had no rest from their lathes in the new factories that had been built at such terrible human cost. There was the rejoicing of the convicts who were still alive and had been given a chance to survive the meat grinder they were being fed into.

If the newspapers are to be believed, songs like this one were sung by the people of Bashkiria:

Сверкают самолеты в небесах
Их крылья сделаны из светлой стали.
Да здравствует руководитель наш.
Великий друг людей – Иосиф Сталин!
На наш любимы праздник – Первый май,
Я в шелковой, я в белой выйду шали.
Блестящим белым шелком вышьем мы
На знамени родное имя Сталин.
Перед моим окошком для цветов

Друг изгородь плетеную поставил
Мы, как цветы в ограде, разрослись:
Садовник наш – родной Иосиф Сталин.
Колхозная пшеница высока.
Она созрела – желтая, густая.
Мы весело, зажиточно живем:
Учитель наш – родной Иосиф Сталин.
Не белые растут в полях цветы, –
Там алые раскинулись кустами.
Ведет нас к солнцу, впереди идет
Цветок наш алый, наш товарищ Сталин.

Planes glisten in the heavens
Their wings made of bright steel.
Hail our leader –
The great friend of people – Joseph Stalin!
On our great holiday, May Day,
I will go out in a white shawl of silk.
With bright white silk we will sew
The dear name of Stalin on our banner.
Before my window a friend has placed
A wattle fence for flowers.
We have grown like protected flowers:
Our gardener is dear Joseph Stalin.
The kolkhoz wheat is high.
It has ripened yellow and dense.
We are living happily and prosperously:
Our teacher is dear Joseph Stalin.
It is not white flowers that grow in the fields,
Crimson ones have spread like bushes.
Leading us to the sun, walking ahead
Is our crimson flower, our Comrade Stalin.

And Ukraine, not to be outdone by Bashkiria, also raised its voice in song:

Никогда так не было
В поле зелено
Небывалой радостью
Все село полно.
Никогда нам не была
Жизнь так весела
Никогда досель у нас

Рожь так не цвела.
По-иному светит нам
Солнце на земле:
Знать, оно у Сталина
Побыло в Кремле.
 Парни есть и девушки не в одном селе,
Те, что речи Сталина
Слышали в Кремле.
Не вмещает вод стольких
Ширь Днепра сама
Сколько есть у Сталина
Светлого ума…

Never before
Have the fields been so green
Nor has the village
Been so filled with joy.
Never before
Has life been so gay
Never before
Has the rye thrived so.
The sun shines on us on Earth
In a new way:
We can tell it has been
To see Stalin in the Kremlin.
There are lads and lasses in many a village,
Honored to have heard the speeches
Of Stalin in the Kremlin.
The breadth of the Dnieper
Could not hold water to equal
The brilliance of mind
That Stalin has…

Factories and collective farms reported that the annual plans had been fulfilled and overfulfilled. Philologists, journalists, and teachers were all preparing for a rather odd celebration – the 100th anniversary of Pushkin's death. The day of the poet's demise was being treated just as ecstatically as the achievements of *Stakhanovites*, the builders of the country's metros, or its Arctic explorers.

Those at the forefront of production were given awards for their feats. Sergo Ordzhonikidze, People's Commissar for Heavy Industry, was meeting with representatives of the industrial sector. (He had only about a month left to live before he would commit suicide.)

On January 1, newspapers ran a long list of soldiers who had been awarded medals. Many of them probably did not live to see another New Year's celebration – the summer of 1937 saw the beginning of a sweeping purge of the army that followed the trial of Marshal Mikhail Tukhachevsky, who was accused of plotting to overthrow the government.

But for now, medals were being handed out left and right. Yakov Serebryansky was singled out, "For special services in the fight against counterrevolution" and awarded the Order of Lenin. Serebryansky's services were truly remarkable. In 1930, he succeeded in kidnapping the leader of the Russian All-Military Union from France, General Kutepov. Serebryansky headed a group dedicated to removing anyone in the West who Stalin felt needed removing. In 1936, he managed to buy fighter planes in France and get them to the Spanish Communists. Serebryansky received word that he was being awarded a medal when he was in the midst of arrangements to kidnap Trotsky's son. Things did not work out the way they were supposed to – his victim died of a botched appendectomy. Although, who knows? Perhaps that was all part of the decorated agent's plan.

Serebryansky, however, did not have many days of freedom left. In November 1938 he was arrested and sentenced to death. However, such a valuable agent was not actually shot. Most likely, he returned to his duties at the intelligence services. In the end, he died in prison, but only after Stalin's death. At the dawn of 1937, Serebryansky was rejoicing with the rest of the Soviet people and trying on his new medal. Perhaps as a *Chekist* and a spy, however, he could already smell the ever stronger stench of blood in the air.

The general jubilation over plans fulfilled, censuses, New Year's trees in the Hall of Columns, and simply the fact that the Great Helmsman Stalin was presiding over the Kremlin, was accompanied by hatred toward those who would not let the Soviet People rejoice and celebrate. Enemies, terrorists, saboteurs, wreckers, and Trotskyites threatened from every corner. Your friend, wife, brother, boss, and even you yourself could turn out to be an enemy of the people, and as surprising as such revelations might be, they were sure to be correct. Mistakes were unlikely in such

Best of Russian Life: History and Culture

matters, and if they did occur, it just meant that "you can't make an omelet without breaking eggs."

The NKVD agents worked tirelessly. The black police wagons set out every evening and in millions of homes, behind millions of doors, people lay awake, listening for footsteps on the stairs – and letting out a sigh of relief when they heard the knock on someone else's door.

With every day, more saboteurs were discovered. In January 1937, it even turned out that well-known Bolsheviks were wreckers: Radek, Pyatakov, and others. They were publicly tried in that same Hall of Columns where the New Year's tree had so recently stood, encircled by frolicking children. Universal rejoicing was replaced with universal anger. The newspapers did not let up for a minute. The front pages yelled: "Blood curdling crimes," "They wanted to sell out our motherland," "A disgusting picture of human disgrace." Radek and Pyatakov acknowledged their guilt, and acknowledged it, and acknowledged it.

Lion Feuchtwanger, a marvelous writer who had fled Fascism, sat in the Hall of Columns taking notes for his book, *Moskau 1937*. This man, who had so insightfully portrayed the mechanisms of German Fascism in his novels, believed every word he heard in Moscow from men terrified for their lives. "When I witnessed the second trial in Moscow, when I saw and heard Pyatakov, Radek, and their friends, I felt all my doubts melt away like salt in water under the immediate impressions of what the accused were saying and how they said it. If all of this was fabricated or rigged, then I don't know the meaning of the word truth." And the entire Soviet people believed, or pretended to believe, everything that was said during the trials. With every day, their fury grew. It was like an Orwellian "Five-Minute Hate" session that stretched into weeks and months.

> К стене, к стене иезуитов!
> С них кировская кровь не смыта,
> Она их душит до сих пор.
> Враги народа – их защита! –
> И в гроб не влезет их позор!
> На свалку человечий сор!

> Up against the wall Jesuits!
> Stained with Kirov's blood,
> They choke on it yet.
> Enemies of the people are their defense!

And their shame won't fit in a coffin!
Onto the garbage heap of human trash!

The sentiments expressed by poet Mikhail Golodny were echoed by the polishing shop at the ball-bearing factory, by the women of the caramel unit at the candy factory, by doctors and teachers, by dairymaids and soldiers. They all obediently attended meetings and cast their votes in support of the death sentence for those who had committed all sorts of savage and monstrous crimes.

It was revealed that the actors in the blood-drenched comedy playing out in the Hall of Columns had wreaked havoc throughout the entire country. They had set off an explosion that killed a host of miners in the Central Mineshaft in Kemerovo. They had permanently crippled workers at the Gorlovsky Factory. And in one small town they had specially arranged an auto accident that resulted in the death of an engineer from the local factory who had been riding his horse down the road. Letters from throughout the country poured in; meeting followed meeting. Word even came from New York that 20,000 American workers were demanding the death sentence for the scoundrels. And their demands would, of course, be met. Radek and Pyatakov would be shot – along with their assistants, secretaries, drivers, relatives, friends, acquaintances, friends of acquaintances, and those who simply were not energetic enough in demanding their execution.

When summer came, Marshal Tukhachevsky was sentenced to death in a single day. Perhaps they were not able to force him to behave himself in a public trial. And a few months later they would shoot almost everyone who had tried Tukhachevsky, and their assistants, drivers, relatives, and simply those who were surprised that such famous heroes of the Civil War could have turned out to be traitors and spies.

People tell stories about a street-car driver, a member of the Communist Party. When all the Party officials at his street-car depot were arrested, he was made depot party secretary. When the directors of all the depots were arrested, he was made a director. When all the deputy transport ministers in his republic were arrested, he was promoted to deputy minister, and then minister. All of this happened over the course of several weeks. Such were also the dizzying ascents of platoon commanders, instantly elevated to the rank of army commander, or lowly bureaucrats transformed into top administrators because everyone above them had been destroyed.

And in the famous House on the Embankment, where all high-ranking government officials and military officers lived, the children from those families that had survived would make morbid sport of riding the elevators of the deserted sections of the building, ringing the doorbells of the sealed apartments whose residents had been led away, and taking the newspapers from the overflowing mail boxes. Those who had subscribed were now far away, and nobody took it upon themselves to cancel their subscriptions.

And so, 1937 was a year of a horrific, bloody harvest of human souls. And when it at last came to an end, those who had survived once again decorated New Year's trees and welcomed in the New Year, hoping for better things to come.

January/February 2007

The Bryansk Forest Sternly Stirred
Laura Williams

*J*ust before the onset of the Second World War, my 83-year-old neighbor Olga Ivanovna had a dream. The wooden chest in her entryway stood empty with the lid open. Clothes and other belongings were strewn out over the floor. She awoke and prodded her husband, Pavel, telling him to go look. He came back and said all was well. She dreamed it again. Waking up, she lit a candle and went to check for herself. Everything was in its place. The next day she asked one of the elder women in the village about the dream. The woman said the dream meant Olga Ivanovna would become a widow. Olga Ivanovna, then 20 and pregnant with her second child, tried to put it out of her head.

On June 22, 1941, Olga Ivanovna, eight months pregnant, was cleaning out the grain mill in the field with some other women when a man from the village of Chukhrai shouted to them to hurry back. All the villagers gathered in front of the store, where the district policeman from Suzemka, a town in the southern Bryansk Province, awaited them.

"I bear sad news," he said. "Hitler has attacked us. The war has begun."

All the able men in the village received notice soon after and were drafted into the Soviet Red Army. Olga Ivanovna's husband Pavel went to the enlistment office and asked to be let off until his child was born.

"At least until I find out if it is a girl or a boy," he pleaded.

They said he could stay until the third and final mobilization on August 12, when the last of the men – the old, the young, the sick, and even the authorities – were to be sent to war.

On July 12, 1941, Olga Ivanovna gave birth to a healthy girl, Anastasia. When Pavel was enlisted a month later, Olga Ivanovna accompanied him as far as the nearby river. Pavel carried their newborn on one arm and their two-year old girl on the other.

At the riverbank, Pavel looked at the infant sorrowfully and said, "I wish God would take you from your mother to unbind her hands."

That was the last time Olga Ivanovna saw him.

THE VILLAGERS OF Chukhrai soon learned that Hitler's army was overrunning Bryansk and the neighboring regions of Oryol and Smolensk, renaming towns and streets as they went and installing Nazi power. By November 1941, the Germans had reached the outskirts of Moscow, taking Tula and Kursk on the way.

The Nazis appointed Russians who had opposed the Soviet regime as Burgomasters of newly-occupied towns and villages. A former *kulak* who had refused to join the collective farm was named head of Chukhrai. Russians working for the Nazis were called *Politsai*. These Nazi collaborators forced people to work in the factories and fields from dawn until dusk. Livestock and grain supplies were seized and sent to Germany. Hundreds of thousands of people were sent there as well – for so-called "voluntary work programs."

But the Nazis did not gain control of Chukhrai or the surrounding countryside. Russians who had been left behind enemy lines, those who had returned home, and boys just learning to fight, created a resistance movement. They formed covert partisan groups that moved under the dense cover of the Bryansk Forest. Czechs, Slovaks, and Hungarians defecting from the Nazi army joined them. The partisans raided villages and towns to remove traitors working for the Germans and attacked Nazi posts and supply depots.

The Soviet government supported the partisan movement, hailing it as an effective way to fight behind enemy lines in occupied territories. Nightly, Soviet airplanes flew over the Bryansk Forest (a belt of dense forest extending 100 miles through the Bryansk Province and into the Ukraine), dropping thousands of parachutes with sacks of weapons, ammunition, food, and army garb. With support from Moscow and assistance from the surrounding villages, partisans – numbering more than 60,000 – began to gain control of the Bryansk Forest. They ousted the enemy from significant areas, forcing them from 500 towns in what was then Oryol Province and freeing more than 200,000 people by April 1942. They created three partisan-controlled zones in the southern, western, and northern portions of present-day Bryansk region.

The village of Chukhrai, where I live with my husband Igor, and neighboring Smelizh, were in the heart of the Southern Partisan Zone.

The villagers assisted the partisans in every way possible. They sewed undergarments from parachutes and jackets from the burlap bags dropped from airplanes. They provided food and shelter. My friend Olga Ivanovna remembers when 22 partisans spent the night on her floor. She made a pot of porridge to feed them. One was a woman. Another night, a group brought a sack of flour and asked her to bake bread. Some of the partisan groups were bandits, Olga said, especially those formed of men from other regions. They would take the last potato from a child and snatch a chicken out of the coop to boot.

Hitler announced that any person caught aiding, supplying, or hiding partisans would be executed and his property destroyed. Chukhrai and other villages in the Bryansk Partisan Zones came under fire. Nazi warplanes flew from the German airbase in Lokot, 30 miles away. They flew over Chukhrai daily, each time dropping bombs. Even today, in our paddock, there are craters left behind by the bombing. They fill with rainwater in the spring, and our horses drink from them. My husband Igor found several bombshells on his land when he first moved here. Now the exploded casings line the stoop by our front door, below a hanging display of other rusted war paraphernalia, such as a Nazi bayonet and folding shovel. Our postman uses one of the hollow bomb casings as an ashtray when he pauses on our porch stoop after delivering the mail.

During the air raids, low-flying planes skimmed the roofs of Chukhrai, firing off rounds of bullets, perforating every house. One small boy was shot through the leg while asleep in bed. Anti-aircraft guns placed around the village managed to shoot down only one Nazi plane in the course of the war. A 65-year-old man from Smelizh known as Belik found the propeller as a boy and later melted it down to make cast-iron pots.

The villagers dug trenches around Chukhrai and sought shelter in them during the bomb raids. I can still see the eroded furrows in the meadow beyond the lake. When it became too dangerous for them to remain near Chukhrai in daylight hours, they hid in the woods. The women took their children and elderly to the cover of the woods before dawn, returning to the village only after dark, stealing out to the garden plots they hastily tended for food.

THE PARTISANS CREATED a makeshift airfield near Smelizh, six miles from our village of Chukhrai, providing a connection to the Red Army stationed in areas to the east. Soviet planes were able to land at night in total darkness, carrying supplies and medicine. The partisans lit fires to mark a dummy airstrip in Chukhrai – where our paddock is today. While the Germans bombed the field where our horses now graze, riddling it with craters, Soviet planes landed in the dark near Smelizh. The planes were quickly pulled under the cover of the trees, where they were unloaded and, if necessary, repaired. Filled anew with the sick and wounded, the planes departed before dawn to Soviet-controlled territory. Despite the harrowing conditions, not a single plane crash was recorded on the Smelizh airfield during the war.

On November 6, 1942, the poet Anatoly Safronov arrived in Smelizh aboard one such airplane. He delivered a song he had written with composer Sigizmund Katz for the Bryansk partisans. They understood that it couldn't be a marching song, because partisans don't march. Nor could stealthy partisans sing loudly. The result was a song that could be sung softly in chorus – an epic hymn that would become well-known throughout Russia and the anthem for the Bryansk Province. Safronov sang the song that November night for the partisans there to greet him. They cheered and hugged him, begging him to sing it again and again, which he did.

> *The Bryansk Forest sternly stirred.*
> *A blue haze descended like a veil.*
> *And all around, the pines heard*
> *How partisans strode down the trail.*
>
> *Down a hidden trail amid the birch,*
> *Hurrying through the dense thickets.*
> *And swung over the shoulder, each*
> *Held a rifle loaded with cast bullets.*
>
> *And in the dark of night, to the enemy,*
> *To the Fascist command they dashed.*
> *And bullets between the tree trunks*
> *In the Bryansk oak woods crashed.*
>
> *In the forest, the foe finds no shelter,*
> *Grenades tear through the trees.*
> *And a commander yells to them after,*
> *"Smash the invaders, boys!"*

The Bryansk Forest sternly stirred.
A blue haze descended like a veil.
And all around, the pines heard
How partisans strode to victory.

As the partisans' new war mantra filtered through the Bryansk Forest, the Nazis escalated the bombing in partisan country, demolishing villages and towns. By the spring of 1943, the villagers of Chukhrai were forced to abandon their homes entirely and move to the woods, where they dug earthen bunkers to shelter their families. They fortified the walls and roof of each pit with logs, shoveling dirt over the top and laying pine bows to camouflage the shelters from above. They stuffed moss into slits and holes to keep the bunkers warm and to muffle the sound of children crying, in case the Nazis came near. They stashed food, weapons, and supplies in pits in the surrounding woods.

Partisans also inhabited such bunkers. One bunker off the road between Chukhrai and Smelizh housed a printing press where an underground partisan newspaper was published. Another nearby bunker served as a partisan hospital, housing the sick and wounded. In the makeshift hospital, cots were made from poles laced together with twine and covered with beds of moss. Doctors, nurses, and even veterinarians performed hundreds of complicated operations on a square wooden platform in the corner near the door, often without medication or anesthesia. With time, these structures gradually decayed, but recognizable bunkers can still be seen in the woods today. The hospital was recently restored as a historical monument. I have ducked inside many times, and I cannot imagine how doctors must have operated, or how wounded partisans recuperated in the dark, damp, and dirty quarters.

IN THE SUMMER of 1943, as the Nazi and Soviet armies prepared for what proved to be a decisive encounter and the greatest tank battle in history, at Kurskaya Duga (Kursk Arch), about 100 miles southeast of Bryansk, the Bryansk partisans escalated their clandestine operations behind enemy lines. Coordinating with the Red Army on the front, the partisans derailed trains and blew up railroad tracks and bridges throughout the region, cutting Nazi supply lines. In the course of the war, the Bryansk partisans would derail more than 1,000 armored trains, shoot down 120 airplanes, destroy 180 miles of railroad tracks and over 4,000 wooden bridges, raid dozens of Nazi command centers and garrisons, and cause some 100,000 Nazi casualties.

The Nazis diverted five divisions from the front lines to expel the partisans from the Bryansk Forest. They formed a chain and combed the woods around Chukhrai and Smelizh, where the Southern Partisan Zone was headquartered. The Nazis hoped to push the partisans out onto the open floodplain of the nearby Desna River, but their adversary placed 230 gunners in a line and breached the Nazi chain. The partisans escaped and headed towards the front. The people from nearby villages weren't so lucky and remained within the Nazi loop.

ON MAY 30, 1943, the Nazis rounded up all those found in the forests near Chukhrai, driving them from their earthen bunkers. The people hastily gathered food and supplies. They wrapped extra clothes around their waists to trade for food. Those who had cows took them along. The Nazis herded them through the village and down the road to Smelizh, burning any remaining houses on the way by throwing blazing bottles into the windows. Anyone who could not keep up with the column was shot on the spot.

The terrified villagers spent the night in the field near Smelizh and were joined the next day by more people evicted from the forests around that village. They then trudged the 30 miles to the Nazi base in Lokot, walking in a guarded, mile-long human column that grew with each partisan village passed. They ate raw potatoes and nibbled on flour. Women carried their infants. Older children walked, but none dared complain. One woman carried a newborn who died in her arms. She carried the dead child 15 miles until the procession paused for a moment, when she buried it on the side of the road.

Some were lucky and escaped from the column that day. As they left partisan country and came to a village under Nazi control on the road to Lokot, one woman leading a cow called to a local villager, "Pretend I am your family and I will give you my cow." The woman took her in for the cow.

People watching the procession cried to those in the column that the Nazis were executing everyone in Lokot. One boy slid out of the column and ducked between two women walking past. A *Politsai* came after him, but the women cried, "He's ours!" The boy stayed with the women for the next year.

When the displaced villagers arrived in Lokot that evening, their captors directed them into a bathhouse to be washed and rid of lice. Men were steered one way and women and children another. Families were split. There was no time for goodbyes. The men and women were driven into separate enclosures with 12 rows of barbed wire. The Nazis seized their cows and other livestock. They slept on the ground. The Nazis gave them boiled potatoes and water. My friend Olga Ivanovna recalls that when a German soldier brought potatoes, he personally handed them out to each individual. However, when a Russian *Politsai* delivered the potatoes, he heaved the whole pot through the fence. The prisoners shoved each other to get to the food. Children were crushed and smothered. If a German brought water, he would ladle it into the tin cans, jars, or cups of each prisoner, but if a *Politsai* brought the water, he would simply spray the crowd and leave.

Soon after the prisoners arrived, the Nazis ordered all the men and boys over 12 at the camp executed. The *Politsai* lined them up along a pit within view of their mothers, wives, children, and grandchildren. The executioners told them, "Stand with your own and you'll lie together." They fired from four machine guns. The men folded into the pit one by one. Then they were buried, some still alive. Witnesses say that the earth groaned and heaved for three days. Partisans were treated differently they were burned alive for all to see.

A few days passed and the *Politsai* handed the remaining women and children shovels and led them from the camp into a field. The prisoners dug a long trench. The *Politsai* told them they would be executed and they should stand near their loved ones. Machine guns were positioned, but before they could be fired, the guard at the camp changed. According to Olga Ivanovna, the German officer stepped down and the new officer, a Hungarian working for the Nazis, called off the execution.

After nearly two months in the Lokot camp, the women and children were loaded into 80 cattle cars and taken to Minsk. From Minsk, some women were sent to Germany to work in forced labor camps. Women with children stayed in the cattle cars for another week, evidently until the Germans figured out what to do with them. A week later, Olga Ivanovna's cattle car was hitched to a locomotive with a dozen other cars and sent to Ukraine. When the train stopped, a stout German officer opened the doors.

"Who wants to go to Germany to work as a volunteer?" he asked. "Food and shelter will be provided."

No one volunteered.

"Then you will all be sent to work in the *kolkhozy* in Nazi-controlled territory."

Dozens of horse-drawn carts rolled down to the train and took them away. The Ukrainian coachmen told them to make sure they were in the same cart as their kin, or they might end up in different villages.

Olga Ivanovna, her sister, two sisters-in-law, and their 15 children ended up in a small Ukrainian village called Kruty, along with nine other families from Chukhrai. They lived in the school and begged for food from the other villagers. For reasons Olga Ivanovna couldn't understand, the *Politsai* collaborators didn't allow them to work in the fields for food. Perhaps the *Politsai* didn't trust them because they were from partisan country. Their only food was potatoes given to them by kindhearted villagers. They cooked them on a fire pit outside the school. One particularly malicious *Politsai* would come by each evening and spit in the kettle. A woman living with them had an infant. The *Politsai* would tear the nursing child away from its mother's breast and spit in its face, saying nastily, "That's a budding partisan." The baby eventually died.

VICTORIOUS AFTER THE Nazi retreat from Kurskaya Duga on July 17, 1943, the Red Army began to push Hitler's troops out of Russia. Suzemka – in the Southern Partisan Zone – was freed from occupation on September 5, 1943. The capital city of Bryansk was freed on September 17. The two dates are still marked annually in the Bryansk Province. Last fall, I joined veterans and partisans as they gathered around the restored field hospital and a monument to the partisans erected near the wartime airfield in Smelizh.

Retreating, some Nazis came to the Ukrainian village where the Chukhrai families were living. They occupied the school, evicting the families. To escape, the women pushed their children out the window and jumped out after them. Some of the villagers let the refugees sleep on their floors. That night in the village, partisans killed two Nazis guarding a hangar where 200 confiscated horses were being held. The next day, the

Nazis sent troops to retaliate for the murders. They tossed shells into a few of the houses, intending to destroy everything and everyone in the Ukrainian village. But the Nazis retreated when the partisans blew up the bridge, mill, and three grain storage silos. The Red Army soon followed, ousting the Nazis further. It was October 1943. The survivors were free.

It wasn't until 1944, however, that the villagers returned to the charred remains of their homes in what was once Chukhrai, to pick up the pieces and begin life anew.

May/June 2005

Siege
Polina Fomina

Do you have any idea what 900 days is?
It is almost three years. Not a long stretch of time, so it seems. But now imagine being deprived of all the basic necessities of life for those three years.
Could you live for three years without water, food, indoor plumbing, electricity, public transport, telephones and everything which you are used to?
There is no question it can be done.
For this is how the inhabitants of Leningrad lived from 1941 to 1944.

*O*n a beautiful summer night in June 1941, the Great Patriotic War began.

No one in Leningrad could have imagined that, by September, war would reach the City of the Revolution.

The first bombing raid on Leningrad took place on the night of June 23, 1941. Soon, the evening bombings became more frequent, started fires and, worst of all, destroyed food supply warehouses. The war proceeded unexpectedly quickly... Germans seized the last rail line connecting Leningrad with the rest of Russia and, on September 8, 1941, the horrifying word "blockade" was first pronounced.

Three months after the start of the war, the city was ringed by German troops.

For the military, the blockade of Leningrad was a strategic maneuver. But for Leningrad's residents, the blockade meant that food, water, arms, clothing, construction materials, etc., no longer flowed into the city.

For three years – until January 27, 1944 – a hungry nightmare ensued. The door was slammed shut and the key was lost for 900 days.

There is a fairy tale by Vladimir Odoyevsky, *Town in a Snuff Box*, in which the town in question can only be observed through a tiny keyhole. Similarly, almost everything we know about life in Leningrad during the blockade we know from the tales of those who lived in the closed city.

These stories are graphic, dramatic and very concrete. Each is about a hero, and therefore a bit unreal. The immeasurable tragedy becomes almost surreal when we try to understand what "normal" life was like under the blockade. What was daily subsistence like for those who wore the mantle of heroes?

Take for example my grandmother and her friends. They were 17 years old. They falsified the dates of birth on their passports so that they could get into the army (for which you had to be 18). Or they stayed in encircled Leningrad in order to work in factories and hospitals.

But soon it was no longer important how old you were. Everyone was called up, except those trapped in Leningrad, surrounded by the enemy. They had no choice but to fight any way they could.

It is said that, when Soviet troops were taking Berlin, Russian army commanders were shocked when boys and girls of the Hitler Youth came out to fight against them. But the Germans had themselves met with this kind of resistance during the blockade of Leningrad. During the second and third winters of the blockade, it was Pioneers – boys and girls – who, with one rifle for every six, rode the trolleys to the front line. The war, which had already claimed so many grown-ups, was that close to their everyday lives...

These boys and girls stood guard on the rooftops, tossing incendiaries down on those who were bombarding the city. Meanwhile, they continued to attend schools, which, despite the hunger, cold and chaos, remained open.

What kind of life was this? How can one adequately describe it in a short journalistic article with words alone?

Well, words is all we have. So let us consider three "blockade words": hunger, cold and bombings.

Hunger

The essence of life under the blockade was that everyone was constantly hungry. In order to eat, you had to work. But working was very difficult... because everyone was constantly weak from hunger.

When the Badayevsky warehouse (which held the city's emergency food reserves) was destroyed by bombing in the spring of 1941, the city had no option but to introduce ration cards. Food could only be obtained with a ration card, and cards were handed out at workplaces. Yet there was not enough work for all. It is rumored that the Badayevsky warehouse was actually empty when it was hit, because of the ineptitude of city administrators. But many blockade survivors recount how they took buckets to the smoking remains of the warehouse and gathered up ashes and earth that was saturated with sugar and butter. And they ate it.

One of the most persistent blockade myths is that there was hunger in the city because some wanted to surrender it, and therefore took all the food out of the city prior to the blockade. Dreadful stories arose that some in the city were well-fed, that city bosses were flying in pears and that they were baking pastries at Smolny. The NKVD dealt harshly with the purveyors of such unpatriotic rumors, summarily executing those who sowed panic. They also dealt swiftly with cases of cannibalism and with those who held romantic notions toward the Germans, such as: "Let them in, at least they will bring food."

But the facts speak for themselves: 97 percent of Leningraders went hungry.

What can a hungry person eat? The blockade menu included such things as leather belts, carpenter's glue, weeds and grasses. Without exception, the food was low in calories and without vitamins. There were huge variations in the rationed norms allotted residents day by day. In the most critical winter months, rations were cut to 125 grams of bread (about two slices) per person per day. And for that share you had to stand in line for six hours.

Hunger was perhaps the most horrible trial, and those who lived through the blockade related to food differently the rest of their lives. During my carefree childhood, my grandmother persistently harangued us to completely clean off our plates and, even more so, to always gather up the breadcrumbs from the table – in memory of the blockade.

Imagine: the power of this massive fear of hunger is such that it survives even after 60 years.

Cold

Unabating cold was a central fear of the three blockade winters. Furnaces did not work.

If the first sign of war in the city was the crosses of paper glued to windows, to protect inhabitants from shattered glass during bombings, then the second sign was narrow tubes sticking out of these same apartment windows. Handy people crafted small, crude stoves – *burzhuykas* – and sold them. People would sell their family heirlooms to buy such a stove. They were small, fit in one room, and would burn up whatever you had. First firewood, then furniture, then books.

Windows blown out by bombs were covered with blankets. But what good does a blanket do over the window, when it is -30° C outside? You would light up the *burzhuyka* and sleep in your coat. Everyone who was still among the living would sleep together in the room with the stove. It was warmer that way. When people could no longer find the energy to climb the stairs, they moved to evacuated apartments on lower floors, or moved in with neighbors. Those who had enough strength took turns emptying the wastewater – the drains also did not work.

There was no water. The water pipes were as broken as everything else. When you wanted water, you went to the Neva.

Here was a typical picture: while her mother is at work, a young girl tows a bucket of water on a sled. To get the water in winter, she had to descend an icy precipice to the water hole, stand in a long line, ladle the water into a pail, haul that pail back up the icy cliff, empty it into her larger bucket, then get in line again. The entire procedure could take several hours.

In spring, it was a bit easier. The sun appeared and the ice melted. People found the strength to remove the corpses and trash from the streets. In the spring, in the very center of the city, on Nevsky Prospekt by Kazan Cathedral, gardens were laid. Life became a bit easier... until the next winter (and there were three of them).

Bombings

Fear was the third element in blockade life. Hunger and cold deadened the nerves. But fear resounded with the cry of air raid sirens and the whines of falling bombs and shells.

Your home could simply disappear in a regular bombing raid. There were ten per day.

The city had bomb shelters, some built before the war. Basements were then added to the list of shelters. There were, for example, 12 bomb shelters in the basements of the Hermitage, which, early in 1942, became the permanent home for 2,000 people. It was safer in the shelters, but what if, because of hunger, one lacked the energy to descend underground?

Gradually, Leningraders became accustomed to the close proximity of the front lines. As it happens, the house where my parents live sits on what was then the front line. In my childhood, we loved to play in the

In the German war plan Barbarossa, Leningrad was identified as one of the main strategic objectives. Moscow was to be taken only after Leningrad was overrun. The city was to be leveled. The German General Franz Halder, in the July 8, 1941, entry of his diary wrote: "It is the unshakable decision of the Führer to level Moscow and Leningrad, in order to completely annihilate the populations of these cities."

According to the most recent data, the number of citizens who died during the blockade was 900,000. At the beginning of the war, the population of Leningrad was 3.2 million. In 1944, when the blockade was completely lifted, just 560,000 persons remained. 700,000 died from hunger and bombings. 600,000 were sent to the front. The remainder were evacuated.

At the beginning of September 1941, an inventory was taken of all food reserves, cattle, poultry and grain in the city. Based on the real needs of the troops and population, on September 12, 1941 there was: flour and grain for 35 days; buckwheat and macaroni for 30 days; meat for 33 days; fat for 45 days; sugar and candies for 60 days. In order to economize on food, *stolovayas*, restaurants and other public eating establishments were closed. The consumption of food products over the established limits without special permission of the Supreme Soviet was strictly forbidden.

The only path for bringing foodstuffs and military goods into the city was over Lake Ladoga, and it was very unreliable. There were few ships on Lake Ladoga and they could not help the starving city. In November, Ladoga would begin to be covered with ice. Road workers would measure the thickness of the ice all across the lake every day. When the ice was 180 mm thick, they could drive trucks on it.

Spacing themselves out, the trucks slowly traversed the ice with their payloads. Everyone hoped that this would save the city's residents. But reality upset all hopes and estimates. The ice turned out to be too delicate. Aside from the fact that the trucks were constantly fired upon, many sunk through the ice because of the weight of their cargo.

At the approaches to the city, at the factories and mills, on the streets, thousands of people were constantly working to turn the city into a fortress. They worked 12-14 hour days, without consideration of who one was – *kolkhoznik* or professor at Leningrad State University. And, in a short period of time, they had created a defensive anti-tank barrier that was 626 km long; they built 15,000 pill boxes, and 35 km of barricades.

trenches – they had not yet been filled in. Then, in 1941-43, soldiers rode the trolleys to the front. The grandmother of one of my friends was a war correspondent for *Komsomolskaya Pravda* and rode the trolley every day to her work on the front lines – to write her reports from the battlefield. That's the kind of work she had: each morning she rode off to war.

German troops advanced into the city as far as the Kirov Factory. Today it is 20 minutes from there to the center of the city. Decisive battles took place here, directly in the factory. On one production line, they were assembling shells, while on another a battle was taking place. This factory, which in peacetime constructed tractors, was converted to production of tanks. Daily, the tanks would drive out the factory gates and head directly to the front. But, after the blockade began, there was not enough material; deliveries of steel were halted. At one point, all the artists and stage hands from the Mariinsky theater who were still living and in the city were summoned to the factory. Their task was top secret: they were to construct a tank division... out of cardboard. In just a few days, tanks filed out of the factory gates one after another, in the plain light of day. The entire intent was that the stage-managed division should be seen by German surveillance. It is said that this trick delayed a German attack on the city for several weeks.

PEOPLE HAVE FIVE senses: smell, hearing, sight, taste and touch. During those 900 days in the middle of the last century, all possible laws for normal human existence were destroyed. Every one of the five senses was assaulted with a fatal dose of "blockade poison." For 900 days, the customary smells were of blood, urine, fire and decomposition. Touch your face and you will feel nothing – just skin and bones, and you can't get warm. Look about you, and you don't recognize your city: buildings are destroyed; cupolas and spires of churches are covered with dark paint and camouflage netting; sculptures are buried and any intact windows are glued over with paper.

The body of the city was suffering. Yet a sound remained. It was like the beating of a heart. It was the sound of a metronome.

Radio was the only link to the outside world and the only possible source of information in the blockaded city. And, during those times when there was nothing to be announced or when there was no strength to carry on a broadcast, the sound of a metronome was broadcast over the radio, counting off the seconds. The dying city was dark, cold and hungry, but still the heart was beating. As long as there was this beating, it meant there was life. Perhaps not visible without, but it was there within.

Truly, life is surprising.

Humans can do anything. If they are without food, heat and light, they will drink spirits and eat grass. They will listen to the radio and tell jokes. The reason is simple: humans love life, even if it means enduring 900 days of horror.

From the Diaries of Leningraders.

V. G. Mantulin (died of starvation, January 24, 1942.)

January 4, 1942

The New Year is here. We greeted it with a cup of tea, a bit of bread and a spoonful of jam... The firewood is running out. There is nowhere to get any more. And there is still all of January and February. Two months yet of freezing cold!..

January 13, 1942

I must, apparently, go for some water. The water is completely frozen everywhere, and I have to carry it 4 kilometers home from the well. There is not even a drop of water left in the apartment to brew tea. Tea! How incredible this word sounds, when one is happy with just boiling water and bread! There is absolutely nothing to make tea with. There is not a crumb of anything sweet, and I have to flavor boiling water with salt. The only thing which we have enough of is salt. There is none in the stores, but we had a small reserve – some 2-3 kilograms, and it is holding out for now.

Well, there you have it. I have to go for some water... I so fear the cold. If I make it back, I will be wonderfully happy.

Mark Finkelstein

I related to my neighbors my theory of the "low probability of death by bombing." The representative of the family's youth, the delightful Masha, followed my example and stopped going to the bomb shelter. If I was at home at these times, I would turn on the gramophone, invite Masha over, and we would dance and, God forgive me, we would kiss. We laughed for the slightest reason and for no reason at all. We were simply happy – they were bombing the city, horror was everywhere, and we went nowhere, remaining upstairs, dancing. I have always loved the dances in fashion then – the foxtrot, the tango, and the Boston waltz.

But I have never experienced the supreme pleasure from dancing that I felt then, when the alarm had been sounded. They were bombing the city and we were dancing. If we were unlucky, it would be our last dance.

Once I was told that Masha was not home, so I did not turn on the gramophone. But she came running into the room and cried: "What happened? Why is the music not on? The alarm sounded ten minutes ago!" I smiled and turned on the gramophone.

In October in Leningrad camouflage work was being organized. We workers of the Narkomat Planning Institute of the Chemical Industry were transferred to barracks. When we worked on military objects, they fed us there. What is more, we did not have to show our food ration cards and, if we were lucky, we could receive food with them at the institute cafeteria. One time we worked at the aerodrome for almost a month. Returning home, we redeemed all our outstanding ration coupons at the cafeteria. For each coupon, they gave us a dessert spoonful of pearl kasha, served in a little dish. I received 22 servings of kasha, arrayed on my tray in several layers. It was a fantastic sight! I sat down at a table by myself and started to eat. I put a spoonful of kasha in my mouth and set aside the empty dish. Everyone watched me with envy. I slowly ate my 22 portions and drank up almost a month's worth of tea. That never happened again.

I was at that time a fearsome, bloated, dying old man of just 32.

Not long before the New Year, I witnessed a tragic episode. I was at the aerodrome, meeting airplanes that had flown in with produce for Leningrad. The unloading was done and suddenly I heard a desperate cry:

"Let me go! I only took a small bit! For my child! He is starving," cried some fellow, who was being dragged away by several other guys. In those severe times there was an ironclad law: execution was the singular punishment for theft of food. The sentence could not be appealed and was carried out the very same day.

Alexei Zorgenfrey

The pigeons and sparrows are disappearing from Leningrad. The dark ones – crows – are next. Signs are appearing in many houses: "Would like to buy a cat," "Who will sell a dog to a good home?" Workers in scientific laboratories – with their experimental animals – and zoo workers are the source of great envy. The last of everything is disappearing from already empty stores – dry mustard, pepper, bay leaves, cornstarch, bone meal. People try to bake cakes or boil up a soup from these things. Castor oil is worth its weight in gold: there is no other fat. But it has already disappeared from pharmacies. Cough drops and all other oral medicines have also been bought up. People learned how to make cutlets from oil cakes. But even oil cakes can not be found anymore.

Leningraders' outward appearance is changing.

Hunger.

"Comrade Bogdanovich, please come to Party Committee Headquarters. You will be given something there."

I went.

"We have succeeded in obtaining for the professorial-teaching group two boxes of carpenter's glue. Here is one pound for you. You can make a soup from it or make a jelly. Be sure to add a bit of pepper."

January/February 2004

Daily Bread
Darra Goldstein

*D*uring the Siege of Leningrad, people had to be creative beyond measure simply to stay alive. They began by slowly braising and softening the tough outer leaves of cabbage they previously had discarded, turning them into a dish called *khryapa*. But soon they had to resort to more desperate acts. They retrieved old flour dust from the cracks in floorboards and licked spattered grease from the kitchen walls. They tore books apart for the glue from their bindings and scraped wallpaper paste from the walls (before the age of synthetics, glue and paste were made from animal protein). These practices were necessitated by a ration that, at its lowest, allowed for only 125 grams of bread a day. And this wasn't even normal bread. In addition to rye flour it also contained "edible" cellulose, cottonseed-oil cake, chaff, and the dust shaken from flour sacks. This siege loaf was damp, heavy, and greenish-brown. Its texture was crumbly, yet gummy on the tongue.

The authorities periodically provided foodstuffs that had been salvaged from industry. Especially distasteful and hard to digest were the hard cakes of pressed seed hulls left over from the processing of oil from sunflower, cotton, hemp, or linseed. Originally meant for cattle fodder, these "oil cakes" were often too hard to break into pieces by hand. A knife or axe blade was used to plane them like wood, and then the shavings were fried like pancakes. Other industrial products included *olifa*, boiled linseed or hempseed oil. Used in classical oil paints, *olifa* could be metabolized like edible oil, with the same nutritional value, but the flavor was vile. Even so, it was preferable to machine oil, which people stole from factories that had ceased production. Although machine oil generally went right through the system and had no nutritional value, there was always a chance that it was based on animal fats or vegetable oil rather than petroleum. Similarly, the coarse siege bread seemed more palatable when fried in paint thinner. The inner side of pig- or calfskin could be boiled for hours to make a kind of soup. Since soup is such an important component of Russian cuisine, an integral part of the daily meal, women often made soup out of the family's bread ration instead of just serving the bread plain. Although it consisted of nothing but breadcrumbs and water, the whole felt like something more than its parts. And it was certainly more appealing than the murky white yeast soup derived from cellulose that was given out instead of a grain ration.

As the Siege continued, and hunger grew, the people of Leningrad grew increasingly desperate and resourceful. Women scoured the city, braving artillery fire in their search for food. At night, dressed in dark clothes, crawling from row to row, they chopped at the frozen ground to dig the potatoes that lay rotting in the fields outside the city. Survivors tell of readily, even avidly, eating the wood shavings, peat, and pine branches they scavenged. Joiner's glue became standard fare for many. Nearly all of the Siege survivors express nostalgia for the "sweet earth" they salvaged from the site of the Badayevsky warehouse fire, in which 2,500 tons of sugar melted onto the ground. For months after the fire they used axes to chop away at the frozen earth and loosen the soil, still saturated with sugar. Retrieved down to a depth of three feet, the soil sold for one hundred rubles a glass; from more than three feet below the surface it cost only fifty rubles. This "sweet earth" could be heated until the sugar melted, then strained through several layers of muslin, or it could be mixed with library paste to make a kind of gummy confection. People often called this concoction "candy" or "jelly" because it seemed like such a treat.

Food has meaning only when it is shared, and in blockaded Leningrad sharing was nearly impossible. The unnatural role into which food was cast represented a particularly debasing aspect of Siege life, one that went against the very idea of hospitality that the Russians hold so sacred.

January/February 2004

Moscow Knights
Nikolai Poroskov

On the morning of June 22, 1941, Hitler unleashed Operation Barbarossa, his invasion plan for the Soviet Union that had been in the works for six months. Over 4.5 million troops invaded the USSR along a 2900 km front. It was the largest military operation in history, both in terms of manpower and eventual casualties. Initially, the blitzkrieg operation in the East delivered swift successes and by the fall Nazi forces were closing on Moscow.

German General Headquarters had worked out their plan for the final offensive on Moscow during their successful battle near Kiev, in late September 1941. Dubbed "Typhoon," the operation was to include 77 army divisions, including 8 motorized and 14 tank divisions, which would sweep through Soviet defenses like a typhoon, the seemingly unstoppable German forces taking Moscow before winter set in. To prepare the offensive against the Russian capital, the Germans unfolded their forces from Kursk in the South to Kalinin in the North. They faced the defense of the Western, Reserve and Bryansk fronts under the respective commanders Ivan Konev, Semyon Budyonny and Alexander Yeremenko.

A month earlier, during the hubris of the early successes of Operation Barbarossa, Hitler had told Goebels that Moscow will be "erased from the face of the earth as the center of Bolshevik resistance." Special equipment was being prepared to inundate the city and create a gigantic lake on its site. From among the 4th German Army a "special team" within the *Einzatsgruppen* SS "B" was to become the police force of Moscow and take control of a fallen Moscow. Several German units had already been distributed special uniforms for a future parade in the Russian capital (notably, however, just one-third of German forces had clothing for winter, as the high command expected the war to be over by then and two-thirds of the German army to be returned to the rear).

German intelligence on Russian capabilities was virtually non-existent prior to the war. And Hitler, overconfident from his easy victory in France, brooked no doubts about German invincibility. When Croatian Defense Minister Kvaternik asserted that the USSR could create new divisions behind the Urals, the Führer just laughed.

Even the USSR's new allies were confident of its imminent collapse. U.S. Naval Secretary Frank Knox estimated that the Soviet Union would crumble in 6-8 weeks. The head of the British General Staff said that "the Soviet armies will be herded like cattle." Only Franklin Roosevelt continued to believe that the USSR would take the heat and withstand the challenge.

Why did the Nazis choose to march on Moscow? After all, for Hitler, the main operational objectives for attacking the Soviet Union were to gain control of the fertile Ukraine and access the Caucasian oilfields. As late as July 1941, Hitler relegated the capture of Moscow to secondary importance, after Leningrad and Ukraine. Moscow, he said, "is merely a mark on a map."

His senior commanders did not agree. General of the Tank Corps Guderian summarized their views when he stressed that "Moscow is not only the head and heart of the Soviet Union. It is also a communication center, a political center, the most industrialized region and a major transportation center. Stalin knows it. He knows that the Moscow variant means a definite defeat. He will thus concentrate all his forces near Moscow. If we win a victory in Moscow and thus turn off the central switching station of the Soviet Union, then its other regions will also fall before us."

But Hitler would not be swayed. On August 24, fully a month after the swift victories in Minsk and Smolensk, with his troops just 200 miles from Moscow at the height of summer, the Führer opted to split the bulk of his forces, simultaneously attacking north toward Leningrad and south toward Ukraine. It would be October before these forces, now even more over-extended, would regroup with Army Group Center and turn their attention on the capital. And by that time, winter was fast closing in.

Meanwhile, in July, the Soviet State Committee of Defense (GKO) ordered that the main line of defense form at Mozhaisk (110 km west of Moscow). It was to consist of three armies headed by the commander of the Moscow Military Region, General-Lieutenant Artemiev. By the end of July, three echelons of forces had been regrouped for the defense of Moscow: the Western Front, the Front of Armies in Reserve and the Front of the Mozhaisk Line of Defense. Interestingly, some of the first significant military actions were to unfold not far from the Borodino field where 129 years previous the Russians had fought Napoleon.

Meanwhile, long anti-tank ditches (stretching over 200 miles on the northern approaches and 160 miles in the West and South, in addition to four semi-circular lines around Moscow) were beefed up with minefields and barricades, largely through the efforts of the 250,000 civilian residents of Moscow and its environs.

In late August, Georgy Zhukov threw the two armies from the left flank of the Reserve Front into a counter-offensive near the town of Yelnya. This helped to disrupt German organization of the impending attack, liquidating the so-called Yelnya ledge, which the Germans had intended to exploit to breakthrough to Moscow. It was the first piece of land in Europe (150-200 km^2) won back from the Wehrmacht. Similar types of counterattacks were launched to the south, unfortunately to little effect.

By late September, German forces at Army Center had been reinforced with reserves and with forces from other fronts. The total center group of armies now numbered 1.8 million soldiers, 1,700 tanks and 1,390 aircraft. This represented a 1.4-2 fold numerical superiority over the Red Army and was the greatest concentration of German forces ever seen. There were more tank and motorized divisions than those Germany lined up in May 1940 against France, Belgium and the Netherlands put together. Over the 203 days of the Battle for Moscow, considering reinforcements, some 7,035,000 soldiers took part on both sides.

Historians divide the Battle for Moscow into two periods: the defensive (September 3 to December 4, 1941) and the offensive (December 5, 1941 to April 20, 1942). Several units of German troops began the assault on Moscow as early as September 26. But the main attack was to be unleashed on October 3. On the night of October 2, the soldiers of the Eastern Front were read Hitler's address. He told the troops that this was "the last great decisive battle of the year." The next day, Hitler announced to the German people that "not before then was he permitted to tell the German people that the foe was already broken and would never rise again."

At dawn on October 3, the main German forces headed east. Employing the by now standard tank-led pincer movement that had encircled Smolensk, Kiev and other cities, German forces pierced Russian defenses in three locations along the front, each separated by some 150-200 km.

Within ten days German forces were in Khimki, northwest of Moscow, had encircled Soviets troops near Vyazma (creating the so-called "Bryansk *kotyol*" – "pot") and had broken through to Kalinin from the Southwest. There was now a 500 km wide gap in the Western Front. The road to Moscow stood open to German tanks, just 40 km from the outskirts.

It was a desperate situation and, for Stalin, it called for desperate measures. In July, Stalin had dismissed General Georgy Zhukov as Chief of the General Staff in favor of the hapless Shaposhnikov. Since that time, Zhukov had been coordinating the Reserve Forces and the defense of Leningrad. Without admitting his error, Stalin on October 10 appointed Zhukov Commander of the Western Front, saying by telephone, "take everything in your hands and act."

Intelligence from Japan, provided by Richard Zorge, indicated that Japan would not join the war against Russia, but was instead preparing for an attack on the U.S. This allowed crucial reinforcement of the western front with "Siberian Divisions" from the Far East, many of them top class marksmen and all well-equipped for winter warfare.

That Hitler's forces were able to come so close to Moscow is largely attributable to Soviet military command's complacency and inability to correctly anticipate German actions. Forces were spread too thin along the front lines and did not correlate with enemy forces. For instance, where the 9th German army broke through Soviet lines, Soviet forces had just 19 tanks against Germany's 591. At the same time, on other, less crucial sectors of the front, a useless balance in Russia's favor was found. Throw in the manifest German superiority in aviation and artillery and it is no surprise that two-thirds of Russian divisions ended up encircled.

The State Defense Committee (GKO) evacuated from Moscow industrial enterprises, state agencies and most of the city's population, having declared the capital under siege. As many as 1,119 sites were prepared for destruction. The most important state establishments and the diplomatic corps were evacuated to Kuybyshev (modern day Samara). A Special Brigade subordinated to the chief of the 4th Diversionary Directorate of the NKVD, General Pavel Sudoplatov, mined buildings which might serve as offices for the Wehrmacht command, should Moscow be occupied. The brigade also mined several government *dachas* near Moscow, excepting Stalin's dacha.

According to numerous memoirs and documents now available, Stalin had in fact envisaged that Moscow could be sacrificed. The Resolution of October 15, 1941, on the evacuation of the capital, testifies that the Supreme Commander (Stalin) was also supposed to leave the capital. On the night of October 15-16, the order was given to evacuate part of the city's population, and to distribute food products from stores to residents. When measures began being implemented, there were cases of disorder on the streets, but these were quickly stopped. Yet, on October 16, cases of panic during mass evacuation had to be quelled again.

On the whole however, Muscovites were quite stoic in the face of difficult odds. Entire divisions of people's militia were formed in Moscow. As many as 440,000 Muscovites built barriers, anti-tank moats and metallic barricades from rails. As Admiral Nikolai Kuznetsov recalled, the artillery from several warships was put on wheels and sent to Moscow, 25 naval brigades arrived near the Russian capital. In no time the city was turned into a fortress.

On November 6, 1941, on the eve of the 24th anniversary of the October Revolution, Stalin called upon his compatriots to wage a patriotic war. Despite the tense situation, on November 7, 1941 troops were found to parade on the Red Square and right after the parade went to the front (all artillery was on the front lines, however, and relics from military museums had to be used in the demonstration).

The Typhoon was losing wind at the Mozhaisk line of defense, and, for the first time, German command was realizing that it was in a dire situation. Vastly overextended, facing serious equipment breakdowns and supply problems, the Wehrmacht was finally realizing that it faced a formidable enemy in Russia, which had a much stronger rear than anticipated and which was the first foe yet capable of grinding the *blitzkrieg* to a halt. And then there was winter, which was arriving early. German equipment was not oiled or prepared for the subfreezing climes; there were insufficient winter uniforms for troops and supply lines were further fractured by cold weather.

Yet, on November 11, notwithstanding the diminished potential of his troops, Hitler signed an order for a new offensive against Moscow – given the over-stressed condition of his troops, it would later be called Germany's "retreat to the East." The offensive was launched on November 15, its intent being the encirclement and blockade of the capital. Initially, there were successes. By November 23, German tanks were in Klin and winding around the capital to the North.

In his book *Reminiscences and Thoughts*, Zhukov wrote about a phone conversation he had with Stalin during the November offensive:

Stalin: "Are you sure we will retain Moscow? I am asking you with pain in my soul. Answer me honestly, like a communist."

Zhukov: "We will no doubt retain Moscow. But then we need no less than two armies and at least 200 tanks," Zhukov answered.

Stalin: "It's not bad you have such assurance. Call the General Staff and ask where to focus the two reserve armies you are asking for. They will be ready by late November. But we cannot give you tanks for now."

Stalin had reason to be worried, for it seemed initially that the German offensive would be successful. In early December, just 12 km separated the Germans from the borders of modern Moscow in the Lianozovo district. From the roofs of houses in the villages Katyushki, Puchki and Krasnaya Polyana, German soldiers could peer into Moscow streets through binoculars. The atmosphere in the Soviet government was extremely tense: Foreign Minister Vyacheslav Molotov, the top Soviet leader after Stalin, threatened to shoot Zhukov. Zhukov, in turn, threatened to shoot commander Konstantin Rokosovsky for any non-ordered withdrawal of troops.

But Russian soldiers continued to fight. Cases of mass heroism were legion. For example, in the Northwest, where the situation was especially dangerous, near the crossroads of Dubosekovo village, the now famous 28 *Panfilovtsy* (i.e. soldiers commanded by General Ivan Panfilov) fought to the last man for four hours, stopping 18 enemy tanks and killing many German soldiers. It was there that the *politruk* (political leader) Vasily Klochkov pronounced his now famous phrase: "Russia is huge, but there is nowhere to retreat to, for Moscow is behind us!"

Meanwhile, behind German lines throughout the Moscow region, partisans were decimating the German forces from the rear. As a result, the Germans were especially merciless to partisan prisoners. On November 28, 1941, they caught one such hero – 18-year old student Zoya Kosmodemyanskaya – in the village of Petrishchevo outside Moscow, as she tried to set fire to an *izba* where Germans were lodged. Zoya was tortured by her captors but never revealed the names of her comrades. Aghast at her stubbornness, the Germans raped her and hanged her in front of the whole village. But rather than deter others, it only spurred further acts of heroism.

The Germans were finally stopped on December 3. On the night of December 5-6, the long-awaited Soviet counter-offensive was launched at Moscow. Simultaneously, the Stavka ordered an offensive in Tikhvin, near Leningrad, and at Rostov-on-Don, to keep the Germans from diverting troops from the South or North to Moscow.

This transition to a counter-offensive without any pause took the Germans by surprise. What is more, the scale of the action was unprecedented, with three Soviet armies on the offensive along a 1000 kilometer front.

The date of the counter-offensive was significant: according to the Orthodox Church calendar, December 5 was the date that Prince Alexander Nevsky defeated the Teutonic (German) knights on Chudskoye Lake in 1142.

Historians have meticulously calculated the correlation of forces on the eve of the Soviet counter-offensive. The Red Army had 1,100,000 soldiers, 7,652 guns and mortars, 415 reactive "Katyusha" artillery rockets, 774 tanks and 1,000 aircraft. The German Center Army Group had 1,708,000 men, 13,500 guns and mortars, 1,170 tanks and 615 aircraft. Yet, notwithstanding their numerical superiority, the Germans were beaten back. The Soviet army liberated Kalinin, Klin and Solnechnogorsk. Their breakthrough to Rzhev posed a threat to the armies from the North. In the South, Kaluga and Naro Fominsk were freed. By January 7, 1942, German forces had been pushed back by some 100-250 km and suffered incredible losses. The threat of Moscow's sack was eliminated.

The Wehrmacht's top commanders paid dearly for the defeat, even though the strategy had been entirely of Hitler's making. On December 19, 1941 Fieldmarshal von Bock, commander of the Center Army Group, lost his position. On December 26, 1941, commander of the 2nd Tank Army, General Guderian was dismissed. In all, Hitler ordered the purge of 177 generals because of the "debacle" near Moscow.

During the most critical moment of the German retreat, General von Bock noted in his diary three reasons for the German defeat at Moscow: "poor roads caused by autumn weather, which impeded maneuverability, paralysis of railroads, and the underestimation of the forces and reserves of the adversary."

In fact, the lattermost reason was decisive. As von Bock wrote in his diary, the adversary, "with its inexhaustible human forces, without sparing it, is switching to the counter-offensive." True enough, Soviet generals did not always spare their soldiers. But then the "zero dead" doctrine was not applicable in those times and extreme circumstances. Russians were fiercely defending the heart of their country at all costs. As a result, again according to von Bock, "in an amazingly short period of time, the Russians could reassemble destroyed divisions."

Hitler was so sure of victory in the East that he did not anticipate a winter campaign. He calculated that surprise and his cruel, ferocious fashion of waging war would break the country's will to resist. But the tactic which paid off in Europe failed against a people whose will was forged by many centuries of trials and tribulations.

At Moscow, Germany suffered its first major defeat in WWII and was no longer considered invincible. The *blitzkrieg's* epitaph was also written, and Hitler could never again marshal the forces for a large-scale surprise attack. In the future, Germany was forced to introduce a system of total mobilization of human and material resources.

Fieldmarshal Keitel (who in May 1945 would sign the act of surrender on behalf of Germany) acknowledged that, after the Battle for Moscow, he could no longer envision a military solution to the campaign in the East. Germany was henceforth faced with a truly People's War. From both sides of the Atlantic, there was a growing awareness that the Moscow battle saved the Free World from the fascist yoke. The confidence of the Axis Powers was also sapped: Japan relinquished its "Northern Variant" and didn't attack the USSR. Turkey also refrained from siding with Germany. The Germans gave up their plans of invading India and the Middle East. Franklin Roosevelt told Stalin about the "overwhelming enthusiasm which swept the people and the country because of the encouraging successes of the Red Army." In mid-December 1941, Winston Churchill wrote to his Chief of Staff that "the main factors in the war now are the defeats and losses of Hitler in Russia."

Indeed, the victory of the USSR in the Battle for Moscow played a decisive role in the creation of the anti-Hitler coalition. Before the USSR proved itself near Moscow against Hitler, its allies, potential and real, were taking a wait and see attitude. The USSR was waging the war against

Hitler alone. The Lend-Lease shipments and the opening of the Second Front were still in the future.

A million Muscovites were decorated with the medal "For the Defense of Moscow." Paradoxically, Georgy Zhukov was not awarded one of these medals. To fathom this injustice, one merely needs to consider the "court psychology" in Stalin's retinue: if the merits of the front commander were highly appreciated, then the contribution of Stalin would surely be diminished.

Zhukov, for his part, led Soviet forces all the way to the seizure of Berlin and the storming of the Reichstag. Yet in his memoirs he stated the matter quite simply: "When I am asked what I remembered best from the past war, I answer, 'the Battle for Moscow.'"

> *Cut the phrases on valor and bravery*
> *Words are just words*
> *We stood here making no step backward*
> *We are laying here. But then Moscow stands tall.*
>
> *– Poet Vladimir Karpeko*

November/December 2001

Stalingrad
Nikolai Poroskov

In the spring of 1942, Soviet troops were in a difficult position. They had survived a difficult winter and snatched victory from the jaws of defeat at Moscow, yet they had not yet been able to turn back the German tide. Against the advice of General Georgy Zhukov, Stalin decided on an ill-fated attempt to attack the Germans in the South, to try to retake Kharkov. It turned into a bloody debacle in which over a quarter of a million Soviet troops were captured, and it led to a German breakthrough. Fascist forces began marching toward the Volga and the stage was set for the most important military battle of the Second World War. Within a few months, the "invincible" German war machine would be broken and the tide of the war finally turned. But only after hundreds of thousands had perished and the city on the Volga bearing the vozhd's name – Stalingrad – was turned into a pile of steaming rubble.

Stalin had expected Hitler's main attack in 1942 to be on the Central Front, directed at Moscow. As a result, Soviet forces in the South were diluted to strengthen the Center, and they were unable to withstand the German onslaught, the main objective of which turned out to be driving to the Volga, cutting off Russia's oil supplies from the Caucasus (and Lend-Lease, supplied through Iran), and cutting Russia in two.

Hitler's task was made easier by the lack of a second front in Western Europe (which would not be opened for two years). Except for England, Hitler had virtually all of Europe quietly subdued, and he was able to send 25 divisions east. On June 28, a month after the failed Soviet counterattack on Kharkov, the German attack in the South began, directed at Voronezh. By July, Soviet forces had been beaten back to the Don River and, on July 28, the infamous Order #227 was issued by the Soviet Supreme Command: *"Ni Shagu Nazad!"* ("Not a single step backward!")

The order harshly declared that the Soviet people were losing their faith in the Red Army, that many damned the army for fleeing east, allowing the people to be subjugated to the German yoke. The document ordered soldiers and officers to defend every meter of their homeland until the last drop of blood. It said the main flaw of the army was a lack of discipline in the troops, and it authorized summary execution of cowards and panic-mongers as traitors.

As a matter of fact, Order #227 drew on German expertise. After their crushing defeat near Moscow, the German army formed over 100 "penalty companies" – made up of soldiers and officers who retreated or panicked – and threw them into the most dangerous segments of the front, so that those "at fault" could be cleansed of their guilt with their blood.

The Red Army established 10 penalty (*shtrafniye*) battalions composed of commanders who showed cowardice. They were stripped of their war medals and ranks and were sent to serve in the hottest, most dangerous spots along the front. The families of these "traitors" fell victim to repressions. As a result, the members of these *shtrafniye* battalions really had nothing to lose (but their lives) and soon became the Germans' worst nightmare. Bard Vladimir Vysotsky, who composed quite a few poignant songs on the Great Patriotic War, later sang: "You're better off cutting down the forest for coffins – the penalty battalions are going into the breach." *("Vy luchshe les rubite na groby – v proryv idut shtrafniye bataliony.")*

Stalin ordered the creation of one to three *shtrafniye* battalions at Stalingrad, with 800 soldiers in each. Barrage (*zagraditelniye*) squads were formed in the rear of "shaky divisions" – another idea stolen from the Germans. Each Russian army was supposed to have three to five barrage squads, each with 200 soldiers.

Shortly after the signing of Order #227, the well-greased Soviet propaganda machine began to tell stories of the heroic deeds and unparalleled courage of Soviet soldiers. The day after Stalin's order was issued, it became known that four soldiers, who had only two armor-piercing rifles between them, engaged battle with 30 enemy tanks and set 15 of them on fire. Such exploits were legion – almost a daily fact – like the pilot Rogalsky who, shot down over Stalingrad, directed his burning aircraft into a mass of German tanks.

"Not a Single Step Back!" was actually very controversial among the troops, and raised quite a few objections. This is plain to see now from the reports of the *osobye otdely* ("Special Departments" – military counter-intelligence). But then the vociferous malcontents were quickly silenced by their transfer to penalty battalions.

By late August, German forces had taken the Donets basin, the Crimean peninsula and had raised the German flag atop Mount Elbrus. On August 23, German planes made some 2,000 sorties attacking Stalingrad. Over 20 ships were hit in the Volga waterway and oil storage tanks were struck, their contents flowing in an infernal stream into the Volga. The whole river was on fire, with flames nearly a kilometer high. Over 300,000 Stalingraders were evacuated beyond the Volga, and on August 25, a state of siege was declared in Stalingrad. Hitler's 6th Army, under General Friedrich von Paulus, encircled the city.

On August 27, General Georgy Zhukov, who had been commander of the Western Front since his decisive victory at the Battle of Moscow, was promoted to Deputy Supreme Commander, second only to Stalin, who held the title of Supreme Commander. Together with the Red Army's Chief of the General Staff, General Alexander Vasilevsky, Zhukov was put in charge of the Battle of Stalingrad.

By early September, the Germans had pierced Soviet defenses, seizing several strategic heights above the city and key positions in the approaches to the city. Only a few kilometers separated them from Stalingrad. On September 13, the Germans began the storming. The central railway station changed hands more than 10 times. The "House of Sergeant Pavlov" – a brick building which occupied a dominant position above the city – was turned into an unassailable point of Russian resistance. Its defenders withstood a 58-day Siege, barring the enemy from reaching the Volga. Here, as Marshal Vasily Chuykov later wrote, the Germans lost more soldiers than during the seizure of Paris. Sergeant Pavlov – the defender of the house – was later awarded the title of Hero of the Soviet Union.

It was not only soldiers who displayed heroism. Generals sacrificed themselves too. The overcoat of Major General V. A. Gladkov, of the 35th rifle division, bore 160 bullet and fragment traces when he died. And the food rations were the same for generals and soldiers alike: 25 grams of dried bread, 12 grams of cereals and five grams of sugar. As to ammunition, 30 cartridges were alloted for each gun. And women fought alongside the men. Maria Ulyanova fought as a defender of Sergeant Pavlov's House from the very first day; Valentina Pakhomova pulled over a hundred wounded soldiers from the battlefield.

As the battle for Pavlov's House raged, Zhukov and Vasilevsky were in Moscow with the Stavka, or Central Command. Stalin told them to come up with a plan to save Stalingrad. They devised a plan that foresaw a prolonged period of "active defense," to wear down the Germans, then a sudden and overwhelming counterattack that would decimate the foe and split their army in two. Success required the utmost stealth and secrecy (codenamed "Uranus," the plan was kept secret for some time from many top generals), and for the next two months, massive amounts of men and material were carefully moved into reserve positions above and to the east of Stalingrad.

Meanwhile, German command threw as many as six divisions into a very narrow portion of the front. Hundreds of aircraft provided air support. The defense provided by the 62nd Russian army was pierced and it ended up being cut off from the units of the Stalingrad Front in the North and the South-East Front to the South. At this very critical point, on September 16, the 13th Division of the Guards, under the command of General Alexander Rodimtsev, broke out of encirclement. Rodimtsev's division took Mamaev Mound (known as Hill 102 at the time) by storm, and the defense of the hill raged for the next 135 days. The steep slopes of Mamaev Mound became much less so from the weeks of bombing and artillery shelling. Some places on the hill bore more metal than dirt. Even in winter, the hill stood out like a blackened eye.

The Germans pummeled the 62nd army day and night. Sometimes the Soviets had to repulse as many as 10 attacks in a day. They were fighting not only for factory workshops but over the debris of buildings. Workers of the Stalingrad Tractor Plant repaired damaged tanks at night, right next to the front lines. A quarter million civilians took part in building lines of defense at radii of 50, 100, 150 and 500 km from the city.

The tenacity of Soviet troops quashed German attempts to carry out a rapid, *blitzkrieg* offensive. In late September, General Franz Halder was fired as head of the German General Staff and General Kurt Zeitzler took over. Hitler sent Jodl to the Caucasus, where he was to use his troops to distract the Red Army from Stalingrad. But Jodl soon saw that the Wehrmacht was exhausted, that the territory they had seized was more than could be held by the size of the army which occupied it. He rightly surmised that a debacle loomed. Jodl also noted, in his report to the Führer, that "U.S. aid to the Soviets" – the vast U.S. supplies sent under Lend-Lease – was having a significant impact. Soviet pilots were flying U.S.-made AeroCobras from Alaska to the Western Front; whole caravans of U.S. ships were delivering foodstuffs and machine tools to Murmansk; U.S.-made jeeps ("Dodges") were shipping in by sea.

Soviet snipers also had a huge impact on the events at Stalingrad, and particularly on morale during this period of "active defense." Vasily Zaitsev personally shot 242 German soldiers; Soviet soldiers who apprenticed themselves to Zaitsev added another 1,106 to that list. "There is no land for us behind the Volga," was Zaitsev's motto. In all, 400 snipers of the 62nd Soviet army liquidated over 6,000 Germans. As retold in the American movie, *Enemy at the Gates*, in response to Zaitsev's decimation of their units, the fascists allegedly sent to Stalingrad the head of the Berlin Sniper School, Major Koenings. Four days later, the Wehrmacht major was killed in a sniper's duel with the Russian.

BY EARLY NOVEMBER, German troops in and around Stalingrad were spent. While they still occupied much of the western portion of the city, an October Nazi offensive to "finally and decisively take Stalingrad" had been successfully repulsed by the 62nd army. Meanwhile, controlled Soviet counterattacks all along the front kept German troops pinned down and unable to redirect forces to the southern battle.

At 7:30 in the morning on November 19, the period of "active defense" of Stalingrad came to an abrupt end. Soviet troops on the Southwest Front surged through defenses occupied by Romanian troops northwest of Stalingrad. Meanwhile, attacks south of Stalingrad and further to the north ensured that Soviet troops would not be flanked and aimed at encircling the German 6th Army.

In his memoirs, Zeitzler cited the following reasons for German defeat on this day: the snowstorm, the -20° C biting frost, and the "crowds of fleeing Romanians" who impeded the activity of Reserve Tank Corps X. Zeitzler saw what the Russians had in mind and urged Hitler to order his 6th Army to abandon Stalingrad in order to strike the Soviets in the West. Hitler went beserk: "I won't leave the Volga!"

Within three days, the Russian plan succeeded in driving back the Germans and encircling Paulus' once invincible 6th Army. Hitler ordered Paulus to establish a circular defense and told the General Staff to stay in the city. Soviet troops then re-directed their strikes westward, to keep German forces from performing a breakout of the encircled army. Hitler ordered that Paulus' army henceforth be referred to as "the troops of the Stalingrad fortress." But that was just linguistic juggling. The area of encirclement actually stretched 40 km west to east and 20 km from north to south, including plenty of barren steppe, a few villages and the majority of Stalingrad. Germans troops were forced to construct defenses in snowstorm and frost conditions without proper construction materials or fuel. They were ordered "to use horse meat for food."

By November 24, the encircled group of German forces consisted of 20 German divisions and two Romanian armies totaling 330,000 soldiers. Of these, 100,000 were later taken prisoner. The remainder died of combat, famine or cold. Only the remnants of General Hoth's tank army and rear services succeeded in breaking out of the encirclement.

Goering promised to send supplies by air. Over 600 German military cargo planes located in the Don steppe were supposed to deliver 600 tons of cargo by air, but the weather and Russian air defenses only allowed half to get through. A last attempt to break the encirclement from outside in December faltered quickly, over 45 km from the city limits.

In early January, Soviet command began its *Koltso* ("Circle") strategy, to dismember and destroy the encircled German troops. On January 8, 1943, emissaries were sent to the embattled German fortress, demanding immediate surrender of the city. Paulus was given a lengthy document that guaranteed safe passage for those who surrendered and the right to return home after the war. The alternative was liquidation. Paulus got in touch with Hitler asking for a carte blanche in negotiations but was resolutely rebuffed.

Hitler had told the German people that the stoic resistance of the 6th Army did not allow the Russians to launch an offensive elsewhere along the front. Only to General Jodl (who was very close to the Führer) did Hitler admit that he had no faith in the salvation of the 6th Army. Nonetheless, Hitler sent a huge number of German orders, medals and promotions to the moribund soldiers marooned in the city.

On January 10, the Soviet army began a general offensive across the Stalingrad front, launched simultaneously from the north, the south and the west. For several days the Soviets tightened the rope around Paulus' neck. German artillery units, short of ammunition, destroyed their guns; German drivers, short of gas, set fire to their vehicles. There were no medical supplies or facilities to treat the wounded and they were left to die.

On January 24, the last German plane flew west and the Soviet army occupied the airport. On January 26, German forces were cut in two, and, on January 31, Paulus – whom Hitler had promoted to the rank of field marshal just the day before – was taken prisoner at his headquarters in the basement of a city department store. Two-thirds of the Germans surrendered. Only the 11th army corps would not lay down its arms, and was fully destroyed by the Soviets.

On February 2 the encircled army capitulated. The last cable sent to Hitler's headquarters read: "Long Live Germany!" But it was the name of Stalingrad that would live on, with streets and towns around the world taking the name of the Russian city that symbolized the turning of Allied fortunes in the Second World War.

THE BATTLE FOR Stalingrad lasted 200 days and ranged over 100,000 square kilometers. Over two million participants employed some 26,000 field guns and mortars, as well as 2,000 tanks and as many aircraft. German losses (killed, wounded, and taken prisoner) totalled 1.5 million persons – one quarter of its total Eastern Front forces. Over sixty divisions were destroyed at Stalingrad, and a three day period of mourning was declared in Germany.

Later, towards the end of the war (in the summer of 1944), many of the Germans taken prisoner near Stalingrad were made to march through the streets of Moscow, so that the Soviet people could see the army which planned to invade their homeland and enslave its people. Following behind the German columns were city trucks, symbolically washing off the streets where the enemies had trod. Authorities on the radio asked the population "to remain calm" during the prisoners' march, and Moscow residents showed no signs of vindictiveness at the sight of the German column, just staring blankly at the march down Tverskaya street. In fact, many gave the prisoners pieces of bread from their scarce food rations.

On December 22, 1942, the Soviet government instituted the medal "For the Defense of Stalingrad." Over 700,000 participants of the battle received the medal.

In May 1944, U.S. President Franklin Roosevelt sent a telegram to the city of Stalingrad, stating: "On behalf of the people of the United States I send this document to the city of Stalingrad to express our admiration of its valiant defenders ... Their glorious victory stopped the wave of invasion and became a turning point in the war of allied nations against the forces of aggression."

In 1961, Stalingrad was renamed Volgograd as part of a de-stalinization of place names and an eradication of the "cult of personality" that surrounded Stalin during his lifetime. The city had actually been founded in 1589 as Tsaritsyn, and was renamed Stalingrad in 1925 in honor of Stalin, who had organized the city's defense during the Russian Civil War.

On October 15, 1967, an impressive monument was unveiled atop Mamaev Mound. A 72-meter high statue of a woman with outstretched arm wields a sword and her face is wrenched into a battle cry – it is a symbol of the Motherland fighting back. The sculptor was Yevgeny Vutechich, who is also known for his monument to the warrior-liberator in Treptov Park in Berlin. For many years, especially during the rule of Leonid Brezhnev (a war veteran himself), the memorial complex at Mamaev Mound was a place of great reverence for millions of Soviets who traveled there to pay homage to the courage of the defenders of Stalingrad – those who broke Hitler's charge to the Volga – many at the cost of their lives.

November/December 2002

1942

A Match at Gunpoint
Nikolai Dolgopolov

The history of a war is not just a recounting of battles, armaments and fallen soldiers. Often, far from the front lines one finds amazing tales of human bravery and honor. This is one of those stories.

In 1942, Kiev had been occupied by Nazi forces for nearly a year. Then a German commander decided he would like to see German and Soviet players face off on a soccer field. This placed the players of Dinamo (Kiev) in a quandary: do they try their hardest to defeat a team comprised of the reviled occupiers, at the risk of losing their lives, or do they intentionally throw the match, at the risk of losing their honor?

Kiev fell to the Nazis on September 19, 1941. After occupation began, many of the soccer players from Kiev's popular Dinamo club tried to fight in the resistance for a time, but soon were cut off from the partisans and the front line. Rather than leave the capital city, they decided to stay together and most took jobs at the Kiev-based Bread Factory Number 1.

Then, in the summer of 1942, the players heard that the Germans wanted to stage a series of "friendly matches" – they even proposed that the *Dinamovtsy* (former Dinamo players) practice at Zenith stadium. The players were incredulous. Why? What for? What matches and what kind of soccer can one talk about with an opponent who is torturing and executing your fellow citizens? And how is one to find enough energy to play on meager war rations?

The very idea of a soccer match in Kiev between occupied and occupier sounded like a page out of Kafka. There was no logical explanation. But then how could there be logic with the fascists?

The military superintendent of the city, Major General Eberhardt, was said to be the "project manager." He saw in the proposed match a chance to further humiliate enslaved Kiev – through an exhibition before the eyes of thousands of observers. What is more, he thought, the occupiers might have a little fun at the expense of weakened Dinamo players.

The *Dinamovtsy* debated amongst themselves. How could they play with the fascist invaders, sullying themselves? How could the *Dinamovtsy* ever face their fans again? But then Dinamo's key players, Alexei Klimenko and Nikolai Trusevich, began to argue for the matches. They would not just play, they said, they would win! The people would come and see the fascists beaten in soccer. It would be a breath of fresh air for Kievans. They would not consider the possibility of defeat. They would just strike and strike. Dangerous? Of course. The risk was huge. But then, was it any safer for those who fight on the front lines or as partisans?

So the *Dinamovtsy* accepted the challenge and named their team "Start." On July 12, 1942, posters were hung all over Kiev: "Soccer Match. German Armed Forces vs. Start Team, Kiev."

Start did not train much. They just kicked the ball around a bit near the bread factory, under the laconic glare of the German police, preserving their precious energy. Yet Ivan Kuzmenko worked hard on honing his free kick – 30 meters from the goal, testing goalie Nikolai Trusevich. Kuzmenko knew what was what. He suffered from some joint problems and knew he could not run much, but wanted to make a contribution. He hid his injury and showed his teammates that, if there was a penalty kick or a free kick, Vanya Kuzmenko would be the one to count on.

A few days prior to the first match, Misha Sviridovsky, the most respected player on the team, dug up some uniforms for his comrades: white shorts, red t-shirts and long red soccer socks. Everyone knew that the color of the jerseys and socks was in defiance of the Germans. But the confident Nazis turned out not to mind the red: it was such a tantalizing prospect to beat the "reds" in soccer.

Yet the first match went a bit differently than the Germans had planned. The Reich's railway unit team was destroyed by Start 9-1. Five days later, the Germans pulled together a somewhat stronger team. But the Kievans trounced them too: 6-0.

Now the Germans were irritated. But they didn't cancel the next match, with the Hungarian club MSG Wal [Hungary was allied with Hitler]. Start crushed the Hungarian squad 5-1 and then again in a rematch, 3-2.

Kievans started to quietly cheer. The players began to be recognized on the streets once again, to be met with a smile: "Thank you, oh, you dears, thank you!" More and more people showed up at the matches.

In the fifth match, the Germans decided to teach the Russians a lesson. They assembled a strong team from the "Flakelf" – German air defense units ... which was also destroyed. During the match, the *Dinamovtsy* could hear the fans shouting *"Davay Krasnye!"* ("Come on Reds!") The shouts were timid, but they were shouts.

The management of the bread bakery where most of the players worked had promised to get them more bread to help them build up energy for the games. But now they had forgotten their promise and were frowning. "Guys, you are walking a tightrope," they said. "They will shoot you! The opposing stands, full of German fans, are already shouting: 'Hang the bastards on the goal, on the crossbar!'"

From the very first matches, the *Dinamovtsy* felt as if they were playing on the edge of a knife. They feared that each entry onto the field could be the last of their lives. Death was not something distant and easily dismissed. It was their close companion. But they resolved to leave their fear in the locker room. Will there be more matches? Will they let us remain among the living? Each player thought about these things more and more often, but they never spoke about their fears with each other. They played as they had decided once and for all: for real.

Meanwhile, the referees – all German – were not doing their job. The fascists were playing rough, but Start refused to answer rough play with more of the same. They would not stoop to that level. The fascists, after all, were acting as one would expect: if one is insidious in deed, thought and philosophy, it follows they could not be gracious on the field. Thus, knowing that Vanya Kuzmenko had problems with his leg, the fascists hunted him down and finally struck his bad leg so that he had to be carried from the field.

THE DECISIVE MATCH was to be played against a team from the German Air Force, the Luftwaffe. But there were not many flyers on this team. Instead, it included several professionals from different German soccer clubs (some of whom even continued their sports careers after the war). A local occupationist newspaper sang the praises of the Luftwaffe team, writing that it enjoyed the patronage of Herman Goering himself.

Meanwhile, the players from Start knew that things could not continue as they had much longer. The fascists would not let them keep winning before thousands of fans. So it was not surprising when an officer in a Gestapo uniform stopped in their locker room before the match and issued an explicit order in clear Russian: when the team goes out onto the field, it should salute the opposing Luftwaffe team with the traditional "Heil Hitler!"

And there was one more thing, the Gestapo officer said. They were not to win the match.

The Russian players were silent. The Gestapo officer showed off his knowledge of Russian: "*Molchaniye – znak soglasiya.*" ("Silence is a sign of assent.") Indeed, the emaciated players did not utter a word before the game. But, after lining up in the central part of the field, on a signal from captain Misha Sviridovsky, they defiantly yelled: "*Fizkult Privet!*" a common Soviet sports salute.

BEFORE THE WAR, the *Dinamovtsy*'s names were known to millions of soccer fans throughout the Soviet Union. Goalie Nikolai Trusevich was king of the air game and excelled in intercepting balls fired at his goal. Defender Mikhail Sviridovsky had actually retired from the sport before the war, but he could not possibly refuse the offer of his teammates to join them. As right defender, he was the linchpin of the team's defense.

The German strikers feared the stocky central defender, Vladimir Balakin, and didn't dare use their rough tactics on him. But they were not so reserved with left defender Alexei Klimenko, who they injured in every match. A fine tactician, Klimenko repeatedly led the charge in Start's attacks. Ivan Kuzmenko, as already mentioned, was limping because of his injury. But even that could not keep Kuzmenko from playing a vital role in "sudden death" playoffs.

Insider Fyodor Tyutchev was the tallest and oldest player on the team. He had quit Dinamo Kiev back in 1937, but he came back into active duty for these matches and gave his all.

Striker Mikhail Putistin also played the role of manager, engaging in rather frightening negotiations with the Germans. But Putistin never lost his cool and proved as able a diplomat as he was a player.

Forward Nikolai Korotkhikh had played for Dinamo Kiev for five seasons and was known by all Kievans. But Kievans also knew that, before the war, Korotkhikh had worn an officer's uniform. So each game against the Germans could easily have become his last, had they found out. But he played all the same.

Right insider Mikhail Melnik was only 27 that year, but he played a very mature game, helping his teammates across the entire field of play.

Defender Vasily Sukharev had turned 30 in 1941. He moved to Dinamo Kiev from the Kievan team Lokomotiv. After the war, Sukharev went on to play several seasons for a revived Dinamo Kiev.

The sociable Makar Goncharenko pierced the German's right flank like a knife, shooting at the goal from unexpectedly sharp angles. He proved to be the Nazi defenders' worst nightmare.

THE LUFTWAFFE TEAM was a different class of players from the previous Nazi teams. Well-fed and muscular, they played a mean brand of soccer. "They were hitting us so hard that we could hear our bones creaking," Makar Goncharenko later recalled. "The referees on the field turned a blind eye to it and even smirked at such roughness."

The Germans' primary target was goalie Trusevich, and a crowd of German forwards was constantly chasing him down. Finally, Trusevich was hit so hard in a melee near his goal that he lost consciousness. But the German referee did not penalize the German team, instead demanding that Start replace Trusevich with a substitute. The problem was that Start had no substitute goalie, so they had to help Trusevich return to his senses and somehow got him to stand upright in the goal. He held his throbbing head in his hands and joked to his team, "Don't turn this bruise into some kind of mortal concussion. I will play." But playing proved difficult. By halftime, the Germans had scored three goals. But Start held fast, scoring two goals of their own. The German fans were celebrating; the Kievan fans kept silent.

In the locker room, the team exchanged encouraging words and came together around a simple thought: we can't shame ourselves in front of our people; we need to prove we are stronger than the fascists. They prepared themselves calmly for the second half, and before running onto the field gathered in a close circle: "We have to try. But without any panicking. We can win. Play for real."

But the German referees did not let them get close to the German goal, whistling "offsides" on the slightest provocation. So it became senseless to make passes too close to the penalty box. Start had to resort to shooting at the goal from afar or outplaying the German defenders one-on-one.

Finally a German defender fouled a Kievan striker so blatantly that even the German judge had to award Start a free kick. It was Vanya Kuzmenko's hour. Limping out onto the field, the veteran scored a free kick from over 30 meters out, tying the game.

The "aviators" of the Luftwaffe called the "guilty" referee every name in the book, and then started stalling, running down the clock, hoping to end the game with a 3-3 draw, pointing to their wrists to signal the referee that it was time to blow the final whistle.

But there was too much time left. The local fans were roaring in support of Start and the local police had to rush in to quiet them down.

Meanwhile, Kuzmenko made a terrific pass to Goncharenko and the latter smashed the ball into the German net with a spectacular header. The German fans began moving toward the exit. After all, who would want to witness yet another German defeat? Then Goncharenko came through again, slalom-dribbling through the German defense and scoring a crushing fifth goal, ending the game 5-3.

THE START PLAYERS had a driving passion: to win today, to spite the enemy, and to bring joy to their compatriots. They knew that for many residents of occupied Kiev it was their only solace. They also knew, however, that this was their last game. That they would have to give their lives for this victory. In the morning, they were all arrested. They were summoned to the office of the bread factory's director, where four Gestapo officers and soldiers armed with automatic rifles were waiting for them. The senior Gestapo officer held a list with the names of wanted players.

There followed 32 long days in the basement of Gestapo headquarters. There were senseless interrogations, accusations, humiliations and threats. The players were all isolated from one another and interrogated individually. The Gestapo officers accused the players of being connected with the local underground and beating the Germans on orders from the partisans. The interpreter in the interrogations turned out to be a traitor; before the war he had worked as a janitor at the stadium, now he slandered the players and sullied their reputations.

The prisoners were taken from the Gestapo dungeon one morning at dawn. Five or six cars were waiting in the courtyard. One of two bleak futures awaited those whose "crime" was having outplayed their opponents: a concentration camp or immediate execution. Gestapo officers burst into the cells telling them to get outside. If they shouted: "Hey, take your things and get out!" then gave the prisoner a piece of bread, it meant the player was to be sent to a concentration camp. If they yelled simply "Hey, get out!" then a death sentence awaited.

Of the players sent to Syretsky concentration camp (later known as Babyn Yar), four were later shot there: goalie Nikolai Trusevich, Ivan Kuzmenko, Alexei Klimenko and Nikolai Korotkhikh. Makar Goncharenko somehow survived. As did Balakin, Sukharev, Melnik, Putistin and Sviridovsky. In fact, Sviridovsky and Goncharenko executed a daring escape from the camp, just as they had once evaded the Luftwaffe defenders.

Goncharenko actually went on to became a respected coach in Ukraine, training such famous players and coaches as Valery Lobanovsky and Oleg Bazilevich.

Interestingly, Lobanovsky, who died in 2002 from a stroke, resurrected the fame of Dinamo Kiev in the 1970s and into the 1990s. He led his team, in 1975, to win the National Cup and then the Super Cup (the Cup of Cup Holders), by defeating the German team "Bayern" in two matches – a fitting epilogue to this astonishing story.

September/October 2002

Lost and Found in Siberia
By Otis E. Hays, Jr.

On August 20, 1944, pilot Richard McGlinn and his crew of ten took off from a base in southern China. Their plane, a B-29 American superfortress dubbed "St. Catherine," was destined for a bombing raid on the industrial target of Yamata, on the Japanese island of Kyushu. Little did they suspect that they would not return from their "routine" bombing raid for over five months, during which they would traverse the entire breadth of the Soviet Union.

After a long flight north, McGlinn and his crew met with fierce Japanese resistance. "Bingo! One of our engines was hit," McGlinn later recalled. In fact, the plane was severely crippled and had no chance of making it back to China.

McGlinn sought cover in the clouds and charted a course for Vladivostok.

Daylight faded. The weather turned turbulent. McGlinn hoped to glimpse Vladivostok's lights very soon. Nothing. Were they too far west, over Northeast Manchuria? If so, the Japanese could be waiting. McGlinn decided to keep the St. Catherine on a northward course as long as possible.

Unknown to McGlinn, they had overshot Vladivostok. His plane was now in the northern portion of the Sikhote-Alin mountain range, which parallels the coast of the Russian Far East, between the Amur river and the Sea of Japan. The region is wild and severe, boasting towering mountain peaks, dense pine forests, swift, log-jammed rivers, and abundant wildlife, including bears and tigers.

As the plane used up the last of its fuel, it became clear that the crew had to bail out. Each man was equipped with an emergency pack containing a few day's food rations, matches, a poncho, knife, machete, whistle, signal mirror, fish hooks, canteen, cooking pan and insect repellant. Each also had a sidearm and ammunition. McGlinn instructed the crew to head north after reaching the ground, toward what would be the wreckage of the plane, which contained a stock of emergency rations and equipment.

McGlinn jumped last into the cold night air, watching the St. Catherine silently drift north while he was pelted by frigid rain. But McGlinn did not quite reach the ground that night. His parachute lodged in the crown of a towering fir tree, where he was suspended in his harness until dawn. Then he managed to drop to the soggy forest floor, uninjured but worried about the safety of his crew.

Right gunner John Beckley had crashed violently into the wilderness and suffered a split nose and bruised ribs. He waited for daylight. When he heard gunshots, he pushed through the underbrush and came face-to-face with radar operator Otis Childs, Jr., who had sprained his knees and ankles. Left gunner Lewis Mannatt also heard the shots and quickly joined the two men.

Elsewhere, bombardier Eugene Murphy, flight engineer Almon Conrath, radio operator Melvin Webb and senior gunner William Stocks located one another soon after dawn. Murphy had injured his back in the jump, but the men nonetheless heeded McGlinn's orders to search for the bomber's wreckage. They soon found, however, that the route north was blocked by high, impassable mountains. They were undecided about how to proceed, but felt the other airmen must be near, so they fired more pistol shots. Beckley, Childs and Mannatt heard them and, within a short time, the seven men were united. They decided to follow a small stream flowing southwest, hoping it would lead them from the wilderness.

Two more airmen, navigator Lyle Turner and copilot Ernest Caudle landed literally side-by-side in the forest. After dawn, they too began struggling north. But when they heard faint shots from the southwest, they turned in that direction. Finding a stream running in the same direction, they decided to follow it.

The eleventh missing airman, tail-gunner Charles Robson, was temporarily knocked breathless when he landed on his back. At daybreak he fired several shots without any response. A nearby stream trickled in a westerly direction. Anxious and alone, he camped for the coming night.

MCGLINN FOUND A small, westward-flowing river that later made a bend toward the northwest. He looked for an animal or man-made trail beside it, but there was none. After camping on the riverbank, he tried and failed to catch some fish. So he brewed a tea of grass leaves and black ants. The sour brew foreshadowed the trials yet before him.

The seven-man group limited themselves to one meal a day from their scant emergency food supplies. The stream that was their guideline to the southwest tumbled over waterfalls and merged with other mountain streams. Slowed by three injured men, they tried to follow the stream's vine-tangled bank. They were cheered when Mannatt shot a squirrel.

Elsewhere, Turner and Caudle endured the fog and rain. They continued through the wilderness along the widening stream. They did not see any animals, not even squirrels. Neither did they find any tracks in the mud to indicate that the fabled Siberian tigers and bears had passed this way.

Meanwhile, on his second day along, Robson battled swarms of insects and massive thorn bushes. He kept walking within sight of the stream. Often he stopped and listened. He heard only the splash and gurgle of water moving from rock to rock.

After a second night's rest, McGlinn was refreshed and ready to begin the search for the crashed bomber. He still believed that his crew members were not far away. He deposited his equipment at his river bank campsite and, in a note that he attached to a nearby bush, explained where he had gone and that he would return. However, after a daylong search, he encountered only mountains and endless forest stretching in every direction.

On his return to his campsite, McGlinn heard a whistle. He blew his own whistle. A whistle answered! The sound came from the direction of his camp, which Robson, following the stream, had found. The two men embraced; they were no longer alone.

At this point, McGlinn decided to abandon his search for the bomber wreckage. Instead, he believed that he and Robson should seek their way out of the wilderness by following the river to a settlement. They had no way of knowing they were starting a race with death.

When the eleven airmen parachuted into the stormy night of August 20, they were at least 100 miles from the Amur river. Nine of them were on the southwestern slope of the Sikhote-Alin mountain range. McGlinn and Robson were on a northwestern slope. The groups were moving in different westerly directions along the headwaters of the Monamo and Khoso rivers. With each step they took, McGinn and Robson were moving further away from the other nine men.

The group of seven continued to follow their stream. Turner and Caudle also struggled to keep their stream in sight. Although they did not yet know it, they were on higher ground behind the other seven men. They were all following the Monamo river.

Days were wet and nights cold. Their emergency rations dwindled and they ate whatever they found – squirrels, wild fowl, frogs, snails, mice, fish, insects, grubs, worms, pine nuts, berries and wild grapes, leaves, moss and grass.

Their strength ebbed. Their despair mounted. Rain widened the rivers to flood levels. Debris and swamps blocked the stream banks. Vines and fallen trees slowed the men's travel. The distance covered each day became shorter and shorter.

MCGLINN AND ROBSON lost track of time as day followed day. Stinging insects made every waking hour miserable. Their search for food was constant.

Concluding that their best chance to survive was by building a raft to float down the Khoso river, they spent three days at slow labor with their machetes, cutting suitable logs for a raft and tying them together with parachute cord. The river seemed calm when they launched the raft and climbed aboard. Later, the river made a sharp turn and suddenly entered a gorge, where the raft was smashed against a massive log jam. McGlinn and Robson escaped with their lives. However, they lost vital personal items, including a pistol, a machete and, most significantly, one of Robson's shoes.

MERGING WITH THE other mountain streams, the Monamo river became wide and deep. Exhausted and hungry, the group of seven decided they should build a raft to float down river. They were not aware, of course, that McGlinn and Robson had already tried and failed to do the same thing on the Khoso.

The raft was a huge undertaking: it had to be large enough to carry seven men. The seven men worked in relays with their machetes to cut enough logs. Yet when they tested the finished raft, they were disheartened to discover that it would only support the weight of three persons.

By this time, the men had been in the wilderness for 13 days. Three of them had still not recovered from their injuries, and none of them had the strength to build a yet larger raft. Time was running out.

It was decided that Beckley, Webb and Murphy, the strongest and healthiest of the seven, would ride the raft downriver.

The stream was at flood stage and the men floated for a time, but were soon caught in a log jam. They used their remaining strength to swim to shore. After resting, they began walking downstream, lessening their hunger pangs with squirrels, frogs, moss and berries.

On the seventh day of walking, they glimpsed an apparently abandoned village on the opposite bank of the river. The very sight of the village boosted their spirits. They knew that they had reached the edge of the wilderness. Then, as they watched, a small child and later a woman appeared. They turned to see a man and a boy paddling an *ulmagda* (a dugout canoe for use on mountain streams) toward them.

After they were ferried across the river, they were fed raw vegetables and then led to a nearby settlement of log and bark huts. Again they were fed, after which the exhausted men fell asleep on the floor of one of the huts.

Twenty days had passed since the eleven airmen had bailed out over Eastern Siberia. Three were now safe.

LIKE THEIR SEVEN comrades ahead of them, Turner and Caudle followed the Monamo river. Desperate for food, they subsisted mainly on frogs and snails. Then, on September 5, (a few days after Beckley, Murphy and Webb had set afloat down the Monamo), they stumbled into the camp where Conrath, Stocks, Childs and Mannatt were waiting.

DOWNRIVER, BECKLEY, MURPHY and Webb awoke after a night of sound sleep in the village. They were then paddled down the river to another village that was only two hours by horseback from the Amur river. Two Soviet Army officers rushed the bed-ragged men to the border patrol headquarters in Troitskoye, where they were finally able to relate their experiences.

It was now September 12; Soviet officials finally found out that eleven American airmen had been missing in the Siberian wilderness since August 20. Was it possible, they wondered, that the other eight men were still alive? Border patrol pilots assembled an aerial search of the upper Monamo river valley. Meanwhile, the three rescued men were put up in the Troitskoye hospital and treated for malnutrition, cuts and abrasions. After four days of bed rest and feeding, they boarded a motor launch and were taken up the Amur river to the border patrol hospital in Khabarovsk.

ON SEPTEMBER 12, the six men at their makeshift camp on the Monamo heard the search planes overhead. But rain and clouds made it impossible to attract the attention of the search party. On the next day, the sun was shining, and when they again heard the sounds of plane engines, they were able to hail the pilots with their signal mirrors. A pilot fired a recognition signal and returned to Troitskoye to report his discovery.

On September 14, another plane located the men's camp and dropped a sack with food and a note assuring them that help was on its way, and that Beckley, Murphy and Webb were safe.

The men waited several days while rescue dugouts were poled and paddled mile by mile upstream, through rapids and around log jams and snags. When the rescue party finally arrived, it was surprised to find not four, but six lost airmen. The men were successfully delivered downstream to Troitskoye where, after several days of rest and feeding, they joined Beckley, Murphy and Webb in the border patrol hospital.

Nine of the men were now accounted for. But where were McGlinn and Robson? Weather permitting, border patrol pilots continued to fly over the nearby mountains, looking for any sign of life in the dense wilderness below. With each passing day, winter drew nearer and hope of finding McGlinn and Robson alive began to fade.

HAVING LOST ONE of his shoes, Robson converted his leather pistol holster into a makeshift sandal, which he tied to his foot with parachute cord. He and McGlinn were thus able to resume their stumbling walk along the Khoso riverbank, eating what wild grapes, berries and edible leaves they could find.

"Things were getting desperate," McGlinn later wrote. "Our clothes were torn, our food a mere taste, and we were very weak."

ALEXANDER POBOZHY WAS camped in the Sikhote-Alin mountains in September 1944. An engineer, he was the head of an expedition that was selecting the route for the future Baikal-Amur Railroad (BAM), to run from the city of Komsomolsk east to the Sea of Japan. On September 20, a messenger from Komsomolsk arrived at Pobozhy's camp with an official order: Pobozhy was to halt his engineering activity and immediately organize a search party to find the remaining two American airmen. He was assigned the area of the Khoso river from its mouth to its headwaters.

Pobozhy and five men established a base camp at the mouth of the Khoso on September 22. They then set out upstream in dugouts, probing the log-jammed river. Privately, Pobozhy wondered how the two men could still be alive over a month after landing in the wilderness. If they had not starved to death, he thought, surely they had been torn to pieces by wild animals by now.

As THE SEARCH began, McGlinn and Robson were trying to bypass a swamp bordering the Khoso. Exhausted, they camped and built a fire. Suddenly, they heard airplane engines for the first time since abandoning the St. Catherine. Above them were two planes. Frantically, McGlinn and Robson threw tree branches onto their fire to make a smoke smudge. At first, the ploy seemed unsuccessful, because the planes continued their course. But then they turned back and began to circle above the men's position. The two planes dived and buzzed the smudge area before departing. Weeping with joy, McGlinn and Robson tried to relax as darkness came. They hardly dared to believe that their prayers for rescue had been answered.

The next morning, September 23, the temperature dropped to below freezing. Pobozhy's search team, moving from the river's mouth, was able to move upstream only very slowly, because of all the fallen trees. In the late afternoon of that same day, a plane again located the two men's camp and dropped a sack containing food and a note that read, in broken English, "Good day, Comrades. You are in USSR. Raise left the hand if you need help." McGlinn later recalled that "we waved everything, no only because we were in desperate need, but for joy."

The next day, planes dropped more bags of food. On the following day, September 25, a new note read: "Stay where you are. Do not move. Our people are coming for you. Nine of your crew are safe and well."

EARLY ON THE morning of September 26, Pobozhy selected three men to continue the search with him in one large dugout. Before long, they saw a thin column of smoke and two men standing near a campfire on the river's bank. When Pobozhy and his men stepped ashore, Pobozhy recalled, "the Americans tried to hug us. They were so weak they could not stand for long.... I didn't know any English words. Not knowing how to greet these people from acros the ocean, I shouted, 'Mister America.'" Both men had beards. McGlinn wore a leather jacket over tattered overalls that barely reached his knees. On his swollen feet were battered shoes. Robson wore overalls that were snagged to shards below his waist. One of Robson's swollen feet was wrapped in rags and his pistol holster was still tied to the other. Their faces and bodies were lacerated and covered with festering insect bites.

The trip downstream was fast. They reached Pobozhy's base camp before dark the same day, September 26. Using the camp's radio equipment, Pobozhy reported the successful rescue to his superiors in Komsomolsk. He also ordered clothing and shoes for the Americans that were dropped in by aircraft the following morning. McGlinn and Robson were now comfortably clothed. In gratitude, McGlinn gave Pobozhy his pistol and the two remaining cartridges.

Two days later, on September 29, Pobozhy delivered the two men to the Komsomolsk military hospital for examination and treatment. The men had defied the odds, surviving for forty days in the wilderness with little more than their wits and some luck.

ON OCTOBER 2, Pobozhy visited the men. It was the last time he would ever see them. Years later, Pobozhy wrote that he wondered "whether Dick (Richard McGlinn) and Charles (Robson) remember our friendship on the bank of the Khoso?"

McGlinn and Robson healed and rested in Komsomolsk until October 5, then made the cold voyage up the Amur river to the Khabarovsk Border Patrol Hospital. Now interned, they were examined, photographed, and allowed to join their nine fellow airmen. Little did they know that their journey home was far from over.

ON APRIL 13, 1941, the Soviet Union and Japan had signed a five-year neutrality pact. The agreement stipulated that the USSR would remain neutral in the event of any war Japan had with other powers.

Soviet neutrality in the U.S.-Japanese war in the Pacific (begun December 7, 1941) was first tested in April 1942, when one of the Doolittle Tokyo raiders landed near Vladivostok. If the Soviet Union simply released the men, they would be aiding Japan's enemy, violating the principle of neutrality. So the five-man crew was to be interned, theoretically for the duration of the war. However, the men were quietly moved across Siberia to Perm, where they spent the winter. Then, in May 1943, after having been moved to Ashkhabad, Turkmenistan, the five men were allowed to "escape" from internment, across the border into Iran.

This was only the beginning of the Soviet Union's internee "problem" during World War II. Over the course of the war, some 286 more American airmen were interned in Russia. In July 1943, the first of what would be 32 Aleutian Island-based army and navy bombers crash-landed on Kamchatka. Four China-based superfortresses, including McGlinn's, crashed or landed in the Soviet Far East.

As the number of internees increased, the Soviets commenced moving them from Petropavlovsk (Kamchatka) and Vladivostok to Khabarovsk's Red Army Rest Camp. Meanwhile, the Soviets organized an internee holding camp at Vrevskaya (now Almazar), near Tashkent, Uzbekistan, thousands of miles from prying Japanese agents.

Internees began arriving at Vrevskaya in late 1943. Soon afterward, the Soviet Foreign Commissariat and the Internal Affairs Commissariat staged the first of four elaborate "escapes" that repatriated the internees to American hands. Sixty-one airmen, accompanied by an American military attaché, escaped to Teheran, Iran, in February, 1944. The Soviets confiscated their cameras, film and souvenirs. American security officers, keen to protect the illusion of Soviet neutrality in the Pacific and mindful that there were other internees, ordered the soldiers to sign pledges that they would not reveal to anyone where they had been while interned in the USSR.

As SNOW DEEPENED and ice formed on the Amur in the winter of 1944, McGlinn and his crew were relocated to the Red Army Rest Camp in Khabarovsk. There they met 28 other internees who had been rescued from Kamchatka. On November 15, the 39 Americans were issued winter clothing and boarded a Trans-Siberian train bound for Novosibirsk. From there, a southbound train carried them to Tashkent. On November 24, they entered the Vrevskaya internee holding camp, where they met 51 other Aleutian airmen and the 11-man crew belonging to Howard Jarrell's B-29, also from China.

On December 5, 100 men were packed onto a train bound for Ashkhabad for an escape over the border into Iran (one was too sick to travel). Three days later, the train deposited the men on a railroad siding near Ashkhabad. The Iranian border lie just 18 miles to the south. Restless, the men waited in vain all day for their escape trucks to arrive and drive them across the border. The next day, the men were informed that American newspapers had reported that the Doolittle five had escaped from Siberia with Soviet help. As a result, Moscow called off the escape to await Japan's reaction to the rumors.

Despite orders to stand fast, 34 of the internees (none of McGlinn's crew) decided to attempt a real escape and headed for the Iranian border on foot. The effort was futile. Most were rounded up within hours, the

---

The Story of a Photo

In 1997, the American Ambassador in Moscow received a surprising letter from Mikhail Ilyich Karlinsky, a war veteran living in Moscow. Karlinsky wrote: "While revising my archives, I discovered a photograph of the American pilots, Richard McGlinn and Charles Robson. In 1944, during a combat operation, they made an emergency landing and were later rescued by the head of our geological expedition, Alexander Pobozhy." Karlinsky reported that "Pobozhy has passed away and I do not know the details of the rescue operation. I believe this photo may be of interest to the pilots themselves or their relatives. I hope you could inform me on the delivery of the photo."

John N. Tefft, the Charge d'Affaires of the American Embassy, later replied to Karlinsky: "Unfortunately, Pilot Richard McGlinn and Tail-Gunner Charles Robson are deceased. We contacted the families of both men and they have stated that they would be delighted to receive the photograph. We will be sending them your photograph with a copy of this letter.

"On behalf of the families of Richard McGlinn and Charles Robson, I would like to extend my thanks to both you and the rescue team members of Alexander Pobozhy's geological expedition. Your efforts to provide this piece of history to the families of the men who served both our countries during that terrible time are appreciated by a grateful nation."

---

remainder the following day. All were sent back to Vrevskaya where, by December 16, the camp's population had swelled to 130, with the arrival of two more B – 29 crews (piloted by Weston Price and William Mickish) and another army crew from the Aleutians.

As it turned out, Japan did not react to the Doolittle rumors. So the Soviets hastened to organize another, bigger escape on January 25, 1945. This time, the train held 130 men and went as far as Kyzil Arvat, Turkmenistan, near the Caspian Sea (the passes from Ashkhabad having been closed by avalanches and snow drifts). They were escorted by Major Paul Hall, assistant military attaché. Ten covered trucks carried the concealed men on the two-day overland trip to Teheran. After again being ordered to observe strict secrecy about their past whereabouts, the men were flown on January 31 to Abadan, Iran, then Cairo, Egypt and then, on February 10, to Naples, Italy. There they became the only passengers on the transport John L. Sullivan, which reached New York on March 6, 1945. The navy airmen were escorted to the naval air station at Floyd Bennett Field, and the army men to Fort Hamilton, NY. Souvenir items and any clothing that were clues to their recent presence in the Soviet Union were confiscated and the men were given yet another set of orders binding them to secrecy.

McGlinn, Turner and Beckley, however, were earmarked for special attention. They were rushed to Washington, where War Department intelligence specialists interrogated them in depth on March 8. Undoubtedly, they wanted to know how American airmen could slip into the Soviet Union unnoticed and roam the wilderness undetected for weeks.

PostScript

After the group of 130 left the Soviet Union, two more groups of American airmen were accommodated at the notoriously escape-prone Vrevskaya internee holding camp. A group of 43 airmen escaped on May 17; a final group of 52 were released August 24, after the war had ended.

In 1992, half a century later, the U.S. Air Force and Navy Departments recognized 291 secret internees as having been prisoners of war and awarded them the military POW medal.

March/April 2003

War With Japan
Tamara Eidelman

*I*f there was one thing the people of the Soviet Union did not want to do in August of 1945, it was enter into a new war. It had been three months since victory over Germany, and everyone wanted to believe that this would be the start of a wonderful new life – in which soldiers would return from war, when wounds, both physical and emotional, would gradually heal, and everything would be just fine. But, as usual, ordinary people did not have any say in the matter. The only way they could express their feelings was using the official formulations handed down from above.

On August 2, the *kolkhozniki* (collective farm workers) of Moscow Region issued a statement "to all *kolkhozniki* and tractor station workers, to all agricultural specialists of the Soviet Union," sharing their joy at the end of the war and their desire to do the best work possible:

> We have decided to hoe our potatoes two or three times; we managed to cover our entire patch during our first weeding, and half of it has even had a second going-over. We will weed our vegetable patches as many times as needed.

It is hard to believe that ordinary peasants would not weed their vegetables as many times as needed in any event, but in the surreal atmosphere of the Stalin era, even such things had to be determined at a higher level. And why not? Such calls were viewed as part of the natural order of things. Peace had been restored and that was good. And they certainly planned to weed their vegetables as many times as was needed.

Several days passed and now it was the turn of the *kolkhozniki* of Rostov Region to speak to the people. They reminded everyone that:

> We have now reached the time of the agricultural year that is most critical, that demands the greatest responsibility: harvesting the grain and preparing it for storage. We *kolkhozniki* of the Soviet Don River basin, we workers of the tractor

TRANSLATION: NORA FAVOROV

stations and of the *sovkhozy* (state farms), all the toilers of the village and the
stations and the farm, will fight with everything in us to fulfill the instructions
of the Party and the government to collect the harvest quickly and without waste
and to fulfill the first duty of the *kolkhoz* – the harvesting of grain.

It seems unlikely that there was anyone in the villages who did not
realize that harvesting grain was the most important thing they did. But it
was not just that they had to harvest the grain. They had to hand it over to
the State – that was the true First Commandment of *kolkhozy*. Going out
into the fields was transformed into a sacred act and violation of the First
Commandment became a mortal sin.

As fate would have it, the appeal to remember the harvest came on the
very same day when the fate not only of Japan, but of the entire world, was
shaken. This was August 6, the day the bomb was dropped on Hiroshima.
There was not a word about this in the newspapers; information came only
after a 24-hour delay.

It was not until August 8 that President Harry Truman's announcement
about the New Atom Bomb was printed on the last pages of Soviet
newspapers, without commentary. Journalists had not yet received
instructions about how to react to what had happened, so they just
provided a brief and dispassionate account, expressing neither approval nor
condemnation. But any attentive reader would have been able to guess that
changes were coming.

On August 5, Stalin had returned from the Potsdam Conference, where
the victorious allies had met. The entire country, naturally, was eager to
welcome him home and show their unanimous support for the decisions
of the Potsdam Conference. Three days later, there were already visitors at
the Kremlin – T.V. Soong, President of the Kuomintang Executive Yuan
and Kuomintang Foreign Minister Wang Shih-chieh. There were probably
many who wondered what sort of urgent business had brought these
Chinese leaders to Moscow. What had happened? But these ruminations
were probably quickly put to the side – 1945 was no time to sit around
discussing the actions of the government. The Chinese can come and go –
it is none of our business.

Meanwhile, echelon upon echelon made their way across Eurasia.
Soldiers were being brought from Berlin and from Prague, from Budapest
and from Warsaw. They spent long weeks traveling across the wasteland
of Europe, over the charred and trampled earth of Belarus, across the

devastation of Ukraine. Many of them passed close to their homes and families, and in most cases their loved ones did not have the slightest idea. Then there was the long, seemingly eternal, passage through Siberia. Mile upon mile of taiga flashed through the train windows. Cities occasionally appeared amidst the endless forest. Some had been there for hundreds of years; others had been built quite recently – right before or even during the war.

A little farther from the train tracks – of course hidden – were a multitude of forced labor camps.

Simultaneously with this deployment, the camps received new residents: echelons of soldiers recently "freed" from Nazi prison camps... Soviet citizens unfortunate enough to find themselves in territory occupied by the Nazis. Did the soldiers know of this? Probably they knew, but preferred to keep these thoughts to themselves. Did they understand where they were being taken? Most likely they understood, or at least were able to guess.

In the end, their long journey ended on the shores of the Pacific Ocean. On August 9, the entire Soviet Union learned of the new war.

On August 8th, the Soviet People's Commissar for Foreign Affairs, V. M. Molotov, received Japanese Ambassador Sato and communicated the following statement in the name of the Soviet Government, to be conveyed to the government of Japan:

"After the defeat and capitulation of Hitler's Germany, Japan is the only great power that insists on a continuation of the war...

"True to its duty to its Allies, the Soviet Government has accepted the proposal of its allies...

"The Soviet Government believes that only such a policy is capable of bringing peace..."

Well, if we must, we must. Everyone rushed to show their approval for the new war.

At Ball-bearing Factory No. 1, night-shift workers held a meeting of the roller-bearing shop, the automatic lathe shop, the separator shop and the forge shop. Foreman Vasin, who took the floor after Party Organizer Ivanov of the roller-bearing shop, who had relayed the contents of Comrade Molotov's statement, said that he – and he was speaking for the entire collective – fully supported the government's decision.

Passionate speeches could be heard in the forge shop. Manager Shemyakin expressed his approval of the Soviet government and pledged to double ring output. Ironsmith Goncharenko concluded his brief statement with a call to increase output and pledged to do just that. Foremen Makarov and Gorliv attested that the shop was ready to fulfill any task set by the government.

Perhaps Foreman Vasin or Party Organizer Ivanov could still recall how several years ago, in the spring of 1941, they had unanimously expressed their approval of the non-aggression pact signed between the Soviet Union and Japan. At the time, this seemed a great achievement. Stalin was so happy about this pact that he even escorted the Japanese diplomats to the train station. Eyewitnesses describe how he walked cheerfully along the platform, joked with the conductors, and said to the Japanese ambassador after hugging him, "We Asians should not fight one another."

Of course, since then, everything had changed. A terrible war had been fought against Germany. Japan had kept its word and had not invaded the Soviet Union. But what else could be done? The USSR had to fulfill the request of its allies. Back in Yalta, Stalin had promised to start a war against Japan no later than three months after the defeat of Germany. Three months had passed and it was time to keep his promise.

Was this how the Allies now wanted the Soviet Union to support them in Japan? Did President Truman – who had barely been able to conceal his sense of triumph as he told Stalin that American scientists had successfully conducted tests of a new bomb – really need this? What was Stalin thinking when he politely congratulated Truman on his success, maintaining a look of complete calm and – to the President's great surprise – not asking a single question about the deadly weapon. Most likely, Stalin immediately sent an order to Igor Kurchatov to speed up efforts to create a Soviet bomb; most likely coded messages were fired off to spies in the U.S., demanding that they urgently obtain information about what was happening in Los Alamos. And, of course, orders were issued to hurry the redeployment of troops to the East, closer to Japan.

At this point, who cared about the forgotten non-aggression pact – who, that is, besides the Japanese military? America and the Soviet Union were faced with quite a different question – who would wind up with a larger sphere of influence in the Far East? This meant that the time to act was now. It was not long before planes were flying to Hiroshima and Nagasaki and echelons were making their way across the vastness of Siberia, and Foreman Vasin and Party Organizer Ivanov were ordered to immediately express their approval of the new war.

And so the war began.

It must have seemed a terrible shame to start fighting all over again so soon after the war with Germany ended. But if we are to believe what journalists wrote, the military stepped into battle without flinching.

> In early morning, the powerful bombers of Officer Nikiforov's detachment took off from the airfield. Their goal: to bomb the military targets around a major Japanese-Manchurian city. The planes head for the East.
>
> Among the pilots of the combat formation are the old, the young, those seasoned in battle and those who have never been under fire. Comrade Svirida flies his plane with confidence... Together with his fellow crew members, he collected money to buy his own plane and requested Comrade Stalin to send him and his plane to the Soviet-German front. The request was approved and Comrade Svirida dropped many a bomb on Fascist Germany from his flying machine. Now he is here again.
>
> Master Sergeant Kuzin is flying toward enemy territory. He chanced to take part in some of the most colossal engagements of the Great Patriotic War. Now he is peering down at the Manchurian earth, which is obscured by morning fog. There, new battles and new glory await our pilots.
>
> Sergeant Kamyshny is flying the first combat mission of his life. The flight commander is following his actions closely and is satisfied. Comrade Kamyshny is calm and attentive. He is ready to carry out the mission.
>
> ...The target has been spotted. The pilots press their eyes to the sights. The bombs fall to the ground. The pilots see pillars of flame rise up out of the military storage depots and the rail yard.
>
> The enemy was not able to do anything to prevent the powerful bomb strike. Having dropped their lethal cargo, the planes head back.

How did Comrade Svirida manage to collect enough money to buy his own plane? How many times were deductions taken from his paycheck, as it was explained to him that this was actually all his idea in the first place, and that this would earn him the great honor of approaching Comrade

Stalin personally. Did his crew make it to the end of the war? What became of them, of Master Sergeant Kuzin, of young Sergeant Kamyshny?

Of course, the journalist who described their flight in such purple prose never came back to see how their lives turned out. What happened to them after the war? Did they stay on to serve in the Far East or were they demobilized? Did any of them wind up in a labor camp for expressing too much enthusiasm for the beauties of Manchuria and Japan? Did they have nightmares about the cities reduced to rubble, or did their consciences tell them that they had just been doing their duty and that they had committed acts essential to the security of the country?

The Emperor announced Japan's surrender and Soviet troops continued to advance. Special explanations were published in the newspapers to the effect that words alone mean nothing, since the Japanese troops were continuing to fight. For two more weeks, the troops marched across Manchuria, still fighting the cornered Japanese, still dying at a time when the war was essentially over.

In Moscow, Physical Education Day was being celebrated. And General Eisenhower arrived in the USSR. Naturally, he was greeted warmly and with enthusiasm – he could certainly have had no inkling of the mockery and insults that would rain down on his name in a few years, after the start of the Cold War. For now, there was to be a reception in his honor in the Kremlin, where a meeting of representatives of the Allied Powers was taking place.

Alongside newspaper articles about the banquet in the Kremlin, there was news of another event of supreme importance: the fourth edition of Stalin's book, *On the Great Patriotic War of the Soviet Union*, had come out in the Kyrgyz language. One has to assume that the other republics were keeping up – no one wanted to be the republic with the fewest number of editions.

The troops kept going. Journalists described their actions, evidently competing to see who could come up with the most fantastic reporting.

The path the invasion followed was a tough one. Chest-deep in water, the soldiers of Captain Safulin's battalion combed every square inch, pulling Japanese scouts out from among the rushes. On an island, our soldiers caught 19 Japanese officers who had dressed themselves in the rags of Manchurian farmers. These "peasants" were photographing our coastline. They stationed radio transmitters in peasant huts, to connect the island with Kwangtung Army Headquarters.

So far, so good. After all, there probably really were scouts in the area of battle, although it is a bit hard to imagine 19 Japanese officers all photographing the coastline at the same time. But if we are going to believe the journalists, there were plenty more surprises. It turns out, for instance, that the nomads of the Mongolian steppe welcomed the Soviet invasion. In fact, they even kept red flags in their yurts, ready to be waved at the victorious invaders.

South of the road, the steppe is just as vast and desolate. But, a few kilometers on, we unexpectedly find ourselves in the midst of a huge encampment of Mongolian nomads. Around us undulate waves of sheep, and among these waves are wagons, covered with white canvas parched by the sun, and people are scurrying and horsemen in colorful dress gallop with long whips.

This entire tribe of Mongolian nomads is traveling down from the Khingan Mountains toward western grazing lands. The Mongolians are herding their livestock across the front line and are headed straight for the Red Army. As a sign of friendship and respect, from horseback and wagons they are waving red flags. Hundreds of such flags rise above the steppe just as soon as the convoy of Soviet officers comes into view.

But whatever lies were told, whatever political games were being played or propagandistic articles written, the troops really were marching on and on, and the war was coming to an end. The newspaper stories became more and more jubilant; the numbers of captured Japanese soldiers and officers became more and more impressive.

And finally there was a communiqué from the battleship *Missouri*:

The Japanese delegation of 11 is ascending the gangway, having been brought to the ship as soon as preparations for the ceremony had been completed. All present are completely silent as the representatives of haughty Japanese diplomacy and rabid militarism approach the table. In front, dressed in black, is the head of the Japanese delegation, the Minister of Foreign Affairs, Mamoru Shigemitsu. Behind him is the short and stout Chief of the Army General Staff, General Umezu. With him are Japanese diplomatic and military officials in motley uniforms and suits.

The entire group makes a forlorn impression.

For five minutes, the Japanese delegation stands under the harsh gaze of the representatives of freedom-loving nations assembled on the ship's deck. The Japanese are forced to face the Chinese delegation...

It is silent as MacArthur addresses the delegates and guests.

MacArthur concludes his speech with a laconic gesture, inviting the Japanese delegation to approach the table.

Shigemitsu walks slowly to the table. After clumsily carrying out his painful duty, Shigemitsu draws away from the table without looking at anyone. General Umezu carefully signs his name.

The Japanese resume their places.

MacArthur walks up to the folders laid out on the table and invites American Generals Wainwright and Percival – the heroes of Corregidor – to join him. Not long before, they had been rescued from Japanese captivity. Just a few days before, Wainwright had been freed by the Red Army in Manchuria.

After MacArthur, the Chinese delegates sign the Instruments of Surrender.

After the Chinese, British Admiral Fraser approaches the table.

The clicking and whirring of innumerable movie and still cameras increase as MacArthur invites the Soviet delegation to the table. It has been the center of attention here. Lt. General Derevyanko, the signer of the Instrument, is accompanied by Air Major General Voronov and Rear Admiral Stetsenko.

Of course, even here the correspondent could not restrain himself; he had to show who was really most important on the Battleship *Missouri*, and who had the most pictures taken. Nonetheless, the magnitude of the moment is clear. The Second World War had come to an end. (Well, not quite. Even now, 60 years on, there is still no peace treaty between Russia and Japan.)

Pilot Svirida and Master Sergeant Kuzin, Sergeant Kamyshny and Captain Safulin were all ordinary people who very much wanted peace to come as quickly as possible so that they could return home to their families and get back to their ordinary peacetime lives. Did they manage to this? Heaven only knows...

July/August 2005

All's Fair in Party Warfare
Valentina Kolesnikova

*I*n 1933, the poet Osip Mandelstam described Stalin's deputies and hangers-on as a "rabble of thin-necked leaders – fawning half-men for him to play with, they whinny, purr or whine as he prates and points a finger." That this proved a prophetically accurate description of Stalin's rule is shown in the many cases where Stalin set one group of his cronies against the other in a battle to the death. A prime example of this is the infamous Leningrad Affair, which came to a head in February 1949.

Interestingly, the substance and events surrounding this allegedly treasonous conspiracy (in which thousands would be sent to the camps) were not made public until Khrushchev's Secret Speech of 1956, and then only superficially. The real story of this post-war purge has only come to light since the fall of the USSR.

The affair revolved around the balance of power Stalin constantly manipulated in his Politburo, as a way to ensure his total dictatorship. And it began with a death. On August 31, 1948, Leningrad Communist Party boss and heir-apparent to the Soviet throne Andrei Zhdanov (whose son was married to Stalin's only daughter, Svetlana) died of an apparent heart attack after months of ill health. Meanwhile, Deputy Prime Minister Georgy Malenkov, a long-time rival of Zhdanov's, had just returned to Moscow from near-disgrace and political exile in Tashkent. Malenkov and his supporters had recently suffered a purge, and it is speculated that, in Zhdanov's death, Malenkov saw an opportunity to redress their losses. Notably, Malenkov had Lavrenti Beria on his side – the latter had convinced Stalin to bring Malenkov back to Moscow.

The target was two key Zhdanov loyalists: Nikolai Voznesensky, a Politburo member and chairman of Gosplan, and Alexei Kuznetsov, head of the Communist Party Central Committee's Personnel Department. But they were only the tip of the iceberg. Other prominent party leaders and Zhdanov protégés were also targetted, such as Mikhail Rodionov,

Chairman of the Council of Ministers of the Russian Federation, and Alexei Kosygin, Minister of Finance (who, amazingly, would survive the purge and rise again). All were younger, up-and-coming party leaders, and their capabilities, particularly on the economic front, were a threat to the "Old Guard."

Joseph Stalin had supported the promotion of "new blood" in the Party after the war. Specifically, he had praised Voznesensky and Kuznetsov, saying they were worthy to lead the party and government after he, Stalin, had departed. Meanwhile, Stalin supported and encouraged Malenkov and Beria in their attempt to compromise the younger leaders. It was a classic case of divide-and-rule.

In October 1948, at a session of the USSR Council of Ministers (headed by Malenkov), the Minister of Trade reported that the country had accumulated R5 billion in unsold goods. To remedy the situation, the Council of Ministers decided to hold interregional wholesale fairs in November-December 1948. Thus, Leningrad leaders decided to hold an All-Russian wholesale fair in their city on January 10-20, 1949. Rodionov wrote to Malenkov, announcing the fair. Malenkov responded in a letter on January 13, saying that the fair was illegal, that Kuznetsov, Mikhail Rodionov, Pyotr Popkov and Yakov Kapustin were conducting the fair without Central Committee approval. This, despite the Council of Ministers' decision (which Malenkov said was not "official"). Beria and Minister of Foreign Trade Anastas Mikoyan stood behind Malenkov. The battle lines were drawn.

Meanwhile, a month earlier, in December 1948, the Central Committee had received an anonymous letter which claimed that, during the most recent Leningrad Party Conference, negative votes against a number of Leningrad leaders were registered (all in all just 10 votes), but that the leaders had nonetheless claimed "unanimous support." Needless to say, for any Soviet leader to allege there was or should be internal party democracy, was ludicrous hypocrisy.

On February 15, 1949, the Politburo issued its resolution "On Anti-Party Actions of Central Committee Member Kuznetsov and Deputy Central Committee Members Rodionov and Popkov." This infamous resolution triggered the Leningrad Affair, accusing the three of "separatism" and "anti-state" actions caused by "a sick and non-Bolshevik deviation." Interestingly, the substance of the accusations were not known widely in the party, even in the Central Committee. Khrushchev, who was the Ukrainian leader at the time and would not be transferred back to Moscow until the end of 1949, said he "never saw the indictments in the Leningrad case," and concluded, based on conversations he overheard between Malenkov and Beria, that the charges were of nationalism and opposition to the Central Committee.

Regardless of the charges, it was a frame-up on all counts. The resolution claimed that the Leningrad fair had resulted in unjustified costs. Stalin fired the accused, then had them arrested (and then their families, protégés, etc.). In typical fashion, the accusations started with "economic crimes," but ended in "espionage" and "contacts with British intelligence." Stalin's hangmen, led by MGB Chairman Viktor Abakumov, arrested party leaders in other regions and Soviet republics. The Leningrad Affair turned into a full-scale purge echoing the Great Terror of a decade previous, with victims humiliated, beaten up and tortured. Over 2,000 leaders at different levels were fired and stripped of their titles and positions, to say nothing of those who were arrested (estimated at over 1300, with some 100 executed).

"Who directed the investigation?" Khrushchev wrote in his memoirs. "Stalin himself did. But if Stalin was the conductor, then Beria was the first violinist. Why do I say that? Because Abakumov, who actually supervised the prosecution, was Beria's man; he never reported to anyone, not even to Stalin, without first checking with Beria."

The court trial preparation lasted more than a year. In January 1950, Abakumov presented Stalin with a list of 44 persons who were arrested and whom he suggested be tried in secret by the Military Collegium of the USSR Supreme Court. The trial (its results predetermined) took place in Leningrad on September 29-30, 1950. On the second day of the trial, Abakumov presented Stalin with another list, this one of six defendants who ought to be executed. Stalin approved the list and on October 1, 1950, the sentence was made public: in addition to those who received different prison terms (mostly 10 and 15 years), Voznesensky, Kuznetsov, Rodionov, Popkov, Kapustin and Pyotr Lazutin were sentenced to death and shot one hour after the sentence was announced. Other arrests and court trials continued throughout the country until August 1952.

In 1951, Abakumov would himself be arrested after being denounced first by a rival, then by a deputy. The latter, Mikhail Ryumin, accused Abakumov of covering up a "Doctor's Plot" to murder Soviet leaders. Abakumov languished in jail for three years – where his patron Beria was unable to help him. Then, after Stalin's death, Abakumov and those complicit in fabricating the Leningrad Affair were tried and convicted. For his part, Abakumov, who said he had merely followed Stalin's orders, was executed in December 1954.

The tyrant was dead by then, but his tactics of pitting his subordinates against one another was still in use. Stalin had brought Khrushchev back to Moscow in late 1949, in the middle of the Leningrad Affair, as a counterbalance to the growing influence of Malenkov and Beria. When Stalin died, Khrushchev used the scandal surrounding the Leningrad Affair to undermine Malenkov and increase his own standing. Ironically, the Leningrad Affair, which Malenkov and Beria spearheaded to strengthen their power, came back to haunt them both and played a large part in their downfall and in Khrushchev's rise.

Interestingly, while, in today's Russia, physical extermination of political adversaries has gone the way of the "leading role" of the communist party, repeated, irrational shake-ups in the Russian political elite continue.[1] Indeed, the present Kremlin leadership's system of "checks and balances" for steadying the influence of "oligarchs" shows that divide-and-rule tactics of pitting apparatchiks against one other remains deep-rooted in the mentality of Russian rulers.

February/March 1999

---

1. The author was referring to a common tactic in Yeltsin's Kremlin. Since 2000, such irrational shake-ups have ceased to be the norm.

Khrushchev's Secret Speech
Tamara Eidelman

Sergo Anastasovich Mikoyan, Ph.D, is a specialist in Latin American history, and the son of Anastas Ivanovich Mikoyan (1895-1978), a Soviet leader with particularly good political skills, having served Joseph Stalin, Nikita Khrushchev and Leonid Brezhnev. In 1956, Sergo Mikoyan was a graduate student at the Moscow State Institute for International Relations (MGIMO); his father Anastas was then first deputy prime minister. Tamara Eidelman interviewed Mikoyan about the twentieth Congress of the Soviet Communist Party, which took place in February 1956, and where Khrushchev delivered his now famous "Secret Speech," exposing the Stalinist Terror and Cult of Personality.

Did you discuss political questions at home?
After Stalin's death, yes. Before Stalin's death, we knew that we were being bugged and did not have unnecessary conversations. If we had to discuss something, we talked outside. [After Stalin's death] they were probably bugging our apartment as well, and even after my father's death, but I no longer paid any attention to it.

Did you sense the coming changes before the Twentieth Congress?
I knew what was happening. I knew the two people who made a huge contribution to Khrushchev's decision to prepare and read the report at the Congress. Unfortunately, historians know almost nothing about these two people: Alexei Vladimirovich Snegov and Olga Grigorevna Shatunovskaya.

Snegov had been a member of the party since 1917, and in his youth was an organizer alongside [Vyacheslav] Molotov's wife and even knew her before Molotov did. Then he was in party work, but in 1937 was working in my father's apparatus and ended up in prison. In 1938, after [Lavrenty] Beria took the post of Narkom at the NKVD, a small number of people were let out of prison, Snegov among them. He came to my father and explained everything that had happened. My father recommended that he go to Sochi and check into a sanatorium and not come back [to Moscow] for as long as possible. He promised to inform Snegov when it would be safe to return, since he understood that Snegov's release might end up being temporary. But Snegov, a confirmed Bolshevik, did something rather stupid. He said that he would go away only after his Party Card was returned to him. He was so insistent, that my father called [Matvey Fyodorovich] Skiryatov in the Party Control Commission and requested the swift return of Snegov's Party Card, as he had just been released from prison. As soon as Snegov showed up to pick up his Party Card, he was once again arrested, and he returned [to freedom] only 17 years later. During this time, he passed through all of the circles of hell. They even led him off to be shot, but then did not shoot him. He was in Butyrka and Sukhanovo prisons. His back was covered with marks from floggings; he was missing a finger on one hand.

Olga Shatunovskaya worked with [Stepan] Shaumyan in Baku in 1918, and therefore knew my father from an early age. Then she worked in Moscow and met Khrushchev, and worked with him from 1936-7 in the Moscow Party Committee. She was also arrested, and spent some 10 years in the camps, then was exiled.

In 1954, both of these people returned to Moscow, and, with the help of Lev Shaumyan [Stepan Shaumyan's son] succeeded in meeting with my father, talked with him and related what went on in the prisons. As strange as it may sound, much of this was unknown to my father. He had not any conception of the massive scale of the repressions. Olga related an interesting story about how, in one of the camps where she had been, there were ten thousand women. A Japanese spy was brought to the prison and she spoke very directly: "I am an actual spy. I know why I am in prison. But you cursed Bolsheviks are in prison for no reason whatsoever..."

Their stories had a great deal of influence on my father, and he related them to Khrushchev. In fact, to Snegov belongs the phrase, which both Khrushchev and my father used in their memoirs: "If you do not dissociate yourself from Stalin at the first Congress after his death, and if you do not recount his crimes, then you will become willing accomplices in these crimes."

I was present when they told their stories, and I saw how my father was surprised and taken aback. When Olga Shatunovskaya spoke of the spy in the camp, he even called in my mother and said, "Ashkhen, come here, listen to what she is saying," and he asked her to repeat her story.

In particular, it was under the influence of these stories that we understood that practically no one who was arrested was guilty of any crime. After the Twentieth Congress, my father created 93 commissions which visited the camps in order to free people. They did not consider individual cases but simply looked at the article of law in question. If an individual had been convicted under Article 58 for sabotage, terror, anti-Soviet opinions or actions, then he or she was immediately set free, because it was clear that there were no guilty parties convicted under this article.

Snegov understood that the public had to be prepared, so he wrote an article which, today, is perhaps not that interesting, but which played a huge role at the time. He wrote his article for the journal *Party Life*, about the Sixth Party Congress, and showed how, on many issues, Stalin differed with Lenin during his lifetime. Prior to the Twentieth Party Congress, it was practically impossible to say anything about this. He caught Stalin in many deviations from the Lenin line. It was quite difficult to get this article published. And here again my father placed an important role, reading through the article in draft form, editing it. And it was published.

It was all part of the preparation for Stalin's unmasking.

Did your father discuss with you how Khrushchev's report on the Cult of Personality was prepared?

Up until the last minute there was a battle over this report. In the Presidium of the Central Committee, Molotov, [Lazar] Kaganovich and [Kliment] Voroshilov all spoke categorically against it being given. They proposed tabling it until a later date. Then they came up with another course of action: to delegate the preparation of this report to the editor of *Pravda* at that time, [Pyotr] Pospelov, thereby hoping to decrease the report's significance. Pospelov was a Stalinist; he had selected materials for Stalin's *Short Course* [*History of the Communist Party of the Soviet Union (Bolsheviks): Short Course*]. But this Stalinist, working with the materials provided by the NKVD, could not hold back his tears. Khrushchev correctly understood the situation, however, that a report of such significance should be given by the top person in the Party, and he decided to deliver it himself.

What was the situation like in the Congress? Did people suspect the changes that were coming?

Prior to the report – some five or six days before – my father spoke at the Congress and sharply criticized Stalin. And there was quiet indignation in the hall. No one cried out, but my uncle, [the aircraft designer] Artyom Ivanovich, was a guest at the Congress. That evening, he came by the house and said: "Your father has made a huge mistake. He spoke critically of Stalin and the Party bosses sitting around me were quite upset. This could end badly for him." He said the same thing to my father: "Anastas, you have made a huge mistake." My father answered that such a reaction in the hall signifies that they even fear a dead man, but that soon they would hear much more. My father's speech was a trial balloon. In truth, Molotov, Kaganovich and Voroshilov fought to the end. Their final condition was that the report be delivered only after the elections to the Central Committee and the Politburo. They feared that their role, as accomplices of Stalin, would have an effect on the outcome of the elections. Therefore, the final session of the Congress was held after elections to the leadership organs. The foreign delegations were not invited. It was a closed session. Representatives of socialist countries were later given a copy of the report in printed form.

Do you recall the evening of that fateful day?

Once again my uncle Artyom Ivanovich came by. We all sat around the table and my father recounted to him and all of us exactly what had happened at the closed session. He said that the report provoked a furor, that everyone sat completely flabbergasted; some were horrified, others were insulted, and still others were indignant on Stalin's behalf. There were of course still many Stalinists in the Party *apparat*. And I can actually relate something from a reception I was personally at, a year after the Congress. Khrushchev obviously understood that Stalinists comprised a certain part of the Party *apparat*, and he himself was an inconsistent person. Perhaps [Mikhail] Suslov said something to him, but at this reception Khrushchev said that "the term 'Stalinist' has come into use, and many consider this to be a bad thing. But what is so bad? For we all worked alongside Stalin for many years. He was our leader. And, in that sense, we are all Stalinists." And the hall was filled with the sound of applause.

How did the country react to what had happened?

A wise decision was made to read Khrushchev's secret speech to every party organization in the country. As a result, the entire country found out about it within the space of a month. Every party member came home and told everyone he could about it. I remember how the speech was read out in our institute. Everyone there was shocked.

How did you start to feel changes after the Twentieth Congress?

The greatest significance was that, after the speech, the great fear disappeared. The great fear became a small fear. Prior to this, people feared that they could disappear with one wrong word. Now there began to be talk of justice, of legality. Articles and publications began to appear. It was quite simply an explosion of sorts.

And how did the students react to the changes? And the graduate students and professors at your institute?

At MGIMO, of course, everything was discussed. But I should note that, at the institute, there were many soldiers. And there were many Stalinists among them. In any event, they remembered how they went off to battle with the words: "For the Homeland, For Stalin!" For them, discussing this was difficult. There were heated debates about Stalin's role during the war. Khrushchev went a bit too far on this when he said that Stalin did not use a map but a globe: "What kind of Supreme Commander was he, if he led in military matters by using a globe?!" Of course, Stalin had maps. There was a globe in his office, but this means nothing. Many military types at that time criticized Khrushchev for saying that.

January/February 2006

The Kitchen Debate
Yale Richmond

*K*itchens in model homes are not normally sites where world leaders debate their differences. Yet that is exactly what happened on July 24, 1959, when U.S. Vice President Richard M. Nixon and Soviet leader Nikita S. Khrushchev squared off while touring the kitchen of a model American home at the U.S. National Exhibition in Moscow's Sokolniki Park.

In that "kitchen debate," as it came to be known, the two leaders vigorously debated not only whether such a well-equipped kitchen – with dishwasher, refrigerator, and range – could be found in the $14,000 home of a typical American worker, but also on the relative merits of their rival political and economic systems. There is no exact record of their remarks, but many Western reporters witnessed the debate, and a reconstructed version was published in the *New York Times* (July 25, 1959).

Neither Nixon nor Khrushchev, moreover, could have foreseen that their verbal sparring would signal not only the start of a series of high-level summit meetings between leaders of their two countries, but also the endorsement of a broad program of cultural and other exchanges, which would lead eventually to profound changes within the Soviet Union.

Nixon had come to Moscow to preside over the opening of a U.S. National Exhibition under the 1958 U.S.-Soviet Cultural Agreement, which provided for national exhibitions in the two countries. A centerpiece of the U.S. exhibition was Buckminster Fuller's 30,000 square foot geodesic dome, which housed the scientific and technical exhibits, and which the Soviets agreed to purchase at the close of the Moscow exhibition. But the success of the U.S. exhibition was due in large part to the many items provided gratis for display by more than 450 American companies, ranging from consumer products to automobiles, trucks, farm machinery, and other mechanized products of U.S. industry, as well as the 75 young American guides, all fluent in Russian, who were assigned to explain the exhibition's products to inquisitive Russian visitors. And it was at Sokolniki that

Khrushchev got his first taste of Pepsi Cola, dispensed free to all visitors in Dixie cups. Khrushchev and other Russians liked it, giving Pepsi a huge head start in the Soviet market over its rival Coca Cola.

More than three million Soviet citizens attended the six weeks of the exhibition. For Soviet visitors, the U.S. exhibition was a cornucopia of consumer products that had never been seen in the Soviet Union. And for most of the Soviet visitors, it was their first and only opportunity to speak with an American. In the reciprocal exchange, the Soviets mounted their own national exhibition in New York City's Coliseum. Unlike the U.S. exhibition, which emphasized consumer goods, the Soviet exhibition was strong in machinery, science, and technology.

Nixon had four encounters with Khrushchev during his Moscow visit. The first was the so-called "courtesy call" on Khrushchev in the Kremlin, where Khrushchev defied diplomatic protocol by railing against the Captive Nations Resolution passed by the U.S. Congress one week earlier, and banging his fist on the table for emphasis. The second was in a television studio at the U.S. exhibition, where, as William Safire reported in the *New York Times* (July 27, 1984), "the bellicose Soviet leader verbally mauled the American Vice President, who was trying to be Mr. Nice Guy." A video tape of that encounter was smuggled out of the Soviet Union and shown on American TV. The third encounter was the so-called "kitchen debate," where the two leaders traded barbs and debated over the $14,000 model American prefab home, with Nixon defending its kitchen as typical for an American worker's home, and Khrushchev arguing that the home on exhibit was within the reach of only rich Americans, while Soviet workers had homes with similar modern appliances. The fourth, and most substantive and important meeting, was a five-hour off-the-record debate that took place at Khrushchev's country dacha, where the two discussed foreign policy issues in a non-bellicose manner, and Nixon repeated President Eisenhower's invitation to Khrushchev to visit the United States, which Khrushchev did for two weeks in September 1959.

Khrushchev, in remarks delivered at the formal opening of the exhibition, admitted that he had felt a "certain envy" while on his informal tour of the U.S. exhibition that morning, but he added that the Soviets would soon "overtake" Americans in peaceful economic competition, and would wave as they passed them, a pledge the Soviets would continue to emphasize in future years, but were unable to fulfill. Not made public was one of those

Soviet jokes (called *anekdoty* in Russian) that soon began to circulate – that the Soviet Union should not try to overtake the United States, because then Americans would see that Russian behinds were bare.

Nixon, in his formal remarks, read a conciliatory statement from Eisenhower regretting the Cold War, which he termed as "so unnecessary," and expressed his hope that the exchange of exhibitions would be the first step in restoring the trust and unity that the two countries had experienced during World War II. And, in an unprecedented radio and TV address to the Soviet people, broadcast at the end of his visit to the Soviet Union, Nixon called for "sharply expanded exchange programs" between the two countries, an end to jamming of foreign broadcasts, and an exchange of regular radio and TV broadcasts by leaders of the two countries.

As Charlotte Saikowski of the *Christian Science Monitor*, one of the U.S. National Exhibition's Russian-speaking guides, has described it:

> To those of us who were there, the American National Exhibition in Moscow in 1959 was an exhilarating, demanding, and heart-warming experience. It represented a breakthrough in Soviet-American cultural relations. After six weeks of talking and arguing with thousands of the some three million Soviet citizens who attended, we left Moscow with an indelible feeling that on a human, personal level, Soviets and Americans can communicate and, despite their differing political systems, find something in common.

Nixon concluded his visit with an exhausting 10-day, 5,000 mile tour of the Soviet Union. This was followed by a stop in Warsaw, where he spent three pleasant days focusing on U.S. relations with Poland and other East European communist countries. The visit to Warsaw was not planned, but when the Soviets refused to give Nixon permission to exit the Soviet Union from Siberia on his return trip to Washington, he seized the opportunity to visit a country which in 1956 had replaced a Stalinist regime with one of "national communism," and was seeking improved relations with the West, and with the United States in particular.

Nixon's plane landed at a Polish military base outside Warsaw, but his route into the city had been broadcast by Radio Free Europe, and, as his convoy of vehicles approached the city, many thousands of Poles turned out to enthusiastically and warmly greet the U.S. Vice President. As the convoy neared the center of the city, Nixon rose and the crowd began to throw bouquets of flowers.[1]

The decision to visit Warsaw was also a signal that the United States henceforth would treat each East European communist country individually, depending on its willingness to reform and to expand contacts with the West. It highlighted the centrality of cultural exchanges in U.S. foreign policy.

When U.S. cultural exchange with the Soviet Union is mentioned, most Americans think of dancers, orchestras, and ice shows that came to the U.S., filling halls with admiring spectators. But cultural exchange consisted of much more: the exchange of ordinary citizens. They fall under the rubric of what we now call Public Diplomacy – talking to another country, not through diplomats, but directly to its people, to influence how they regard one another.

Under Stalin, the Iron Curtain was almost impenetrable. Information about the West was tightly controlled. Foreign travel was limited – only officials, trusted newspaper reporters, and KGB agents were allowed to travel beyond the Soviet Bloc.

But over 30 years (1958-1988), more than 50,000 Soviets came to the United States under the 1958 U.S.-Soviet Cultural Agreement, and many thousands more traveled to Western Europe. They came as scholars and students, scientists and engineers, writers and journalists, government and party leaders, musicians, and athletes. They came, they saw, they were conquered, and the Soviet Union would never again be the same. Those exchanges prepared the way for Gorbachev's *glasnost, perestroika*, and the end of the Cold War.

THE CULTURAL AGREEMENT was actually an agreement for long-term exchanges in science and technology, agriculture, medicine and public health, radio and television, motion pictures, exhibitions, publications, government, youth, athletics, scholarly research, culture, and tourism. Why an agreement? What did we hope to accomplish?

An agreement was necessary because the Soviets made it a requirement, although many of the activities covered by the agreement were not the

....

1. I was driving my Ford sedan in the third vehicle of the convoy, as our embassy's cultural attaché in Warsaw, and I had to stop several times to push aside the bunches of flowers piling up on the hood of my car and obstructing my view.

responsibility of the U.S. government. But President Eisenhower wanted exchanges with the Soviets, and his role was very important. He was a national hero, had great prestige, and had been to Moscow after World War II. Eisenhower originally wanted to receive 10,000 Soviet students, pay all their expenses, and not require any reciprocity for American students. FBI's J. Edgar Hoover concurred, but the State Department, in its negotiations with Moscow, tried for just 100 students, and the Soviets eventually agreed to exchange only 20 a year for each of the first two years. After the Soviets withdrew three of their nominees, only 17 were exchanged in academic year 1958-59.

U.S. objectives, published in National Security Council directive 5607, included the following: to broaden relations by expanding contacts between people and institutions of the two countries; involve the Soviets in joint activities and develop habits of cooperation with the U.S.; end Soviet isolation and inward orientation by giving it a broader view of the world and of itself; improve U.S. understanding of the USSR through access to its institutions and people; and obtain the benefits of cooperation in culture, education, science and technology.

For most Russians who came to the United States in those years – and most *were* Russians – their visits were a form of shock therapy. When the first Soviet students were shown a U.S. supermarket, they thought it was a Potemkin village created to impress them. But perhaps the most important impression Soviets brought back from the United States was not amazement at our consumer goods but a redefinition of what is "normal," a word with special meaning for Russians who want to live in a normal society.

Over the next 30 years, several thousand Soviet graduate students and young scholars studied in the United States, and an equal number of Americans went to the Soviet Union. For the United States, the exchanges created a pool of people knowledgeable about the Soviet Union who, having lived there, were able to distinguish fact from fiction. Most American professors in Russian studies today are alumni of those exchanges.

The Soviets likewise accumulated a growing number of scholars who had seen the West, who recognized how far behind the Soviet Union was, that communism had failed them, and that the Soviet media were not telling the truth. Here it is worth mentioning just one of them: Alexander Yakovlev, who studied at Columbia University in 1958-59, the first year of the exchanges.

Yakovlev has been described as the architect of *glasnost* and *perestroika*, the twin policies of Mikhail Gorbachev to promote "openness" and a "restructuring" of the Soviet Union. His rise from a small peasant village to the Politburo in Moscow and a senior adviser to Gorbachev was not unprecedented for an ambitious and bright young Russian. But Yakovlev was different from the run-of-the-mill party official. He read voraciously, had an open mind, and, in addition to his year at Columbia, had served ten years as Soviet ambassador to Canada. That lengthy exposure to the West differentiated Yakovlev from other rising Russian leaders whose backgrounds were more insular.

Yakovlev was one of four Soviet graduate students at Columbia in the fall of 1958. He studied modern American history, in particular the foreign policy of Franklin D. Roosevelt. Greatly affected by his year at Columbia, Yakovlev has described it as more meaningful to him than the 10 years he later spent as Soviet ambassador to Canada. When I asked him what he had gotten from his year at Columbia, Yakovlev said "I spent most of my time in the library, where I read more than 200 books that I could not have read in the Soviet Union."

Yakovlev later earned a reputation as the protector of the Soviet liberal intelligentsia that emerged during Gorbachev's reforms. And, as a foreign policy adviser, he was at Gorbachev's side during each of the Soviet leader's five summit meetings with President Reagan.

To reach the mass audience, the Cultural Agreement also provided for the exchange of motion pictures. During the years of the agreement, four or five U.S. films were purchased by the Soviets each year. Most were pure entertainment – comedies, adventure stories, musicals, and science fiction – which met the interests of Soviet audiences. Among the more popular over the years were *Some Like it Hot*, *The Apartment*, and *Tootsie*. Although the number of purchased films was small, hundreds of copies were made for distribution to cinemas throughout the Soviet Union. Other American films, although not purchased by the Soviets, were clandestinely copied and screened at "members-only" showings in professional clubs of Soviet writers, scientists, architects, journalists, cinematographers, and other privileged persons.

From foreign films, Soviet audiences learned that people in the West did not have to stand in long lines to purchase food, did not live in communal apartments, dressed fashionably, enjoyed many conveniences not available in the USSR, owned cars, and lived the normal life so sought by Russians. Audiences were not listening to the soundtrack or reading subtitles, but watching the doings of people in the films – in their homes, on the streets, the clothes they wore, the cars they drove. And when refrigerators were opened in Western films, they were always full of food. Such details of how people lived in the West were very revealing for Soviet audiences.

Meanwhile, Soviet performing artists – symphony orchestras, ballet troupes, individual artists, as well as circuses and ice shows – were good box office attractions in the United States, and big dollar earners for the Soviet state. In exchange, the State Department sent major symphony orchestras, jazz bands, dance ensembles, and even once a circus.

Sending a performing arts group required the approval of both parties to the agreement. The United States exercised its veto several times when the State Department, fearing protests by émigré groups after the Soviet suppression of the 1956 Hungarian revolution, said that it would not grant visas for tours by the Soviet Army Chorus. Goskontsert, the Soviet state concert agency, reflecting the conservatism of Russian officials and ideologists, rejected many of the modern dance groups and jazz ensembles proposed by the State Department as "too avant garde." And, until the late 1980s, rock music was out of the question.

An old Russian proverb has it that, "It is better to see once than hear a hundred times," and Russians heeded that advice in flocking to see the 23 thematic exhibitions produced by U.S. Information Agency under the 1958 Cultural Agreement. What they had heard a hundred times about the United States from their own media was negated by a single visit to one of the USIA touring exhibitions, which gave them a glimpse of the United States and its people. The U.S. exhibitions, like the 1959 National Exhibition, drew huge crowds, with lines stretching for blocks awaiting admittance, and were seen, on average, by some 250,000 visitors in each city. All told, more than 20 million Soviet citizens visited the 23 U.S. exhibitions over a 30-year period.

Many of the American guides would go on to make careers in the Soviet area as scholars, professors, diplomats, and journalists. With their first-hand knowledge of life in the Soviet provinces, they became a national asset during the years when U.S. knowledge of the Soviet Union was minimal.

The more than 50,000 Soviets who came to United States over the 30-year period of the Cultural Agreement, plus the tens of thousands who went to Western Europe during those years, prepared the way for Gorbachev's *glasnost* and *perestroika*, and the end of Cold War. Equally important, the exchanges prepared the way for agreements with the Soviet Union on arms control and other important issues, as the Soviets learned that they could accept more Americans on their territory without risk to their national security.

It is fascinating to consider that it all traces back to a makeshift kitchen.

July/August 2009

Digging Up the Past
Christopher Marcisz

In 1962, Soviet police fired on a crowd of demonstrators in the industrial city of Novocherkassk. It was one of the biggest domestic disturbances of the Soviet era. Yet even today the event is shrouded in misinformation, rumor and myth.

*O*ur cab is headed into the center of Novocherkassk. We are on our way to visit the city's museum dedicated to the 1962 riot. At first our driver does not believe such a museum exists (it *is* rather small), but then he recounts the version of the "truth" as he knows it. Apparently, the father of a friend was there that June day and saw everything: the bodies stacked up like firewood, the blood flowing into the drains like it was raining, the kids who'd climbed up into the trees and who dropped like hunted birds. Of course, his witness has been dead for years.

"I hope they tell the real story," he says, casually flipping an obscene hand gesture at someone who had cut him off.

We mention the work of researcher Irina Mardar, who has spent two decades working with a group of researchers to put together the truth – or the closest thing to it – of what happened. The best number she has come up with, after years of digging through documents, interviews with policemen, doctors, government officials, and even several clandestine excavations at secret cemeteries around Rostov region, is that 26 people died that day, with dozens more injured.

Our driver is unconvinced. He explains how in the Soviet Union there were never any airplane crashes, and that, officially, there were no maniacs running the streets, even as Andrei Chikatilo from nearby Rostov-on-Don murdered 52 people around the region and near Moscow. "I know this type of counting," he says.

THE NOVOCHERKASSK TRAGEDY of 1962 remains one of the most neglected chapters in Soviet history. It was one of the rare cases of overt domestic dissent during seven long decades of systemic political repression. It was a moment when common workers took Soviet rhetoric about the workers' paradise at face value, honestly believing that a peaceful demonstration was the best way not to overthrow or challenge their rulers, but simply to be heard.

On June 1, 1962, thousands of workers at the Budyonny Locomotive Plant on the outskirts of this industrial town walked off their jobs in response to price increases for meat and bread. The next day, bearing portraits of Lenin and led by Young Pioneers carrying flowers, they marched to Communist Party headquarters in the center of town to voice their demands. They were met there by units of Interior Ministry troops, who had been trucked in overnight. After a brief standoff, for reasons lost to history, shots were fired. There were 26 killed, another 59 seriously wounded. In the aftermath, 112 alleged "ringleaders" were rounded up and put on trial. Seven were executed.

In a way, it almost makes sense that it was in Novocherkassk that Soviet power faced its most serious domestic riot in 40 years. This small provincial city of about 180,000 is located just 25 miles from the region's capital, Rostov-on-Don. It was founded in 1805 by Matvei Platov – the Cossack *hetman* who became famous in the war against Napoleon – as the new capital for the Don Cossacks.

The Cossacks were always an unruly element of Russia's imperial rule. As free refugees from serfdom, they were a vibrant subculture on the empire's edge, an uneasy part of the nation's vertical power structure. Theirs has been a history punctuated with both violent revolts and fierce support of the tsarist regime against its enemies. During the Civil War (1918-1922), Novocherkassk was a center of White resistance. Soviet rule was not firmly established until January 1920.

During the 1930s, the city became an important industrial center. The population tripled as increasing numbers of former peasants found work at the city's plants and factories. Among them was the Budyonny Electric Locomotive Factory, a sprawling operation 12 kilometers from the city center. The factory made railroad cars and employed thousands of workers.

Fast forward three decades. Khrushchev's "Thaw" was hitched to a mindless political and economic optimism that did not reflect reality. By 1962, rising costs of production on collective farms meant that it cost these farms more to produce goods than the state was paying for them. So, the more they produced, the more money they lost. To surmount this deficit, Khrushchev and the Politburo decided – for the first time in decades – to raise food prices, by as much as 25-35 percent. Meanwhile, in an effort to boost economic growth, production quotas had been increased, creating *de facto* wage cuts.

The price increases went into effect on Friday, June 1. Riots and strikes broke out all across the Soviet Union – in Murom, Alexandrovsk, Tbilisi, Novosibirsk, Leningrad, Dnepropetrovsk and Grozny. But nowhere were they as large – or would they turn as violent – as in Novocherkassk.

The workers at the Budyonny factory were angry about the price increases. A small group went to management to complain about the situation. Eyewitnesses have said the origins of the events were spontaneous – subsequent Soviet propaganda made much about the plotting that preceded the events. During a meeting with management (notably, the factory boss had recently been changed from someone the workers liked, to one who was widely seen as worthless), it was clear that no progress was forthcoming. In exasperation, when workers said they couldn't even afford *pirozhki* with meat at the price it was being offered in the factory cafeteria, one manager replied, *a la* Marie Antoinette, that they go enjoy a pastry with liver (*pirozhki c liverom*), an expensive treat out of reach of the increasingly strapped workers.

The knot of workers called a strike, and, within a matter of hours, it spread to various parts of the factory. Workers threw down their tools, walked away from the production lines, and began to gather and mill around the open courtyards between the factory's buildings. Managers exhorted them to get back to work, to no avail.

Throughout the day, plant managers frantically called the local Communist authorities. But the real turning point took place halfway through the afternoon, when a group of strikers broke down a nearby fence and blocked a major rail artery that linked Rostov with Saratov. That event, more than anything else, got the Kremlin's attention.

By the end of the day, the strikers' ranks had swelled to several thousand and limited attempts by local KGB troops to put down the riot were unsuccessful. Yet, as darkness fell, the workers had no real sense of how best to proceed, and so they went home. Overnight, troops from the Interior Ministry and Red Army began to arrive, along with the KGB.

The authorities identified who they suspected were the "ringleaders," and began arresting them around town.

On Saturday, many of the workers again gathered at the plant. Still unclear about how to proceed, they opted to march on the Party headquarters, which was located in the former Hetman's Palace of the Don Cossacks in the center of town, about 12 kilometers away.

The spirit of the march was festive. The workers carried portraits of Lenin, and were led by schoolchildren carrying flowers. They made their way along the main thoroughfare. It was unclear how many actually set out, but it was likely over 1,000. The first sign of trouble came on a bridge over the Tuzlov River, where regular troops of the Red Army had been ordered to set up a blockade with tanks. The marchers supposedly greeted the soldiers as comrades, urging them to "make way for the working class!" The military commander on the scene was Matvei Kuzmich Shaposhnikov, deputy commander of the North-Caucasus Region, who reported to his superiors that "he couldn't see the enemy."

The demonstrators forded the river or climbed over the tanks on the bridge, and headed along the city's main thoroughfare, Moskovskaya Street, soon arriving at the tree-lined square in front of the squat former palace. In front of the building was a large cordon of heavily armed Interior Ministry (MVD) troops, bussed in from Chechnya and Ingushetia (it was thought that troops from other regions would be less likely to sympathize with the locals).

WHAT HAPPENED NEXT is unclear. The official version that would come out later was inherently flawed, and the versions that were passed along as hearsay and rumors for decades are not much better. It seems that at some point, some of the protesters broke into the Hetman's Palace, which had been abandoned earlier in the day. They may have rifled through some offices and possibly destroyed some furniture.

But in the midst of it, at some point, troops fired into the crowd (later reports would indicate that most of the shooting may have been by KGB snipers). Children who had been hiding in the trees watching jumped down quickly, the group scattered back onto the main streets. A 23-year old woman from a nearby village, Alexandra Moskalchenko, had just stepped out of a hair salon and was hit by two bullets in the leg, which had to be amputated. In the end, 26 people were killed on the square, and another 59 were seriously wounded. Three died later from their wounds.

The chaos gave birth to countless rumors. All of the kids jumping down from nearby trees led to the belief that the troops had tried to fire warning shots and accidentally slaughtered many children. The fact that no children were among the dead did not assuage the rumors – a large orphanage is located nearby, and many just assumed that the dead were orphans that no one was looking for.

Another persistent rumor, heard in various forms through the years, is that one of the MVD officers was so distraught when he saw what had happened that he began shouting at his troops in rage, and became so upset that he shot himself in the head. Researchers have been unable to find any proof that this happened.

The police made quick work of the square. The bodies were gathered up onto trucks and rushed away, and the square was washed down by fire trucks that had been on hand throughout (the stains, Lady Macbeth-like, would not wash out, however, and the street was hastily repaved). Meanwhile, the injured were rushed to the city hospital, which was inundated. Already the heavy hand of the state was at work, KGB agents were visible everywhere, keeping their ears open for any potential dissent.

Word of the events instantly became the talk of the region, and the news somehow managed to get to the wider world as well. Radio Free Europe and the BBC began broadcasting reports about the massacre. A briefing paper from the Central Intelligence Agency dated June 1963 reported that health authorities had closed the entire province to outsiders, alleging a cholera outbreak. The airport in Rostov-on-Don was taken over by the military, and the province was sealed off for the rest of the month. In October, *TIME* magazine reported an exaggerated variation of the rumor in a brief article describing "a wild night of rioting and pillaging," killing "several hundred" students and workers.

The inevitable roundups began. Hundreds were arrested and put on trial at a nearby military base, facing charges of treason, coup plotting, liaisons with foreigners, and hooliganism. The authorities produced piles and piles of photographs. KGB agents had thoroughly infiltrated the group of protesters, and took thousands of photographs of people in the crowd. In a chilling touch, photos were produced at the trials of small groups of people with ominous "X's" marked throughout. Agents testified that the workers were overheard slandering Soviet authorities, and inciting people to riot and property damage. In the end, 112 so-called "ringleaders" were given prison terms, and seven were executed.

Many arrests were arbitrary. Valentina Vodyanitskaya was a 19-year-old worker at the foundry who had recently moved to the city from the provinces. She was hardly a troublemaker: she claimed she showed up at the city center late in the day, and only came to the demonstrations as a way of "reporting to work." In the aftermath of the shooting, she was arrested and accused of vandalism for breaking into the party building and destroying some pictures. She was sentenced to 19 years in prison, but was released a few years later, after Khrushchev fell from power.

Today, Vodyanitskaya is a volunteer at the museum. Clearly, the events shaped her distrust for Soviet authority permanently, even though she still refers to the marchers in the third-person. "They wanted someone to listen to them," she said. "But the government was afraid."

When I visited the museum last summer, it was a quiet day. One visitor arrived, and struck up a conversation with Vodyanitskaya about the events. He said he had come to the city shortly before the events, to attend the Polytechnical Institute. He and some friends had been on the square for a little while that afternoon, and had left to get lunch when the shooting started. He laid the blame for everything squarely on Khrushchev, whose inept handling of the economy had sparked the unrest in the first place, and whose paranoid overreaction was unwarranted. Vodyanitskaya disagreed, saying that Khrushchev simply believed what he was told: that a gang of bandits and troublemakers were running riot in the city. The blame, she said, belongs to local authorities and the security services for lying.

OFFICIALLY, ACCORDING TO Soviet authorities, the event never took place. But the memory of what happened persisted in those living in or near Novocherkassk. Through the years, the magnitude of the crime seems to have gotten worse, with more and more people recalling hearing (from someone who is now dead) about bodies stacked like cordwood, about rivers of blood, about children being shot in the trees.

The cover-up began just after the shooting started. In the chaotic aftermath, the authorities couldn't figure out what to do with the bodies. They were taken out of town and left buried in heaps of hay. Summer had already arrived, with temperatures over 30° C (86° F). And when dogs began to get at the bodies, the authorities realized they needed a more permanent solution. They had the bodies buried in unused portions of existing cemeteries around the province. The work was done in the middle of the night, with the gravediggers hiding from passing headlights when they passed.

The event lived on in murk and confusion. It appeared briefly in Alexander Solzhenitsyn's epic account of Soviet crimes, *The Gulag Archipelago*. One local man, Peter Siuda, ran a one-person campaign to tell the truth. Siuda was an employee at the plant who was among the planners of the first day's events. He was arrested while on his way home that night, and was charged as a ringleader. He spent years in prison, and for the rest of his life was obsessed with the events. He claimed that he had compiled an extensive oral history of what happened, but it vanished, allegedly taken when he was attacked in the street in spring 1990.

It wasn't until the 1980s, when Mikhail Gorbachev's *glasnost* began to loosen the ties of state secrecy, that people began to demand answers. Among them was Irina Mardar, a journalism student in Rostov who later worked at Novocherkassk Polytechnic Institute. In the spirit of getting to the bottom of a local secret, they assembled stories of eyewitnesses in a student journal called *Covered Yard*, dedicated to the 1962 tragedy. It appeared in 1988, and sold out almost immediately.

In 1990, she and a group of historians, frustrated by the continued official silence, decided to take matters into their own hands. Along with historian Tatyana Bocharova and archaeologist Mikhail Kraysvetny, they wanted to dig further. In the face of bureaucratic opposition, they decided to seek physical evidence to force authorities to acknowledge their work. That meant digging, literally. With modest information, they were able to identify some of the cemeteries where they believed the bodies had been interred.

Wherever possible, the group tried to get official permission for their work. Once, when Mardar and Bocharova showed up to search for remains in Tarasovka, north of Novocherkassk, the official in charge was baffled. His first instinct, as a Soviet bureaucrat in good standing, was to simply say "no." Surely things could not have happened as they claimed; they were just rabble-rousers. But, on the other hand, he had lived in the region for years, and had heard all the stories. In the end, his curiosity got the better of him, and he granted them permission.

Their work was also aided by the uncertain lines of authority of a Russia in chaos. Bocharova determined that, if things were not officially forbidden, they would go ahead and do their work anyway. Usually, no one stopped them. But inevitably the local KGB would make an appearance in the form of a mysterious Volga car that drove back and forth past the digs.

Finally, possessing evidence – the remains of unaccounted for bodies, Mardar and Bocharova decided to present them to the State Prosecutor's Office in Moscow (local prosecutors insisted they couldn't reopen the case). Bocharova left for the capital with stacks of photos and human remains in her luggage. In the end, she convinced the authorities to open an investigation. Once that process was underway, she and her team were able to extract more information from the Interior Ministry about locations and trials. The KGB never opened their files, but the researchers suspect that the KGB did pass some of its information along to the public via the MVD.

IN THE END, the investigation turned up 26 people in three cemeteries around the province. Twenty-four of the bodies were identified as belonging to individuals whose death certificates had been doctored. Two remain unidentified. Yet to this day, many insist that there were many more deaths.

Photographic evidence from the KGB and MVD might illuminate that claim, but those sources are not forthcoming. Indeed, the number of photographs the KGB and MVD produced at the trials suggest that this may have been the most photographed public event in the nation in 1962, and credible rumors that a full film of what happened is buried somewhere in the KGB archives are impossible to dismiss.

The path to discovery was also harder than it needed to be. The investigators wanted to secure pension increases for those who were wounded that day, which would be very simple to prove if they were able to check the hospital's medical records from that time. Yet, strangely, a doctor at the Novocherkassk hospital took stacks of records with him when he retired, including details about who was wounded and how. And although approached several times by the team of researchers, he declined to relinquish them, for reasons he would not reveal. The team had to bring doctors from Rostov to "confirm" that the participants' injuries were caused by gunshot wounds 40 years previous.

They also received help from an unexpected quarter. Early in their work, the investigators tracked down former police officials, to get their first-hand accounts. At the time, policemen who were involved in the events had been required to sign a release stating that they understood that, if they ever spoke out about their role in the cover-up, it would be considered a capital offense. But when the researchers caught up with them, most expressed relief, saying they had been waiting decades for someone to ask them about what had happened.

Interestingly, as prosecutors were in the early stages of convincing officials to open an investigation, they got an unexpected boost by the reformist mayor of St. Petersburg, Anatoly Sobchak, who visited to look over their work, along with a young aide, a former KGB man named Vladimir Putin.

Throughout the 1990s, the investigators were lucky and probably learned as much as the authorities were willing to allow. But, beginning in 2000, the archives slammed shut, and they have been unable to gain much more information. So the group began to think about ways to preserve and shape the memory of what happened. Applying for and receiving a grant from the Open Society Institute, they opened a museum.

Today, the museum fills two ground-floor rooms of an old building on Karl Marx Street, overlooking the square where the shooting took place. It faces the former Hetman's Palace, which itself is a museum to Cossack history. The exhibits are rather simple – one room is dedicated to the research effort, the other to the events themselves. There are copies of articles about the incidents, including a lengthy article from 1989 that appeared in the huge-circulation Moscow daily *Komsomolskaya Pravda*, from which most Russians first learned about the events of 1962. Along the walls are photos of the dead and injured and cards that tell their stories. One ghastly display shows personal items like bullets and buckles that were pulled from the graves; another wall chronicles life in the Soviet prison system for those who were sentenced.

The museum's director is Yelena Gubanova, a schoolteacher who met Mardar in 2000 in connection with a history project she was organizing in schools. Gubanova estimates that the museum receives about 2,000 visitors each year, most of them school groups from the surrounding region.

Yet Gubanova said she fears that an interest in the past is ebbing. She recalled how, in the summer of 1990, she and a huge crowd of people stood stock still on a train platform in Rostov, listening to the proceedings of the first freely elected Congress of People's Deputies on someone's transistor radio. It was, she said, "a very interesting time, because all kinds of things were starting to come out."

But today, it can be hard for Gubanova and others like her to recreate the excitement and inquisitiveness of those times. High schoolers, she said, once they start getting worried about exams and the future, have little interest in what happened decades ago. So Gubanova aims for younger students. Ninth grade is ideal, she said. Even so, many students come to the museum with little more than stereotypes about the past. They accept without question the Soviet Union's heroic role in the Second World War, but have few critical thoughts about the Soviet experience in general. Without a connection to the people and narratives of the time, "for them, [what happened here] is just irrelevant."

July/August 2008

On Moscow's Orders
Nikolai Cherkashin

> *In 1967-8, Captain Nikolai Shashkov, commander of a submarine carrying nuclear warheads, had a mission in what was then the most troubled region of the planet, the eastern Mediterranean, scene of the Arab-Israeli conflict. It was no secret that the USSR gave not only moral, but also military support to its Arab allies.*
>
> *I have no doubt whatsoever that Captain Shashkov would have carried out any order from Command if this local conflict had grown to global proportions. That was the reality of the time, the reality of Cold War and the opposition of military blocs. And I hope that we have finally departed from such a balance on the thin line between war and peace.*
>
>   – *Fleet Admiral Vladimir Chernavin,*
>   *President of the Union of Submariners*

Shashkov's mission was none other than the destruction of Israel. He was to fire eight P-6 (SS-12) rockets with nuclear warheads at the shore, thus causing a minimum of eight "Hiroshimas." And all this on the eve of or during Passover 1968. The captain tells his story.

Russian Life: ...*a minimum of eight "Hiroshimas?"*

Nikolai Shashkov: There could have been more. The American atom bomb dropped on Hiroshima was the equivalent of 20,000 tons of TNT. I could have been fitted with megaton warheads.

RL: You mean you didn't know the strike power of your own rockets?

N.S.: Not one commander of a submarine carrying nuclear warheads knows exactly. Warheads are fitted by specialists from another department entirely. All I have is initial data to calculate the trajectory. For me that's considered enough.

RL: Was a special order given?

N.S.: There could have been. We expected it. Just before I started my service I received an oral instruction from the Commander-in-Chief of the USSR Navy, Fleet Admiral [Sergei] Gorshkov, to "be ready to make a rocket strike on the coast of Israel." Of course this was only in the event of the Americans and Israelis launching a beachhead in friendly Syria. In fact it was there near the shores of Syria that was my main position...

I was restricted by the flight distance of my rockets, which did not exceed 600 km, so I was forced to "loiter"... dangerously close to three U.S. aircraft carrier strike groups headed by the nuclear carriers *America*, *Forrestal* and *Enterprise*. Each had 20-30 escort ships, almost every one of which was equipped with submarine search systems. And I was alone. The Americans also had patrol planes in the air. At times there were as many as 17 submarine hunting aircraft hammering the entire eastern Mediterranean with their radar. There was always a signal on the [radar detector] antenna. They were looking for an entire underwater Soviet screen, while in fact there was only my one K-172...

This was war, and most definitely not a "cold" one. No one knew what would happen the next day. This was the first time since the [1960 U2 crisis] that the international situation had worsened to the point of potential nuclear exchange, i.e. nuclear war on a worldwide scale. I was supposed to start it on the first signal from Moscow. And so as not to miss this signal, I had to get on the radio every two hours...

We kept having to dive away from approaching aircraft. Around us it was basically business as usual: dry cargo ships, liners, fishing boats. And we meanwhile spent most of our time at periscope depth, more dangerous for a submarine than further down because you can get hit by someone's bow. We were also very concerned about... sonars. Our intelligence really put the wind up us: "look out," [they said,] "they can pick up a boat at 200 miles, whatever the conditions." They never picked up a thing. We heard them, but they didn't hear us.

RL: *Are you sure?*

N.S.: Well if they had I wouldn't be talking to you today. That would have been the end of my career as a commander... If they had discovered me, I'd have had half a dozen anti-submarine ships down on me, Sea Kings flying overhead and a nuclear torpedo boat on my tail, ready to launch a full salvo if I so much as opened the lids of my rocket containers. That's why I'm 100 percent sure that we didn't blow our cover.

RL: *Did the Arabs know of your presence?*

N.S.: Well, of course they didn't know which boat and where exactly it was. But they knew that, if it came to the crunch, the Soviet Union would support them using any means available, including nuclear. As for where the strike against Israel would be made from, they were also aware that it would be from the sea.

RL: *Please describe your vessel.*

N.S.:... the K-172 (NATO classification Echo-2) was for its time a very modern vessel. Soviet sailors called it the "folding bed," because of the rocket containers, arranged in pairs along the sides, which rose out of its light body. The launchers were raised to an angle of 15 degrees... Its surface displacement was 5,800 metric tons, underwater displacement 6,200 tons, length 199 meters. It had ten compartments and two reactors, an underwater speed of 24 knots, and a crew of 90. It was built in Severodvinsk in the mid 60s.

We considered it a "one-time" sub, i.e. only fit for firing one salvo. After all, we could only fire when surfaced, and the time between surfacing and launching is 20 minutes. This would have been more than enough to find us and destroy us immediately after the salvo was fired.

RL: *Did you realize you were hostages of power politics, and that you were effectively kamikazes?*

N.S.: I understood perfectly well the whole risk of our venture. But war is war. You take risks every day, and under the water with two nuclear reactors, twenty odd torpedoes and eight rockets you take risks every hour, if not every minute. But we are servicemen, we took an oath to carry out any orders of the Party and government, even if they meant our own lives were threatened...

RL: *And the whole world.*

N.S.: Do you suppose the Americans didn't behave in exactly the same way? I can name for you the commanders of those American nuclear-powered vessels which had Moscow and the industrial areas of the Urals in their sights. They could also have had the honor, or rather misfortune, of starting the Third World War.

And the Americans knew that, in the event of developments which were extremely unfavorable for us in the Middle East, the USSR was just as capable of making a nuclear strike as American strategists defending their geopolitical interests. That was the dangerous absurdity of the Cold War, that any local crisis – whether it be off Cuba, in Indonesia or in the Middle East – could grow immediately into thermonuclear war, with all its monstrous consequences for mankind.

Personally I have not and do not feel any hostility towards Israel itself.

And another thing. It's one thing when you're, say, a marine, and see your opponent's face, and aim at a living individual; it's another when you have in front of you a remote control device, instruments, lamps and arrows. You can see neither blood, nor destruction, nor explosions nor fires. Just the usual work with the usual equipment, and nothing more. A whole country could disappear, and you would never see anything because you were under water or in an underground bunker. Techniques of mass destruction are now such that the direct executor of nuclear apocalypse bears no personal responsibility. He is just a link in the chain in the war machine. Wars are begun not by admirals but by civilians. It is they who give the fatal orders.

RL: Doesn't it scare you, when you look back and are conscious of the danger which you, like it or not, put yourself and the whole world in?

N.S.: You see, I've had so many dangerous moments in my life... Doctors say that all the stresses stay in the subconscious and then make themselves known. The dreams I have sometimes... But on the whole I have a clear conscience. I did my military duty honestly, and I am not ashamed of those years... My son Alexander followed in my footsteps and served as an officer on a new generation rocket-carrying submarine. He would also carry out such orders. It's a matter of military honor, whether Soviet or American.

RL: Did you have any Jews on the sub at the time you were in the Middle East?

N.S.: Yes, there were Jews, and Georgians, and Ukrainians... It was a normal international crew, like on all the other Soviet ships.

RL: Did they know that you had been appointed to destroy Israel?

N.S.: No. Only I knew about the order to be ready to strike. But they too must have guessed that we hadn't come to Haifa for a friendly visit.

RL: And how did they behave?

N.S.: There were no breaches of discipline.

RL: Why did the choice fall on you in particular?

N.S.: I had battle experience in the Mediterranean. I... received top marks for all the missions I had been assigned. You could call it fresh experience.

But I think my biographical details played a major role too. My father was in the secret service, head of a special department of the 2nd Strike Army.

RL: The same one as General Vlasov [who later headed Russian forces fighting for the Nazis]?

N.S.: Yes. My father tried to break out of encirclement with Vlasov, and when things became critical, he shot himself, while Vlasov surrendered.

Whatever people say about the secret services now, I am convinced that among them were absolutely honest people, like my father... I recently found his grave in the woods near Novgorod. Unfortunately a symbolic one.

RL: *Do you believe that today's Russian navy would be capable of repeating that 1968 mission which you participated in?*

N.S.: Quite recently a nuclear *Akula* class submarine on battle patrol entered the North Pole area. There, on top of the world, the commander was given the order to launch one of his rockets. The target was a polygon in Arkhangelsk Region. All the battle blocs of the RSM-52 rocket reached their target within the given coordinates. And this was just one rocket. In fact the *Akula* is capable of launching a nuclear "hail" of 200 separate warheads. For its hurricane-like power, this strategic underwater rocket complex was called "Typhoon."

Draw your own conclusions.

October 1996

1969

30 Years Under the Winter Sun
Mikhail Ivanov

In April 1969, maverick Russian film director Vladimir Motyl finished his movie White Sun of the Desert. Despite the efforts of ideologues and bureaucrats, the movie came to be Russians' most beloved film, and it propelled Motyl to nationwide fame.

In 1968, just a few months after Soviet troops invaded Czechoslovakia to quell the Prague Spring, another crisis was brewing in the Kremlin. At the Kremlin dacha, to be more exact...

General Secretary Leonid Brezhnev was having a party with his acolytes. The appointed hour came to screen the Western movie traditional at such parties. But somehow the featured film had gone missing. It was Sunday, nobody was working. The mortified representative of Goskino (State Committee for Cinema) recalled that there was a "Russian Western" sitting on the censor's shelf. God Save the Goskino! After all, The Tsar is Permitted Everything. This weekend, instead of an American Western, Brezhnev previewed an uncut version of *White Sun of the Desert*.

In the middle of the night after the screening, the Goskino minister was woken by a phone call from Brezhnev. "You're making good movies out there," Leonid Ilyich told him. "You really know how to please me."

This auspicious turn of events "saved" *White Sun of the Desert*. Shortly before the Brezhnev showing, the film's director, Vladimir Motyl, had been told to make some 27 "corrections" to the film. After the incident at the dacha, the number of edits was whittled to three. One change the kino commissars insisted on was that Motyl "edit out the naked buttocks of Katerina Matveyevna" in a scene where the film's protagonist, Sukhov, dreams of his wife after a long absence from home. Still, Motyl, who was famous for "never bowing his head to anyone," balked. "Brezhnev is happy," he said, "what else do you want?!" But the *apparatchik* replied with an unassailable argument: "Volodya! No naked a-- could ever deviate the party and the government. But you can easily deviate the Soviet people." If only he knew how close he was to the truth...

White Sun of the Desert (*Белое солнце пустыни*, 1969) went on to become one of a handful of Soviet-era films known and loved by all Russians, not just for its ironic tone and Western-style plotline, but also because it was different (or, in the view of the censors, "ideologically shaky"). Some years later, when Brezhnev was readying for a détente-inspired trip to the U.S., he ordered Goskino to prepare the five best Soviet films to be shown in Carnegie Hall. He was quick to notice that the *apparatchiks'* list did not include *White Sun*, so he added it to the list himself. The film came to America, where it received positive reviews.

By any measure, *White Sun* was a mega-hit, seen by over 100 million Soviets in its first year alone. But Motyl saw no financial windfall, despite the fact that Soviet directors benefited financially and otherwise from successful films. He would not find out the reason for this until some years later, when a representative of Glavkinoprokat (the Soviet institution which oversaw film distribution) revealed the secret over a shot of vodka. It had been decided by the ideological watchdogs that this "politically incorrect" film must not be ranked in the top ten Soviet movies shown. So it was always ranked lower: 11th or 12th; its ticket sales were attributed to more ideologically acceptable films. "They loved me," Motyl said, "because I helped them to overfulfill the plan for many years. Each year, data and figures relevant to the *White Sun* were lowered on order from Goskino and the Central Committee of the CPSU... mediocre movies, which failed commercially but which were done by officially endorsed directors, were stealing figures from us."

Exportfilm cheated on figures for the same reason. Over 100 countries bought the *White Sun*, but Exportfilm paid for only 20 sales.

Later, Mosfilm took over the copyright on *White Sun*. Motyl saw nothing from the huge, legal video sales of the film all over the world. Moreover, *White Sun* is shown on TV at least 4-5 times a year on different channels, bringing in lucrative commercial contracts. Mosfilm receives $10,000 and $18,000 for each showing. Motyl gets nothing.

The only chance Motyl has been offered to obtain long overdue financial compensation was on a proposed sequel of *White Sun*. Numerous "people of substance," including then Prime Minister Viktor Chernomyrdin, have offered support for a sequel. But Motyl bristles at the idea – such a venture, he said, would surely spoil the legend of the original. Besides, he said, "the actors are almost 30 years older... the only thing I would maybe agree to would be a remake with younger actors."

But even this compromise, Motyl said, makes him cringe. "I understand that, commercially, the film would work well. Each of the millions of previous viewers would watch the new version at least once. But then I thought to myself: 'What price shall I set for silencing my conscience?' which was whispering to me – 'Don't do this.' For I am fatalist – if a film has to be done, it is going to happen anyway, by will of fate. That's the way I have produced all my films."

The Road to Karakum

Fate has played a large role in Motyl's life and career. As a young boy growing up in the Urals in the 1930s, he was mesmerized by the new cinema. His mother, Berta Levin, had been exiled to the region after her husband was arrested. Films shown in a local club were the only local distraction and Motyl's only window to the outside world. Glued to the screen, he says he swore to his mother: "I will make movies." Despite her meager salary, his mother, a nurse at an orphanage, bought her son a subscription to an illustrated film magazine.

After high school, Motyl failed to enter a film institute, so he became a theater director instead. And it was there, in Sverdlovsk (now Yekaterinburg) that he had a fateful clash with a local *Komsomol* boss. The *apparatchik* banned two of Motyl's theater performances because they were impregnated with the spirit of Khrushchev's Thaw. In a bizarre twist worthy of a movie script, this party boss would dog Motyl throughout his career.

Motyl made the jump from theater to film when a director in Tadzhikistan was fired from a film team. Motyl reworked the script, replaced the actors and broke through with his team to the hitherto inaccessible Pamir. His finished film, *Children of Pamir (Дети Памира*, 1963), was a smashing debut. It earned him a State Prize in the Soviet Republic of Tadzhikistan as well as the title Honorary Citizen of Dushanbe (the Tadzhik capital). Still, the film commissar from Sverdlovsk used his influence to ensure that the film did not participate in the International Class A Festival in Venice. There, Soviet films for children had a strong track record for bringing home the coveted Golden Lion award.

Motyl's next film project was quashed when party bosses disallowed both of his screenplays for a film about the Decembrists – the scripts apparently had "too much of a touch of dissidence." So the embattled director turned to a lighter subject, an ironic comedy about the Second World War, *Zhenya, Zhenechka, Katyusha* (*Женя, Женечка и «катюша»*, 1967). But this only added fuel to the fire. Back then, irony was not a tone used to portray the Great Patriotic War. Motyl was dressed down and blacklisted for making "pacifist films denigrating the heroism of the Soviet Army."

Yet, this setback had a silver lining. *Zhenya, Zhenechka, Katyusha* attracted the attention of famous Soviet director Pavel Chukhrai, who headed the Experimental Studio, which Motyl said was an "oasis of common sense amidst the absurdity of socialist cinema production." At the Experimental Studio, there was unheard of artistic freedom: the studio head was authorized to hire scriptwriters and directors at his discretion and there were even financial incentives for writers, contingent upon a film's performance.

Chukhrai asked Motyl to direct the movie that would become *White Sun*. But Motyl accepted the offer only half-heartedly. When he read the first script – the story of a soldier who saves a harem from a bandit, he turned the project down. "I didn't want to do an adventure movie," he said. Yet the writers, Yezhov and Ibragimbekov, were persistent: Motyl was the only director they wanted to work with and they explained to him that, because of the scandal with his war comedy, Chukhrai's Experimental Studio was his only chance.

Backed into the corner, Motyl secured an important concession: he would have carte blanche to rewrite the script, change the dialogue and the plot, etc. This was no small achievement at a time when a script was a sacred document requiring signatures and stamps at every stage.

The film was shot on location in the Karakum desert. "I worked under stress in a suffocating heat, realizing it was my last resort," Motyl said. "But I worked easily, as if the scenarios were dictated to me from the heavens... many catch-phrases were born off-the-cuff."

Notwithstanding the film's huge public success and the significant revenues it brought the state, Motyl received only scorn from the Soviet film elite (despite the fact that the head of the party, General Secretary Brezhnev, loved the film). They labeled the film "an ideologically alien imitation of Hollywood," good only for distraction and replenishing the state coffers.

The fate of *White Sun* may actually have been preordained. Motyl's long-time party nemesis from Sverdlovsk had since risen to the position of head of Goskino. "*The White Sun of the Desert* was not sent to any international film festivals," Motyl said, "because of my 25-year-old conflict with the Minister of Cinema." (It took another Sverdlovsk communist party alum, Boris Yeltsin, to right this wrong. In 1997, Motyl was awarded the State Prize and the Award of Honor. That same year, a new general director at Mosfilm decided to begin paying some royalties from their *White Sun* TV earnings to the film's authors and director.)

So it was that even after *White Sun of the Desert*, Motyl had to push his next film like a debutante. It took him nearly five years to get permission to shoot his romantic-historical saga dedicated to the Decembrists, *The Star of Captivating Happiness* (*Звезда пленительного счастья*, 1975). But the result was as stunning artistically as *White Sun*. And the film, while on a more somber topic, was commercially successful and is still frequently aired.

This movie, about revolutionaries and the wives that followed them to exile in Siberia, was, Motyl said, a tribute to his parents. His father was a Polish political émigré "who arrived in Soviet Russia, believing in the Bolsheviks, only to fall prey to their guillotine... He was soon arrested and perished in Solovki [labor camp], so [my parents] lived together for only two-and-a-half years... My maternal grandfather – a Jew from Belarus – was dekulakized in the 1930s and exiled with eight children to a permafrost area in the North, where my mother's young sister went insane..."

His next film, *The Forest* (*Лес*, 1980), inspired by Russian playwright Alexander Ostrovsky, was banned after being labeled a distortion of the Russian classic and an insult to the Russian people. This sealed Motyl's fate. For the next decade he was a pariah in Russian cinema. He was only able to work on TV movies, write scripts, teach, consult young directors, stage theater plays and lecture. Only the collapse of the communist regime would enable Motyl to return to film-making.

Aiming at Viewers' Hearts

So what is it about *White Sun* that makes it popular even today, over 30 years after its release? How can a film situated in Soviet realities strike a chord with post-Soviet Russians?

Lenkom theater director Mark Zakharov, a long-time friend of Motyl's (he also wrote the script for Sukhov's dream letters to Katerina Matveevna), said he thinks it is because *White Sun* "is a huge social and state phenomenon, a success from heavens... Everything is great there – the actors, the scripts, the editing of the film. There are no delays, good dynamics, lots of professional merit. Plus there is nothing from our day-to-day life, there are great quotes and a great song by [Bulat] Okudzhava. It is a great, deeply Russian movie using the laws of a U.S. Western."

Political "heavyweight" Alexander Lebed certainly agrees. When he recently met Motyl, he called *White Sun* a movie that "will last for centuries." Lebed was himself beholden to *White Sun*: a famous line from the movie: "I feel sorry for the country" ("*Za derzhavu obidno*") was the title of Lebed's autobiography. (Not surprisingly, Motyl expressed a reciprocal affection for Lebed. "I do see some traits of [*White Sun's* main character] Sukhov in him... He is natural, strong, brave and self-abnegated man like Sukhov," he said, citing Lebed's role in stopping the war in Chechnya.)[1]

Of course, phrases like "*Za derzhavu obidno*" strike a patriotic chord with Russians. And the landscape and scenery of the movie is a modern Russia in miniature: a desolated customs point ignored by bandits and smugglers, but rife with ethnic problems and aching for a folk hero of Sukhovian proportions. Russians unite in their love of the film's simple themes of honor, bravery and trust – much more than they might around some elusive "national idea."

But it is the film's focus on eternal themes and human values that won it its initial admiration by the public. "Our people," Motyl said, "lost a lot as a result of this godless Soviet propaganda, which caused the country's moral decay... No matter how hard our propaganda tried to stigmatize American pragmatism, in fact we were faced with the monstrous, Soviet "scratch my back" type of pragmatism... We were perverting our country by this approach to life: how to get some goods and benefits by cozying up to the higher-ups and kissing-up to those working in our deficit-based system of trade. It was tough to survive in that immoral system. So I liked the fact that

1. General Alexander Lebed perished in a helicopter crash in 2002.

the hero is not subordinated to anyone. And the fact that he was already demobilized and returning home. He obviously didn't need anything from these women from the harem – he dreams only of his Katerina Matveyevna. But, on the other hand, he risks his life. In the name of what? Just because he is such a fairytale hero. He doesn't get burned in fire, nor is he drowned in water, as we say in Russian folklore."

The movie takes place in the aftermath of the Civil War (1918-1922), but Motyl readily admits that he did not seek to make the movie an authentic reflection of that war. "My Sukhov was not fighting with national extremists or with the White Guards," Motyl said. "He was just fighting with bandits. That's why I introduced the character of this customs officer, to make this conflict between Sukhov and the bandit Abdulah purely criminal, not ideological. So, one didn't need to know well the country's history, but rather to accept the story with one's heart. And it was precisely the heart of the viewer that I was targeting with my film."

An additional attraction of *White Sun* is that Motyl strayed from the uni-dimensional characters of Socialist Realist films. Here the characters are more complex. Even the bandit, Abdulah, is somehow charming and attractive. Wrong, yes, but still capable of change and repentance. The point, Motyl said, was "to show how a stranger (Sukhov) arrived with his own rules at somebody else's monastery. I wanted to show that the best intentions in a foreign country can't become an imperative. Abdulah is a cruel husband towards his harem, but these are *their* customs and traditions. Therefore I always remember the words of Kipling about the East and the West."[2] In marked contrast to the prevailing ideology of Soviet film at the time, Sukhov's good intentions do not end happily. In fact, the end result is largely tragic. Sukhov's aide is killed, the customs officer perishes and his wife goes insane, Abdulah's most beloved wife is strangled and Sukhov himself is wounded. As Motyl said, because he made his Abdulah a "courageous, charming, strong hero... the price of my hero Sukhov's victory over Abdulah increased."

These sentiments of *White Sun* were perhaps best summarized by Sukhov's famous line in the movie, "the East is a very subtle thing" ("*Vostok – delo tonkoye*"). And it is a theme which was also at the center of

---

2. "Oh, East is East, and West is West, and never the twain shall meet, / Till Earth and Sky stand presently at God's great Judgment Seat; / But there is neither East nor West, Border, nor Breed, nor Birth, / When two strong men stand face to face, / tho' they come from the ends of the earth!" From *The Ballad of East and West,* Rudyard Kipling.

Motyl's first post-Soviet production. The film, *Let's Part While You are Kind* (Расстанемся, пока хорошие, 1991*),* inspired by a short story by Fazil Iskander, focuses on betrayal and Russia's blind interference in the Caucasus. The film was shot before the Chechen war and showed "how clumsily the Russians interfered in affairs in the Caucasus," Motyl said. In the film's finale, Russians act on a false signal and send troops and artillery into a village against one man, an Abkhaz who is fighting with a local prince to defend his dignity.

Russia and the Caucasus, Motyl said, is a "painful historical theme... we have been conquering the Caucasus for over half a century... Today you can't solve these issues with a truncheon. That we sent our troops to Chechnya was a terrible crime perpetrated by our ex-Defense Minister [Pavel Grachev], who said he could take care of Chechnya with just one regiment of paratroopers. He was just ignorant and showed no knowledge of history. The ruler of the Caucasus under the tsar, General Yermolov, noted long ago that the Chechens are the most warlike, cruel and ferocious people. They can be liquidated, but not conquered."

Let's Part While You Are Kind met with its share of difficulties, indicative of the post-Soviet order of things. The nouveau riche "wild capitalist" producer who underwrote the film had earned a fortune in video sales while Motyl was filming in the difficult conditions of the war-torn Caucasus. After the film was finished, the jaded producer turned out to be little interested in promoting something with uncertain prospects. The film also fell victim to the very types of mindless conflict it spoke out against. Georgian intellectuals boycotted the film because, in it, Georgian actors played Abkhazians, their sworn enemies.

Motyl's latest film, *Gone with the Horses* (Несут меня кони..., 1996), takes on the themes of loyalty and repentance. Based on several Chekhov stories, it stars Andrei Sokolov (star of *Little Vera*) as an inveterate womanizer. After becoming disenchanted with his latest "conquest" (played by Agneshka Wagner), a sudden crisis (a duel) brings him to the brink of physical death, and face-to-face with his emptiness. "When he finds himself in this deep spiritual crisis," Motyl said, "when he looks deep into his soul, he realizes he is alone in the world and all he has as a refuge is [Wagner]. He comes back to her spiritually. He looks at her as if he sees her for the first time."

The film's plot echoes events in the director's own life. Motyl left his family to live with another woman for three years, during which he became increasingly depressed that his child was growing up without him. "This poisoned the happiness I found with this other woman," he said, "and finally led to our alienation, as she began to feel my inner, second life... And then I began helping my family financially... then I began meeting with my daughter, then my wife, who was such a loyal friend. During my entire absence, whenever someone spoke ill of me, she defended me with passion. She simply won me back with her generosity. I didn't expect it, so I came back to her."

The critics have not been so universally kind to *Gone with the Horses*. While more traditional, mainstream critics have praised the movie, younger critics have savaged the film as a creative failure, one even suggesting that "certain directors should be shot after they reach a certain age." Commercially, the movie was no *White Sun*, but has done "quite okay," Motyl said, and was invited to the Montreal Film Festival.

WHILE HE IS not a wealthy man these days, Vladimir Motyl is doing better than in the difficult days when he was ostracized by the Soviet film bureaucracy. He receives a modest stipend from the state that allows him freedom to write. But his greatest wealth is that of the love of several generations of Soviet – and now Russian – viewers. As journalist and cinema critic Ishtvan Yulash wrote, "the circle of admirers of his cult film is not limited by differences in age, profession, political views, nationality, educational level, or even intellect or temperament." At a recent Russian TV festival, *White Sun of the Desert* was awarded the title "Russian Viewers' Most Loved Film."

Many of the film's lines have become proverbial in Russian, used in media articles and headlines, cited by politicians, advertisers and marketers. For 25 years Russian cosmonauts have made it a ritual to watch the film before blast-off. Cosmonauts even took a video of *White Sun* into space. According to Alexei Leonov, a member of the Soyuz-Apollo flight, his American colleagues were delighted with the film.

There have been some unique perks for Motyl as well. GAI officers let him go in peace once they find out he is the author of *White Sun*. In the 1990s, the Federal Customs Service bestowed on Motyl a unique corporate watch as thanks for the character of the incorruptible customs officer. The watch serves as a special talisman that lets him pass through Russian customs smoothly.

"Not so long ago," Motyl recalled, "I helped a producer who accompanied me on a trip to Italy. This lady had far exceeded her duty-free limit of $500 and was about to be stopped by the customs. But she was let go as soon as I waved my hand at the customs officer, intimating she was with me."

Even in Soviet times, Motyl compensated for a lack of official recognition using his wits, not unlike his hero Fyodor Sukhov. He said his "favorite pastime" has always been traveling – not something enabled on a fixed income. So he tagged along with groups of filmmakers sent on lecture trips throughout the USSR by the Soviet Bureau of Film Propaganda. "But my wildest dream," he said, "was to see the Kommandor Islands – the ones neighboring the Kamchatka Peninsula. But there was no affiliate of the Film Propaganda Bureau in those closed, secret areas ..."

Not one to give up easily, Motyl found out how to call the Border Guards division of the KGB in Moscow. As soon as he mentioned *White Sun of the Desert*, an appointment was set.

"I paid a visit to the KGB general supervising the Border Guards. I told him I love travelling and offered to distract the border guards of these areas with my lectures and film excerpts. The general looked at me with human eyes like I have never seen in a KGB officer. He said, 'It's great that you have such a spiritual, noble thrust. So go ahead, fly to Kamchatka. There, the commander of the local political department of the Border Guards will meet you and satisfy your every wish. You will have a helicopter, a patrol boat... anything.'"

The reality surpassed Motyl's wildest dreams. A naval destroyer was put at his disposal. The Soviet border guards not only showed him the geysers near Petropavlovsk-Kamchatsky, but also provoked a scrambling of American fighter planes and let him witness the search of a Japanese fishing boat.

"This huge destroyer approached a miniscule boat and for the first time I saw Japanese at close quarters. The Japanese captain came out in casual sportswear, glanced at us, then turned his back and sat in an oriental, Zen-like pose throughout the search. But I could read a lot in this glance of his... The boat was shortly released after a document check. So I told the captain: 'you should not have.' But he said, 'Don't worry, we saw them let the poached fish go from their special holding tank.'"

Later, Motyl met some Japanese poachers under arrest on Shikotan Island (in the disputed Kuril chain). He was told that, in cases where there were really gross violations, they would detain the poachers and make them sit in a library full of Lenin's and Brezhnev's works in Japanese, which each poacher was required to read. "I think it was the worst torture they had to endure," he said.

Today, when so many creative types in the Russian arts are focused on international awards and working in the West, Vladimir Motyl remains firmly rooted in Russian soil. If he had total creative and financial freedom, he said, he would make a film about Tsar Alexander I, the reformer whose epoch reminds him of the Gorbachev era. Then, as now, he said, there was this "frenzied resistance to reform from the corrupt and greedy aristocracy on the one hand, and a no less frenzied resistance from the ignorant, backward lower classes on the other." To bring the story to film, he envisions telling the tale through the lives of three couples. Indeed, not waiting for an idyllic time of "total creative and financial freedom" to fall in his lap, he has already written one-third of the script. Obviously, those local critics who questioned Motyl's continued worth got it wrong. The white sun of this director's creativity continues to burn brightly.

April/May 1999

Postscript: Since this article was published, Motyl has directed just one film, Crimson Snow (Багровый цвет снегопада, 2009), *a romantic historical saga that takes place against the backdrop of the First World War and the Bolshevik Revolution. In 2003, Motyl was awarded the title "People's Artist of the Russian Federation."*

The Strangely Lucky Flight of Mathias Rust
Tom Lecompte

In Mathias Rust's neat, two-bedroom apartment outside Berlin there are no mementos, no photographs, no framed newspaper headlines – nothing to indicate that, for a few short weeks 18 years ago, he was the most famous pilot in the world. On May 28, 1987, Rust took off in a small Cessna from Helsinki, Finland, turned southeast toward the border of the then-Soviet Union, and flew 450 miles into the center of Moscow, landing next to the Kremlin.

*R*ust's stunt was an international sensation. Newspapers all over the world splashed photos of his plane sitting under the distinctive onion domes of St. Basil's Cathedral. Dubbed "the new Red Baron" and the "Don Quixote of the Skies," Rust's name was mentioned in the same breath as Charles Lindbergh and Chuck Yeager.

The political backdrop made his exploit even more sensational. No one knew it yet, but the Cold War was winding down. Gorbachev was pushing *glasnost* and *perestroika*. He and U.S. President Ronald Reagan were in the middle of delicate arms negotiations.

Into this flew a naïve, idealistic young man who decided to build "an imaginary bridge of peace" by flying solo to Moscow and personally delivering a goodwill message to the Soviet leader. Rust never met Gorbachev. But within days of Rust's landing, the Soviet defense minister and the Soviet air defense chief were sacked. A wide-ranging firing of military leadership followed. Within a year, Reagan and Gorbachev signed a major nuclear arms reduction treaty. Within two and a half years, the Berlin Wall came down. Within five years, the Soviet Union disappeared.

Today Rust, 37, seems the same earnest, idealistic young man he was 18 years ago. Though he has not piloted a plane since 1987, and in fact has spent many years trying to distance himself from his famous flight, the memory is fresh. "It seems like it happened yesterday," he said. "It's alive in me."

Genesis

As Rust remembered it, two things preoccupied him during his high school years in Hamburg: flying and Nuclear Armageddon. Not long after his seventeenth birthday in 1986, Rust joined a flying club. Between his job as a data processor at a local mail-order company and with his parents' help, Rust spent all of his money and most of his time taking flying lessons. He received his license in August 1986.

Rust's interest in politics, he remembers, began around 1983 – a boiling point in the Cold War when Europeans felt Ronald Reagan's bellicose anti-Sovietism put them at risk. "There was a real sense of fear," Rust said, "because if there was a conflict, we all knew we would be the first to be hit."

Gorbachev's ascendancy to the Soviet leadership in 1985 offered a glimmer of hope, but the Reagan-Gorbachev summits in Geneva and Reykjavik were bitter disappointments. Reykjavik in particular, because Gorbachev had boldly proposed the elimination of all strategic weapons, but Reagan refused to give up his Strategic Defense Initiative ("Star Wars") ABM system, so no deal was reached.

Rust felt a chance had been squandered. He felt Reagan's reflexive mistrust of the Soviet Union had blinded him to Gorbachev and the historic opportunity he presented. Rust decided he must do something, something big.

He decided to build an "imaginary bridge" by flying to Moscow. "I realized [that I needed] to go there to prove that Moscow is the source of peace. If I was be able to reach there, [if I could] pass through the Iron Curtain without being intercepted, it would show that Gorbachev was serious about new relations with the West. How would Reagan continue to say it was the 'Empire of Evil' if me, in a small aircraft, can go straight there and be unharmed? This way, they couldn't just ignore me."

Of course, Rust had little reason to believe he could actually make it to Moscow. In the past, the Soviets had shown little hesitation in shooting down aircraft intruding into their airspace. Tensions still lingered over the 1983 downing of Korean Airlines Flight 007 by a Soviet MiG, after the airliner strayed into Soviet airspace near the Kamchatka Peninsula. For years, the Soviets maintained the airliner was part of spy mission.

"I thought my chances of actually getting to Moscow were about fifty-fifty," Rust said. "Gorbachev was saying that he really wanted to open a new chapter of peace. If he means it, he must react differently than his predecessors... he can't give orders to shoot me down." Of course, it was presumptive to think Gorbachev would even be the one to give the order, Rust admits, but, "I was young, I knew it was a big risk, but I was convinced I was doing the right thing. I just had to dare to do it."

So he quietly started making plans.

He decided to make the trip the following spring, when the weather was generally good. At the time, he barely had 50 hours total flight time, and had only done a few short cross-country flights around Germany, and one longer flight to Denmark with his family, to celebrate receiving his license. So he figured he needed to test himself, to prove to himself that he was capable of making the flight.

He would fly to Reykjavik, the inspiration of his plans. But more to the point, Rust said, "flying to Reykjavik is a difficult flight, a long-distance flight, a long time flying over open water with very little navigation aids. But it would also put me under a lot of pressure, pressure I would receive flying to Moscow. I figured if I succeeded, I would be able to cope with the pressure of flying to Moscow."

Rust's Hamburg flying club owned four aircraft, one of which was a Cessna Skyhawk. The four-seat, single-engine plane had a full complement of radios and navigation equipment for instrument flight. More importantly, the plane had a set of auxiliary fuel tanks that boosted fuel capacity and extended the aircraft's range from a standard 575 nautical miles to 750 nautical miles, range Rust would need to reach Reykjavik and later Moscow.

For weeks, Rust meticulously planned all the routes. From Hamburg, he would fly across northern Europe and the North Atlantic to Reykjavik, then back and across lower Scandinavia to Helsinki. He made sure he had all the maps. He worked out alternate routes in case he had to divert around weather.

Rust told the flying club he needed to charter the aircraft for three weeks. The club didn't ask him where he was going, and Rust didn't say. To his mother, Monika, and father Karl-Heinz, a mild-mannered engineer, Rust simply said he was flying to Iceland, then to Helsinki and back home. "I just told them I wanted to do it because it was a very challenging flight, a very interesting flight," Rust said. There was no point in telling them his true intentions, Rust said, because at that point he was not sure himself if he would make the flight to Moscow. So he kept it to himself.

For the trip, Rust packed a small suitcase, a satchel with his maps and flight planning supplies, a sleeping bag, a box containing 15 quarts of engine oil, and a life vest. "I tried to get a lifeboat," Rust said, "but they didn't have any to rent at that time, so I bought a life vest." Rust knew the vest would be of limited use in the frigid waters of the North Atlantic, but he brought it anyway. "If I had to land in the sea I wouldn't drown," Rust said. "I might freeze, but I wouldn't drown." As a final precaution, Rust packed a motorcycle crash helmet. The helmet was for his final leg to Moscow, "because I didn't know what [the Soviets] would do, and if I was forced down it would give me extra protection [in case of a crash-landing]." Considering the risks he was taking, such precautions might seem ludicrous, but they do show that, as crazy as Rust's flight might seem, he wasn't suicidal.

"Just a turn to the left"

From Uetersen Airfield outside Hamburg, Rust took off on May 13 at 10:51 AM. Flying across the Baltic and North seas, he reached the Shetland Islands north of Scotland late in the day, after nearly five-hours flying over open water. The next day, he flew to Vagar, in the Danish Faroe Islands, in the middle of the North Atlantic.

On May 15, Rust flew to Reykjavik, where he decided to stay a few days. He visited Hofdi House, the white villa that was the site of the Reagan-Gorbachev summit. "It was locked," Rust said, "but I felt I got in touch with the spirit of the place. I was so emotionally involved then, and was so disappointed with the failure of the summit and my failure to get there the previous autumn. So it gave me motivation to continue."

Rust departed Reykjavik on May 22, arriving at Helsinki's Malmi airport on May 25 after stops in Hofn, Iceland, the Shetland Islands and Bergen, Norway. Since leaving Hamburg, he had covered nearly 2,600 miles and had nearly doubled his total flight time to more than 100 hours. He had proven to himself he had the flying skills he needed, but he still had doubts about his nerve. His resolve constantly wavered. Yes, it was something he had to do. No, it was crazy. Yes. No. Yes. No... He could not make up his mind.

"The whole flight had a huge question mark," Rust said. "There were so many unknowns. Would they shoot me down as soon as I crossed the border? Or would they wait until I reached Moscow? Would they intercept me and force me to land? Even if I got to Moscow and Red Square, would there be a place to land? But it didn't do me any good to ask all these questions, because I really didn't have any answers. The only real question was, would I do it?"

Rust spent a restless night the evening of May 27. The next morning, he still was unsure. "I just decided to go through my pre-flight routine," he said. "I just decided that, at the moment I had to make the decision, when I'm airborne, then I would decide."

After showering, Rust put on his red overalls. He got breakfast. He drove to Malmi airport. He got the airplane fueled, paid his fees, and checked the weather. A briefing officer later said Rust had appeared calm but "absorbed in his thoughts." Rust filed a flight plan for Stockholm, a two-hour trip to the southwest. "You might say that Stockholm was my alternate if I chickened out," Rust said. He then checked in with customs, did his final pre-flight inspection of the aircraft, and buckled himself into the pilot's seat.

At about 12:21 pm, Rust's airplane lifted off the runway. Controllers at Malmi had Rust turn west towards Stockholm, asking him to keep the plane low to avoid other traffic. Though the plane was equipped with a transponder, a radio device that allows controllers to identify a particular aircraft on radar, Helsinki controllers had Rust depart without giving him a transponder setting, so the device was turned off. Rust held course for about 20 minutes, at which point controllers radioed Rust to say he was leaving their control area. Rust thanked them and said goodbye, tuning his communications radio to 121.5 megahertz, the international frequency for emergency communications.

Rust recalled that he was about to reach his first waypoint, when, "all of a sudden, I just turned the plane to the left. It wasn't really even a decision. It was like I was having an out-of-body experience, like I was in the passenger seat watching myself. I wasn't nervous. I wasn't excited. It was almost like the plane was on autopilot. I just turned and headed straight across [the Gulf of Finland] to the border."

At the Tampere air traffic control facility, Finnish air traffic controllers noticed Rust's nearly 180-degree change of course. As the radar blip headed south and east across the water, passing through restricted military airspace, controllers reportedly tried and failed to contact Rust. At about 1 PM, Rust's plane reportedly disappeared from their radar screens, meaning

472   *Best of Russian Life: History and Culture*

either it was flying too low to be detected or had crashed. Assuming the worst, controllers asked other aircraft in the area to search for signs of a crash. At about 1:15 PM, a helicopter pilot radioed that he spotted an oil slick and some debris on the surface of the water near where Rust's plane was last detected on radar. A search and rescue operation was activated. That search was later called off when it was learned Rust had landed in Moscow.[1]

Meanwhile, at a radar station about 90 miles from Riga, in the small town of Skrunda, Soviet military personnel manning radar screens were also tracking Rust. Soviet controllers thought at first that the unidentified blip was a flock of birds, but quickly realized that the target was moving too fast to be birds and must be an aircraft.[2]

Occasionally, small aircraft from the West might approach the border, only to turn around once they realized where they were. All foreign aircraft flying into the Soviet Union were required to get a permit and to fly along special corridors, so this was obviously not an approved flight. As the unidentified aircraft neared the coastline at around 2:10 PM Moscow time (an hour ahead of Helsinki), controllers assigned the radar target the number 8255. In addition, three missile units were automatically put on alert.

Rust put on his crash helmet. Awaiting him was the most formidable air defense system in the world. Over 40 years in the making and in a constant state of expansion and upgrade, Soviet air defenses comprised an impressive network of radars, missile batteries and anti-aircraft artillery, backed by hundreds of fighter-interceptors.

After crossing the coastline near the town of Kohtla-Jarve, Estonia, he climbed to his planned altitude of 2,500 feet above sea level, a standard altitude for cross-country flight, which would keep him at least 1,000 feet above the surface for the entire route.

"As I headed inland," Rust said, "the whole time I was just sitting in the aircraft, focusing on the dials. It felt like I wasn't really doing it. Sometimes

1. Rust contends he climbed to 1,000 feet as he began crossing the Gulf of Finland, which should have made him visible to radar. Years later, Finnish aviation authorities investigated a series of incidents in which airliners mysteriously disappeared from Tampere radar screens for up to several minutes while in the same area.
2. Most of what is known about the Soviet reactions to Rust's flight is from an April 2001 article by retired general Volter Kraskovsky in *Nezavisimaya Gazeta.*

I had the impression that I was seeing myself – like I left my body and was sitting in the passenger seat, like it was beyond my ability to cope."

Soviet controllers continued to monitor the unidentified plane's progress. Duty officers, perhaps afraid of being penalized for raising a false alarm, waited until Rust was well inland before deciding to scramble a pair of fighter-interceptors from nearby Tapa Air Base to investigate. The weather at that time was partly cloudy, with the lower edge of clouds at 1,300 to 1,900 feet above the ground, winds out of the west and occasional rain. After being directed to the area where the unidentified aircraft was detected, one of the Soviet pilots looked through a hole in the clouds and reported seeing a plane that looked similar to a Yak-12, a single-engine, high-wing Soviet trainer that from a distance does in fact look very similar to a Cessna. The plane, the pilot said, was white with a dark stripe along its fuselage.

Not long after first being seen by the Soviet fighter pilot, Rust descended to avoid some low clouds. For a brief period, his blip disappeared from Soviet radar screens. Once the weather cleared, Rust climbed back to 2,500 feet, and reemerged on radar screens. The commander of the radar center ordered two more fighter-interceptors to investigate.

Nearly two hours into his flight, Rust said the sun was shining when suddenly, "I remember just seeing a shadow – a black shadow shooting in the sky and then disappear. I wondered what it was and then I realized it was an aircraft." A few moments later, from out of a layer of clouds hovering in the sky in front of him, an aircraft appeared. At first, it was just a small speck, but it grew rapidly in size. The plane, Rust said, "was coming at me very fast, and dead-on. And it went, whoosh! Right over me.

"I remember how my heart felt, beating very fast. This was exactly the moment when you start to ask yourself: Is this when they shoot you down?" There was nothing he could do but wait: "It was like the hands of time stuck on the clock."

After what seemed an eternity, Rust saw, in the corner of his eye, below and to the left, a MiG-23 fighter-interceptor. It was pulling up beside him. Designed to fly at over twice the speed of sound, the swing-wing fighter had to be put into full landing configuration, with its gear and flaps extended and its wings swung outward, in order slow it enough to fly alongside the Cessna. Its nose rode high in the air as it hovered near the edge of a stall.

Rust's investigators later told him that the Soviet pilot attempted several times to raise Rust over the radio, but that there was no response. Rust explained that his radio was turned on. They could have talked to him at any time. Only later did Rust realize that the Soviet fighter communicated over military channels on a higher frequency band than Rust's radio, and that the two aircraft were probably incapable of communicating with each other.

After a minute of eyeing each other, the Soviet pilot retracted his jet's gear and flaps. The jet accelerated, peeled away and disappeared. After a few more anxious minutes, Rust saw the MiG again. This time it circled from a distance of about a kilometer, drawing a long arc around Rust's plane. Once. Twice. Then disappearing for good.

Unbelievably, Rust was allowed to continue. This despite the fact that the Soviet pilot could clearly tell that the plane was not a Yak, and that, by its registration number (D-ECJB) and flag, it was clearly of West German origin. The official account has it that the pilot never found anything. But Marshal Sergei Akhromeyev, chief of staff of the Soviet armed forces, admitted in 1990 that the fighter pilot's commander either did not believe his pilot's report or did not think it was significant, thus the information was never passed up the chain-of-command.

Since the fiasco surrounding the KAL 007 tragedy, strict orders were given that no hostile action be taken against civilian aircraft without orders from the highest level of the Soviet military. As it happened, at this time the Soviet Union's top military commander, Defense Minister Sergei Sokolov, along with a number of other top military commanders, was accompanying Gorbachev on a trip to East Berlin, to meet with other Warsaw Pact states to discuss new military policies.

From UFO to Friend

By 3 PM, the weather had improved. The rain stopped, and Rust climbed back to an altitude of 2,500 feet. As he did, he entered an area where an air force training regiment was performing flight-training exercises. At the time, from seven to 12 aircraft, all with similar performance characteristics and radar signatures to Rust's, were in varying stages of flight. Some were doing maneuvers, some were landing, others were taking off, so that the number of planes on radar screens was constantly changing.

Soviet military aircraft, like military aircraft around the world, are equipped with a radio transponder that sends out a signal that identifies them to controllers and other aircraft as being "friendly" (the Identification Friend or Foe system, similar to the civilian transponder that Rust had aboard his aircraft, but which was turned off). Radar controllers on the ground can override the system and flag the aircraft as "friendly" in order to prevent the aircraft from being accidentally targeted and fired upon.

Common procedures for Soviet air forces were for all ground radar and aircraft to reset their transponder codes at prearranged times. On this day, 3 pm was one of those times. Those who failed to make the switch would have their radar signature go from "friendly" to "hostile." As Rust proceeded, a commander looking over the shoulder of a radar operator – apparently thinking Rust's radar return was that of a student pilot who had forgotten to make the transponder switch – ordered the officer on duty to change all the planes' radar signatures to "friendly."

"Otherwise we might shoot some of our own," he explained.

But the officer refused, explaining to his superior that to do so was a violation of established rules and regulations.

The irritated commander dismissed the duty officer, replacing him with a younger officer who, unfamiliar with the situation, carried out the order. Rust, now officially sanctioned as a "friendly" aircraft, continued on.

By 4:00 PM, Rust crossed radar sectors near Lake Seliger, a popular summer retreat near the town of Ostashkov, about 230 miles from Moscow. As the radar return for Rust's plane popped up on a new set of radar screens, controllers again took note of the unidentified aircraft. Once again it was tracked, and once again a pair of fighter-interceptors was launched to investigate. But because of low clouds, commanders considered it too dangerous for the planes to descend through the cloud deck to intercept Rust. Visual contact was never made. Rust was now a little more than two and one-half hours away from his destination.

A bit further on, about 40 miles west of the city of Torzhok, a pair of helicopters had been doing search and rescue operations following the crash of a plane the previous day. The helicopters had been skimming the surface, landing and taking off, for much of the day. As Rust passed through the region, another radar controller saw his plane's signal and assumed it was one of the helicopters. On his radar screen, he flagged it as such, thus for the second time marking Rust as a "friendly" flight.

As Rust flew on, military jurisdiction changed from the Leningrad Military District to the Moscow Military District. In the hand-off, the Leningrad commander reported to his Moscow counterpart that his controllers had been tracking a Soviet plane flying without its transponder turned on. There was nothing about tracking an unidentified plane from the Gulf of Finland, nothing about fighter-interceptors seeing a West German aircraft and nothing about an unidentified aircraft tracking a steady course to Moscow. As such, no one thought much about the report.

Although new radar and communication systems had been installed around Moscow, they were not integrated with the systems nearer the Soviet border. Had they been, Moscow commanders might have been able to evaluate the situation for themselves, rather than rely on reports from their Leningrad colleagues.

"Let it be birds"

But as radar controllers continued to track the unidentified target, an amazing conference call took place. As Michael Dobbs related the episode in his book, *Down with Big Brother*, based on a 1992 *Pravda* account, the generals argued about what to do and about what was flying around up there.

"I'm afraid it was birds, small birds," said Major General Gvozdenko, one of the commanders of the national air defense system.

"No," objected Major General Reznichencko, in charge of Moscow's air defenses that day. "The pilots saw it."

"They didn't see anything. Those pilots are always seeing things."

"But the pilot is very insistent. A plane appeared from somewhere."

Frustrated at his colleague's stubbornness. Gvozdenko tried a different approach. "Do you realize if we say it's a plane, the higher-ups are going to badger everybody? They're going to say, 'If you saw a plane, then look for it.'"

Reznichenko's superior, Lieutenant General Brazhnikov, joined the conversation. "It's a weather formation, or birds. That's the most likely."

"It would be nice if it really were a weather formation," said Reznichenko. "But what if it's a plane? And it comes down because it runs out of fuel. Then [the higher-ups] will really start yelling at us, 'What did you do, and why did you do it this way and not that way?'"

"So it comes down," argued Gvozdenko, still thinking about ways to cover himself. "We tracked it consistently. We sent fighters up."

As the senior general among the group, Brazhnikov realized it was time to make a decision. "Okay, we have to make a report. What is it to be: birds, a weather formation, or a target?"

Another general listening in, Aleksandr Gukov, the general in charge of the radar system, chimed in. "I can't make a decision," he told Brazhnikov. "I doubt it is a weather formation. It's moving too fast."

A few minutes later, Gukov came back on line. A good soldier, he knew how to please his superiors. "Our conclusion is that it is a weather formation," he reported.

"But, Alexander Ivanovich, you're so contradictory," said Brazhnikov, exasperated. "Two minutes ago you said it couldn't be a weather formation. You made a decision. It's up to us to work these things out."

Taking a few moments, Brazhnikov decided he preferred the birds explanation. "Try to remember what the North and Siberia are like at this time of year," he told Gukov. "Do geese fly for a long time?"

"Yes, they do. The Leningraders decided it was birds."

"Well, there you are," Brazhnikov said to Gukov, "and you were saying a weather formation. Why should weather formations stand out against such a cloudy background? It seems very doubtful."

"We should go along with the decision of the Leningraders and show solidarity," agreed Gukov. "There's just one thing that confuses me. Birds fly north in the spring. But this is coming from the North."

"I still think we will conclude that it was geese," said Brazhnikov firmly, bringing the debate to a close. "So, Alexander Ivanovich, it will be birds."

"Yes, sir, understood," Gukov conceded. "Let it be birds."

Chief Air Marshall Alexander Koldunov, who commanded Soviet air forces and whose office was in the same building as the Moscow controllers then watching Rust's steady progress toward Moscow, went home that evening without knowing anything was wrong.

Meanwhile, from Rust's viewpoint, his flight was going flawlessly. The weather had improved, and, despite overcast skies, visibility was quite good. He had no problem identifying the landmarks he had chosen as waypoints on the map, and he felt confident his goal was within reach. Considering the circumstances, Rust felt oddly safe. "I had a sense of peace. Everything was calm and in order." During the flight, he ate some chocolate.

Moscow Center

Forty miles outside Moscow, Rust flew through the outermost belt of Moscow's vaunted "Ring of Steel," an elaborate network of anti-aircraft defenses that, according to defense analyst John Pike, was "one the great engineering feats of the twentieth century." Beginning in the 1950s, in response to the United States's build-up of its bomber fleets, the Soviets started building a network of anti-aircraft and anti-missile missiles along a ring road that circled the city at a distance of about 10 miles. Over the next 40 years, the Soviets kept expanding the system, creating two more rings at a distance of 25 nautical miles and 45 nautical miles. "It's big," said Pike. "The Soviets, and the Russians, like to do things in a big way. And this was big. The scale of it was enormous... They poured a lot of concrete, with many, many hundreds of missiles poised to fend off an attack." It was one reason that the PVO, the national Air Defense Forces, with 630,000 troops under its command, was a separate military service. The system, however, was designed to fend off armadas of American bombers flying low and fast, not tiny, slow-flying Cessnas.

Just after 6 PM, at about 25 miles out, Rust reached the outskirts of Moscow. The city was enjoying spring-like weather, with mild temperatures, light winds and a high overcast. Moscow itself was a restricted area, with all overflights – both military and civilian – prohibited. As Rust approached the city, his investigators later told him, radar controllers suddenly realized something was terribly wrong. Passing near Sheremetyevo Airport, the Cessna crossed the path of a departing Lufthansa flight, causing it to be diverted.

But it was too late. Not only was there no one around with the authority to make a decision, there was simply very little anyone could do. If the Soviets brought down Rust's plane, he might endanger people below, and who knows how the world (or worse, their superiors) might react. Besides, no one knew anything about the pilot or his intentions. Was he lost? Was he incapacitated? Was he a defector? Or perhaps the plane was some officially sanctioned flight that they happened not to know about?

As the tiny radar blip headed toward the center of Moscow, those in command decided, as Rust's investigators later put it, "to just let it happen."

Rust removed his crash helmet and began to search for Red Square. Moscow had no skyline of glittering office towers. The only structures breaking the relatively flat horizon were Stalin's hulking "Seven Sisters," which rise up like giant wedding cakes topped with red stars. Unsure of where to go, Rust headed from building to building, first to the Hotel Ukraine, then south toward Moscow State University, then east and north toward the Leningrad Hotel.

"As I maneuvered around, I sort of narrowed in on the core of the city," Rust said. Then, as he flew toward the Leningrad Hotel, he saw it: the distinctive crenelated wall of the Kremlin. Turning toward it, Rust began a descent from about 500 feet and started looking for a place to land. "I didn't need much space. After all, I was flying light, with only a couple hours fuel on board, so even with the obstacle clearance, if I brought the plane in at full flaps I could bring the plane to a stop in 800 meters.

"At first, I thought maybe I should land inside the Kremlin Wall, but then I realized that, although there was plenty of space, I wasn't sure what the KGB might do with me. If I landed inside the wall, only a few people would see me, and they could just take me away and deny the whole thing. But if I landed in the Square, plenty of people would see me, and the KGB couldn't just arrest me and lie about it. So it was for my own security that I dropped the idea [of landing inside the Kremlin wall]."

Rust made a gentle left-hand turn around Red Square, looking for a place to land. "There was a long line of people extending into the Square waiting to go into the mausoleum of Lenin's Tomb. It wasn't like St. Peter's Square in Rome, where people can go all over the place. There were just lines of people, and later I noticed they were only allowed to walk across Red Square in certain directions. But without those people [in the way], there was plenty of space to land."

He decided to make a low pass over the square to warn the crowd of his intentions to land. He descended to about 20 feet off the ground, about the height of the Kremlin wall, and flew directly over the square. The people scattered all right, some ducking as Rust passed, but rather than clear a space for Rust to land, they all ran back into the middle of the square to see what he was doing. Rust decided to make another pass. He came in again, this time even lower, but he misjudged the amount of space available. At the end of the square was a large construction crane. Rust pulled up quickly, just missing it.

"My leg was shaking like mad," Rust said, "and I thought to myself, 'Now I think I [need to] stop this, because that felt very bad.' I realized I needed to look for another landing spot."

As he circled, Rust noticed that, adjacent to the square, between the Kremlin and the Hotel Rossia, was a roadway leading into the square from a bridge crossing the Moscow River. The bridge [Bolshoy Moskvoretsky Bridge] was about six lanes wide. Traffic was light, and from above Rust could see that the only obstacles were some wires strung across the road at each end of the bridge and another set across the middle. He figured there was enough space to come in over the first set of wires, drop down, land and run under the other wires into the square.

As Rust set up for his approach, a pair of alert policemen on the ground realized what was happening and moved to block traffic to clear the roadway. Rust came in steeply, with full flaps, his engine idling. As planned, he came in over the first set of wires, dropped down, and flared for landing. Suddenly, he noticed a car in front of him, traveling in the same direction. It must have already been on the bridge when the police blocked traffic. It was an old Volga. As Rust overtook it, he looked over and saw the old man driving it wearing a look of utter disbelief. Rust hoped the man wouldn't panic and lose control of the car, endangering them both.

Passing under the last set of wires, Rust came off the bridge, slowed, and began looking for a place to park. He wanted to pull the plane into the middle of Red Square, in front of Lenin's Tomb. But St. Basil's Cathedral was surrounded by a small fence, with a chain strung across, blocking his path. As he taxied around, he considered taking off and leaving. But the moment passed. He told himself, "I can't do that. I'm here for a purpose. I need to be serious." Seeing no way to get around the fence, he pulled up in front of the church, and shut down his engine.

Rust closed his eyes and sucked in a deep breath. "There was this great feeling of relief, like I had gotten this big load off my back. It was like I had climbed this big mountain."

Rust unbuckled himself, opened the cockpit door, climbed out and looked at the Kremlin clock tower. The time was 6:43 PM, almost five and one-half hours since his take-off from Helsinki. He leaned against the side of the aircraft, took another deep breath, and waited.

Nothing happened. Rust was alone.

Beautiful Hooliganism

He had expected his plane to be stormed by armed troops and KGB agents. But all around the square, people seemed nervous or stunned, not sure what was going on. Some thought Rust's plane might be Gorbachev's private aircraft. Others thought it all might all be part of a movie production, or perhaps some sporting event. Once they realized both the plane and pilot were foreign, and that whoever was at the controls had just pulled off one of the most magnificent exploits they had ever witnessed, they drew closer.

"A big crowd had formed around me," Rust recalls. "People were smiling and coming up to shake my hand or ask for autographs."

There was much chatter, but little communication. Rust spoke no Russian and most of the crowd spoke no German or English. A young man approached Rust, a street artist who sold paintings to tourists waiting in line at Lenin's Mausoleum. He spoke English, and, after determining that Rust did as well, he approached.

Rust explained that he had flown from the West and that he wanted to talk to Gorbachev, that he had a goodwill message to deliver to the Soviet leader. He wanted to show the world that Gorbachev was a man of peace.

The young man told Rust he could not help arrange a meeting with Gorbachev, but he was happy to act as an interpreter, fielding questions from the growing crowd.

Rust went on to explain how he had flown from Helsinki, how, after he crossed the border, a Soviet interceptor had pulled alongside him, looked him over, and then let him continue.

The crowd could hardly believe what they were hearing. "They all wanted to talk to me," Rust said. "One woman came up and gave me a piece of bread." The young artist explained to Rust that he had just received a special gift. He said it was a Russian custom to give a new friend a piece of bread.

"Now," he told Rust, "you have a new friend."

Everyone was smiling. The atmosphere was festive.

Among the onlookers were many in army uniforms, cadets from a nearby academy. But they were just part of the crowd. One cadet approached Rust and told him that, while he admired his courage and initiative, Rust should have applied for a visa and made an appointment with Gorbachev. The cadet then thought for a moment, saying of course that such a request would have been refused.

"Instead of putting him in prison," said another onlooker, "they should give him a medal, not Hero of the Soviet Union, just Hero."

One old man complained that the young man was crazy, that the plane could have "landed on their heads."

Another man denounced the stunt as "hooliganism," saying "there are laws, after all." But, the man then added. "it was beautiful hooliganism."

Though Rust may not have seen them, KGB agents were nearby. As he chatted with onlookers and waited for the inevitable, plainclothes agents moved through the crowd, interviewing people and confiscating cameras and notebooks. A British tourist traveling with a group happened to have a video camera, and taped one of Rust's passes. The man hid the camera under his jacket and snuck it back onto his tour bus. After smuggling the camera out of the country, he sold the tape to a television network.

Nearly a half-hour had passed. A large, black ZiL drove up. Seeing the car, Rust thought that the KGB had finally arrived to take him away. Out of the car stepped an enormously tall, powerfully built man wearing a dark blue overcoat. Medals covered his chest and he wore a dress military cap. He strode forward, trailed by his deputies, waving the crowd aside and stepping right up to Rust. The huge man then began speaking in Russian. Through his makeshift interpreter, Rust learned that the man was Police Commissioner of Moscow. The commissioner said he had gotten a call just a few minutes before from one of his policemen, saying that an aircraft from abroad had landed in Red Square. He said he couldn't believe it, that he figured his men were pulling his leg, so he came over to see for himself.

He then asked to see Rust's passport. After examining it, he handed it back.

"Very fine, you are a West German citizen, but where is your visa stamp?"

Of course, there wasn't one.

"Oh that will be a very confusing matter to be solved."

He then offered Rust some cigarettes. Rust told him he didn't smoke.

"Oh, you don't smoke. Well then, would you like some vodka?"

Rust said he didn't drink, either.

"What is this? You don't smoke. You don't drink. I hope you at least like sex."

Rust said he had no problem with sex.

"Well, I can't offer you a woman right now," joked the commissioner. "Maybe later."

Rust could not believe it. "I expected to be quickly surrounded by police. I expected more hostility. After all, these were the first Russians I had ever met. I was surprised at how warm and friendly they all seemed." He had grown up thinking Russians were all gruff and unfriendly. "I never would have expected this warmth."

More than an hour passed before a pair of army trucks carrying soldiers arrived. They leapt out of the trucks and began clearing the crowd, which had grown to about 200. Many, however, did not want to leave, and began to complain. The soldiers started shouting at them and, holding their rifles against their chests, began shoving them roughly aside. Other soldiers started putting up metal barricades around the plane.

With the crowd dispersed, Rust was left with just a few officers. At around 8 PM, three men in plainclothes approached. One was younger, perhaps 30 years old, and the other two were 45-50 years old. The younger man acted as interpreter, speaking to Rust in German. He asked to see Rust's passport. The older man looked it over but didn't say anything. He handed it to the third man, telling Rust they needed to keep it for a while. Rust was asked if he was carrying any weapons. No. Could they look inside the aircraft? Sure. After peering through the glass, they asked Rust to open the plane. Because Rust had covered all his baggage with a blanket, they asked if Rust would pull back the blanket to show them. They then asked him for the keys, and directed him to a small sedan parked nearby. Don't worry, Rust was told, they would take care of the plane.

Rust was driven to a beige-colored building, an unimposing structure that looked as if it could be an apartment block or a minor governmental ministry. The car pulled up to a security gate. The front gate opened. The car drove in and stopped. The gate closed behind it and another gate opened. The car drove into a small yard and parked. Rust was escorted from the car and taken inside.

He had arrived at Lefortovo prison, the notorious complex used by the KGB to hold political prisoners. Among its more recent residents at that time were the dissident Natan Sharansky and American journalist Nicholas Daniloff. The prison and interrogation center would be Rust's home for the next 14 months.

Confusion and Speculation

Military analyst John Pike was at the U.S. embassy in Moscow on business, he recalled, when he looked out the window and saw a small airplane circling over Red Square. "Gee, that's peculiar," he thought. "There's no private aviation in the Soviet Union. Hell, there's no private anything."

Valery Boldin, Gorbachev's chief of staff, said he was in his office at the Kremlin when he, too, looked out and saw the small plane circling over the square. But he thought nothing of it, as recently a number of helicopter and airplane flights over the city had been authorized to shoot footage for historical and documentary films. When, a short time later, he got a call from the Interior Ministry saying that a German sports plane had landed next to the Kremlin, he could not believe it, so he demanded confirmation.

Word spread quickly through the city. An American journalist working in Moscow received an excited call from a Soviet friend asking if it was true that a foreign plane had landed in Red Square. It seemed impossible, the journalist thought, but he decided to have a look for himself, "just for the hell of it." Sure enough, at the base of St. Basil's Cathedral, cordoned off by barriers and guarded by militiamen, was a small airplane. The reporter went up to one of the guards and asked what kind of plane it was. Without a trace of irony, the officer answered, "What plane?"

The landing quickly became the fodder of jokes. U.S. Ambassador to the Soviet Union Jack Matlock was hosting a reception at his residence, Spaso House, when he learned of Rust's landing.

"Have you heard? They've renamed Red Square."

"Really. To what?"

"Why, Sheremetyevo III, of course."

German Foreign Minister Hans-Dietrich Genscher confessed to reporters in Bonn that, "I laughed my head off" when told of the landing. Officially, however, the West German government was more coy. Spokesman Friedhelm Ost told reporters the landing must have been a mistake. "It appears this involves a pilot who has made a mistake in navigation."

TASS, the official Soviet news agency, waited a full day before issuing a statement, an indication of the level of confusion and embarrassment the landing had caused within the highest levels of the government. The following day, Soviet television read the statement on its evening news program, but it was buried deep into the show, the last item before the sports report. The statement simply said that a small plane from the West had intruded into Soviet airspace 120 miles west of Leningrad and that the plane had landed in Moscow – without specifying exactly where.

In Hamburg the next morning, Rust's parents, his mother Monika and father Karl-Heinz, were at home. Karl-Heinz had had taken the day off in order to enjoy a long weekend. Around 9 PM, the phone rang. It was Mathias' flight instructor, Rüdiger Heise. "Did you hear anything about this German guy who landed in Moscow last night?" asked Heise. No, answered Rust's parents, they had not watched the television news. After telling them what he knew, Heise asked, "You don't think it's Mathias?"

"No," answered Monika. "I just talked to him the other day. He was about to fly back from Helsinki."

About two hours later, Rust's name was released.

"Oh God," Monika said, "it's true."

Almost immediately, their phone started ringing. Journalists descended on their house. Why did he do it? Did they know about it in advance? Who helped him?

Rust's parents had nothing to say. Desperate for news of their son, they got on the phone. They called the Defense Ministry in Bonn. Directed to a public affairs officer, they asked what he knew about the German plane landing in Moscow.

"What! A German aircraft landed in Moscow? My God! What military unit? What type of aircraft? A fighter? A helicopter?"

No, it was a private aircraft, Rust's parents explained.

"Well, that's none of our business," the officer said. "We have nothing to do with that!" He hung up the phone.

Next they called the Foreign Minister's office. A spokesman told them they were in touch with the German embassy in Moscow and were trying to find out the details for themselves. The embassy would call them when they had more information.

The story was front-page news around the world, but with little official information available, reporters struggled to describe what had happened, and why. Most assumed that Rust must have hedgehopped his way across Soviet territory, flying low enough to evade Soviet radar. Some figured he must have followed rail lines linking Leningrad to Moscow. One newspaper printed that Rust did the stunt on a bet, another that he did it to impress a girl. Yet another said he dropped leaflets calling for the release of Rudolf Hess, the nonagenarian Hitler lieutenant, from jail. *Pravda* wrote that Rust was a patsy in an international plot: he was supposed to be shot down and killed in order to provoke an international incident.

Some experts said the landing pointed to the vulnerability of Soviet air defenses to bomber or cruise missile attacks. A few realized the whole thing was simply a fluke, and that, militarily, the landing meant nothing. "It must have been a Stealth Cessna," joked one U.S. Air Force official. Another diplomat said he was actually encouraged the Soviets didn't shoot Rust down, as they had four years earlier with KAL 007. He speculated that perhaps it was an indication of improved relations.

Soviet citizens took great delight in Rust's stunt. After all, for years the Soviet military had been practically immune to criticism, and had grown accustomed to treating the general public in a haughty, high-handed manner. Many were only too glad to see the military brass brought down a notch or two.

But it was no laughing matter for the Soviet military. That night, while the city enjoyed a massive fireworks display that lit up the sky for – irony of ironies – Border Guards Day, Soviet authorities considered how to treat this crisis.

Gorbachev Takes Charge

Stepping down from his plane at Vnukovo airport after flying back early from a Warsaw Pact summit, Gorbachev greeted his Politburo colleagues with the usual smiles and comradely bear hugs. But his eyes were filled with anger.

Gorbachev led the Politburo members and Central Committee secretaries into a small room off the terminal's reception hall. "It's a national shame," he fumed. "This is as bad as Chernobyl" [the 1986 nuclear power plant disaster].

The Soviet leader had, until this point, been careful to avoid any direct confrontation with his military commanders. Instead, he hoped he could achieve large-scale cuts in military expenditures by successfully negotiating arms reductions with the West. But that was about to change. Gorbachev's wife Raisa smelled a conspiracy, staged by the military to embarrass her husband and damage his standing in the eyes of the public and foreign leaders.

Gorbachev's chief of staff, Valery Boldin, said the Rust affair permanently hardened his boss's attitude toward the military. "Now he was filled with savage hatred for them and never forgave them for their little 'joke,'" Boldin wrote. From then on, Boldin said, Gorbachev took every opportunity to denounce the military.

"They have disgraced the country, humiliated our people," Gorbachev said of his commanders. "But fine, at least everyone here, and in the West, will know where power lies. It is in the hands of the political leadership, the Politburo. This will put an end to gossip about the military's opposition to Gorbachev, that he's afraid of them, and they're close to ousting him."

After an hour and a half, the group emerged. Gorbachev, flushed and glowering, grumbled, "Politburo meeting tomorrow at eleven," and walked to the car.

The Investigation

At around 9 AM the next morning, the guards woke Rust up and brought him back to the investigation center. In a routine that would delineate his life for the next three weeks, Rust was questioned for eight hours, breaking once when he was returned to his cell for lunch, usually some porridge or bread.

The questioning was very repetitive: Are you sure you didn't do this with anybody? Did you drop off anybody en route? Did you bring anything in with you? Did you throw anything out of the plane?

Given the level of planning put into the flight, and the number of apparent coincidences and lucky breaks that Rust benefited from, the investigators could not believe this was the work of one man, much less an idealistic boy. In their mind, Rust had to be part of a larger plot.

Take the date itself, May 28, Border Guards Day. Many speculated Rust chose that day thinking the border would be more lightly defended, or perhaps to maximize the embarrassment it would cause the military.

"I heard about that afterwards," Rust said. "I said, 'I'm a West German. How should I know about your holidays?' It was just a lucky circumstance. I didn't know."

His interrogators pulled out the maps Rust used. They pointed to the airfields and navigation frequencies and told him he must have obtained them from the CIA or the German military. They asked him whom he had contacted. "I told them, 'No, I didn't contact anyone from the German government or the CIA.'" Rust said. "I just filled out the order form from the German company and I received them in the mail to my home."

So they sent the maps to the Soviet consul general in Hamburg. The consul general was then asked to place an order for the same maps from the same company. Sure enough, the consul general received them in the mail just as Rust had. The investigators then returned to Rust and said, "Yes, we know you are telling the truth."

The plane itself was put on the back of a flatbed truck and hauled to a hangar at Sheremetyevo Airport, where it was broken down completely. The investigators found the plane's emergency locator transmitter, a beacon device required on most general aviation aircraft. It activates automatically after a crash, to assist search and rescue crews trying to locate the wreck. Not knowing this, the investigators told Rust they believed he installed the device to send a signal to someone so they could follow where he was going.

"That's not so," Rust said. "The device is required as a safety precaution." But the investigators did not believe him. Later on, they returned and said to Rust, "Yes, you were right."

Rust's investigators showed him photos of Bolshoi Moskvoretsky Bridge. In the photos were many sets of wires stretched out across the bridge, each about two meters apart. They asked Rust how he could possibly land with so many wires in his way. Perplexed himself, Rust explained that when he landed he could only see three sets of wires. Upon further investigation, the Soviets learned that the morning Rust landed a public works crew had removed all the wires for maintenance purposes, replacing them all the day after Rust landed – another bizarre coincidence.

"You must have been born in a shirt," investigators told Rust, using a Russian expression to say he was lucky.

On June 23, the investigation was completed. Shortly afterward, Soviet prosecutors charged Rust with illegal entry, violation of flight laws and "malicious hooliganism." Rust pleaded guilty to all but the last charge. There was, he argued, nothing malicious in his intentions.

A Quiet Coup

By long-standing tradition, Politburo meetings took place every Thursday on the third floor of the government building in the Kremlin, beginning at the stroke of 11:00 AM. The large conference hall, located directly above the office once used by Stalin, was a gloomy room dominated by a large table covered in green felt. Perpendicular to this table was the chairman's table, on which rested an inkstand, a clock, a bell and a control panel for a series of maps hidden behind a movable wall. The seating arrangement was based strictly on status and seniority.

Anatoly Chernyaev, Gorbachev's chief foreign policy advisor, recounted in his memoir, *My Six Years with Gorbachev*, the events of May 30 Politburo meeting.

Gorbachev opened the meeting with a scorching attack on "the complete helplessness of the Defense Ministry, which still has to explain this extraordinary incident to the Party and the people." Gorbachev then sat stone-faced as Defense Minister Marshal Sergei Sokolov and Air Defense Chief Alexander Koldunov tried to explain through their aides how the world's most vaunted air defense system managed to allow a deluded boy to fly straight into the heart of Moscow.

General Ivan Lushev, deputy defense minister, told the gathering that Rust presented a situation military planners had never prepared for and which they could never have predicted. The elaborate radar and anti-aircraft systems, he said, were designed to intercept military aircraft, not slow-flying small planes at low altitudes. If anything, he argued, Rust proved the system did work. He was picked up and tracked on radar. Fighter-interceptors were sent aloft. It was simply a fluke he was allowed to proceed unchallenged.

No one bought it. As a growing chorus of Politburo members stood to voice their opinion, Gorbachev sat scowling at his defense ministers. Finally, he took the floor.

Exactly how Rust managed to get through the country's supposedly impregnable air defenses didn't really matter, Gorbachev said. The real issue was leadership and accountability. The problem was an army whose top leaders were "apprehensive of the party's turn toward *perestroika* and the new thinking." He demanded stronger leadership at the defense ministry "to increase the military establishment's sense of political responsibility." Then, turning to defense minister Sokolov, he said, "I don't question your personal integrity, Sergei Leonidovich, but under the present circumstances, if I were you, I would resign at once."

Sokolov, a former tank commander and a hero of the Great Patriotic War against the Nazis, looked shaken. He stood at attention and resigned on the spot. Gorbachev did not hesitate to accept the resignation "on behalf of the Politburo," adding that it would be announced as a retirement, sparing Sokolov total public humiliation. After a 15-minute break, Gorbachev returned and announced the appointment of Dmitry Yazov, a little-known general whom Gorbachev had plucked from the Soviet Far East earlier that year and appointed deputy defense minister in charge of personnel. In picking Yazov, Gorbachev bypassed dozens of more senior officers, violating the pecking order and long-standing tradition, but gaining a defense minister whose loyalty was assured (at least until the August 1991 coup, when Yazov would side against Gorbachev as a member of the State Emergency Committee).

Also fired was Air Defense Chief Koldunov. The Politburo statement released for the television news that evening was unusually harsh, saying that Sokolov and Koldunov "had shown intolerable indecision and lack of concern" during the incident, which testified to the "serious shortcomings" in the air defense forces in general.

In subsequent days and weeks, the "Rust Massacre," as it came to be called, would see about 150 officers brought to trial. Hundreds of others were fired or forced to retire. By the end of 1988, in addition to Sokolov and Koldunov, all deputy ministers but two, all the first deputy chiefs of the General Staff, the commander and the chief of staff of the Warsaw Pact forces, all the commanders of the groups of forces and fleets, and all military district commanders had been changed.

The swiftness of Gorbachev's actions stunned many. Gorbachev had, noted career diplomat Anatoly Dobrynin, "accomplished a quiet coup." For this, Rust should be awarded, one senior official added only half-jokingly, the Order of Lenin – the nation's highest decoration.

More important than the replacement of specific individuals, analyst John Pike said, was the change Rust's flight precipitated in the public perception of the military. The myth of Soviet military superiority had been punctured, and with it the almost iconic reverence the public had held for the military. One former Soviet colonel described walking around in uniform in the city where he was stationed and sensing the feeling of scorn by ordinary civilians. After all, the Soviet public had made enormous economic sacrifices to support the military-industrial complex.

For decades, Pike said, Soviet citizens had been led to believe "the West was poised to destroy them and that... if they let their guard down for an instant they would be obliterated." It was this logic that perpetuated the Cold War. Now, Pike said, "the challenge was how do you turn it off? How do you turn it off without things flying apart." Gorbachev had talked about changes in the military, changes that hinted the Soviet Union could let down its guard without being destroyed by external forces. Letting Rust land, Pike argues, "was an initial test of that hypothesis."

In retrospect, Gorbachev was right. External forces would not destroy the Soviet Union. Ultimately, the main threat would come from within.

As it became increasingly clear that Rust had acted alone, some in the leadership urged Gorbachev to put Rust on a plane and send him home with but a scolding.

Gorbachev responded to this idea furiously at a Politburo meeting after the investigation was completed. "What is this? So he wanted to meet me? Many people meet with me… No, it was a clear provocation! We took 150 officers and generals to court, discharged the minister of defense. Maybe we shouldn't have? And now we're to tell him 'go on, fly home.' No, democracy does not mean weakness. He broke the law three times, and so by those laws must be punished. The investigation is finished, right? Let's have a trial then. Everything as it should be. The law said one to ten years. The court will decide. And then we'll see."

Trial and Aftermath

On September 4, 1987, after a three-day trial, a panel of three judges found Rust guilty of all charges and sentenced him to four years at Lefortovo Prison. The prison, though starker and more restrictive than a labor camp, ensured Rust's safety. He spent his time there quietly and was afforded special privileges: He was allowed to work in the garden and receive visits by his parents every two months.

But jail is still jail. Rust was allowed just one shower a week. The barren cell had no window, just a milky pane of glass that let in light. The antiquated heating system meant it was always frigid in winter and sweltering in summer. The lone light bulb in the ceiling burned day and night, and most meals consisted of bread and bland soup (Rust lost 22 pounds in jail).

On June 1, 1988, during a summit in Moscow, President Reagan and General Secretary Gorbachev signed a treaty to eliminate intermediate nuclear forces in Europe. From his jail cell, Rust heard the news and took quiet satisfaction knowing that maybe, in a small way, he had had a hand in it. Two months later, on August 3, Rust was released by an order of the Supreme Soviet in what TASS described as a "goodwill gesture."

After serving his 14 months in a Moscow jail, Rust returned home, but not as a hero. The West German press, initially enamored with "the new Red Baron," had since turned on him. For his part, Rust did not help his situation. He refused to play up to the press, and repeatedly snubbed them. In return, he was hounded and ridiculed. The stiff, seemingly arrogant young man was called everything from a dangerous fool to a madman or even a traitor. Among the hundreds of letters he received, many were death threats. Outside his parent's apartment building, vandals had painted: "Go Back to Siberia!"

Rust struggled to readjust. While working in a hospital in Hamburg in 1989, he suffered a breakdown. In an episode his lawyer later likened to post-traumatic stress syndrome, Rust stabbed a young woman, seriously injuring her. Of course, the German press loved it. "To them, it only confirmed to them that I was mad," Rust said. "They said the flight to Moscow was the first indication, but now I had blood on my hands. Who knows what he'll do next?"

Prosecutors sought to put Rust away for eight years for attempted murder. Rust's attorney, however, discovered documents proving the Soviets had drugged Rust with a powerful truth serum during his detention and interrogation. The drugs had long-lasting psychological effects, his attorney alleged, and thus he convinced the court that Rust was not entirely culpable for his actions. Rust got off relatively lightly, sentenced to 15 months. He was released in 1993.

Upon his release, unable to work, unable to even go out without people pointing at him or calling him a murderer, Rust's life fell to depths he could not imagine. He left Germany and moved to the Caribbean island of Trinidad, a place where no one had heard of him or his famous flight. He got a job, met a girl and got married.

But controversy followed him wherever he went. During a visit home for Christmas in 2000, Rust found himself back in court facing a shoplifting charge. Rust denied the charge, but was fined 2,000 euros. He returned to Trinidad.

Even *in absentia*, Rust became a popular topic of rumor and innuendo. He was said to have returned to live in Russia, to have married the daughter of an Indian sultan and converted to Hinduism, to have lost millions and gone bankrupt, to have died. As a result, he avoided the press, gave few interviews and did everything he could to distance himself from his famous flight.

In 2001, he moved back to Germany, settling in Berlin. "I got tired of the warm weather and the single season. That, and I thought I was just killing time there." And, by then, the German press seemed to have lost interest in him.

"I had a friend in London who did investments through a firm in Luxembourg, and while I was in Trinidad, he asked me to help him make contacts and work out some deals. So I did. I would try and find investors for his business deals. I did, and it worked out, so I have continued. It's nice."

Rust never flew a plane again, but he never lost his idealism. In 2002, he started a new enterprise, Orion and Isis, a mediation service designed to "fight violence by providing proper redress." Unlike traditional mediation services that try to resolve labor or business disputes, Rust spent much of his time in the occupied territories of Israel, negotiating hostage releases. In 2004, Rust suspended the service to work full-time doing business deals.

Now divorced, Rust looks back on his flight and says, "It gave me new respect for life, my life. I've experienced both aspects of life: the greatest feeling of achievement and happiness by flying to Moscow, and the absolute bottom, where I fell to the depths of the darkest corner of my soul. There was an odd balance."

One of the few items Rust saved from his flight to Moscow is his pilot's logbook. The final entry lists the flight between Bergen, Norway and Helsinki on May 25, 1987. There is no entry for his flight to Moscow. Asked why, Rust shrugs and said, "because I never completed my mission."

He never got to meet Gorbachev.

November/December 2005

1999

The Secret Life of a Russian Santa Claus
Alexei Pospelov

The New Year's Eve visit of Father Frost (Ded Moroz – Russia's version of Santa Claus) is a cherished tradition in Russia. At least once in their young lives, little children are kept up late to see a masqueraded friend or relative come around and hand out toys to good little boys and girls... And while the kids' and parents' side of this tradition's "story" are easy to imagine, much less is known about those who are imposed upon to don the red robe and white beard...

*I*t was my 13th stop and, as Father Frost for the Moscow design bureau *Salyut*, I was as red as my costume. Not that I minded the ominous number 13. I am never superstitious, not even on New Year's Eve! It was just that the hosts were being far too hospitable. Instead of the routine *ugoscheniye* (treat) at the entrance to the apartment (a shot of vodka, plus a salty snack picked from a plate with a fork), they insisted on offering Marina (my *Snegurochka*, or Snowmaiden) and I two seats of honor at the New Year's table.

Of course, I had only myself to blame for the dinner invitation. Sure, the vodka shot had gone down easily. But, after twelve previous "treats," I had a hard time spearing a marinated mushroom from a bowl full of juicy marinade. So the young host, Irina, took pity on me. "Hey, take your time! Why don't you sit with us for a while? The *kuranty* [Kremlin tower bells] have already struck 12! No sweat."

"No sweat"?! Easy for her to say. This *Ded Moroz* was baking in his thick wool suit.

I loosened my long cotton beard and dreamed of a session in the *banya*. But that would have to wait. It was half past midnight and I had two more visits to make on my rounds. Both were in the neighborhood, so I dropped my half-full sacks of gifts on the pine needle-covered parquet, resigning myself to my fate.

I knew what was to come. Irina's children were anxious to perform their "homework" so that they could earn the gifts brought by *Ded Moroz*. And by this thirteenth stop, truth be told, I wasn't sure I could get through it. The repertoire rarely varied from house to house.

Of course, I would rather be playing my guitar and singing with friends or watching *Ogonyok's* TV party or... But no, the show must go on! Kids are kids and they need to have their party.

Twelve-year-old Masha was timid and stumbled over her first line of Pushkin: "*Moroz i Solntse den chudesny...*" ("Frost and sun, it was a miraculous day.) Oops. That did it. My reddened mug must have frightened her – she burst into tears. Thankfully, Marina, the able Snowmaiden, pulled a pirated Barbie doll and some Red October chocolates from my bag and the jittery Masha was quickly consoled.

Younger brother Kostya was not old enough to be so nervous. He was happy and excited and had no trouble singing a capella: "*V lesu rodilas yolochka, v lesu ona rosla.*" ("Once upon a time a fur-tree was born, in a forest she grew...")

"*Zimoy i letom stroynaya, zelyonya byla,*" ("Green and slim it was in winter and in summer") I interjected with a quick wink in Marina's direction. Wasn't I clever now! Happy with myself for this flourish, I drank down a shot of cognac, "to polish the whole thing," and pulled a coveted plastic saber with shield from the bottom of my sack. Kostya was enthralled and immediately forgave my interruption of his performance.

Having completed the compulsory exercises, I knew this was the perfect time to make for the door and finish off those last two clients. But then Ira, alas, came traipsing in with the *goryachee* (main course): duck with apples. The temptation was overpowering. I had tasted more than my share of Stolichny salads and been stuffed with every salty snack imaginable tonight, but had not been offered anything hot. I hesitated and was lost...

"*Nikakhikh 'nyet'*" ("I won't take 'no' for an answer"), Irina declared, ever so sweetly, while blocking my only exit. The scent of baked duck wafted over me. All hope was lost.

"You want to offend my mother?" Irina continued. "This duck was made with her famous Antonovkas." Irina nodded meaningfully toward the head of the table. There sat the apple grower in question, Galina Petrovna, obviously not a force to be trifled with.

Well, far be it for me to offend my host (or her *mother*), much less my stomach. Were it not for this coat and beard, I could truly en—

But wait! Irina, the angel, is sending the little ones off to bed. I guess every littlest dream *can* come true on New Year's!

The fairy tale was over. I tossed off my beard, opened my coat, gave a meaningful glance in Marina's direction and attacked the juicy duck "with all proletarian hatred," as Gennady Petrovich Guskov, the head of our bureau's trade union committee, loved to say.

As a matter of fact, if it were not for Gennady Petrovich, I might have been sitting home with friends on New Year's. "There is the market now, Petrovich," I said after being informed of the trade union's decision. "You can even order a *Baba Yaga* to come visit, let alone a Father Frost."

"Oh, sure, we're going to have one of these new, private *Ded Morozes*," Petrovich parried. "The ones that look more like a Santa Claus than one of our trusted Father Frosts. And how many of our employees could afford this 'market alternative,' eh? You tell me."

"Not many," I sheepishly admitted.

Before the trade union at *Salyut* had selected me as Father Frost, I thought of calling one myself. But to get a *Ded Moroz* to visit the kids would cost two to three hundred rubles. That's half mother's pension. I earn decent enough money, when you add in some moonlighting doing drawings for technical institute students. But 200 rubles just like that for a fairy tale? The moral costs alone are disabling – this money could buy fifteen, if not 20, lunches in the local canteen (dessert included!). Or five bottles of vodka...

So, despite the expansion of all sorts of private businesses offering *Ded Moroz* services, *Salyut* employees stuck to the tried and true traditions. Our *Ded Moroz* would pay his visits thanks to the trade union's "Holiday Fund." And the bureau director would "sacrifice" his personal car for the night – easy enough when you are going to be sitting cozily at home around the New Year's table...

The hard part was to pick a *Ded Moroz* and *Snegurochka* who would willingly sacrifice their New Year's to the common cause. Volunteerism had long since faded from memory, so *Salyut* tackled the problem in the usual way – by drawing a name from a fur hat. As the duty was taxing to health and hearth, last year's *Ded Moroz* was automatically exempted from the drawing. But it seemed plenty others had negotiated other exemptions

– this one was traveling, this one's wife had the flu, this one was too old. So even before the paper was drawn, I knew my number was up. Needless to say, my kids were not happy with this turn of events...

Irina's duck was indeed delicious. The sour *Antonovkas* added just the right flavor to the meat and the potatoes roasted in duck fat simply melted in my mouth. Surely this would provide a good, protective layer for my stomach against the combined forces of the champagne (stops 6, 9 and 10) and vodka (all stops). Of course, I should have skipped the cognac...

By now, the party at home is surely revving up. They must have taken the guitar from the wall and begun to sing...

"Do you have a guitar?" I ask Irina. She returns with an old six-string *Leningradskaya* that had been hidden in a cupboard.

"It's my dad's," she says. "I'm not sure it's in tune. We thought Masha would play, but it turned out she hasn't got the ear for it."

I wiped the duck grease from my hands and lost myself in tuning the old guitar. I thought for a moment what to strum and the song came out before I myself had time to answer... everyone knows Okudzhava's *Miss Luck*... and what is more important on New Year's than luck?

Truth be told, I am of the Grebenshchikov or Time Machine generation. But it was Okudzhava's night tonight. A night of sweet melodies and poignant lyrics. Irina asked for *The Grape's Stone*. Galina Petrovna pined for *My Arbat*.

The cranberry *nalivka* (liqueur) – straight from Galina Petrovna's dacha, someone murmured – had mysteriously appeared in the center of the table, glowing red in a chiseled glass carafe.

"Oh Arbat, my Arbat – you are my religion..."

Galina Petrovna was won over. She cut the honey pie and placed the first slice right in front of me. Irina filled a small glass with the ruby colored *nalivka*...

"Hello... Alexei!... you there?"

"What the – Petrovich?! It's you, is it? The one I have to thank for lying here on my death bed?" I looked over at the clock. Eight-o'clock. In the evening. I had slept through the first day of the new year.

"So, how was it?" Petrovich asked. "I heard that duck with apples played a bad trick on you, eh?"

I didn't even have the strength to respond to the taunt. Holding up the phone was all I could muster and that was going fast.

"Never mind the Lukins and the Maslovs," he continued. "Marina visited them today and delivered the gifts."

"Akkhhhh, I never made it to the last two stops..." As if I didn't feel miserable enough as it was.

"Take heart, Lyosha, last year the *Ded Moroz* had four no-shows. Everybody says you were great, really! Maybe you can make up for it by trying again next year, though, eh?"

I caught myself before replying with a tirade that I would later regret. Barely. "Sure," I said, "if you play the Snowmaiden for me."

"Me?! C'mon, how would a Snowmaiden look with a moustache and my ugly mug? And it's not like the disguise of a man as a woman is a fresh joke."

"Well," I said, "after the first couple of visits, what difference does it make anyway?"

January/February 2000

The Cats Who Guard the Hermitage
Anna Tarasova

If you think that St. Petersburg's Hermitage Museum is famous only for its great collections and masterpieces, you are mistaken. It is a little-known fact outside St. Petersburg that this city's most prestigious museum has the largest feline museum staff in the world – estimated at about a hundred souls. It is their daily duty to protect the Hermitage's treasures from rats and other uneducated vermin who cannot tell the difference between a fifteenth century tapestry and a husk of corn. The furry custodians have done such a fine job that they enjoy the protection of museum officials and especially its director, Professor Mikhail Piotrovsky.

*I*t is believed that the first cats appeared at the royal palace under Empress Elizabeth, daughter of Peter the Great. At least first historical evidence dates to her time, when Elizabeth requisitioned 30 neutered cats from the governor-general of Kazan. Elizabeth, a beautiful woman obsessed with fashion, obviously had a need to protect her tremendous wardrobe from predators. The cats were sent to court and served the crown faithfully until the end of their days.

As far as the history of mice at the Hermitage is concerned, the first person who wrote about them was Catherine the Great. In her correspondence with Voltaire, the mighty empress once complained that the only admirers of the Hermitage treasures were herself and the mice.

Certainly, today's feline inhabitants of the Hermitage basements and courtyards are not direct descendants of Elizabeth's royal mousers. In the years of the Leningrad blockade, many cats died or left the city to escape starvation, and the Hermitage was no an exception. Cats appeared again in the museum only after the end of the Second World War.

"It smells like cats," visitors commonly exclaim upon venturing into the Hermitage basements for the first time. To which museum staffers reply, "cats smell better than rats."

The cats regard the Hermitage basements and courtyards as their territory, particularly the basements, because they are heated.

Every museum workshop – restorers, joiners, electricians, plumbers and others – has its favorite cats. "They make us better than we are," said a plumber. Cats are not allowed in the exhibition halls, however, but Hermitage workers speak of the legendarily elusive Maria Vasiliyevna, who liked to bear her kittens under the throne in the Throne Room and pestered museum security workers by setting off motion detectors.

In fact, cats are favored characters in the museum's unwritten history. Each cat has its personal character, many their personal names. While traditional names (Masha, Vasily, Barsik, Murzik) prevail, only in the Hermitage could you meet a cat known as Van Dyck. She got her nickname because she got stuck in the ventilation duct of the Van Dyck room. "I've never heard such haunting cries before," recalled a museum guard. It took several hours to rescue the howling cat.

Katerina, who lives near the director's office, is named for Catherine the Great, who founded the Hermitage's art collection.

Muska (dimimutive of Maria), a lame mother-cat with a dozen kittens, showed uncommon persistence in fighting for her living space, slated to be destroyed during reconstruction of the museum's entrance. Muska never became reconciled with the new architecture, and left her "marks" in ticket-offices and even by the administrator's desk. Thus did nature take vengeance on civilization.

Pirate, a big, great, one-eyed cat, lost his eye in a fight, and is deserving of T.S. Eliot's poetic description: "a real fiend in feline shape, a monster of depravity."

During the crisis years of *perestroika*, the Hermitage was in danger of becoming a shelter for cats. As many museum room guards are female pensioners of very modest means, some brought their pets to the Hermitage, hoping that they would be better fed there. Still other employees brought sick and orphaned cats into the museum from the streets. As a result, the cat population multiplied. Something had to be done.

To begin with, most of the cats were sterilized and many were placed in new homes. But, even with lower numbers, the food problem remained; leftovers from the canteen were no longer enough to feed the cat army.

At that time, the Drawing Studio of the Hermitage School Center made an important contribution toward the cats' social safety net.

Founded in 1957, the world famous Drawing Studio teaches art to about 100 children aged 5-11. About half have whiskered pets at home, so it was only natural that the children's hearts were moved by the "cat issue." One boy came up with the idea of a charity auction and was enthusiastically supported by the Studio's director, Dr. Boris Kravchunas.

"Cats are most significant for children in a megalopolis," Dr. Kravchunas said, "because for many little boys and girls, they are the only piece of nature around them. I found the idea of an auction very important, not only because of its moral significance, but also because it was another chance for the children to get in touch with nature through their creative work."

Young participants prepared for the auction in earnest, creating feline-themed paintings and sculptures. The event took place at the end of 1997. Though the works were bought chiefly by the artist's parents, the profit was spent on cat food and on a dinner-party in the basement. But this turned out to be just the beginning...

On April 1, 1999 (April Fools Day during the Year of the Cat, according to the Chinese Zodiac) the Hermitage opened an extraordinary exhibition in the reading room of the museum's Scientific Library. The one-day show was entitled "Cats: Friends of Science and Sensuality" and consisted of the young painters' work of their own cats and those in the Hermitage basements. Actually, the title referred back to Charles Baudelaire's *Les Fleurs du Mal*, or rather it is a line from *Spleen et Idéal, LXVI*. *"Les Chats: Amis de la science et de la volupté..."* It was the Hermitage's first entirely philanthropic exhibition: visitors could place a donation in a cat-shaped box. The money gained was used to buy cat food and flea collars..

This youthful enterprise threw down a challenge to adult artists. As a result, on March 7, 2001, a special one-day show took place in a Hermitage basement. Two contemporary artists from St. Petersburg, Yuri Lukshin and Vera Pavlova, together with the Hermitage photographer Yuri Molodkovets, presented portraits of the museum's feline protectors. It was a closed event for museum staff and mass media (and the cats, who proved not to be easily frightened by camera flashes). This public relations blitz resonated in the city and attracted the attention of compassionate citizens eager to help the cats that help the Hermitage.

Today, the "cat problem" is under museum officials' control. The cats have a "curator" and press-attaché: Maria Khaltunen, secretary to Director Mikhail Piotrovsky. In addition to the usual kitchen leftovers, the cats now receive a special monthly allowance from the staff. Every month on payday there appears at the director's office an envelope with a whiskered muzzle drawn on it. Inside are the proceeds from the "cat tax" on staff, affixed at one ruble per person. Not a high fee, but, considering the number of staffers in this huge institution, it assures that the cat guards will be safe and comfortable. The money is not only spent on cat food, but also pays for visits by a veterinarian.

Petersburgers have gotten used to being proud of this unusual feature of their greatest museum's life. And those who have adopted kittens from the Hermitage's cellars do not miss an opportunity to mention the royal provenance of their pets.

"Cats," said Kravchunas, "are like the Penates – Roman patron gods of the home and, especially, of storerooms."

Indeed, the cats take care of the Hermitage and the museum takes care of its cats.

March/April 2003

Duck Devil and Little Wolf
Christine Seashore

*W*e threaded our way down the aisle of the stuffed Yak-40 airplane, between bundles of dried fish and bags of onions, to claim the last three empty seats. Incongruously, a huge bouquet of crimson, long-stemmed roses occupied in its own seat.

We were flying to Tilichiki, a small town on the east coast of Kamchatka. But our ultimate destination was the tiny Koryak village of Vvenka, and the only way to get there in April was a two-hour snowmobile ride south from the airport.

The summer before, Jon (my husband) and Misha had been storm-bound in Vvenka for three days during their sea kayak journey from Petropavlovsk-Kamchatsky to Alaska. After the storm, while Jon and Misha were loading up their kayaks to continue their journey, Moolynaut, the grandmother and shaman of the village, hobbled down to the beach. She urged them to return for the spring festival and to help her adopted sons, Oleg and Sergei, buy some reindeer for Vvenka. It's not everyday one is invited on a pilgrimage by a Siberian shaman, so Jon and Misha accepted immediately and asked me to come along.

As the airplane started to descend, the flight attendant announced that the temperature in Tilichiki was -17° C (+1° F), with a 50 km/hour northerly wind. Swirling snow gave the asphalt runway an ephemeral appearance as our huge balloon tires touched down. I quickly donned anorak, hat, and gloves to wait on the frigid runway as baggage was passed from hand to hand down the narrow stairs that extended from the tail section. The other passengers stood calmly without hats or gloves, as if -17° was normal for the sixth of April. I watched the roses, inside their silver and blue foil wrapper, flap frantically as a man in a fur hat whisked them into the terminal.

Our Koryak friends, Sergei and Oleg, stood out from the Russian-looking crowd waiting on the other side of the gate. They wore sealskin mukluks, deerskin pants and boxy canvas anoraks. They were dressed in the muted colors of the land, but for their colorful *malahi* hats. The hats gave them a canine look: their top corners standing up like dog's ears. Sewn of sheepskin, the hats are dyed dark brown or black, trimmed with dog hair, and decorated with brightly beaded medallions. Loopy, beaded garlands connected the medallions like the shills on a Las Vegas dancer.

We gathered our mountain of gear and hauled it to the snowmobiles parked outside the gate. Oleg opened the flapping canvas tarp on a sled of hand-carved wood and Sergei loaded it with our duffels. Then their machines roared to life and they sped off through the iced-over streets of Tilichiki. We walked, following the lingering smell of two-cycle engine exhaust. Five minutes later, we caught up with them in front of Sergei's sister's apartment where he tinkered with his ancient, red *Buran* snowmobile, the workhorse of Siberia.

Jon, Misha, and Oleg went off to buy a few provisions in the big city, while Sergei tied another sled behind the one filled with camping gear. Sergei's sister spied me from her apartment window, and signaled me to come up for tea. Twenty minutes later, the others returned with bulging bags of fresh onions, eggs, milk, and other goodies for the folks in Vvenka. We then packed all our things and ourselves onto the snowmobiles and sleds and began the drive south.

After an hour of bumping over sea ice and frozen tundra, we climbed over a divide and descended to the Vvenka River, which meandered like a smooth white highway all the way to the village.

Oleg's wife Lydia met us in front of her house with a small shovel full of glowing coals. Before even saying hello, she picked small pieces of lint from our jackets and put them into the coals. While I rubbed my frozen cheeks, Lydia explained that burning a small piece of our clothing was a Koryak custom – it was meant to frighten off any evil spirits that might have arrived with us. She was following every custom so that we would be purified when Grandmother Moolynaut came to greet us.

Within five minutes, the old woman limped into the room. She took off an ordinary looking coat and hat just as would any old woman. I started to wonder if Jon's imagination had cooked up this whole expedition. Then Moolynaut turned to face me. While hardly imposing at four and half feet tall, her deeply-lined Koryak face and intense eyes seemed to probe the depths of my soul.

Now ninety-six, Moolynaut has been Vvenka's cultural mentor and healer for over 70 years. Through the upheavals caused by the change into and out of the Soviet system, Moolynaut has healed the sick, herded reindeer, fished in the sea, and raised displaced children like Sergei and Oleg. Locals claim she kept wolves away from the reindeer herds by whispering spells. And she remembers when the last American ships came to trade with her father before the Cold War. Most importantly, Moolynaut now believed that the post-*perestroika* despair in modern Vvenka could only be cured if the Koryak – *the people of the deer* – were reunited with the reindeer.

The last of the Vvenka herds were killed off a year ago. Once, this region and neighboring Chukotka were home to the world's largest domesticated reindeer herds. But, decimated by poaching, predation by wolves, and newer, more difficult economic conditions (including a steep fall in demand for reindeer meat during the 1990s), domesticated reindeer have dwindled to a few small herds hidden in the vast Siberian tundra.

Without deer, the Koryak lifestyle has lost its compass. Moolynaut said that, although the younger generation will adapt to new ways and new foods, the older villagers have a difficult time living without the reindeer. The villagers want to start herding again, and Oleg and Sergei hoped that, if we traveled west and north, we could find one of the remaining herds and bring reindeer back to Vvenka.

Jon had theorized that mountain bikes would be the perfect way to travel across the frozen tundra. Two days after the spring festival, we assembled the bicycles in the tiny kitchen of our borrowed apartment. Lydia sat near the stove and wistfully told stories of how the Koryak had lived with their herds on the tundra. She also told us that Oleg's Koryak name translates to "Duck Devil" and that he is the most successful hunter in the village. His hunting skill isn't confined to shooting ducks. Because there were no deer to eat, he had killed two moose, numerous ptarmigan, and hares to feed the village and his family during the winter.

Very early the next morning, Oleg drove up on his snowmobile. With a rifle strapped across his broad shoulders, his *malahi* hat, and a pair of Russian flight goggles, he looked very much the demon. A small gray dog, a husky named Little Wolf – *Volchuk* in Russian – perched on the seat behind him. We loaded our gear on the sleds and helped lash on the three, 55-gallon drums of fuel for the journey. Then Jon, Misha, and I pedaled out of town in hope that the snow would be firm enough to support the bikes.

But the theory that it might prove possible to ride mountain bikes on the frozen tundra did not pan out. Little snow had fallen during the winter and the snow pack was unconsolidated and spotty. Less than a kilometer from the village, we left the firm snowmobile track. Our wheels broke through the surface and churned down to the hubs. We pedaled and pushed, but, by the end of day, we had pedaled only one of the 33 kilometers that we gained.

Duck Devil, Little Wolf, and Sergei left ten hours after we did, but caught up to us just before we reached a hunter's shack where we spent the night. Over the next several days, we tied the bikes on the sleds and tried skiing, but a lack of snow and rough country also made skiing difficult and slow. Then a blizzard held us down for two days, and we all realized that, in order to find the reindeer people before we ran out of gas and food, we had to move faster. I climbed on the passenger's seat behind Duck Devil. Little Wolf jumped up and wiggled his way in between us and the three of us shared this seat for the rest of the 500 kilometer journey. Misha and Jon perched on one of the sleds that Sergei towed behind his snowmobile. They bumped along only slightly cushioned by a reindeer hide on top of an extra motor, an ice drill, a shovel, and a spare ski for the snowmobile.

Misha called this big, open expanse of the snow-covered "tundra" – the white desert. But it seemed more like being on an immense, white ocean. When I sat nestled on the rear seat of the snowmobile, I felt as though I was traveling on a snow yacht. Captain Duck Devil navigated us through wind-sculpted snow that undulated in wave-like mounds in every direction. There were no trees, no buildings, nothing but rolling white and blue sky. Without anything vertical to use as a reference point, a tiny alder bush looked from a distance like a house or a rock. When Sergei, Jon, and Misha traveled ahead of us, they soon became small dots on an infinite white plain.

Fruitlessly, we wandered around for a week looking every place where Duck Devil and Sergei expected to find reindeer people. When another blizzard blew in from the north, we quickly pitched our canvas-walled tent in a sheltered gully.

After two days, the storm let up. Duck Devil did a short reconnaissance on his snowmobile, and returned to tell us we were only 10 minutes away from an abandoned geology village. The next morning, we followed the smoke coming from the chimney of a dilapidated house. Constantine and Anatoli, caretakers for the mining company, were the only inhabitants.

Constantine was also a hunter, and knew the exact migration route of a group of herders. Earlier in the winter, they had hired him to trap a wolf that threatened their herd. We pulled out the map and he pointed out the route to their base.

By early afternoon, we had turned up the third stream that flows into Talovka Lake, and followed it toward the Parapalsky Mountains. The Parapalsky Valley lies about 200 kilometers southeast of Manily on the west coast of Kamchatka. We stopped on a small rise to scan the horizon with binoculars. The day wore on and I felt like we were looking for the proverbial needle in a haystack. We continued driving toward the mountains. Then suddenly Little Wolf's ears perked up, and I noticed that Duck Devil was staring intently toward a thicket of bushes near a small stream. He stopped the snowmobile and pointed to brown spots beyond the brush and all but shouted an enthusiastic, "*oleyn, oleyn!*" My less-trained eyes required binoculars to see the well-hidden reindeer herd.

Four herders met us at the stream. They crowded around us to share their excitement about a tiny deer that had just been born. The still wet baby deer wobbled on long, gangly legs to hide behind its mother. Transfixed, we watched until one of the herders offered to lead us to the herding base. He tied his small sled to the toboggan of extra fuel we were towing behind the snowmobile, and careened back and forth whenever Duck Devil hit the throttle.

We skirted the base of the mountains, crossed a stream, and climbed to the top of a vast plateau. When we arrived, a cluster of people had gathered outside a one room, squared-log cabin covered with tarpaper. The reindeer herders were amazed to meet Americans. They had only seen foreign visitors once before, when a Japanese photographer had helicoptered to their base camp in 1997. He shot photos of their funeral ceremony and two hours later disappeared into the sky.

Nikolai, the leader, beckoned us into the cabin that the clan uses as its permanent base, which is situated at the best birthing place on their migration. By the time my eyes adjusted to the darkness of the room, Nikolai's oldest daughter Lucia had cleared a low table, filled cups with tea, and dished up plates of moose meat and *kasha*. A younger woman, Nadia, continued her daily task of making bread dough in a metal bucket. After we were served the meat and *kasha*, the women formed the dough into flat rounds that they fried in a pan fitted directly over the flame of a wood-fired iron stove.

The herding group moves with their herd of 800 deer over a 300-kilometer migration. During the coldest months of the year, they travel between three different cabins that align with their route. The birth of the new deer had brought them to this small enclave of buildings and corrals. The rest of the year they travel with the herd, staying in small canvas tents, with a larger hide tent for cooking. Nikolai's brigade, (the name has stuck since Soviet times) is composed of 12 adults and two little girls. About half of the group is from Nikolai's immediate family.

The next day we walked out into the bright, icy sunlight and the herders gave me a handful of dried fish with which to tempt a flock of sled deer into a small corral. These deer had been selected from the main herd and were trained to pull sleds. Nikolai supervised the selection of six deer. The herders hitched two deer each to three small wooden sleds and led them to where we stood. A herder sat on the front of the sled and motioned me to sit behind him. Then he whipped the sled deer into a trot and we jostled along, back to the main herd. The jingle of bells and the soft click of hooves crunching through the snow was muffled by the hood of the deerskin anorak that the women insisted I wear against the cold. When we got to the herd, Nikolai's son-in-law, Vladimir, stiffly stood up to greet us. He had been out with the deer all night. He welcomed us to sit by his fire, which he had built in the lee of a sled tipped on edge and covered with a sheet of plastic as a windbreak. Even on the coldest, stormiest nights of winter, the herders sit without a tent or even a sleeping bag, watching over the herd.

On our thirty-hour flight to Kamchatka, I had read George Kennan's classic *Tent Life in Siberia*, about scouting for a Trans-Siberian telegraph line in the 1860s. Kennan traveled with the wandering Koryak herders for months and his book described the herder's life almost exactly as it still exists today. While watching and moving the herds, the herders still prefer to wear skin clothing made by the women. Sleds and herding equipment are also made by hand. Besides herding deer, the men hunt for moose, ptarmigan and bear (and fish and seals when their migration takes them close to the Sea of Okhotsk).

Today, the *sovkhoz* – a remnant of the herding cooperatives of Soviet times – provides very little money for food and equipment to keep the group going. Nikolai's herd migrates over the second largest platinum deposit in the world. Last year, mining companies removed over \$180 million in ore from the region. To keep relations friendly, the companies who want to mine the rich ore of the Koryak Autonomous Region have started to contribute money to preserve the herding lifestyle. Nikolai's brigade uses the money to buy tea, rice, kasha, flour, materials, and gasoline.

Sergei and Oleg had planned to ask Nikolai about deer to restart the Vvenka herd. But, after five days, it was obvious that the brigade would not sell any of their deer. Nikolai explained that during Soviet times, his clan had herded 2000 deer. But today the herd stood at just 800. He would not sell deer until he was able to build the herd back to its original size. However, we did not go back to Vvenka empty-handed. The women piled hides in shades of creamy tan and rich coffee to send back to the old people.

That evening, they prepared a special dinner with stacks of fried bread, huge kettles of boiled moose, plates filled with dried salmon and salted wild onion, dishes of cloudberries and blueberries, and cup after cup of dark black tea and sugar. We joked and chatted. Nikolai told how much of the Koryak tradition had been destroyed during the Soviet era.

"Before, we had many, many ceremonies and festivals and contests where we would race our deer and make sacrifices to our gods. I don't think that we will ever get back everything that we lost, but I hope that things will be better now. Three of my four children still want to live the herder's life and these two granddaughters enjoy our life here at Parapalsky Valley."

At dawn, we packed the sleds for our return to Vvenka. As we got on the snowmobiles, one of the little girls came out carrying a small shopping bag and handed it to Sergei. Inside was a husky puppy curled up in a furry ball on a small piece of deerhide.

"Come back when the puppy grows up and then we can talk about herding some deer to Vvenka," Nikolai said.

Moolynaut did not seem surprised when we returned to Vvenka without any reindeer. The villagers say that seeing the future is another one of her many powers. Her equanimity about the events of the last 96 years is amazing. Again we sat in the small kitchen and Lydia translated Moolynaut's memories of the wonderful Winchester rifles that the American traders had brought in the 1930's, and how Moolynaut had cried when she saw traders put live deer into a boat to take them away to the American ship. She told us of her nomadic life with the four husbands she has survived.

All the while, villagers kept coming by to welcome us back to Vvenka with plates of food. Soon, an impromptu banquet was spread across a tablecloth on the floor. The children inflated the balloons we had given them and after dinner the whole group batted them around in a giggling version of "hot potato." Moolynaut rocked back on her haunches and swatted a green balloon. Her eyes sparkled with joy and mirth – a smile that seemed to say that Vvenka's people of the deer would one day soon get their reindeer and their lives back.

January/February 2002

Keeping a Sweet Tradition Alive
Laura Williams

Beekeepers in Russia's Bashkirian Republic are saving the Burzyan honeybee and the ancient tradition of keeping bees.

Sagit Galin, 69, saddles up his chestnut mare, strapping a long, braided leather rope and small wooden vat to the horn. He calls to his son, Sabit, 35, who is readying a horse in the next stall. Together, the two Bashkirians, descendents of semi-nomadic keepers of wild bees, lead the horses out of the small barnyard encircling their log home.

They gallop out of the village and through a rolling meadow flowering with fireweed, angelica, and buttercup. Soon they disappear into the surrounding woods, which extend up the gentle slopes of the ancient Urals. Securing their horses beneath a towering pine tree, Sabit hangs a jumble of handmade tools over his shoulder and from his waist. He throws a braided rope around the massive tree, slightly above his head, catching it with his free hand, and pulls himself up. He grabs a foothold in a subtle notch in the tree's trunk. He releases the rope and quickly snaps it around the tree higher still. With the swiftness of a startled bear cub, he scales the tree in seconds. Sending the rope around the tree one last time – just below his feet – he attaches a narrow wooden footrest. Now supported by a sturdy platform 30 feet above ground, he turns to tend his wild bees.

Sabit learned the art of keeping wild bees from his father, who learned it from his father. Wild beekeeping has endured for nearly 1000 years in these remote forests of the southern Ural Mountains – passing from father to son. Wild beekeeping in Bashkiria was at its peak in the eighteenth century, but the art was nearly lost by the middle of the twentieth century. Exiled and purged by Stalin in 1936, killed on the front lines during World War II, and enticed to leave forest villages for more promising livelihoods in burgeoning cities in the 1970s, few beekeepers remained in Bashkiria to carry on the tradition.

Survival of the distinct population of wild honeybee the Bashkirians depended on for their honey was also problematic. The Burzyan honeybee, found only in Bashkiria, is known for its resistance to disease, its uncanny ability to survive in cold climates, and its extreme proficiency in gathering large amounts of nectar from the linden tree, which blooms for only three weeks in July. Sweet linden honey is prized all over the world, and Bashkiria harbors 36 per cent of all linden forests in Russia.

Like the Bashkirian beekeepers, the wild bees came under fire in the twentieth century. The large trees the bees require for their nests fell to make way for agricultural fields and development. Other, less resilient subspecies of honeybees from the Carpathian and Caucasian Mountains were introduced to the region, causing the bees to hybridize. Weakened populations began to die out. Thus, the future of the honeybee and the wild beekeeping tradition were at stake.

In 1958, Russian scientists created a protected area at the core of the bee's natural range to save the distinct population of Burzyan honeybees. Originally a division of the Baskhiria Zapovednik (strict nature reserve), the protected area was reorganized in 1986 as the Shulgan Tash Zapovednik to preserve the last remaining habitat of purebred populations of Burzyan honeybees.

Just saving the bees was not enough for Mikhail Kosarev, however, now Director of Shulgan Tash Zapovednik. Kosarev sought to save the local tradition as well. Kosarev knew that Burzyan honeybees occupy natural cavities in trees but are readily attracted to dens carved out by experienced beekeepers. By maintaining artificial hives in the forest, more families of bees could be supported within the protected bounds of the nature reserve. Yet, creation of a federally-run, strictly protected nature reserve limits the types of activities permitted within its boundaries. Consequently, many beekeepers were precluded from tending the specific trees their forefathers cultivated.

To preserve ancient tradition and win the support of the local community, Kosarev created a new position in the reserve: ranger-beekeeper. He hired 12 ranger-beekeepers, all descendants of Bashkirian keepers of wild bees, to tend bee trees in the reserve and to protect the forests and its inhabitants from poachers and other intruders. Sabit Galin is one of the reserve's ranger-beekeepers and cares for the same trees that his family harvested for centuries. Today, because they are within the nature reserve, the trees are granted protection in perpetuity from loggers and developers. Since good bee trees take centuries to mature, Kosarev says that drawing on local experience and resources was crucial for saving both the bees and the tradition.

Climbing down from the tree with a vat full of golden honeycomb, Sabit Galin describes how his great-grandfather must have picked out this pine tree for his progeny nearly 100 years ago. He would have selected a tree that was 150 to 200 years old, making sure that sufficient flowering plants and fresh water were nearby. Next he lopped off the crown of the tree 15 feet from the top and capped it with a flat stone, forcing it to grow in circumference rather than height. After carving the family's insignia into the trunk to lay unofficial claim to the future bee tree, he opened up a clearing to let in the light.

Seventy years passed and the pine tree grew broad enough to house a beehive. That is when Sabit's father carved out a hollow cavity high up in the tree, using traditional instruments that have remained virtually unchanged for 1000 years. He made the den nearly three feet high and a foot wide, smoothing out the inside with a sharp blade. He carved a small entry hole for the bees on one side and a removable door on the other to allow access to the hive and its honey. He rubbed the inside of the den with grasses to give it a natural smell, and hung lattices of honeycomb to attract wild bees.

Evidently, the Galin dynasty has a knack for attracting bees, because over the years wild bees have occupied all of their more than 30 trees at one time or another. When Sagit became too old to scale the trees himself, he passed the trade on to his son. Now Sabit cares for the bees, while readying new trees for his own sons and grandsons. The Galins are grateful that their trees are now protected in the reserve. Logging and roads would have surely destroyed them by now.

To save the Burzyan bee and beekeeping tradition, more is needed than simply protecting the land where the trees are located. Today, the Zapovednik is taking proactive measures to shape the future. The reserve's head ranger-beekeeper, Fidrat Yumaguzhin, is dedicated to preserving the genetic integrity of the hardy Burzyan honeybee. His research and breeding efforts are helping the Burzyan bee regain its foothold in the region and resettle its former range.

With encouragement from Yumaguzhin and the Shulgan Tash Zapovednik, the Republic of Bashkiria passed a law in 1995 prohibiting the import of other strains of bees. Yumaguzhin provides local people with Burzyan bee "starter kits" – a queen bee laden with eggs and a few of her workers. By encouraging local beekeepers to use the hardy Burzyan bee to make honey, the population of Burzyan bees in the region is increasing and its range is expanding. This approach keeps locals from using other strains of bees, which can hybridize with Burzyan bees and weaken the population. In addition, some bees kept by locals will inevitably escape and move to the dens in trees maintained by the reserve or to natural dens to help boost the wild bee population.

Thanks to the efforts of the Shulgan Tash Zapovednik and generations of keepers of wild bees, people now understand the importance of saving the Burzyan honeybee. They value these bees, which are more resistant to disease and pests than domestic bees, and which produce award-winning honey. The reserve's honey has won gold medals at international beekeeping exhibitions in France, Germany, and Russia. Preservation of these hardy and proficient bees and their forest habitat is in turn saving the ancient tradition of wild beekeeping in Bashkiria. Hard work and courage are needed to tend wild bees. These two traits, always valued in Bashkirian culture, are now paying off for the bees and their keepers.

July/August 2002

Peculiarities of Russia's National Mushroom Hunt
Mikhail Ivanov

Come late August through early September, millions of Russians rush to the woods in search of their prized forest fungi – the *griby*. But Russia's fall fascination with mushrooms is not just about a weekend in the country. It has a practical basis too: it adds seasonal variety to the diet; autumnal feasting on mushrooms is quite a healthy indulgence. What is more, mushrooms are a very affordable meal for those who take the trouble of picking them themselves. For buying mushrooms in Russian markets is a very "expensive pleasure" as Russians say. And the so-called *shampiniony*, the white mushrooms artificially grown in humid basements or at special mushroom farms, are not the real thing.

Russia's ancient forest culture developed a myriad of uses for this delicacy. Fresh mushrooms have always figured in local soups and garnishes. They are also pickled for the long winter months. And that says nothing about the delicious pies with mushroom filling or the exquisite meal "*gribnaya ikra*" ("mushroom caviar"), made from finely diced fungi. Salted or marinated mushrooms are also a great snack (*zakuska*) to go along with a shot of ice cold vodka.

Every Russian housewife knows how to pickle or dry mushrooms. Traditionally collected in a woven basket (*lukoshko*, to use the ancient Russian word) then cleaned of leaves, twigs and moss, the mushrooms are soaked in salt water to rid them of any possible worms, then sun-dried on the second floor of one's dacha (or *izba*). In urban conditions, you can also oven-dry them. The result is the strings of dried mushrooms (*sushyonye griby*) one sees babushkas selling in underpasses, by metro entrances or near train stations.

The secrets of how to find mushrooms and tips on how best to discern the dozen or so time-tested varieties of edible mushrooms from their poisonous cousins, are passed from generation to generation within Russian families. This training begins early, with fairy tales of mushrooms' magical powers and continues through the peaceful hours that families spend together in "the silent hunt."

It is best to start your mushroom hunt at sunrise or even earlier, when the air is humid and the mushrooms are juicy and full of flavor. Mushrooms like to nest in humid yet sun-warmed places. An experienced, gray-haired mushroom hunter who is about to step into a sunny glade surrounded by birch trees can already smell mushrooms in the air: they typically hide on moss growing under the birch tree. "*Nashyol!*" ("I found it!") his grandson shouts in triumph, rushing to show grandpa his prey – a huge mushroom almost as big as his little head. The shrewd elder smiles, then pats the kid on the back, urging him to remember the sort of place where the mushroom was hiding. Quite often, for the sake of training, parents and grandparents falsely overlook obvious patches, letting the children savor their first trophies, longed for since they started hearing about mushroom picking in Russian fairy tales.

> *Жили-были дедушка да бабушка. Была у них внучка Машенька. Собрались раз подружки в лес – по грибы да по ягоды. Пришли звать с собой и Машеньку.*
>
> – *Сказка "Маша и Медведь"*

> *Once upon a time, there was a grandpa and a grandma. And they had a granddaughter, little Masha. One day, her friends decided to go to the forest to pick mushrooms and berries. So they came to take little Masha along...*
>
> – *From the fairytale, "Masha and the Bear"*

If you are ever invited by your Russian friend on a mushroom hunt, you should extend your deepest gratitude to your host. Such an invitation is truly an honor. But be sure you control yourself ... The hero of Georgy Daneliya's film comedy *Autumn Marathon*, upon meeting a visitor from Denmark invites him on a mushroom hunt as an ultimate sign of hospitality. The hunt, needless to say, ends up in a huge drinking bout, so much so that the next morning the Dane wakes up in a Soviet *vytrezvitel* (sobering-up station).

Back in the Gorbachevian days of *perestroika* and anti-alcohol campaigns, some Russians desperate to get high used semi-toxic or psychotropic mushrooms. They did not employ the "pale toadstool," as this toxic variety causes nearly instant death. But the red and white *mukhomor* ("fly-killer") was a good candidate, as its effects are somewhat less severe. It is, in fact, food for moose.

The most prestigious mushroom in Russia is the "Tsar of All Mushrooms" – the *bely grib* ("white mushroom"). It is called this because of the white meat under its brown cap. This premium mushroom is also often called *borovik*. The next best varieties in the Russian mushroom pantheon are the *podosinovik* and *podberezovik* (literally, "under the aspen tree" and "under the birch tree"). These three varieties are often catalogued as *blagorodny* ("noble") mushrooms, as they take very little processing and are fit for any type of consumption – in soups, fried, dried or marinated.

In many mushroom-rich regions – Karelia, for instance – mushroom pickers are so jaded that they won't pick anything but the three *blagorodnys*; some are even so "snobbish" that they refuse to pick *podosinoviki* or *podberyozoviki* and only pay attention to *belys*. In Karelia, one can afford such snobbery – a single hunt can easily turn up 50 or 100 *belys*. The untouched nature of the region is fertile soil for mushrooms. But then, in a good mushroom year in the Moscow region (like 1999), there are plenty of premium mushrooms as well. In years when summers are hot, fungal growth is discourage; when peat fires rage, prime mushroom undergrowth is damaged.

The most "democratic" and common mushroom is the *syroyezhka* ("eat-it-raw"). Granted, Russians don't consider it the most delicious mushroom, but its yellow, green, pink or blue caps make your collection of mushrooms so much merrier and colorful. And, frankly, the *syroyezhka* is very good for frying and could even be used in soup in a bad mushroom year.

The *maslyata* ("buttery ones") get their name from the buttery texture of the yellow meat under their light brown cap. Perfect for marinades and pickles, they are also very tasty fried.

Another excellent frying mushroom is the *lisichka* ("little fox"), so named because of its orange and red fox-like coloring.

A number of mushrooms are good only for pickling and marinades – the rosy *volnushka* ("little wave"), the solid white *gruzd*, the black and yellow *chernushka* ("blacky") and the somewhat slippery and wet *valuy*.

Finally, the king of Russian fall is the *opyonok*. *Opyata* (plural for *opyonok*) grow mainly from September through mid-October, when one finds the so-called *pozdniye* ("late") *opyata*, This is a mushroom perfect for impatient hunters, those who are not interested in combing the forest only to find three or four *belys* – who would rather fill a bucket or two with *opyata* in just ten minutes. Or, as some local hunters do, fill the trunk of a Volga car with them. If you find the right glade – tree stumps are the key – then chances are you will bring home at least couple of buckets of *opyata*. When there is an abundance of *opyata*, mushroom pickers say they can "*kosit kosoy*" the *opyata* ("cut them with a scythe").

Sadly, the *opyata* season is the last hurrah for the mushroom fan. It augurs the end of mushroom picking for the year. The sport resumes only in spring – when the first mushrooms, known as *smorchki* (morels) pop up, in April and May.

Granted, the wrinkled *smorchok* it is not your typical Russian *bely*, but if you are too impatient to wait till the peak of the mushroom hunt, it can't hurt to pick a few morels to tide you over until fall…

September/October 2002

Kolyma Gold
Alexei Dmitriev

*W*ithout slave labor there would be no Kolyma.

Since the late nineteenth century, prospectors have ventured to this inhospitable and remote region in the distant Northeast of Russia, searching for gold. But severe climate and geographic isolation prevented colonization. For their part, the indigenous people – Evenk reindeer herdsmen – believed that Kolyma's gold was inadvertently left behind when the Great Spirit sought to deliver Earth from gold, because the metal sowed wickedness among people. Little did they know about the magnitude of evil Kolyma was to see in the twentieth century because of its gold.

VLADIMIR ILYICH CAME to Kolyma thirty years ago as a young geologist. Today, he works for a Moscow bank, trading in precious metals and looking after the bank's interests in Kolyma and Yakutia. Every month, he makes a bone-rattling, 1,500-mile "tour of duty" of the region in his Toyota Land Cruiser. He invited us – myself and Sergei – along for the ride.

Our trip began in Magadan, 4,500 miles from Moscow, where, outside the air terminal a billboard proclaims: "Welcome to Kolyma – the Golden Heart of Russia."

The road to town from the airport is part of the legendary Kolyma highway – built by Gulag prisoners and known as the "Road of Bones." Every settlement here began as a labor camp. Every facility dating back more than 50 years was built and initially manned by prisoners. Under Stalin, every sort of "enemy of the people," from alleged spies and traitors, to POWs and *kulaks*,[1] were sent here to mine gold.

Prisoners who survived an arduous sea passage in cargo holds from Vladivostok to Magadan landed in a frozen wilderness (temperatures rarely

1. Kulaks were private farmers opposed to collectivization.

rise above -30° F from November to March) and had to survive on daily rations of 500 grams of bread, two bowls of watery soup and a serving of *kasha* (for "under-achievers" and during "slow" winter months these were scaled down to 400 grams). Harassed by guards and common criminals who were assigned "privileged" jobs such as cooks and orderlies, housed in unheated barracks with virtually no medical care (wounds were routinely treated with gasoline), political prisoners worked 12-hour days, armed with nothing but shovels, pickaxes and wheelbarrows. Official records say that almost two million persons were sifted through the Kolyma camps between 1932 and 1953, and more than 200,000 died here – victims of hunger, sickness or execution. Some historians argue that the number of dead was three times higher.

On the wave of the post-Stalinist "thaw," young Communist enthusiasts rushed to Kolyma to de-stigmatize the place (most of the Kolyma camps had been closed down, but the Gulag system remained) and turn it into a romantic symbol of new beginnings. Prisoners and romantics had much in common: both could survive for a time without schools, theaters, hairdressing salons, hospitals, and libraries. But as the romantics put down roots and started families, their taste for deprivation ebbed. To keep the gold flowing, the state had to offer higher salaries and create a civil infrastructure to keep people from leaving. Soon, the government was pumping up to six percent of its GDP into its Northern and Far Eastern regions to sustain economic activity there.

State subsidies to Kolyma ended with the arrival of *perestroika*. Soon, state enterprises became burdened by debt and unpaid wages, and were eventually shut down. Annual gold production declined from 160 tons to slightly over 100. Russia, previously the world's second largest gold producer (after South Africa), fell to seventh place.

Then, in 1993, the Russian government took a drastic step: in an attempt to breathe life into the stagnating industry, it denationalized gold mining. Local governments were given authority over concession licenses, production volumes, and foreign investment. Instead of improving social conditions, the move kindled "Wild East" capitalism and attracted adventurers in search of quick riches. Over the past decade, some 270 licenses have been given to prospector cooperatives – known in Russian as "*artels*." But only 180 *artels* delivered gold to a local refinery. The rest could

not make it without state subsidies or went bankrupt, unable to repay loans
to commercial banks, like, for instance, Vladimir's.

MOST GOLD MINING occurs along the circular Road of Bones that runs 400
miles north to Susuman and then turns back via Ust-Omchug for another
450 miles to Magadan. Beyond Susuman, a 240-mile stretch runs to Ust-
Nera in Yakutia. From there, drivers take chances and continue to Yakutsk
for another 600 miles over a packed snow tract – there is no year-round
road to the rest of Russia, which adds to the heightened sense of isolation
and the islander mentality of Kolyma residents – they call the rest of Russia
"the mainland."

Winter driving requires special skill, since heavy trucks compact the
snow into solid ice. Steep mountain passes and hairpin turns normally
reveal a wreck or two rusting in the ditch below. Trucks never travel solo
and always carry easily ignitable materials to start a fire – to keep the driver
warm in case of a winter breakdown. And breakdowns happen. Trucks are
old, maintenance is costly and thus most often performed by drivers, with
improvised replacement parts. Diesel engines are run continuously during
stops and overnight, when the temperature drops below minus -40° F.

On average, trucks lose one tire to unpaved roads and extreme cold for
every 350 miles traveled. We could hardly drive 100 yards without seeing a
discarded tire by the side of the road. Equally noticeable (and only slightly
less frequent) were roadside graves of drivers killed in accidents. These are
usually marked by a steering wheel or a tire, with a photo of the deceased
in a wreath of plastic flowers. Despite these solemn reminders, truckers, as
a rule, drive recklessly and at high speeds.

Our driver, who we called by his patronymic, Yevgenich, was a handsome
man of reserved demeanor. Yevgenich took his smoking breaks seriously: we
stopped religiously every 40 miles. Like most people who came to Kolyma
in the 1980s, Yevgenich was drawn here by the prospect of money: while an
average salary on the mainland was R120 per month, here it started at R330.
He thought he would save some money and go home to central Russia in
three years, but was sucked in by the promise of doubling his earnings in
seven years. A dream of buying a R5,000 Lada suddenly became a reality.
With R160 airfares to Crimea, Yevgenich vacationed at Black Sea resorts
every summer. His savings account was growing fatter at a time when few
consumer goods were available. Then one August day in 1998 the Yeltsin

government devalued the ruble and Yevgenich's savings evaporated. This was a blow to many Russians, but it was an even greater tragedy in Kolyma, where people had managed to save large sums. Yevgenich and thousands like him were stranded, unable to book passage to the mainland and start a new life there.

We met another marooned soul at a place called Atka. Some eight years ago, Atka was a warehousing center with a population of about 2,000, supplying food to the outback mines and settlements from a huge truck depot. Today, all that is left are collapsed or burned-out houses, barns with caved-in roofs, truck skeletons rusting away in high grass and thousands of crushed, empty wooden crates once used to transport vegetables. Huge mosquitoes and gadflies appeared to be Atka's only inhabitants, but Vladimir suggested we stop here for lunch. Apparently, nearly 200 people still live in Atka and it boasts a little canteen for truckers, which turned out to be a ramshackle wooden cabin sunk into the permafrost. There we met Anya, a robust, crimson-faced, 40-something chef who served us a hearty meal of cabbage soup and *blini*.

Everyone who had a chance to leave Atka took it. Anya stayed because she could not afford the move to the mainland. She had been offered a one-time grant of R50,000 ($1,650) to help her and her son move to Magadan, but she calculated this would only cover five months of food and rent. During the school year, her son lives with relatives in Magadan, because the school in Atka closed a couple of years ago. Having a husband would help, but most single men are gone for five months, prospecting for gold, and can't pull their own weight the rest of the year. "My life has no space for courtship," Anya said. "I am in a love-hate relationship with this canteen!" Her laughter was younger than her years.

We reached the base of the Belichan mine near Susuman after eleven butt-numbing hours. The lot around a huge equipment repair and storage hangar was littered with rusted bulldozers, graders and trucks in varying degrees of disassembly. The derelict village, with its yawning black holes of burned out windows, and smoke from distant forest fires crawling over surrounding hills, created the eerie feel of a recently-emptied battlefield. It looked like the Belichan "infantry" was losing its fight.

It turned out the infantry was enjoying a smoke between 12-hour shifts. We were introduced to Fasil, the owner of the *artel*, a stocky man in black dress shoes and a shiny polo shirt. We shook hands with Ivan Ivanovich, a gray-haired, lanky foreman with a Popeye face. A real pro, Ivan has been mining gold for 25 years. He had recently started his own *artel*, only to be swindled by an unscrupulous partner. "He would not be toiling here now if he didn't have a new wife at home," announced Rustam, a swarthy fellow with a mouth full of gold teeth. "She must be so-o-o-o bored alone," winked a short, bald, bearded man in rubber boots and an unbelievably dirty quilted winter jacket, which he wore without a shirt. We asked if they got any gold today. "Could be better," Ivan Ivanovich said, spitting on the ground. "Last week we got a 700-gram nugget, but today's take is just over a kilo."

The new shift was about to board the bus. "Come, I'll show you the works," said Ivan Ivanovich, opening the door of his beat-up Toyota. We followed the bus around waterlogged pits and gravel mounds to what Ivan Ivanovich laconically referred to as the "*pribor*" (the "device"). We were driving through an immense desert of "tailings" – rocks and gravel left behind after the gold has been extracted. Magenta willow herb was the only vegetation that this scarred wasteland had produced in 60 years. There was not a patch of grass to be seen.

"They collected a lot of gold when this claim was first mined 60 years ago. A lot of lives to spare back then, but the gold recovery rate was poor. One of our devices here re-processes the tailings. The yield may not make us rich by the end of the season, but it sure keeps costs down," Ivan Ivanovich chuckled.

Belichan is a "placer" gold mine, which means that loose gold is present in alluvial sand, gravel and clay. When the mine was developed in the 1940s, prisoners removed six to ten feet of topsoil and vegetation to expose the gold-bearing "pay-dirt" underneath. This hard work was done in the winter, when water for sluicing gold was unavailable. Once the ice melted, the pay-dirt was washed with massive quantities of water over a grate of parallel bars called a "grizzly." The bars caught larger stones, but the mix of gravel, sand and water ran down the sluice-box, a 30-foot-long trough with metal ridges – "riffles" – along its bottom to trap the gold. Gold is 19 times heavier than water and would deposit at the bottom, while soil would be carried through and disgorged at the end of the sluice to form heaps of tailings. This is how gold was mined in California in the 1850s and in Kolyma in the 1940s.

The *pribor* in Belichan operated on the same principle. Every four minutes, monstrous 25-ton trucks backed up to the edge of a pit and emptied their holds of gravel and sand over a mechanized grizzly, its plates moving in waves, pushing larger boulders into the pit. A giant sprinkler sprayed water over the pay-dirt and the watery soil rushed down into three parallel sluice-boxes. The *pribor* resembled a ravenous creature that devoured and expelled hundreds of cubic feet of earth every minute. A couple of bulldozers pushed mounds of tailings away from the sluice-boxes, challenging nature with a new, barren landscape. The roar of bulldozers and trucks, the clanking sound of the chains that moved the grizzly plates and the noise of stones banging against the metal of the sluice-boxes silenced us. We watched in awe as the earth was raped for the sake of a handful of the yellow metal.

On the way back we stopped at a second, slightly different *pribor*. A water cannon propelled water at pay-dirt that bulldozers moved within its range. A young fellow, a cigarette glued to his lip, was playfully aiming the nozzle at huge boulders. The jet stream, apparently strong enough to kill a man, hurled the boulders away, allowing gravel and sand to pass through the grizzly below. The mixture of water, gravel and sand was then pumped up the rig equipped with a sluice-box at the top. The tailings were disgorged below, forming high mounds to be levelled. "Tomorrow you can watch the requisition. That's when they clean the sluice-boxes and pick the gold," said Ivan Ivanovich motioning us to the car. It was getting dark.

OUR HOME IN Susuman was a former hostel where Soviet bureaucrats stayed when they flocked to attend training sessions on how to be better Communists. Other than a sauna, it was a typical five-story apartment building. But in Kolyma they sit on concrete stilts to prevent the permafrost from melting and the building from sinking. The town was entwined by a web of huge heating and sewer pipes wrapped in shabby insulation.

Susuman is the second largest town in the region, after Magadan. It had a forlorn look; half of its population, primarily the younger, better-educated professionals, has left over the last decade. The pensioners, the sick and the dispossessed have stayed, subsisting on pensions averaging R1,800 ($60) a month. The airport, which used to have a daily flight to Magadan, was closed – a symbolic reminder that getting out may be a tricky endeavor. The 12-hour bus trip to Magadan costs about R800; a one-way ticket to

Moscow R12,000. Susuman's population would be even smaller, if not for the inflow from outlying villages, where municipal authorities, saddled with costs of maintaining the crumbling infrastructure, shut off heat and electricity to places with fewer than half of its original inhabitants.

A 2002 $80 million World Bank migration program to finance the outsettlement of pensioners and invalids upsets many able-bodied locals. "I don't want to rot here while I still have a good chunk of my life and health left," said Lyudmila, a stout woman I met at a 24-hour grocery store, where 50 percent of the shelf space is taken by vodka, and a billboard outside advertises Cuban cigars. "Why not accommodate everyone who wants to leave? Look at these prices – we have to pay twice what people on the mainland pay, but our pensions and salaries are not what they used to be. Once they get rid of the old people, they will cut the heat in our apartments and force us into barracks. It will be a camp, just like before."

Two respectable buildings rise out of the ruin that is Susuman. One is the company headquarters of Susumanzoloto ("*zoloto*" means "gold"), the second largest gold mining company in Kolyma, which has 1,100 employees who mined 5.8 tons of gold in 2002. Director General Vladimir Khristov has overseen the company's difficult transition. Paradoxically, the August 1998 default that swept away the savings of millions of Russians lent the industry a helping hand. The collapse of the ruble while having gold as an asset made it easier to pay off ruble loans. Helped by lower production costs, lax gold production and export controls, and stabilizing global gold prices, the profitability of gold mining appealed to investors. Small companies and *artels* began merging into larger groups such as "Susumanzoloto" to better adapt to a shift from seasonal placer mining to year-round and more capital-intensive lode mining. Realizing that returns from extraction of placer gold are diminishing, Khristov negotiated a $13 million credit line from Sberbank to develop the Vetrenskoye lode deposit. The company's most valuable asset, however, is the license for the development of the largest gold-ore deposit in Magadan region – Natalkinskoye, which holds an estimated 245 tons of gold in residual reserves. After investments of about $220 million, the deposit could produce up to 10-15 tons of gold a year.

The second well-kept building is the local police headquarters, with parking spots (not that Kolyma is scarce on parking space) designated for the Head of Hard Currency and the Head of OMON, the Special Police

Force. These are not typical police jobs in Russia, but Susuman is not a typical town. "Stakes are high," commented Yevgenich. "Officially, Kolyma produces about 30 tons of gold per year. A National TV program recently stated that another third gets stolen. I think this is way too high; I'd say one-fifth. With 30 percent of the locals living below the poverty line, panning for gold illegally may be the only chance for some to make ends meet. We call these prospectors *khishchniki* (predators). If the police find gold on them, they seize it, beat them up and then arrest them. Nobody knows how much gold is stolen and how much the police recover, if you know what I mean."

There is no shortage of middlemen willing to buy gold from "predators." Some of the middlemen are Ingush, a Muslim people from the Caucasus. We saw Ingush women in Susuman dressed in colorful ethnic gowns. They acted as if they owned the place. "Most of them are officially unemployed. They run their own company – 'Ingushzoloto'!'" Yevgenich laughed at his own joke. "They are close-knit and not afraid of the police because they pay everybody off. Many of the Ingush buy a license to a claim, get a loan from a commercial bank to buy equipment and go into the business of... buying gold from illegal prospectors at ridiculously low prices. I heard about desperate 'predators' swapping gold for canned meat. The Ingush then sell the gold to the bank at official rates, pay back the loan and pocket the difference. This way, they don't have to worry about shipping the metal to the mainland inside wheelchairs or cans of red caviar. They say the Ingush use the profits to finance the Chechens' war for independence. I believe it. All people from the Caucasus are like brothers."

The next morning, when Rustam, sporting his fatigues and a shiny golden smile, drove up in a beat-up Russian jeep, we realized that he had not slept since last night. "It's OK. Come October, all we'll do is sleep... Yesterday you were asking about predators. Come, I'll show you their lair."

A twenty-minute off-road drive took us into the far end of the tailings field, with islands of bushes and grass among water-filled gullies. "I saw them yesterday and hopefully did not chase them away," said Rustam, pulling the jeep to a stop. We walked the last 100 meters. All we found was a smoldering fire, empty food cans and tools. "They are around here somewhere. They dig in a few places and move between them when they sense danger. This is no joke: if OMON spots them, they may not get out of here alive." Rustam slapped a mosquito on his neck. "These predators must be a desperate and hardy bunch. Look, they are making preparations for winter," he pointed to piles of firewood covered with oil drums cut into halves and a few old tires. "They will burn tires and wood to melt snow in these oil drums, in order to sluice the gold. In -40° cold! You should see them in early spring, faces black from tire smoke, clothes reduced to oily shreds," Rustam got tired of the swarm of mosquitoes hovering around him and lit a cigarette.

"Can we try it to get a feeling of what it's like?" I asked, a wave of anticipation ran through my body. "Suit yourself. I'll tell you what to do." Rustam looked amused.

The principal tool of the predator is a *prokhodnushka*, a cradle-like box three to four feet long and two feet wide with one end open to allow water and earth to escape. The bottom is lined with riffled rubber mats and small wooden planks to hold them in place. We propped the *prokhodnushka* at an angle and placed the hopper, a huge scoop made out of a sawed-off oil drum with a perforated bottom, over its elevated end. Sergei and I were ready for some serious gold mining.

I filled a pail with gravel and sand, and emptied it into the hopper. After two more pail loads, I scooped water from a nearby hollow and poured it over the earth in the hopper. Sergei's job was to rock the hopper and mix its contents with a stick. The mixture of muddy water, small stones and sand ran through the holes into the cradle-box, over the riffled mats and out through the open lower end. We poured in more water. When only large stones were left in the hopper we set it aside and inspected the riffles. Nothing. More pails of earth and water and – could it be happening – tiny yellow specks shone on the mat.

Feeling encouraged, we worked for twenty more minutes and ended up with roughly half a gram of gold. The sun was shining brighter, the mosquitoes were kinder, and the pulsating thought was to dig, haul, and wash until the first snowfall. Call it beginner's luck or the highest concentration of gold in Kolyma, but if a dozen pails bring in this much, what would the yield be from 25-ton trucks that come in every four minutes? Conservative calculations produced a daily take from the big *pribor* in the range of 25 kilograms. We asked Rustam how off we were. The clever Ingush just gave us his golden smile: "The requisition will start in half an hour; you'll see...." The last thing we wanted at that moment, however, was to part with the *prokhodnushka*, the pail and the shovel.

On the ride back, Rustam told us about the Ingush people. "We take care of each other. This is our strength. At first, Russian foremen were suspicious of us, because we are different. Then they saw that we do not drink and are not afraid of hard work. Many Ingush became foremen or even *artel* directors like Fasil, but would be listed as Russians. When the war in Chechnya started, many problems began for us. We have lived side by side with the Chechens for centuries. We are Muslim, too, and empathize with them, but we do not want to fight the Russians. I deal just fine with the Russians in the *artel*. But many Russians think that the Ingush loathe work and live off gold smuggling. When the Governor of Magadan was gunned down in Moscow in 2002, many fingers were pointed at us. Life is tough for many here and with Russian soldiers being killed in Chechnya, it just takes one little spark..." he left the sentence unfinished.

When we returned, Ivan Ivanovich, two fellows in high rubber boots, and a roly-poly, AK47-toting guard were waiting for us. With trucks gone and the giant grizzly stopped, the place no longer looked like hell's waiting room. Ivan opened the seals on the three sluice-boxes one by one and the two guys started cleaning rocks and sand out of them. After about 15 minutes, we could see tiny nuggets and gold sand caught in the riffled rubber mats at the bottom. "Should be about a kilo and a third," estimated Ivan Ivanovich matter-of-factly. Later we learned that his margin of error was less than 50 grams. One after another, the mats were placed into a round red canister and rinsed. The canister was then sealed. The catch did not come close to our guesstimate, made on the pinnacle of our gold-mining luck. Apparently, Mother Earth does not always bestow her gifts in a predictable manner.

I asked the men how prospectors decide where to mine gold. Aside from estimating the total reserves in a particular deposit and the purity of the gold, the big factor is the gold-to-dirt ratio. If our math could still be trusted, in the last 24 hours the Belichan *artel* went through about 9,000 tons of dirt to get 1,300 grams of gold, averaging about 1.4 grams per ton. "We break even at about 1.2 grams per ton," Ivan explained. "Processing tailings rarely gets you more than 5 grams. Placer deposit yields are generally low compared to lode deposits, where gold is embedded in solid rock. Exploration drilling is expensive and most *artels* use data from 1960's geological surveys which are often inaccurate."

"Why don't you invest in reliable exploration if it means so much for your bottom line?" I asked the miners.

"You remind me of Lord Judd, this British parliamentarian who visited Chechnya," said Rustam. "He thought he had stopping the war all figured out. There was just one problem: none of his proposals made sense in Chechnya! We have a geologist on staff. You can ask *her* this question," said Rustam, emphasizing the gender.

An area of the base surrounded by barbed-wire fencing and with a viciously barking dog inside is the "golden heart" of the Belichan *artel*. Inside were a tiny hut – the geologist's office – and a second fence. Through a door with a barred peephole we entered the *sanctum sanctorum*. It was a shack where two teenage boys and a somber but amply maquillaged matron washed nuggets and golden sand from tenacious earth on a vibrating table. Looking at the silently moving brushes in the washers' hands, I thought how gold's beauty and value result from such unattractive multiples as thousands of square miles of defaced land, predators with faces black from tire soot, and these hands dancing for hours in icy water.

It was past lunchtime and we walked to the mess hall to grab a bite to eat. Andrei, a Ukrainian who had just been hired as a welder, joined us. We sat at a long table covered with an oilcloth and the ubiquitous flies. Ads for imported food aspired to give the drab walls a homey look. After serving us a meal of soup, rice with tiny pieces of meat, and a dried fruit compote, the cook wiped her hands on an apron and started warmly reminiscing about the Communists while cursing the new life. "We are like slaves. We can't leave and the jobs are few, so we are stuck with what's available. If I am lucky, by the end of the season the management will pay me whatever they feel like."

"But don't you have a contract with them?" The Lord Judd in me raised his stately head once again.

"What do we know about contracts? I signed a piece of paper today, but there was nothing there about money," interjected Andrei. The major scars on his scalp could tell a few chilling stories. "If the *artel* does well at the end of the season, we get paid. But the management may say that the cost of diesel went up or that the price of gold went down and that there is no money left. We can't say anything. We are the slaves." He thanked the cook and left.

Back at the base, Vladimir was pacing impatiently in his slippers. Once inside the car, he vented his frustration: "How will they pay back the loan in the fall, mining less than two kilos per shift? I told them to look into developing new claims. Sure, they can always buy gold on the side. Either way Fasil won't lose his shirt over it... The bank will have the headache of liquidating the dozers and trucks to get some money back... Oh well, it's only gold, right? Are you hungry? We have been invited for dinner." I was thinking about the cook and the welder and their slim chances of eating well this winter.

After a short drive, we reached the village of Kholodny, Russian for "cold." The village looked deserted and had an appropriately cold and desolate look about it. Yevgenich pointed at a huge eagle sitting motionless on a concrete fence: "That's Vitaly's pet. It's always there." An ordinary looking man dressed in a plaid shirt came out to shake hands with Vladimir Ilyich. We were introduced to Vitaly, the owner of the Fortuna *artel* and a successful gold mining entrepreneur.

"Of course, I was scared when I decided to go on my own," Vitaly said, "but the situation was so bad that I really didn't have much choice. I didn't want to leave Kolyma. You may think I'm nuts, but I like it here. Going to the mainland meant starting a new life in a new place. I said to myself, 'I know this land. I know gold mining.' So I chose to start a new life at the old place." Vitaly was talking to us at his office – a wagon-like house on wheels that is often used in Russia to house workers at construction sites. Geological maps, log books and machinery parts occupied all the free space. "I got a loan through Vladimir Ilyich and bought the machinery. I repaid the loan in one year and took another one. I borrowed only what I needed for mining, not a ruble for myself. I do not sleep well when I owe money." He had a good smile.

"Come, I'll show you something," Vitaly motioned. We stepped outside and walked to the far side of the lot. We heard them before we saw them: a dozen or so piglets were feeding next to their mothers. Adjacent was an enclosure with goats and a chicken coop. Behind it were greenhouses with tomatoes, cucumbers and squash.

Vitaly proudly showed us around. "We grow our own food. The boys are happy. I bought a grocery store in the village that my wife runs, so she can sell any excess produce. You know, the ground we are standing on is the site where I first prospected 12 years ago. When I started this *artel* I wanted the base to be here. I had to bring a lot of topsoil for greenhouses and livestock and to insulate the soil so that the permafrost does not slow down the growth."

The dinner table was set outside with vodka and deliciously tender salmon caught and smoked by our host. The main course was boiled caribou hunted by Vitaly. "Caribou are easily scared and dash for the woods before you can come close enough to take a shot. I chase them from an ATV, but never kill more than what we can eat. I got two this time and gave one to the boys in the field." The caribou meat was chewy, but tasty, and the broth, spiced with local herbs, was robust and fragrant. "You may hear people say that Kolyma's days are numbered and that it is just a matter of time before Russia gives it to the Chinese or Japanese as a concession or sells it, just like Alaska. We'll bite our elbows if we do. I feel I own a claim on this land in more senses than one, and I'm staying put."

When we were leaving, Vitaly's eagle turned its head and gave us a stern look. The vodka and the warm evening light must have had something to do with it, but the empty streets and lopsided houses of Kholodny did not look quite as cold. But that was not the only reason. I was thinking about Vitaly. His grandfather was exiled here as a *kulak*. His father stayed because, after Stalin's death, life in Kolyma did not seem that bad. Two generations later, Vitaly was building wealth in the land where his grandfather had been forced to toil for the benefit of those who had taken away everything he had worked for.

THE NEXT DAY, Yevgenich took us to the Shkolnoye underground mine. Nikolai, our guide on the track inside the mountain, gave us orange helmets with headlamps and battery packs. A fellow with a face that betrayed a lifelong affair with alcohol handed us padded jackets: "Take these, or you'll freeze your a-- off," he blurted. Dark and cold, the mountain's innards felt alive with muffled noises. As we went further, condensation painted every surface in shades of white, giving the place an eerie, out-of-this-world look. We came across a welder strengthening the ceiling supports. The light of his torch illuminated an endless tunnel with numerous branches.

In eleven years as a miner, Nikolai has worked throughout Siberia and the Russian Far East, but Kolyma was his favorite. "It must be the hardship and the climate that make people here so unique. Have you heard the joke that winter is here for twelve months and the rest is summer? Well, it does take a special kind of a person to live here. It also takes a special type of friendship, because a man can't survive here by himself. I can be making the same kind of money [$620-680 a month] elsewhere in Russia, but it won't be the same. You have to live here to understand. I know guys who left and came back after a year or two. I guess Kolyma conditions humans a certain way."

We clearly fell short of the Kolyma spirit: with gold veins still a mile ahead, Sergei and I turned back, overcome by cold and by what we later found out were residual explosive gases. The smell of the outside air and the light at the end of the tunnel suddenly took on new meaning. I stepped out into the warm sunlight and acknowledged to myself that I was indeed a warm-blooded, diurnal animal. My frozen fingers resisted attempts to unbutton the loaner jacket. My mind reeled as it grappled to understand how inured to hardship one has to be to commit to not seeing the light of day for weeks on end.

The visit continued at a processing plant, where ore from the mine is crushed into powder in giant cylindrical mills by eight-inch steel balls. Dust was everywhere. Crushed ore is mixed with water and circulated through tanks containing a weak solution of sodium cyanide, to dissolve the gold. The solution is then separated from the rock pulp, which is filtered off to a tailings lake lined with 1/16-inch thick plastic – the only barrier between low-concentration cyanide and the environment. Zinc powder is mixed into the solution to make gold, silver and copper precipitate. Gold is then removed by filtration, melted down and cast into so-called gold doré bars containing about 90 percent fine. The solution is sent back to the leaching circuit. The doré bars are then sent to an off-site refinery near Magadan, where they are smelted into bullion.

"Are you turning into mining pros?" joked Vladimir Ilyich back in the car.

"Getting to know what Kolyma is all about?" Yevgenich played along.

This stretch of the Road of Bones had plenty of sharp turns and passes. The name of one of them surprised us – the "Rio Rita Pass." Yevgenich told us the story. The prisoners who built the road over this pass in 1949 had a gramophone with only one record, which happened to be from the soundtrack to the Abbot and Costello film. I imagined starved and exhausted men in scruffy clothes pushing heavy wheelbarrows to foxtrot music. This little glimpse into what Kolyma was all about moved me more than Magadan's colossal "Mask of Mourning" Memorial to the Victims of Stalinism.

Behind the next curve, two men were squatting by the side of the road. A flatbed truck carrying an ATV was lying on its side in a ditch 15 feet below, apparently the result of an accident. Yevgenich made no sign of slowing down. Through the rear window I saw the two men, their posture unchanged, looking lost yet resolute.

"Should we stop and offer help?" I asked Vladimir.

"They did not motion us to stop, so we shouldn't," he said, sounding as if he was explaining the obvious. "They may be drunk, or their documents may not be in order, or they may need to be elsewhere right now. The last thing they want is to attract the attention of strangers. It is their problem and they will take care of it the way they know. In this part of the world, you stay out of other people's business. And forget about insurance – they can't afford any," added Vladimir Ilyich, anticipating a Lord Judd type of question.

"What about people helping each other and that special Kolyma spirit?" I knew I was pushing it.

"We drive the wrong type of car and that's where the spirit stops. It is not a classless society anymore." The finality in his voice told me the topic had run its course.

We took a detour to check some equipment Vladimir Ilyich's bank had a lien on because an *artel* went insolvent. A half a dozen Komatsu and Caterpillar trucks and bulldozers slept under the watchful eyes of two guards who were cooking lunch over an open fire and who almost jumped to attention upon seeing the Land Cruiser.

On the way back, I saw something moving in the distance and asked Yevgenich to stop. "Predators," he said without much emotion. "They ducked when we first passed here, but didn't expect us to come back that fast and did not take cover." Sergei and I exchanged glances. "Look, if you want to get whacked over the head with a shovel..." Yevgenich started. But we were already out of the car and walking towards the two men who stopped whatever they were doing and were just staring at our cameras and camcorder. Then we saw the dog, a big German shepherd one of them was holding by the collar.

"Your dog will not hurt us if we come closer, will it?" I asked, making the first attempt at dialogue. They did not encourage us to, so we stayed a few feet away while talking with them.

Their day is off to a good start when they get a lift. If not, it is a 40-minute walk along the main road and another 40-minute shortcut to the site. Then it is 14 hours of digging and shoveling. Pavel used to be a metal worker. Vladimir used to work at a school that closed down. Both dig for gold mainly to support their families. They actually have an official permit to "explore," but not to mine gold. The punitive raids of the OMON made illegal panning too dangerous.

"If you didn't have papers, they would start by breaking or burning your gear. Then they'd beat you up 'for preventative measures' if they didn't find gold on you." Between the two of them, Pavel was the talker. "Otherwise, one gram of gold means one year in jail. But now they realize that our grams are nothing compared to the hundreds of kilos funneled through organized crime routes, so first-time offenders get a suspended sentence."

"The water is way too far from here, but this old river bank is a decent spot, so we pick at its side with metal sticks, looking for larger specks and small nuggets," Pavel explained, letting go of the dog to show us their instruments. "On a good day, we get four grams that we can sell for about R200 ($6.50) per gram.[2] To whom? We do not really care, as long as they pay. Of course, it isn't much. We'll be in really good shape if we could get seven grams per day."

Would they switch to something else? Yes, if the job paid well, which automatically excludes going back to metalworking or teaching. Would they move? Moving to another village makes no sense, as any village can become a candidate for demolition. Moving to Magadan and beyond is unrealistic. What are their plans for winter? "We'll shovel coal at the central boiler that heats the village. We may get lucky next summer, though. A couple of settlements nearby will be razed to the ground and rumor has it that they sit on some placer gold."

Pavel and Vladimir are but two of the many faceless captives of liberal reforms for whom the change of seasons means a change of shovels. The paradoxical misnomer of "predators" with which they have been branded betrays the reversal of attributes that has always been handy for

....
2. At the time this article was published, the world market price for gold was about $13 per gram.

manipulating the perception of the masses. Even today, enigmatic Kolyma has a relentless hold over its inhabitants.

THE LAST DETOUR of the trip proved to be one of the most memorable. After an almost idyllic drive on a dry riverbed, we came to the ruins of the Butugychag Uranium Mining Camp. Decades ago, prisoners mined tin and uranium in the surrounding hills and then brought the blasted ore down to the valley for processing. Railroad beds, ore wagon cars and mine workings were visible at the summit. "There is a little graveyard halfway up the hillside," Vladimir Ilyich spoke slowly. "It took a lot of effort to dig graves in the permafrost, so most bodies were stacked in the unused shafts. When the shafts were full, the camp administration would blow up the entrance. After the Americans dropped their [atomic] bombs on Japan, we had to have our own [uranium], whatever the price."

Although the wooden structures of the camp had been burned when the mines were abandoned in 1953, it was easy to see where they stood. We came across a stone barrack with grilled windows, overgrown with willow herb. Here and there we stumbled upon a boot sole, an aluminum plate or an empty food tin.

"See this white building in the middle of the valley?" Vladimir said. "It used to be an uranium-processing factory and barrels leaking uranium were found there. I am not sure they've cleaned them up since. I suggest we don't hang around here for too long." We hesitated to leave and continued to wander about the site, unable to satisfy our compulsion to find a conduit into the past, to understand what it was like to be a prisoner here fifty years ago.

We were flying back to the mainland the next morning. The sign, "Welcome to Kolyma – the Golden Heart of Russia" still greeted new arrivals at the airport. Its cruel irony was now readily apparent. What sign greeted the Gulag prisoners when they walked ashore in Magadan after a gut-wrenching voyage in cargo holds? What slogans greeted those who came here in the 1960s, full of youthful ardor and a belief in Communism's human face, only to realize a generation later that they had given their best to a country that was no longer and that the new Russia does not have a place for these prisoners of freedom.

Where in fact is the Golden Heart of Russia if not in Kolyma? Is it in Moscow, where you can casually spend for lunch what a laborer elsewhere in Russia makes in a week? When you get off the eight-hour flight from Magadan, Moscow feels like another country. In fact, being just 50 miles out of Moscow feels like another country. What empathy can it then have for the rest of Russia?

Take away Kolyma's gold, Yakutia's diamonds and Siberia's oil and gas, and Moscow's $300-an-hour spas will run out of steam. For now, Moscow seems oblivious to the needs of the hand that feeds it. Eventually it will have to face the consequences. What will happen by then to the 200,000 people (down from 300,000 in 1989), still calling Kolyma home and cursed to live through interesting times?

July/August 2004

May the Earth Be as Soft as Feathers
Laura Williams

My neighbor Yevdokia Balakhonova, known by her patronymic Trofimovna, died on November 9. But no one noticed that day. A blizzard, the first of winter, raged over the village of Chukhrai. Three days later, my husband Igor passed her house and noticed that no smoke was coming from the chimney. Trofimovna always stoked up the stove in the early morning, just before dawn.

Igor knocked on the door, but there was no answer. He peered in the window. The overstuffed bed with overstuffed pillows where she usually slept was empty, the covers pulled back.

Silence loomed. Suddenly a cat appeared in the window and began to scratch feverishly, trying to get out. Igor bent back the nails holding in one of the small panes, and the cat shot out. That's when Igor told me Trofimovna was dead.

Not a week earlier, I had watched from my window the old lady sawing wood. She heaved a large log onto a sawhorse and began to ply at it with her two-man saw, pushing it forward and back. The long saw bent and shuddered as Trofimovna pushed, then grew taut as she pulled.

The villagers find Trofimovna in the foyer, lying on her back, her stockinged feet wedged up against the door, her arms splayed out to the sides. Her long, gray hair is fanned out around her head. Rats have eaten half her face. One eye stares at the ceiling. Her yellow teeth are clenched together.

A man from the village makes a coffin. Two of the women wash and dress Trofimovna in a never-before-worn blue suit from her wardrobe. Trofimovna always wore an old ragged jacket, which had been patched and mended in a dozen places. It hung loosely over her humped back and the long cloth for a skirt she wrapped around her small waist. On her feet she donned rubber boots. In the winter, she added a dirty gray jacket of wadded cotton and several layers of thick, wool stockings under her skirt.

She pulled *valenki* over her feet, warm boots made of thick pressed felt. That was her entire line of apparel, which changed only with the seasons, not with the fashions.

The two village drunks are commandeered to dig the grave. They are assured a sufficient allowance of moonshine, to be paid for out of Trofimovna's bequest. (The villagers found 9,000 rubles – $300 – stashed under her floorboards). I am asked to host the wake, as Trofimovna's house is too small and cold. Igor and I make *borsch*, *blini*, and *kisel* (berry juice thickened with starch).

When everything is ready, four men carry the coffin – a plain box of pine boards crudely nailed together – out of her house. Small and narrow, it is scarcely big enough to house Trofimovna's body, shrunken with age and pulled down by gravity. The coffin is placed on a sleigh pulled by two men. I am directed to the front of the procession with a wreath of fake flowers, just behind my other neighbor Glukhaya (Deaf Woman), who holds an icon wrapped in a white cloth. The rest of the villagers follow. Two men toss spruce bows along the way to the cemetery, to help the soul find its way home.

We arrive at the small cemetery, which is enclosed by a wooden fence falling down in places. I walk over to the freshly dug pit. A pile of brown dirt flanks one side, dark in contrast with the white snow. Several bones jut from the pile of dirt. A cracked skull watches from the ground next to the pile. My 83-year-old friend Olga Ivanovna tells me that they are the bones of Trofimovna's ancestors. Each family has their own section in the cemetery, so no one has to rest eternally with the bones of someone with whom they weren't on speaking terms. People have been buried here for 300 years, she explains, and the cemetery has always been the same size.

The villagers approach the now open coffin for one last farewell, quietly saying, *"Pust tebe pukhom budet zemlya"* ("May the earth be as soft as feathers"), then cross themselves and move away. I hold back, afraid I might do something out of protocol. All I can see are Trofimovna's hands, lying on her midriff, the fingers of one hand cupping the fingers of the other. They are not pale or blue, but seemingly full of blood, full of life. Her hands are muscular, yet bony. The fingers are crooked, yet graceful in the way they arch. These are the hands that she lived by, the hands that sowed seeds, plucked weeds, kneaded bread, chopped firewood, milked the cow. At last, her hands have come to rest.

The men loudly nail the lid on the coffin, then lower it slowly into the pit. They shovel the dirt onto the plain wooden box and toss the bones back in the hole. Two men thrust a cross made of thick oak beams into the newly formed mound. No words are said.

We file out of the cemetery to our house for the wake. This was the moment the men had been waiting for. The booze would flow to honor the dead woman. The 18 villagers funnel into our small kitchen.

I dish out the *borsch*, only one ladle in each bowl to make sure there is enough. Igor fills the glasses with moonshine. The villagers begin to drink without a word.

Then Igor interjects, "To Trofimovna – she was a hard worker."

Yes, they agree. She was a difficult woman, but she was a hard worker.

The men drain their glasses, mopping their mouths with bread. When the food is gone, they depart one by one. Some of them wobble from drink, and one falls and nearly shatters the glass in the kitchen window.

On the ninth day after Trofimovna's death, when God is said to pass judgment on the soul, we hold another wake at the cemetery. I spread a tablecloth over Trofimovna's grave and cut bread and sausage. There are only three glasses for the whole village, so we fill them with drink and pass them around. No words are said. It saddens me that most of the villagers have come not to remember Trofimovna, but to drink at her expense.

January/February 2004

The Coldest Village on Earth
Nick Allen

*I*s there no Russian winter in Russia anymore? After weeks of the mercury hovering around zero in a slushy, filthy Moscow, it was looking that way.

So, in preparation for the day when youngsters in the family line would sit on my knee and ask about my time in Russia ("What did you do in the cold, grandpa?"), I set course for the worst Siberia has to offer: Oymyakon, Yakutia. Oymyakon holds the title of the world's coldest permanently inhabited settlement. In 1926, a ferocious -71.2° Celsius (-96.2° F) was registered there.

It is said that, in this log cabin village of some 1,000 souls, spit freezes into a pellet in mid-flight, breath crystallizes and audibly tinkles to the ground, plastic carrier bags stiffen and snap in two.

It sounded perfect.

AFTER A SIX-HOUR flight to the republican capital of Yakutsk, I find the locals are baffled why anyone would spend their vacation time pursuing monster frosts in remote climes.

"Normal people don't come here, only the scum of the earth," said Seva, a 30-year-old heating engineer who said he fled the law in his homeland of Ukraine, for reasons he would not clarify.

Meanwhile, Yakutsk's respectable -40° C already produces some bizarre phenomena: the earbuds of my CD player freeze stiff on the wire and bounce around in front of my face like a pair of deely-boppers. I hear reports of -60° C in Eastern Yakutia two days previous. This is starting to look promising.

Another two-hour flight leads to the Oymyakon district center, Ust-Nera, a rundown shanty town of crumbling apartment blocks, snaking outdoor heating pipes, frozen rubbish tips and shells of jeeps and buses that serve as sheds. The town's only claim to fame appears to be a lavish visit in distant Soviet times by the son of the Iranian Shah. The heir apparent booked the town's entire hotel (now dismally dilapidated) for his entourage during a hunting trip, hoping to bag one of the region's prized spiral-horned mountain rams.

Today, Ust-Nera exists largely as a staging post for workers in the gold-mining industry and for offbeat travelers on their way to the *Polyus Kholoda*, or "Cold Pole," as Oymyakon is proudly known.

Visitors to the Cold Pole in recent years have hailed from Germany, Britain, the Czech Republic and Japan, arriving by plane, car and even bicycle to confront the infamous temperatures.

"These are people who are prepared to rough it, they don't need luxury hotels, but stay with families, go hunting, ride reindeer," said Vitaly Kondakov, head of tourist development in the district.

Kondakov motions to a poster of a resplendent, silver-bearded figure on the wall: this is Chishaan, the Yakutian Santa Claus, who is now charged with the task of attracting more tourists to the Cold Pole for its annual festival in March. Beyond diamonds, gold, timber and oil, Yakutia has evidently cottoned on to the potential of another of its plentiful natural resources: the cold. All the festival needs now is a star guest from overseas, hence the hopeful invite sent this year by the republic to California's Governor Arnold Schwarzenegger.

I ARRANGE A $40 ride in one of the ubiquitous UAZ minivans to travel 400 kilometers to Tomtor, the next village to Oymyakon. It's an uncomfortable eight-hour haul, lurching through the taiga forest and over frozen rivers in the knowledge that a truck hurtling the other way can bat you down the hillside to join the other wrecks.

The onset of a warm front is equally disturbing. The mercury infuriatingly rises to -30° C, which, if it holds, will be like diving at Sharm el-Sheikh and seeing no fish.

I spend the night in Tomtor, 40 kilometers from my goal, where I am introduced the next morning to the head of the Oymyakon village administration and given the red carpet treatment on the last leg of the journey. Like a few dozen foreign guests before me, I am accommodated in a private home for a very market-wise $25 a day, and the locals attentively take me under their wing in this most unlikely of tourist destinations.

Initially, I feel somewhat conspicuous – within a few hours everyone knows who I am and what I am doing here, such is the lightning speed of the local grapevine. But the Yakuts are now accustomed to the appearance of thermometer-fixated foreigners, and not just those in their prime.

"Here I successfully experienced an air temperature of minus 51 degrees," 84-year-old Japanese tourist Ishiko Honzo wrote in a visitor's book last February, while visiting with a group of octogenarians wishing to test their mettle.

"Minus 50 or 60 is unthinkable for most people and they come to see how it is possible to live in such conditions," said Albina Vinokurova, director of studies at the village school.

Paradoxically, "Oymyakon" means "river that doesn't freeze" in Evenk. A tiny tributary of the Indigirka river in the village never freezes, because warm springs bubble up underneath it.

Situated 350 kilometers from the Arctic Circle, Oymyakon's latitude and continental climate combine with its valley location some 2000 meters above sea level to produce a pocket of intense cold, earning it the Cold Pole status. Winter temperatures usually plummet to the mid – 60s, but not today. I glumly note that it is still only a paltry -38°. As the population happily goes about its daily business, remarking how "warm" it is, doubts start to arise: "Where am I and what am I doing here?"

Perhaps a friend in Moscow was right when he declined an invitation to travel with me, saying, "Why would I go halfway round the world just to see people with frozen moustaches?"

Mercifully, the natural spirits revered by the pagan Yakuts apparently heeded my silent prayers. A day later, a searing -56° shroud drops on the village, and its foggy paths beckon.

If Oymyakon basks in unspoiled nature in summer, there is little to see in winter except for the monument to the lowest temperature, measured 78 years ago by Russian geographer Sergei Obruchev. But tramping around in multiple layers of clothing is an adrenalin-pumping exercise in itself. The temperature is a few degrees lacking for the full range of cold phenomena like freezing spit and breath, but exhaled gusts thicken with a gratifying roar, as if I am blowing in the embers of a fire. My cheeks start to burn and my eyebrows turn to small thickets of frost. I am without furs and *unty* reindeer skin boots, so the cold penetrates to my bones in just a few minutes. Daytime forays are therefore kept short, not to mention the unavoidable ones at night. After Oymyakon, people riding bicycles over canyons or groping around in vats full of snakes no longer impress – the true "fear factor" is a trip to an unlit outhouse when it is -50° C.

THIS CHALLENGE MET, I offer thanks to the vast night sky. The stars are vivid here as in few places on Earth. As an unexpected bonus, the aurora borealis, or Northern Lights, spread out in a salad green display. The most spectacular lightshows coincide with the coldest spells. More northerly towns in Yakutia like Tiksi are blessed with a greater frequency of lightshows, so much so that a hotel was built there to cater to Japanese couples who seek out the lights, in the belief, said tourism chief Kondakov, that a child conceived beneath their tumbling columns will grow up to be a genius.

Beyond the rigors of the cold, the local diet is also not for vegetarians or the faint-of-heart. A mid-morning snack of horsemeat and bread may be followed by a lunch of moose and macaroni, and a supper featuring cow entrail soup and rabbit. Fresh vegetables and fruit are luxuries that have to be brought in from the South.

Inbound transport has been limited since the suspension of regular flights to Tomtor from Yakutsk in the 1990s, due to rising costs. Special runs by twin-propped Antonov-24 planes service the Cold Pole festival, but otherwise travelers must come the round-a-bout route via Ust-Nera, or drive from Yakutsk, jolting 18 hours along 1000 kilometers of ice-clad taiga road and dizzying mountain passes.

A calendar highlight is the annual motor rally along the route from Yakutsk to Oymyakon, a chilly alternative to the Paris-Dakar race that is drawing an increasing number of competitors from overseas. Oymyakon and Tomtor will this year hold their fourth Festival of the Cold Pole, capping the road rally with a program of festivities that feature Chishaan, Santa Claus and Russia's Grandfather Frost, if not Governor Schwarzenegger. And, of course, the frosts, which are slightly abated by March, but still formidable.

Last year's harshest period brought -65° C. "We'll never get -71° again, because of global warming," said Valery Vinokurov, a weather monitor for the regional meteorological service.

OYMYAKON'S ICY SUPREMACY is challenged by the Yakut town of Verkhoyansk, located 400 kilometers further north, inside the Arctic Circle. It has a well-documented winter low of -68° C, and some say Obruchev's reading of -71.2° C was not properly witnessed. This year, Oymyakon hoped for an exceptionally bitter winter in the presence of a visiting team of German meteorologists. "We are counting on them," Vinokurov laughed. "If they record -68°, then there will be no more discussion."

Oymyakon is remote but not completely cut off from the fads and troubles of the *materik,* or mainland, as they say here, meaning Moscow and European Russia. In the chaotic general store, shotgun cartridges are piled in a box with bubble gum, and chunks of animal fat are sold alongside Ninja Turtle toys. A few kilometers outside the village, I think I've found a timeless snapshot of Yakutia, as I sip tea with two horse farmers in their cabin, which is lined with skins and has only a hurricane lamp for light. But, sensing an additional presence, I glance over my shoulder and see Frodo gazing down at me from a glossy Lord of the Rings poster.

Drugs and HIV are not established problems yet, but alcohol abuse is, said social worker Aksenia Sibtseva. The village's three young men who did combat tours in Chechnya all started drinking heavily when they returned. One died in a fishing accident on the river last year, another hanged himself a few days before I arrived. The third is in a rapid downward spiral.

Generally, however, people here enjoy sturdy health and live to a ripe old age, even though the climactic fluctuations are hard on the body. The main natural cause of death is stroke caused by sudden pressure changes in winter, as the temperature soars and plummets. By contrast, the short summers in the valley are stifling, as temperatures rise to +35° C (95° F). Thus, the temperature span between the record high and low readings in this remote village is a staggering 109°.

But even in summer, Yakutia's icy mantle is never far away. Dig down a meter and you hit the concrete that is permafrost. Many homes in the republic improvise an additional refrigerator in the form of a pit under the floor, ensuring that food products stay cool even in the baking heat.

In winter, the ground is rock solid to the surface, posing problems for funerals, for which fires are lit in the cemetery to defrost the soil deep enough to dig a grave. It's a race against the clock, however, as, according to local beliefs, the dead must be buried within three days.

The effects of the cold on the human body intrigue the village doctor, Alexandra Yakovleva, who runs the village's 10-bed hospital. "I have worked all over Yakutia," she said, "and can say that people are very healthy here in

Oymyakon, they live a long time. Evidently, there is some kind of link with the frosts. In Southern Yakutia, where it's warmer, the children are more prone to sickness. But, for example, we don't get flu epidemics here."

There are practically no cases of cancer, Yakovleva said, and surprisingly few intestinal complaints, despite the fatty, meat-intensive diet. But the doctor does point to a worrying increase in alcoholism, which is blamed for many of the unruly incidents that occur in the village.

Apart from the occasional drunk and disorderly outbursts, though, crime is said to be generally limited to domestic fights and altercations between neighbors. There is no policeman here and most matters are sorted out by the local administration. More serious cases are referred to two Russian officers based in Tomtor, and to the prosecutor's office in Ust-Nera if necessary, said deputy administration head Gavril Gotovtsev.

The crime situation was far worse in the 1990s, when, like rural communities all across Russia, Oymyakon foundered after the Soviet collapse. Most of its services were cut and the town reverted to a largely hunter-gatherer existence.

"It was a terrible period," recalled teacher Vinokurova. "We received no wages, the shop was empty, there was lots of crime, theft, even murder. Now life is normalizing; young people are having more children; classes at the school are growing."

Last year, the village finally got some real money from the republican budget and things are slowly on the mend. It is just in time, it would seem, as the local landscape and fauna show the strain.

"We can't live on hunting like we used to, there are too many people and not enough animals," said villager Mariana Tylgina. "Now the hunters have to go farther and farther."

Funds and work may be appearing, but unemployment still rises and falls with the seasons. Some of the men get summer jobs at the region's gold mine, located about 30 kilometers up the river Indigirka; others work as stokers at the coal-fired heating plant, or they might save for a second-hand UAZ van and earn a living driving goods and passengers to and from Yakutsk. The average monthly wage here is less than $150, but most families supplement their income and larder by keeping a few head of cattle. Creature comforts are limited, but everyone tells of projects to improve their homes and village life in general. The town has just completed a large new school, and now plans to resurrect the post office, which was shut down in the last decade.

People are also counting the days until the installation of a modern, outbound phone line and internet connection. The enthusiasm here contrasts starkly with other villages I've visited in Russia, where people have wearily retreated into a bottle and are waiting for the community to die.

Perhaps there's just too much to do to simply quit. The short summer is spent fishing and hunting moose, ram and bear, gathering firewood and making hay for the grueling months ahead. Winter means full combat with the elements, keeping the homes heated, repairing burst pipes, tending cattle in all temperatures and coaxing life from frozen vehicles for the supply runs to Yakutsk. In short, the year in Oymyakon is every bit as busy as in the Russian capital, 5,000 kilometers away.

"Life here is a constant bustle, like being on a wheel," said Gotovtsev. "But we like this bustle, this life of ours."

At the end-of-term sports competition for the region's teachers, a microphone is thrust into my hand at the closing banquet. Before I leave this far corner of the country, apparently I am expected to share my impressions both orally and musically. I manage a rusty version of "You are my Sunshine," and improvise a toast to cold climes and warm people.

Now, back in Moscow's slush-drenched rat race, I can confirm that Real Russian Winter lives on in Oymyakon – all nine months of it.

March/April 2004

Their Lives for Their Art
Maria Antonova

$\mathcal{J}$ust 20 kilometers outside hectic Moscow sits the tiny village of Zhostovo, unfazed by its proximity to the busy capital. Houses that line the main street have picture-perfect wooden lattices, carefully tended gardens, and it is clear that most who live here are not victims of the daily commute to the megapolis. In fact, even on a weekday one hears saws ringing in garages and can watch wood carvings taking shape in front yards.

The saws and sculptures hint at the magic at work in this rural oasis: most of Zhostovo's residents are artists and craftspeople, connected to the nearly two centuries of folk craft tradition that goes into the making of Zhostovo metal trays.

In 1825, two serfs bought their freedom and organized a tray painting business. The Vishnyakov brothers had an entrepreneurial streak: they rapidly expanded, opening workshops in nearby villages, and selling their products as far afield as Moscow and Nizhny Novgorod. Special orders were even rushed to St. Petersburg.

Zhostovo is just one of hundreds of Russian towns that specialize in a specific folk or artisan craft. Fedoskino lacquered miniatures, Gzhel blue-white pottery, Vologda lace and Rostov enamelware – every region has some specialty; every natural resource has some niche. In most instances, the crafts were developed by peasants and were highly practical items like children's toys, spinning wheels, and kitchenware. Their enchanting and unpretentious designs were often inspired by folk tales, Orthodox religion, nature, and daily life, and the skill at making them was handed down from generation to generation, traditions and canons well-preserved by the insular artisan communities.

Walk a little further down the main road in Zhostovo and a dusty, gray, three-story building rises before you like a spaceship inserted among the small houses. This is the Zhostovo Factory, village eyesore and source of the famous trays. During the peak of their popularity in the 1980s, many traditional folk crafts were produced in factory conditions – in bare rooms and tiled corridors with fluorescent lights, all but severing their traditional roots. Today, many of the factories stand empty or half-idle, while a quiet renaissance of small-scale producers tries to take hold outside their walls.

LOCATED AT THE other end of the Moscow region from Zhostovo is the town of Gzhel. The word *"gzhel"* comes from *"glinu zhech"* or "firing clay." The cluster of villages here is home to a distinctive blue-and-white patterned ceramic pottery, a popular Russian souvenir, a poor cousin of Dutch Delft or British Wedgwood, and a maverick of sorts in the world of traditional Russian crafts.

Prior to the 1917 revolution, Gzhel was popularly known as "the Russian Staffordshire," referring to Britain's famous porcelain center. Gzhel produced massive amounts of porcelain, yet no decorative style dominated. The best individual craftsmen were instead known for their majolica pottery decorated with colorful scenes from daily village life. After the revolution, Lenin's New Economic Policy allowed both state and private workshops to trade in folk crafts, and a cooperative workshop with the optimistic name, "Forward, Ceramics!" briskly sold little figurines made of red clay, as well as other small items of little artistic value.

The blue-and-white style was not introduced until after World War II, when, due to post-war scarcities, the only color glaze to be had was cobalt. Yet it became the cornerstone of Gzhel crafts as they exist to this day. While postwar training programs and upscaling of production and employment gave Gzhel new life, it would not be quite correct to call Gzhel porcelain "traditional."

In its golden years in the 1970s and 1980s, the United Gzhel factory employed some 2,300 people and was the poster child for successful Soviet artisan producers. Children in local schools began painting blue birds and flowers as early as kindergarten, finishing their education in the nearby ceramics institute. Most aspects of life for area residents revolved around the craft in one way or another, and the style gained popularity and artistic acceptance.

So successful was the town that plans were put forward to create a National Folk Craft Center: a theme park with cultural centers, hotels, restaurants, and artist boarding schools. Those ambitions never got beyond the blueprint stage.

Meanwhile, the factory is little changed since its heyday. There are the "Wall of Fame" photos, a bust of Lenin, and echoing, stark hallways. Yet there is one important difference: today there are only about 200 employees left at United Gzhel. Salaries are low and late, and bankruptcy proceedings have been thrice started and stopped. Women in the painting room sigh as they look through old Gzhel catalogs and photo albums. Director Vladimir Loginov spends a good deal of his time and energy filing lawsuits against local government representatives, who he says are illegally selling off the factory's clay-rich land, in the process ravaging local culture.

"They are knowingly destroying our heritage and restraining the production of the factory. For example, we recently had to close down our factory shop in Moscow," Loginov said, unable to pinpoint whether the cause of his struggles was the authorities or the imitation Gzhel producers.

Loginov and his factory are an example of how a successful Soviet enterprise can dysfunction in today's market environment. In the Soviet era, artists never had to worry about sales or marketing. They had just one customer, the state, and no competitors in their field. But today the market is awash in cheap counterfeits and the former state enterprise needs subsidies just to limp along. As for the artists, many have changed careers, while others have learned new crafts that can be done at home.

Loginov is quick to criticize those who left the factory to open their own Gzhel manufacturing operations: they are traitors interested only in self-enrichment; they are diluting traditional Gzhel canons with their irresponsible designs, and they can often sell more cheaply because of their tax avoidance. Critics, meanwhile, say that Loginov, who has been in charge of the factory for 30 years, is incapable of adapting, that he seeks to fix new problems with tired old tools like reintroduction of state subsidies and monopolies.

One of the "traitors" from United Gzhel is Valentin Rozanov, head artist at the nearby Gzhel Porcelain factory. A recognized master, Rozanov started his career at United Gzhel and rose to become head artist there, but eventually left in the turbulent 1990s, due to perennially late salary payments. Under his leadership, Gzhel Porcelain is doing quite well (its output even winning praise from art experts), despite the onslaught of cheap counterfeits and high taxes that plague all craft producers.

ZHOSTOVO FACTORY WENT through many of the same problems as United Gzhel, struggling to make electricity and land tax payments on its inefficient Soviet-sized factory, constantly running behind on artists' salaries. After stumbling through the 1990s, the state-run enterprise went bankrupt. Artists moved their painting operations to their homes but struggled for lack of a distribution model or adequate equipment.

Three years ago, an investor bought the Zhostovo factory and sent in Natalia Logvinova to be its director. She reports that orders are now plentiful and salaries are paid on time. The only thing lacking, she said, is new artists. "I think there was a lost generation during the transition period of the 1990s, when folk crafts weren't prestigious," Logvinova said. "But children who are very young today are likely to take on the old traditions."

The village is the perfect environment for that – every family in Zhostovo seems to have something to do with the craft. Even everyday signs like "Beware of Dog" or house numbers are painted on trays. And the artists in the main studio of the factory are mostly local women. "My mother was also a painter, and my grandfather worked at the factory as a driver," said Natalia, one of the women, as she etched a precise golden border on a round tray.

Although there are also individual artists in Zhostovo that work outside the factory, Logvinova said the company does not consider them a threat to the craft. "The interesting thing about traditional folk crafts is that they have to be done in a group," she said. "People that splinter off keep working for a while, using their skill, but they stop developing as artists." And while individuals may veer right and left from the canons of the Zhostovo bouquet, she said, the group at the factory holds the center. Yet the outlines of that center can be a bit fuzzy. While factory artists specialize in trays, they also take special orders to decorate mobile phones, drum sets and even cars. Clearly there are compromises to be made when running a traditional folk craft business in the modern world.

Indeed, there is a perennial conflict between art and the business of art. What is good for the tradition? What is good for the artist? What is good for the enterprise? Did the struggling factories provide the best atmosphere for artisans in the late Soviet era, keeping traditions alive? Or did mass production stunt artistic growth?

The decision to put artists in factory conditions was actually criticized by art historians at the time, even in the circumscribed atmosphere of

Soviet discourse. Today, while old-timers like Loginov advocate the factories' protection, the buildings seem atavistic. "Factories today are not necessary, they are unprofitable and meaningless," said art historian Natalia Gayevskaya of the Russian Museum of Decorative and Folk Art. "For crafts like Gzhel, there are some benefits in industrializing the process, since it requires very high temperatures. But most other crafts were traditionally done at home, where artisans wove or carved and took care of their household at the same time, selling craft items to wandering merchants."

A perfect example of such home-spun craft is the Bogorodskoye carved toy. This tradition began in fifteenth century Sergiyev Posad, a town just north of Moscow that is home to the famous monastery founded by Sergiy of Radonezh. Legend has it that Sergiy made wooden spoons and toys and gave them away to children who visited the monastery. Bogorodskoye, which is 22 kilometers north of Sergiyev Posad, eventually developed its own carving tradition: toys often feature a peasant *muzhik* or a bear, and sometimes the two of them together. Bogorodskoye toys are never painted and have strings and levers to make the characters come alive, chopping wood or drinking tea. Masterfully carved and humorous, they embody traditions of Russian village life.

Bogorodskoye village carvers united into a cooperative in 1913. In 1960, the factory building was constructed to commemorate the 300th anniversary of the craft. Yet, since carving work is done exclusively by hand, the benefits of a factory are not immediately clear. Today, the building is almost totally deserted and acts mostly as the middle-man between carvers and potential clients, with a small museum and shop on the first floor. Where once 300 employees worked here, today only a handful still sit at the factory benches, and most rooms are let out to firms that have nothing to do with carving. Salaries range from 1,500 to 2,500 rubles a month, and, though many employees still bring their work to the factory, it is no secret that they earn most of the money through other contracts.

Mikhail, the only person carving in the second-floor workshop of the main building on a Friday afternoon, said he holds down another job and comes only for a few hours a week. Sergei, a carver at the factory's nearby artists' workshop, was working on an individual project – a sculpture of an angel for his apartment. "After we finish remodeling, I will have a workplace on the balcony at home. Until then, I come here," he said, adding that most carvers would prefer to work in rural studios, rather than apartments or the factory. After all, the best artisans of Bogorodskoye were inspired by the views from their village homes, looking out onto the forest and meadows.

In the 1970s, Bogorodskoye's quaint village life and traditions were inundated when GAES, the country's largest hydropower station, was sited right next door. Thousands of workers poured in from all over the USSR. A new town was built, and many of the rural houses were destroyed to make room for cookie-cutter, five-story concrete apartment buildings. The artists took this in stride, carving statues and carousels for playgrounds and hoping that the children using them would some day help to carry on the local craft.

AT THE TIME, the corralling of Russian folk crafts into factories was presented as natural and necessary. Artists could concentrate on their work in a single, designated place, receive critical reviews from their peers, educate younger employees, and at the same time produce items on a mass scale, while popularizing a Russian national tradition. Although there were definite benefits in this arrangement, it obviously restricted artists' freedom and creativity. Factory-ization made them employees, subject to the deadlines and productivity demands of the irrational five year plans. Moreover, in the departmental tossup of the Soviet bureaucracy, factories were slotted into illogical governmental hierarchies. For example, silver jewelry artisans in Tver region were subordinated to the Ministry of Instrument Making, home to bureaucrats with no artistic training.

Today's challenges are different: skilled labor is expensive, which drives up prices on authentic artisan items. Intellectual property laws are loosely applied, so consumers look to inexpensive, counterfeit souvenirs as an alternative (artists complain that everything at Moscow's popular Izmailovo market is counterfeit, for example). As well, artists searching for financial well-being are tempted to compromise the integrity of traditions and canons. Is it okay to decorate mobile phones with traditional Zhostovo designs? How about making Bogorodskoye Santa Clauses instead of bears? How far can artists wander into innovation without losing touch with a centuries-old craft?

Natalia Gayevskaya recognizes that some form of outside support is needed for authentic crafts, whether from the government or from foundations. Artists, she said, need a chance to breathe and to create without constant financial pressure. She is less worried about watering down traditions: "The more artists work in a certain type of craft, the better for the craft, even if they don't all strictly follow the canons," she said. One cannot be too protective of a certain style, she said, since a craft lives on only as long as it springs from the artist's heart, not from a textbook.

At the Bogorodskoye factory, children on a school fieldtrip gather around Mikhail, who is demonstrating the use of a special carving knife. Carving instruments are very personal, and have to be sharpened by the artist himself. The room fills with wows and ahhs as kids watch a chunk of linden wood slowly turn into a bear. When the guide asks who wants to grow up to be a carver, all of the hands shoot up.

November/December 2007

2006

Gypsies, Tramps and Thieves
Laura Williams

Old man Kudinyonok, as he is known in our village, approached me in the yard one afternoon as I was saddling our mare to go for a ride.

"Laura, can you call my cousin in Smelizh? Here's the number," he pleaded, extending a piece of paper toward me. "Some gypsies just robbed my house, and maybe she can do something to stop them on their way to town. They've only been gone about an hour. They were on foot. Three women and a man."

"Shouldn't we call the police?" I asked. "What did they steal?"

"They broke into our trunk in the main room and took 40,000 rubles ($1,500) and all of our documents!"

I went to tell my husband Igor what happened. Igor phoned the police in the district center of Suzemka, 60 kilometers away. The police said they would send a car to intercept the perpetrators.

Igor threw on his coat and grabbed the rifle out of the safe, loading it as he went out of the house. As an inspector in the nature reserve where we live, he has a permit to carry a rifle.

"Where do you think you're going?" I called after him, as he barged out the door.

"I might still be able to catch them," he called back. "They can't have gotten far on foot along the forest road with all the mud and puddles."

He grabbed the horse I was fixing to ride and jumped on, saying that he could sneak up on them on horseback, whereas they would be able to hide if they heard the jeep.

Gypsies are notorious for descending upon remote Russian villages, selling odds and ends or promising to cure the sick with their charms. When they sell an item of clothing to local villagers, the gypsies follow them into the house to see where they take their money from to pay for the wares. Last summer, learning that a woman sold her house in the next village of Smelizh, gypsies convinced her to let them in to treat her ailments. After hypnotizing her, they stole 60,000 rubles (over $2,000). Sometimes gypsies steal horses and cattle, leading them away at night and selling them to the sausage factory. Several times they had attempted to steal our horses, which graze freely in the fields around our village. But our horses are wary of anyone but me, Igor, and our caretaker Sergei, and shy away when approached.

Igor galloped down the muddy road, the rifle slung over his shoulder. Every so often, he stopped to study the tracks. Small puncture-like imprints in the mud testified that one woman wore heels. Another wore flip-flops. Igor followed them. Soon he met our caretaker Sergei on his way back to the village in the jeep after a weekend away. Sergei stopped to ask Igor what happened. Igor explained that the gypsies had robbed Kudinyonok. Sergei said he hadn't met anyone on the road. They must have hid in the woods upon hearing the car. Igor told Sergei to turn around and lend him a hand, and then galloped on. Sergei found a place on the narrow road to turn, but got stuck as he maneuvered the jeep about.

Up ahead, Igor heard a car. Soon he saw four people climbing into a yellow Lada. The driver noticed Igor and quickly put the car in motion. Evidently the gypsies had driven the car as far as they could down the muddy road and walked the rest of the way to our village. Now they meant to escape. As their car emerged from the forest, it dipped into a mud-filled gully and the front wheels sank into the mire. Realizing they were stuck, the gypsies abandoned the car and ran down the road. Igor galloped after them and rounded them up with the horse, taking the rifle from his shoulder.

"Don't move," he said, "The police are on their way."

The three women and man waited with Igor guarding them. At first they waited silently, but soon began to protest. First they tried pleading with Igor, saying they were sick and had children at home. Then the women began to chant various curses, damning Igor and his kin for generations to come. They tried to hypnotize him. Seeing it was no use, they began to threaten him. One of the young women, who must have been about 16, said she would tell the police that Igor raped her. She said she was pregnant, and she would claim the baby was his. Igor laughed, hiding his distress that the police had yet to arrive. Using his cell phone, which worked only from the raised clearing, he called the police again.

They said they had sent a car an hour earlier. It should have been here by now. They promised to send another.

Seeing that Igor was without reinforcements, the gypsies decided to make a run for it. They scattered in all different directions, running across the field and through the woods. Igor ran after them on the horse, but then leapt from the horse and fired his rifle in the air, yelling at them to stop. They stopped, but the mare bolted upon hearing the gunshot and made a beeline down the road toward home. In about a mile, she came upon Sergei digging out the jeep. Sergei intercepted the horse and jumped on, galloping back to Igor.

Sergei arrived on the horse as Igor rounded up the gypsies. Together they guarded them, until the police car finally arrived from Suzemka. The police loaded the gypsies into the vehicle, and wrote down Igor's statement.

The next day, as I was cleaning up in the kitchen, there came a knock at the door. I knew it couldn't be one of the villagers, as they didn't knock. I opened the door to see three Russian men dressed in civilian clothes and two small, colorfully-clad young gypsy women. One, about 16, wore an old fleece sweater, a long colorful skirt and pink flip-flops with socks, even though the temperature outside was below freezing. The other woman was slightly older and bundled more warmly, wearing spiky heels.

Saying they were looking for Igor, the men walked right into the door, the gypsy women trailing behind. I blocked the entryway, saying that Igor was out. The men said they were policemen and needed to talk to Igor. I asked what right they had to bring the thieves into my house, where they could size up their next job. Realizing their mistake, they directed the two young women to wait outside.

One of the policemen stank of alcohol. I told them Igor would be returning from town soon, and they would probably meet him on their way down the road out of the village. I walked them out, seeing that they all made it out the gate. On the way to Smelizh, they met Igor on the road, and got his signature for the statement. The gypsies showed the police where they had tossed the documents and stashed the money. In Smelizh, the woman who had been hypnotized by gypsies the summer before identified the perpetrators as those who had stolen her money.

Later I heard that the older of the two women took the blame and was put in jail for two years, while the other two went free. Meanwhile, other members of their extended family continued to comb the countryside for vulnerable peasants. While Chukhrai would remain vigilant, in all likelihood stories of the armed horseman would spread through the gypsies' ranks, and they will give Chukhrai a wide berth for some time to come.

July/August 2007

2007

A Floating Confessional
Alexander Mozhayev

Increasingly, the Orthodox Church is using itinerant churches to feed the spiritual needs of Russians living in distant regions and not otherwise served by parish churches. Three floating churches are active in the Volgograd eparchy. One of them, named St. Innokenty, has been plying the Don for eight years.

I.

Donskaya *stanitsa* (a large Cossack village) is submerged in a deep, post-prandial dream. It is so hot that not a soul is wandering the streets. Even the chickens are hiding in the shade. I peer into fenced yards for quite awhile, trying to find someone who might be able to point me toward the missing church. I finally find a grey-haired old fellow sitting on a bench.

"Excuse me sir, they say that a church is sometimes tied up around here. Have you not seen it?"

"Nah, what'm I gonna do there? I'm too old for such nonsense. Lived my whole life without priests, why start now...? Why don'cha ask at the store? Maybe somebody there knows."

A handwritten notice hangs on the iron doors of the store: "The floating church has arrived. It is moored at the pumping station." I ask a young guy in an overstretched muscle shirt for directions.

"Somewhere over thattaway," he answers. "Haven't seen it myself. Nut'n for me there, I was baptized ages ago."

Circling around the brick buildings of the pumping station, I emerge near the shore of the Don and immediately spot the sparkling silver cross of St. Innokenty. It is an ordinary barge with an iron cupola on the roof; in the stern hangs a row of copper bells. Before the church stretches a small sandy beach, where the locals are relaxing. Young pioneer-aged girls are belting out a song: "Tonight will be so easy, I love you so sweetly." Nearby, three guys are boozing it up and I catch a fragment of their conversation.

"Tolya, don't you say nothing about my mama, that's sacred."

TRANSLATION: PAUL E. RICHARDSON

"Sacred is floating over there, and, as for your mama…"

II.

I board the St. Innokenty by a wooden gangplank. A lock hangs on the doors of the church, with a note warning: "No smoking, swimming or fishing on board the church." Powerful snoring emanates from a round porthole. I knock on the window: "Is Father Gennady at home?" The snoring stops abruptly and a cry rings out: "Team, get up, guests have arrived!"

The sleep-heavy crew of the floating sanctuary appears through the rear doors of the barge: the priest (and captain) Gennady Khanykin, sexton Sergei, sailor Andrei and his son, the ship's boy Sasha. The sailor, if truth be told, was in a bad way and smelled of smoke. He moaned something incomprehensible and collapsed back onto his bunk. Father Gennady stroked his beard, put on sunglasses and commented in an official tone: "Yesterday we had a bit of bad luck. Andrei went up on deck last night and the locals saw him. They were celebrating someone's birthday on shore, invited our comrade to their table, and filled him up with 25-ruble vodka. He's really hurting now."

We sit down at a table in the refectory (a ward room, actually) and discuss the evening's schedule. Services are not planned for today – owing to the small number of visitors, services are only held on holidays and Sundays. There are no plans to set sail in the coming days either, as the ship is immobilized. A week before, the St. Innokenty stumbled into a storm on Tsimlyansky Reservoir. The waves dashed the church's tug onto the rocks and it had to be sent for repairs.

"So what exactly will you do?" I ask the priest.

"We'll fish a bit in the morning, then swim and sleep again. There is really nothing else you can do in heat like this. In the evening, when it gets dark, we'll have a procession of the cross on deck. We do that all the time, without outsiders, for our own peace of mind. We are, after all, travelers."

Father Gennady has been plying the Don since 1998, when he purchased a used barge from a river construction crew with money provided by the international aid fund, "Church in Trouble." At one point he was abbot of all the Don's floating churches, but the work became too demanding, so he gave it up. Father Gennady has lived in Moscow, Lipetsk and Volgograd – all "ant-hills," he says. Apparently his soul was meant for the slower-paced life of a floating priest. His annual travels along the Don begin in the spring and continue until the end of the navigation season. In the winter, the church is tied up at a small village, acting as a regular parish church, with a priest from Volgograd serving on weekends.

"My whole family has served the Church," Father Gennady says. "My great-grandfather was a hermit, leading the life of a recluse in a forest hut near Tobolsk. There's plenty of seclusion here as well, because of the surprising peace and quiet on the river. But, in general, I have to do missionary work, to awaken the people. For without churches it is impossible to show people what is good in faith. Only in confession, in the liturgy, do people understand what this is all about. Therefore, we bring our church here, to the countryside, where there weren't even churches before the revolution – to show people how to live another life, to commune with God. We try to show how good it is to be with God: just ask Him and He will always help. When we do, people begin to see how their prayers create their world.

"You know, the best time for discussing such things is after evening prayers, in the silence, when we go out onto the deck and chat. We'll continue this then. Right now we have to go and get some water from the well. Meanwhile, perhaps you could pop into the store and buy a beer for our ailing sailor? It really wouldn't look right if I went."

III.

We go down onto dry land, climb into Father Gennady's Niva jeep and head off to refill the water barrels. As we drive through the *stanitsa*, it seems larger and less desolate than it felt at midday. Along the way, *batyushka*[1] describes his complex relationship with the shore-dwelling aborigines.

"The people here are neglectful and lazy. They consider themselves to be Cossacks and therefore feel that their lives should be carefree and stable. The Don gives you everything you need, even if you don't work at all. Sit for half an hour and you'll catch a little roach for dinner – you'll not starve here. They even feed fish to the chickens. The women, meanwhile, are bent over housework without a break.

"A Cossack considers it an insult if he confesses – he is his own god. They often say to me, 'Come by here again and I'll punch your face in.' It's 70 kilometers to the nearest church, but if 12 people attend service,

---

1. A term of endearment for a priest: "little father."

that's not a bad turnout. Refugees from Asia attend more often than locals. Yet, of course it's not a question of quantity. Once I baptized a person not far from here, knowing full well that he was a criminal. Then, six years later, he came to me and I am telling you, up 'til then, I had no idea what a real confession was. How he repented and what he became… he is now an excellent, Orthodox, honest working person. This is of course a rare thing, yet completely true. Miracles like that are what keep you working."

<h2 style="text-align:center">IV.</h2>

Poor Andrei awaits us on board the barge. He hastily seizes the bottle of Baltika, takes a gulp and finally speaks, as if continuing a fragmentary phrase:

"…and they invited me. You refuse, and they're gonna say, 'What, are you too good to drink with villagers?' Well, we had a good time. Ye-e-a-ah, they're good people. One of them was a bit strange, though, trying to mess with me and pick a fight. But they calmed him down. Seryozha, I'm dying."

"You're not dying, but you could have if I hadn't saved you yesterday," replies Seryozha, the tow-headed sexton. "Do you remember falling off the gangway?"

"I fell from the gangway? And you pulled me out? Well, what kind of sailor never falls off a gangway!"

"A sober one, Andryush, doesn't fall off."

"Nah, Seryozh, that's not a real sailor."

"Look, the correspondent is listening to this, and he's gonna write: 'How sad, our churches have still not rid themselves of the repulsive vice of drunkenness.'"

"But I'm not a priest, I'm a sailor! The real thing!"

"People will say, 'as with the parish, so with the priest.' If they have drunken sailors sprawled on the church steps, then what do you expect to see in the sanctuary?"

Andrei suddenly let out a loud snigger, remembering something from last night's binge on shore.

"Get this, one of the local chicks says to me: 'Are you the one selling the costume jewelry in the church store? Give me a silver necklace and I'll give you anything you like.' Right. Crazy people."

Sergei the sensible sexton heads to the galley. Time to make soup. He peels a potato and tells his story:

"I actually finished seminary. I could serve, but I don't want to just yet. It's a big responsibility. I only talk with non-believers now if they are childhood friends. Otherwise, what's the point? To listen to them swear? To talk about life? As soon as they start talking, everything is clear to me."

On the door of Sergei's cell hangs a sheet of paper with a quote copied out in a careful hand: "If someone lives in a place and does not bear fruit which benefits that place, then that place will reject him as something that takes up space and does not bear fruit."

V.

In the evening, Father Gennady welcomes a treasured guest on board, a middle-aged fellow named Yuri Nikolayevich. A local law enforcement official, he spent three years working as a sheriff in America (prolonging an employment exchange program). Now he teaches at the Volgograd Police Academy. In Donskaya he has a private plot with 15 chickens, a rooster, 10 cats and two dogs. He is one of the region's most active visitors of St. Innokenty.

A table is pulled out onto the deck. A bucket with boiled crabs appears alongside five bottles of *kagor*.[2] *Batyushka* cheerfully raises his glass.

"Look around, there is such beauty here, such peace! What more could a man want? Only that this moment would last longer, because it reveals to us the essence of the universe. For now, we are free of all earthly worries, so let's drink to the hope that, at least for this moment, we all experience the surprising unity of God and man. Yuri Nikolayevich, what would you like? Would you like a sip of wine? Help yourself. Would you like a bit of fish? Help yourself. Or perhaps both, all things are blessed."

The heat finally subsides. The loud voices on the beach have died down; we hear only the chirping of cicadas and the splashing of fish in the river. The fact that we are not simply on a moored ship, but in a church yard, is as surprising as the fact that this is not simply a church on the water, but a real ship. Yuri Nikolayevich recounts with pleasure the history of his overseas training, expressing his greatest astonishment at the contrasts between the Cossack and American worldviews.

"I can't even tell you how hard it was for me at times over there. Of course, everything is upside down. Our day is their night. So I would wake up, as I usually do, at four AM and look out the window. But there were

---

2. A red dessert wine.

these blinking, colored lights. And I would sit, almost crying, thinking: 'Lord, save my sinful soul! Just let me return, and I will immediately stop being unfaithful to my wife and will completely turn my life around.' And then I returned. I came out of Sheremetyevo airport and everywhere there was snow, dirt, and greedy taxi drivers. And again I shed tears, thinking, 'Lord, I must have lost my head. How am I supposed to turn my life around here, when everyone looks at you with crazed eyes and no one ever smiles?' Back in America, everyone smiles. You step on someone's foot, and he says 'Excuse me.' Only it is all fake. Here, they look at you like wild animals, but at least it's honest! Later, American sheriffs came to Volgograd on their exchange visit – 50 people from different states. And I welcomed them here, at my place, *batyushka*, and it was something! They gobbled up caviar by the bucketful, drank, danced – as you would expect. But you know what surprised them most? 'You have huge liberties here,' they said, 'you are a free people!' In America, if you toss a cigarette butt on the ground, they immediately issue you a fine. But here, toss it wherever you like… you can fall asleep with your face in the salad and no one will say a word! Our Don is a free land."

"You know, I could sit here with you all night, Yuri Nikolayevich, with pleasure," *batyushka* says. "Because life in Christ is sheer joy. I don't do anything because it is required of me, but only to make myself and others happy. If a person is depressed, it means he is not a complete Christian. And for our part we have nothing to be depressed about: we still have three bottles of wine. I confess, I love this stuff, because I feel wine is bliss. My wife sometimes curses me, but when I arrive home from my travels, I always say as I cross the threshold, '*Matushka*, why are we out of wine?!' You can't binge on wine, its purpose is to make a person feel fine, talkative. Yuri Nikolayevich, why have you not emptied your glass? Does that mean you don't like it? You don't find it blissful here? Or perhaps you are not accustomed to it?"

"I am accustomed, *batyushka*, to sleeping at night, as God intended."

"So-o-o, that means you are not staying? Well, Christ be with you. But let's at least finish this glass."

After escorting his guest to land, *batyushka* returns to the table and pours me and himself full glasses (the rest of the crew have long since gone off to bed).

"And now, Alexander, let's get to the bottom of things – who are you and what worries your soul?"

VI.

Our conversation drags well past midnight. I should say that *batyushka* and I did not come to a meeting of the minds on certain issues. That sort of thing happens in even the best of company, often with one's more elderly acquaintances. The conversation accidentally slips onto a dangerous topic like the nationality question or birth control. And you unexpectedly realize that you and this very nice person not only have different priorities, but entirely different conceptions of Good and Evil. And you have no idea how to continue the conversation in a civilized manner. Therefore, somewhere during the third bottle *batyushka* narrows his gaze and says:

"I have a combative character, everyone here knows that. And now I am going to raise you up and slam you down on the table, to break you of the habit of arguing with this priest!"

Luckily, we agree to find Truth through a bloodless arm wrestling contest. Father Gennady sweeps the dishes from the table with his mighty right arm and utterly destroys me. Then he says:

"There. Tomorrow, you're not going anywhere. I will give you a severe preaching to. We may even skip the procession of the cross tomorrow as well. Hey, Andryusha, get up, put on the teapot!"

"Oh, what are you doing, *batyushka*? Have mercy on the sick!"

"Nevermind, it will remind them who is in charge on this ship. Akh, I have to do everything myself."

Father Gennady heads to the galley. A few minutes later I hear the by now familiar throb of snoring, floating out of his cabin window.

May/June 2008

The Lighthouse Master
Natalya Beskhlebnaya

*T*here is a reason it is called the White Sea (or the Icy Sea). Winter lasts for about eight months up here, and for much of that time, the water is covered by ice and snow.

When the sea is open for navigation, the color of the White Sea, as in other seas, changes depending on the weather and the sky. But the sky here is austere and often completely colorless; the deep, cold water is opaque and for the most part has a characteristically grayish-blue tint. At sunset it resembles melted silver.

The water is so bitterly cold that White Sea sailors don't bother with life jackets. If you are not pulled out of the sea immediately, you will not survive. Then again, there are no special lifeboat stations on the White Sea; those functions are performed by the lighthouses.

There are numerous islands in the White Sea. The ten or so situated along important shipping routes have lighthouses perched atop them. The lighthouse keepers are in constant contact with one another via radio, but they otherwise live solitary lives and never visit one another.

Take for example Pavel Petrovich Trofimov, a lighthouse keeper on Rombak Island. He has never been to the nearby island of Zhuzhmuy. What is more, if you don't count his annual vacation and the short periods when workers from the lighthouse service stay on the island, the keeper of the Rombak lighthouse lives on his island completely alone. His predecessor, unlike Pavel Petrovich, lived here with his family. In 2005, he and his wife were found dead on the island, shot by a hunting rifle. Soon after, the lighthouse keeper's job was offered to Pavel Petrovich. He accepted.

This was all we knew about life on Rombak when our group approached the island, enveloped in a mysterious fog. No one came out to greet us, which was rather strange, since, despite the fog, we could see the bright yellow building of the lighthouse on the hill right before us. All the island's buildings were close, and surely we could be seen from above. On the other

TRANSLATION: SUSANNA NAZAROVA

hand, we could see almost nothing but the shore. Having been warned that there could be dogs and that lighthouse keepers are generally an unpredictable sort, we didn't hurry to go ashore. The island lay right before us, the sea was absolutely calm, and yet we waited.

After a while, we fired a shot from a signal pistol; it exploded the illusory atmosphere of tranquility. A large seagull let out a piercing cry, as if woken from a nightmare, and took wing from the water. But that was the end of it. In an instant, the bird disappeared into the fog, and the suspenseful stillness returned. After waiting a bit longer, we decided to go ashore.

As soon as we stepped on shore, a thin-faced, tanned, wiry man somewhere on the other side of 40 appeared out of the fog. He said that he had been busy on the other side of the island, then introduced himself, before asking us to explain who we were and what we were doing there. Satisfied, he quickly became amicable and agreed to talk to us.

In his abrupt and controlled gestures, in his rare but charming smiles, in the awkward way he invited us to tea, and in his attempts to be hospitable, there was the air of a real hermit. He was a true northern lighthouse keeper: independent and extremely austere, yet also open, a person whom you could ask anything of, though not quite everything. The one question I didn't ask, and that wished I had, was why he lives alone, and whether he had ever married...

Can you tell me what happened to the previous lighthouse keeper?

I don't know the conclusion of the expert commission, but we were told that he supposedly did it himself – I don't know the details – that he shot his wife and then shot himself. Nobody knows why it happened here. And, by the way, this is not my first time here. Nine years ago I worked here as a technician, but I didn't get along with the lighthouse keeper, so I decided to get out of harm's way. We didn't work well together, didn't get along; all the same, you need to have a certain temperament here...

What kind of temperament?
What?

What sort of temperament does one need to have here?

In short, that of a lone wolf. You can't be gazing and howling at the other shore, but must have everything you need in you and where you are. Over there, on the mainland, yes, there are some things you need from there, of course, but...

You mean people here need to be somewhat special?
Yes, of course. For example, would you be able to live here? Like this, without ever leaving?

Not me, that's why I'm asking.
But I, on the other hand, can't spend more than three days there [on the mainland], there's too many problems there. There's fewer here. You rub your eyes in the morning, and that's it – you're already at work.

And what's next?
Well, that's how the day starts – I come out, walk around, watch the lighthouse – turn it on, turn it off, check the lighthouse's conditions, well everything, I have to do literally everything. If a rail falls off the fence, I have to nail it back on, it's my job, I can't step over it, I need to lift it, put it away... everything needs to be done around the house, right? For example, you live at home, you go to work, come back home, sweep a little something, clean, boil some potatoes, or cabbage soup, wash some clothes – it's the same here, everything is just like at home, but then you also have your work, and everything's right here...

And where does your home end?
The whole island is my home. Everything here is mine, everything. When I come out in the morning, I don't know what I'm going to do. No, of course, I do have plans sometimes; suppose I need to do this and that urgently, I can't put it off, because of the weather or something else. Today the weather is like this, and I try to do something outside, and if there is rain or, say, wind, then – there's something inside, in the house, and sometimes in the repair shop. Like just now, I went to remove a board and got distracted by some other work, and so what – the board can wait, but I'll do this now since the weather is cooperating. And then I was walking by here and I saw you. I look out and see a boat – what is this Flying Dutchman doing here? I didn't even hear you pull in...

ROMBAK IS SITUATED in the White Sea, in the Onega Bay. It is one of the Kem skerries – a string of islands stretching from the White Sea port of Kem, in Karelia.

The island is a large, granite crag completely void of trees. The crag is knobby, with piles of stones spread about; it's wet in places, and it's difficult to walk quickly. What is more, you can't see the ground clearly: the stones are covered by multicolored moss, berries, and other northern groundcover. From Rombak Island you can see the neighboring island, Little Rombak. In good weather, other islands are visible as well. It is eight miles from Rombak Island to the town of Kem, or the mainland (*Bolshaya Zemlya*, in Russian).

The island lies along the ancient route that stretches from Kem to the famous Solovetsky Islands ("Solovki") – an archipelago famous for many aspects of its history and geography, as well as for being the home of famous stone labyrinths, monuments to a 4000-year-old megalithic culture. Little is known about the labyrinth's builders, aside from the fact that they didn't live on Solovki permanently, but would sail over from the continent, from the upper reaches of the Kem River. The ancient sailors hopped from island to island and surely did not bypass Rombak. The most convenient route of navigation from the Kem skerries passes by here; on contemporary sailing maps of the White Sea, it is called the *Korabelny* ("shipping") or *Poperechny* ("crossing") route. At Rombak, the complicated navigation between the islands ends, and there's no land for many miles.

And the sea also belongs to you?

Yes, the sea is also mine. I went out, put out some nets, fed a fish to the cat, but while I was catching the fish, the cat caught himself a bird and made a mess somewhere around here, the feathers...

Yes, I saw. And the ships are also yours?

The ships... depends how you look at it... They don't travel near me any longer; before, they passed right by here, but now they've changed their route a little, made it a bit more convenient, they've calculated it with modern equipment, but if they pass close by, they always signal me. And, if they can see me, I wave my hat at them.

Has a lot changed recently?

Not really, no, everything is generally the same, lighthouses are still lighthouses.

But now, in the era of GPS, there is no real need for lighthouses, don't you think?

I think that, all this GPS, who knows for how long all these satellites are going to keep flying around, and if, for example, a war starts, they'll turn all that stuff off. And then what? Turn on the lighthouses again, look for lighthouse keepers? Right? And explain to them, ask them, "Come back, we've turned everything off, we've got some problems in space." Is that how to do it? No, lighthouses need to always be kept in working condition.

IT WAS FOUNDED in 1903, on the precipice of the southernmost elevated point of Rombak Island. The light is 34 meters above sea level and is visible from 15 miles off, helping to determine the accuracy of a ship's bearing en route to the Solovetsky Islands. Last year, new equipment was delivered for the beacon, but it was the wrong size. Now it's stored next to the working lighthouse, still functioning fine with its old French lens.

The lighthouse building has been made suitable for habitation; there is a yellow, wooden house with a red roof, the northern point of which holds the tower and the beacon. In recent years, vinyl siding was added to the building, but its colors did not change, and the lighthouse keeper moved to live in the neighboring wooden cottage. When technicians and pilots come to the island, they stay in the lighthouse itself. There is also a sound-signal system on the island, a wind-power station, navigational signs, and several functional wooden buildings, the smallest of which once held a bell. In times of fog, the lighthouse keeper had to ring the bell every three minutes, and, if he received a return signal from a ship, the ringing had to become more frequent, almost non-stop. Fog on the White Sea can last for days.

Isn't it scary here all alone?

What's there to be scared of? The seven of you came here, and I don't know how many are still in the boat, do you feel scared?

Well, a little scared, I guess.

And I am not scared. It's scarier when there are seven of you, and everybody is worrying about each other. I am alone, I don't have to be scared for anybody. That's it. Only for myself.

You are saying that, if you were here with a family, it would be more difficult?

Well, yes, you have to think more, your own health doesn't matter, but you worry about your loved ones. What if something really happens, even appendicitis, but nowadays it's good that we have a cell phone connection; if something happens, one can call on the phone, they'll send a helicopter or deliver something. But before, there was a time when we didn't even have radio communication, I remember those times; it's only later that we got radio transmitters. We go on the air every day to communicate with all the lighthouses and with the authorities. Oh, do you hear that signal? They are signaling to me, someone is going by. But when you approached, I didn't hear, and I even feel bad that I somehow missed you. The island is big, you know, I can't always watch every part of it… But really, such stillness is very rare. You might have been unable to pull in to the shore, would be circling the island, there would be wind even just seven or eight meters offshore, and you would be hard put to figure out where to pull in, where to leave the boat, you would have to pull it out of the water, couldn't have left it on the water like that…

And do you sometimes feel bored here?

No, I never get bored, I always find something to do. I am not saying that I have to look for something to do, but, on the contrary, the day is too short to do everything. I never plan, but there's always a pile of work, the day is not enough. One day, the boat needs to be fixed, or the nets untangled and put away, or they are lying around dirty, so you don't put it off till tomorrow but get it done now. So, I come out, and that's it, there's always work to do. I walk along and see some tangled cable I'd forgotten about, and if I don't straighten it out now, then what am I going to do when I really need it to pull the boat up in bad weather, for example? I am going to start untangling it then, right? The boat will be smashed up by then, so, no, let me untangle this cable today, even though I don't need it today. So, I walk on the shore and check whether I left something loose, and, oh hell,

yes, I did, and if the weather turns bad, it'll all be washed away – so, I need
to put it away. That's how things are…

And what are you doing now?

Right now I am waiting for a ship, there's food coming, some other
stuff… They're bringing it by GS [a hydrographic ship], and I need to
receive it. I've been waiting for it for two weeks already, still no ship.

And in winter, do you have contact with the shore?

It depends on the winter, on the winds, the temperatures; the water
doesn't freeze every year, this winter it didn't, so there was no contact;
there's no boats going by in the winter. In the spring, when the ice-breaker
comes, navigation begins. And when it freezes, you can ride a snowmobile
on it. But this year I never even started the snowmobile, so there was no
way you could travel over there.

And does anybody come to visit you by way of the ice?

Sometimes wolves come. It happens.

Are you afraid?

Well, a wolf is afraid of a man, they stay away when they pass by, but you
can see them. But this winter, a fox came over. I don't know how it got here,
maybe it drifted on the ice, so now it lives here with me.

And what kind of relationship do you have with it?

What kind of relationship… It doesn't interfere with me, but my cat
can't stand having it around. My cat is very timid. I brought him here on
a snowmobile when he was still a blind kitten, and he has never seen the
mainland. That was such a stressful journey for him – the wind, the noise –
so he doesn't like noise now.

THE EMERGENCE OF navigation in Russia and everything associated with it
is commonly linked to Peter the Great. This is not quite accurate, since the
history of Russian navigation stretches into a more distant past: residents of
the Russian North not only went to sea on fishing karbasses but settled the
Arctic and were famous among northern European seafarers.

Recently, interest in this period of the country's history has been on
the rise, and there are seafaring enthusiasts who annually organize difficult

archaeological expeditions along the country's northern borders. The center for such activity is the Solovetsky Islands in the White Sea. Every summer, members of the Association of Northern Seafaring (*Tovarishchestvo Severnovo Morekhodstva*: solovki.info) travel from throughout Russia to work in the Solovetsky Oceanic Museum (museum.solovki.info). The museum is just two years old, but is one of the most original museums in the country, founded by individuals and located directly on the docks, in an old storehouse once used for renovating rowboats. The museum offers a wealth of information on active lighthouses and on boatbuilding using ancient techniques. According to the museum, in ancient times coastal bonfires performed the function of modern lighthouses, as navigation of the Baltic Sea also predated Peter the Great.

The first Russian lighthouse is thought to have been built on Kopu (in present-day Estonia), at the beginning of the sixteenth century. Still, Peter the Great started extensive lighthouse construction in the Baltic and in the North. There was also a lighthouse built in the South, in the Sea of Azov.

For a long time, private individuals could also build and maintain lighthouses. This led to numerous problems. Since lighthouse fires were of wood or coal, they looked exactly like regular fires, and thus, by lighting a false fire, one could easily cause a shipwreck. In the beginning of the nineteenth century, all lighthouses became the purview of the government. At the same time, stone lighthouses began to replace wooden ones, and the system of beacon-lights with reflectors was introduced.

There are some 350 lighthouses in Russia today. With the break-up of the Soviet Union, many Baltic and Black Sea lighthouses are now owned by the newly independent states. Besides lighthouses in the North of Russia, there are many in the Far East. However, the number of operating lighthouses is on the decline since their international significance is waning, and there are plans to abolish many of them. For instance, some want to decommission the famous Solovetsky lighthouse, situated in the island's Cathedral of the Ascension. The lighthouse's beacon had already been abandoned as a navigational bearing, but the monks continued to maintain the lighthouse in working condition and succeeded in proving its value, after which authorities returned it to official status. New equipment was delivered, along with solar panels; but the modern electrical equipment turned out to be too powerful for the ancient lighthouse structure, and so, for a full navigation season, the lighthouse stood idle, awaiting the necessary cable. In the summer of 2009, the lighthouse was finally back in operation.

The phenomenon of the deserted lighthouse causes another problem. In places where there is no other power source, lighthouses draw their power from radioisotope thermoelectric generators (RTGs), which are in effect small nuclear power plants, powered by highly-radioactive strontium cores. According to the International Atomic Energy Agency, RTGs are classified as a first class danger. More than 1000 RTGs were manufactured during the Soviet era, and many have reached the effective end of their working life. In the last two decades, there have been incidents where RTGs have been vandalized or stolen, with the expected environmental and human costs. More recently, international programs have been begun to replace RTGs with solar batteries. Still, traveling to a northern lighthouse can be a risky venture; the traveler is advised to take along a dosimeter.

And does this island suit you? Do you ever think about other islands? Would you, for example, up and exchange this island for a better one?
Somehow this island I... I've known it since my childhood. I have lived around here on the shore all my life and often went to Solovki as a boy. I just used to go there for a day, there and back, I would go there, run around and... I had family there, an aunt and uncle... I would go there, show myself and leave... And I always passed this island on the old route, and it has always been right here and always seemed interesting to me – how do they live, what do they do?... I'd see the boats pulled up on the shore, see them walking around, wondered what they did here and always dreamed of coming here, just to take a look. I never thought about any job, I was just thinking as a kid – how can I get here, who are these people?

The lighthouse keeper during those days was this Chichenin, and I really wanted to get a look at him – what's he like – I thought I'd see him, look him over, and everything would become clear. But he was the same as everyone else, it's all the same here like everywhere. And then many years passed, and fate brought me here. And I've never thought about any other islands, though I was offered many times, there were other vacancies, but I didn't... to have a look maybe – yes, that would be interesting, I haven't been to any other lighthouse, even to these closest ones, and I would like to have a look at their lives, what they are doing over there, I should go take a look. But this is not my first time here, you see. That time we didn't hit it off, and I left, and it turned out I only lived on the shore for a short time, and they all died out here. And everybody used to say to me, "you see, if you had stuck it out then and hadn't left, you would have stayed on the island without a break," and when this emergency happened, and they offered me the job again, I immediately accepted, without giving it another thought…

And do you have anything to defend yourself with here?
What do you mean?

Do you have a rifle?
No, that's not stipulated. Against the rules. Defend myself from whom? From mosquitoes?

Well, you never know who might pull up to the shore.
Well, it's actually a prohibited zone, and it's not allowed to pull up here; only with permission from the lighthouse authority.

But you're the only one who can send them away.
Well, I would first ask nicely, and if they don't understand, I have a phone and I can inform someone on the shore who would do something about it. Yes, it's happened before… And I had to apply force; they don't understand "not allowed" around here. And other times, they are so polite, they come, they ask for some water, and sometimes, if something breaks, they ask, "could we please pull in, stay for a while," and, of course, I let them. But others come and begin, "Who are you?" and stuff like that. They see that I am all alone here, and they start demanding something. But I am not afraid of you, since you don't even know what I have, right? Yes? You just asked me if I had something to defend myself with, but maybe I lied to you. How would you know? You come and you don't know anything, but I am protected. Why would I be afraid?

And aren't you afraid of yourself?
And why would I be afraid of myself?

Well, you are always alone with yourself, the same landscape, sunrise-lighthouse-sunset, sunrise-lighthouse-sunset, one could go mad here all alone. Aren't you scared?

They often ask me about this, and I never know what to say, how to explain. No, I'm not scared.

As we were sailing away, the fog had lifted, it was evening, and not far from the shore we saw a large ship, from which a small boat separated and started moving in the direction of Rombak. It turned out to be the very supplies Pavel Petrovich had been expecting for so long. We didn't hear the words with which he greeted the new arrivals, though from the sea we witnessed one of the most life-affirming scenes I have ever seen.

There was the lonely figure of the lighthouse keeper on the empty island; he was holding his hand to his forehead, peering intently into the distance. And then, having noticed the boat, he shows it where to pull in; fanning off the mosquitoes and clomping along the pier, he hurries to meet the approaching boat. And then finally, in the rays of the evening sun, a dozen sailors, with Pavel Petrovich rushing about between them, are amicably unloading large white objects onto the shore.

We argued about what they might be, but couldn't agree. In the evening sun, the most plausible story seemed to be that they were humongous chunks of white sugar, and, really, how else could one entertain oneself during the long winter evenings? Later, we were told that those were just mundane ration boxes; each box contained a specific portion of essential provisions and items. We were also told that the delay in delivery was due to excessive drinking by the person responsible for the delivery.

November/December 2009

Index

Made in the USA
Charleston, SC
25 June 2011